Language ESSENTIALS

Grammar and Writing

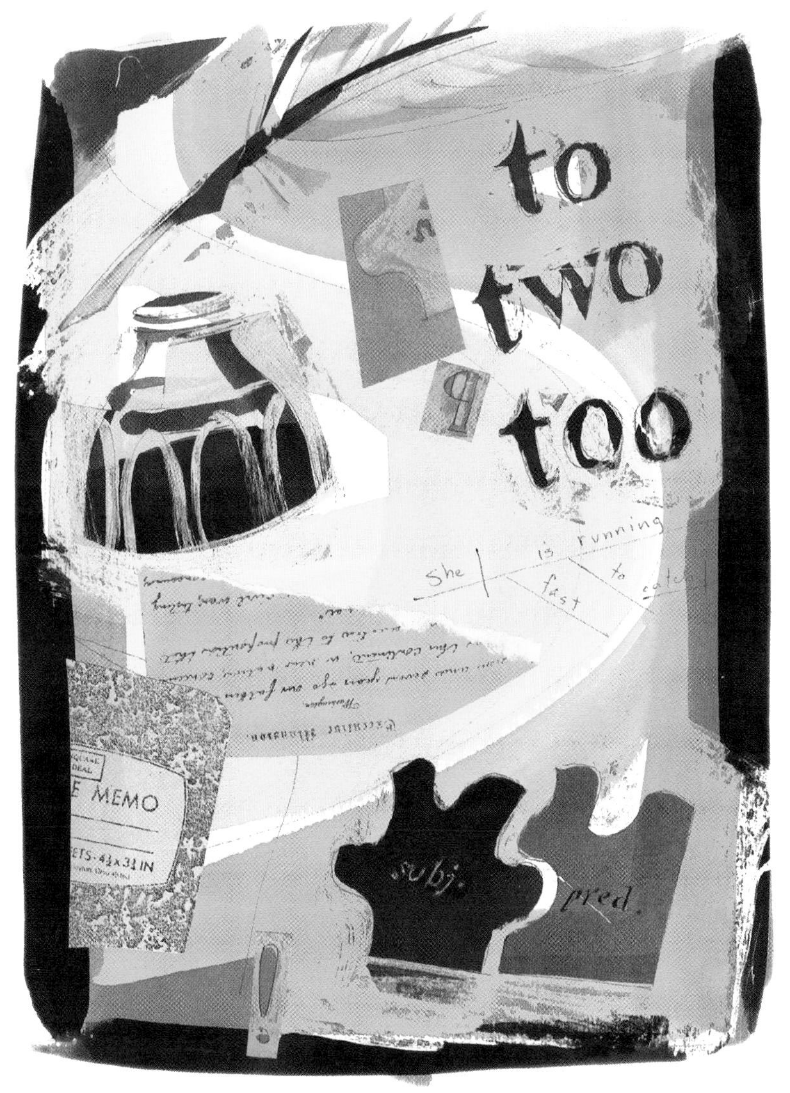

THE EMC MASTERPIECE SERIES • PINE LEVEL

Staff Credits

Editorial

Laurie Skiba
Managing Editor

Brenda Owens
Editor

Nichola Torbett
Associate Editor

Becky Palmer
Associate Editor

Jennifer Joline Anderson
Assistant Editor

Valerie Murphy
Editorial Assistant

Lisa S. Torrey
Educational Writer

Paul Spencer
Art and Photo Researcher

Senior Editorial Consultant

Dr. Edmund J. Farrell
Emeritus Professor of English Education
University of Texas at Austin
Austin, Texas

Design and Production

Shelley Clubb
Production Manager

Jennifer Wreisner
Text and Cover Designer

Matthias Frasch
Production Specialist

Sharon O'Donnell
Proofreader

Terry Casey
Indexer

Julie Delton
Cover Artist

ISBN 0-8219-3032-X Teacher's Edition
ISBN 0-8219-2528-8

Published by EMC/Paradigm Publishing
875 Montreal Way
St. Paul, Minnesota 55102
www.emcp.com
E-mail: educate@emcp.com

Printed in the United States of America
11 10 9 8 7 6 5 4 3 2 XXX 10 09 08 07 06 05 04
11 10 9 8 7 6 5 4 3 2 1 XXX 10 09 08 07 06 05 04 Teacher's Edition

Language

ESSENTIALS

Grammar and Writing

REDWOOD LEVEL

BIRCH LEVEL

CEDAR LEVEL

WILLOW LEVEL

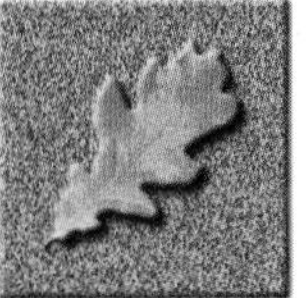
OAK LEVEL

PINE LEVEL

MAPLE LEVEL

CONTENTS IN BRIEF

CONTENTS

PART I LANGUAGE

Unit 1 The English Language

PART II GRAMMAR

Unit 2 The Sentence

ASSESSMENT
Grammar Pretests and Comprehensive Tests are available at www.emcp.com.

Unit 3 The Parts of Speech

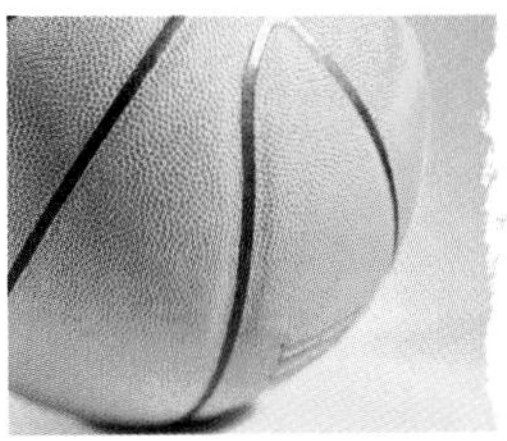

LANGUAGELINK
Print exercise worksheets or have students complete exercises online with the LanguageLINK CD.

UNIT 4 NAMERS: NOUNS

UNIT 5 NAMERS: PRONOUNS

UNIT 6 EXPRESSERS: VERBS

Unit 7 Sentence Completers: Complements

Unit 8 Subject-Verb Agreement and Usage

ASSESSMENT
Grammar and Usage Test is available at www.emcp.com.

Unit 9 Modifiers

UNIT 10 LINKERS AND JOINERS: PREPOSITIONS AND CONJUNCTIONS

UNIT 11 INTERRUPTERS

UNIT 12 PHRASES, CLAUSES, AND COMPLEX SENTENCES

Unit 13 Diagramming Sentences

Unit 14 Common Usage Problems

PART III STYLE

Unit 15 Punctuation

ASSESSMENT
Style Pretest, Style Comprehensive Test, and Punctuation and Capitalization Test are available at www.emcp.com.

Unit 16 Capitalization

ASSESSMENT
Spelling Test is available at www.emcp.com.

Unit 17 Spelling

UNIT 18 ELECTRONIC COMMUNICATIONS: ETIQUETTE AND STYLE

PART IV WRITING

UNIT 19 WRITER'S WORKSHOP: BUILDING EFFECTIVE SENTENCES

UNIT 20 WRITER'S WORKSHOP: BUILDING EFFECTIVE PARAGRAPHS

ASSESSMENT
Writing Comprehensive Test, Writing Rubrics, and Writing Evaluation Forms are available at www.emcp.com.

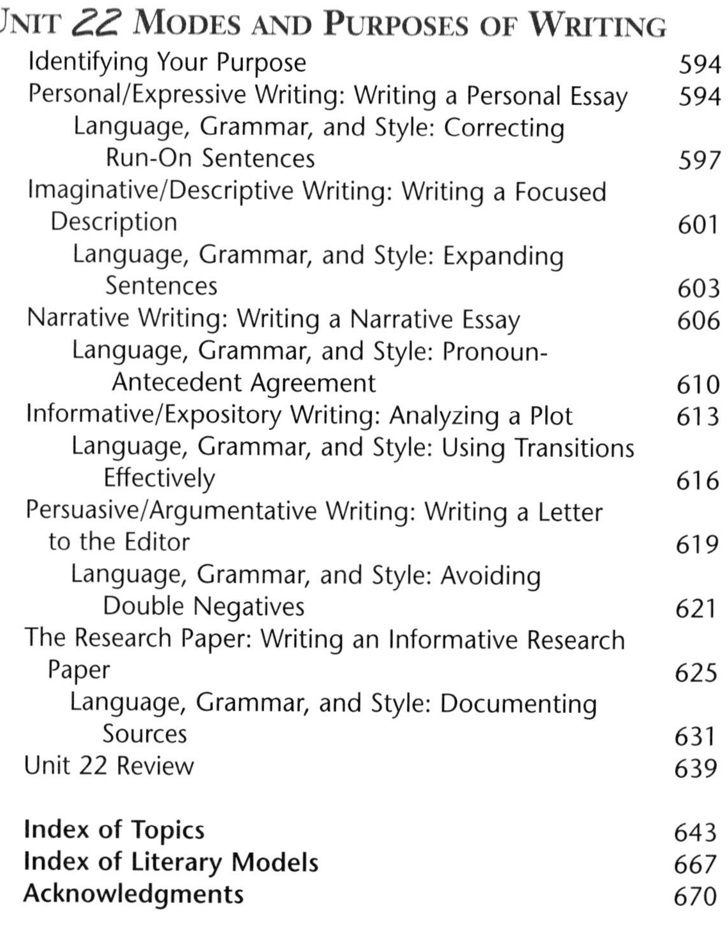

UNIT 21 THE WRITING PROCESS

UNIT 22 MODES AND PURPOSES OF WRITING

Literature Models

PART ONE

Language

UNIT 1 THE ENGLISH LANGUAGE

UNIT OVERVIEW

THE ENGLISH LANGUAGE

THE DEVELOPMENT OF THE ENGLISH LANGUAGE

Chances are that you know some words unfamiliar to people older than you. In every generation, the language changes. These changes accumulate over time until an entirely new language emerges. Over the centuries, the development of the English language has been divided into three stages: Old English, Middle English, and Modern English.

Old English

When the Anglo-Saxons invaded England in the fifth century, they brought with them the West Germanic dialects (spoken languages), which are known today as **Old English.** The English language, descended from Old English, is related to modern Danish, German, Norwegian, Icelandic, and Dutch. Old English was spoken in Britain from roughly A.D. 450 to A.D. 1100. Look at the following examples of Old English.

MODEL

Hwaet we Gar-Dena in gear-dagum,
Yes, we of the Gar-Danes in days of old,

þeod-cyninga, þrym gefrunon:
The great kings' renown have heard of,

Hu ðа æþelingas ellen fremendon.
How those princes bravery displayed.

from *Beowulf*
Anonymous

A thousand years ago, that's what the English language looked like. Today, because of the changes in the language over time, it is impossible to read Old English without special training. However, it is still possible to make out many words. Compare the following words:

MODERN ENGLISH	OLD ENGLISH
come	cuman
fiend	feond
folk	folc
heaven	heofon
holy	halig
king	cyning
love	lufu
mind	mynd
see	seon
sit	sittan
work	weorc
what	hwæt

As you see, there are many Old English words that you can still recognize. A thousand years from now, speakers of English or of a language descended from it will probably be able to recognize a few words from the language that you speak today.

Middle English

Middle English, which developed from 1100 to 1500, was strongly influenced by the Norman French language spoken by the ruling class after the Norman Conquest of Britain in 1066. As a result of the borrowings from French that began in the Medieval Period, today it is almost impossible to write an English paragraph without using many words of French origin.

EXAMPLES

French words

assembly	boutique	debut	fatigue	forfeit
government	parlor	parquet	property	

Modern English

The version of English that we use today, known as **Modern English**, emerged in the two-hundred-year period from roughly 1400 to 1600. Of great importance to the development of the language currently spoken was the introduction by scholars during the early Modern period of thousands of new words from Latin and Greek.

EXAMPLES

Latin words

benign	creed	flex	grateful	lateral
levity	mentor	museum	script	

Greek words

benefit	character	crisis	esophagus	exist
geriatric	hegemony	icon	psyche	

In addition to borrowing from Latin and Greek, early Modern English borrowed heavily from other European languages, especially from French, Spanish, and Italian.

USAGE tip

Etymology is the study of the origins of words and how they evolved. When you look up a word in the dictionary the etymology of the word is given in brackets: *pasta [It (Italian), fr. (from) LL (Late Latin)].*

EXAMPLES

French words

cache	coupon	entrance	fillet
limousine	mustache	technique	trophy

Spanish words

alligator	avocado	embargo	guitar
platinum	vanilla		

Italian words

artichoke	grotto	motto	opera
porcelain	portfolio	spaghetti	villa

American English

Beginning around 1600, the English colonization of North America resulted over time in the creation of a distinct American dialect. The English language we speak today in the United States has developed and changed as we have adopted new pronunciations and spellings of words and borrowed words from the languages of other peoples of our country, such as American Indians, African Americans, Asian Americans, and immigrants from around the world, to form our own unique **American English** language.

EXAMPLES

African words

banana	cola	kudu	mamba
voodoo	yam	zombie	

American Indian words

chipmunk	hickory	kayak	maize
peccary	savanna		

Arabic words

admiral	alcohol	alcove	coffee
magazine	saluki	sash	zero

Chinese words

chow	kowtow	kung fu	
tea	yen		

East Indian words

bandanna	cheetah	curry	jungle
pajamas	sari	shampoo	yoga

Japanese words

bonsai	hibachi	judo	kamikaze
kudzu	origami	samurai	

FORMAL AND INFORMAL ENGLISH

To write or speak effectively, you must choose your language according to your audience, purpose, and the occasion or situation. **Formal English** contains carefully constructed, complete sentences; avoids contractions; follows standard English usage and grammar; uses a serious tone; and uses sophisticated vocabulary. **Informal English** contains everyday speech and popular expressions, uses contractions, and may include sentence fragments. Formal English is appropriate for school essays, oral or written reports, interviews, and debates. Informal English is appropriate for conversations with friends, personal letters or notes, and journal entries.

EXAMPLES

formal English	I am very impressed with your new automobile.
informal English	That is one nice set of wheels you've got.

Standard English is the variety of the English language taught in English-language school systems and characterized by universally accepted and understood words, phrases, and pronunciations. Standard English enables all speakers of English to communicate and understand the spoken and written word in a common language.

Dialects

There are many different varieties of informal English, developed from the use of dialects, including slang, colloquialisms, and idioms. A **dialect** is a kind of English spoken by a particular group of people in a particular area or place. Dialects are characterized by differences in pronunciation, word choice, grammar, and accent. They are usually based on regional or social differences. In the United States, the major regional dialects are northern, southern, midland, and western. Everyone speaks with some type of dialect.

Differences in dialect show up especially in the terms people use to describe or refer to things. For example, depending on which region of the United States you live in, you may say the word *potato*, *tater*, or *spud* when referring to a starchy, edible tuber plant.

EXAMPLES

regional dialect	We found nary a cent inside the box.
standard English	We did not find any money in the box.

Writers sometimes use dialects in dialogue to make their characters' voices sound realistic. In the following excerpt from "The Outcasts of Poker Flat," notice how Bret Harte uses standard English for narration and a regional dialect for the character's voice.

> Mr. Oakhurst's calm, handsome face betrayed small concern of these indications. Whether he was conscious of any predisposing cause, was another question. "I reckon they're after somebody," he reflected; "likely it's me." He returned to his pocket the handkerchief with which he had been whipping away the red dust of Poker Flat from his neat boots, and quietly discharged his mind of any further conjecture.
>
> from "The Outcasts of Poker Flat"
> Bret Harte

Literature MODEL

Slang is a form of speech made up of invented words or existing words given a new meaning.

EXAMPLES
Can you dig it, dog?
We'll score a nice chunk of change from this gig!

USAGE tip

Keep in mind that slang is inappropriate language except for the most informal forms of writing or speaking, such as a personal note or an informal discussion.

A **colloquialism** is a word or phrase used in everyday conversation. An **idiom** is a common expression that has come to have a meaning different from the literal meaning of the individual words within the expression.

EXAMPLES

colloquialisms

This expedition was a **bust**.
I hope mother doesn't get **steamed** about the broken window.

idioms

There is more than one way to **skin a cat**.

Scott likes to make sure all his **ducks are lined up** before starting a project.

LANGUAGELINK
Print exercise worksheets or have students complete exercises online with the LanguageLINK CD.

Try It Yourself

EXERCISE 1

Identifying Formal and Informal English

Identify each of the following sentences as an example of formal or informal English.

1. We have been operating in the red since last January.
2. You can question Dane if you would like, but you are barking up the wrong tree.
3. When hiking after dark, be sure to apply a generous amount of bug repellent.
4. While watching Tino round the bases, Kerry realized he had gone to the well once too often with his fastball.
5. The voters rejected both bond issues that were on the ballot this year.
6. That man who lives across the street from you is a rare bird.
7. While tying my shoe, I spotted a silver dollar underneath the park bench.
8. Before you can help someone else, you need to put your own house in order.
9. Let's ditch your little brother and go cruise by the lake.
10. The neighbor was fit to be tied when she saw you hop the fence.

EXERCISE 2

Understanding Formal and Informal English

Revise to formal English the sentences in Exercise 1 that are written in informal English.

EXERCISE 3

Using Formal and Informal English in Your Writing

Write a dialogue between two new students who meet for the first time on the first day of school. Pretend that these students are from different places or regions of the country. In your dialogue, include at least two examples of slang, two examples of idioms, and at least one example of dialect. Use formal English in the narrative sections between the lines of dialogue. Be prepared to share your dialogue with a classmate.

EXERCISE 1
1. informal
2. informal
3. formal
4. informal
5. formal
6. informal
7. formal
8. informal
9. informal
10. informal

EXERCISE 2
Responses will vary.
Sample responses:
1. We have been operating with a deficit since last January.
2. You can question Dane if you would like, but that will not yield any useful information.
3. formal
4. While watching Tino round the bases, Kerry realized that he had thrown too many fastballs.
5. formal
6. That man who lives across the street from you is quirky.
7. formal
8. Before you can help someone else, you need clarity and stability in your own life.
9. Let's leave your little brother here and go for a ride by the lake.
10. The neighbor was very upset when she saw you climb over the fence.

APPROPRIATE USES OF ENGLISH

Language is a powerful and complex tool. What you say, and how you choose to say it, matters. Think about the great number and variety of messages you communicate in one day to friends, family members, classmates, teachers, and others. Language helps you to communicate the meaning of your message—whether in a chatty phone conversation with your best friend or in a persuasive editorial for your school newspaper. To communicate your messages effectively, however, you need to think about who your audience is and make choices, such as whether to use formal or informal language. You also need to consider whether other elements—such as sarcasm or slang—are appropriate and how they might affect your message.

Consider the following examples. Which do you think would be appropriate to communicate to a group of friends, and which would be appropriate to communicate in a book review in your local newspaper?

EXAMPLES

Dig this! I just read a kickin' book! It's called *The Time Machine.* H. G. Wells is where it's at when it comes to science fiction. The world he creates is filled with gnarly creatures. You need to jump on this book before the summer ends.

The novel *The Time Machine* tells a compelling story about what Earth could be like in the distant future. The book, written by H. G. Wells, remains a science fiction classic, despite its having been written over 100 years ago. Wells's vivid descriptions place his readers in a world over 800,000 years from today.

As the examples illustrate, the audience and your purpose for writing will shape the language you use to communicate your message. Before writing or talking about your topic, ask yourself these questions:

EXERCISE 3

Responses will vary. Students' dialogues should include at least two examples of slang, two examples of idioms, and at least one example of dialect. Most likely, students will use examples of informal English in the scene's dialogue. Students should use formal English in the narrative portion of the scene.

EXERCISE 4
Responses will vary. Same responses:

1. a toast at a relative's wedding reception—humorous, teasing but complimentary language
2. an e-mail to a sibling—informal, highly personal language; private; spontaneous
3. a set of directions to your house—clear, brief, highly specific, sequential
4. a letter praising the work of a crew that painted your house—clear and direct; explanatory; respectful, complimentary description
5. a letter to a manufacturer explaining why you are returning a product—clear, respectful but gently critical, specific in requesting action
6. an editorial for your town newspaper—persuasive; serious and detailed; informative about the debated issue; formal language but directed at an audience of peers
7. an e-mail requesting information—clear and direct language; brief
8. a list of items to bring on a weekend trip—brief, specific, highly informal
9. a Web page for jai alai players—informative and engaging; helpful to jai alai players
10. an amusing anecdote—relatively short; playful, somewhat informal use of language

- What is my purpose for communicating? (to inform? to entertain? to persuade?)
- Who is my audience?
- What are the audience members' ages, backgrounds, values, and interests?
- What does the audience already know about the topic?
- What do they need to know about the topic?

Try It Yourself

EXERCISE 4

Understanding Appropriate Language

Consider each example of communication listed below. Then in your own words, describe for each the kind of language you would use that would be appropriate to the audience and purpose.

EXAMPLE
a historical essay about the Reconstruction era
(formal language; informative; logically organized; complete sentences; serious tone)

1. a toast at a relative's wedding reception
2. an e-mail to a sibling
3. a set of directions to your house
4. a letter praising the work of a crew that painted your house
5. a letter to a manufacturer explaining why you are returning a product
6. an editorial for your town newspaper
7. an e-mail requesting information
8. a list of items to bring on a weekend trip
9. a Web page for jai alai players
10. an amusing anecdote

EXERCISE 5

Using Appropriate Language in Your Writing

Write two separate paragraphs reviewing a book you've recently read. In the first paragraph, use language appropriate to peers with similar cultural references and reading interests. In the second paragraph, use language appropriate to an older audience, such as a parent, who might be unfamiliar with the book. In both cases, try to persuade your audience to read the book.

EXERCISE 5

Responses will vary. In the first paragraph, students should use language appropriate for peers who share cultural references and reading interests. In the second paragraph, students should use language appropriate for an older audience, such as a parent, who might be unfamiliar with the book. In both cases, students should try to persuade the audience to read the book. You might invite some students to read their paragraphs aloud and discuss as a class the differences in appropriate language for the two audiences.

REGISTER, TONE, DICTION, AND VOICE

Have you ever heard the terms *upper*, *middle*, and *lower register* in music? In a slow, jazzy tune, for example, the lower register is more appropriate than the high, brassy register. The term *register* has a similar application in the English language.

Register refers to language appropriate for a specific relationship between people. For example, when talking with a friend, you speak in a register that is warm, open, and informal. When speaking to a young child, you speak in a register that is nonthreatening and simple to understand. When speaking with a parent or other adult, you probably use a register that is warm, but respectful. By suiting the register you use to the specific situation and audience, you will neither offend someone by being too familiar, nor puzzle or confuse your friends by being too formal.

Tone is a writer's or speaker's attitude toward a subject and an audience. A writer shapes the tone of the message by carefully choosing words and phrases that convey his or her feelings about the topic. The tone of the following excerpt, for example, written by Robert E. Lee to his soldiers, conveys the general's admiring attitude.

Literature
MODEL

I need not tell the survivors of so many hard-fought battles, who have remained steadfast to the last, that I have consented to this result from no distrust of them; but, feeling that valor and devotion could accomplish nothing that could compensate for the loss that would have attended the continuation of the contest, I have determined to avoid the useless sacrifice of those whose past services have endeared them to their countrymen. . . .

You will take with you *the satisfaction that proceeds from the consciousness of duty faithfully performed*; and I earnestly pray that a merciful God will extend to you his blessing and protection. With an unceasing admiration of your constancy and devotion to your country, and a grateful remembrance of your kind and generous consideration of myself, I bid you an affectionate farewell.

from "Farewell to His Army"
Robert E. Lee

Mostly, a writer's tone is determined by **diction**, or choice of words. By using specific nouns and verbs, a writer shapes the tone as well as the meaning of his or her words. Compare the following two examples. How does the use of the specific noun and verb change the tone and meaning of the sentence?

USAGE tip

A writer's voice usually takes years of experience and practice to develop. Don't be discouraged, though. Write honestly and choose your words carefully, and your voice will shine through.

EXAMPLES

general	The **man walked** down the stairs to the dark cellar.
specific	The **thief sidled** down the stairs to the dark cellar.

Voice refers to a writer's personal style. Voice—the collective effect of many elements, including diction and tone—makes a written work unique and tells you that one person in particular wrote it. Read the following two excerpts, each of which discusses writer Zora Neale Hurston, the first by Hurston herself and the second by a well-known contemporary American author.

But I am not tragically colored. There is no great sorrow dammed up in my soul, nor lurking behind my eyes. I do not mind at all. I do not belong to the sobbing school of Negrohood who hold that nature somehow has given them a lowdown dirty deal and whose feelings are all hurt about it. Even in the helter-skelter skirmish that is my life, I have seen that the world is to the strong regardless of a little pigmentation more or less. No, I do not weep at the world—I am too busy sharpening my oyster knife.

from "How It Feels to Be Colored Me"
Zora Neale Hurston

After all, with her pen she had erected a monument to the African-American and African-AmerIndian common people both she and I are descended from. After reading Hurston, anyone coming to the United States would know exactly where to go to find the remains of a culture that kept Southern black people going through centuries of white oppression. They could find what was left of the music; they could find what was left of the speech; they could find what was left of the dancing . . . they could find what was left of the work, the people's relationship to the earth and to animals; they could find what was left of the orchards, the gardens, and the fields; they could find what was left of the prayer.

from "The Resurrection of Zora Neale Hurston and Her Work"
Alice Walker

Literature MODELS

Try It Yourself

EXERCISE 6

Understanding Register, Tone, Diction, and Voice

In language appropriate for the school literary magazine, write a paragraph comparing and contrasting the register, tone, diction, and voice in the two excerpts printed above from Zora Neale Hurston and Alice Walker.

EXERCISE 6
Responses will vary. Sample response:
Both excerpts discuss Zora Neale Hurston's connection with racial issues. The excerpt from Alice Walker has a respectful, admiring tone, which celebrates her literary achievements. The excerpt from Zora Neale Hurston is written with a playful but determined tone. Walker's diction, or word choice, is meant to inspire awe ("with her pen she had erected a monument") and respect ("they could find what was left of the prayer"). In comparison, the simple but personal diction ("I am not tragically colored" and "I do not weep at the world") in the Hurston passage creates a tone that is playful, yet inspiring ("I am too busy sharpening my oyster knife").

EXERCISE 7
Responses will vary. Students' paragraphs should reflect an understanding of register, tone, diction, and voice. You might invite students to read their paragraphs aloud and analyze the register, tone, diction, and voice created in each.

EXERCISE 7

Using Register, Tone, Diction, and Voice in Your Writing

Interview a classmate about his or her interests, family, travels, habits, and plans for the future. Then write two separate paragraphs describing the individual. In each paragraph, use register, tone, and diction to create a unique voice—as if each paragraph were written by a different author. Have the classmate you interviewed then select the paragraph that he or she believes best describes him or her.

FIGURATIVE LANGUAGE

Language that suggests a meaning beyond or different from the literal meanings of the words is called **figurative language**. A **figure of speech** is meant to be understood imaginatively instead of literally. Many writers, especially poets, use figures of speech to create vivid, memorable images and to help readers see and understand things in new ways. Think about the difference in meaning in the following two examples.

EXAMPLES

literal meaning	George **raced** his pacer car around the track.
figurative meaning	George's heart **raced** with excitement as he opened the letter.

In the first sentence, the verb *raced* conveys its literal meaning "to cause to run, move, or go swiftly." In the second sentence, the verb is used figuratively to illustrate the emotional effect of an anticipated event.

Three common figures of speech are **simile, metaphor,** and **personification.**

A **simile** compares one thing with another using the word *like* or *as*. What two things are being compared in each of the following similes?

EXAMPLES

The cat crept toward its supper dish **like** a lion stalking its prey.

With this new padlock installed, our cellar will be as secure **as** a medieval castle.

USAGE tip

Some similes are overused and become clichés, such as "He is as quiet as a mouse," "She was as happy as a clam," or "It was an cold as ice." Avoid using clichés in your writing.

A **metaphor** compares one thing to another without using the word *like* or *as*. In a metaphor, one thing is spoken or written about as if it were another. Metaphors can be especially helpful when describing difficult or abstract ideas, such as love, joy, sorrow, truth, and so forth.

EXAMPLES

Her sense of dread was a dark shadow that trailed her wherever she went.

Dozens of responsibilities crowded me, threatening to knock me down.

Personification is a figure of speech in which something not human—an animal, object, place, or idea—is given human qualities and characteristics.

EXAMPLES

The stars awake at night, blinking their luminous eyes.

As we crossed the desert, the sun gazed relentlessly at us.

Try It Yourself

EXERCISE 8

Identifying Figurative Language in Literature

Identify at least three figures of speech in the following excerpt as simile, metaphor, or personification. Then tell what two things are being compared in the simile or metaphor. Also tell what is being personified and what human characteristics or features have been given to nonhumans.

EXERCISE 8

Responses will vary. Sample responses:

1. metaphor: "with the balanced heaviness and lightness of a pendulum in a grandfather clock"

> She was very old and small and she walked slowly in the dark pine shadows, moving a little from side to side in her steps, with the balanced heaviness and lightness of a

CONTINUED

2. simile: "like the chirping of a solitary little bird"
3. personification: "that seemed meditative"
4. In the metaphor, the woman's gait is compared to a pendulum. In the simile, the tapping of the cane is compared to the chirping of a solitary bird. The tapping cane is also personified; it is described as meditative.

pendulum in a grandfather clock. She carried a thin, small cane made from an umbrella, and with this she kept tapping the frozen earth in front of her. This made a grave and persistent noise in the still air, that seemed meditative like the chirping of a solitary little bird. . . . Her eyes were blue with age. Her skin had a pattern all its own of numberless branching wrinkles and as though a whole little tree stood in the middle of her forehead, but a golden color ran underneath, and the two knobs of her cheeks were illumined by a yellow burning under the dark.

from "A Worn Path"
Eudora Welty

EXERCISE 9
1. personification
2. simile
3. metaphor
4. simile
5. personification/ metaphor
6. personification
7. simile

EXERCISE 9
Identifying Figurative Language in Literature

Tell what figure of speech is used in each of the following excerpts: *simile*, *metaphor*, or *personification.*

1. The yellow fog that rubs its back upon the window panes. . . . —from "The Love Song of J. Alfred Prufrock" by T. S. Eliot
2. Mother whose heart hung humble as a button / On the bright splendid shroud of your son. . . . —from "Do not weep, maiden, for war is kind" by Stephen Crane
3. I believe a leaf of grass is no less than the journey-work of the stars. . . . —from "Song of Myself" by Walt Whitman
4. Love set you going like a fat gold watch. —from "Morning Song" by Sylvia Plath
5. How much the timid poem needs / the mindless explosion of your rage. . . . —from "For the Last Wolverine" by James Dickey
6. Acres of sunflowers brighten the land in summer, their heads alert, expectant. —from "Seeing" by Kathleen Norris
7. Her face is closed as a nut, / closed as a careful snail. . . . —from "House Guest" by Elizabeth Bishop

8. The spotted hawk swoops by and accuses me, he complains of my gab and my loitering. —from "Song of Myself" by Walt Whitman
9. into that rushing beast of the night. . . . —from "The Starry Night" by Anne Sexton
10. And the muscles of his brawny arms / Are strong as iron bands. —from "The Village Blacksmith" by Henry Wadsworth Longfellow

8. personification
9. metaphor
10. simile

EXERCISE 10

Understanding Figurative Language

Write a sentence that describes each thing by using a simile, metaphor, or personification as directed.

EXAMPLE
mountain (personification)
(As we approached the mountain, it stared us down, daring us to climb its rocky slope.)

1. dancer (simile)
2. rain (personification)
3. fear (metaphor)
4. conversation (metaphor)
5. furnace (personification)
6. laborers (simile)
7. regret (personification)
8. water (metaphor)
9. headache (simile)
10. time (simile)

EXERCISE 10
Responses will vary. Sample responses:
1. The dancer floated like a dust mote across the stage.
2. The rain ran its long, cool fingers through the trees.
3. Her chronic fear was a ball and chain that she carried through life.
4. Their conversation was a dance of words and laughter.
5. Downstairs, the furnace threw another temper tantrum.
6. The laborers toiled like beasts in the summer heat.
7. Every now and then, regret tapped her on the shoulder.
8. Water is the elixir of life.
9. His headache gripped him like a steel clamp, refusing to let go.
10. Time is like a hurried friend who forever arrives too early for a date.

EXERCISE 11

Using Figurative Language in Your Writing

Write a descriptive paragraph in which you recount to a friend a difficult task that you completed as part of a group. Include descriptions of the others in the group, the tools/materials you used, and any hindrances to your group's progress. In the paragraph, use at least two examples each of simile, metaphor, and personification.

EXERCISE 11
Responses will vary. Students should use two examples each of simile, metaphor, and personification in their descriptive paragraphs.

THE IMPORTANCE OF GRAMMAR AND SYNTAX

Grammar is something you know, even if you have never studied it. Inside the head of every person is a sophisticated device that works, all by itself, to learn how to put words and phrases together grammatically. Read this sentence:

Skiers filled frosty slope cold wind spread a snowy tentacles over a with.

Does it make sense to you? The sentence is muddled because it doesn't follow the rules of English grammar and syntax. You probably already know more about grammar and syntax than you think you do; otherwise you wouldn't be able to communicate and make your meaning clear. You have already learned, unconsciously, many thousands of rules governing how words can be put together and how they can't.

When you study grammar, what you are really learning is not the grammar of the language—for the most part, that's something you already know. What you are learning is terminology for describing what you know so that you can more consciously and effectively communicate with others.

Grammar refers to the rules and conventions for organizing words into meaningful sentences. **Syntax** refers to the order of the words in the sentences, or *word order*. When the words in the nonsensical sentence are reorganized according to the rules of grammar and syntax, then the sentence conveys a clear meaning.

EXAMPLE

Skiers filled frosty slope cold wind spread a snowy tentacles over a with.

A frosty wind spread cold tentacles over a snowy slope filled with skiers.

Different languages have different rules about word order. In the English language, most sentences follow the word order of subject-verb-object. In contrast, other languages such as German and Japanese place the verb at the end of a sentence.

EXAMPLES

A frosty **wind** (subject) **spread** (verb) cold **tentacles** (object) over a snowy slope filled with skiers.

Jeff (subject) **volunteers** (verb) his **time** (object) as a mentor.

As you can see, grammar and syntax make the meaning of a sentence clear. Word order in a sentence can affect or change meaning, too. Consider how the different word order in the following two sentences affects meaning.

EXAMPLES

The batter struck the ball.
The ball struck the batter.

The use of modifiers is also ruled by grammar and syntax. In the English language, adjectives usually come before the noun or pronoun they modify.

EXAMPLES

She found his **tattered orange** baseball cap.
The **menacing** cloud of insects harried the **weary** travelers.

Try It Yourself

EXERCISE 12

Understanding Grammar and Syntax

Reorganize the word order in the following sentences so that each makes sense.

EXAMPLE

The tripped Joseph cat sleeping over.
(Joseph tripped over the sleeping cat.)

1. Inside burning firefighters the rushed building.
2. Sinking shark lifeboat ominously circled the hungry the sleek.
3. Plagued drought Midwest extreme the.
4. Lost into a the compound dog wandered.
5. Incriminating the executive shredded greedy the documents.
6. Jet the Jerry boarded and jumbo Iris.
7. Porch found I ring a diamond underneath the.
8. Route another take the snake caused us to hissing.
9. Afternoon shed the painted yesterday wooden they.
10. The dog brother already her youngest fed overweight.

EXERCISE 12
1. Firefighters rushed inside the burning building.
2. The hungry, sleek shark ominously circled the sinking lifeboat.
3. Extreme drought plagued the Midwest.
4. A lost dog wandered into the compound.
5. The greedy executive shredded the incriminating documents.
6. Jerry and Iris boarded the jumbo jet.
7. I found a diamond ring underneath the porch.
8. The hissing snake caused us to take another route.
9. They painted the wooden shed yesterday afternoon.
10. Her youngest brother fed the already overweight dog.

EXERCISE 13
Using Grammar and Syntax Correctly

Write at least three sentences using only the following words. Then discuss how different word order in each sentence affects meaning.

1. frightened
2. the bird
3. the cat
4. stalked
5. imposing

EXERCISE 13
Responses will vary. Students' sentences should include at least three of these five different word orders:

The imposing cat stalked the frightened bird.

The imposing bird stalked the frightened cat.

The frightened cat stalked the imposing bird.

The frightened bird stalked the imposing cat.

The imposing bird frightened the stalked cat.

UNIT 1 REVIEW

TEST YOUR KNOWLEDGE

EXERCISE 1

Identifying Formal and Informal English

Identify each of the following sentences as an example of either formal or informal English. (10 points)

EXAMPLE
Can you dig it? (informal)

1. I'm going to hit the hay when this show is over.
2. Before leaving on your trip, remember to check the oil in the car.
3. The flowerbeds look much better after they have been watered.
4. This new Tom Petty CD rules!
5. After finishing the test, Marcia gathered her books and walked home.
6. Aunt Bessie's behavior has been rather squirrelly, don't you think?
7. Are you picking up on what I'm laying down?
8. Randy is as cool as a cucumber when driving in heavy traffic.
9. A bird flew in the window and landed on the piano.
10. Peel me off another Benjamin will you?

EXERCISE 1
1. informal
2. formal
3. formal
4. informal
5. formal
6. informal
7. informal
8. informal
9. formal
10. informal

EXERCISE 2

Identifying Figurative Language

Tell whether each of the following sentences contains an example of simile, metaphor, or personification. (10 points)

EXAMPLE
The abandoned home sagged with the weight of loneliness. (personification)

EXERCISE 2
1. simile
2. personification
3. simile
4. simile
5. metaphor
6. personification
7. metaphor
8. simile
9. personification
10. simile

1. Unfortunately, Sam's negative attitude spread through the team like a flu virus.
2. The campfire's warmth enveloped us in its soft, glowing arms.
3. Like winged dancers, a trio of butterflies fluttered above the purple blossoms.
4. The wrinkles on the old storyteller's face were as deep and craggy as ancient rivers.
5. Experience and education are the currency most valued in the working world.
6. The river meandered across the state, pausing here and there to take in the scenery.
7. Summer is a ripening peach, delicious and sweet, then gone.
8. With his pen as his weapon, he retaliated with a sharp response.
9. The fox cub, suddenly shy, did not accept our offer of strawberries.
10. Her heart was like an ice cube, cold and hard one moment, melting the next.

EXERCISE 3
Responses will vary.
Sample responses:
1. We will be in trouble if we do not meet our sales quota this month.
2. If you turn on the electricity, the Christmas tree will light up.
3. At the meeting, we presented the idea to the committee, but it was rejected.
4. Wouldn't you like to know what is happening behind that closed door?
5. It is very hot outside today.

EXERCISE 3

Understanding Formal and Informal English

Revise each of the following sentences so that it is written in formal English. (20 points)

EXAMPLE
It's a dependable car, but it will cost you an arm and a leg.
(It's a dependable car, but it will cost a great deal of money.)

1. Heads will roll if we do not meet our sales quota this month.
2. If you turn on the juice, the Christmas tree will light up.
3. At the meeting, we floated the idea by the committee, but it quickly sank.
4. Wouldn't you like to be a fly on the wall behind that closed door?
5. You could fry an egg on the sidewalk today.

6. Investigators quickly discovered that Kenneth had been cooking the books.
7. Do you think that I was born yesterday?
8. My dad hit the roof when he saw last month's phone bill.
9. Hey, chill out, okay?
10. At the office tomorrow, I plan to hit the ground running.

EXERCISE 4
Understanding Figurative Language
Write a simile or metaphor describing each of the following things by comparing it with something else. (20 points)

EXAMPLE
talent *(Talent is a seed that needs to be watered and fed.)*

1. appetite
2. harmony
3. brothers and sisters
4. despair
5. grasshopper
6. ice storm
7. running water
8. hope
9. misunderstanding
10. a secret

EXERCISE 5
Understanding the Importance of Grammar and Syntax
Revise the word order in the following sentences so that each makes sense. (20 points)

EXAMPLE
Lost for pen the searched we. *(We searched for the lost pen.)*

6. Investigators discovered that Kenneth engaged in illegal accounting practices.
7. Do you think I am that naive?
8. My dad became very upset when he saw last month's phone bill.
9. Relax, all right?
10. At the office tomorrow, I plan to start on my work right away.

EXERCISE 4
Responses will vary. Each sentence should use either a simile or a metaphor to describe each item.

EXERCISE 5
Responses may vary slightly. Sample responses:
1. A pungent odor caught our attention.
2. He mowed his neighbor's weedy and overgrown backyard.
3. The exhausted dancer gazed appreciatively at the applauding audience.
4. Angry hornets disrupted our picnic along the riverbank.
5. The inexperienced new employee made several mistakes on his first day.
6. A glowing harvest moon floated above the horizon.

7. Five rats scurried across the floor of the abandoned building.
8. Voters showed only an apathetic interest in the election.
9. A gusty wind lifted my homework into the sky.
10. She arrived safely home sometime after midnight.

1. Attention odor a caught our pungent.
2. Weedy mowed his and he backyard neighbor's overgrown.
3. Appreciatively applauding at dancer exhausted the gazed the audience.
4. Riverbank our the along disrupted hornets angry picnic.
5. First his mistakes on day employee new the made several inexperienced.
6. Moon above floated harvest a horizon the glowing.
7. Building floor the the of across rats scurried five abandoned.
8. Interest the election voters apathetic showed only in an.
9. Wind a sky my lifted the homework into gusty.
10. Sometime midnight after home arrived she safely.

EXERCISE 6
Responses will vary. Students should use appropriate language in their letters. They should write in a natural voice that strikes a balance between formal and informal language. The letters should be written in an admiring yet respectful tone and use at least two different examples of figurative language.

EXERCISE 6

Using Appropriate Language in Your Writing

Write a letter to the editor nominating someone in your community for the local newspaper's annual "Person of the Year" contest. In a respectful and admiring tone, describe your nominee's contributions to the community, and explain why he or she is qualified to win the award. Use at least two different examples of figurative language to describe the person and his or her accomplishments. (20 points)

PART TWO

grammar

UNIT 2 THE SENTENCE

ASSESSMENT
Grammar Pretests and Comprehensive Tests are available at www.emcp.com.

UNIT OVERVIEW

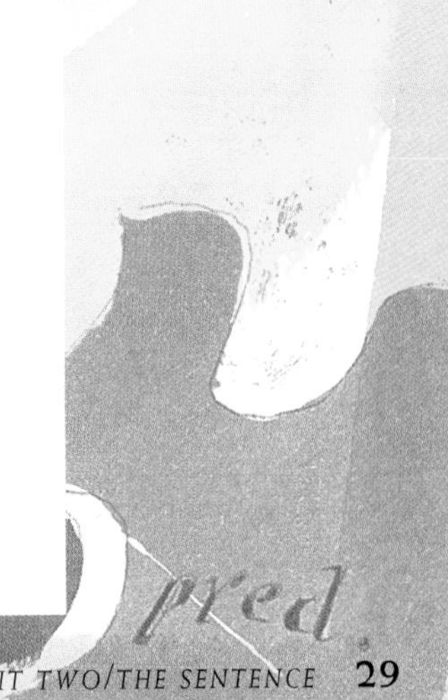

THE SENTENCE

THE SENTENCE: THE BASIC BUILDING BLOCK OF THE ENGLISH LANGUAGE

From the time you entered school, you probably have been speaking and writing in sentences. In the English language, the sentence is the basic unit of meaning.

A **sentence** is a group of words that expresses a complete thought. Every sentence has two basic parts: a subject and a predicate. The **subject** tells whom or what the sentence is about. The **predicate** tells information about the subject—what the subject is, what the subject does, or what happens to the subject.

EXAMPLE

sentence	An etymologist	specializes in the origins and historical development of words.
	(subject)	**(predicate)**

A group of words that does not have both a subject and a predicate is called a **sentence fragment**. A sentence fragment does not express a complete thought.

EXAMPLES

sentence fragment	Mrs. Buchanan. (The fragment does not have a predicate. The group of words does not answer the question *What did Mrs. Buchanan do?*)
sentence fragment	Presented a slide show. (The fragment does not have a subject. The group of words does not answer the question *Who presented a slide show?*)

CONTINUED

sentence fragment	About Modern art. (The fragment does not have a subject or predicate. The group of words does not tell what the sentence is about or what the subject does.)
complete sentence	Mrs. Buchanan presented a slide show about Modern art.

Try It Yourself

EXERCISE 1

Identifying Sentences and Sentence Fragments

Identify each of the following groups of words as either a complete sentence or a sentence fragment. Write *S* for sentence or *F* for fragment.

1. Jogging through the park will help you release stress from the day's worries.
2. Could very well lead you into a spiral of credit card debt.
3. For many young people, the game of golf has been revitalized by Tiger Woods.
4. Seeking a new challenge.
5. Soccer season begins at the start of the school year.
6. A curriculum that stresses fitness and a positive self-image.
7. Available either at the bookstore or online.
8. Call Adam.
9. The ability to understand, reflect, and respond.
10. They were known as the "Three Graces" in Greek mythology.

EXERCISE 1
1. S
2. F
3. S
4. F
5. S
6. F
7. F
8. S
9. F
10. S

LANGUAGELINK
Print exercise worksheets or have students complete exercises online with the LanguageLINK CD.

EXERCISE 2

Understanding Sentences and Their Basic Parts

Some of the following groups of words are missing a subject or predicate or both. Tell what part is missing; then revise the sentence to include the missing part. If the group of words contains both a subject and a predicate, write *sentence*.

EXERCISE 2
Revised sentences will vary.
1. subject missing
2. sentence
3. subject missing
4. subject and predicate missing
5. sentence
6. subject and predicate missing
7. predicate missing
8. subject missing
9. sentence
10. sentence

EXAMPLE
Courageously throughout the night.
(subject and predicate missing; *The volunteers battled the flood waters* courageously throughout the night.)

1. Heard splashing in the basement.
2. Emily feared the worst.
3. Believes she should investigate if any damage has been done.
4. Before opening the door.
5. She noticed her sofa floating, unbelievably, near the door.
6. Cold, murky water.
7. For the rest of this gloomy morning.
8. Sat in the rocking chair and waited.
9. Discovering water in the basement is a depressing way to start the day.
10. It was a long and difficult week.

EXERCISE 3
Responses will vary. Each sentence in students' paragraphs should contain a subject and a predicate.

EXERCISE 3
Using Complete Sentences in Your Writing
Write a first-person column for your school newspaper describing a recent weather occurrence, such as a storm, a flood, or a heat wave. Where were you at the time? What damage occurred? How did the event affect you? What do you think citizens can do to prepare for such an event in the future? Make sure that each sentence in your paragraph contains a subject and predicate.

FUNCTIONS OF SENTENCES

There are four different kinds of sentences: *declarative*, *interrogative*, *imperative*, and *exclamatory*. Each kind of sentence has a different purpose. You can vary the tone and mood of your writing by using the four different sentence types. Read the example sentences aloud and notice how your voice changes to express each sentence's different meaning.

- A **declarative sentence** makes a statement. It ends with a period.

EXAMPLE
Pete will be traveling to Europe this summer.

- An **interrogative sentence** asks a question. It ends with a question mark.

EXAMPLE
Does he have an updated passport?

- An **imperative sentence** gives an order or makes a request. It ends with a period or an exclamation mark. An imperative sentence has an understood subject. The understood subject is often *you*.

EXAMPLES
(You) Tell Pete that he needs a passport.
(You) Please remind him.

- An **exclamatory sentence** expresses strong feeling. It ends with an exclamation mark.

EXAMPLE
Hey, I'm finally going to Europe!

Try It Yourself

EXERCISE 4

Identifying Different Kinds of Sentences in Literature

Identify each of the seven sentences in the literature passage as *declarative*, *interrogative*, *imperative*, or *exclamatory*.

> That man over there says that women need to be helped into carriages, and lifted over ditches, and to have the best place everywhere. Nobody ever helps me into carriages, or over mud-puddles, or gives me any best place! And ain't I a woman? Look at me! Look at my arm! I have ploughed and planted, and gathered into barns, and no man could head me! And ain't I a woman?
>
> from "Ain't I a Woman?"
> Sojourner Truth

EXERCISE 4

1. That man over there says that women need to be helped into carriages, and lifted over ditches, and to have the best place everywhere. (declarative)
2. Nobody ever helps me into carriages, or over mud-puddles, or give me any best place! (exclamatory)
3. And ain't I a woman? (interrogative)
4. Look at me! (imperative)

Literature MODEL

5. Look at my arm! (imperative)
6. I have ploughed and planted, and gathered into barns, and no man could head me! (exclamatory)
7. And ain't I a woman? (interrogative)

EXERCISE 5
Understanding the Functions of Sentences

Identify the following sentences as *declarative*, *imperative*, *interrogative*, or *exclamatory*. Then revise each sentence according to the directions in parentheses.

EXAMPLE
Will we be studying Sojourner Truth's autobiography this week? (Change into a declarative sentence.)
(interrogative—declarative; *We will be studying Sojourner Truth's autobiography this week.*)

1. Tell me what Sojourner Truth's given name was. (Change into an interrogative sentence.)
2. Did Sojourner Truth travel extensively, speaking for the abolition of slavery and women's rights? (Change into a declarative sentence.)
3. Will you read her autobiography, *Narrative of Sojourner Truth: A Northern Slave?* (Change into an imperative sentence.)
4. I think Sojourner Truth's speech must have had a tremendous impact on the audience. (Change into an exclamatory sentence.)
5. Identify the colloquial expressions that she uses in her speech. (Change into an interrogative sentence.)
6. Sojourner Truth was put up for auction as a slave when she was only nine years old! (Change into a declarative sentence.)
7. Did you know that she could neither read nor write? (Change into an exclamatory sentence.)
8. Please explain Sojourner Truth's arguments for women's rights. (Change into an interrogative sentence.)
9. This speech was given at a women's rights convention in 1851. (Change into an interrogative sentence.)
10. You might want to create a time line illustrating major events in the suffrage movement. (Change into an imperative sentence.)

EXERCISE 5
Sentence revisions will vary.
Sample responses:
1. imperative; interrogative sentence: What was Sojourner Truth's given name?
2. interrogative; declarative sentence: Sojourner Truth traveled extensively, speaking for the abolition of slavery and women's rights.
3. interrogative; imperative sentence: Read her autobiography, *Narrative of Sojourner Truth: A Northern Slave.*
4. declarative; exclamatory sentence: Sojourner Truth's speech must have had a tremendous impact on the audience!
5. imperative; interrogative sentence: Will you identify the colloquial expressions that she uses in her speech?
6. exclamatory; declarative sentence: Sojourner Truth was put up for auction as a slave when she was only nine years old.
7. interrogative; exclamatory sentence: She could neither read nor write!
8. imperative; interrogative sentence: What were Sojourner Truth's arguments for women's rights?
9. declarative; interrogative sentence: Was this speech given at a women's rights convention in 1851?
10. declarative; imperative sentence: Create a time line illustrating major events in the suffrage movement.

EXERCISE 6

Using Different Kinds of Sentences in Your Writing

Write a brief article about a historical figure you greatly admire. Describe when the person lived and his or her accomplishments and characteristics. Also include two questions you wish you could ask the person about his or her life and times. Use all four kinds of sentences in your article. Then take turns with your classmates reading your articles aloud. Consider how the four kinds of sentences make your articles more expressive.

EXERCISE 6
Responses will vary. Students should use all four kinds of sentences to write their paragraphs.

SUBJECTS AND PREDICATES: THE BASIC BUILDING BLOCKS IN A SENTENCE

Just as the sentence is the basic building block of the English language, the subject and predicate are the basic building blocks in a sentence. Every sentence has two basic parts: a subject and a predicate. The **subject** tells whom or what the sentence is about. The **predicate** tells information about the subject—what the subject is, what the subject does, or what happens to the subject.

EXAMPLE

sentence	My stubborn brother	apologized finally for the mistake.
	(subject)	**(predicate)**

To find the subject, ask who or what performs the action of the verb.

Who apologized for the mistake? (*my stubborn brother*, subject)
What did the stubborn brother do? (*apologized finally for the mistake*, predicate)

EXERCISE 7
A **counterswirl** | **had caught** Farquhar and **turned** him half round; **he** | **was** again **looking** into the forest on the bank opposite the fort. The **sound** of a clear, high voice in a monotonous

MODEL

singsong | now **rang** out behind him and **came** across the water with a distinctness **that** | **pierced** and **subdued** all other sounds, even the beating of the ripples in his ears. Although no soldier, **he** | **had frequented** camps enough to know the dread significance of that deliberate, drawling, aspirated chant; the **lieutenant** on shore | **was taking** a part in the morning's work.

EXERCISE 8
Responses will vary. Students' sentences should contain a subject and a predicate as well as any further details needed to create complete sentences.

Try It Yourself

EXERCISE 7
Identifying Subjects and Predicates in Literature
Write each sentence from the literature passage and draw a vertical line between the subject and predicate.

> A counterswirl had caught Farquhar and turned him half round; he was again looking into the forest on the bank opposite the fort. The sound of a clear, high voice in a monotonous singsong now rang out behind him and came across the water with a distinctness that pierced and subdued all other sounds, even the beating of the ripples in his ears. Although no soldier, he had frequented camps enough to know the dread significance of that deliberate, drawling, aspirated chant; the lieutenant on shore was taking a part in the morning's work.
>
> from "An Occurrence at Owl Creek Bridge"
> Ambrose Bierce

EXERCISE 8
Understanding Subjects and Predicates
Write a sentence for each subject or predicate listed, adding the missing part and any other details to create a clear, complete sentence.

1. The whirling water below the bridge
2. Every student in the eleventh grade
3. Were tossed into the recycling bin
4. A bouquet of zinnias, daisies, and larkspur
5. Someone you've never met before
6. Finds loose change on the sidewalk
7. The tapping of branches against the windowpanes
8. Wore a sweater made of pink cotton
9. Persuaded us to volunteer
10. Hesitates before answering a question

EXERCISE 9

Using Subjects and Predicates in Your Writing

Write a short letter to a pen pal in which you describe a chance event that has somehow affected your life, whether in a small or large way. Make sure each sentence includes a subject and predicate.

EXERCISE 9

Responses will vary. Each sentence should include a subject and predicate; the overall paragraph should clearly describe a chance event and the impact—whether small or large—that the event has had on the student's life.

SIMPLE AND COMPLETE SUBJECTS AND PREDICATES

In a sentence, the **simple subject** is the key word or words in the subject. The simple subject is usually a noun or a pronoun and does not include any modifiers. The **complete subject** includes the simple subject and all the words that modify it.

The **simple predicate** is the key verb or verb phrase that tells what the subject does, has, or is. The **complete predicate** includes the verb and all the words that modify it.

In the following sentence, a vertical line separates the complete subject and complete predicate. The simple subject is underlined once. The simple predicate is underlined twice.

EXAMPLE

(complete subject)		(complete predicate)
A fast-moving river with clear blue water	|	blocked our progress through the forest.

USAGE tip

Every word in a sentence is part of a complete subject or complete predicate.

Sometimes, the simple subject is also the complete subject, and the simple predicate or verb is also the complete predicate.

EXAMPLE

Hours | passed.

USAGE tip

The complete subject can be replaced by a single pronoun—*I, you, he, she, it, we,* or *they.*

To find the simple subject and simple predicate in a sentence, first break the sentence into its two basic parts: complete subject and complete predicate. Then, identify the simple predicate by asking yourself, "What is the action of this sentence?" Finally, identify the simple subject by asking yourself, "Who or what is performing the action?"

In the following sentences, the complete predicate is in parentheses. The simple predicate, or verb, appears in boldface. Remember, verbs may have more than one word, and as many as four.

EXAMPLES

one-word verb A man with a moustache (**listens** at the library door.)

two-word verb A man with a moustache (**is listening** at the library door.)

three-word verb A man with a moustache (**has been listening** at the library door.)

four-word verb A man with a moustache (**might have been listening** at the library door.)

EXERCISE 10

1. The campaign staff | has worked for two weeks on this important speech.
2. Pollsters | canvassed the city seeking to gauge public opinion.
3. Voter apathy | may have begun to appear at the last election.
4. Inspired supporters | eagerly volunteered to support the campaign.
5. Patriotic songs | are played at the start of the rally.
6. A popular hometown sports hero, Jack Samson, | is selected to introduce the candidate.
7. Political coverage | has been increasing in the local newspapers.
8. The candidate's detractors | have become increasingly vocal during the last week.

Try It Yourself

EXERCISE 10

Identifying Simple and Complete Subjects and Predicates

Draw a vertical line between the complete subject and predicate in each sentence. Then, underline once the simple subject. Underline twice the simple predicate or verb.

EXAMPLE

The politician on the stage | waved to her cheering supporters.

1. The campaign staff has worked for two weeks on this important speech.
2. Pollsters canvassed the city seeking to gauge public opinion.
3. Voter apathy may have begun to appear at the last election.
4. Inspired supporters eagerly volunteered to support the campaign.
5. Patriotic songs are played at the start of the rally.
6. A popular hometown sports hero, Jack Samson, is selected to introduce the candidate.
7. Political coverage has been increasing in the local newspapers.
8. The candidate's detractors have become increasingly vocal during the last week.

9. More than two thousand citizens assembled at the town square for the rally.
10. The politician spoke for over an hour about her foreign policy concerns.

9. More than two thousand citizens | assembled at the town square for the rally.
10. The politician | spoke for over an hour about her foreign policy concerns.

EXERCISE 11

Understanding Simple and Complete Subjects and Predicates

Each of the following sentences contains a simple subject and predicate. Revise each sentence by adding details to the simple subject and predicate to create a more specific and clearer sentence. Then draw a vertical line between the complete subject and predicate you've created. Underline once the original simple subject. Underline twice the original simple predicate.

EXAMPLE
Ships sailed.
(Ships belonging to the British Navy | sailed across the Atlantic Ocean.)

1. The river swelled.
2. A balloon was floating.
3. The soldiers might have been hoping.
4. Flowers bloom.
5. The candles are melting.
6. Lights have been beaming.
7. Expectations heightened.
8. Visitors will be arriving.
9. Leah laughs.
10. The mystery might have been solved.

EXERCISE 11
Students' revisions of original sentences will vary. Students should add adjectives, adverbs, and prepositional phrases to create detailed sentences.

1. The river | swelled.
2. A balloon | was floating.
3. The soldiers | might have been hoping.
4. Flowers | bloom.
5. The candles | are melting.
6. Lights | have been beaming.
7. Expectations | heightened.
8. Visitors | will be arriving.
9. Leah | laughs.
10. The mystery | might have been solved.

EXERCISE 12

Using Simple and Complete Subjects and Predicates in Your Writing

Imagine that the editor of your school literary magazine has asked you to write a mystery or suspense story. Write your first paragraph, adding details to simple subjects and predicates to help your readers visualize the subject and the action.

EXERCISE 12
Responses will vary. Students' opening paragraphs should demonstrate their understanding of how to build on simple subjects and predicates to create complete subjects and predicates that help readers picture the subject and action that is taking place.

COMPOUND SUBJECTS AND PREDICATES

A sentence may have more than one subject or predicate. A **compound subject** has two or more simple subjects that have the same predicate. The subjects are joined by the conjunction *and*, *or*, or *but*. A **compound predicate** has two or more simple predicates, or verbs, that share the same subject. The verbs are connected by the conjunction *and*, *or*, or *but*.

EXAMPLES

compound subject

Richard and Lois | jogged through the park.

compound predicate

Four playful dolphins | splashed and swam around the boat.

The conjunctions *either* and *or* and *neither* and *nor* can also join compound subjects or predicates.

EXAMPLES

compound subject

Either Ann *or* Nancy | plays a guitar solo at the end of the concert.

Neither Germany *nor* France | sent representatives to the conference.

compound predicate

They | *either* shredded *or* burned the incriminating evidence.

The alert guard | *neither* saw *nor* heard anything unusual.

A sentence may also have a compound subject and a compound predicate.

EXAMPLE

compound subject and compound predicate

Tammy and Patti | mowed the lawn and trimmed the hedges.

Try It Yourself

EXERCISE 13

Identifying Compound Subjects and Predicates

Underline once all of the simple subjects in each sentence. Underline twice all of the simple predicates in each sentence. Then tell whether the sentence has a compound subject, compound predicate, or compound subject and predicate.

EXAMPLE
The baseball player drove to the stadium and walked down the corridor. (Compound predicate)

1. The ballplayer enters the stadium, brushes past the autograph seekers, and takes batting practice.
2. "The Slump" was written by John Updike and published in *Esquire* magazine in 1968.
3. The coach and the newspaper reporters blame the ballplayer's slump on his reflexes.
4. As the ball flies toward the plate, the batter sees it in vivid detail and even identifies details such as the pitcher's thumbprint.
5. In Florida, the ballplayer and his wife lie on the beach and imagine the sun as a high fly ball.
6. Opposing pitchers and catchers are confident about the game and their respective teams.
7. Philosophy and reflection have not helped the batter with his slump.
8. The player's hunger for the game blurs, skips, and fades.
9. John Updike graduated from Harvard and joined the staff of the *New Yorker* magazine.
10. *Rabbit, Run* and *The Poorhouse Fair* are two of Updike's early works.

EXERCISE 13
1. The ballplayer enters the stadium, brushes past the autograph seekers, and takes batting practice. Compound predicate
2. "The Slump" was written by John Updike and published in *Esquire* magazine in 1968. Compound predicate
3. The coach and the newspaper reporters blame the ballplayer's slump on his reflexes. Compound subject
4. As the ball flies toward the plate, the batter sees it in vivid detail and even identifies details such as the pitcher's thumbprint. Compound predicate
5. In Florida, the ballplayer and his wife lie on the beach and imagine the sun as a high fly ball. Compound subject and compound predicate
6. Opposing pitchers and catchers are confident about the game and their respective teams. Compound subject
7. Philosophy and reflection have not helped the batter with his slump. Compound subject
8. The player's hunger for the game blurs, skips, and fades. Compound predicate
9. John Updike graduated from Harvard and joined the staff of the *New Yorker* magazine. Compound predicate
10. *Rabbit, Run* and *The Poorhouse Fair* are two of Updike's early works. Compound subject

EXERCISE 14

Responses may vary slightly.

Sample responses:

1. Denmark Vesey and Nat Turner resisted slavery by organizing revolts.
2. Many Northerners and some Southerners opposed slavery.
3. William Lloyd Garrison and Frederick Douglass published newspapers calling for the end of slavery.
4. Slaves were fed meagerly, whipped, and separated from their families.
5. In 1852, Harriet Beecher Stowe's novel *Uncle Tom's Cabin* became a bestseller and helped turn Northern public opinion against slavery.
6. The Missouri Compromise, the Compromise of 1850, and the Kansas-Nebraska Act were attempts to keep the Union together.
7. Stephen Douglas, Abraham Lincoln, John Breckinridge, and John Bell ran for president in 1860.
8. Slavery's spread to the territories and its continued existence in the states were big issues in the election.
9. Eleven states seceded from the Union and formed a separate nation called the Confederate States of America.
10. Robert E. Lee initially opposed secession, but he did not want to fight against his home state of Virginia and therefore became a general in the Confederate Army.

EXERCISE 14

Using Compound Subjects and Predicates to Combine Sentences

Combine each pair of short, choppy sentences by joining simple subjects, simple predicates, or both with the appropriate conjunction. Remember to change other parts of the sentence so that they agree with the combined subjects or verbs.

EXAMPLE

In the 1800s, many people in the North moved to the cities. They also worked in factories.

(In the 1800s, many people in the North moved to the cities and worked in factories.)

1. Denmark Vesey resisted slavery by organizing a revolt. Nat Turner also started a slave revolt.
2. Many Northerners opposed slavery. Some Southerners did, too.
3. William Lloyd Garrison published a newspaper calling for the end of slavery. Another abolitionist paper was started by Frederick Douglass.
4. Slaves were fed meagerly. They were also whipped and separated from their families.
5. In 1852, Harriet Beecher Stowe's novel *Uncle Tom's Cabin* became a bestseller. It helped turn Northern public opinion against slavery.
6. The Missouri Compromise and the Compromise of 1850 were attempts to keep the Union together. The Kansas-Nebraska Act was another attempt to avoid a civil war.
7. Stephen Douglas and Abraham Lincoln ran for president in 1860. John Breckinridge and John Bell also sought the nation's highest office that year.
8. Slavery's spread to the territories was a big issue in the election. Slavery's continued existence in the states also interested voters.

9. Eleven states seceded from the Union. They formed a separate nation called the Confederate States of America.
10. Robert E. Lee initially opposed secession. He did not want to fight against his home state of Virginia and became a general in the Confederate Army.

EXERCISE 15

Using Compound Subjects and Compound Predicates in Your Writing

Write a letter to a pen pal in a foreign country and describe a local or national political issue that interests you. In your paragraph, explain why you find this issue relevant and describe the opinions of your peers. Use compound subjects and compound predicates to vary your sentence structure and to remove short sentences that might cause choppiness in your writing.

EXERCISE 15
Responses will vary. Students' letters should explain why they find the issue relevant, as well as what their peers think about the issue. They should use compound subjects and compound predicates to vary their sentence structure.

SENTENCE STRUCTURES: SIMPLE, COMPOUND, COMPLEX, AND COMPOUND-COMPLEX SENTENCES

A **clause** has a subject and a verb. An **independent clause** expresses a complete thought and can stand alone; a **subordinate clause** doesn't express a complete thought and can't stand alone. A **simple sentence** consists of one independent clause and no subordinate clauses. It may have a compound subject and a compound predicate. It may also have any number of phrases. A simple sentence is sometimes called an independent clause because it can stand by itself.

EXAMPLES

The author Richard Wright was born on a farm in Mississippi.

Wright and the young schoolteacher shared a love for stories.

Wright graduated as valedictorian of his high school class, moved to Chicago, and worked with the Federal Writers' Project.

A **compound sentence** consists of two sentences joined by a semicolon or by a coordinating conjunction and a comma. Each part of the compound sentence has its own subject and verb. The most common coordinating conjunctions are *and*, *or*, *nor*, *for*, *but*, *so*, and *yet*.

EXAMPLES

Wright's autobiography *Black Boy* was published in 1945; it is considered to be his most important work.

He had a difficult childhood of poverty, **but** he found escape, release, and inspiration in literature.

A **complex sentence** consists of one independent clause and one or more subordinate clauses. The subordinate clauses in the following examples are underlined.

EXAMPLES

Before he moved to New York, Richard Wright lived and worked in Chicago.

Whenever Wright sought refuge in fiction, his grandmother disapproved because she considered novels to be "the Devil's work."

If you combine a compound sentence and a complex sentence, you form a **compound-complex sentence**. This kind of sentence must have two or more independent clauses and at least one subordinate clause. In the following examples, the subordinate clauses are underlined.

EXAMPLES

Ella, who lived with Wright and his grandmother, read stories aloud, but she stopped when Mrs. Wright stepped onto the porch.

Reading, which Wright's grandmother feared, enthralled the young boy, and he vowed to buy and read every novel that had been published.

Try It Yourself

EXERCISE 16

Identifying Simple, Compound, Complex, and Compound-Complex Sentences in Literature

Label each of the following sentences in the literature passage as *simple*, *compound*, *complex*, or *compound-complex*.

She whispered to me the story of *Bluebeard and His Seven Wives* and I ceased to see the porch, the sunshine, her face, everything. As her words fell upon my new ears, I endowed them with a reality that welled up from somewhere within me. She told how Bluebeard had duped and married his seven wives, how he had loved and slain them, how he had hanged them up by their hair in a dark closet. The tale made the world around me be, throb, live. As she spoke, reality changed, the look of

CONTINUED

MODEL

EXERCISE 16

1. She whispered to me the story of *Bluebeard and His Seven Wives* and I ceased to see the porch, the sunshine, her face, everything. (compound)
2. As her words fell upon my new ears, I endowed them with a reality that welled up from somewhere within me. (complex)
3. She told how Bluebeard had duped and married his seven wives, how he had loved and slain them, how he had hanged them up by their hair in a dark closet. (complex)
4. The tale made the world around me be, throb, live. (simple)
5. As she spoke, reality changed, the look of things altered, and the world became peopled with magical presences. (compound-complex)

Literature MODEL

6. My sense of life deepened and the feel of things was different, somehow. (compound)
7. Enchanted and enthralled, I stopped her constantly to ask for details. (simple)

8. My imagination blazed. (simple)
9. The sensations the story aroused in me were never to leave me. (complex)
10. When she was about to finish, when my interest was keenest, when I was lost to the world around me, Granny stepped briskly onto the porch. (complex)

things altered, and the world became peopled with magical presences. My sense of life deepened and the feel of things was different, somehow. Enchanted and enthralled, I stopped her constantly to ask for details. My imagination blazed. The sensations the story aroused in me were never to leave me. When she was about to finish, when my interest was keenest, when I was lost to the world around me, Granny stepped briskly onto the porch.

from *Black Boy*
Richard Wright

EXERCISE 17
Responses will vary. They should pay close attention to all elements specified in the directions.

EXERCISE 17
Understanding Sentence Structure

Write sentences containing the elements described in each of the directions below.

1. simple sentence with simple subject and simple predicate
2. simple sentence with compound subject and compound predicate
3. compound sentence using conjunction *and*
4. compound sentence using conjunction *yet*
5. compound sentence with one independent clause having a compound subject and the other independent clause having a compound predicate
6. compound sentence using semicolon
7. complex sentence using one independent and one subordinate clause
8. complex sentence using one independent and two subordinate clauses
9. compound-complex sentence using two independent and one subordinate clause
10. compound-complex sentence using two independent and two subordinate clauses

EXERCISE 18

Using Different Sentence Structures in Your Writing

For a special section in your school newspaper titled "Defining Moments," write a vivid description of a defining moment in your life. Include the circumstances, the other people involved (if any), and the feelings and emotions you experienced at the time. Use a variety of simple, compound, complex, and compound-complex sentences in your description.

EXERCISE 18
Responses will vary. They should include circumstances, people, feelings, and emotions to create a vivid description of the moment. Students should use a variety of sentence structures in their descriptions.

ASSESSMENT
Grammar Pretests and Comprehensive Tests are available at www.emcp.com.

UNIT 2 REVIEW

TEST YOUR KNOWLEDGE

EXERCISE 1
1. sentence
2. sentence
3. sentence fragment
4. sentence
5. sentence
6. sentence fragment
7. sentence fragment
8. sentence fragment
9. sentence
10. sentence fragment

EXERCISE 1
Identifying Sentences
Identify each of the following groups of words as either a *sentence* or a *sentence fragment*. (10 points)

EXAMPLE
Yesterday is forgotten. (sentence)

1. I was so embarrassed.
2. Who knocked?
3. Hoping for an opportunity and a better life.
4. After all the commotion and disruption passed, we ate.
5. Don't forget to write!
6. The first software glitch of the day.
7. Everyone in the crowded, stuffy auditorium.
8. A great day for scientists around the globe.
9. It left a lasting impression.
10. Because we really need to understand.

EXERCISE 2
Identifying the Functions of Sentences
Identify each of the following sentences as *declarative*, *imperative*, *interrogative*, or *exclamatory*. (10 points)

EXAMPLE
Bernard Malamud's renown as a writer rests on his short stories. (declarative)

EXERCISE 2
1. declarative
2. imperative
3. exclamatory
4. interrogative

1. In the story an antihero searches for love with the help of a matchmaker.
2. Never mind!
3. These arrangements are ridiculous!
4. Which Yiddish folk tales influence Malamud's stories?

5. High expectations often clash with the harsh realities of life.
6. Matchmaking is Pinye Salzman's profession.
7. You cannot be serious!
8. Why does Leo reject Sophie, Lily, and Ruth?
9. This story will explore the nature of love.
10. Listen to his good news.

EXERCISE 3
Identifying Simple and Complete Subjects and Predicates

Draw a vertical line between the complete subject and predicate. Then underline once the simple subject, and underline twice the simple predicate. (10 points)

EXAMPLE
Novelist and short story writer Nathaniel Hawthorne | was born in Salem, Massachusetts.

1. Hawthorne's ancestors participated in the Salem witch trials in the seventeenth century.
2. Hawthorne met Henry Wadsworth Longfellow at Bowdoin College in Maine.
3. Franklin Pierce, who later became president of the United States, also knew Hawthorne at Bowdoin.
4. After graduating, Hawthorne studied the Puritans and published short story collections.
5. You probably have not heard of *Fanshawe*, his first novel.
6. For a few years, Hawthorne worked as a surveyor at the Salem Customs House.
7. The novel *The Scarlet Letter* eventually became Hawthorne's best-known work.
8. Many of his later works were written for children.
9. In 1853, President Pierce appointed his old friend American counsel at Liverpool and Manchester, England.
10. Hawthorne died in 1864, leaving several of his works unfinished.

5. declarative
6. declarative
7. exclamatory
8. interrogative
9. declarative
10. imperative

EXERCISE 3

1. Hawthorne's ancestors | participated in the Salem witch trials in the seventeenth century.
2. Hawthorne | met Henry Wadsworth Longfellow at Bowdoin College in Maine.
3. Franklin Pierce, who later became president of the United States, | also knew Hawthorne at Bowdoin.
4. After graduating, Hawthorne | studied the Puritans and published short story collections.
5. You | probably have not heard of *Fanshawe*, his first novel.
6. For a few years, Hawthorne | worked as a surveyor at the Salem Customs House.
7. The novel *The Scarlet Letter* | eventually became Hawthorne's best-known work.
8. Many of his later works | were written for children.
9. In 1853, President Pierce | appointed his old friend American counsel at Liverpool and Manchester, England.
10. Hawthorne | died in 1864, leaving several of his works unfinished.

EXERCISE 4
1. simple
2. compound
3. complex
4. compound
5. compound
6. compound-complex
7. simple
8. compound
9. compound
10. complex

EXERCISE 4

Identifying Simple, Compound, Complex, and Compound-Complex Sentences

Label each of the following sentences as *simple*, *compound*, *complex*, or *compound-complex*. (10 points)

EXAMPLE
Jamestown, founded in 1607, was the first English colony in North America to survive. (simple)

1. Sailing several hundred years before Christopher Columbus, the Norse Vikings were the first Europeans to reach North America.
2. Seeking to find a shorter travel route to Asia, Columbus received funding from Spain, and he sailed across the Atlantic in 1492.
3. Believing that he had reached India, Columbus called the people he met on the Caribbean islands "Indians."
4. Spain claimed much of North and South America in the 1500s, but other European powers would soon challenge them for supremacy.
5. Hoping to acquire wealth, English settlers established a colony on the coast of North America in 1587, but it mysteriously disappeared in less than three years.
6. The Virginia Colony started to grow in the early 1600s, and large numbers of Puritans, who broke away from the Church of England, settled in Massachusetts in the 1630s.
7. The arrival of Europeans brought hardship and destruction to the Native Americans.
8. Settlers drove tribes from their ancestral lands, and European diseases wiped out millions of Native Americans.
9. Columbus Day stirs controversy each October, for many people today view his voyage in 1492 as a great disaster.
10. Historians often disagree with each other when they interpret important events of the past.

EXERCISE 5

Understanding Subjects and Predicates

Tell whether the subject, predicate, or both subject and predicate are missing from the following groups of words. Then revise each group to include the missing part or parts. (20 points)

EXAMPLE

Found a dime. (missing subject; *The boy found a dime.*)

1. Inside the empty stadium
2. Two of the most mischievous boys
3. Saw it on the evening news
4. A most impressive display of power
5. Oppressive heat of the attic
6. Five simple directions
7. Dwell in a damp cave
8. CDs from my uncle's collection
9. On a minor detail of little consequence
10. Four hundred houses in the city

EXERCISE 6

Understanding Different Kinds of Sentences

Write sentences containing the elements described in each of the directions below. Underline subject elements once, and underline predicate elements twice. (20 points)

EXAMPLE

simple subject *(His presentation was inspiring.)*

1. simple sentence
2. compound subject
3. compound predicate
3. compound subject and compound predicate
4. compound sentence using conjunction *yet*
5. compound sentence using conjunction *for*
6. compound sentence using conjunction *and*
7. compound sentence using semicolon

EXERCISE 5

Responses will vary. Sample responses:

1. Missing subject and predicate: The coach walked inside the empty stadium.
2. Missing predicate: Two of the most mischievous boys climbed a tree during recess.
3. Missing subject: Geoff saw it on the evening news.
4. Missing predicate: A most impressive display of power could be seen at the ballpark today.
5. Missing subject and predicate: We quickly escaped the oppressive heat of the attic.
6. Missing predicate: Five simple directions were posted on the bulletin board.
7. Missing subject: Your cousins dwell in a damp cave.
8. Missing predicate: CDs from my uncle's collection will provide the music for the party.
9. Missing subject and predicate: Marie was focused on a minor detail of little consequence.
10. Missing predicate: Four hundred houses in the city collapsed in the earthquake.

EXERCISE 6

Responses will vary. Students should write a sentence indicative of each sentence element. They should also identify the subject with a single underscore and the predicate with a double underscore.

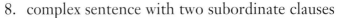

8. complex sentence with two subordinate clauses
9. complex sentence with three subordinate clauses
10. compound-complex sentence with two independent and two subordinate clauses

EXERCISE 7

Responses will vary. Students' narratives should recreate the learning of the lesson or the impact of the lesson. Students should have made every effort to include at least two examples of the eight different kinds of sentences in their essays, thereby reflecting a successful attempt at sentence variety.

EXERCISE 7

Using Different Kinds of Sentences in Your Writing

Imagine that you are a Big Brother or a Big Sister to a student in the sixth grade and that you want him or her to learn from your experiences. Write a brief personal narrative about a lesson you had to learn the hard way and how learning this lesson affected your life. Explain who or what was involved in the experience and when, where, and why it occurred. In your narrative, include at least two examples of each of these kinds of sentences: declarative, interrogative, imperative, and exclamatory; and simple, compound, complex, and compound-complex. (20 points)

UNIT 3 THE PARTS OF SPEECH

ASSESSMENT
Grammar Pretests and Comprehensive Tests are available at www.emcp.com.

UNIT OVERVIEW

THE PARTS OF SPEECH

IDENTIFYING THE PARTS OF SPEECH

Each word in a sentence performs a basic function or task. Words perform four basic tasks: they name, modify, express action or state of being, or link. By the arrangement of words in a sentence and the task that each word performs within a sentence, you can understand a sentence's meaning. To illustrate how parts of speech work together, try to decipher the following nonsense sentence.

EXAMPLE
A squirgishy rhodorum thanapoppop prantoloped on the lunashine's stratus.

What nonsense noun is the subject of the sentence? What adjectives modify the word *thanapoppop*? Which nonsense verb expresses the action in the sentence? Which noun is possessive?

If you substitute real words for the nonsense words, but keep the same arrangement of words, you can identify the nouns, verb, adjective, and adverb in the sentence.

EXAMPLE
A silver mechanical robot perambulated on the moon's surface.

There are eight different parts of speech. Each part of speech is defined in the following chart.

Part of Speech	Definition	Example
noun	A **noun** names a person, place, thing, or idea.	A frog-jumping **contest** provided excellent **material** for a humorous **tale.**
pronoun	A **pronoun** is used in place of a noun.	The inspector twirled **his** moustache as **he** kept **his** thoughts to **himself.**
verb	A **verb** expresses action or a state of being.	I **suspect** that you **nibble** on chocolate bars while you **work.**

CONTINUED

adjective	An **adjective** modifies a noun or pronoun. The most common adjectives are the articles *a, an,* and *the.*	**Plump** tomatoes hung from **tangled** vines in **the vegetable** garden.
adverb	An **adverb** modifies a verb, an adjective, or another adverb.	The gymnast **gracefully** executed an **extremely** difficult jump.
preposition	A **preposition** shows the relationship between its object—a noun or a pronoun—and another word in a sentence. Common prepositions include *after, around, at, behind, beside, off, through, until, upon,* and *with.*	Sitting on the corner, we waited **for** the marching band to come **down** the street.
conjunction	A **conjunction** joins words or groups of words. Common conjunctions are *and, but, for, nor, or, so,* and *yet.*	The weather has been **either** too hot **or** too dry, **so** many crops have been damaged.
interjection	An **interjection** is a word used to express emotion. Common interjections are *oh, ah, well, hey,* and *wow.*	**Say!** Haven't we met before?

Try It Yourself

EXERCISE 1

Identifying the Parts of Speech in Literature

Identify the part of speech of each underlined word in the following excerpt.

> "Oh, no, they're stuffed and preserved, dozens and dozens of them," said the ornithologist, "and I have shot or snared every one myself. I caught a glimpse of a white heron three miles from here on Saturday, and I have followed it in this direction. They have never been found in this district at all. The little white heron, it is," and he turned again to look at Sylvia with the hope of discovering that the rare bird was one of her acquaintances."
>
> from "A White Heron"
> Sarah Orne Jewett

EXERCISE 1

1. *Oh, no*—interjection
2. *dozens*—noun
3. *and*—conjunction
4. *of*—preposition
5. *them*—pronoun
6. *ornithologist*—noun

Literature
MODEL

7. *or*—conjunction
8. *myself*—pronoun
9. *caught*—verb
10. *glimpse*—noun
11. *white*—adjective
12. *three*—adjective
13. *from*—preposition
14. *Saturday*—noun
15. *it*—pronoun
16. *this*—adjective
17. *They*—pronoun

18. *in*—preposition
19. *district*—noun
20. *little*—adjective
21. *again*—adverb
22. *at*—preposition
23. *with*—preposition
24. *hope*—noun
25. *rare*—adjective
26. *one*—pronoun
27. *her*—pronoun
28. *acquaintances*—noun

EXERCISE 2
Responses will vary.

LANGUAGELINK
Print exercise worksheets or have students complete exercises online with the LanguageLINK CD.

EXERCISE 2

Understanding the Parts of Speech

Use each word and its designated part of speech in a sentence.

EXAMPLES

past (adverb)	*We walked past in a hurry, so we didn't notice the new shop.*
past (preposition)	*Practice often runs past dinnertime on week nights.*
past (noun)	*Stories about the past often offer insights about the present.*

1. inscribed (adjective); inscribed (verb)
2. through (preposition); through (adverb)
3. both/and (conjunction)
4. uniform (noun); uniform (adjective)
5. well (interjection)
6. themselves (pronoun)
7. question (noun); question (verb)
8. slight (adjective); slight (noun); slight (verb)
9. command (noun); command (verb)
10. quite (adverb)

EXERCISE 3
Responses will vary. Students' opening paragraphs should include and correctly use at least two examples of each of the eight parts of speech.

EXERCISE 3

Using the Parts of Speech in Your Writing

Write the opening paragraph for a children's book called *Stranger Things Have Happened.* The genre may be fiction, nonfiction, or fantasy. Begin your paragraph, "Who would have thought that . . ." Include at least two examples of each part of speech. Be prepared to share your paragraph with classmates.

GRAMMAR REFERENCE CHARTS

Parts of Speech Overview

Use these charts as a quick reference guide to different parts of speech, definitions, and examples.

Type of Noun	Definition	Examples
common noun	names a person, place, idea, or thing	siblings, highway, equality, examination
proper noun	names a specific person, place, or thing; begins with a capital letter	Saskia, Mississippi River, English horn
concrete noun	names a thing that can be touched, seen, heard, smelled, or tasted	linen, fog, conversation, cleanser, pineapple
abstract noun	names an idea, quality, concept, or feeling	peace, economy, Baroque, melancholy
singular noun	names one person, place, idea, or thing	mirror, scarf, bunch, pants
plural noun	names more than one person, place, idea, or thing	mirrors, scarves, bunches, pants
possessive noun	shows ownership or possession of things or qualities	*Bartlett's Familiar Quotations,* Holly's laughter, glass's reflection
compound noun	made up of two or more words	laptop, string bean, great-granddaughter
collective noun	names groups	pack, ensemble, cabinet

Type of Pronoun	Definition	Examples
personal pronoun	used in place of the name of a person or thing	I, me, we, us, he, she, it, him, her, you, they, them
singular pronoun	used in place of the name of one person or thing	I, me, you, he, she, it, him, her
plural pronoun	used in place of more than one person or thing	us, you, we, they, them
possessive pronoun	shows ownership or possession	my, mine, your, yours, his, her, hers, its, our, ours, their, theirs

CONTINUED

demonstrative pronoun	points out a specific person, place, idea, or thing	this, that, these, those
indefinite pronoun	points out a person, place, or thing, but not a particular or definite one	anyone, someone, anything, everyone, nobody, nothing many, any, some, none
reflexive pronoun	refers back to a noun previously used; adds *–self* and *–selves* to other pronoun forms	myself, herself, himself, itself, yourself, themselves, ourselves
intensive pronoun	emphasizes a noun or pronoun	me *myself,* he *himself,* you *yourself,* they *themselves,* we *ourselves*
interrogative pronoun	asks a question	who, whom, whose, which, what
relative pronoun	introduces an adjective clause	that, which, who, whom, whose, what

Type of Verb	Definition	Examples
action verb	names an action	complain, waddle, disappear, divide
helping verb	helps a main verb express action or a state of being	Leah *may* travel to Atlanta next week. Sam and Max *have been* taking guitar lessons.
linking verb	connects a noun with another noun, pronoun, or adjective that describes or identifies it; the most common linking verbs are formed from the verb *to be*	Jane Campion *was* the director of the film. That fashion model *looks* much too thin.
transitive verb	has a direct object	Katrina *studies* French and Spanish.
intransitive verb	does not have a direct object	Katrina is *studying* at the library.
irregular verb	has a different past tense form and spelling	catch/caught keep/kept swing/swung

Type of Adjective	Definition	Examples
adjective	modifies nouns and pronouns; answers the questions *what kind? which one? how many?* and *how much?*	*gusty* wind *minor* key *seventeen* years *one* penny
article	*a* and *an* refer to an unspecified person, place, thing, or idea; *the* refers to a specific person, place, thing, or idea	Let's ask *a* clerk for help. *An* honest answer would be appreciated. *The* play was fabulous.
proper adjective	is formed from proper nouns; is capitalized; often ends in *–n, –an, –ian, –ese,* or *–ish*	Russian language Burmese culture Byzantine Empire Scottish terrier Byronic characteristics

Type of Conjunction	Definition	Examples
coordinating conjunction	joins words or groups of words of equal importance; coordinating conjunctions are *and, but, for, nor, or, so, yet*	Maxine *and* Mary are identical twin sisters. They may look alike, *but* they have different interests.
correlative conjunction	word pairs that join words or groups of words; correlative conjunctions include *both/and, neither/nor, either/or*	However, *both* Maxine *and* Mary enjoy reading.
subordinating conjunction	introduces a subordinate clause and joins it to an independent clause; subordinating conjunctions include *after, although, as, as if, because, before, if, since, unless, till, when,* and *while*	*When* their schedules permit, the twins eat lunch together.

ASSESSMENT
Grammar Pretests and Comprehensive Tests are available at www.emcp.com.

EXERCISE 1
1. noun, preposition
2. noun, verb
3. adjective, adverb
4. pronoun, verb
5. preposition, adverb
6. pronoun, verb, adjective
7. adjective, adjective
8. adjective, noun
9. noun, adverb, conjunction
10. interjection, noun, pronoun

EXERCISE 2
1. noun—*Hemingway's;* noun—*stories,* adjective—*major;* noun—*Place,* adjectives—*a, Clean, Well-Lighted*
2. noun—*selection,* adjective—*the;* noun—*waiters,* adjective—*two;* noun—*café,* adjectives—*a, Spanish;* noun—*clients,* adjectives—*their, regular;* noun—*man,* adjectives—*an, elderly*

UNIT 3 REVIEW

TEST YOUR KNOWLEDGE

EXERCISE 1

Identifying the Parts of Speech

Identify the part of speech of each underlined word in the following sentences. (20 points)

EXAMPLE
Unusual for women of her time, Anne Bradstreet had the advantage of an education. (noun)

1. At the age of seventeen, Anne sailed to the New World with her husband, Simon Bradstreet.
2. Simon, a graduate of Cambridge University, became governor of the Bay Colony.
3. Because of a childhood illness, Anne was already in a weakened state when they arrived in Massachusetts.
4. Anne, who had begun writing poetry as a child, continued to write.
5. At first, Anne shared her poetry only with family and friends.
6. One of her poems is titled, "To My Dear and Loving Husband."
7. The poem begins with these words: "If ever two were one, then surely we."
8. The poem expresses the sustaining and transforming power of love.
9. Life in the New World was very difficult at times, but Anne lived to see her sixtieth birthday.
10. Alas, she did not live to see the publication of her second edition of poems.

EXERCISE 2

Identifying Nouns and Adjectives

Identify the nouns in the following sentences and any adjectives that modify them. (20 points)

EXAMPLE
Ernest Hemingway was part of the large community of expatriate artists and writers who lived in Europe.
(*Ernest Hemingway,* noun; *community,* noun, *large,* adjective; *artists, writers,* nouns; *expatriate,* adjective; *Europe,* noun)

1. Among Hemingway's major stories is "A Clean, Well-Lighted Place."
2. In the selection, two waiters at a Spanish café discuss one of their regular clients, an elderly man.
3. An internal monologue reveals the older waiter's private thoughts and his feelings about human existence.
4. Two important motifs are introduced in the opening sentences, and other references to them appear throughout the story.
5. After publishing three collections, Hemingway became one of America's most admired writers of short fiction.
6. Hemingway began his writing career as a reporter for a midwestern newspaper.
7. His short story collections include *The Fifth Column*, *Winner Take Nothing*, and *First Forty-Nine Stories.*
8. By stripping verbal interactions to their barest essentials, Hemingway produced the illusion of actual speech.
9. An eye problem prevented Hemingway from joining the American army, so he served as an ambulance driver with the Italian army.
10. Hemingway began his serious writing career after the war, when he returned to Europe as a journalist.

3. noun—*monologue,* adjectives—*an, internal;* noun—*waiter's,* adjectives—*the, older;* noun—*thoughts,* adjective—*private;* noun—*feelings,* noun—*existence,* adjective—*human*
4. noun—*motifs,* adjectives—*two, important;* noun—*sentences,* adjectives—*the, opening;* noun—*references,* adjective—*other;* noun—*story,* adjective—*the*
5. noun—*collections,* adjective—*three;* noun—*Hemingway;* noun—*America's;* adjective—*admired;* noun—*fiction,* adjective—*short*
6. noun—*Hemingway;* noun—*career,* adjective—*writing;* noun—*reporter,* adjective—*a;* noun—*newspaper,* adjectives—*a, midwestern*
7. noun—*collections,* adjective—*short story;* nouns—*The Fifth Column, Winner Take Nothing, First Forty-Nine Stories*
8. noun—*interactions,* adjective—*verbal;* noun—*essentials,* adjective—barest; noun—*Hemingway;* noun—illusion; noun—*speech,* adjective—*actual*
9. noun—*problem,* adjectives—*an, eye;* noun—*Hemingway;* noun—*army,* adjectives—*the, American;* noun—*driver,* adjective—*an, ambulance;* noun—*army,* adjectives—*the, Italian*
10. noun—*Hemingway;* noun—*career,* adjectives—*serious, writing;* noun—*war,* adjective—*the;* noun—*Europe;* noun—*journalist,* adjective—*a*

EXERCISE 3

1. adverb—*also,* modifies verb—*provided*
2. adverb—*highly,* modifies adjective—*experimental;* adverb—*characteristically,* modifies verb—*challenged*
3. adverb—*closely,* modifies verb—*related;* adverb—*such,* modifies adverb—*severe;* adverb—*severe,* modifies adjective—*economic*
4. adjective—*many,* modifies adjective—*interrelated*
5. adverb—*so,* modifies adverb—*appropriately;* adverb—*appropriately,* modifies verb—*called;* adverb—*truly,* modifies adjective—*modern*
6. adverb—*first,* modifies verb—*were featured*
7. adverb—*sometimes,* modifies verb—*called;* adverb—*artistically,* modifies verb—*were influenced;* adverb—*such,* modifies adjective—*Modernist*
8. adverb—*long,* modifies verb—*associated;* adverb—*daily,* modifies verb—*walked;* adverb—*away,* modifies verb—*had been thrown*
9. adverb—*best,* modifies adjective—*known*
10. adverb—*very,* modifies adverb—*effectively;* adverb—*effectively,* modifies verb—*were included*

EXERCISE 3

Understanding Adverbs

Identify the adverbs in the following sentences and tell whether they modify a verb, an adjective, or another adverb. (20 points)

EXAMPLE

The trilogy *U.S.A.* often is considered John Dos Passos's major contribution to Modernism.
(*often,* adverb; modifies verb *is considered*)

1. Like Hemingway, Dos Passos's wartime experiences also provided material for his writing.
2. Modernism, a highly experimental twentieth-century artistic movement, characteristically challenged traditional culture and art forms.
3. "Newsreel LXVIII," the third volume in *U.S.A.*, focuses on issues closely related to the Great Depression, when millions of Americans faced such severe economic hardship.
4. The trilogy is comprised of many interrelated stories and creates an epic portrait of American life.
5. Personal commentaries, so appropriately called "The Camera Eye," appear in the truly modern trilogy.
6. Newsreels were featured first in movie houses, before the advent of television.
7. Dos Passos's newsreels, sometimes called collages, were influenced artistically by the work of such Modernist painters as Picasso and Braque.
8. Kurt Schwitters—an artist long associated with the Dada movement—daily walked the streets, collecting trash that had been thrown away.
9. With this trash, Schwitters created his best known collages, which combined numerous visual and verbal elements.
10. Bits and pieces of popular culture were very effectively included in the works created by the Modernists.

EXERCISE 4

Understanding the Parts of Speech

Use each word and its designated part of speech in a sentence. (20 points)

EXAMPLE
but (conjunction)
(We searched for her lost contact lens, *but* we couldn't find it.)

1. shivering (adjective)
2. casually (adverb)
3. encouraged (verb)
4. Puerto Rican (adjective)
5. Sojourner Truth (noun)
6. yes (interjection)
7. reflected (verb)
8. painfully (adverb)
9. beneath (preposition)
10. valid (adjective)
11. flying (noun)
12. later (adverb)
13. yet (conjunction)
14. hey (interjection)
15. shadow (noun)
16. modern (adjective)
17. someone (pronoun)
18. troubled (adjective)
19. against (preposition)
20. express (verb)

EXERCISE 4
Responses will vary. Students should use each part of speech specified. In some cases, you may want to invite suggestions of other ways in which the word might be used in a sentence.

EXERCISE 5

Using the Eight Parts of Speech in Your Writing

Write a vivid description of an object, but do not name the object in the paragraph. From your description of the object's size, texture, purpose, and so forth, a peer reader should be able to identify the "mystery" object. In your description, use each of the eight parts of speech at least three times. (20 points)

EXERCISE 5
Responses will vary. Students should create a vivid description of a "mystery" object, using each of the eight parts of speech at least five times.

UNIT 4 NAMERS *Nouns*

UNIT OVERVIEW

ASSESSMENT
Grammar Pretests and Comprehensive Tests are available at www.emcp.com.

NAMERS: NOUNS

NOUNS

A **noun** is a part of speech that names a person, place, idea, or thing. In this unit, you'll learn about the different kinds of nouns and what they name.

EXAMPLES

people	Sabrina, photographer, tourist, daughter
places	garden, dining room, Algonquin Hotel, Minneapolis
ideas	theory, ambivalence, democracy, friendship
things	doorway, brook trout, sapphires, cantaloupe

USAGE tip

Every noun is:
- common or proper
- concrete or abstract
- singular or plural

Types of Nouns	Definition	Examples
common noun	names a person, place, idea, or thing	avocado, backpack, slippers, volunteer
proper noun	names a specific person, place, or thing; begins with capital letter	F. Scott Fitzgerald, Paris, *Tender Is the Night*
concrete noun	names a thing that can be touched, seen, heard, smelled, or tasted	plum, knickknack, allergy, fence post
abstract noun	names an idea, a theory, a concept, or a feeling	imagination, despair, understanding, respect
singular noun	names one person, place, idea, or thing	princess, sun room, calamity, bread loaf
plural noun	names more than one thing	princesses, sun rooms, calamities, bread loaves
possessive noun	shows ownership or possession of things or qualities	T. S. Eliot's, Miss Moore's, communities', hoaxes'
compound noun	made up of two or more words	birdseed, flight deck, attorney-at-law, ball-and-socket joint
collective noun	names groups	community, class, flock, tribe

COMMON AND PROPER NOUNS

The two basic kinds of nouns are *common nouns* and *proper nouns*. A **common noun** names *any* person, place, thing, or idea. Common nouns are usually not capitalized.

EXAMPLES

common nouns

any person	The **novelist** lived in Greenwich Village during the 1920s.
any place	Many bicyclists and joggers use the path along the **lakefront**.
any thing	Workers remained on the **assembly line** for nearly ten hours each day.
any idea	**Individualism** is a basic American ideal.

A **proper noun** names a *specific* person, place, or thing, and begins with a capital letter.

EXAMPLES

common nouns	poet, novel, dance
proper nouns	Edna St. Vincent Millay, *The Age of Innocence,* the Charleston

Try It Yourself

EXERCISE 1

Identifying Common and Proper Nouns in Literature

Identify the underlined nouns in the passage as either common or proper. Then identify each noun as a person, place, thing, or idea.

> On a damp afternoon in September of the following year a young man with his face burned to a deep copper glow got off a train at a city in Tennessee. He looked around anxiously, and seemed relieved when he found that there was no one in the station to meet him. He taxied to the best hotel in the city where he registered with some satisfaction as George O'Kelly, Cuzco, Peru.

CONTINUED

EXERCISE 1

1. *afternoon*—common, thing
2. *September*—proper, thing
3. *year*—common, thing
4. *man*—common, person
5. *face*—common, thing
6. *glow*—common, thing (or idea)
7. *train*—common, thing
8. *city*—common, place
9. *Tennessee*—proper, place
10. *station*—common, place
11. *hotel*—common, place
12. *satisfaction*—common, idea
13. *George O'Kelly*—proper, person
14. *Peru*—proper, place
15. *room*—common, place
16. *minutes*—common, thing
17. *window*—common, thing
18. *street*—common, place
19. *hand*—common, thing
20. *receiver*—common, thing
21. *number*—common, thing

Literature MODEL

22. *Miss Jonquil*—proper, person
23. *voice*—common, thing
24. *formality*—common, idea

Up in his room he sat for a few minutes at the window looking down into the familiar street below. Then with his hand trembling faintly he took off the telephone receiver and called a number.

"Is Miss Jonquil in?"

"This is she."

"Oh—" His voice after overcoming a faint tendency to waver went on with friendly formality.

from "The Sensible Thing"
F. Scott Fitzgerald

LANGUAGELINK
Print exercise worksheets or have students complete exercises online with the LanguageLINK CD.

EXERCISE 2
Responses will vary. Students should correctly capitalize their examples of proper nouns.

EXERCISE 2

Understanding Common and Proper Nouns

For each of the following common nouns, write two proper nouns on your own paper.

1. baseball team
2. river
3. newspaper
4. political party
5. philosopher
6. cathedral
7. island
8. historical era
9. actor/actress
10. galaxy
11. museum
12. author
13. restaurant
14. automobile
15. mythical character
16. continent
17. religion
18. clothing brand
19. desert
20. inventor

EXERCISE 3

Using Common and Proper Nouns in Your Writing

Assume that you are the author of a children's history book. Write a brief narrative that introduces an important era in American history, such as the Civil War, the Roaring Twenties, or the Great Depression. Provide information about some of the key figures of the era, as well as places where important events took place. In your description, underline and label five common nouns and five proper nouns. Notice how the use of proper nouns helps to make your description of the historical era more specific.

EXERCISE 3

Responses will vary. Each narrative should correctly use and identify at least five common nouns and five proper nouns.

CONCRETE AND ABSTRACT NOUNS

A **concrete noun** names a thing than can be touched, seen, heard, smelled, or tasted—something that can be perceived with any of your five senses.

An **abstract noun** names an idea, a theory, a quality, a feeling, or a characteristic—something that *cannot* be touched or seen.

EXAMPLES

concrete nouns	stranger, mailbox, canyon, echo
abstract nouns	poverty, delusion, independence, adoration

Try It Yourself

EXERCISE 4

Identifying Concrete and Abstract Nouns in Literature

Identify the underlined nouns in the following passage and indicate whether each is either concrete or abstract.

Literature MODEL

> Her face deeply moved him. Why, he could at first not say. It gave him the impression of youth—spring flowers, yet age—a sense of having been used to the bone, wasted; this came from the eyes, which were hauntingly familiar yet absolutely strange. He had a vivid impression that he had met her before, but try as he might he could not

CONTINUED

EXERCISE 4

1. *face*—concrete
2. *youth*—abstract
3. *flowers*—concrete
4. *age*—abstract
5. *sense*—abstract
6. *bone*—concrete
7. *eyes*—concrete
8. *impression*—abstract
9. *name*—concrete
10. *handwriting*—concrete
11. *beauty*—abstract
12. *feature*—concrete
13. *ladies*—concrete
14. *photographs*—concrete
15. *heart*—abstract (can also be concrete)
16. *light*—concrete
17. *realms*—abstract
18. *possibility*—abstract

place her although he could almost recall her name, as if he had read it in her own handwriting. No, this couldn't be; he would have remembered her. It was not, he affirmed, that she had an extraordinary beauty—no, though her face was attractive enough; it was that *something* about her moved him. Feature for feature, even some of the ladies of the photographs could do better; but she leaped forth to his heart—had *lived*, or wanted to—more than just wanted, perhaps regretted how she had lived—had somehow deeply suffered: it could be seen in the depths of those reluctant eyes, and from the way the light enclosed and shone from her, and within her, opening realms of possibility: this was her own.

from "The Magic Barrel"
Bernard Malamud

EXERCISE 5
Responses will vary. Sample responses:
1. success, security
2. friendship, trust
3. destruction
4. inspiration
5. journey
6. justice
7. splendor, fragility
8. communication
9. exuberance, power
10. life, freedom

EXERCISE 5
Understanding Concrete and Abstract Nouns

For each concrete noun in items 1–10, write an abstract noun that names an idea, quality, or characteristic with which the concrete noun can be associated. For each abstract noun in items 11–20, write a concrete noun that has the quality of the abstract noun.

EXAMPLES
cathedral (concrete); faith (abstract)
deceit (abstract); lie (concrete)

1. portfolio
2. handshake
3. tornado
4. candle
5. map
6. scale
7. crystal
8. telephone
9. waterfall
10. highway

11. wisdom
12. authority
13. perception
14. frugality
15. majesty
16. patriotism
17. gluttony
18. desolation
19. comfort
20. serenity

11. judge, owl
12. badge, parent
13. eyes
14. penny, miser
15. crown, velvet
16. flag
17. pig
18. desert
19. quilt, pillow
20. blue sky, yoga

EXERCISE 6

Using Concrete and Abstract Nouns in Your Writing

In the short story "The Magic Barrel," the main character undergoes an experience that helps him focus his thoughts about love. For a special Valentine's Day issue of the school literary magazine, write a paragraph in which you complete the statement, "Love [should/should not] be . . ." Use at least five concrete and five abstract nouns in your paragraph.

EXERCISE 6
Responses will vary. Students' paragraphs should include at least five concrete and five abstract nouns.

SINGULAR AND PLURAL NOUNS

Nouns that represent one person, place, idea, or thing are called **singular nouns.** Nouns that represent more than one person, place, idea, or thing are called **plural nouns.**

Most nouns can be made plural simply by adding *–s* to the end of the word. The spelling of some nouns changes slightly when the words are made plural, depending on how the word ends.

USAGE tip

Some nouns have the same spelling in both the singular and the plural forms, such as *sheep, moose, species,* or *catfish.* Other nouns form plurals in special ways, such as *men, geese,* or *oxen.*

EXAMPLES

plural nouns

For most nouns, to form the plural add *–s* to the end of the word.

calendar = calendars
patio = patios
course = courses
truth = truths

CONTINUED

If a noun ends in *s, sh, ch, x,* or *z,* add *–es.*

gloss = glosses | crash = crashes
twitch = twitches | hoax = hoaxes
waltz = waltzes | buzz = buzzes

If a noun ends in *o* preceded by a consonant, add *–es.*

hobo = hoboes | cargo = cargoes
tomato = tomatoes | echo = echoes

If a noun ends in *y* preceded by a consonant, change the *y* to *i* and add *–es.*

community = communities | frailty = frailties
lobby = lobbies | society = societies

For some nouns that end in *f* or *fe,* change the *f* to *v* and add *–es* or *–s.*

self = selves | leaf = leaves
knife = knives | hoof = hooves

EXERCISE 7
1. *musicians*—plural
2. *places*—plural
3. *stir*—singular
4. *anticipation*—singular
5. *interest*—singular
6. *rail*—singular
7. *grouping*—singular

Try It Yourself

EXERCISE 7

Identifying Singular and Plural Nouns in Literature

Identify the nouns in the following passage. Indicate whether they are singular or plural.

> When the musicians came out and took their places, she gave a little stir of anticipation, and looked with quickening interest down over the rail at that invariable grouping, perhaps the first wholly familiar thing that had greeted her eye since she had left old Maggie and her weakling calf. I could feel how all those details sank into her soul, for I had not forgotten how they had sunk into mine when I came fresh from ploughing forever and forever between green aisles of corn, where, as in a treadmill, one might walk from daybreak to dusk without perceiving a shadow of change.

from "A Wagner Matinee"
Willa Cather

8. *thing*—singular
9. *eye*—singular
10. *Maggie*—singular
11. *calf*—singular
12. *details*—plural
13. *soul*—singular
14. *ploughing*—singular
15. *aisles*—plural
16. *corn*—singular
17. *treadmill*—singular
18. *daybreak*—singular
19. *dusk*—singular
20. *shadow*—singular
21. *change*—singular

EXERCISE 8

Correcting Singular and Plural Nouns

For each singular noun in items 1–10, write the correct plural form. In items 11–20 correct any error in the plural nouns listed. Write *correct* if the plural form is correct.

1. liability
2. swatch
3. veto
4. ox
5. survey
6. history
7. superhero
8. thief
9. solo
10. species
11. beliefs
12. taxs
13. factorys
14. moose
15. churches
16. halfs
17. ex-wifes
18. shelves
19. tooths
20. potatos

EXERCISE 8
1. liabilities
2. swatches
3. vetoes
4. oxen
5. surveys
6. histories
7. superheroes
8. thieves
9. solos
10. species (no change from singular to plural)
11. correct
12. taxes
13. factories
14. correct (no change from singular to plural)
15. correct
16. halves
17. ex-wives
18. correct
19. teeth
20. potatoes

EXERCISE 9

Using Singular and Plural Nouns in Your Writing

The narrator in Cather's "A Wagner Matinee" recalls the time he first heard an orchestra play. As part of a letter to a pen pal, write a paragraph describing a moment or experience that affected you profoundly. Include details about the experience and its effect on you. Be sure to use descriptive details that provide a specific portrait of the moment, so that a peer reader will understand its impact on you. Use at least five singular and five plural nouns in your description.

EXERCISE 9
Responses will vary. Students' paragraphs should correctly use at least five singular and five plural nouns.

POSSESSIVE NOUNS

Nouns that show ownership or possession of things or qualities are called **possessive nouns.** A possessive noun names who or what has something. Possessive nouns can also be singular or plural.

Both common nouns and proper nouns can be possessive in form.

EXAMPLES

common nouns

The **prosecutor's** argument influenced the jury.

The **short story's** ending surprised all of us.

proper nouns

Wisconsin's dairy farms produce much of the nation's milk products.

Vinnie's homegrown tomatoes are plump and juicy.

USAGE tip

Singular nouns that end in *s* still need an apostrophe and an *s* added at the end of the word.

glass **glass's**

Ms. Nichols
Ms. Nichols's

An apostrophe is used to form the possessive of nouns. To form the possessive of a singular noun, add an apostrophe and an *s* to the end of the word.

EXAMPLES

singular possessive nouns

My **sister's** sense of humor is infectious and high-spirited. (sister + **'s** = sister'**s**)

Henry's winter coat needs to be dry cleaned. (Henry + **'s** = Henry's)

The possessive of a plural noun is formed two different ways. If the plural noun does not end in –*s*, you add an apostrophe and an *s* to the end of the word. If the plural noun ends with an *s*, add only an apostrophe.

EXAMPLES

plural possessive nouns

A new **women's** health clinic will open in our town this fall. (women + **'s** = women's)

The **daisies'** cheerful blossoms brightened the hospital room. (daisies + ' = daisies')

Try It Yourself

EXERCISE 10

Identifying Possessive Nouns

Indicate whether the underlined nouns in the following sentences are plural or possessive or both.

1. Nathaniel Hawthorne's short story "Rappaccini's Daughter" was published in 1844.
2. The author, whose ancestors participated in the Salem witch trials, studied the Puritans' way of life.
3. Many critics have pointed out the author's preoccupation with good and evil—a recurring theme in many of his stories.
4. This particular story's use of symbolism, fantasy, and allusion are characteristic traits of his works.
5. Strange, poisonous plants grow in Beatrice's father's garden.
6. The garden's mysteries, including the beautiful Beatrice, can be viewed from Giovanni's window.
7. Baglioni and Rappaccini are both teachers of medicine and each other's archrival.
8. Giovanni does not heed Baglioni's "grave objections" regarding his rival's personal character.
9. The characters' different degrees of evil challenge readers to define the nature of evil.
10. The poison's deadly effect is swift, and Beatrice—"the poor victim of man's ingenuity"—dies at her father's feet.

EXERCISE 10

1. *Hawthorne's*—possessive; *Rappaccini's*—possessive
2. *ancestors*—plural; *trials*—plural; *Puritans'*—both
3. *critics*—plural; *author's*—possessive; *stories*—plural
4. *story's*—possessive; *traits*—plural; *works*—plural
5. *plants*—plural; *Beatrice's*—possessive; *father's*—possessive
6. *garden's*—possessive; *mysteries*—plural; *Giovanni's*—possessive
7. *teachers*—plural; *other's*—possessive
8. *Baglioni's*—possessive; *objections*—plural; *rival's*—possessive
9. *characters'*—both; *degrees*—plural; *readers*—plural
10. *poison's*—possessive; *man's*—possessive; *father's*—possessive

EXERCISE 11

Understanding How to Form Possessive Nouns

Write the correct possessive form of each of the first words in each group below.

EXERCISE 11

1. musicians' instruments
2. children's laughter
3. history's legacy
4. Mr. Adams's letter
5. crisis's outcome
6. chief's speech
7. church's steeple
8. Chris's presentation
9. hoax's originator
10. country's leaders
11. bees' buzzing
12. natives' dialect
13. tresses' waves
14. geese's flight
15. people's confidence
16. alto's tone
17. melodrama's characteristics
18. Italy's artisans
19. heroes' medals
20. Mississippi's width

1. musicians instruments
2. children laughter
3. history legacy
4. Mr. Adams letter
5. crisis outcome
6. chief speech
7. church steeple
8. Chris presentation
9. hoax originator
10. country leaders
11. bees buzzing
12. natives dialect
13. tresses waves
14. geese flight
15. people confidence
16. alto tone
17. melodrama characteristics
18. Italy artisans
19. heroes medals
20. Mississippi width

EXERCISE 12

1. the knives' sharpness
2. the libraries' collection
3. the handkerchiefs' monogram
4. the dishes' pattern
5. the coach's frustration
6. the tomatoes' flavor
7. the oxen's yoke
8. an hour's wait
9. the veto's effect
10. the jelly's fruit

EXERCISE 12

Using Possessive Nouns

Rewrite each of the following groups of words so that the singular possessive nouns are plural and the plural possessive nouns are singular.

1. the knife's sharpness
2. the library's collection
3. the handkerchief's monogram
4. the dish's pattern
5. the coaches' frustration
6. the tomato's flavor
7. the ox's yoke
8. several hours' wait
9. the vetoes' effect
10. the jellies' fruit

COMPOUND NOUNS

A **compound noun** is a noun made up of two or more words. Some compound nouns are written as one word, some as two or more words, and some as hyphenated words.

EXAMPLES

one word	wonderland, swordfish, typeface, fingerprint
two or more words	United States, motion pictures, sea horse
hyphenated	Johnny-on-the-spot, attorney-at-law, fifteen-year-old

USAGE tip

To form the plural of compound nouns made up of one word, add *–s* or *–es.*

handcuffs
hotdishes

To form the plural of compound nouns written as more than one word or hyphenated, make the most important part plural.

brothers-in-law
family trees

Try It Yourself

EXERCISE 13

Identifying Compound Nouns

Identify the compound nouns in the following sentences.

1. Common in North America, joe-pye weed is a tall plant with small, purplish flowers.
2. The bright moonlight dazzled the stargazers, who were awestruck by the sparkling display of starlight, each constellation a precious gem in the night sky.
3. A crackdown on leaf litter helped to reduce the blight on the crab apple trees.
4. The secretary of state held a press conference to discuss the administration's foreign policy.
5. Lady's-slipper is only one type of orchid that my great-grandmother grows in the sunroom, where she also stores raincoats, seashells, hatboxes, and an old, dusty player piano.
6. One of the houses in our neighborhood, a unique piece of real estate, features a widow's walk, which is a railed gallery on the rooftop.
7. Henry Ford's mass production of automobiles introduced the assembly line and revolutionized the auto industry.

EXERCISE 13

1. Common in North America, joe-pye weed is a tall plant with small, purplish flowers.
2. The bright moonlight dazzled the stargazers, who were awestruck by the sparkling display of starlight, each constellation a precious gem in the night sky.
3. A crackdown on leaf litter helped to reduce the blight on the crab apple trees.
4. The secretary of state held a press conference to discuss the administration's foreign policy.
5. Lady's-slipper is only one type of orchid that my great-grandmother grows in the sunroom, where she also stores raincoats, seashells, hatboxes, and an old, dusty player piano.

8. The masthead in our newspaper identifies the editor in chief and other information about the staff.
9. After eleventh grade, Max will apply for an internship with a printmaker whose masterpieces are collected around the world.
10. During World War II, many Native Americans served as code talkers, sending and translating secret code in their native languages.

EXERCISE 14

Understanding Plural Compound Nouns

Write the plural form of the compound noun in parentheses to complete each sentence.

1. Three (maid of honor), dressed in petal pink silk dresses, slowly walked down the aisle.
2. At the national journalism conference, (editor in chief) discussed issues relevant to their profession.
3. Several of Melanie's (coworker) carpooled to the office three days a week.
4. Imprinted on their impressive stationery were the words ("Attorney-at-law.")
5. The queen's (lady-in-waiting) all had royal lineage.
6. The contest's two (runner-up) each received a savings bond and bouquet of flowers.
7. Always a prankster, my little brother has pulled many (double cross) on family members.
8. Many (vice president) have played a quiet, behind-the-scenes role in the White House.
9. The archers pulled back their bows and pointed their arrows toward the row of (bull's-eye).
10. For how many months should consumers save their (bill of sale)?

6. One of the houses in our neighborhood, a unique piece of real estate, features a widow's walk, which is a railed gallery on the rooftop.
7. Henry Ford's mass production of automobiles introduced the assembly line and revolutionized the auto industry.
8. The masthead in our newspaper identifies the editor in chief and other information about the staff.
9. After eleventh grade, Max will apply for an internship with a printmaker whose masterpieces are collected around the world.
10. During World War II, many Native Americans served as code talkers, sending and translating secret code in their native languages.

EXERCISE 14

1. maids of honor
2. editors in chief
3. coworkers
4. "Attorneys-at-law"
5. ladies-in-waiting
6. runners-up
7. double crosses
8. vice presidents
9. bull's-eyes
10. bills of sale

EXERCISE 15

Using Compound Nouns

Write a sentence using each of the compound nouns listed below.

1. shoelace
2. pole vault
3. theater-in-the-round
4. double bass
5. jigsaw puzzle
6. father-in-law
7. timber wolf
8. jumping jack
9. campfire
10. hospital bed

EXERCISE 15
Responses will vary. You may want to have students write sentences for both singular and plural forms of the compound nouns.

COLLECTIVE NOUNS

Collective nouns name groups—such as *class*, *audience*, and *staff*—that are made up of individuals. A collective noun may be either singular or plural, depending on how the group acts. When the group acts together as one unit to do something, the group is considered *singular*. When individuals within the group act differently or do different things at the same time, the collective noun is *plural*.

USAGE tip

If you can substitute the word *it* for a collective noun, it is singular. If you can substitute the word *they*, the collective noun is plural.

EXAMPLES

singular The election **committee meets** before the primary to review procedures.
A **family** in our neighborhood **volunteers** on weekends at the animal shelter.

plural Our election **committee disagree** about the correct balloting procedures.
During the week, the **family pursue** their individual interests and tasks.

Try It Yourself

EXERCISE 16

Identifying Collective Nouns

Identify the collective nouns in the following sentences.

1. The newborn kit of fox cubs cry in unison to be fed.
2. American society holds dear the ideal of the "self-made" person.
3. The talented trio delights the audience with familiar folksongs.
4. A lone rabbit will not survive the deadly persistence of a murder of crows.
5. With our binoculars we could see a pod of whales swim together in the ocean.
6. Dogs of Endearment is a group of dedicated human-canine teams who work with people who are elderly or disabled.
7. Our community now has more than a dozen book clubs that meet regularly at the library.
8. As a swarm of wasps descends from the roof rafters, the painting crew scrambles down the scaffolding.
9. The counseling staff offers individual guidance and support to interested students.
10. After hearing the closing remarks, the jury is sequestered until it reaches a verdict.

EXERCISE 17

Understanding Collective Noun-Verb Agreement

Identify the collective noun in each of the following sentences. Then complete each sentence by using the correct form of the verb in parentheses.

1. On September 11, our nation (remembers, remember) those who lost their lives in the terrorist attacks.
2. Humanity (benefits, benefit) when there is peace and security throughout the world.
3. A local theater troupe (performs, perform) annually at the summer art fair.

EXERCISE 16

1. The newborn kit of fox cubs cry in unison to be fed.
2. American society holds dear the ideal of the "self-made" person.
3. The talented trio delights the audience with familiar folksongs.
4. A lone rabbit will not survive the deadly persistence of a murder of crows.
5. With our binoculars we could see a pod of whales swim together in the ocean.
6. Dogs of Endearment is a group of dedicated human-canine teams who work with people who are elderly or disabled.
7. Our community now has more than a dozen book clubs that meet regularly at the library.
8. As a swarm of wasps descends from the roof rafters, the painting crew scrambles down the scaffolding.
9. The counseling staff offers individual guidance and support to interested students.
10. After hearing the closing remarks, the jury is sequestered until it reaches a verdict.

EXERCISE 17

1. remembers
2. benefits
3. performs

4. The family (was reading, were reading) their favorite books in the living room.
5. After a play closes, the stage crew (is, are) always eager to tear down the sets.
6. Only a minority of citizens (is exercising, are exercising) their right to vote.
7. The student council (has met, have met) every Friday morning for the past month.
8. During the holidays overseas, the troop (is calling, are calling) their families and friends back home.
9. Unfortunately, the faculty (is disagreeing, are disagreeing) with one another about the proposed dress code.
10. A police squad (responds, respond) as quickly as possible to any emergency calls.

4. were reading
5. is
6. are exercising
7. has met
8. are calling
9. are disagreeing
10. responds

EXERCISE 18

Using Collective Nouns in Your Writing

For a pen pal from another culture, write a paragraph about a group with which you are familiar—a congregation, a club, a committee, a pack, a herd, or some other group. Describe the group and its activities, using the collective noun you choose and synonyms to replace it. Use each collective noun once in its singular form and once in its plural form. Check your subject-verb agreement when you edit your paragraph.

EXERCISE 18
Responses will vary. Students should use their collective nouns or appropriate synonym replacements in both singular and plural forms. In each case, subjects should agree with verbs.

UNIT 4 REVIEW

TEST YOUR KNOWLEDGE

EXERCISE 1

Identifying Nouns

Identify the nouns in each sentence. (10 points)

EXAMPLE

Anne Bradstreet was the first New World resident to have a published volume of poems.

1. Married to a graduate of Cambridge University, Bradstreet sailed to the New World in the seventeenth century.
2. Because a childhood illness had left Anne in a weakened state, life in the Bay Colony was difficult.
3. When her husband, Simon Bradstreet, became governor, she maintained her many obligations and found time to continue writing poetry.
4. Unusual for a woman living in her time, Anne had the advantage of an education.
5. In "To My Dear and Loving Husband," the speaker prizes her husband's love more than gold and more than all the riches of the East.
6. In a comparison, the poem's speaker claims that even rivers are unable to "quench" her love.
7. By persevering in the difficulties of this life, she suggests that they will be rewarded in the afterlife.
8. The speaker's hopeful view and clearly evident happiness mirror Bradstreet's own beliefs.
9. Some readers may think that the relationship between the speaker and her husband presents an idealized portrait of marriage.
10. The second edition of Anne Bradstreet's work was not published until after her death.

EXERCISE 1

1. Married to a graduate of Cambridge University, Bradstreet sailed to the New World in the seventeenth century.
2. Because a childhood illness had left Anne in a weakened state, life in the Bay Colony was difficult.
3. When her husband, Simon Bradstreet, became governor, she maintained her many obligations and found time to continue writing poetry.
4. Unusual for a woman living in her time, Anne had the advantage of an education.
5. In "To My Dear and Loving Husband," the speaker prizes her husband's love more than gold and more than all the riches of the East.
6. In a comparison, the poem's speaker claims that even rivers are unable to "quench" her love.
7. By persevering [gerund] in the difficulties of this life, she suggests that they will be rewarded in the afterlife.
8. The speaker's hopeful view and clearly evident happiness mirror Bradstreet's own beliefs.
9. Some readers may think that the relationship between the speaker and her husband presents an idealized portrait of marriage.
10. The second edition of Anne Bradstreet's work was not published until after her death.

EXERCISE 2

Identifying Common, Proper, Compound, Collective, Abstract, and Concrete Nouns

Identify each underlined noun in the following sentences as common or proper. Then tell whether it is concrete or abstract. Finally, make two lists, one of all compound nouns among the underlined words, and one of all collective nouns among the underlined words. (20 points)

EXAMPLE

During the Jazz Age, an alienated younger generation challenged the traditions and ways of life of the older, more conservative generation.

(*Jazz Age*, proper, abstract; *generation*, common, abstract; *traditions*, common, abstract; *life*, common, abstract; compound noun is *Jazz Age*; collective noun is *generation*)

1. New York City became a center for avant-garde, attracting bohemian writers, artists, and intellectuals.
2. This was also the era of Prohibition, which banned the manufacture or sale of alcohol.
3. Many writers, particularly F. Scott Fitzgerald, chronicled the breakdown of a disillusioned class of people.
4. After the stock market crashed in 1929, many other writers questioned basic ideals about free-market capitalism held by the majority of Americans.
5. Some American writers moved to Paris or London and became part of a group of expatriates that met and exchanged ideas.
6. Their views, now referred to as Modernism, rejected the popular culture and artistic conventions of the past.
7. Modernism, an international movement, found expression in many experiments in form—both literary and artistic.
8. Free verse and stream-of-consciousness are two examples of forms characteristic of Modernist literature.
9. In a speech, the poet Robert Frost said, "Writing free verse is like playing tennis with the net down."
10. A dramatic change that occurred during the early twentieth century was the increased role of women in the arts.

EXERCISE 2

1. *New York City*—proper, concrete; *center*—common, abstract; *avant-garde*—abstract; *writers*—common, concrete; *artists*—common, concrete; *intellectuals*—common, concrete
2. *era*—common, abstract; *Prohibition*—proper, abstract; *alcohol*—common, concrete
3. *F. Scott Fitzgerald*—proper, concrete; *breakdown*—common, abstract; *class*—common, abstract
4. *stock market*—common, concrete; *ideals*—common, abstract; *capitalism*—common, abstract; *majority*—common, abstract; *Americans*—proper, concrete
5. *Paris*—proper, concrete; *group*—common, concrete; *expatriates*—common, concrete; *ideas*—common, abstract
6. *views*—common, abstract; *Modernism*—proper, abstract; *culture*—common, abstract; *conventions*—common, abstract; *past*—common, abstract
7. *movement*—common, abstract; *expression*—common, abstract; *experiments*—common, concrete; *form*—common, abstract
8. *Free verse*—common, abstract; *stream-of-consciousness*—common, abstract; *examples*—common, concrete; *literature*—common, concrete
9. *speech*—common, concrete; *poet*—common,

concrete; *tennis*—common, concrete; *net*—common, concrete
10. *change*—common, abstract; *century*—common, abstract; *role*—common, abstract; *women*—common, concrete; *arts*—common, concrete
11. *period*—common, abstract; *Great Depression*—proper, concrete; *nation*—common, collective, concrete; *millions*—common, collective, concrete; *jobs*—common, concrete; *families*—common, concrete; *hunger*—common, abstract; *hope*—common, abstract
12. *feelings*—common, abstract; *hopelessness*—common, abstract; *renewal*—common, abstract
13. *people*—common, concrete; *occurrences*—common, concrete; *farmlands*—common, concrete; *towns*—common, concrete
14. *William Faulkner*—proper, concrete; *plot structure*—common, concrete; *point of view*—common, concrete; *novels*—common, concrete; *setting*—common, concrete
15. *African American*—proper; *South*—proper, abstract
16. *publications*—common, concrete; *Mules*—common, concrete; *Men*—common, concrete; *Eyes*—common, concrete; *God*—proper, abstract
17. *Jungle*—common,

11. The period known as the Great Depression profoundly affected the nation; millions of Americans lost their jobs, families lived with hunger, and many lost hope.
12. Some writers responded to people's feelings of hopelessness by looking for sources of renewal.
13. Robert Frost and Sherwood Anderson focused on the local people and occurrences in the rural farmlands and towns where they lived.
14. Others, such as William Faulkner, experimented with plot structure and point of view, but placed his mythical novels in a regional setting.
15. Zora Neale Hurston, an African American, wrote novels about the rural South.
16. Two of her publications are *Of Mules and Men* and *Their Eyes Were Watching God*.
17. In *The Jungle*, author Upton Sinclair exposed the horrific practices of meatpackers in the grossly unsanitary slaughterhouses in the early 1900s.
18. Sinclair's novel shocked readers, including President Theodore Roosevelt, who invited Sinclair to the White House.
19. In the 1930s the effects of the depression were intensified by severe droughts in Oklahoma, which caused the migration of workers to California.
20. John Steinbeck eloquently described the plight of one migrant family in *The Grapes of Wrath*.

EXERCISE 3

Identifying Singular, Plural, and Possessive Nouns

Identify the type of noun underlined in each sentence as either singular, plural, possessive, or plural possessive. (20 points)

EXAMPLE
The centuries-old Iroquois Constitution joined together peoples who lived on the shores of the Great Lakes.
(Constitution, singular; *shores*, plural*)*

1. The five nations that originally formed the confederacy included the Mohawk, Oneida, Onondaga, Cayuga, and Seneca.

2. The <u>league's</u> political <u>system</u> was a model form of representative government.
3. Fifty male <u>chiefs</u>, who were chosen by the Iroquois <u>women</u>, presided over the league.
4. Each league member had one vote, and all Iroquois <u>nations</u> had to agree before any <u>action</u> was taken.
5. The Iroquois Constitution says that a <u>leader</u> should possess the <u>qualities</u> of peace, good will, patience, and calm deliberation.
6. It also says that a <u>leader's</u> mind should be focused not on himself but on his <u>people's</u> welfare.
7. The Iroquois lived in <u>longhouses</u>, which were covered with elm bark and housed several <u>families</u>.
8. The Iroquois <u>nation's</u> <u>livelihood</u> was dependent on hunting, trading, and farming.
9. <u>Diseases</u> such as <u>smallpox</u> killed large numbers of Native American <u>populations</u>.
10. During the American Revolution <u>Washington's</u> troops destroyed Iroquois <u>settlements</u>.

EXERCISE 4

Understanding Compound, Collective, Plural, and Possessive Nouns

Write the word in parentheses that correctly completes the sentence. (10 points)

EXAMPLE
Our (voices, voice's) echoed through the (canyon's, canyons') walls and disappeared in the wind. *(voices, canyon's)*

1. Twentieth-century leaders in the (woman's, women's) movement included Gloria Steinem, Betty Friedan, and Shirley Chisholm.
2. My three (brother-in-laws, brothers-in-law) helped us repair the dilapidated dairy barn.
3. While exploring the pasture, the (calfs, calves) ate the (blackberrys, blackberries) in the hedgerow.
4. Research data (proves, prove) that shared evening meals have positive effects on (families, family's).
5. Many (churchs, churches) in our community participate in the shelter program for the homeless.

concrete; *meatpackers*—common, concrete; *slaughterhouses*—common, concrete

18. *readers*—common, concrete; *President Theodore Roosevelt*—proper, concrete; *White House*—proper, concrete
19. *effects*—common, concrete; *depression*—common, abstract; *droughts*—common, concrete; *Oklahoma*—proper, concrete; *migration*—common, concrete
20. *plight*—common, abstract; *family*—common, concrete; *The Grapes of Wrath*—proper, concrete

EXERCISE 3

1. *nations*—plural; *confederacy*—singular
2. *league's*—possessive; *system*—singular
3. *chiefs*—plural; *women*—plural
4. *nations*—plural; *action*—singular
5. *leader*—singular; *qualities*—plural
6. *leader's*—singular possessive; *people's*—plural possessive
7. *longhouses*—plural; *families*—plural
8. *nation's*—possessive; *livelihood*—singular
9. *Diseases*—plural; *smallpox*—singular; *populations*—plural
10. *Washington's*—possessive; *settlements*—plural

EXERCISE 4

1. women's
2. brothers-in-law
3. calves, blackberries

4. proves [or prove—*data* is traditionally plural but is increasingly used as singular], families
5. churches
6. music boxes
7. waits, maids of honor
8. story's, sheeps'
9. children, parents'
10. People's

6. The collector of (music box's, music boxes) lovingly listened to each tune.
7. The congregation patiently (waits, wait) for the appearance of the bride, while the (maids of honor, maid of honors) walk down the aisle.
8. Jamie didn't understand the (story's, stories) moral, which had something to do with someone hiding in (sheep's, sheeps') clothing.
9. The well-mannered (childs, children) who live next door are their (parent's, parents') pride and joy.
10. (People's, Peoples') jobs and economic future have been threatened by the sluggish economy.

EXERCISE 5
Responses will vary. Students' sentences should use each type of noun correctly, capitalizing and punctuating where necessary.

EXERCISE 6
Responses will vary. Students' paragraphs should include details about the contribution, audience, and background to help others envision what happened. They should make an effort to use examples of all types and forms of nouns.

EXERCISE 5
Using Nouns

Write a sentence using each of the types of nouns listed below. Underline the noun in each sentence. (20 points)

1. common noun
2. proper noun
3. concrete noun
4. abstract noun
5. singular noun
6. plural noun
7. singular possessive noun
8. plural possessive noun
9. compound noun
10. collective noun

EXERCISE 6
Using Nouns in Your Writing

Respond to criticism of teenagers' behavior by writing a paragraph for a community newspaper describing a worthwhile contribution made by a group of teenagers. You can include details about the significance of the contribution, the people involved, and any background information you think your readers will need to understand what happened. Use each of the kinds of nouns listed in Exercise 5 at least once. (20 points)

UNIT 5 NAMERS
Pronouns

ASSESSMENT
Grammar Pretests and Comprehensive Tests are available at www.emcp.com.

UNIT OVERVIEW

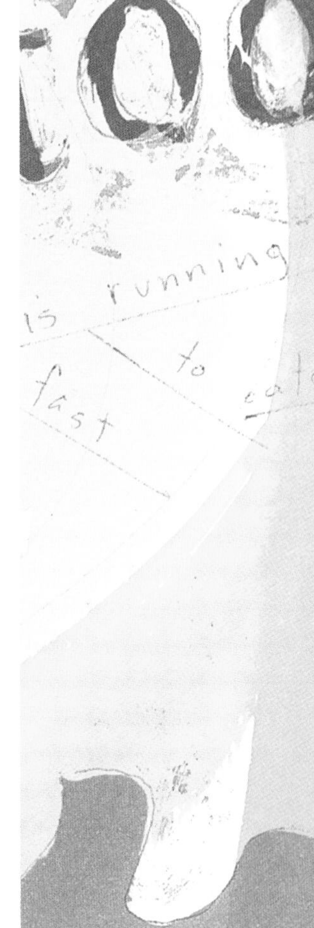

NAMERS: PRONOUNS

PRONOUNS

A **pronoun** is used in place of a noun. Sometimes a pronoun refers to a specific person or thing.

Pronouns can help your writing flow more smoothly. Without them, writing can sound awkward and repetitive. Take a look at the following examples, which show the same sentence written without and with pronouns.

EXAMPLES

without pronouns	Jenny started **Jenny's car** and drove away before **Jenny** remembered that **Jenny's car** needed gas.
with pronouns	Jenny started **her car** and drove away before **she** remembered that **it** needed gas.

The most commonly used pronouns are *personal pronouns*, *reflexive* and *intensive pronouns*, *demonstrative pronouns*, *indefinite pronouns*, *interrogative pronouns*, and *relative pronouns*.

Types of Pronouns	Definition	Examples
personal pronoun	used in place of the name of a person or thing	I, me, we, us, he, she, it, him, her, you, they, them
indefinite pronoun	points out a person, place, or thing, but not a specific or definite one	one, someone, anything, other, all, few, nobody
reflexive pronoun	refers back to a noun previously used; adds –*self* and –*selves* to other pronoun forms	myself, herself, yourself, themselves, ourselves
intensive pronoun	emphasizes a noun or pronoun	me *myself,* he *himself,* you *yourself,* they *themselves,* we *ourselves*
interrogative pronoun	asks a question	who, whose, whom, what, which

CONTINUED

demonstrative pronoun	points out a specific person, place, idea, or thing	this, these, that, those
relative pronoun	introduces an adjective clause	that, which, who, whose, whom
singular pronoun	used in place of the name of one person or thing	I, me, you, he, she, it, him, her
plural pronoun	used in place of more than one person or thing	we, us, you, they, them
possessive pronoun	shows ownership or possession	mine, yours, his, hers, ours, theirs

PERSONAL PRONOUNS

A **personal pronoun** is used in place of the name of a person or thing. Personal pronouns are singular, plural, or possessive.

EXAMPLES

personal pronouns

singular I, me, you, he, she, it, him, her

plural we, us, you, they, them

possessive my, mine, yours, his, hers, ours, theirs

Use personal pronouns to refer to yourself (first person), to refer to people to whom you are talking (second person), and to refer to other people, places, and things (third person).

EXAMPLES

first person the speaker or speakers talk about themselves: *I, me, my, mine, we, us, our, ours*

second person the speaker talks about the person talked to: *you, your, yours*

third person the speaker talks about someone or something else: *he, him, his, she, her, hers, it, its, they, them, their, theirs*

If subjects are of different numbers, the verb should agree with the subject nearest the verb.

Try It Yourself

EXERCISE 1
The old woman and her daughter were sitting on their porch when Mr. Shiftlet came up their road for the first time. The old

Literature MODEL

woman slid to the edge of her chair and leaned forward, shading her eyes from the piercing sunset with her hand. The daughter could not see far in front of her and continued to play with her fingers. Although the old woman lived in this desolate spot with only her daughter and she had never seen Mr. Shiftlet before, she could tell, even from a distance, that he was a tramp and no one to be afraid of.

USAGE tip

When pronouns replace common nouns, they replace the common noun and all of its modifiers.

EXERCISE 2
Responses may vary slightly.
Sample responses:

1. Flannery O'Connor was born in Savannah, Georgia. At age twelve, she moved to Milledgeville, Georgia, with her family.
2. O'Connor knew from an early age that she wanted to write.
3. After graduating from Georgia State College for Women, O'Connor left her home state to study writing at the University of Iowa.

EXERCISE 1
Identifying Pronouns in Literature

Identify the personal pronouns in the following passage.

> The old woman and her daughter were sitting on their porch when Mr. Shiftlet came up their road for the first time. The old woman slid to the edge of her chair and leaned forward, shading her eyes from the piercing sunset with her hand. The daughter could not see far in front of her and continued to play with her fingers. Although the old woman lived in this desolate spot with only her daughter and she had never seen Mr. Shiftlet before, she could tell, even from a distance, that he was a tramp and no one to be afraid of.
>
> from "The Life You Save May Be Your Own"
> Flannery O'Connor

EXERCISE 2
Understanding Pronouns

Rewrite each of the following sentences or sentence pairs. Use pronouns in place of any repetitive nouns or groups of nouns.

1. Flannery O'Connor was born in Savannah, Georgia. At age twelve, Flannery O'Connor moved to Milledgeville, Georgia, with Flannery O'Connor's family.
2. O'Connor knew from an early age that O'Connor wanted to write.
3. After graduating from Georgia State College for Women, O'Connor left O'Connor's home state to study writing at the University of Iowa.
4. O'Connor published O'Connor's first story, "The Geranium," while at Iowa. O'Connor later moved to a writer's colony in Saratoga Springs, New York, to gain perspective on contemporary culture.

5. O'Connor's stories have been called "dark," "bizarre," and "grotesque." O'Connor's stories often contain characters who are con artists and criminals.
6. Last semester Nick and Sara read O'Connor's story "The Life You Save May Be Your Own." Nick and Sara plan to read "The Life You Save May Be Your Own" again during summer vacation.
7. Nancy and I worked together on a book report of O'Connor's first novel, *Wise Blood.* Nancy and my teacher, Mr. Leonard, gave Nancy and me an A for that report.
8. Mr. Leonard later told Nancy, "I think Nancy should consider majoring in English in college."
9. My father read O'Connor's works when my father was in high school. My father has given me three of O'Connor's books to read.
10. Mr. Leonard and my father both enjoy literature. Mr. Leonard and my father have encouraged Nancy and me to study literature. Nancy and I will probably read twenty books this summer.

EXERCISE 3

Using Pronouns in Your Writing

For a local public access television program called "Believe It or Not," write a brief news clip about a strange or bizarre event that recently occurred in your town. The event may be real or imaginary. Describe the people involved, what happened and where, and who was affected. Use at least five different pronouns in your news clip.

PRONOUNS AND ANTECEDENTS

As you know, a *pronoun* is a word used in place of one or more nouns. The word that a pronoun stands for is called its **antecedent.** The antecedent clarifies the meaning of the pronoun. The pronoun may appear in the same sentence as its antecedent or in a following sentence.

4. O'Connor published her first story, "The Geranium," while at Iowa. She later moved to a writer's colony in Saratoga Springs, New York, to gain perspective on contemporary culture.
5. O'Connor's stories have been called "dark," "bizarre," and "grotesque." They often contain characters who are con artists and criminals.
6. Last semester Nick and Sara read O'Connor's story "The Life You Save May Be Your Own." They plan to read it again during summer vacation.
7. Nancy and I worked together on a book report of O'Connor's first novel, *Wise Blood.* Our teacher, Mr. Leonard, gave us an A for it.

8. Mr. Leonard later told Nancy, "I think you should consider majoring in English in college."
9. My father read O'Connor's works when he was in high school. He has given me three of them to read.
10. Mr. Leonard and my father both enjoy literature. They have encouraged Nancy and me to study literature. We will probably read twenty books this summer.

EXERCISE 3

Responses will vary. Students should use at least five different pronouns in their paragraphs.

EXAMPLES

Where is **Joseph**? **Bobby** believes that **he** heard **him** working in the garage. (*Joseph* is the antecedent of *him. Bobby* is the antecedent of *he.*)

The rusty **car** does not have a reliable set of brakes, and **it** might leak oil. (*Car* is the antecedent of *it.*)

When you use a pronoun, be sure that it refers clearly to its antecedent. A pronoun should agree in both number (singular or plural) and gender (masculine, feminine, or neutral) with its antecedent.

EXAMPLES

number

singular	**John Dewey** wrote many articles about psychology. "The Reflex Arc" is one of **his** most influential essays.
plural	The **psychologists** thought **they** might be better off working together.

gender

masculine	**Dr. Phil McGraw** has had a successful practice for many years, but **he** did not become famous until appearing on *Oprah.*
feminine	**Oprah Winfrey** started hosting **her** talk show in the mid-1980s in Chicago.
neutral	The **topic** for today is "soap opera addiction," and **it** always sparks a lively debate.

Singular pronouns are used with some nouns that are plural in form but refer to a single entity, such as *economics*, *electronics*, *gymnastics*, *linguistics*, *mathematics*, *measles*, *news*, and *physics*.

EXAMPLES

My grandmother knows everything there is to know about **electronics. It** is her area of expertise.

Do you plan to study **linguistics** in college? I think **it** will be helpful for your career.

Plural pronouns are used with some nouns that are plural in form but refer to single items, such as *pliers*, *eyeglasses*, *pants*, *scissors*, and *shorts*.

EXAMPLES

Do you remember where you put the **pliers**? I think you left **them** on the picnic table.

Those **pants** do look sharp on you, but **they** are not currently in style.

Agreement between a relative pronoun—*who*, *whom*, *whose*, *which*, and *that*—and its antecedent is determined by the number of the antecedent.

EXAMPLES

Betty, who spends two hours each day in **her** garden, is teaching a horticulture class. (*Who* is singular because it refers to the singular noun *Betty. Her* is used to agree with *who.*)

All who want to cross the bridge must take off **their** gold medallions and give **them** to the troll. (*Who* is plural because it refers to the plural pronoun *All. Their* is used to agree with *who. Them* is used to agree with *medallions.*)

LANGUAGELINK
Print exercise worksheets or have students complete exercises online with the LanguageLINK CD.

Try It Yourself

EXERCISE 4

Identifying Pronouns and Antecedents

Identify the personal pronoun(s) in each of the following sentences or sentence pairs. Then identify the antecedent to which each pronoun refers.

1. Last semester, Jane wrote a report about Sweden. It is located on the Scandinavian peninsula in Europe.
2. In 1973, Carl XVI Gustaf became the King of Sweden. He ascended to the throne after Gustav VI Adolf died.
3. About nine million people live in Sweden. Their primary language is Swedish.

EXERCISE 4

1. antecedent—*Sweden*, pronoun—*It*
2. antecedent—*Carl XVI Gustaf*, pronoun—*He*
3. antecedent—*people*, pronoun—*Their*

4. antecedent—*country*, pronoun—*it*
5. antecedent—*Sweden*, pronoun—*its*; antecedent—*exports*, pronoun—*they*
6. antecedent—*farmers*, pronoun—*They*
7. antecedent—*Sweden*, pronoun—*its*
8. antecedent—*Jane*, pronoun—*her*; antecedent—*grandmother*; pronoun—*her*
9. antecedent—*Jane*, pronoun—*her*; antecedent—*grandparents*, pronouns—*they*, *their*
10. antecedent—*Jane*, pronoun—*her*; antecedent—*teacher*, pronoun—*she*; antecedent—*report*, pronoun—*it*

EXERCISE 5

1. their—Svear
2. they—Swedes and Norse people
3. It—Christianity
4. her, she—Christine
5. they—people
6. them—classmates
7. she—Susan
8. his—Alan
9. our—My parents and I
10. its—European Union

4. The country is considered a constitutional monarchy because it has a king, a prime minister, and a three-branch government.
5. Sweden derives much of its income from exports. They include machinery, automobiles, paper products, wood, iron products, and steel products.
6. Swedish farmers also play an important economic role. They grow grain, sugar beets, and potatoes.
7. Sweden imports about 70 billion dollars' worth of products from its primary trading partners.
8. Jane's grandmother is of Swedish descent. Her grandmother can trace her lineage as far back as the seventeenth century.
9. Jane's grandparents showed her a number of artifacts from Swedish history that they have in their basement.
10. Jane's teacher liked her report. She gave it a good grade.

EXERCISE 5
Understanding Pronouns and Antecedents

Complete the following sentences by using the correct pronoun in each blank. Then write the pronoun's antecedent.

1. The earliest Swedes consisted of the Svear, who merged with _____ neighbors, the Gotar.
2. In the tenth century the Swedes allied with other Norse people, and _____ began to dominate a large trading empire.
3. St. Ansgar introduced Christianity to Sweden in 829; _____ did not become a fully established religion in the country until the twelfth century.
4. Christine told _____ father that _____ wants to learn more about his Swedish heritage.
5. Several people of Swedish descent live in our neighborhood and _____ decided to build a community center last year.
6. My classmates also wrote reports about a country, but none of _____ chose a Scandinavian nation.

7. Susan asked Marie to proofread her report about Egypt before _____ turned it in.
8. Did Alan ever make a decision about the topic of _____ report?
9. My parents and I talked about spending _____ family vacation in Sweden next year.
10. Sweden is part of the European Union, an economic alliance that promotes trade among _____ members.

EXERCISE 6

Using Pronouns and Antecedents in Your Writing

Write a letter to a friend about a site in a country that you have visited or would like to visit. Describe the site's features and major attractions. Use at least five different pronouns in your paragraph. Check your writing for correct pronoun-antecedent agreement. Then draw an arrow from each pronoun to the antecedent to which it refers.

EXERCISE 6
Responses will vary. Students' letters should include at least five different pronouns and use correct pronoun-antecedent agreement. Students should draw an arrow from each pronoun to the antecedent to which it refers.

PRONOUN CASES

Personal pronouns take on different forms—called *cases*—depending on how they are used in sentences. Personal pronouns can be used as subjects, direct objects, indirect objects, and objects of prepositions. In the English language, there are three case forms for personal pronouns: *nominative*, *objective*, and *possessive*. The following chart organizes personal pronouns by case, number, and person.

Personal Pronouns

	Nominative Case	Objective Case	Possessive Case
Singular			
first person	I	me	my, mine
second person	you	you	your, yours
third person	he, she, it	him, her, it	his, her, hers, its
Plural			
first person	we	us	our, ours
second person	you	you	your, yours
third person	they	them	their, theirs

The Nominative Case

A personal pronoun in the **nominative case** is used when the pronoun functions as the subject of a sentence.

EXAMPLES
I talked to Laurie at the store yesterday.
She will be leaving for college in late August.

A pronoun in the nominative case is also used in compound subjects. Use the nominative pronoun *I* last when it is part of the compound subject.

EXAMPLES
Joel and **I** will be performing a comedy routine.
(*Joel* and *I* form the compound subject.)

Writers sometimes confuse the nominative and objective cases when a pronoun is used in a compound subject.

EXAMPLES

incorrect	Joel and me wrote all of the jokes for the comedy routine.
correct	**Joel and I** wrote all of the jokes for the comedy routine.

To choose the correct pronoun case for a compound subject, try each part of the compound subject alone in the sentence.

EXAMPLES
(She, Her) and (he, him) sang a lovely ballad.

incorrect	Him sang a lovely ballad.
	Her sang a lovely ballad.
correct	**He** sang a lovely ballad.
	She sang a lovely ballad.
correct case	**He and she** sang a lovely ballad.

A **predicate nominative** is a word or group of words that follows a linking verb and identifies the subject or refers to it. When a personal pronoun is used as a predicate nominative, it usually completes the meaning of the form of the verb *be—am, is, are, was, were, be, been,* or *being.*

EXAMPLES
The anonymous caller *could be* **he.**
Could the mysterious strangers *have been* **they**?
It *was* **she** who found the missing bracelet.

The Objective Case

A personal pronoun in the **objective case** is used when the pronoun functions as a direct object, indirect object, or object of the preposition.

USAGE tip

Reminder: A **direct object** receives the action in the sentence. An **indirect object** is the receiver of the direct object. An **object of the preposition** is the noun or pronoun that follows the preposition.

EXAMPLES

direct object	Buck warned **us** yesterday about the challenges.
indirect object	He sent **me** a list of potential problems that could arise.
object of the preposition	Buck doesn't trust any plans that haven't been reviewed by **him.**

Pronouns are also used in the objective case when they are part of a compound object.

EXAMPLES

compound direct object	Francine noticed **Theresa and me** hiding under her desk.
compound indirect object	We gave **Francine and him** quite a scare.
compound object of the preposition	This story never went beyond **her and me.**

The Possessive Case

A personal pronoun in the **possessive case** is used to show ownership or possession. A possessive pronoun may stand alone and function as a pronoun. It may also be used before a noun or gerund and function as an adjective.

EXAMPLES

pronoun	The green backpack in the corner is **mine**. **Hers** is red with a blue stripe. The locker at the end of the hall is **ours**.
adjective before a noun	Read **your** book after school. **My** pencil is not sharpened. Frank mailed **his** payment to the treasurer.
adjective before a gerund	**Her** painting is much better than it was a year ago. If we are not careful **our** laughing is going to get us in trouble. **Their** thinking has become muddled.

USAGE tip

Do not confuse possessive pronouns and contractions. Some possessive pronouns and contractions sound alike, but they have different meanings and spellings. Possessive pronouns do not contain an apostrophe.

your/you're
their/they're
theirs/there's
its/it's

Try It Yourself

EXERCISE 7

1. *her*—possessive pronoun
2. *she*—nominative pronoun
3. *her*—possessive pronoun
4. *her*—possessive pronoun
5. *her*—possessive pronoun
6. *her*—objective pronoun

MODEL

7. *she*—nominative pronoun
8. *she*—nominative pronoun
9. *her*—possessive pronoun
10. *she*—nominative pronoun
11. *I*—nominative pronoun
12. *I*—nominative pronoun
13. *she*—nominative pronoun

EXERCISE 7

Identifying Pronoun Cases in Literature

Identify each of the underlined words as a nominative, objective, or possessive pronoun.

> Putting her right foot out, she mounted the log and shut her eyes. Lifting her skirt, leveling her cane fiercely before her, like a festival figure in some parade, she began to march across. Then she opened her eyes and she was safe on the other side.
>
> "I wasn't as old as I thought," she said.
>
> from "A Worn Path"
> Eudora Welty

EXERCISE 8

Understanding Pronoun Cases

Complete each of the following sentences with an appropriate personal pronoun in the nominative, objective, or possessive case.

1. I am certain that the keys you found in the backyard are _____.
2. The last act in the revue will be performed by _____ and _____.
3. Joe and _____ worked all night to finish the project on time.
4. The Johnson sisters believe _____ gave the best performance at the talent show.
5. Bob brought home cheeseburgers and fries for his brother and _____.
6. Tiger birdied the last three holes and it is _____ who will be taking home the trophy again.
7. Jeff is a great baseball player, yet few fans ever ask for _____ autograph.
8. _____ car needs a new muffler; could we borrow _____ this afternoon?
9. _____ negative behavior is not going to make _____ feel any better.
10. That booming voice of _____ is easily heard even in a crowded room.

EXERCISE 8
Responses may vary in pronoun choice, but the correct case must be used.
1. mine
2. him, her
3. he
4. they
5. him
6. he
7. his
8. Our, yours
9. Her, her
10. his (In this instance, *his* is a possessive pronoun, although it appears to be used as the object of a preposition. This form is called the predicate possessive; in essence, it is a double possessive, since both *of* and *his* imply possession. This form must be used when another modifier precedes the noun, in this case *that*. A native speaker would never say *that his voice* or *his that voice*.)

EXERCISE 9

Correcting Pronoun Case Errors

Rewrite the following sentences, correcting any errors in pronoun cases. If the sentence correctly uses pronouns, write *correct*.

1. The four hobbits who visited your village last week were them.
2. He and her made an ill-fated decision to get matching tattoos.
3. Him and I had better start driving if we are to make it home before dark.
4. Jeff and her caused the greatest amount of frustration for the substitute teacher.
5. A fine example of a citizen and a soldier is he.
6. Them apples were picked by she yesterday afternoon.
7. The person who was calling you each morning was me.
8. Rachel overheard Tracy and she planning the surprise party.

EXERCISE 9
1. The four hobbits who visited your village last week were they.
2. He and she made an ill-fated decision to get matching tattoos.
3. He and I had better start driving if we are to make it home before dark.
4. Jeff and she caused the greatest amount of frustration for the substitute teacher.
5. correct
6. Those apples were picked by her yesterday afternoon.

7. The person who was calling you each morning was I.
8. Rachel overheard Tracy and her planning the surprise party.
9. Neither we nor they want to make the first move toward reconciliation.
10. Sandy bought ice cream and candy for him and them.

EXERCISE 10
Responses will vary. Students should correctly use pronouns in the nominative, objective, and possessive cases.

9. Neither us nor them want to make the first move toward reconciliation.
10. Sandy bought ice cream and candy for he and they.

EXERCISE 10

Using Subject and Object Pronouns in Your Writing

For the "Local Humor" column in your student newspaper, write a brief description of an amusing event in which you and your friends were involved. Correctly use at least two examples of pronouns in each of the cases: nominative, objective, and possessive.

INDEFINITE PRONOUNS

An **indefinite pronoun** points out a person, place, or thing, but not a particular or definite one. The indefinite pronouns are listed below.

Singular	Plural	Singular or Plural
another	both	all
anybody	few	any
anyone	many	more
anything	several	most
each	others	none
each other		some
either		
everybody		
everyone		
everything		
much		
neither		
nobody		
no one		
nothing		
one		
one another		
somebody		
someone		
something		

EXAMPLES

singular

Does **anyone** understand what I have been talking about?

At this point, **nothing** you say matters to her anymore.

plural

Few are able to tell the difference between a genuine and an imitation gemstone.

Despite strong evidence to the contrary, **several** believe the defendant is guilty.

Don't be confused if a phrase comes between an indefinite pronoun and the verb in a sentence. When an indefinite pronoun is the subject of a sentence, it must agree in number with the verb. In these two examples, the indefinite pronoun and its verb are now in boldface. The interrupting phrase is between them.

EXAMPLES

Someone in this house **hid** the chocolate chip cookies.

One of the zinnias **seems** to be blooming later than usual this year.

The indefinite pronouns *all*, *any*, *more*, *most*, *none*, and *some* may be singular or plural, depending on their meaning in the sentence.

EXAMPLES

singular

Most of the backyard **remains** covered with snow.

plural

Most of the carrot and celery sticks **remain** untouched by the party guests.

USAGE tip

Indefinite pronouns may also be used as adjectives to modify nouns.

Many politicians visit this town before the primary election.

Some water accumulated in our basement.

Try It Yourself

EXERCISE 11

Identifying Indefinite Pronouns

Underline the indefinite pronouns in the following sentences.

1. Someone suggested that we spend more time studying the life of Frederick Douglass.
2. Everybody in class had at least heard of this great abolitionist.
3. One of the students had read Douglass's autobiography, but most of us had only a cursory knowledge of the civil rights leader.
4. Most history textbooks today devote more attention to Douglass than they have in years past.
5. Harriet Tubman is another who helped many slaves escape to freedom.
6. Everybody in our class wanted to learn more about Douglass and Tubman.
7. After all of our class time expired, some of my classmates wanted to meet after school to continue the discussion.
8. I think everyone was pleased with our discussion today.
9. Each in the class was assigned to learn several little-known facts about Douglass to share in class tomorrow.
10. Some historical topics are interesting to most of the students, but few inspire everybody.

EXERCISE 12

Understanding Indefinite Pronouns

Identify the indefinite pronoun in each of the following sentences. Then choose the word or words in parentheses that correctly complete the sentence. Tell whether the indefinite pronoun is singular or plural.

EXAMPLE

One of my friends (studies, study) Civil War history in his spare time. (*One, studies,* singular)

EXERCISE 11

1. Someone suggested that we spend more time studying the life of Frederick Douglass.
2. Everybody in class had at least heard of this great abolitionist.
3. One of the students had read Douglass's autobiography, but most of us had only a cursory knowledge of the civil rights leader.
4. Most history textbooks today devote more attention to Douglass than they have in years past.
5. Harriet Tubman is another who helped many slaves escape to freedom
6. Everybody in our class wanted to learn more about Douglass and Tubman.
7. After all of our class time expired, some of my classmates wanted to meet after school to continue the discussion.
8. I think everyone was pleased with our discussion today.
9. Each in the class was assigned to learn several little-known facts about Douglass to share in class tomorrow.
10. Some historical topics are interesting to most of the students, but few inspire everybody.

1. Few slaves (was, were) allowed to read or write.
2. Either Sam or Tara (visits, visit) a Civil War battlefield site each year.
3. Every semester, somebody always (writes, write) a term paper about the Civil War.
4. Few (displays, display) much interest in writing about Reconstruction.
5. Most available videos (depicts, depict) the war rather than what happened afterward.
6. Some teachers (restricts, restrict) their students from writing about well-known topics.
7. Nothing but the Civil War (interests, interest) my friend George.
8. All topics (offers, offer) something enlightening to the diligent student of history.
9. Neither of us (understands, understand) the other's viewpoint.
10. Most of my favorite authors (is, are) historians.

EXERCISE 12
1. *Few, were,* plural
2. *Either, visits,* singular
3. *Somebody, writes,* singular
4. *Few, display,* plural
5. *Most, depict,* plural
6. *Some, restrict,* plural
7. *Nothing, interests,* singular
8. *All, offer,* plural
9. *Neither, understands,* singular
10. *Most, are,* plural

EXERCISE 13
Using Indefinite Pronouns

Write ten sentences using the indefinite pronouns below.

1. either
2. nothing
3. several
4. both
5. another
6. everyone
7. much
8. others
9. none (singular)
10. none (plural)

EXERCISE 13
Responses will vary. Students should correctly use each indefinite pronoun in a sentence.

REFLEXIVE AND INTENSIVE PRONOUNS

A **reflexive pronoun** refers back to a noun previously used and can be recognized because *–self* and *–selves* have been added to other pronoun forms.

EXAMPLES
I consider **myself** the victim in this little tragedy.
Aunt Silvia often portrays **herself** as a martyr.
The union leaders left **themselves** little room to negotiate.

An **intensive pronoun** is used to emphasize a noun or pronoun already named in a sentence. Intensive pronouns and reflexive pronouns use the same forms.

EXAMPLE
The king **himself** led the assault on the city.

Adding *himself* to *king* emphasizes that the king led the assault; he didn't send someone else to lead the attack.

EXAMPLE
I **myself** do not like popcorn, but my friends all consider it a tasty treat.

Adding *myself* stresses that I do not like popcorn whereas my friends think it is tasty.

USAGE tip

Reflexive and intensive pronouns should never be used as the subject of a sentence.

incorrect
Shelly and myself plan to sell the canoe.
correct
Shelly and I plan to sell the canoe.

Reflexive and Intensive Pronouns		
	singular	**plural**
first person	myself	ourselves
second person	yourself	yourselves
third person	himself, herself, itself	themselves

Try It Yourself

EXERCISE 14

Identifying Reflexive and Intensive Pronouns

Identify the reflective and intensive pronouns in each of the following sentences and indicate whether each is *reflexive* or *intensive.*

1. I bought myself a new pair of sunglasses for our trip to the beach.
2. The soldiers themselves do not want to attack the enemy fort.
3. You can choose a lawyer yourself or one will be selected for you.
4. Charles himself will be piloting this aircraft across the Atlantic.
5. Because she wanted to be like her sister, Renee forced herself to practice each day.
6. I suggest that you yourselves figure out how to resolve this dispute.
7. After rescheduling three meetings, the president herself conducted the meeting.
8. The accountants perjured themselves when testifying before Congress.
9. When Tim saw the battleship itself, he knew that he had chosen the right profession.
10. I consider myself fortunate to have escaped before the house collapsed.

EXERCISE 15

Understanding Reflexive and Intensive Pronouns

Complete each of the following sentences with the correct reflexive or intensive pronoun. Then identify the pronoun as either reflexive or intensive.

EXAMPLE

Julie _____ is coming here tonight. (*herself,* intensive)

EXERCISE 14

1. I bought myself a new pair of sunglasses for our trip to the beach. (reflexive)
2. The soldiers themselves do not want to attack the enemy fort. (intensive)
3. You can choose a lawyer yourself or one will be selected for you. (reflexive)
4. Charles himself will be piloting this aircraft across the Atlantic. (intensive)
5. Because she wanted to be like her sister, Renee forced herself to practice each day. (reflexive)
6. I suggest that you yourselves figure out how to resolve this dispute. (intensive)
7. After rescheduling three meetings, the president herself conducted the meeting. (intensive)
8. The accountants perjured themselves when testifying before Congress. (reflexive)
9. When Tim saw the battleship itself, he knew that he had chosen the right profession. (intensive)
10. I consider myself fortunate to have escaped before the house collapsed. (reflexive)

EXERCISE 15

1. *myself*—reflexive
2. *themselves*—reflexive
3. *himself*—intensive
4. *itself*—intensive

USAGE tip

Do not mistakenly use *hisself* for *himself* and *theirselves* for *themselves.*

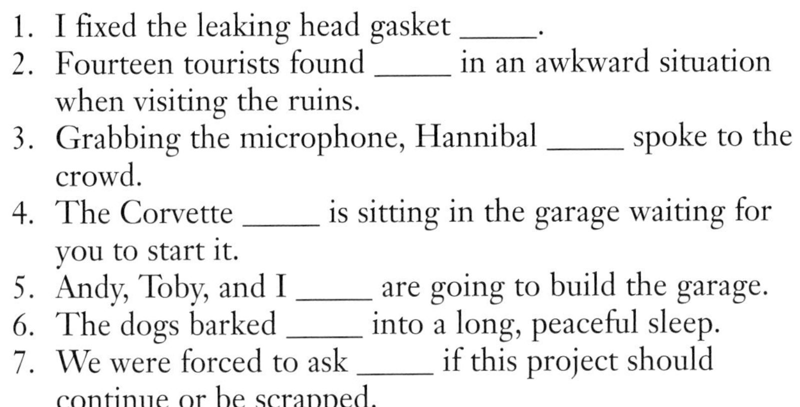

1. I fixed the leaking head gasket _____.
2. Fourteen tourists found _____ in an awkward situation when visiting the ruins.
3. Grabbing the microphone, Hannibal _____ spoke to the crowd.
4. The Corvette _____ is sitting in the garage waiting for you to start it.
5. Andy, Toby, and I _____ are going to build the garage.
6. The dogs barked _____ into a long, peaceful sleep.
7. We were forced to ask _____ if this project should continue or be scrapped.
8. Brooke likes to read _____ to sleep.
9. I'm guessing that you _____ will be responsible for fixing the damage.
10. The Smiths and we consider _____ honored to be invited on this trip.

5. *ourselves* or *myself*—intensive
6. *themselves*—reflexive
7. *ourselves*—reflexive
8. *herself*—reflexive
9. *yourself*—intensive
10. *ourselves*—reflexive

EXERCISE 16
Responses will vary. Students should correctly use reflexive and intensive pronouns in their paragraphs.

EXERCISE 16

Using Reflexive and Intensive Pronouns in Your Writing

Write a paragraph to be shared with a classmate about a goal that you recently achieved. Describe the accomplishment and how you achieved it. Correctly use at least five examples of reflexive and intensive pronouns in your paragraph.

INTERROGATIVE AND DEMONSTRATIVE PRONOUNS

USAGE tip

Who is used when the interrogative pronoun is the subject of a sentence. *Whom* is used when the interrogative pronoun is the object of a verb or a preposition.

An **interrogative pronoun** asks a question. *Who, whom, whose, what,* and *which* are interrogative pronouns.

EXAMPLES

Who planted the trees? (subject)
Whom did you ask? (direct object)
From **whom** did you receive that check? (object of preposition)
Whose lunchbox is on top of the building?
What fell into the potato salad?
Which of the fish likes to devour the others?

A **demonstrative pronoun** points out a specific person, place, thing or idea. The demonstrative pronouns are *this*, *that*, *these*, and *those*.

EXAMPLES

singular	**This** is a well-researched proposal.
plural	**These** are well-researched proposals.
singular	**That** was an agonizingly long meeting.
plural	**Those** were agonizingly long meetings.

Try It Yourself

EXERCISE 17

Identifying Interrogative and Demonstrative Pronouns

Identify and label the interrogative and demonstrative pronouns in the following sentences.

1. From whom did you purchase this six-string guitar?
2. That is a monstrously large automobile you are driving.
3. Whose lawnmower is making such an infernal racket?
4. Are these available in a size 9?
5. Who thought this up in the first place?
6. What will you do to keep the water from rushing into the basement?
7. This is the tartest lemonade you have ever made.
8. Which of the tourists looks the most gullible?
9. Those were the most ferocious bears we ever saw in the forest.
10. Whom did you ask about the reorganization?

EXERCISE 18

Understanding Interrogative and Demonstrative Pronouns

Complete each sentence with the correct word in parentheses.

1. (Who, Whom) did you tell about the surprise party?
2. (This, That) was the worst part of the auditing process.

EXERCISE 17

1. From whom did you purchase this six-string guitar? (interrogative)
2. That is a monstrously large automobile you are driving. (demonstrative)
3. Whose lawnmower is making such an infernal racket? (interrogative)
4. Are these available in a size 9? (demonstrative)
5. Who thought this up in the first place? (*Who*—interrogative; *this*—demonstrative)
6. What will you do to keep the water from rushing into the basement? (interrogative)
7. This is the tartest lemonade you have ever made. (demonstrative)
8. Which of the tourists looks the most gullible? (interrogative)
9. Those were the most ferocious bears we ever saw in the forest. (demonstrative)
10. Whom did you ask about the reorganization? (interrogative)

EXERCISE 18

1. Whom
2. That
3. Who
4. What
5. This
6. whom
7. Those
8. These
9. these
10. Which

3. (Who, Whom) is the first person to enter the building each morning?
4. (What, Which) are the names of your sister's children?
5. (This, That) is the last time I am going to bail you out.
6. To (who, whom) were these gag gifts sent?
7. (These, Those) were among the finest soldiers who ever served in our military.
8. (This, These) are the phrases you should memorize before your trip.
9. Are (these, those) the officers we elected last week?
10. (What, Which) cereal would you like me to buy at the store?

EXERCISE 19
Responses will vary. Students should correctly use each interrogative and demonstrative pronoun in a question or statement.

EXERCISE 19
Using Interrogative and Demonstrative Pronouns

Choose a person representing you in school, local, state, or national government. Write a list of questions you would like to ask him or her. Then write a list of statements about the person and his or her responsibilities. Use each of the interrogative and demonstrative pronouns listed below.

1. who
2. (with) whom
3. (for) whom
4. whose
5. what
6. which
7. this
8. these
9. that
10. those

RELATIVE PRONOUNS

A **relative pronoun** introduces an adjective clause that modifies a noun or pronoun in the main clause. The relative pronouns are *who*, *whom*, *whose*, *which*, and *that*.

EXAMPLES

Abigail Adams, **who** was the second First Lady in American history, was born in Massachusetts in 1744.

Dane Hanson, **whom** you met at orientation, is the professor **who** wrote an article about Adams.

David McCullough is the writer **whose** biography of John Adams is frequently cited by Hanson.

Truman, **which** is another book by McCullough, also won the Pulitzer Prize.

Writing a biography requires research **that** can become very time consuming.

EXERCISE 20

1. Weymouth, which is a town in Massachusetts, is the town in which Abigail Adams was born.

USAGE tip

Relative pronouns use some of the same words as interrogative pronouns, but they do not ask a question.

Try It Yourself

EXERCISE 20

Identifying Relative Pronouns

Identify the relative pronoun and the adjective clause it introduces in each of the following sentences. Be careful not to confuse relative pronouns and interrogative pronouns.

1. Weymouth, which is a town in Massachusetts, is the town in which Abigail Adams was born.
2. She married John Adams, who succeeded George Washington as president of the United States.
3. Adams's correspondence, which provides insight into her relationship with her husband, is of great interest to historians.
4. Her letters provide valuable source material that describes daily life during the American Revolution.
5. Adams, who opposed slavery, was an early champion of women's rights.

2. She married John Adams, who succeeded George Washington as president of the United States.
3. Adams's correspondence, which provides insight into her relationship with her husband, is of great interest to historians.
4. Her letters provide valuable source material that describes daily life during the American Revolution.

USAGE tip

Relative pronouns indicate that a clause is a subordinate clause. A subordinate clause cannot stand by itself.

5. Adams, who opposed slavery, was an early champion of women's rights.
6. After the Revolution, she spent part of her time living in Philadelphia, a city that served as the temporary capitol of the United States.
7. The Adams family, which produced two U.S. presidents, is sometimes referred to as an American dynasty.
8. Adams's son, John Quincy Adams, whom you learned about last week, was the sixth president of the United States.
9. John Adams, whose status as a great president is often debated, seemed to have a loving relationship with his wife.
10. The letter from Abigail to John that I read is dated May 7, 1776.

EXERCISE 21
Responses will vary. Sample responses:
1. who taught my American history course
2. which was written by David McCullough
3. that interests me the most
4. who signed the Declaration of Independence
5. which was assigned three weeks ago
6. whose election was controversial

6. After the Revolution, she spent part of her time living in Philadelphia, a city that served as the temporary capitol of the United States.
7. The Adams family, which produced two U.S. presidents, is sometimes referred to as an American dynasty.
8. Adams's son, John Quincy Adams, whom you learned about last week, was the sixth president of the United States.
9. John Adams, whose status as a great president is often debated, seemed to have a loving relationship with his wife.
10. The letter from Abigail to John that I read is dated May 7, 1776.

EXERCISE 21

Understanding Relative Pronouns

Complete each of the following sentences using the relative pronoun in parentheses and an adjective clause.

1. He was the professor (who) _____.
2. She bought the book *John Adams*, (which) _____.
3. This is a topic of study (that) _____.
4. All of the leaders (who) _____ risked their lives.
5. While researching this report, (which) _____, I learned that historians often disagree with each other.
6. Her son John Quincy, (whose) _____, is not as widely remembered as his father.
7. Andrew Jackson, (whom) _____, often overshadows John Quincy Adams.
8. The era in American history (that) _____ has many similarities to today.
9. Samuel Adams, (who) _____, was a cousin of John.
10. It is the date that John Adams died (that) _____.

EXERCISE 22
Using Relative Pronouns
Write a sentence using each of the relative pronouns listed below.

1. who
2. whom
3. whose
4. which
5. that

7. whom you already read about
8. that we studied this week
9. who was governor of Massachusetts
10. that attracts curiosity

EXERCISE 22
Responses will vary. Students should correctly use each relative pronoun in a sentence. Be certain students do not confuse a relative pronoun with an interrogative pronoun.

PRONOUNS AND APPOSITIVES

An **appositive** is a noun or pronoun that identifies or renames another noun or pronoun. When a pronoun is used as an appositive, in an appositive, or with an appositive, the pronoun should be in the same case as the word to which it refers.

EXAMPLES
nominative case
The tour guides—**she** and **I**—rarely hear a question that we are unable to handle. (Because the pronouns *she* and *I* refer to the subject *tour guides,* the pronouns are in the nominative case.)

The best fielders on the team should be the highest paid players, Scott and **he**. (Because the pronoun *he* refers to the predicate nominative *players,* the pronoun is in the nominative case.)

objective case
I believe that this victory can be attributed to only one man—**me**! (Because the pronoun *me* refers to the direct object *man,* the pronoun is in the objective case.)

The professor gave the students, **them** and **us**, a study guide for the final exam. (Because the pronouns *them* and *us* refer to the indirect object *students,* the pronouns are in the objective case.)

CONTINUED

Paulette bought expensive presents for her two siblings, **her** and **him**. (Because the pronouns *her* and *him* refer to *siblings*, the object of the preposition *for*, the pronouns are in the objective case.)

The pronoun *we* or *us* is sometimes followed by an appositive.

EXAMPLES

We catchers have to wear more equipment than anybody else on the field. (Because *we* is the subject, the pronoun is in the nominative case.)

The drill instructor motivated **us** recruits with copious amounts of yelling and push-ups. (Because the pronoun *us* is the direct object, the pronoun is in the objective case.)

Try It Yourself

EXERCISE 23

1. *him and her; grandchildren;* objective
2. *We; miners;* nominative
3. *she; nurses;* nominative
4. *him and her; culprits;* objective
5. *us; players;* objective
6. *she and he; performers;* nominative
7. *them and us; parties;* objective
8. *us; parents;* objective
9. *me; hires;* objective
10. *they and we; armies;* nominative

EXERCISE 23

Identifying Pronouns and Appositives

Identify pronouns used as appositives, in appositives, or with appositives in each of the following sentences. Identify the word to which the pronoun(s) refers. Then identify the pronoun's case as either nominative or objective.

1. Doris bought her grandchildren, him and her, a pair of watches.
2. We miners have little interest in returning to the partially collapsed shaft.
3. The nurses on duty tonight, Cheryl and she, are the two best we have on staff.
4. Following the trail of crumbs leads to the culprits, him and her.
5. Why are the fans so unsympathetic toward us players?
6. The big losers in the whole fiasco are the performers, she and he.
7. Do you think an agreement is possible between the two parties, them and us?
8. The speakers distributed helpful literature to us parents at the seminar.

9. Alexis looked in the closet and found a couple of uniforms for the new hires, Tom and me.
10. The opposing armies, they and we, maneuvered into position and prepared to battle.

EXERCISE 24

Understanding Pronouns and Appositives

Complete each of the following sentences by choosing the correct pronoun form in parentheses.

1. Delegates selected (she, her) to represent the state at the national convention.
2. The referee read a list of regulations to the two teams, (they, them) and (we, us).
3. Shawn's two favorite performers that he heard today are (she, her) and (he, him).
4. Captain Farello interrogated the two primary suspects, Otto and (I, me).
5. (We, Us) civilians do not understand any of the jargon you are using.
6. The medal winners in attendance, Sara and (I, me), waved to our adoring fans.
7. From a large flat rock, a green turtle watched (we, us) joggers thunder down the road.
8. The most courageous soldiers I have ever served with are (they, them).
9. A witness for the prosecution identified the two bank robbers, (he, him) and (I, me).
10. A cloud of uncertainty settled in among (we, us) astronauts.

EXERCISE 24
1. her
2. them, us
3. she, he
4. me
5. We
6. I
7. us
8. they
9. him, me
10. us

EXERCISE 25

Responses will vary. Students should correctly use pronouns as appositives, in appositives, or with appositives in the nominative and objective cases.

EXERCISE 25

Using Pronouns and Appositives in Your Writing

Write a paragraph for the school literary journal about a recent family outing. Explain who participated and describe the activities you and they took part in. Use at least three pronouns as appositives, in appositives, or with appositives. Correctly use three pronouns in the nominative case and three in the objective case.

FORMS OF *WHO* AND *WHOM*

You've already learned about the pronoun *who* earlier in this unit in the sections on interrogative and relative pronouns. *Who* and *whom* can be used to ask questions and to introduce subordinate clauses. Knowing what form of *who* to use can sometimes be confusing. Just remember that the case of the pronoun *who* is determined by the pronoun's function in a sentence.

nominative case	who, whoever
objective case	whom, whomever

USAGE tip

To determine whether to use *who* or *whom* in a question, rewrite the question as a statement.

statement
We are following (who, whom)?

Then figure out how the pronoun functions in the sentence. Since the pronoun in the sentence above is the direct object, the pronoun should be in the objective case—*whom.*

question
Whom are we following?

EXAMPLES

Who tracked mud onto the new carpet?
(Because *who* is the subject in the sentence, the pronoun is in the nominative case.)

Did you see **who** ran across the lawn?
(Because *who* is the subject of the subordinate clause, the pronoun is in the nominative case.)

Whoever wishes to volunteer will not be disappointed.
(Because *whoever* is the subject in the sentence, the pronoun is in the nominative case.)

Whom did you invite?
(Because *whom* is the direct object in the sentence, the pronoun is in the objective case.)

From **whom** did you hear this bit of information?
(Because *whom* is the object of the preposition *from*, the pronoun is in the objective case.)

Mr. Douglas is a teacher **whom** I revere.
(Because *whom* is the direct object in the subordinate clause, the pronoun is in the objective case.)

Whoever receives this position will face a monumental challenge.
(Because *whoever* is the subject in the sentence, the pronoun is in the nominative case.)

Try It Yourself

EXERCISE 26

Understanding *Who* and *Whom*

Complete each of the following sentences by choosing the correct pronoun form in parentheses.

1. With (who, whom) did you devise this strategy?
2. (Whoever, Whomever) borrowed my shovel has not returned it yet.
3. (Who, whom) will be attending the seminar with you?
4. Your Spanish teacher is (who, whom)?
5. Should (whoever, whomever) is called, respond immediately?
6. Don believes (whoever, whomever) takes this job will quit two weeks later.
7. Ray is one politician (who, whom) we admire.
8. Kyle is a golfer (who, whom) never gives up until the eighteenth hole.
9. For (who, whom) did Shirley buy this new stereo?
10. (Who, Whom) mowed the lawn and trimmed the hedges?

EXERCISE 26
1. whom
2. Whoever
3. Who
4. who
5. whoever
6. whoever
7. whom
8. who
9. whom
10. Who

EXERCISE 27
Responses will vary. Students should correctly use at least two examples each of the pronouns *who, whom, whoever,* and *whomever* in their letters.

EXERCISE 27

Using *Who* and *Whom* in Your Writing

Write a letter to a relative or friend who lives in another state. Update this person with news about members of your family and ask how his or her family is doing. Use at least two examples each of the pronouns *who, whom, whoever,* and *whomever* in your letter.

UNIT 5 REVIEW

ASSESSMENT
Grammar Pretests and Comprehensive Tests are available at www.emcp.com.

TEST YOUR KNOWLEDGE

EXERCISE 1

Identifying Types of Pronouns

Identify the type of pronoun underlined in each sentence by writing *personal*, *possessive*, *indefinite*, *reflexive*, *intensive*, *interrogative*, *demonstrative*, or *relative*. (10 points)

EXAMPLE
Where did you put her tarantula? (possessive)

1. When Gregory's goldfish died, his parents bought another at the pet store.
2. The professor herself seemed puzzled by the question.
3. Would you like to go for a ride in our boat?
4. I drove to the mall to buy myself a new set of work clothes.
5. Your lamp, which is low on oil, will probably go out soon.
6. Everyone in the audience enjoyed the comedy routine.
7. This doesn't belong to me.
8. Will she be enrolling in a degree program this fall?
9. With whom will you be attending the opera?
10. I let Tim borrow the accounting book that I used last semester.

EXERCISE 1
1. indefinite
2. intensive
3. possessive
4. reflexive
5. relative
6. indefinite
7. demonstrative
8. personal
9. interrogative
10. relative

EXERCISE 2

Identifying Pronouns and Antecedents

Identify the pronoun or pronouns in each sentence. Then identify the antecedent to which each pronoun refers. (10 points)

EXAMPLE
Jed and his dog Samson ran across the meadow.
(*his,* pronoun; *Jed,* antecedent)

EXERCISE 2
1. pronoun—*you,* antecedent—*Tony*
2. pronoun—*he,* antecedent—*Tony*
3. pronoun—*it,* antecedent—*base*
4. pronoun—*his,* antecedent—*Tony;* pronoun—*they,* antecedent—*Jodie and Iris*
5. pronoun—*their,* antecedent—*Jodie and Iris;* pronoun—*they,* antecedent—*Jodie and Iris*
6. pronoun—*his,* antecedent—*Tony*
7. pronoun—*him,* antecedent—*Tony*

1. Phil asked Tony, "What do you plan to do after graduation?"
2. Tony enlisted in the Army, and then he boarded a bus for Basic Training.
3. The Army base is located in Colorado; it was 700 miles away from Tony's hometown.
4. Soon after Tony departed, his sisters Jodie and Iris decided they should write him a letter.
5. Jodie and Iris asked several questions in their letter, since they did not know anything about Basic Training.
6. The Army welcomed Tony by shaving off all of his flowing blonde locks.
7. Drill Instructor Hanson made Tony feel at home by giving him endless opportunities to do push-ups.
8. Seeking to motivate his new recruit, Sergeant Hanson asked Tony, "Were you born lazy or do you have to work at it?"
9. Tony excelled at target practice and told his sisters that it was the best part of Boot Camp.
10. At the end of Basic Training, Sergeant Hanson gathered his recruits and told them they would miss his constant yelling.

8. pronoun—*his*, antecedent—*Sergeant Hanson*; pronouns—*you*, *you*, antecedent—*Tony*
9. pronoun—*his*, antecedent—*Tony*; pronoun—*it*, antecedent—*target practice*
10. pronoun—*his*, antecedent—*Sergeant Hanson*; pronoun—*them*, antecedent—*recruits*; pronoun—*his*, antecedent—*Sergeant Hanson*

EXERCISE 3

Understanding Pronoun Cases

Complete each sentence with the correct pronoun in parentheses. Think about the pronoun's function in the sentence and then tell whether the pronoun is in the nominative, objective, or possessive case. (20 points)

EXAMPLE
Fred and (I, me) painted the house in our spare time.
(*I*, nominative)

1. True to form, it is (she, her) who earned the highest score in the class.
2. The pit bull terrier cast an eye at (we, us) before deciding that supper was more interesting.

EXERCISE 3
1. *she*, nominative
2. *us*, objective
3. *they*, nominative
4. *me*, objective
5. *My*, possessive
6. *her*, objective; *me*, objective
7. *He*, nominative
8. *him*, objective
9. *their*, possessive
10. *they*, nominative; *we*, nominative

3. Does Sheila and (they, them) support your decision to go to art school?
4. Both of the ash bats in the rack belong to (I, me).
5. (My, mine) main challenge this semester will be to pass quantum physics.
6. If the principal finds out about Kelli's shenanigans, he will create a world of trouble for (she, her) and (I, me).
7. (He, Him) and Paul performed for the crowd for three hours.
8. The drenched puppy was dried off and fed by Jodie and (he, him).
9. Fifteen of (they's, their) cows escaped when the storm knocked out a section of the fence.
10. Mother suspects that (they, them) and (we, us) played a role in the chocolate cake disappearing.

EXERCISE 4

1. him
2. We
3. they
4. him
5. I
6. us
7. he
8. him, her
9. them
10. she

EXERCISE 4

Understanding Pronouns and Appositives

Choose the pronoun that correctly completes each of the following sentences. (10 points)

EXAMPLE

The two candidates, Simon and (she, her), spoke about the need for fiscal responsibility. *(she)*

1. Ron's athletic skills and knowledge of the game impressed the coaches, Frank and (he, him).
2. (We, Us) mimes do not spend a lot of time studying the thesaurus.
3. Your sisters and (they, them) finally found the restaurant at nine o'clock.
4. A flock of pigeons gathered around the elderly couple, Agnes and (he, him).
5. There is only one crime-fighting duo in this town—you and (I, me)—who can stop the nefarious Red Scorpion.
6. Grandma Skinner gave (we, us) a taste of her superb baking skills.

7. An interesting pair, Tina and (he, him), opened the evening's festivities.
8. Gary persuaded his children, (he, him) and (she, her), to behave for the rest of the service.
9. The director told the actors—(they, them)—to memorize all of their lines.
10. Clearly, a citizen of great integrity has been selected to be grand marshal—(she, her).

EXERCISE 5
Pronoun corrections are underlined:
1. You and I will win 50 or more this season.
2. From whom did you buy that book of elevator passes?
3. She and Sherry operate the cash register when Sid collects the mail.
4. Abandoned by his friends, Jack himself set out to find the chest.
5. Our new professor, who graduated from Princeton in 1980, assigns twelve books every semester.
6. Someone would like to fill his or her car with premium unleaded.
7. The shiny new Corvette in the driveway is theirs.
8. David and she believe that ghosts dwell in the town cemetery.
9. correct
10. Whose plate and glass are still sitting on the table?

EXERCISE 5
Correcting Pronouns

Rewrite the following sentences, correcting any errors in pronouns or pronoun use. If the sentence correctly uses pronouns, write *correct*. (10 points)

EXAMPLE
Three mice gave I quite a fright last night.
(Three mice gave *me* quite a fright last night.)

1. You and me will win 50 or more this season.
2. From who did you buy that book of elevator passes?
3. Her and Sherry operate the cash register when Sid collects the mail.
4. Abandoned by his friends, Jack hisself set out to find the chest.
5. Our new professor, whom graduated from Princeton in 1980, assigns twelve books every semester.
6. Someone would like to fill their car with premium unleaded.
7. The shiny new Corvette in the driveway is there's.
8. David and her believe that ghosts dwell in the town cemetery.
9. The P51 Mustang is one aircraft that proved indispensable during World War II.
10. Who's plate and glass is still sitting on the table?

EXERCISE 6
Responses will vary.
Sample responses:
1. She still wants to drive to Memphis.
2. I found a turtle in my backyard today.
3. Hank quizzed them about their assigned reading.
4. His coat is hanging in the closet.
5. Can anybody hear us?
6. Ted will have to think for himself at college.
7. Shelly herself emerged from the house and began shoveling the sidewalk.

8. For whom did you purchase that package of cookies?
9. If the earrings over there are yours, those must be mine.
10. The sandwich, which costs over six dollars, is loaded with meat and cheese.

EXERCISE 7
Responses will vary. Students should correctly use at least two examples each of the pronouns *who, whoever, whom,* and *whomever* in their paragraphs.

EXERCISE 6
Using Pronouns

Write a sentence using each of the types of pronoun listed below. Underline the pronoun in each sentence. (20 points)

1. personal pronoun
2. nominative pronoun
3. objective pronoun
4. possessive pronoun
5. indefinite pronoun
6. reflexive pronoun
7. intensive pronoun
8. interrogative pronoun
9. demonstrative pronoun
10. relative pronoun

EXERCISE 7
Using *Who* and *Whom* in Your Writing

Write a paragraph describing a comic sidekick for a novel you might one day write. Who is she or he? What makes this character funny? Use at least two examples each of the pronouns *who*, *whoever*, *whom*, and *whomever*. (20 points)

UNIT 6 EXPRESSERS
Verbs

ASSESSMENT
Grammar Pretests and Comprehensive Tests are available at www.emcp.com.

UNIT OVERVIEW

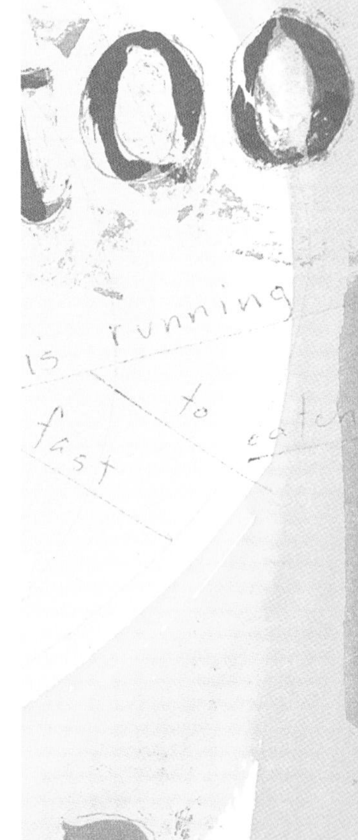

EXPRESSERS: VERBS

PREDICATES—VERBS

In Unit 2 you learned that subjects and predicates are the two basic building blocks in a sentence. Every sentence can be divided into two parts: the **subject** and the **predicate**. The following sentence is divided between the complete subject and the complete predicate.

EXERCISE 1
On the day that President Kennedy was shot, my ninth grade class had been out in the fenced playground of Public School Number 13. We had been given "free" exercise time and had been ordered by our P.E. teacher, Mr. DePalma, to "keep moving." That meant that the girls should jump rope and the boys toss basketballs through a hoop at the far end of the yard. He in the meantime would "keep an eye" on us from just inside the building.

EXAMPLE
The malevolent **goblin** | **paced** back and forth in front of the cavern entrance.

The subject of a sentence names whom or what the sentence is about. The predicate tells what the subject does, is, or has. A **verb** is the predicate without any complements, linkers, or modifiers. In other words, the verb is the simple predicate.

Verbs are the expressers of the English language. **Verbs** are used to express action or a state of being. They work hard to tell whether the action is completed, continuing, or will happen in the future. Verbs also express all kinds of conditions for the action. Verbs in the English language can be from one to four words long.

USAGE tip

Remember: A sentence can have more than one verb.

The malamute **ran** across the street, **barked** at the mole, and **chased** it into a hole.

EXAMPLE
Moles **dig** burrows in the backyard.
Moles **are digging** burrows in the backyard.
Moles **have been digging** burrows in the backyard.
Moles **might have been digging** burrows in the backyard.

Try It Yourself

EXERCISE 1

Identifying Verbs in Literature

Identify each of the verbs in the following literature passage.

On the day that President Kennedy was shot, my ninth grade class had been out in the fenced playground of Public School Number 13. We had been given "free" exercise time and had been ordered by our P.E. teacher, Mr. DePalma, to "keep moving." That meant that the girls should jump rope and the boys toss basketballs through a hoop at the far end of the yard. He in the meantime would "keep an eye" on us from just inside the building.

from "American History"
Judith Ortiz Cofer

Literature
MODEL

ACTION VERBS AND STATE OF BEING VERBS

A **verb** is a word used to express action or a state of being. An **action verb** may express physical action or mental action. The action may or may not be one that you see, but either way an action verb tells you that something is happening, has happened, or will happen.

USAGE tip

Use action verbs in your writing to create strong images and convey a clear picture for your readers.

EXAMPLES

physical action	The sorrel horse **swatted** flies with its tail.
	Mrs. Farrell **lectures** her students about the importance of good hygiene.
mental action	Florence **considered** all of the alternatives.
	Understandably, she **chose** the calling plan with the lowest monthly fee.

LANGUAGELINK
Print exercise worksheets or have students complete exercises online with the LanguageLINK CD.

A state of being verb does not tell about an action. A **state of being verb** tells you when and where someone or something exists. State of being verbs are formed from the verb *to be.*

Forms of *Be*							
am	be	being	was	are	been	is	were

EXAMPLES
A letter **is** in the mailbox.
The calf **may be** in the barn.

Try It Yourself

EXERCISE 2

Identifying Action Verbs and State of Being Verbs in Literature

Tell whether each of the underlined verbs is an action verb or a state of being verb.

Literature MODEL

EXERCISE 2
1. *walked*—action verb
2. *issued*—action verb
3. *rushed*—action verb
4. *was*—state of being verb
5. *was sitting*—action verb
6. *was drowned*—action verb
7. *emerged*—action verb
8. *was*—state of being verb

The next day he walked into town and returned with the parts he needed and a can of gasoline. Late in the afternoon, terrible noises issued from the shed and the old woman rushed out of the house, thinking Lucynell was somewhere having a fit. Lucynell was sitting on a chicken crate, stamping her feet and screaming, "Burrddttt! bddurrddtttt!" but her fuss was drowned out by the car. With a volley of blasts it emerged from the shed, moving in a fierce and stately way. Mr. Shiftlet was in the driver's seat, sitting very erect.

from "The Life You Save May Be Your Own"
Flannery O'Connor

EXERCISE 3

Understanding Action Verbs and State of Being Verbs

Complete each of the following sentences. Include in the predicate an action verb or state of being verb, as indicated.

EXAMPLES

Scores of crows (state of being verb)	Scores of crows **are** on the telephone wires.
Scores of crows (action verb)	Scores of crows **descended** on the sunflower patch.

1. My two favorite uncles (state of being verb)
2. Vaccinating the cows (action verb)
3. The ominous creaking sound (state of being verb)
4. Billowing smoke (action verb)
5. The heavy oak chest (state of being verb)
6. Behind the truck the goat (action verb)
7. Grandma's freshly baked ginger cookies (state of being)
8. Income from last year's harvest (state of being verb)
9. Each morning the faithful rooster (action verb)
10. Sleeping hens (action verb)

EXERCISE 4

Using Action Verbs and State of Being Verbs in Your Writing

Imagine that you will be submitting to the school literary magazine a short story about a mysterious happening in a desolate place. Write an introductory paragraph describing the setting. Include sensory and spatial details that will help your peer readers visualize the scene and feel its desolation. Use at least three different state of being verbs and three different action verbs in your descriptive paragraph.

LINKING VERBS

Like a state of being verb, a linking verb does not express an action. A **linking verb** links, or connects, the subject with a word or words in the predicate that describe or rename the subject.

EXERCISE 3
Responses will vary. Sample responses:
1. My two favorite uncles **are** in the garage fixing the car.
2. Vaccinating the cows **requires** skill and patience.
3. The ominous creaking sound **may be** in the attic.
4. Billowing smoke **rose** high above the city.
5. The heavy oak chest **was** at the foot of the bed.
6. Behind the truck the goat **devoured** the farmer's boots.

7. Grandma's freshly baked ginger cookies **are** on the table.
8. Income from last year's harvest **is** already in the bank.
9. Each morning the faithful rooster **wakes** the entire family.
10. Sleeping hens **make** little noise.

EXERCISE 4
Responses will vary. Students' paragraphs should include at least three different state of being verbs and three different action verbs. Students should carefully choose the verbs to help the audience visualize the desolate setting.

EXAMPLES

A samisen **is** a three-stringed guitarlike instrument. (The verb *is* connects the subject *samisen* with the words that rename it—*a three-stringed guitarlike instrument.*)

Its musical tone **sounds** soothing and melodious. (The verb *sounds* connects the subject *tone* with words that describe it—*soothing* and *melodious.*)

USAGE tip

Some linking verbs are formed from the verb *to be*, but do not confuse a linking verb with a state of being verb. Remember: A linking verb describes or renames the subject.

state of being verb
Ike's horse **was** in the stable.

linking verb
Ike's horse **was** too large for Sally to ride.

Linking verbs can be formed from the verb *to be.*

EXAMPLES

am be being was are been is were

The common linking verbs are listed below.

Linking Verbs			
forms of *be*	feel	remain	sound
become	grow	seem	taste
appear	look	smell	

EXAMPLES

Russell **seems** arrogant and surly, but he **is** actually quite shy. (The linking verb *seems* connects the subject *Russell* with words that describe him—*arrogant* and *surly*; the linking verb *is* connects the subject *he* with another word that describes him—*shy.*)

Lauren **became** animated on the telephone. (The linking verb *became* connects the subject *Lauren* with a word that describes her—*animated.*)

Note that some linking verbs can also be used as action verbs.

EXAMPLES

linking verb The crocodile **grew** unruly after the show began.
action verb The crocodile **grew** a foot longer this fall.

linking verb The filet mignon **tasted** tough and dry.
action verb Bob **tasted** the sauce before pouring it on his steak.

Try It Yourself

EXERCISE 5

Identifying Linking Verbs in Literature

Identify the three linking verbs in the following literature passage. Then identify what each linking verb connects—the subject and the word or words in the predicate that rename or describe the subject.

> By mid-afternoon you are tired of this road, though it has served you well, and you come upon a smaller, unpaved road that evidently leads to your city, though in a convoluted way. After only a moment's pause you turn onto this road, and immediately your automobile registers the change, the chassis bounces, something begins to vibrate, something begins to rattle. This noise is disturbing, but after a while you forget about it in your interest in the beautiful countryside. Here the trees are enormous. There are no villages or houses. For a while the dirt road runs alongside a small river, dangerously close to the river's steep bank, and you begin to feel apprehension.
>
> from "Journey"
> Joyce Carol Oates

EXERCISE 5
1. *are* links *you* and *tired*
2. *is* links *noise* and *disturbing*
3. *are* links *trees* and *enormous*

Literature MODEL

EXERCISE 6

Understanding Linking Verbs

Use each of the following linking verbs in a sentence. If you wish, you may change the form of the verbs.

EXAMPLE
look *(Fred looked worried after receiving the urgent message.)*

EXERCISE 6
Responses will vary. Students should correctly use each linking verb in a sentence.

1. become
2. appear
3. is (form of *be*)
4. taste
5. feel
6. sound
7. smell
8. look
9. seem
10. grow

EXERCISE 7
Responses will vary. In their narrative paragraphs, students should include each of the following linking verbs: *seem, feel, appear, become,* and *grow.* Students should use one of these verbs twice, once as a linking verb and once as an action verb.

EXERCISE 7

Using Linking Verbs in Your Writing

Write the opening three paragraphs for a children's story in which the narrator wakes up one morning and finds that he or she has become a fifteen-foot-tall giant. Describe what the narrator's world is like and how he or she feels about the change in perspective. Include each of the following linking verbs: *seem*, *feel*, *appear*, *become*, and *grow*. You may include other verbs as well. Use one of these verbs twice, once as a linking verb and once as an action verb.

HELPING VERBS, OR AUXILIARY VERBS

A **helping verb**, also called an **auxiliary verb**, helps the main verb to tell about an action. One or more helping verbs followed by a main verb is called a **verb phrase**. In the following examples, the verb phrases are underlined and the helping or auxiliary verbs appear in boldface.

EXAMPLES

Nelson <u>**has** scrubbed</u> the floors of all the mansion's bathrooms.

We <u>**are** planning</u> to visit each of the fifty states in the next three years.

Her dog <u>**had been** trained</u> to bark whenever he smells smoke.

The common helping or auxiliary verbs and their forms are listed in the following chart.

Helping Verbs				
Forms of *be*	**Forms of *do***	**Forms of *have***	**Other helping verbs**	
am	do	have	can	shall
is	does	has	could	should
are	did	had	may	will
was			might	would
were			must	
be				
being				
been				

Some auxiliary verbs—called **modal auxiliaries**—are used to create questions or to express possibility, permission, or obligation. Modal auxiliaries are *can*, *could*, *may*, *might*, *must*, *shall*, *should*, *will*, and *would*. Modal auxiliaries do not change form in the third-person singular, and they have no participial forms. The verb that follows a modal must be in the base form. In the following examples, the verb phrases are underlined and the modal auxiliary verbs appear in boldface.

EXAMPLES

He **can** pitch on three days' rest without any problem.

I **will** need three extra workers to finish building the house on schedule.

Mother **could** hear you talking on the telephone last night.

One of the girls **may** audition for the lead in the musical.

Sometimes helping verbs and main verbs are separated by other words.

EXAMPLES

Fran **will** always **bring** her potato casserole to potluck events. (The modal auxiliary verb *will* and the main verb *bring* are separated by the word *always*.)

CONTINUED

EXERCISE 8
He was infuriated with the marriage broker and swore he would throw him out of the room the minute he reappeared. But Salzman did not come that night, and when Leo's anger had subsided, an uncontrollable despair grew in its place. At first he thought this was caused by his disappointment in Lily, but before long it became evident that he had involved himself with Salzman without a true knowledge of his own intent. He gradually realized—with an emptiness that seized him with six hands—that he had called in the broker to find him a bride because he was incapable of doing it himself. This terrifying insight he had derived as a result of his meeting and conversation with Lily Hirschorn. Her probing questions had somehow irritated him into revealing—to himself more than her—the true nature of his relationship to God, and from that it had come upon him, with shocking force, that apart from his parents, he had never loved anyone.

Scott **may** understandably **decide** to enter the draft following his junior year. (The modal auxiliary verb *may* and the main verb *decide* are separated by the word *understandably*.)

Note that some helping verbs can also be used as main verbs.

EXAMPLES

main verb	Jeff **has** three pieces of pizza on his plate.
helping verb	He **has** always **loved** pepperoni pizza.

Sometimes a helping verb becomes part of a contraction with a pronoun or a negative word.

EXAMPLES

He has not been the first person to ask that question.
He's not been the first person to ask that question.

She will have had thirty credits in psychology when she graduates.
She'll have had thirty credits in psychology when she graduates.

They could have had front-row tickets to the show.
They could've had front-row tickets to the show.

Try It Yourself

EXERCISE 8

Identifying Helping Verbs in Literature

Identify the ten verb phrases that contain a helping verb and a main verb in the following literature passage. Remember that a word or group of words might separate a helping verb and main verb.

Literature MODEL

He was infuriated with the marriage broker and swore he would throw him out of the room the minute he reappeared. But Salzman did not come that night, and when Leo's anger had subsided, an unaccountable despair grew in its place. At first he thought this was caused by his disappointment in Lily, but before long it became evident that he had involved himself with Salzman without a true knowledge of his own intent. He gradually realized—with an emptiness that seized him with six hands—that he had called in the broker to find him a bride because he was incapable of doing it himself. This terrifying insight he had derived as a result of his meeting and conversation with Lily Hirschorn. Her probing questions had somehow irritated him into revealing—to himself more than her—the true nature of his relationship to God, and from that it had come upon him, with shocking force, that apart from his parents, he had never loved anyone.

from "The Magic Barrel"
Bernard Malamud

EXERCISE 9

Understanding Helping Verbs

Complete the following sentences by adding one or more helping verbs that fit the meaning. Then identify the complete verb phrase.

EXAMPLE
Her sister ___ washing dishes in the kitchen all afternoon.
(had been washing).

1. Flossing after supper ___ become part of your daily routine.
2. Climbing ten flights of stairs to reach your office ___ be an exhausting experience.
3. If you do not change the oil regularly, you ___ cause permanent damage to the engine.
4. The neighbors' dogs ___ barking all night.

EXERCISE 9
Responses will vary. Sample responses:

1. Flossing after supper should become part of your daily routine.
2. Climbing ten flights of stairs to reach your office must be an exhausting experience.
3. If you do not change the oil regularly, you could cause permanent damage to the engine.
4. The neighbors' dogs have been barking all night.

5. You finally realized what the counselor has been telling you for the past three months.
6. I don't know if Edna would like to travel to Greece next year.
7. The alligator may look sleepy, but he is actually keeping a close eye on you.
8. These figurines have been meticulously painted by her great-grandfather.
9. A visitor to the general store will always be greeted by a friendly old beagle.
10. Hank could not understand the complicated assembly directions in the manual.

5. You finally realized what the counselor ___ telling you for the past three months.
6. I don't know if Edna ___ like to travel to Greece next year.
7. The alligator ___ look sleepy, but he is actually keeping a close eye on you.
8. These figurines ___ meticulously painted by her great-grandfather.
9. A visitor to the general store ___ always ___ greeted by a friendly old beagle.
10. Hank ___ not understand the complicated assembly directions in the manual.

EXERCISE 10

Using Helping Verbs in Your Writing

Write a journal entry about something you did recently that you would do differently if you had the opportunity. Explain your reasons for making the original decision and why you would now choose a different path. Use at least five different helping verbs in your paragraph.

EXERCISE 10
Responses will vary. Students' journal entries should include at least five different helping verbs.

TRANSITIVE VERBS AND INTRANSITIVE VERBS

An action verb that has a direct object is called a **transitive verb.** An action verb that does not have a direct object is called an **intransitive verb.**

EXAMPLES

transitive verb	Howard **pruned** the **trees** in the backyard. (The trees receive the action; therefore, they are the direct object of the transitive verb *pruned.*)
intransitive verb	Howard **pruned** all afternoon so that his shrubs would impress his guests. (There is no direct object; therefore, *pruned* is an intransitive verb.)

Don't confuse a direct object with an object of a preposition. A direct object never appears in a prepositional phrase.

EXAMPLES

direct object of a verb	Arthur **quieted** the **baby** with a song.
object of a preposition	Arthur quieted the baby with a **song**.

Try It Yourself

EXERCISE 11

Identifying Transitive and Intransitive Verbs in Literature

Identify the underlined verbs in the following literature passage as either transitive or intransitive. If a verb is transitive, identify its direct object.

> She cast her sights about—her daughters ducked—and found her husband's office in need. Several days a week, dressed professionally in a white smock with a little name tag pinned on the lapel, a shopping bag full of cleaning materials and rags, she rode with her husband in his car to the Bronx. On the way, she organized the glove compartment or took off the address stickers from the magazines for the waiting room because she had read somewhere how by means of these stickers drug addict patients found out where doctors lived and burglarized their homes looking for syringes.

from "Daughter of Invention"
Julia Alvarez

EXERCISE 11

1. *cast*—transitive; direct object—*sights*
2. *ducked*—intransitive
3. *found*—transitive; direct object—*office*
4. *rode*—intransitive
5. *organized*—transitive; direct object—*glove compartment*
6. *took*—transitive; direct object—*stickers*
7. *had read*—transitive; direct object—*how . . . syringes* (noun clause)
8. *found*—transitive; direct object—*where doctors lived* (noun clause)
9. *burglarized*—transitive; direct object—*homes*

Literature MODEL

EXERCISE 12

Understanding Transitive and Intransitive Verbs

Write a sentence using the transitive or intransitive verb indicated. Underline the verb. If the verb is transitive, then underline its direct object as well.

EXERCISE 12
Responses will vary. Students should use direct objects with all transitive verbs.

1. I had traveled for four hours to hear the speaker.
2. I bought a new DVD player to replace our broken VCR.
3. Ushers will gather the congregations' votes at the end of the meeting.
4. Father could construct a birdhouse in less than an hour.
5. She had meant to lock the door but at the last minute had forgotten.
6. His counselor was urging Terrance to attend summer school.
7. The arson investigator believed the testimony of the property owner.
8. The paper carrier could have been paid yesterday.
9. Iris and her daughter flew a kite in the park Saturday afternoon.
10. The union might have agreed to your offer had you been less antagonistic.

EXERCISE 13
Responses will vary. Students should use at least five transitive verbs and five intransitive verbs in their brief articles.

EXAMPLES

found (transitive)	*She found the money in the couch, but still needed more for the fare.*
can look (intransitive)	*You can look in the cellar yourself if you don't believe me.*

1. traveled (intransitive)
2. bought (transitive)
3. will gather (transitive)
4. construct (transitive)
5. had forgotten (intransitive)
6. was urging (transitive)
7. believed (transitive)
8. could have been paid (intransitive)
9. flew (transitive)
10. might have agreed (intransitive)

EXERCISE 13

Using Transitive and Intransitive Verbs in Your Writing

Write a brief article for your local newspaper reporting on an important local sports event, either real or imagined. Be sure to report who participated (teams or individuals), who won, where and when it took place, and how the victors emerged triumphant. Use at least three transitive verbs and three intransitive verbs in your article.

VERB TENSES

The Simple Tenses

Verbs have different forms, called **tenses**, which are used to tell the time in which an action takes place. In your writing and speaking, you most commonly use the simple tenses. The **simple tenses** of the verb are **present, past,** and **future.**

The **present tense** tells that an action happens now—in the present time.

EXAMPLES

present tense singular	A prophet **announces** future events.
present tense plural	Prophets **announce** future events.
present tense singular	The chrysanthemum **blooms** in the autumn.
present tense plural	The chrysanthemums **bloom** in the autumn.

The **past tense** tells that an action happened in the past—prior to the present time. The past tense of a regular verb is formed by adding *–d* or *–ed* to the present verb form.

EXAMPLES

past tense singular	A prophet **announced** the fall of the city.
past tense plural	Prophets **announced** the fall of the city.
past tense singular	The chrysanthemum **bloomed** in the autumn.
past tense plural	The chrysanthemums **bloomed** in the autumn.

The **future tense** tells that an action will happen in the future. The future tense is formed by adding the word *will* or *shall* before the present verb form.

EXAMPLES

future tense singular	A prophet **will announce** the fall of the city.
future tense plural	Prophets **will announce** the fall of the city.

The Perfect Tenses

The **perfect tenses** of verbs also express present, past, and future time, but they show that the action continued and was completed over a period of time or that the action will be completed in the present or future. The perfect tense is formed by using *has*, *have*, or *had* with the past participle.

EXAMPLES

present perfect singular	James **has written** his report. The report **has been written** by James.
present perfect plural	James and Diane **have written** their reports. (*have* or *has* + past participle)
past perfect singular	James **had written** his report yesterday. The report **had been written** yesterday by James.
past perfect plural	James and Diane **had written** their reports yesterday. (*had* + past participle)
future perfect singular	James **will** (shall) **have written** his report by now. The report **will** (shall) **have been written** by now.
future perfect plural	James and Diane **will** (shall) **have written** their reports by now. (*will have* or *shall have* + past participle)

The Progressive and Emphatic Verb Forms

Each of the six tenses has another form called the progressive form. The **progressive form** of a verb is used to express continuing action or state of being. The progressive form is made of the appropriate tense of the verb *be* and the present participle of a verb. The following are examples of the six progressive forms.

USAGE tip

The present progressive is often used with an adverb to indicate the time of the action.

Joey **is singing** showtunes now. Her sister **is walking** to school today.

EXAMPLES

present progressive	I **am jogging**. He **is jogging**. They **are jogging**.

CONTINUED

past progressive	I **was jogging.** They **were jogging.**
future progressive	I **will (shall) be jogging.**
present perfect progressive	He **has been jogging.** They **have been jogging.**
past perfect progressive	I **had been jogging.**
future perfect progressive	I **will (shall) have been jogging.**

The **emphatic form** of a verb is used to express emphasis. Only the present and past tenses have the emphatic form.

EXAMPLES

present emphatic	I **do believe** we will be late. It **does seem** to be chilly outside.
past emphatic	I **did send** a thank-you note.

USAGE tip

The emphatic form is often used to correct or contradict. It is also often used in questions and negative statements.

Why **does** the rain **continue** to fall?
Boomerangs sometimes **don't return** to the same location.

Try It Yourself

EXERCISE 14

Identifying Verb Tenses in Literature

Identify the tenses of the underlined verbs in the following literature passage.

> A rising sheet of water curved over him, fell down upon him, blinded him, strangled him! The cannon had taken a hand in the game. As he shook his head free from the commotion of the smitten water he heard the deflected shot humming through the air ahead, and in an instant it was cracking and smashing the branches in the forest beyond.
>
> "They will not do that again," he thought; "the next time they will use a charge of grape. I must keep my eye upon the gun; the smoke will apprise me—the report arrives too late; it lags behind the missile. That is a good gun."
>
> from "An Occurrence at Owl Creek Bridge"
> Ambrose Bierce

EXERCISE 14

1. *curved*—past
2. *blinded*—past
3. *had taken*—past perfect
4. *shook*—past
5. *heard*—past
6. *was cracking*—past progressive
7. *will do*—future
8. *thought*—past
9. *will use*—future
10. *must keep*—present
11. *will apprise*—future
12. *arrives*—present
13. *is*—present

Literature MODEL

EXERCISE 15
1. had intrigued
2. have been analyzing
3. are reading
4. did see
5. have debated
6. engaged
7. will be reenacting
8. decimated
9. have been reading
10. have inspired

EXERCISE 15

Understanding Verb Tenses

Complete each of the following sentences with the correct form of the verb given in parentheses. Remember that the verb must agree in number and gender with its subject.

EXAMPLE

Soldiers (present tense of *clean*) their weapons each day to ensure optimum performance. *(clean)*

1. Even in the early 1900s, the Battle of Gettysburg (past perfect of *intrigue*) Civil War scholars.
2. Scholars of the conflict (present perfect progressive of *analyze*) the decisions of generals at the battle.
3. When opening these diaries from the Civil War, we (present progressive of *read*) the words of young men and women who lived 140 years ago.
4. Combatants on both sides (emphatic form of *see*) themselves as fighting for a noble cause.
5. Historians (present perfect of *debate*) whether General Robert E. Lee should have invaded Pennsylvania or not.
6. The Army of Northern Virginia (past tense of *engage*) the Army of the Potomac at Gettysburg in July 1863.
7. Civil War enthusiasts (future progressive of *reenact*) Pickett's charge for decades to come.
8. The Battle of Gettysburg (past tense of *decimate*) over one-third of Lee's army.
9. Schoolchildren (present perfect progressive of *read*) Lincoln's Gettysburg Address for 140 years.
10. Lincoln's words (present perfect of *inspire*) Americans for generations.

EXERCISE 16

Using Verb Tenses in Your Writing

Imagine that your class will be reenacting a battle from the Civil War and that your job is to assign roles for each student. Describe who will be playing each role. In addition, write directions for the opening scene of the battle; establish where and when the action takes place, who is involved, and what each person will do when the battle begins. In your directions, use all six of the verb forms at least once and include one example each of the progressive and emphatic forms.

EXERCISE 16

Responses will vary. Students' paragraphs should include at least one example of each of the six verb tenses: present, past, future, present perfect, past perfect, and future perfect, as well as one example each of the progressive and emphatic forms.

PASSIVE VOICE AND ACTIVE VOICE

Did you know that verbs have voices? The **voice** of an action verb tells whether the subject of the sentence performs or receives the action. When the subject performs the action of the verb, the verb is in the **active voice**. When the subject receives the action of the verb, the verb is in the **passive voice**.

EXAMPLES

active voice	The bugler **blew** his freshly shined horn.
passive voice	The freshly shined horn **was blown** by the bugler.

USAGE tip

A sentence written in the passive voice uses some form of *be* as a helping verb, followed by a past participle.

The active voice is used more frequently than the passive voice. Active verbs express your ideas more directly. The passive voice is usually used when the receiver of the action is emphasized or the performer of the action is unknown or indefinite. In the following example sentence, knowledge of the army's movements is emphasized.

EXAMPLE

The army's movements **have been spotted** by enemy spies.

A sentence written in the passive voice can usually be revised to the active voice.

EXERCISE 17
1. *wore*—active
2. *were performed*—passive
3. *were performed*—passive
4. *wore*—active
5. *conspired*—active
6. *was called*—passive
7. *were esteemed*—passive
8. *was associated*—passive
9. *could be*—active

EXAMPLES

passive voice Cemetery Ridge **was rocked** by the thunderous artillery barrage.

active voice The thunderous artillery barrage **rocked** Cemetery Ridge.

Try It Yourself

EXERCISE 17

Identifying Passive and Active Verbs in Literature

Identify the underlined verbs in the following literature passage as either active or passive.

Literature MODEL

The home plantation of Colonel Lloyd wore the appearance of a country village. All the mechanical operations for all the farms were performed here. The shoemaking and mending, the blacksmithing, cartwrighting, coopering, weaving, and grain-grinding, were all performed by the slaves on the home plantation. The whole place wore a businesslike aspect very unlike the neighboring farms. The number of houses, too, conspired to give it advantage over the neighboring farms. It was called by the slaves the *Great House Farm.* Few privileges were esteemed higher, by the slaves of the out-farms, than that of being selected to do errands at the Great House Farm. It was associated in their minds with greatness. A representative could not be prouder of his election to a seat in the American Congress, than a slave on one of the out-farms would be of his election to do errands at the Great House Farm.

from *Narrative of the Life of Frederick Douglass, an American Slave, Written by Himself*
Frederick Douglass

EXERCISE 18

Understanding Passive and Active Verbs

Revise each of the following sentences so the verb is in the active voice.

1. Income for plantation owners had been generated by the labor of slaves.
2. Persons of African descent were denied an education by state law in the South.
3. The children of slaves were often sold away from their parents by owners.
4. A slave could be separated from his or her spouse at any time by a Southern planter.
5. The system of slavery was criticized by abolitionists such as Frederick Douglass.
6. Frederick Douglass could not be silenced from speaking out against the institution by slave owners.
7. Slaves numbered one-third of the population of the South in 1860.
8. The beginning of the end of slavery was not marked until the outbreak of the Civil War in 1861.
9. Slaves living in rebel-occupied lands were freed by the Emancipation Proclamation in 1863.
10. The abolition of slavery was extended to all parts of the nation in 1865 by the Thirteenth Amendment.

EXERCISE 18

Responses may vary slightly.

Sample responses:

1. The labor of slaves had been generating income for plantation owners.
2. State law in the South denied persons of African descent an education.
3. Owners often sold the children of slaves away from their parents.
4. A Southern planter could separate a slave from his or her spouse at any time.
5. Abolitionists such as Frederick Douglass criticized the system of slavery.
6. Slave owners could not silence Frederick Douglass from speaking out against the institution.
7. The number of slaves made up one-third of the population of the South in 1860.
8. The outbreak of the Civil War in 1861 marked the beginning of the end of slavery.
9. The Emancipation Proclamation freed slaves living in rebel-occupied lands in 1863.
10. The Thirteenth Amendment extended the abolition of slavery to all parts of the nation in 1865.

EXERCISE 19

Using Passive and Active Verbs in Your Writing

Imagine that your history class will publish an anthology called *Hard-Won Rights*. Select a group of people in American history that had to fight for civil rights. In an informative paragraph for the anthology, identify the group and explain why and how its campaign was significant. Use at least three passive verbs and three active verbs in your paragraph.

IRREGULAR VERBS

USAGE tip

Participles are verb forms that are action adjectives. There are two kinds of participles: *present participles* and *past participles.* Present participles end in *–ing.* Past participles end in *–ed.*

EXERCISE 19
Responses will vary. Students should use at least three passive verbs and three active verbs in their informative paragraphs.

As you know, verb forms change to show when an action happened. The many forms of the verb are based on its three principal parts: the present, the past, and the past participle. For all regular verbs, *–d* or *–ed* are added to form the past and the past participle.

EXAMPLES

present	answer	close
past	answered	closed
past participle	(has, have) answered	(has, have) closed

Some regular verbs change their spelling when *–d* or *–ed* is added. (See Unit 17 Spelling, page 457–458.)

EXAMPLES

present	marry	omit
past	married	omitted
past participle	(has, have) married	(has, have) omitted

Verbs that do not follow the regular pattern of adding *–d* or *–ed* are called **irregular verbs**. Some of these irregular verbs have the same spelling for their past and past participle forms. Some have the same spelling in all three principal parts. Other irregular verbs have three different forms.

EXAMPLES

present	do	set	feel
past	did	set	felt
past participle	(has, have) done	(has, have) set	(has, have) felt

When you're not sure whether a verb is regular or irregular, look up the verb in a dictionary. Many of the common irregular verbs are listed in the following chart.

Pattern	Present	Past	Past Participle
Three different forms	begin	began	(has, have) begun
	drink	drank	(has, have) drunk
	grow	grew	(has, have) grown
	know	knew	(has, have) known
	ring	rang	(has, have) rung
	shrink	shrank or shrunk	(has, have) shrunk
	sing	sang	(has, have) sung
	spring	sprang or sprung	(has, have) sprung
	swim	swam	(has, have) swum
	throw	threw	(has, have) thrown
	write	wrote	(has, have) written
Same past and past participle form	bring	brought	(has, have) brought
	buy	bought	(has, have) bought
	catch	caught	(has, have) caught
	creep	crept	(has, have) crept
	feel	felt	(has, have) felt
	get	got	(has, have) got/gotten
	keep	kept	(has, have) kept
	lay	laid	(has, have) laid
	lead	led	(has, have) led
	leave	left	(has, have) left
	lend	lent	(has, have) lent
	lose	lost	(has, have) lost
	make	made	(has, have) made
	pay	paid	(has, have) paid
	say	said	(has, have) said
	seek	sought	(has, have) sought
	sell	sold	(has, have) sold
	sit	sat	(has, have) sat
	sleep	slept	(has, have) slept
	swing	swung	(has, have) swung
	teach	taught	(has, have) taught
	think	thought	(has, have) thought
	win	won	(has, have) won

Try It Yourself

EXERCISE 20

Identifying Regular and Irregular Verbs in Literature

Identify each of the underlined verbs as either regular or irregular.

EXERCISE 20

1. *seated*—regular
2. *look*—regular
3. *grew*—irregular
4. *glowed*—regular
5. *was steeped*—regular
6. *have said*—irregular

Literature MODEL

Ascending to his chamber, he seated himself near the window, but within the shadow thrown by the depth of the wall, so that he could look down into the garden with little risk of being discovered. All beneath his eye was a solitude. The strange plants were basking in the sunshine, and now and then nodding gently to one another, as if in acknowledgment of sympathy and kindred. In the midst, by the shattered fountain, grew the magnificent shrub, with its purple gems clustering all over it; they glowed in the air, and gleamed back again out of the depths of the pool, which thus seemed to overflow with colored radiance from the rich reflection that was steeped in it. At first, as we have said, the garden was a solitude.

from "Rappaccini's Daughter"
Nathaniel Hawthorne

EXERCISE 21
1. found
2. bit
3. hurt
4. shown
5. paid
6. drank, bought
7. taught
8. grew
9. crept
10. drunk

EXERCISE 21

Understanding Irregular Verbs

Write the correct past or past participle form of the irregular verb given in parentheses.

1. Nate has always (find) great joy in gardening.
2. The lizard (bite) the unsuspecting visitor.
3. Beatrice had been (hurt) by her friend's sharp comments.
4. She will have (show) you the garden by tomorrow afternoon.
5. Giovanni has (pay) for his previous shortsightedness.
6. After he (drink) too much, he (buy) more than he could afford.
7. The professor has not yet (teach) us everything he knows about botany.
8. The multicolored plant (grow) quickly in the spring.
9. Vines from several different sources (creep) up the side of the building.
10. Beatrice may have (drink) all of the liquid in the vial.

EXERCISE 22

Using Irregular Verbs in Your Writing

A fantasy is a literary work that contains highly unrealistic elements. Write the introductory paragraph for a young adult short story containing fantastic elements in which you use at least five irregular verbs in the past and past participle forms. In your introductory paragraph, try to capture your readers' imaginations.

EXERCISE 22
Responses will vary. Students should correctly use at least five irregular verbs in the past and past participle forms in their introductory paragraphs.

MOOD FORMS OF VERBS

The **mood** of a verb indicates the status of the action or condition it expresses. Verbs have three mood forms: *indicative*, *imperative*, and *subjunctive*.

The **indicative mood** is used to express a fact, an opinion, or a question.

EXAMPLES

fact	Brenda **is** an accountant.
opinion	Her employers **think** she **is** hardworking and resourceful.
question	**Have** you ever **hired** an accountant to figure your taxes?

The **imperative** mood is used to make a request or give a command. The subject *you* is understood in the imperative mood form.

EXAMPLES

request	[You] Please **bring** the book to me.
command	[You] **Look** out!

The **subjunctive mood** is used to express a wish or state a condition that is contrary to fact.

EXAMPLES

wish	Francine wishes she **were** a millionaire.
contrary to fact	If I **had** wings, I could fly to Hawaii.

Try It Yourself

EXERCISE 23
1. indicative
2. subjunctive
3. indicative, subjunctive
4. imperative
5. imperative
6. subjunctive
7. indicative
8. indicative
9. indicative
10. indicative

EXERCISE 23

Identifying Mood Forms of Verbs

In each of the following sentences, identify the mood of the underlined verb as indicative, imperative, or subjunctive.

1. My nephew had found the lost keys under the sofa.
2. If Mary had seen a preview, she would not have gone to the movie.
3. Ever the optimist, Raymond hoped his team would overcome a large fourth-quarter deficit.
4. Read the instructions before trying to program the VCR.
5. Wash the dishes that are sitting in the sink.
6. I would like to believe that little fairy tale you just told.
7. Jonathon longed to return to his home in Scotland.
8. Those empty cardboard boxes provide hours of entertainment for the children.
9. Remove your hat when entering a building.
10. Did you understand the lyrics to that song?

EXERCISE 24
Responses will vary slightly.
Sample responses:
1. Take the kids to the park this afternoon.
2. I wish somebody would answer the phone.
3. You will come home over Christmas break.

EXERCISE 24

Understanding Mood Forms of Verbs

Rewrite the following sentences as indicated. You may have to alter the wording on occasion.

EXAMPLE
I don't have to earn any more credits to graduate. (Change from indicative to subjunctive.)
(I wish I didn't have to earn any more credits to graduate.)

1. She would love to take the kids to the park this afternoon. (Change from subjunctive to imperative.)
2. Somebody had better answer the phone. (Change from indicative to subjunctive.)
3. Do you think you could come home over Christmas break? (Change from subjunctive to indicative.)

4. Only three more words are needed to complete the crossword puzzle. (Change from indicative to subjunctive.)
5. Finish reading the book so we can discuss it tomorrow night. (Change from imperative to subjunctive.)
6. You can climb out of debt if you budget your money more effectively. (Change from indicative to imperative.)
7. If you'd landed the Nelson account, I'd have given you a big bonus. (Change from subjunctive to indicative.)
8. You will have an accident if you don't keep your eyes on the road. (Change from subjunctive to imperative.)
9. Jiggling the handle will stop the toilet from running. (Change from indicative to imperative.)
10. After you finish shoveling, throw down some salt so that ice does not form on the walk. (Change from imperative to subjunctive.)

4. If only I had three more words, I could complete the crossword puzzle.
5. If you had finished reading the book, we could have discussed it tomorrow night.
6. Budget your money more effectively so you can climb out of debt.
7. I will give you all a big bonus for landing the Nelson account.
8. Keep your eyes on the road so you won't have an accident.
9. Jiggle the handle to stop the toilet from running.
10. If you had thrown down some salt after you finished shoveling, ice

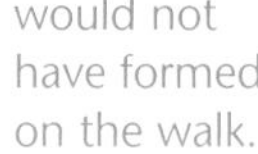
would not have formed on the walk.

EXERCISE 25

Using Mood Forms of Verbs in Your Writing

For an "Alternative Lives" issue of the school literary journal, write an introductory paragraph to an essay about how your life could have been different if you had done something slightly differently. Begin by completing the following statement: "If I had only . . ." Use two examples of each of the indicative, imperative, and subjunctive mood forms of verbs.

EXERCISE 25
Responses will vary. Students should use two examples of each of the three mood forms of verbs in their essays.

ASSESSMENT
Grammar Pretests and Comprehensive Tests are available at www.emcp.com.

UNIT 6 REVIEW

TEST YOUR KNOWLEDGE

EXERCISE 1

Identifying Verbs

Identify each of the underlined verbs in the following sentences as either an action, state of being, linking, or helping verb. (10 points)

EXAMPLE
In 1828, Andrew Jackson was elected president.
(helping verb)

1. In the opinion of some scholars, Jackson could be the nation's best president.
2. Few can dispute that "Old Hickory" was one of the strongest chief executives.
3. However, any assessment of Jackson must take into account his Indian policies.
4. The election of Jackson in 1828 marked the start of the second two-party system in American politics.
5. Soon after taking office, Jackson faced the nullification crisis in South Carolina.
6. John C. Calhoun was the vice president during Jackson's first term.
7. In 1832, Henry Clay of the Whig Party challenged Jackson for the presidency.
8. Jackson sought to remove Indian tribes that were in the South.
9. The government's Indian Removal policy of the 1830s remains one of the darkest incidents in American history.
10. Two other controversies in Jackson's presidency were the Bank War and the Peggy Eaton affair.

EXERCISE 1
1. linking verb
2. linking verb
3. helping verb
4. action verb
5. action verb
6. linking verb
7. action verb
8. state of being verb
9. action verb
10. linking verb

EXERCISE 2

Identifying Transitive and Intransitive Verbs

Identify the verb in each of the following sentences. Tell whether the verb is transitive or intransitive. If a verb is transitive, identify its direct object.
(10 points)

EXAMPLE
Millions of Americans bought television sets in the 1950s.
(*bought,* verb, transitive; *television sets,* direct object)

1. In 1957, more Americans owned television sets than refrigerators.
2. The radio industry was the precursor to the television industry.
3. Advertisers such as GE and Proctor and Gamble determined most programming decisions.
4. College and professional sports became more popular because of television.
5. New fashions and product markets were created by advertising.
6. Programming of the 1950s and early 1960s featured situation comedies such as *Ozzie and Harriet* and *Leave It to Beaver*.
7. Television replaced movies and the radio as the chief source of diversion for Americans.
8. Programming inadvertently created conditions that helped foster social conflict.
9. Groups outside the white middle-class world portrayed on television felt alienated and powerless.
10. Television news covered the social upheavals of the 1950s and 1960s.

EXERCISE 2
1. verb—*owned*: transitive; direct object—*television sets*
2. verb—*was*: intransitive
3. verb—*determined*: transitive; direct object—*decisions*
4. verb—*became*: intransitive
5. verb—*were created*: intransitive
6. verb—*featured*: transitive; direct object—*comedies*
7. verb—*replaced*: transitive; direct object—*movies, radio*
8. verb—*created*: transitive; direct object—*conditions*; verb—*helped*, direct object—*[to] foster social conflict*
9. verb—*felt*: intransitive
10. verb—*covered:* transitive; direct object—*upheavals*

EXERCISE 3

Identifying Verb Tenses

Identify the tense of each of the underlined verbs as present, past, future, present perfect, past perfect, or future perfect.
(10 points)

EXERCISE 3
1. past
2. future (conditional)
3. past perfect
4. past perfect
5. future perfect
6. past
7. present
8. past perfect
9. present perfect
10. future

EXAMPLE
Theodore Roosevelt <u>served</u> as president from 1901 to 1909. (past)

1. In 1900, Theodore Roosevelt <u>was selected</u> by the Republican Party to be their candidate for vice president.
2. Roosevelt <u>would</u> eventually <u>become</u> one of the most respected presidents in U.S. history.
3. William McKinley <u>had won</u> a second term as president in 1900.
4. Roosevelt <u>had been celebrated</u> as a national hero for his role in the Spanish American War in 1898.
5. In 1900, nobody could predict that McKinley <u>will have been assassinated</u> by the end the following year.
6. At forty-two years of age, Roosevelt <u>was</u> the youngest man to assume the presidency.
7. Most historians <u>consider</u> Roosevelt a champion of moderate change.
8. Rosevelt <u>had wanted</u> to use the federal government to be a mediator of the public good, so he engaged in a few highly publicized campaigns against corporate abuse.
9. Though Roosevelt <u>has maintained</u> a reputation as a trust-buster, his administration did not reverse the trend of concentration in the industrial economy.
10. Roosevelt's legacy <u>will continue</u> to fascinate Americans in the twenty-first century.

EXERCISE 4
Responses will vary.
Sample responses:
1. Our new neighbors are gregarious and loquacious.
2. The snow from last week's storm is still in the yard.
3. Cars following a detour route hit speed bumps on our street.
4. Ursula's two boys race up and down the sidewalk.

EXERCISE 4
Understanding Verbs

Complete each of the following sentences using in the predicate the type of verb indicated in parentheses. (10 points)

EXAMPLE
The Nelson's oak tree (linking verb)
(The Nelson's oak tree is at least two hundred years old.)

1. Our new neighbors (linking verb)
2. The snow from last week's storm (state of being verb)
3. Cars following a detour route (transitive verb)
4. Ursula's two boys (action verb)

5. She (transitive verb)
6. Randy and Renee (intransitive verb)
7. Our backyard deck (intransitive verb)
8. Under the bushes, there (helping verb)
9. At the cookout they (transitive verb)
10. This neighborhood (linking verb)

EXERCISE 5

Understanding Verb Tenses and Progressive and Emphatic Verb Forms

Complete each of the following sentences with the form of the verb given in parentheses. Underline the verb phrase. (10 points)

EXAMPLE

Once the workers are finished, everyone (future progressive of *admire*) our new roof.

(Once the workers are finished, everyone will be admiring our new roof.)

1. We (past perfect progressive of *discuss*) reshingling the house for several months.
2. I must admit, we (emphatic form of *need*) a new roof.
3. If we do not select the higher grade of shingle, we (future progressive of *regret*) that decision for the next twenty years.
4. Jeff (present perfect of *call*) several companies to provide estimates.
5. Hanson Roofing (past of *do*) a nice job on the Swanson's house last year.
6. Betty Smith (emphatic form of *warn*) us about hiring Treetop Roof Company despite its low bid.
7. By next week, we (future perfect of *decide*) which company we want to hire.
8. The foreman (past progressive of *think*) that the job would take a little more than a week.
9. I hope the crew (future of *remember*) to clean up the yard at the end of each day.
10. We (emphatic form of *hope*) that this roof will last twenty years or more.

5. She bakes Dutch apple pie on Saturdays.
6. Randy and Renee sit on their front porch in the evenings.
7. Our backyard deck bleaches in the sunlight.
8. Under the bushes, there must be a rabbit hiding.
9. At the cookout they served steaks and hamburgers.
10. This neighborhood is quiet and pleasant.

EXERCISE 5

1. had been discussing
2. do need
3. will be regretting
4. has called
5. did
6. did warn
7. will have decided
8. was thinking
9. will remember
10. do hope

EXERCISE 6
Responses will vary slightly.

EXERCISE 6

Understanding Passive Voice and Active Voice

Revise the following paragraph, changing any passive verbs to active verbs. (10 points)

> The stadium was still being filled with fans when the first ball was thrown by the pitcher. Garrison was asked by the manager to start this game after only three days' rest. The team's number four starter had been injured by a line drive in his previous outing. Garrison had been hailed as the team's savior by the press all season long. A long fly ball from the leadoff hitter was caught by Tony, the speedy left fielder. In the dugout sat the manager nervously chewing sunflower seeds. He geared up for another tense October battle.

EXERCISE 7
Responses will vary. In their paragraphs students should correctly use the following irregular verbs in the present, past, and past participle forms: *buy, bought, has/have bought; pay, paid, has/have paid; bring, brought, has/have brought; keep, kept, has/have kept; cost, cost, has/have cost; see, saw, has/have seen.*

EXERCISE 7

Using Irregular Verbs in Your Writing

For a reporter interested in young adults' shopping habits, write a description of a recent shopping trip you took with friends. Be sure to include details about stores, other customers, and items that you purchased. Use the present, past, and past participle forms of each of the following irregular verbs in your paragraph: *buy*, *pay*, *bring*, *keep*, *cost*, and *see*. (20 points)

EXERCISE 8
Responses will vary. Students' descriptions should include two examples each of the indicative, imperative, and subjunctive mood forms of verbs.

EXERCISE 8

Using Mood Forms of Verbs in Your Writing

For your yearbook, write a description of an event or experience during the year that holds special meaning for you. Include in your description information about the event, why it was important to you, and how you think the event or experience affected your perception of your junior year. In your description use two examples each of the indicative, imperative, and subjunctive mood forms of verbs. (20 points)

UNIT 7 SENTENCE COMPLETERS
Complements

UNIT OVERVIEW

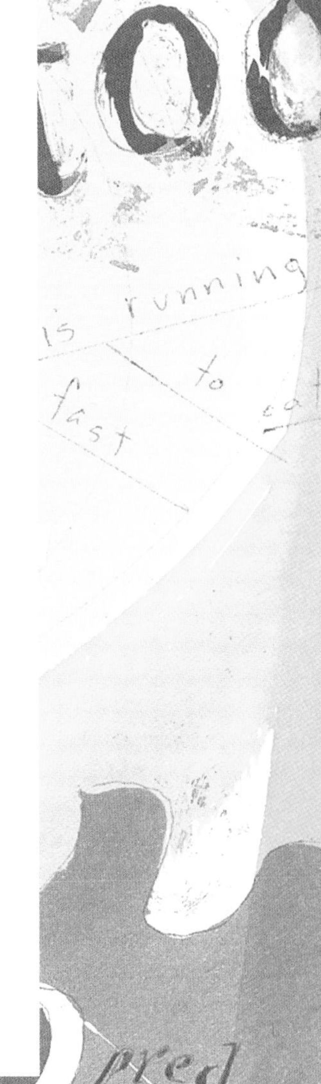

SENTENCE COMPLETERS: COMPLEMENTS

COMPLETERS FOR ACTION VERBS

A sentence must have a subject and a verb to communicate its basic meaning. In the following sentences, the subject and verb express the total concept. There is no receiver of the verb's action.

EXAMPLES
The furnace roars.
The baby contentedly gurgles.
Some purple grapes glowed in the fruit bowl.

Many sentences that include action verbs, however, need an additional word or group of words to complete the meaning.

EXAMPLES
Fiona quickly grabs.
Fiona quickly grabs the last muffin.

The group of words *Fiona quickly grabs* contains a subject *(Fiona)* and a verb *(grabs)*. Although the group of words may be considered a sentence, it does not express a complete thought. A word is needed to tell what Fiona grabs, such as *Fiona grabs the last muffin.* The word *muffin* completes the meaning expressed by the verb *grabs*. Therefore, *muffin* is called a **complement** or a completing word. The **completers** for action verbs are **direct objects** and **indirect objects.**

Direct Objects

A **direct object** receives the action in the sentence. It usually answers the question *what?* or *whom?* To find the direct object, find the action verb in the sentence. Then ask *what?* or *whom?* about the verb.

EXAMPLES

The potter **loaded** the **tray** into the kiln. (*Loaded* is the action verb. What did the potter load? *Tray* is the direct object.)

Noah **twisted** his **ankle**. (*Twisted* is the action verb. What did Noah twist? *Ankle* is the direct object.)

Remember to use object pronouns for a direct object.

singular me, you, him, her, it
plural us, you, them

EXAMPLES
Rachel-Ann teased **me**.
You should assist **her**.

USAGE tip

A direct object is usually a noun or a pronoun. It is never an adjective or an adverb and it is never in a prepositional phrase.

Indirect Objects

Sometimes the direct object is received by someone or something. This receiver is called the **indirect object**. It comes before the direct object and tells *to whom* the action is directed or *for whom* the action is performed. Only verbs that have direct objects can have indirect objects.

EXAMPLE

Graham **gave** his **mother** an orange **begonia**. (*Gave* is the action verb. *Begonia* is the direct object because it tells what Graham gave. *Mother* is an indirect object. It tells to whom Graham gave the begonia.)

USAGE tip

An indirect object is used after certain verbs, such as *get, give, lend, offer, read, tell, buy, send, show, make,* and *pay.*

There are two tests that you can use to identify the indirect object: (1) Look for a noun or a pronoun that precedes the direct object. (2) Determine whether the noun or pronoun following closest after the verb seems to be the understood object of the preposition *to* or *for.*

EXAMPLE
Nicole **lent me** her graphing **calculator**. (The noun *calculator* answers the question *What did Nicole lend me,* so it is the direct object. The understood preposition *to* can be inserted into the sentence before the pronoun *us: Nicole lent to me her graphing calculator.* Therefore, *me* is the indirect object of the sentence.)

Do not confuse direct and indirect objects with objects of prepositions. For example, the words *to* and *for* are prepositions. If the word order of the above sentence was changed to include the preposition *to*, then the sentence would read this way: *Nicole lent her graphing calculator to me*. In this new sentence, the word *me* is the object of the preposition *to*; it is not the indirect object.

Remember to use object pronouns for indirect objects.

singular	me, you, him, her, it
plural	us, you, them

EXAMPLES
Francisco owes **me** three dollars.
Show **him** the secret handshake.

Try It Yourself

LANGUAGELINK
Print exercise worksheets or have students complete exercises online with the LanguageLINK CD.

EXERCISE 1

Identifying Completers for Action Verbs: Direct and Indirect Objects

For each of the following sentences, write and label the direct and indirect objects. Not all sentences will have both a direct and an indirect object.

1. The donkey munched some thistles.
2. Li-Young brought us some baseball souvenirs.
3. They made fantastic decorations out of cut-up soda cans.
4. The war veteran told the class tales of his exploits.
5. Rebecca sent me an illegible postcard from somewhere in Canada.
6. The women in the camping group hauled the canoe to shore.
7. A video store clerk recommended this classic Buster Keaton movie.
8. Grandmother gave Celeste a Victorian birdcage for her room.
9. The junior class held a very successful carwash in the parking lot.
10. The woman on the train kindly offered me a section of her newspaper.

EXERCISE 2

Understanding Completers for Action Verbs: Direct and Indirect Objects

Supply a direct object, an indirect object, or both to complete each of the following sentences. You may need to provide a group of words so that the sentence makes sense.

1. The teacher told ___ ___ about the Chinese Cultural Revolution.
2. On the first day of summer vacation, we rode ___ in the country.
3. Can you give the ___ some ____?
4. Mr. Mackenzie, a woodworker, made the ___ some ____ .
5. Ellie broke her little ___ .
6. The silversmith engraved ___ on the baby's cup.
7. Every evening, Michel reads ___ ___ .
8. The banker showed ___ ___ in his checkbook.
9. At the graduation ceremony, the principal awarded ___ ___ for Greatest Academic Improvement.
10. In our city, police officers give ___ ___ for failing to wear helmets.

EXERCISE 1
1. *thistles*—direct object
2. *us*—indirect object; *souvenirs*—direct object
3. *decorations*—direct object
4. *class*—indirect object; *tales*—direct object
5. *me*—indirect object; *postcard*—direct object
6. *canoe*—direct object
7. *movie*—direct object
8. *Celeste*—indirect object; *birdcage*—direct object
9. *carwash*—direct object
10. *me*—indirect object; *section*—direct object

EXERCISE 2
Responses will vary. Sample responses:
1. The teacher told the students facts about the Chinese Cultural Revolution.
2 On the first day of summer vacation, we rode horses in the country.
3. Can you give the lifeguard some water?
4. Mr. Mackenzie, a woodworker, made the library some bookshelves.
5. Ellie broke her little finger.
6. The silversmith engraved initials on the baby's cup.
7. Every evening, Michel reads his grandmother the news.
8. The banker showed Mr. Rioux the error in his checkbook.
9. At the graduation ceremony, the principal awarded Angel the prize for Greatest Academic Improvement.
10. In our city, police officers give bicycle riders tickets for failing to wear helmets.

EXERCISE 3
Responses will vary. Students' paragraphs should be well organized and clearly explained. They should show an understanding of the way in which direct and indirect objects complete the thoughts conveyed by action verbs.

EXERCISE 3

Using Direct and Indirect Objects in Your Writing

Think about ways family members support each other. Consider how they offer practical and emotional support in ordinary daily life, in times of crisis, and in times of celebration. For a class anthology of writing about family relationships, write a paragraph that describes a particular incident, real or imagined, in which one family member supported another. Use at least five direct objects and at least three indirect objects in your paragraph.

USAGE tip

Some verbs can be linking or action verbs, depending on their meaning. *Grow, look, feel, sound, smell, taste, appear, remain,* and *stay* can be both. By mentally supplying the verb *to be* after the verb, you tell whether it has a linking or action function.

You **look** [to be] pale and ill this morning.

You **look** through this viewfinder on the video camera.

COMPLETERS FOR LINKING VERBS

A **linking verb** connects a subject with a noun, pronoun, or adjective that describes it or identifies it. Linking verbs do not express action. Instead, they express state of being and normally need a noun, a pronoun, or an adjective to complete the sentence meaning.

In each of the following sentences, the subject and verb would seem incomplete without the words that follow them.

EXAMPLES

The Jungle **is** a classic work of social realism.

Upton Sinclair's descriptions of the meat-packing industry **remain** shocking to this day.

Most linking verbs are forms of the verb *to be*, including *am, are, is, was,* and *been*. Other words that can be used as linking verbs include *appear, feel, grow, smell, taste, seem, sound, look, stay, feel, remain,* and *become*. When *to be* verbs are part of an action verb, they are helpers.

Predicate Nouns and Predicate Pronouns

A **predicate noun** is a noun that completes a sentence that uses a form of the verb *to be*. Similarly, a **predicate pronoun** is a pronoun that completes a sentence that uses a form of the verb *to be*. In fact, the relationship between the subject and the predicate noun or pronoun is so close that the sentence usually suggests an equation. Such sentences can often be reordered without changing the meaning.

EXAMPLES

predicate noun

Duke Ellington was a great composer, bandleader, and musician. (*Duke Ellington* = composer, bandleader, and musician)

A great composer, bandleader, and musician was Duke Ellington. (composer, bandleader, and musician = *Duke Ellington*)

predicate pronoun

The originator of the prank was she. (originator = *she*)

She was the originator of the prank. (*she* = originator)

To find a predicate noun or pronoun, ask the same question you would ask to find a direct object.

EXAMPLES

Mr. Milardo is a great **coach**. (Mr. Milardo is a what? *Coach* is the predicate noun that renames or identifies *Mr. Milardo*, the subject of the sentence.)

The winner of the Latin prize is **he**. (The winner of the Latin prize is who? *He* is the predicate pronoun that renames or identifies *winner*, the subject of the sentence.)

CONTINUED

USAGE tip

Remember to use subject pronouns after linking verbs.

singular:
I, you, he, she, it

plural:
we, you, they

EXAMPLES

The family member in charge of feeding the rabbits this week is **I.** (Think: I am the family member in charge of feeding the rabbits this week.)

The founders of the band were **he and Malena**. (Think: He and Malena were the founders of the band.)

Predicate Adjectives

A **predicate adjective** completes a sentence by modifying, or describing, the subject of a sentence. To find a predicate adjective, ask the same question you would ask to find a direct object.

EXERCISE 4
1. *depressed*—predicate adjective
2. *hot*—predicate adjective
3. *sultry*—predicate adjective
4. *own*—predicate adjective (You might point out to students that the sentence could be written *The life you save could be your own life,* in which case *life* would be a predicate noun.)
5. *ball*—predicate noun

EXAMPLE

The butter in the butter dish is **rancid**. (The butter is what? *Rancid* is the predicate adjective that describes *butter,* the subject of the sentence.)

Try It Yourself

EXERCISE 4

Identifying Predicate Nouns and Predicate Adjectives in Literature

Identify the underlined words in the following passage as predicate nouns or predicate adjectives.

He was more depressed than ever as he drove on by himself. The late afternoon had grown hot and sultry and the country had flattened out. Deep in the sky a storm was preparing very slowly and without thunder as if it meant to drain every drop of air from the earth before it broke. There were times when Mr. Shiftlet preferred not to be alone. He felt too that a man with a car had a responsibility to others and he kept his eye out for a hitch-hiker. Occasionally he saw a sign that warned: "Drive carefully. The life you save may be your own."

CONTINUED

The narrow road dropped off on either side into dry fields and here and there a shack or a filling station stood in a clearing. The sun began to set directly in front of the automobile. It was a reddening ball that through his windshield was slightly flat on the bottom and top.

from "The Life You Save May Be Your Own"
Flannery O'Connor

EXERCISE 5

Identifying Completers for Linking Verbs: Predicate Nouns, Predicate Pronouns, and Predicate Adjectives

Write the predicate nouns, predicate pronouns, or predicate adjectives in each of the following sentences. If a sentence does not contain a predicate noun, predicate pronoun, or a predicate adjective, write *none.*

1. For many centuries, the ruler of Russia was the czar.
2. Of all the czars, Peter the Great was the most famous.
3. When Peter became czar in 1682, the poor boy was only nine.
4. When he grew to his adult height of six foot eight, Peter seemed a giant compared to most of his peers.
5. By the early 1900s, the czarist system was considered corrupt by many Russians.
6. Some of the reformers were believers in Marxism.
7. Marxism was a political philosophy dedicated to improving the fate of impoverished workers.
8. When revolution broke out in 1917, the czar reacted poorly.
9. Russia's political condition appeared chaotic, with various factions fighting for control.
10. Despite official policies after the revolution, many Russian workers remained destitute.

EXERCISE 5

1. *czar*—predicate noun
2. *famous*—predicate adjective
3. *czar*—predicate noun; *nine*—predicate adjective
4. *giant*—predicate noun
5. *corrupt*—predicate adjective
6. *believers*—predicate noun
7. *philosophy*—predicate noun
8. none
9. *chaotic*—predicate adjective
10. *destitute*—predicate adjective

EXERCISE 6

Understanding Completers for Linking Verbs: Predicate Nouns, Predicate Pronouns, and Predicate Adjectives

Complete each of the following sentences with a predicate noun, predicate pronoun, or a predicate adjective. You may add a word or a group of words to help the sentence make sense. Identify your addition to the sentence as a predicate noun, predicate pronoun, or a predicate adjective.

1. The castle looked ___ in the moonlight.
2. Isadora's most prized possession is her electric-blue ___ .
3. My brother Nate becomes ___ whenever he travels on a boat, bus, or train.
4. The chef grew ___ when some customers criticized the soup as too salty.
5. Elizabeth has been away from home for several years, but her room remains ___.
6. As lava began to pour down the side of the mountain, inhabitants of the village below became ___.
7. The symbol on the cover of the band's CD is a(n) ___.
8. Aphids, slugs, and beetles are all ____ that a gardener must contend with.
9. Parking your car at the farthest edge of a parking lot is a simple ___ to get a little more exercise.
10. Saturday's televised wrestling match was ___!

EXERCISE 7

Using Predicate Nouns, Predicate Pronouns, and Predicate Adjectives in Your Writing

Imagine you are the entertainment reporter for your student newspaper. Write a paragraph about a celebrity whom you find especially interesting, for either positive or negative reasons. Tell who the person is, what you like or dislike about him or her, and why. Use a total of at least five predicate nouns, predicate pronouns, and predicate adjectives in your paragraph about this person.

EXERCISE 6

Responses will vary. Sample responses:

1. The castle looked eerie in the moonlight. Predicate adjective
2. Isadora's most prized possession is her electric-blue scooter. Predicate noun
3. My brother Nate becomes seasick whenever he travels on a boat, bus, or train. Predicate adjective
4. The chef grew irate when some customers criticized the soup as too salty. Predicate adjective
5. Elizabeth has been away from home for several years, but her room remains unchanged. Predicate adjective
6. As lava began to pour down the side of the mountain, inhabitants of the village below became panicky. Predicate adjective
7. The symbol on the cover of the band's CD is a phoenix. Predicate noun
8. Aphids, slugs, and beetles are all pests that a gardener must contend with. Predicate noun
9. Parking your car at the farthest edge of a parking lot is a simple way to get a little more exercise. Predicate noun
10. Saturday's televised wrestling match was awesome! Predicate adjective

EXERCISE 7

Responses will vary.

UNIT 7 REVIEW

TEST YOUR KNOWLEDGE

EXERCISE 1

Identifying Direct and Indirect Objects

Identify the direct and indirect objects in the following sentences. (10 points)

EXAMPLE
Architects design houses, schools, museums, and other buildings. (*houses, schools, museums, buildings*, direct objects)

1. A good client gives the architect a clear set of needs and preferences.
2. A successful building fits its environment rather than standing out like an alien presence.
3. The consultant reads the client a list of applicable local building codes.
4. An engineer might study the soil to determine the best sort of foundation to lay.
5. Which design magazine awarded your neighbors first prize for their barn renovation?
6. An architect can guarantee the owner a spectacular view by orienting a house toward the ocean or a mountain.
7. The Pennsylvania Conservancy offers visitors daily tours of Fallingwater, a famous house designed by Frank Lloyd Wright.
8. Architect Frank Gehry uses materials in unusual ways and includes wild, curving shapes in his celebrated museums.
9. In traditional North African neighborhoods, buildings have thick walls to keep out the blistering heat.
10. This guide offers readers eight great walking tours of the architecture of New Orleans.

EXERCISE 1

1. *architect*—indirect object; *set*—direct object
2. *environment*—direct object
3. *client*—indirect object; *list*—direct object
4. *soil*—direct object
5. *neighbors*—indirect object; *prize*—direct object
6. *owner*—indirect object; *view*—direct object
7. *visitors*—indirect object; *tours*—direct object
8. *materials*—direct object; *shapes*—direct object
9. *walls*—direct object
10. *readers*—indirect object; *tours*—direct object

EXERCISE 2
1. none
2. *beads*—predicate noun
3. *respected*—predicate adjective
4. *warlike*—predicate adjective
5. *boy*—predicate noun
6. *gentle, pathetic, shy*—predicate adjectives
7. *he*—predicate pronoun
8. *Hiawatha*—predicate noun
9. *logical*—predicate adjective
10. *peaceful, strong*—predicate adjectives

EXERCISE 2
Identifying Predicate Nouns, Predicate Pronouns, and Predicate Adjectives

Identify and label any predicate nouns, predicate pronouns, and predicate adjectives in the following sentences. If there are no predicate nouns, predicate pronouns, or predicate adjectives in the sentence, write *none*. (10 points)

EXAMPLE
The Iroquois were a great Native American tribe divided into five groups, or nations. (*tribe,* predicate noun)

1. The Iroquois recorded their history with wampum.
2. Wampum were tiny shell beads that could be strung on leather cords and then woven into designs.
3. In traditional Iroquois society, women were highly respected.
4. In the distant past, the Iroquois were warlike and the five nations constantly fought each other.
5. Deganwidah was a fatherless boy from the Huron tribe.
6. Deganwidah seemed gentle and rather pathetic because he was so shy.
7. Yet it was he who developed a successful plan for uniting the five Iroquois nations into one confederation.
8. His ally was Hiawatha, an orator who could take Deganwidah's plans and present them to the public.
9. The plan that Hiawatha outlined so eloquently seemed logical to his listeners.
10. The Iroquois grew peaceful and strong under the new government.

EXERCISE 3
Identifying Sentence Completers: Complements

Identify and label any direct and indirect objects, predicate nouns, predicate pronouns, and predicate adjectives in the following sentences. If a sentence has no direct or indirect objects and no predicate nouns, pronouns, or adjectives, write *none*. (20 points)

EXAMPLE
The first postage stamp was the brainchild of Rowland Hill, a British schoolteacher. (*brainchild*, predicate noun)

1. In medieval Germany, workers blew on a horn to announce the mail.
2. The Cape of Good Hope 1853 Four Pence stamp is triangular.
3. Long ago, on the remote Scottish island of St. Kilda, islanders sent letters to the mainland by placing them in an inflated sheep's bladder and tossing it into the ocean!
4. Stamps are both useful and beautiful.
5. Stanley Gibbons was one of the world's first stamp collectors.
6. Some sailors sold Gibbons a bag full of the valuable triangular stamps!
7. The person who steamed the stamp off that letter from Norway was I.
8. You should use tweezers instead of your bare hands to pick up stamps.
9. Grandpa gave Lea his collection of stamps from Samoa.
10. Great Britain is the only country that doesn't include its name on its stamps!

EXERCISE 3
1. none
2. *triangular*—predicate adjective
3. *letters, them, it*—direct objects
4. *useful, beautiful*—predicate adjectives
5. *one*—predicate pronoun
6. *Gibbons*—indirect object; *bag*—direct object
7. *stamp*—direct object; *I*—predicate pronoun
8. *tweezers*—direct object
9. *Lea*—indirect object; *collection*—direct object
10. *country*—predicate noun; *name*—direct object

EXERCISE 4
Correcting Pronouns Used in Complements

Correct pronoun errors made in the following sentences. If there are no errors, write *correct*. (20 points)

EXAMPLE
They gave Gerry and he the directions.
(They gave Gerry and *him* the directions.)

1. The fastest grocery-bag packer at the supermarket is me!
2. Please give Samantha and I some of that saltwater taffy.
3. Mark lent she the Spanish dictionary for exactly twenty-three minutes
4. The only people who obtained the player's autograph were we.
5. The tornado actually picked us up and set us back down in the neighbor's yard.

EXERCISE 4
1. The fastest grocery-bag packer at the supermarket is I.
2. Please give Samantha and me some of that saltwater taffy.
3. Mark lent her the Spanish dictionary for exactly twenty-three minutes.
4. correct
5. correct

6. correct
7. A police officer motioned Jack and <u>him</u> to slow down for the roadwork ahead.
8. The people who found the shipwreck were <u>they</u>.
9. correct
10. It was <u>I</u> who found the lost parrot in the park.

EXERCISE 5
Responses will vary. Students should use each noun, pronoun, or adjective in its stipulated role in a sentence.

EXERCISE 6
Responses will vary. Although the emphasis should be on using predicate nouns, pronouns, adjectives, and direct and indirect objects, students' analyses of the effect of computers should make sense.

6. The bus driver told us kids to sit down.
7. A police officer motioned Jack and he to slow down for the roadwork ahead.
8. The people who found the shipwreck were them.
9. Hand me your dripping umbrella while you run into the restaurant.
10. It was me who found the lost parrot in the park.

EXERCISE 5
Using Complements in Your Writing
Write a sentence for each of the following kinds of complements. Underline the complement in each sentence that you write. (20 points)

EXAMPLE
pronoun as an indirect object
(My younger cousin played <u>me</u> her recital piece in the living room.)

1. direct object
2. indirect object
3. predicate noun
4 predicate adjective
5. predicate pronoun
6. pronoun as a direct object
7. compound predicate noun
8. compound indirect object
9. compound predicate pronoun
10. compound predicate adjective

EXERCISE 6
Using Complements in Your Writing
How do computers affect the lives of you and your peers? How do you use computers for fun, school, and communication? Do you see any drawbacks to having computers? How do you imagine your life would be different if computers were suddenly unavailable? Write a three-paragraph editorial for the local newspaper on the effects of computers on high school students. Use as many predicate nouns, pronouns, and adjectives, as well as direct and indirect objects, as you can. (20 points)

UNIT 8 SUBJECT-VERB AGREEMENT AND USAGE

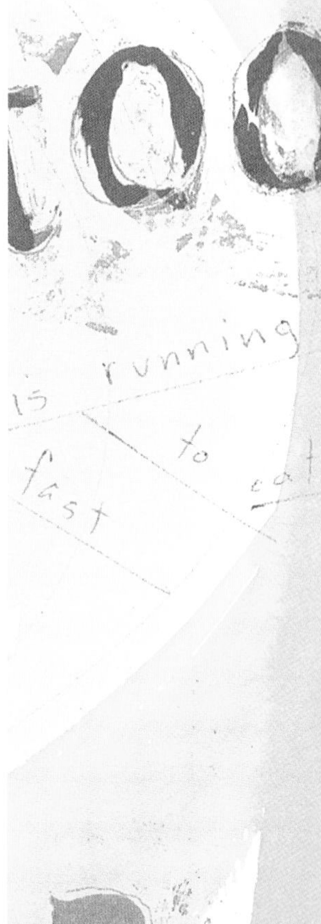

UNIT OVERVIEW

SUBJECT-VERB AGREEMENT AND USAGE

SUBJECT AND VERB AGREEMENT

A **singular** noun describes or stands for *one* person, place, thing, or idea. A **plural noun** describes or stands for *more than one* person, place, thing, or idea.

EXAMPLES

singular nouns	teapot	flame	pheasant	jury	goose
plural nouns	teapots	flames	pheasants	juries	geese

In a sentence, a verb must be singular if its subject is singular and plural if its subject is plural. In other words, a verb must agree in number with its subject.

EXAMPLES

singular subject and verb	A **flame ignites** the dry kindling.
plural subject and verb	The **flames ignite** the dry kindling.
singular subject and verb	The **jury ponders** the incriminating evidence.
plural subject and verb	The **juries ponder** the incriminating evidence.
singular subject and verb	A **goose waddles** across the town square.
plural subject and verb	The **geese waddle** across the town square.

Subject-Verb Agreement with Intervening Expressions

Usually, a verb directly follows the subject in a sentence. Sometimes, however, a prepositional phrase or clause will separate the subject and verb. Even though the subject and verb may be separated, they must still agree in number.

EXAMPLES

The **jury** of twelve local citizens **ponders** the incriminating evidence.

The **teapot**, along with the other old pots and pans, **is** in a box in the attic.

USAGE tip

When a phrase or clause separates a subject and verb, mentally delete or cover up the phrase or clause so that you can more easily identify subject-verb agreement.

Subject-Verb Agreement with Contractions

As you know, a **contraction** is a shortened form of a word, a group of words, or a numeral. The apostrophes in contractions show where letters, words, or numerals have been left out. Contractions should agree in number with their subjects. If you're unsure about the agreement, write out the full form of the words in the contraction. If the contraction includes a negative word, such as *not*, treat the negative word as an intervening expression.

EXAMPLES

She **doesn't** worry about the future. (She **does not** worry about the future.)
They **don't** worry about the future. (They **do not** worry about the future.)

He's the fastest runner on the team. (**He is** the fastest runner on the team.)
They're the fastest runners on the team. (**They are** the fastest runners on the team.)

Subject-Verb Agreement with Linking Verbs

A linking verb agrees with its subject, not the predicate noun or predicate adjective that follows it.

USAGE tip

Remember that the verb *be* has three forms to match person and number in the present tense.

singular I am, you are, he is
plural we are, you are, they are

EXAMPLES

incorrect	My favorite treat **are** fresh blueberries drenched in thick cream!
correct	My favorite treat **is** fresh blueberries drenched in thick cream!
incorrect	Fresh blueberries drenched in thick cream **is** my favorite treat.
correct	Fresh blueberries drenched in thick cream **are** my favorite treat.

Subject-Verb Agreement with Special Subjects

Collective nouns, such as *audience*, *class*, *flock*, *group*, *family*, *the press*, and *the public*, name a group of people or things. Use a singular verb when you think of a collective noun as a single unit. Use a plural verb when you think of a collective noun as multiple members.

EXAMPLES

singular	The audience **roars** as the singer bounds onto the stage.
plural	The audience **leave** in ones and twos when the show is cancelled.

Nouns ending in –*s* are sometimes plural in form but singular in meaning. *News*, *economics*, *measles*, *mumps*, *mathematics*, and *physics* refer to a single thing or to a unit and therefore take a singular verb. Notice that removing the *s* does not make the noun singular.

EXAMPLES

Physics is a field in which astounding discoveries are being made.

Mumps is a viral disease.

Other nouns ending in *–s* always take a plural verb, even though they are understood to refer to one thing. These nouns include *scissors*, *pliers*, *pants*, *trousers*, *slacks*, *eyeglasses*, *binoculars*, *clothes*, *thanks*, and *congratulations*.

EXAMPLES

Eyeglasses are an important fashion accessory this season.

Do you think her **thanks were** sincere?

Some nouns ending in *–s* may be singular or plural, depending on their meaning in the sentence. Words like *politics*, *acoustics*, *statistics*, and *headquarters* depend on their use in the sentence.

EXAMPLES

plural	All of the **headquarters are** located in city centers.
singular	**Headquarters sends** a monthly newsletter to all the branch locations.

The **title of an artwork** (painting, literature, sculpture, or music) is always singular.

EXAMPLES

***Porgy and Bess* is** an opera by the composer George Gershwin.

Great Expectations, a novel by Charles Dickens, **has** been made into a movie.

Words of amount or time may be singular or plural.
Use a singular verb with words and phrases that refer to single units: fractions, measurements, amounts of money, weights, volumes, or specific intervals of time when the intervals refer to a specific unit.

EXAMPLES

Eight glasses of water is the daily amount recommended by some nutritionists. (Eight glasses is equivalent to one daily amount.)

Twenty dollars is a good price for that old chair. (Twenty dollars is equivalent to one price.)

EXERCISE 1

In spring it is a joy to discover, amid snow and mud and pale, withered grass, the delicate lavender of pasqueflower blooming on a ridge with a southern exposure. There is variety in the emptiness; the most prosaic pasture might contain hundreds of different wildflowers along with sage, yucca, and prairie cactus. Coulees harbor chokecherry, buffalo berry, and gooseberry bushes in their gentle folds, along with groves of silvery cottonwoods and Russian olive. Lone junipers often grow on exposed hillsides.

This seemingly empty land is busy with inhabitants. Low to the ground are bullsnakes, rattlers, mice, gophers, moles, grouse, prairie chickens, and pheasant. Prairie dogs are more noticeable, as they denude the landscape with their villages. Badgers and skunk lumber busily through the grass.

Use a plural verb when the amount or the time is considered to be a number of separate units.

EXAMPLES

Seven one-dollar bills were left in the tip jar.

Three decades have gone by since Grandma sold the dairy farm.

When you use the words *the number* or *the variety* as a subject, use a singular verb. When you use *a number* or *a variety* as a subject, use a plural verb.

EXAMPLES

The number of masterpieces in the collection **is** impressive.
The variety of possible diagnoses **is** bewildering.

A number of the athletes in the games **are** professionals.
A variety of courses **are** available over the summer.

Try It Yourself

EXERCISE 1

Identifying Subject-Verb Agreement in Literature

Identify the subjects in each sentence by underlining them once. Identify the verbs in the sentences by underlining them twice. Note how the verb agrees in number with its subject.

Literature MODEL

In spring it is a joy to discover, amid snow and mud and pale, withered grass, the delicate lavender of pasqueflower blooming on a ridge with a southern exposure. There is variety in the emptiness; the most prosaic pasture might contain hundreds of different wildflowers along with sage, yucca, and prairie cactus. Coulees harbor chokecherry, buffalo berry, and gooseberry bushes in their gentle folds, along with groves of silvery cottonwoods and Russian olive. Lone junipers often grow on exposed hillsides.

CONTINUED

This seemingly empty land is busy with inhabitants. Low to the ground are bullsnakes, rattlers, mice, gophers, moles, grouse, prairie chickens, and pheasant. Prairie dogs are more noticeable, as they denude the landscape with their villages. Badgers and skunk lumber busily through the grass. Jackrabbits, weasels, and foxes are quicker, but the great runners of the Plains are the coyote, antelope, and deer.

from "Seeing"
Kathleen Norris

Jackrabbits, weasels, and foxes are quicker, but the great runners of the Plains are the coyote, antelope, and deer.

EXERCISE 2

Understanding Subject-Verb Agreement with Intervening Expressions and Linking Verbs

From the verbs in parentheses, choose the correct verb form that agrees in number with the subject of the sentence.

1. The sharp-tailed grouse, with its mottled brownish feathers, (blends, blend) into the prairie grasses.
2. Louise, like many folks from out East, (thinks, think) the Midwest is too flat.
3. The fields, still hidden under a blanket of snow, (is, are) beginning to thaw.
4. Moles, which spend most of their time underground, (has, have) poor eyesight.
5. Dried grasses, which have been gathered from the prairie, (is, are) made into bouquets.
6. Russian olive, like many other shrubs, (serves, serve) as a windbreak.
7. Among land birds, the prairie chicken (is, are) one of the least common.
8. Coulees, or ravines, (provides, provide) interesting places to explore.
9. Skunks, members of the weasel family, (is, are) avoided because of their smell.
10. Prairie dogs, like ants, (lives, live) in underground communities.

EXERCISE 2
1. blends
2. thinks
3. are
4. have
5. are
6. serves
7. is
8. provide
9. are
10. live

LANGUAGELINK
Print exercise worksheets or have students complete exercises online with the LanguageLINK CD.

EXERCISE 3
1. has thrilled
2. fill
3. appears
4. is
5. are
6. travels
7. visit
8. boggles
9. were
10. attracts

EXERCISE 3
Understanding Subject-Verb Agreement with Special Subjects

From the verbs in parentheses, choose the correct verb form that agrees in number with the subject of the sentence.

1. Arthur Conan Doyle's masterpiece *The Hound of the Baskervilles* (has thrilled, have thrilled) readers for a hundred years.
2. Pennies (fills, fill) the fountain in the middle of the mall.
3. The royal family (appears, appear) every day on the balcony at noon.
4. "The West Virginia Hills" (is, are) one of three state songs for West Virginia.
5. Poorly refrigerated foods (is, are) a common cause of food poisoning.
6. The group (travels, travel) on a fully equipped tour bus.
7. Ten thousand individuals (visits, visit) this website each week.
8. The number of stone blocks in the Great Pyramid (boggles, boggle) the mind!
9. Unfortunately, some of the ornaments (was, were) broken during shipment.
10. Economics (attracts, attract) more students now than in past years.

EXERCISE 4
1. line
2. don't
3. correct
4. makes
5. is
6. correct
7. doesn't
8. was
9. correct
10. seems

EXERCISE 4
Correcting Subject-Verb Agreement

Read each of the following sentences. If the subject and verb in a sentence agree in number, write *correct.* If the subject and verb do not agree in number, write the correct verb form.

1. Hundreds of immigrants lines up at the border crossing.
2. Mr. and Mrs. Kerr doesn't appreciate kids running through their garden.
3. The variety of butterflies in the collection amazes me.
4. *Chariots of Fire*, a film that won an Academy Award, always make me want to go running!

5. Twenty-five hundred dollars are the blue book price for that used car.
6. Binoculars are a necessity when you sit at the back of a large theater.
7. The new mayor don't like to attend local social events.
8. Paul McCartney, one of the Beatles, were recently knighted by Queen Elizabeth II.
9. Hula dancers, with their elaborate hand movements, tell stories when they dance.
10. Three seconds seem like a long time when your tooth is aching!

EXERCISE 5

Using Subject-Verb Agreement in Your Writing

For a community history, write a description of your block, apartment building, or neighborhood. Describe the physical aspects of the area (size, main features) and also some of the people that live there. Use at least one example of subject-verb agreement with a linking verb, with an intervening phrase, and with special subjects. Make sure that each of your verbs agrees with its subject.

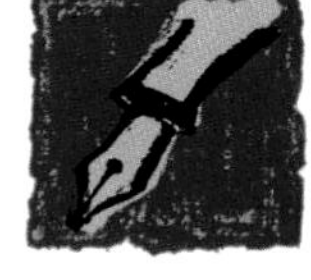

EXERCISE 5
Responses will vary. Students should use at least one example of subject-verb agreement with a linking verb, with an intervening phrase, and with special subjects. They should exhibit correct subject-verb agreement in each case.

INDEFINITE PRONOUN AND VERB AGREEMENT

In Unit 5 you learned about different types of pronouns, including indefinite pronouns. An **indefinite pronoun** does not refer to a specific person, place, or thing. Some indefinite pronouns are always singular and take singular verbs: *anybody, anyone, anything, each, either, everybody, everyone, everything, much, neither, nobody, no one, nothing, one, somebody, someone, something.*

EXAMPLES
singular
Somebody certainly **likes** this hot sauce!
Everything looks beautiful in the moonlight.

Some indefinite pronouns are always plural and take plural verbs: *both, few, many, others, several.*

EXAMPLES
plural
Few think before they speak.
Several of the shuttle missions **were delayed.**

Some indefinite pronouns can be either singular or plural, depending on their use in the sentence: *all, any, most, none, some.* They are singular when they refer to a portion or to a single person, place, or thing. They are plural when they refer to a number of individual persons, places, or things.

EXAMPLES

singular	**All** of the water **has drained** out of the bathtub.
plural	**All** of the football players **are** on the field.

Try It Yourself

EXERCISE 6
1. possesses
2. keeps
3. is
4. believe
5. is
6. have
7. find
8. lines
9. enjoys
10. operate

EXERCISE 6

Identifying Correct Indefinite Pronoun-Verb Agreement
Complete each sentence by identifying the correct form of the verb in parentheses.

1. Each of the twins (possesses, possess) a distinctive, hoarse voice.
2. Someone (keeps, keep) calling the house and hanging up.
3. Neither of the CDs (is, are) one I'd consider buying.
4. Many (believe, believes) in UFOs.
5. Some of the pancake mixture (is, are) oozing over the side of the bowl.
6. Most of the diamonds (has, have) already been mined.
7. Others (finds, find) Cecile charming, but I mistrust her.
8. Everybody (line, lines) up for the new roller coaster as soon as the amusement park opens.
9. Neither the dog nor the cat (enjoy, enjoys) this hot, humid weather.
10. Both of the workers (operate, operates) heavy equipment.

EXERCISE 7

Correcting Indefinite Pronoun-Verb Agreement

Read each of the following sentences. If the subject and verb in a sentence agree in number, write *correct*. If the subject and verb do not agree in number, write the correct verb form.

1. Nobody in my family willingly volunteer to fold the laundry.
2. None of the journalists in the group has ever before visited Peru.
3. Some of the water leaks out through a hole in the hose.
4. Anything go at the summer festival.
5. Someone in our class regularly cause disruption by telling jokes.
6. Several of the forecasters has predicted a glorious weekend.
7. Much are asked of firefighters and others who protect public safety.
8. Both of the skiers seems to be making it down the course in record time.
9. Most of the birds have flown south for the winter.
10. Nothing is the best thing to say sometimes.

EXERCISE 7

1. volunteers
2. have
3. correct
4. goes
5. causes
6. have
7. is
8. seem
9. correct
10. correct

EXERCISE 8

Using Indefinite Pronoun-Verb Agreement in Your Writing

Imagine that you are requesting funding to make a movie or music video. Write a proposal describing the project you would like to make. Start by describing the basic concept, or plot. Then describe details, such as the characters you would create, the actors or singers you would cast, the setting you would choose, and the atmosphere you would try to evoke. Use at least five different indefinite pronouns in your paragraph. Check your paragraph to make sure that the verbs agree in number with the indefinite pronouns.

EXERCISE 8

Responses will vary. Students should include a basic idea and relevant details. They should also use correct indefinite pronoun-verb agreement.

AGREEMENT WITH RELATIVE PRONOUNS IN ADJECTIVE CLAUSES

When a relative pronoun, such as *who*, *whom*, *whose*, *which*, or *that*, is the subject of an adjective clause, decide whether the verb of the adjective clause should be singular or plural by finding the antecedent of the relative pronoun. The verb of the adjective clause and the antecedent of the relative pronoun must agree in number.

EXAMPLES

She is the chef **who is famous for creating** the exciting all-catfish menu. (The adjective clause *who is famous* modifies the singular noun *chef.* Therefore, the verb in the adjective clause, *is,* is singular.)

The dikes **that were built to hold back possible floods** are enormous. (The adjective clause *that were built to hold back possible floods* modifies the plural noun *dikes.* Therefore, the verb in the adjective clause, *are,* is plural.)

Try It Yourself

EXERCISE 9

Identifying Agreement with Adjective Clauses

Choose the correct verb form in parentheses for each adjective clause in the sentences below. Then underline the antecedent of each pronoun that begins an adjective clause.

1. Global warming, which (results, result) to a large extent from the burning of coal and oil, is changing the world in many ways.
2. Glaciers that (seem, seems) a permanent part of the landscape are melting quickly.
3. Dr. Peter Gleick, who (directs, direct) an environmental research center, discusses changes in rainfall related to warming trends.
4. Texas, which (is, are) a big farming state, has less water from underground sources than it used to have.

EXERCISE 9

1. Global warming, which (results, result) to a large extent from the burning of coal and oil, is changing the world in many ways.
2. Glaciers that (seem, seems) a permanent part of the landscape are melting quickly.
3. Dr. Peter Gleick, who (directs, direct) an environmental research center, discusses changes in rainfall related to warming trends.
4. Texas, which (is, are) a big farming state, has less water from underground sources than it used to.
5. The monsoons that (strikes, strike) South Asia every year have become more fierce.
6. According to some scientists, the global weather system, which (has, have) always had its ups and downs, is just exhibiting temporary fluctuations.
7. Glaciers that (melts, melt) rapidly may cause avalanches.
8. Parts of Africa that (has, have) always been arid are now becoming desert.
9. Farmers, whose lives (is, are) dramatically affected by weather, discuss what to do.

5. The monsoons that (strikes, strike) Southeast Asia every year have become more fierce.
6. According to some scientists, the global weather system, which (has, have) always had its ups and downs, is just exhibiting temporary fluctuations.
7. Glaciers that (melts, melt) rapidly may cause avalanches.
8. Parts of Africa that (has, have) always been arid are now becoming desert.
9. Farmers, whose lives (is, are) dramatically affected by weather, discuss what to do.
10. Environmentalists who (works, work) in Nepal and Bhutan notice that glacier-fed lakes now look swollen and likely to flood.

10. Environmentalists who (works, work) in Nepal and Bhutan notice that glacier-fed lakes now look swollen and likely to flood.

EXERCISE 10

Correcting Agreement with Adjective Clauses

Read each of the following sentences. If the verb in the adjective clause agrees in number with the antecedent of the relative pronoun, write *correct*. If the antecedent and verb do not agree in number, rewrite the sentence with the correct verb form.

1. Hilary, who works at a local health club, assist people in regaining strength and mobility after injuries.
2. The elliptical training machine, which exercises muscles gently, is very popular.
3. Mark, whose training program are overly ambitious, is starting to look like the Hulk.
4. The machine that sit in the corner is broken.
5. The deltoids, which are large triangular muscles, covers the shoulders.
6. Athletes who stretch before exercising injures themselves less frequently.
7. Muscle fibers, which actually breaks down during weight training, need time off to repair themselves.
8. Yoga, which is an ancient form of exercise from India, emphasizes rhythmic breathing, gentle stretching, twisting, and balance.

EXERCISE 10

1. Hilary, who works at a local health club, assists people in regaining strength and mobility after injuries.
2. correct
3. Mark, whose training program is overly ambitious, is starting to look like the Hulk.
4. The machine that sits in the corner is broken.
5. The deltoids, which are large, triangular muscles, cover the shoulders.
6. Athletes who stretch before exercising injure themselves less frequently.
7. Muscle fibers, which actually break down during weight training, need time off to repair themselves.
8. correct
9. The exercise program that generally produces the best results combines a cardio-vascular workout with weight training.
10. correct

9. The exercise plan that generally produce the best results combines a vigorous cardiovascular workout with weight training.
10. People who walk at least thirty minutes, three times a week, will feel and look healthier.

EXERCISE 11
Responses will vary. Some students will know more about design and materials than others, but all students should envision and describe meaningful components and features of a school classroom. Students should use at least four adjective clauses that begin with relative pronouns. In each case, their subjects and verbs should agree.

EXERCISE 11

Using Subject-Verb Agreement in Adjective Clauses in Your Writing

How would you design the perfect high school classroom? What would the layout be like? What materials would you use? What colors would you select? What amazing special features would you include? Describe your ultimate high school classroom in a vivid paragraph to be shared with your classmates. In your paragraph, include at least four adjective clauses. Make sure that the verbs in these clauses agree with their antecedents.

COMPOUND SUBJECT AND VERB AGREEMENT

A **compound subject** consists of two or more subjects that share the same verb.

EXAMPLE

Jess and Trevor skateboard at the park. (The nouns in the compound subject—*Jess and Trevor*—share the verb *skateboard.*)

A compound subject must have either a singular or a plural verb, depending on how the parts of the subject are connected.

Use a singular verb:

- when the compound subject is made up of singular nouns or pronouns connected by *either/or* or *neither/nor*.

EXAMPLES

singular verb

Either jazz or classical music **sounds** good.

Neither Jacque nor Norman **plays** the tuba.

Use a plural verb:

- when the compound subject is connected by the coordinating conjunction *and*.
- when the compound subject is formed from plural nouns or pronouns.

EXAMPLES

plural verb

Ice pops and watermelon **taste** refreshing on a hot day.

Either mobiles or rattles **amuse** the baby.

Neither the necklaces nor the rugs **are** authentic Native American products.

When a compound subject consists of a singular subject and a plural subject connected by *or* or *nor*, use a verb that agrees in number with the subject closer to it in the sentence.

EXAMPLES

Either the mayor or some council members **attend** graduation. (*council members attend,* plural)

Neither the custodians nor the principal **appreciates** the senior class prank. (*principal appreciates,* singular)

Try It Yourself

EXERCISE 12

Identifying Compound Subject-Verb Agreement

Identify the correct verb in parentheses to agree with the compound subject in each sentence.

1. Maps and globes (provides, provide) very different views of the world.
2. Beads and wire (is, are) used to make attractive jewelry.

EXERCISE 12
1. provide
2. are

3. are
4. constitutes
5. are
6. appear
7. contain
8. fills
9. litter
10. comes

EXERCISE 13
Responses will vary. Sample responses:
1. Architects and engineers design structures for a living.
2. Either the students or their teacher contacts a speaker for the final class.
3. Some flowers, fruit, and a card sit on the table beside the hospital bed.
4. Either the briefcase or the handbag holds the tickets for the tennis match.
5. Bats and owls fly at night.
6. The surgeon and the nurses prepare the patient.
7. Both elephants and zebras inhabit the African Sahara.
8. Neither Maxine nor Eliot chooses to play computer games right now.
9. Either the captain or the sailors identify the approaching ship.
10. Neither the train nor the airplanes wake me at night.

3. Aggies and steelies (is, are) types of old-fashioned marbles.
4. Either lettuce or spinach (constitutes, constitute) the main ingredient in the salad.
5. In swimming competitions, the crawl and the butterfly (is, are) common strokes.
6. The humorous characters Rosencrantz and Guildenstern (appears, appear) in Shakespeare's *Hamlet.*
7. Neither almanacs nor dictionaries (contains, contain) the information you seek.
8. Either many small flowers or one large bloom (fill, fills) the vase.
9. Baubles and confetti (litters, litter) the streets after the big parade.
10. Neither the goats nor the cow (comes, come) when called the way the pig does.

EXERCISE 13
Understanding Compound Subject-Verb Agreement

Write a sentence for each of the compound subjects and verbs listed below. Make sure that you use the correct verb form to agree with the compound subject.

1. architects and engineers (design)
2. either the students or their teacher (contact)
3. some flowers, fruit, and a card (sit)
4. either the briefcase or the handbag (hold)
5. bats and owls (fly)
6. the surgeon and the nurses (prepare)
7. both elephants and zebras (inhabit)
8. neither Maxine nor Eliot (choose)
9. either the captain or the sailors (identify)
10. neither the train nor the airplanes (wake)

EXERCISE 14

Using Compound Subject-Verb Agreement in Your Writing

Write the opening paragraph for a children's book set in an environment in which animals live. The setting might be a rainforest, a northern woodland, a farm, or a zoo. Describe the animals, their surroundings, and their behaviors. Include at least four sentences with compound verbs, one of which must contain *either/or* or *neither/nor*. Be sure to use compound subject-verb agreement correctly in your paragraph.

EXERCISE 14
Responses will vary. Students should use correct compound subject-verb agreement.

INVERTED SENTENCES

Usually, the subject appears *before* the verb in a sentence. The subject-verb word order is called **natural order**. In an **inverted sentence**, the subject comes after the verb.

EXAMPLES

natural order	The agile **athlete leaped** over the hurdles.
inverted sentence	Over the hurdles **leaped** the agile **athlete**.

When working with inverted sentences, first identify the subject and then make the verb agree with it in number. Saying the sentence aloud or rewriting the sentence in natural order often helps.

USAGE tip

Inverted sentences often begin with a prepositional phrase.

Most sentences that begin with *Here* or *There* are inverted sentences. The subject of the sentence is never *Here* or *There*. Like other inverted sentences, you can rearrange the words into natural order so that the subject comes first.

USAGE tip

To make it easier to find the subject and verb in an inverted sentence or question, rearrange the words into natural order.

EXAMPLES

inverted sentence	There are some clean socks in the dryer.
	Here is the letter from your grandmother.
natural order	Some clean socks are in the dryer.
	The letter from your grandmother is here.

EXERCISE 15
1. *dozens*—subject; *are*—verb
2. *fish*—subject; *swim*—verb
3. *Dad*—subject; *did*—helping verb; *record*—main verb
4. *last*—subject; *goes*—verb
5. *kayakers*—subject; *come*—verb
6. *you*—subject; *have*—helping verb; *contacted*—main verb
7. *sunscreen*—subject; *is*—verb
8. *you*—subject; *can*—helping verb; *remember*—main verb
9. *moth*—subject; *flutters*—verb
10. *sounds*—subject; *pound*—verb

Some questions—interrogative sentences—are written in inverted order. Usually a helping verb appears before the subject. You'll find the subject between the helping verb and the main verb.

EXAMPLES

Did Ms. Henri **give** a quiz? (The subject *Ms. Henri* appears between the helping verb *Did* and the main verb *give.*)

Will trees and shrubs **grow** again after the forest fire? (The compound subject *trees and shrubs* appears between the helping verb *Will* and the main verb *grow.*)

Try It Yourself

EXERCISE 15

Identifying Subjects and Verbs in Inverted Sentences

Underline and label the subject(s) and verb(s) in each of the following inverted sentences.

1. In the drawer are dozens of rusty, broken tools.
2. Below the pier swim some huge fish.
3. Did Dad record the school musical on video?
4. There goes the last of the maple syrup from Vermont.
5. Out of the river come the exhausted kayakers.
6. Have you contacted the travel agent about the tickets?
7. Here is some sunscreen to put on at the beach.
8. Can you remember your password?
9. Against the screen flutters a moth.
10. Throughout the day pound the sounds of construction.

EXERCISE 16
1. rush

EXERCISE 16

Understanding Subject-Verb Agreement in Inverted Sentences

Complete each of the inverted sentences by choosing the correct form of the verb in parentheses.

1. Away from the tsunami (rushes, rush) the terrified villagers.

2. (Does, do) anyone know how to start a fire without a match?
3. Beneath the floorboards (lurks, lurk) all sorts of spiders and bugs.
4. In the closet (is, are) your new flannel comforter.
5. According to Martha, there (is, are) only one way to make fried chicken.
6. Will the network (broadcasts, broadcast) the show at a later date?
7. Over the hillside (swarms, swarm) detectives hunting for clues.
8. Here (is, are) the diagram you need for your report.
9. Can anyone (describes, describe) the stray dog?
10. Between the foothills and the ocean (lies, lie) the ancient village.

2. Does
3. lurk
4. is
5. is
6. broadcast
7. swarm
8. is
9. describe
10. lies

EXERCISE 17
Responses will vary. Students should use at least three inverted sentences with correct subject-verb agreement. One of the inverted sentences should be a question.

EXERCISE 17

Using Inverted Sentences in Your Writing

Write a brief letter to a prospective employer describing your suitability for a summer job or internship. Before explaining your qualifications, specify the job for which you are applying. In your letter, use at least three inverted sentences, one of them a question, to provide variety and interest.

UNIT 8 REVIEW

TEST YOUR KNOWLEDGE

EXERCISE 1
1. are
2. add
3. spends
4. makes
5. is
6. darts
7. stock
8. have
9. climbs
10. doesn't

EXERCISE 1

Identifying Subject-Verb Agreement

Choose the verb in parentheses that agrees in number with the subject or compound subject in each of the following sentences. (10 points)

EXAMPLE

The tank full of seahorses (draws, draw) everyone's attention.
(draws)

1. Neither shorts nor tank tops (is, are) permitted under the new dress code.
2. The dollars needed for lunches (adds, add) up to quite a big sum over the years.
3. The family (spends, spend) a week in the Adirondacks every July.
4. The variety of colors and patterns (makes, make) the carpet dizzying.
5. *Antony and Cleopatra* (is, are) a play by William Shakespeare.
6. Into the hole in the wall (darts, dart) a tiny field mouse.
7. Clothes from the 1960s and 1970s (stocks, stock) the vintage shop on Main Street.
8. The singer and the drummer (has, have) given a funny interview to the hometown newspaper.
9. A group of eager tourists (climbs, climb) to the top of the Mayan pyramid.
10. Ivan (doesn't, don't) understand the appeal of Saturday-morning cartoons.

EXERCISE 2

Identifying Indefinite Pronoun-Verb Agreement

Identify the indefinite pronoun in each of the following sentences. Then choose the verb in parentheses that agrees in number with the indefinite pronoun in the sentence. (10 points)

EXAMPLE
Someone in the crowd (has, have) a cell phone
(*Someone,* indefinite pronoun; *has,* correct verb)

1. Many of the colleges (offers, offer) financial aid to qualified students.
2. Most of the gold paint (has, have) worn off the old picture frame.
3. Some of the marathoners (drops, drop) out of the race if the temperature gets too high.
4. Everybody (vies, vie) for free tickets to the movie opening.
5. Few (chooses, choose) the stew instead of the tacos.
6. Others (prefers, prefer) hip-hop music, but I love jazz.
7. Somebody (claims, claim) to have seen the ivory-billed woodpecker.
8. Nothing (surpasses, surpass) the value of a good friend.
9. All of the carnival rides (is, are) tested at regular intervals.
10. Anyone (is, are) allowed to borrow audiotapes from the library.

EXERCISE 2
1. indefinite pronoun—*many;* correct verb—*offer*
2. indefinite pronoun—*most;* correct verb—*has*
3. indefinite pronoun—*some;* correct verb—*drop*
4. indefinite pronoun—*everybody;* correct verb—*vies*
5. indefinite pronoun—*few;* correct verb—*choose*
6. indefinite pronoun—*others;* correct verb—*prefer*
7. indefinite pronoun—*somebody;* correct verb—*claims*
8. indefinite pronoun—*nothing;* correct verb—*surpasses*
9. indefinite pronoun—*all;* correct verb—*are*
10. indefinite pronoun—*anyone;* correct verb—*is*

EXERCISE 3

Identifying Inverted Sentences

Identify the subject and verb in each of the following sentences. Then identify each of the sentences as either *natural* or *inverted*. (10 points)

EXAMPLE
Into the mummy's tomb creep the archaeologist and her assistant.
(*the archaeologist and her assistant,* subject; *creep,* verb; inverted)

EXERCISE 3
1. subject—*president;* verb—*comes;* inverted
2. subject—*Taxis;* verb—*race;* natural
3. subject—*Bit;* verb—*floats;* inverted
4. subject—*sweater;* verb—*is;* inverted
5. subject—*Marisabel;* verb—*competes;* natural
6. subject—*frogs;* verb—*sing;* inverted
7. subject—*stores;* verb—*raise;* natural
8. subject—*keys, wallet;* verb—*go;* inverted
9. subject—*they;* verb—*hold;* natural
10. subject—*shirt;* verb—*is;* inverted

EXERCISE 4
1. subject—*addresses;* verb—*have*
2. subject—*protesters;* verb—*march*
3. subject—*toys;* verb—*are*
4. subject—*bottles;* verb—*drop*
5. subject—*dozens;* verb—*stand*
6. subject—*clown;* verb—*stalks*
7. subject—*board games;* verb—*are*
8. subject—*flower girl;* verb—*smiles*

1. Out of *Air Force One* comes the president.
2. Taxis race through the city streets.
3. Through the air floats a bit of dandelion fluff.
4. There in the drawer is the missing red sweater.
5. During the summer, Marisabel competes in a lot of riding contests.
6. Loudly sing the tree frogs at night.
7. The stores in the town center raise money for charity.
8. Into Dad's pocket go his keys and his wallet.
9. Over in Abilene they hold a chili contest.
10. Here is your shirt from the dry cleaner's.

EXERCISE 4

Understanding Subject-Verb Agreement with Intervening Expressions and Inverted Order

Underline the subject in each of the sentences. Then choose the correct form of verb in parentheses to complete each sentence. (10 points)

EXAMPLE
A <u>monument</u> to those Americans who died in Vietnam (graces, grace) the Mall in Washington, D.C. *(graces)*

1. The addresses on the letter (has, have) been blurred by some raindrops.
2. Across the bridge (marches, march) the protesters.
3. Here (is, are) some felt toys for the kitten.
4. Into the recycling machine (drops, drop) the empty soda pop bottles.
5. On the bookstore shelves (stands, stand) dozens of volumes of advice.
6. A clown on stilts (stalks, stalk) through the crowd.
7. There (is, are) board games for every age from preschool to adult.
8. The flower girl, flinging rose petals from her basket, (smiles, smile) at all the wedding guests.

9. All over the floor of the theater (lies, lie) empty popcorn containers.
10. Filling the shopping cart (is, are) delicious snacks for the picnic.

9. subject—*containers;* verb—*lies*
10. subject—*snacks;* verb—*are*

EXERCISE 5

Understanding Subject-Verb Agreement with Special Subjects

Choose the correct verb to agree with the subject in each of the following sentences. (20 points)

EXAMPLE
Jewels (is, are) a famous American ballet. *(is)*

1. The evening news on television (is, are) not always appropriate for young children.
2. A flock of starlings (descends, descend) noisily on the lawn.
3. *Diana and Her Companions*, painted by Vermeer, (belongs, belong) to The Hague in the Netherlands.
4. Three months (has, have) passed since Rick started painting the shed.
5. A number of the recordings (features, feature) musicians from Cuba.
6. The variety of housing styles in the new development (surprises, surprise) visitors.
7. The pliers (needs, need) to be put back in the toolbox.
8. *Harry Potter and the Goblet of Fire* (is, are) the fourth volume in the series.
9. The class (says, say) goodbye to each other before embarking on their futures.
10. Twenty-six miles and three hundred and eighty-five yards (is, are) the distance of the Olympic marathon.

EXERCISE 5
1. is
2. descends
3. belongs
4. have
5. feature
6. surprises
7. need
8. is
9. say
10. is

EXERCISE 6

Correcting Subject-Verb Agreement

If the subject and verb in each of the following sentences agree in number, write *correct*. If they do not agree, correct the verb. (20 points)

EXERCISE 6
1. correct
2. has
3. correct
4. correct
5. belong
6. are
7. correct
8. need
9. correct
10. is

EXAMPLES

The number of hurricanes seems to increase each year. *(correct)*

My sweatshirt, as well as my rain jacket, are at home on my bed. (My sweatshirt, as well as my rain jacket, *is* at home on my bed.)

1. Across the soft carpet crawls the baby.
2. Somebody have taken my sweatshirt by mistake.
3. The baker who made those incredible pies deserve first prize.
4. This theater's acoustics are wonderful.
5. My kneepads and the field hockey stick belongs in the trunk between games.
6. Plastic bags is a nuisance if not properly disposed of.
7. There are the missing wedding gifts!
8. The batteries in the fire alarm needs to be checked.
9. Either the salt or the eggs have tarnished the silver fork.
10. The dock, which was built twenty years ago, are being repaired.

EXERCISE 7
Responses will vary. Students' paragraphs should include at least five different examples of subject-verb agreement with indefinite pronouns, compound subjects, inverted sentences, intervening expressions, linking verbs, adjective clauses beginning with relative pronouns, and special subjects. Throughout the paragraph, students should use correct subject-verb agreement.

EXERCISE 7

Using Subject-Verb Agreement in Your Writing

Write a persuasive paragraph to your parents or guardian describing a vacation you would like to take. Tell where you would like to go and why you would like to go there. Include details such as how you would get there and what you would do once you arrived there. In your paragraph, include at least five different examples of subject-verb agreement with indefinite pronouns, compound subjects, inverted sentences, intervening expressions, linking verbs, adjective clauses beginning with relative pronouns, and special subjects. (20 points)

UNIT 9 MODIFIERS

UNIT OVERVIEW

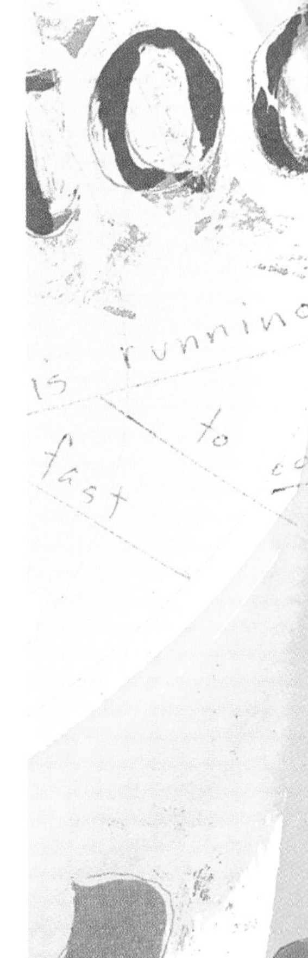

MODIFIERS

ADJECTIVES AND ADVERBS

Adjectives and adverbs—two kinds of **modifiers**—add meaning to nouns, adjectives, verbs, and adverbs.

An **adjective** modifies a noun or pronoun. An **adverb** modifies a verb, adjective, or another adverb.

EXAMPLES

adjective	The **dark** clouds cloaked the town in a **gloomy** dimness. (*Dark* modifies the noun *clouds; gloomy* modifies the noun *dimness.*)
adverb	I remain inside my house when the sky becomes **eerily** dark. (*Eerily* modifies the adjective *dark.*)
	Neighborhood kids run **very** haphazardly home as clouds overhead spread darkness **slowly** across the town. (*Very* modifies the adverb *haphazardly; slowly* modifies the verb *spread.*)

To determine whether a modifier is an adjective or an adverb, you can follow these steps.

1. Look at the word that is modified.
2. Ask yourself, "Is this modified word a noun or a pronoun?" If the answer is yes, the modifier is an adjective. If the answer is no, the modifier is an adverb.

In the following example, the word *cannons* is modified by the word *booming*. The word *cannons* is a noun; therefore, the word *booming* is an adjective.

EXAMPLE

The **booming cannons** bombarded the beleaguered fort.

In the next example, the word *darted* is modified by the word *swiftly*. The word *darted* is a verb, so the word *swiftly* is an adverb.

EXAMPLE
When the hound moved toward it, the rabbit **darted swiftly** out of its hiding place.

LANGUAGELINK
Print exercise worksheets or have students complete exercises online with the LanguageLINK CD.

Try It Yourself

EXERCISE 1
Identifying Adjectives and Adverbs in Literature

Identify each of the underlined words or phrases in the literature passage as either an adjective or an adverb.

I looked around the room, amazed. There were paintings, bronzes, tapestries, all beautifully arranged. I was dazzled and so taken aback that I almost dropped my brief case when I heard a voice say, "And what would your business be?"

I saw the figure out of a collar ad: ruddy face with blond hair faultlessly in place, a tropical weave suit draped handsomely from his broad shoulders, his eyes gray and nervous behind clear-framed glasses.

from *Invisible Man*
Ralph Ellison

EXERCISE 1
1. *beautifully*—adverb
2. *almost*—adverb
3. *collar*—adjective
4. *ruddy*—adjective

Literature MODEL

5. *blond*—adjective
6. *faultlessly*—adverb
7. *topical*—adjective
8. *handsomely*—adverb
9. *gray*—adjective
10. *nervous*—adjective
11. *clear-framed*—adjective

EXERCISE 2
Using Adjectives and Adverbs in Your Writing

Write a paragraph to a pen pal describing your favorite place to spend a weekend afternoon. Use adjectives and adverbs in your paragraph to describe what you do, how it makes you feel, and why you like the place.

EXERCISE 2
Responses will vary. Students' paragraphs should use adjectives and adverbs to describe a favorite place.

ADJECTIVES

Adjectives modify nouns by telling specific details about them.

EXAMPLES

noun	professor
a little more specific	history professor
more specific yet	dedicated history professor
even more specific	meticulous, dedicated history professor

USAGE tip

Use a comma between multiple adjectives if the word *and* makes sense between them: *the meticulous and dedicated history professor.*

Some adjectives tell *how many* or *what kind* about the nouns or pronouns they modify.

EXAMPLES

The scholar devoted **five** years of his life to this project.

After interpreting the **ancient** scrolls, he began developing a **new** theory about Egyptian culture.

Other adjectives tell *which one* or *which ones.*

EXAMPLES

Next year, **his** book will be published.

Those professors are somewhat jealous of his accomplishments.

Articles

The articles *a*, *an*, and *the* are the most commonly occurring adjectives. *A* and *an* refer to any person, place, or thing in general. *The* refers to a specific person, place, or thing.

EXAMPLES

A teaching assistant will grade your exams. (*A* refers to a teaching assistant in general.)

The book on reserve at **the** library is required reading. (*The* refers to a specific book in a specific library.)

Predicate Adjectives

Adjectives usually precede the words they modify, but they may also follow linking verbs. A **predicate adjective** follows a linking verb and modifies the subject of a clause.

USAGE tip

You might want to review predicate adjectives in Unit 7, pages 160–162.

EXAMPLES

adjective preceding noun	**The meticulous, dedicated history** professor entered the library.
predicate adjective	The professor was **meticulous** and **dedicated.**

USAGE tip

You might want to review proper nouns in Unit 4, pages 67–69.

Proper Adjectives

A **proper adjective** is formed from a proper noun. Proper adjectives are capitalized and often end in *–n*, *–an*, *–ian*, *–ese*, *or –ish*.

EXAMPLES

The **British** poet amazed his audience during his reading.

Most of the **Canadian** population lives in the southern part of the country.

Other Words Used as Adjectives

A number of other classes of words can also be used as adjectives.

EXAMPLES

nouns
sky blue, **iron** grip, **concrete** plans, **cat's** eyes

possessive pronouns
your home, **my** desk, **his** car, **their** driveway

demonstrative pronouns
this month, **that** barrel, **these** reports, **those** pears

indefinite pronouns
few customers, **several** diamonds, **some** disagreement, **each** decision

CONTINUED

USAGE tip

You might want to review demonstrative and indefinite pronouns in Unit 5, pages 100–108.

EXERCISE 3
1. my—experiment
2. the—direction
3. his—dreams
4. the—life
5. a—success
6. common—hours
7. some—things
8. an, invisible—boundary
9. new, universal, liberal—laws
10. old—laws
11. his—favor
12. a, liberal—sense
13. the—license
14. a, higher—order

MODEL

EXERCISE 4
Responses will vary. Students should replace such overused adjectives as *good, interesting,* and *many*. They can add or replace adjectives where they think they can improve the paragraph. Sample response:

Henry David Thoreau was a talented writer. He used his numerous essays and books to promote his strong individualist position. His neighbors knew him as an educated man. Thoreau traveled to various places in New England and other northern locations. He hoped to strengthen his tubercular lungs. He wrote many thought-provoking works about abstract ideals such as individualism and libertarianism. Thoreau frequently wrote in his voluminous journals, which he used as sources for his intriguing lectures. In 1854, he published *Walden*, establishing his reputation as a thoughtful writer.

participles
falling snow, **glowing** expression, **dampened** hopes, **departed** travelers

numbers
four weeks, **nine** cents, **million** reasons

Try It Yourself

EXERCISE 3
Identifying Adjectives in Literature
Identify the adjectives in the passage below. Tell which noun or pronoun each adjective modifies.

I learned this, at least, by my experiment; that if one advances confidently in the direction of his dreams, and endeavors to live the life which he has imagined, he will meet with a success unexpected in common hours. He will put some things behind, will pass an invisible boundary; new, universal, and more liberal laws will begin to establish themselves around and within him; or old laws be expanded, and interpreted in his favor in a more liberal sense, and he will live with the license of a higher order of beings.

from *Walden*
Henry David Thoreau

EXERCISE 4
Understanding Adjectives
Rewrite the paragraph below, replacing general, overused adjectives with more colorful and precise choices and adding adjectives that bring the writing to life.

Henry David Thoreau was a good writer. He used his many essays and books to promote his strong individualist position. His neighbors knew him as a smart man. Thoreau traveled to many places in New England and other northern locations. He hoped to strengthen his sick

CONTINUED

lungs. He wrote many interesting works about complex ideals such as individualism and libertarianism. Thoreau frequently wrote in his many journals, which he used as sources for his intriguing lectures. In 1854, he published *Walden*, establishing his reputation as strong writer.

EXERCISE 5
Using Other Words as Adjectives
Write a sentence including the identified word as an adjective.

1. orange (noun)
2. an (article)
3. her (possessive pronoun)
4. Italian (proper adjective)
5. comical (predicate adjective)
6. these (demonstrative pronoun)
7. fleeing (participle ending in *–ing*)
8. ripened (participle ending in *–ed*)
9. every (indefinite pronoun)
10. eight (number)

EXERCISE 6
Using Adjectives in Your Writing
Imagine that you are creating a time capsule to be opened in the year 2200. For the time capsule, write a paragraph about one of your most well-used possessions. The possession may relate to entertainment, education, personal growth, or recreational pursuits. Use vivid adjectives to create a clear description of the possession and why you value it.

ADVERBS

Adverbs modify verbs, adjectives, or other adverbs. Many times adverbs will tell us *how*, *when*, *where*, or *to what extent;* nouns and pronouns tell us *who* or *what*.

EXERCISE 5
Responses will vary. Sample responses:
1. The marigolds retained their orange blooms through October.
2. You should eat an apple for dessert.
3. We found her horse eating grass near the covered bridge.
4. For many years he read an Italian newspaper on the way to work.
5. The play is more comical than I had imagined.
6. I grabbed these documents before we left the building.
7. The fleeing rabbit did not look back at its pursuer.
8. A ripened tomato would taste good on that sandwich.

9. That noise returns every night to haunt us.
10. Duchess gave birth to a litter of eight puppies.

EXERCISE 6
Responses will vary. Students should use vivid adjectives to create a clear description of a possession they use frequently.

EXAMPLES

adverbs modify verbs	Bears sauntered **leisurely** into our camp. (*Leisurely* tells how they sauntered.)
	Bears **often** walk toward the tent with the food. (*Often* tells when they walk to the food.)
adverbs modify adjectives	The lake is **unusually** choppy this morning. (*Unusually* tells to what extent the lake is choppy.)
	This area is subject to **extreme** warming in the afternoon. (*Extreme* tells the extent of the warming.)
adverbs modify adverbs	The water level rises **very** quickly when the tide rolls in. (*Very* tells to what extent the water level rises quickly.)
	This beach has been **so** thoroughly combed that no treasures remain. (*So* tells how thoroughly the beach has been combed.)

USAGE tip

Many adverbs are formed by adding *–ly* to adjectives, such as *strangely, surprisingly*, and *regretfully*. Note, though, that you cannot depend on *–ly* to identify adverbs, since some adjectives have the same ending, as in *fatherly, homely, comely,* and *stately*.

Position of Adverbs

An adverb can be placed before or after a verb it modifies. Sometimes an adverb can be separated from a verb by another word or words.

EXAMPLES
The boxer **forcefully punched** his opponent.
His glove **smashed forcefully** into the chin of the challenger.
He **knocked** his opponent **forcefully** into the ropes.

Note, however, in the following examples, how changing the position of an adverb changes the meaning of the sentence.

USAGE tip

Many common adverbs do not have a consistent ending, such as *always, forever, here, not, now,* and *far*. The only sure way to distinguish between adjectives and adverbs is to determine how the individual word functions in its sentence.

EXAMPLES
She **only** wanted a brown pony. (She did nothing else but want a brown pony.)

She wanted **only** a brown pony. (She wanted nothing except a brown pony.)

Relative Adverbs

A **relative adverb** is used to introduce an adjective clause. The relative adverbs are *where*, *when*, and *why*.

EXAMPLES
This is the field **where** the battle was fought. (*Where* relates the adjective clause to the noun *field.*)

March is the month **when** I start itching to play ball again. (*When* relates the adjective clause to the noun *month.*)

He provided a reason **why** he no longer bowls on Monday night. (*Why* relates the adjective clause to the noun *reason.*)

USAGE tip

Relative adverbs can also be used to introduce adverb clauses:

He threw the ball *where* no one could find it.

He gets spanked *when* he is bad.

Conjunctive Adverbs

A **conjunctive adverb** is used to express relationships between independent clauses.

EXAMPLES

accordingly	furthermore	otherwise
also	hence	similarly
besides	however	still
consequently	instead	therefore
finally	nevertheless	thus

EXAMPLES
Determined to go to the concert, I arrived at the box office at five in the morning; **however,** a line of more than three hundred people had already formed.

I stood in an unmoving line for over three hours; **finally** the ticket office opened at eight o'clock.

Try It Yourself

EXERCISE 7

Identifying Adverbs in Literature

Identify the adverbs in the following literature passage.

> Leo was silent, amused at how he had entangled himself. But Salzman had aroused his interest in Lily H., and he began seriously to consider calling on her. When the marriage broker observed how intently Leo's mind was at work on the facts he had supplied, he felt certain they would soon come to an agreement.
>
> Late Saturday afternoon, conscious of Salzman, Leo Finkle walked with Lily Hirschorn along Riverside Drive. He walked briskly and erectly, wearing with distinction the black fedora he had that morning taken with trepidation out of the dusty hat box on his closet shelf, and the heavy black Saturday coat he had thoroughly whisked clean. Leo also owned a walking stick, a present from a distant relative, but quickly put temptation aside and did not use it. Lily, petite and not unpretty, had on something signifying the approach of spring.

from "The Magic Barrel"
Bernard Malamud

EXERCISE 8

Identifying Adverbs

Identify the adverbs in the following sentences and tell whether each modifies a verb, an adjective, or another adverb, or whether it is a relative or a conjunctive adverb.

1. Lex carefully shaved as part of his preparation for the date he eagerly anticipated.
2. Lucy's apartment was not very far from the neighborhood where he grew up.
3. Believing he was late, Lex drove so speedily that he did not see the police car on the side of the road.

EXERCISE 7

Leo was silent, amused at how he had entangled himself. But Salzman had aroused his interest in Lily H., and he began <u>seriously</u>

Literature MODEL

to consider calling on her. When the marriage broker observed <u>how</u> <u>intently</u> Leo's mind was at work on the facts he had supplied, he felt certain they would <u>soon</u> come to an agreement.

Late Saturday <u>afternoon</u>, conscious of Salzman, Leo Finkle walked with Lily Hirschorn along Riverside Drive. He walked <u>briskly</u> and <u>erectly</u>, wearing with distinction the black fedora he had that <u>morning</u> taken with trepidation out of the dusty hat box on his closet shelf, and the heavy black Saturday coat he had <u>thoroughly</u> whisked clean. Leo also owned a walking stick, a present from a distant relative, but <u>quickly</u> put temptation <u>aside</u> and did not use it. Lily, petite and not unpretty, had on something signifying the approach of spring.

EXERCISE 8

1. *carefully*—verb; *eagerly*—verb
2. *not*—adjective; *very*—adjective; *where*—relative adverb; *up*—verb
3. *so*—adverb; *speedily*—verb; *not*—verb

4. Noticing the flashing lights in his rearview mirror, Lex muttered, "I always have bad luck on the most important days of my life."
5. The officer, however, was a childhood friend; therefore Lex received only a warning.
6. Finally Lex arrived at Lucy's apartment.
7. Although he never paid much attention to women's fashion, Lex found Lucy's dress exceptionally stunning.
8. She smiled when he politely opened the door of his car for her.
9. Lex's mood changed dramatically when he accidentally stepped in a sizeable wad of gum.
10. Lucy laughed uncontrollably as her date struggled so valiantly to remove the pink blob from his shoe.

4. *always*—verb; *most*—adjective
5. *however*—verb; *therefore*—conjunctive adverb; *only*—verb
6. *Finally*—verb
7. *never*—verb; *exceptionally*—adjective
8. *when*—relative adverb; *politely*—verb
9. *dramatically*—verb; *when*—relative adverb; *accidentally*—verb
10. *uncontrollably*—verb; *so*—adverb; *valiantly*—verb

EXERCISE 9

Understanding Adverbs

Write a sentence using each of the following words as an adverb.

1. early
2. extremely
3. more
4. rarely
5. perhaps
6. otherwise
7. when
8. tragically
9. finally
10. annually

EXERCISE 9

Responses will vary. Sample responses:

1. We arrived early and found seats in the front row.
2. Our dog runs away extremely fast when it is time for her bath.
3. If I read more quickly I could finish the novel by Saturday.
4. Hans rarely washes his car.
5. I think we could perhaps come to an agreement at this session.
6. Return the book today; otherwise, you will be charged a fine.
7. Morning is the time of day when I have little or no energy.

EXERCISE 10

Using Adverbs in Your Writing

As part of an e-mail to a friend or relative, write a brief description of how you spent last Saturday. In your description, use adverbs to modify verbs, adjectives, and other adverbs.

8. Tragically, our team lost the game in the ninth inning.
9. We finally made the last payment on our mortgage.
10. That bird returns annually to our garden.

EXERCISE 10
Responses will vary. Students' descriptions should include a variety of adverbs that modify verbs, adjectives, and other adverbs.

APPOSITIVES

An **appositive** is a noun that is placed next to or near another noun to identify it or add information about it. In these examples, the noun *Sue Simpson* identifies the noun *vice president*, and the noun *boss* gives more information about the noun *Sue*. Both *Sue Simpson* and *boss* are appositives.

EXAMPLES
I met the regional vice president **Sue Simpson.**
Sue, our new **boss,** is a stickler for detail.

An **appositive phrase** is a group of words that includes an appositive and words that modify it, such as adjectives and prepositional phrases. The group of words adds information about the noun it modifies. In the next example, the appositive phrase *an island in the South Pacific* gives further information about the noun *Guadalcanal.*

EXAMPLE
Guadalcanal, **an island in the South Pacific,** was a World War II battle site.

If the information in an appositive specifically identifies the noun that precedes it, then the appositive is called **essential** (or **restrictive**) and is not set off with commas. In the following sentence, *Ralph Waldo Emerson* specifically identifies which writer promoted the Transcendentalist movement.

EXAMPLE
The writer **Ralph Waldo Emerson** promoted the Transcendentalist movement.

If the information in the appositive is not necessary to identify the noun that precedes it, then the appositive is called **nonessential** (or **nonrestrictive**) and is set off with commas. The following two sentences will help you see the difference between essential and nonessential information in an appositive.

EXAMPLES

essential The essay "Self-Reliance" has been read by a wide audience. (The appositive *"Self-Reliance"* specifically identifies which essay and thereby restricts the meaning of *essay* to this specific one.)

nonessential "Self-Reliance," an essay written by Ralph Waldo Emerson, expresses ideas about individualism. (The appositive phrase *an essay written by Ralph Waldo Emerson* is not necessary to identify which particular essay, since the essay has already been named.)

USAGE tip

Before punctuating appositives ask yourself: *Is the appositive essential or not essential to identifying the noun that precedes it? Does it restrict the meaning of the sentence, or does it simply provide extra information?* If it is essential, or restrictive, do not use commas. If it is not essential, or nonrestrictive, set it off with commas.

Try It Yourself

EXERCISE 11

Identifying Appositives

Identify the appositives and appositive phrases in the sentences below. Then write the noun or pronoun the appositive identifies or renames.

1. George Herman Ruth, the Babe, became a cultural icon in the 1920s.
2. In 1920, the owner of the Boston Red Sox, Harry Frazee, sold Ruth to the Yankees.
3. He played for baseball's most successful franchise, the Yankees, until 1934.
4. Yankee Stadium, "the House That Ruth Built," opened in April 1923.
5. New York sportswriter Fred Lieb gave the stadium its famous title.
6. Ruth's teammate Lou Gehrig was a rookie for the Yankees in 1925.
7. The nickname "the Sultan of Swat" was especially appropriate after Ruth hit 60 home runs in 1927.
8. Yankee rivals the Philadelphia Athletics won the American League pennant from 1929 to 1931.

EXERCISE 11

1. the Babe—George Herman Ruth
2. Harry Frazee—owner
3. the Yankees—franchise
4. "the House That Ruth Built"—Yankee Stadium
5. Fred Lieb—sportswriter
6. Lou Gehrig—teammate
7. "the Sultan of Swat"—nickname
8. the Philadelphia Athletics—rivals

9. the Chicago Cubs—champions
10. the last-place team in the league—Boston Braves

EXERCISE 12

1. Vince was encouraged to play baseball by his brother Sid.
2. Their uncle Gene pitched for a minor league team in the 1970s.
3. Vince liked to play second base, his favorite position in the field.
4. Tryouts for the high school team, the Stallions, would be held in February.
5. Sid gave Vince his favorite bat, an ash club that had long terrorized opposing pitchers.
6. Tobias, the youngest boy in the family, wanted to watch the tryouts.
7. By the end of the practice, Vince was the starting second baseman for his school, Coolidge High.
8. The brothers raced home to tell the good news to their parents, Thomas and Rachel.
9. That evening, Vince dreamed of playing for his favorite pro team, the Seattle Mariners.
10. His youngest sister, Bernice, could not understand what all the fuss was about.

9. In 1932, Ruth's team won the pennant and defeated the National League champions, the Chicago Cubs, in the World Series.
10. Ruth spent his final season as a member of the Boston Braves, the last-place team in the league.

EXERCISE 12
Understanding Appositives

On your paper, copy the following sentences. Identify the appositive or appositive phrase in each sentence by underlining it. Then insert a comma or commas where they are needed to show information that is not essential.

1. Vince was encouraged to play baseball by his brother Sid.
2. Their uncle Gene pitched for a minor league team in the 1970s.
3. Vince liked to play second base his favorite position in the field.
4. Tryouts for the high school team the Stallions would be held in February.
5. Sid gave Vince his favorite bat an ash club that had long terrorized opposing pitchers.
6. Tobias the youngest boy in the family wanted to watch the tryouts.
7. By the end of the practice, Vince was the starting second baseman for his school Coolidge High.
8. The brothers raced home to tell the good news to their parents Thomas and Rachel.
9. That evening, Vince dreamed of playing for his favorite pro team the Seattle Mariners.
10. His youngest sister Bernice could not understand what all the fuss was about.

EXERCISE 13

Using Appositives in Your Writing

Write a journal entry describing a goal that you achieved after being encouraged by someone else. Use appositives and appositive phrases to identify and provide more information about this person and how he or she helped you achieve your goal. Be sure to punctuate your appositives correctly.

EXERCISE 13

Responses will vary. Students should include appositives and appositive phrases in a descriptive paragraph about a goal they achieved. Students should correctly punctuate appositives that are not essential to the meaning of the sentence.

POSITIVES, COMPARATIVES, AND SUPERLATIVES

Modifiers—adjectives and adverbs—can be used to compare two or more people, places, or things. The form of an adjective or adverb is often changed to show the extent or degree to which a certain quality is present. There are three degrees of comparison—**positive, comparative,** and **superlative.**

EXAMPLES

positive

An adjective or adverb modifies one word.

Edgar is an **intelligent** politician. (The adjective *intelligent* shows that the quality is present.)

comparative

Two persons, places, or things are compared.

Edgar is **smarter** than Greg. (The quality expressed by the adjective *smarter* exists to a greater degree in one of the two people or things being compared.)

superlative

Three or more persons, places, or things are compared.

Edgar was the **brightest** of all students in his graduating class. (The quality expressed by the adjective *brightest* exists to a greater degree in one of more than two people or things being compared.)

USAGE tip

Use *than,* not *then,* when making comparisons. *Then* tells when.

Regular and Irregular Comparisons

Each modifier has a positive, comparative, and superlative form of comparison. Most one-syllable modifiers and some two-syllable modifiers form their comparative and superlative degrees by adding *–er* or *–est.* Other two-syllable modifiers and all modifiers of more than two syllables use *more* and *most.*

Regular Comparisons

- Add *–er* or *–est* to one-syllable words.

EXAMPLES

positive	**comparative**	**superlative**
full	fuller	fullest
cold	colder	coldest
cute	cuter	cutest
small	smaller	smallest

- Add *–er* or *–est* to most two-syllable words or use *more* and *mostly* to form the comparative and superlative degrees.

EXAMPLES

positive	**comparative**	**superlative**
subtle	subtler	subtlest
freeing	more freeing	most freeing
early	earlier	earliest
hopeful	more hopeful	most hopeful

- Use *more* or *mostly* for most words of more than two syllables and words ending in *–ly.*

EXAMPLES

positive	**comparative**	**superlative**
furious	more furious	most furious
difficult	more difficult	most difficult
haltingly	more haltingly	most haltingly
quickly	more quickly	most quickly

Some modifiers, however, have irregular comparative and superlative forms. Check the dictionary if you are unsure about the comparison of a modifier.

EXAMPLES

positive	Since the boss is really stressed, it would be a **bad** time to ask for a raise.
comparative	After this project is finished, he will be in a **better** mood.
superlative	Friday afternoon will provide your **best** opportunity for success.

Irregular Comparisons

EXAMPLES

positive	**comparative**	**superlative**
well	better	best
bad	worse	worst
ill	worse	worst
many	more	most
much	more	most
little	less, lesser	least
far	farther	farthest
far	further	furthest

USAGE tip

Some words are absolute and cannot logically be compared. The positive form of such words as *perfect, unique, dead, impossible,* and *infinite* describes their only state. They are not capable of greater or lesser degrees.

Decreasing Comparisons

To show a decrease in the quality of any modifier, form the comparative and superlative degrees by using *less* and *least*.

EXAMPLES

positive	**comparative**	**superlative**
flooded	less flooded	least flooded
beautiful	less beautiful	least beautiful
august	less august	least august

Problems with Using Comparative and Superlative Forms

It is sometimes easy to mistakenly make a double comparison or an illogical or unclear comparison.

- Avoid using double comparisons. A **double comparison** is incorrect because it contains both *–er* and *more (less)* or both *–est* and *most (least)*.

EXAMPLES

incorrect	Mother becomes more angrier if you lie about your misdeeds.
correct	Mother becomes **angrier** if you lie about your misdeeds.
incorrect	I feel **most sleepiest** right after my alarm rings in the morning.
correct	I feel **sleepiest** right after my alarm rings in the morning.

- Use the word *other* or *else* when comparing one member of a group with the rest of the group.

EXAMPLES

illogical	California is more populous than any state in the union. (Since California is a state in the union, and it cannot logically be more populous than itself, this sentence doesn't make sense.)
logical	California is more populous than any **other** state in the union.
illogical	Fritz is taller than anyone in his class. (Since Fritz is a member of the class, and he cannot logically be taller than himself, this sentence doesn't make sense.)
logical	Fritz is taller than anyone **else** in his class.

- Make sure your comparisons are clear and complete.

EXAMPLES

confusing	Nicole loves to fish more than her brother. (The sentence suggests that Nicole loves to fish more than she loves her brother.)
clear	Nicole loves to fish more than her brother **does**.

CONTINUED

confusing	Homemade spaghetti tastes better than a can. (The taste of homemade spaghetti is unintentionally compared to the taste of a can.)
clear	Homemade spaghetti tastes better than **that from** a can.

Try It Yourself

EXERCISE 14

Identifying Positives, Comparatives, and Superlatives

Identify the underlined words in the following sentences as positive, comparative, or superlative.

1. Jeremy is the most popular boy in school.
2. He is the fastest runner on the track team.
3. When he competes, the event attracts more fans than the stadium can hold.
4. If Jeremy continues to win, he will have a better chance to win a college scholarship.
5. His sister Sara is among the smartest students in the school.
6. However, her many academic achievements have not brought her much admiration.
7. Sara and Jeremy's mother is the politest woman I have ever met.
8. Their father is a quiet man who tends to be boring when he does start talking.
9. Jeremy and Sara's many accomplishments make them look like the wisest parents in town.
10. The family also seems to be happier than most others I have encountered.

EXERCISE 15

Understanding Degrees of Comparison

For each incorrectly used adjective or adverb in the following sentences, write the correct positive, comparative, or superlative form. Write *correct* if all adjective or adverb comparisons in the sentence are used correctly.

USAGE tip

If you are unsure of the clarity of a comparison, completely state both parts of the comparison.

unclear
Sara performs onstage more often than Jamie.

clear
Sara performs onstage more often than Jamie performs onstage.

clear
Sara performs onstage more often than Jamie does.

EXERCISE 14
1. superlative
2. superlative
3. comparative
4. comparative
5. superlative
6. positive, positive
7. superlative
8. positive, positive
9. positive, superlative
10. comparative

EXERCISE 15
1. most inspiring
2. correct
3. bloodiest
4. least
5. correct
6. nobler
7. more trying
8. deeper or deep
9. saddest
10. finest

EXERCISE 16
Responses will vary. Reviews should make comparisons between two short stories, allowing students to use the positive, comparative, and superlative degrees of modifiers.

1. My uncle believes the Gettysburg Address is Lincoln's inspiringest speech.
2. Lincoln served as president during the nation's worst crisis.
3. The Civil War was the more bloodiest conflict in U.S. history.
4. After his election in 1860, Lincoln appeared to be the man less likely to preserve the Union.
5. Although he had little previous political experience, Lincoln rose to the challenge of secession.
6. Lincoln, who initially wanted only to preserve the Union, later embraced the more nobler goal of ending slavery.
7. The war became tryinger to the president with each Confederate victory.
8. He also gained a deepest understanding of human suffering during the conflict.
9. When Lincoln was killed, it was one of the more saddest days in American history.
10. Today, many historians consider Lincoln the finer leader who has ever served in the White House.

EXERCISE 16

Using Comparisons Correctly in Your Writing

Write a brief review for the school newspaper comparing and contrasting two short stories that you have recently read. Use the positive, comparative, and superlative forms of adjectives and adverbs to express your opinions about the stories.

NEGATIVES AND DOUBLE NEGATIVES

Negatives such as *not* and *never* are adverbs because they add to the meaning of the verb. The verb tells what an action is, and the negative says that the writer or speaker means the opposite of that.

EXAMPLES
She is an inspiring storyteller.
She is **not** an inspiring storyteller.

Edith will teach drivers' education.
Edith will **never** teach drivers' education.

USAGE tip

Some negatives contain a contraction. A **contraction** combines two words by shortening and joining them with an apostrophe. You'll learn more about contractions in the next section in this unit.

doesn't = does not
hadn't = had not
wouldn't = would not

Make sure to use only one negative in each sentence. A **double negative** is the use of two negative words together when only one is needed. Check your writing to be sure that you have not used a negative word such as *not, nobody, none, nothing, hardly, can't, doesn't, won't, isn't,* or *aren't* with another negative word. Correct double negatives by removing one of the negative words or by replacing one of the negative words with a positive word.

EXAMPLES

double negative	There isn't nothing like lemonade on a hot summer day.
corrected sentence	There is nothing like lemonade on a hot summer day.
double negative	Marshall didn't hear none of the speech.
corrected sentence	Marshall heard none of the speech.
corrected sentence	Marshall didn't hear any of the speech.
double negative	It hardly never rains here in the summer.
corrected sentence	It hardly ever rains here in the summer.
corrected sentence	It almost never rains here in the summer.

Try It Yourself

EXERCISE 17

Identifying Negatives

Write the negative words in the following sentences.

1. We found nothing of interest when we went to the mall.
2. I did not have much money to spend anyway.

EXERCISE 17
1. nothing
2. not

3. barely
4. nowhere
5. never
6. hadn't (had not)
7. scarcely
8. no one
9. won't (will not)
10. cannot

3. I barely had enough money to buy lunch at the food court.
4. A great deal on clothes in my size was nowhere to be found.
5. We should never go shopping the day after a big clearance sale.
6. I hadn't remembered the weekend sale until after we arrived at the mall.
7. The stores had scarcely refilled their shelves and racks when we arrived.
8. It seemed like no one else besides us missed the weekend sale.
9. I won't make the same mistake twice.
10. Both of us cannot wait until the mall has another big clearance sale.

EXERCISE 18

Responses may vary slightly.

Sample responses:

1. Wes hadn't read anything about the golf course closing.
2. Last week the owner reassured golfers that he would never close the course.
3. The only other course in the county is hardly worth the long drive for most golfers.
4. correct
5. Wes called city hall but never talked to anybody who cared about the issue.
6. When we moved here, I couldn't ever imagine this problem arising.
7. This is not a matter that Wes will drop easily.
8. He was so mad yesterday that he could scarcely say a sentence without cussing.
9. No one could say anything to get him to settle down.
10. Neither Tom nor Wally had any success diverting his attention.

EXERCISE 18

Understanding Double Negatives

Rewrite the following sentences to remove the double negative. Remember that you can either remove one of the negative words or replace it with a positive word. If a sentence does not contain a double negative, write *correct*.

1. Wes hadn't read nothing about the golf course closing.
2. Last week the owner reassured golfers that he wouldn't never close the course.
3. The only other course in the county isn't hardly worth the long drive for most golfers.
4. Now nobody in our town will have anyplace to go golfing.
5. Wes called city hall but never talked to nobody who cared about the issue.
6. When we moved here, I couldn't never imagine this problem arising.
7. This is not no matter that Wes will drop easily.
8. He was so mad yesterday that he couldn't scarcely say a sentence without cussing.

9. No one couldn't say anything to get him to settle down.
10. Neither Tom nor Wally hadn't any success diverting his attention.

EXERCISE 19
Responses will vary. Sample responses:
1. Nobody understands the gravity of this situation.
2. We will not be finished with this mural today.
3. I couldn't go to the football game this weekend because of my cold.
4. We scarcely ate anything on the trip to California.
5. After that Sunday, I never saw her again.

EXERCISE 19

Using Negatives

Write a sentence for each of the five negative words below. Be careful to avoid using any double negatives.

1. nobody
2. not
3. couldn't
4. scarcely
5. never

CONTRACTIONS

Contractions combine two words by shortening and joining them with an apostrophe. When you are trying to determine subjects and verbs in a sentence, write out contractions into the two words that they represent. After the contraction is written out, each word should be considered separately. Remember that a negative is never part of a verb but is an adverb.

EXAMPLES

Teri **wasn't** in the office all afternoon. (*was* = verb; *not* = adverb)

She'll be at a meeting tomorrow morning. (*She* = subject; *will be* = helping verb and verb)

She **couldn't** see you until the afternoon. (*could see* = helping verb and verb; *not* = adverb)

USAGE tip

Contractions are common in speech and in informal writing. Your teacher may want you to write out the words represented by contractions when your topic, purpose, and audience are formal.

USAGE tip

Don't confuse the pronouns *its, their, your,* and *whose* with the contractions *it's, they're, you're,* and *who's.*

EXERCISE 20

1. I've; I have; have got
2. haven't; have not; have
3. You're; You are; are
4. you're; you are; are going
5. Don't; Do not; Do tell
6. I'm; I am; am going
7. I'm; I am; am

MODEL

8. It's; It is; is
9. can't; can not; can hurt

EXERCISE 21

The instructional designers *did not* stop working on the project until midnight. *They will* make their presentation to the board at 9:00 A.M. *We had* tried to move back the starting time of the meeting. The board members *will not* accept any more delays. *It is* important to convince them of the utility of this project. If they are impressed, *you will* probably be in line for a big raise later this year. If they *are not* impressed, our division could be the target of major budget cuts. This *is not* a meeting for the faint of heart.

Try It Yourself

EXERCISE 20

Identifying Contractions in Literature

Identify the contractions in the following literature excerpt. Write out each contraction as the two words it represents. Then write the verb or verb phrase.

> "Well, Missy, excuse me," Doctor Harry patted her cheek. "But I've got to warn you, haven't I? You're a marvel, but you must be careful or you're going to be good and sorry."
>
> "Don't tell me what I'm going to be. I'm on my feet now, morally speaking. It's Cornelia. I had to go to bed to get rid of her."
>
> Her bones felt loose, and floated around in her skin, and Doctor Harry floated like a balloon around the foot of the bed. He floated and pulled down his waistcoat and swung his glasses on a cord. "Well, stay where you are, it certainly can't hurt you."
>
> from "The Jilting of Granny Weatherall"
> Katherine Anne Porter

EXERCISE 21

Understanding Contractions

Revise the following paragraph to make it more formal by removing all contractions.

> The instructional designers didn't stop working on the project until midnight. They'll make their presentation to the board at 9:00 A.M. We'd tried to move back the starting time of the meeting. The board members won't accept any more delays. It's important to convince them of the utility of this project. If they are impressed, you'll probably be in line for a big raise later this year. If they aren't impressed, our division could be the target of major budget cuts. This isn't a meeting for the faint of heart.

EXERCISE 22

Using Contractions in Your Writing

Imagine that you are keeping a learning log in which you reflect on what you learn. Write a summary of one of your classes. Describe the information your teacher presented and what you did to practice it. Tell what you learned about the topic. Use at least five contractions in your summary.

EXERCISE 22 *Responses will vary.* Students' reviews should include details about the class and the teacher. Check to be sure that students have maintained an informal tone and have used at least five contractions correctly.

DANGLING AND MISPLACED MODIFIERS

Dangling modifiers and misplaced modifiers are words, phrases, or clauses that confuse the meaning of a sentence. A **dangling modifier** does not clearly modify another word in a sentence because the word it should modify has been omitted. A **misplaced modifier** seems to modify the wrong word in the sentence because it is located too far from the word it should modify. You can edit dangling and misplaced modifiers by moving the modifier within the sentence or by rewording the sentence.

USAGE tip

Sometimes when you move the misplaced or dangling phrase or clause closer to the word it modifies, you may have to do some additional rewording of the sentence.

EXAMPLES

dangling modifier	Grilling the steaks outside, a jet flew overhead. (It sounds as if the jet is grilling the steaks.)
corrected sentence	Grilling the steaks outside, I heard a jet fly overhead. (*Grilling the steaks outside* now modifies *I*. Notice how the wording of the sentence changes slightly.)
dangling modifier	After waking up in the morning, a strange creaking sound distracted her for a few minutes. (It sounds as if the strange creaking sound is waking up.)
corrected sentence	A strange creaking sound distracted her for a few minutes after she woke up. (*After she woke up* tells when she was distracted.)

CONTINUED

misplaced one-word modifier	The friendly poodle almost jumped on the mail carrier every day. (The poodle almost—but not quite—jumps.)
corrected sentence	The friendly poodle jumped on the mail carrier almost every day. (The poodle jumps often, but not quite every day.)
misplaced phrase	Arrange the chairs in middle of the classroom in a semicircle. (The misplaced prepositional phrase suggests that the classroom is in a semicircle.)
corrected sentence	Arrange the chairs in a semicircle in the middle of the classroom. (The chairs are in a semicircle in the middle of the classroom.)
misplaced clause	Houses provide extra security for city residents that have motion detectors installed. (The misplaced clause suggests that it is the residents, not the houses, that have motion detectors installed.)
corrected sentence	Houses that have motion detectors installed provide extra security for city residents. (Some houses have motion detectors installed, and they provide extra security for city residents.)

Try It Yourself

EXERCISE 23
1. MM
2. DM
3. MM
4. DM
5. MM
6. MM
7. DM
8. DM
9. DM
10. MM

EXERCISE 23

Identifying Dangling and Misplaced Modifiers

Identify the dangling modifiers in the following sentences by writing *DM*. Identify the misplaced modifiers by writing *MM*.

1. The professor lectured on three Mongolian conquerors in class today.
2. Paddling down the river, bears eyed our canoe but quickly lost interest.

3. Scholars met at the university conference center to discuss nuclear disarmament from six universities.
4. The front yard of our house looked like a war zone pulling into the driveway.
5. The salesperson really wanted us to test drive the green sedan with the long, red beard.
6. Cutting the grass every week, Gerard keeps a professional look to his yard with a self-propelled lawnmower.
7. To provide contact information to her students, her office phone number was displayed on the overhead.
8. Walking out to the piano onstage, the audience applauded loudly.
9. While washing the car in the driveway, my sister took a nap on the back porch.
10. To inspire us, the coach recounted his greatest gridiron achievement before the game.

EXERCISE 24

Correcting Dangling and Misplaced Modifiers

Revise the sentences in Exercise 23 so that the modifiers are placed as close as possible to the words they modify.

EXERCISE 25

Understanding Dangling and Misplaced Modifiers

Combine each pair of sentences below by making one sentence into a modifier. Check your sentences to be sure that you didn't create any dangling or misplaced modifiers.

1. Gina got out of bed and turned on the television. She was unable to sleep.
2. The coyote hastily retreated into the brush. He did not want to tangle with our Doberman.
3. Roland was filling out the lineup card. He smoked a cigar.
4. We enrolled in a cartooning class. The class meets at the community college.
5. Julie read poetry at the coffee house. It was packed with admirers of her verse.

EXERCISE 24

Responses will vary. Sample responses:

1. In class today, the professor lectured on three Mongolian conquerors.
2. As we paddled down the river, bears eyed our canoe but quickly lost interest.
3. Scholars from six universities met at the university conference center to discuss nuclear disarmament.
4. Pulling into the driveway, I thought the front yard of our house looked like a war zone.
5. The salesperson with the long, red beard really wanted us to test drive the green sedan.
6. Cutting the grass every week with a self-propelled lawnmower, Gerard keeps a professional look to his yard.
7. To provide contact information to her students, our teacher displayed her office phone number on the overhead.
8. While the musician was walking out to the piano onstage, the audience applauded loudly.
9. While I was washing the car in the driveway, my sister took a nap on the back porch.
10. To inspire us before the game, the coach recounted his greatest gridiron achievement.

EXERCISE 25
Responses will vary. Sample responses:
1. Unable to sleep, Gina got out of bed and turned on the television.
2. Not wanting to tangle with our Doberman, the coyote hastily retreated into the brush.
3. Roland, smoking a cigar, was filling out the lineup card.
4. We enrolled in a cartooning class that meets at the community college.
5. Julie read poetry at the coffee house packed with admirers of her verse.
6. At 5:30 P.M., the boss asked me to start on a new filing project.
7. After he saw the flashing lights behind him, Bobby pulled his car over to the side of the road.
8. Some place kickers who have strong legs can kick field goals of 60 yards or longer.
9. As Patrick stood in his foxhole during the rainstorm, he felt the water around his ankles.
10. Surprisingly, our daughter Amy does not like watching cartoons.

6. The boss asked me to start on a new filing project. It was 5:30 P.M.
7. Bobby pulled his car over to the side of the road. He saw the flashing lights behind him.
8. Some place kickers can kick field goals of sixty yards or longer. They have strong legs.
9. Patrick stood in his foxhole during the rainstorm. He felt the water around his ankles.
10. Surprisingly, our daughter does not like watching cartoons. Her name is Amy.

CHOOSING THE CORRECT MODIFIERS

In everyday conversation, people often use adjectives in place of adverbs. For example, someone might say, "Go quick!" instead of "Go quickly." When you write, make sure that you use adjectives to modify nouns and pronouns and adverbs to modify verbs, adjectives, and other adverbs. In the following sentence, the choice between the adjective and adverb affects the meaning of the sentence.

EXAMPLES

adjective Joaquin felt a sudden, chilly breeze in the night. (The breeze was both sudden and chilly. The adjectives *sudden* and *chilly* modify the noun *breeze*.)

adverb Joaquin felt a suddenly chilly breeze in the night. (The chilliness was sudden. The adverb *suddenly* modifies the adjective *chilly*.)

Try It Yourself

EXERCISE 26

Identifying Modifiers in Literature

Tell whether each underlined modifier in the following passage is an adjective or an adverb.

With these words, the beautiful daughter of Rappaccini plucked one of the richest blossoms of the shrub, and was about to fasten it in her bosom. But now, unless Giovanni's draughts of wine had bewildered his senses, a singular incident occurred. A small orange-colored reptile of the lizard or chameleon species, chanced to be creeping along the path, just at the feet of Beatrice. It appeared to Giovanni—but, at the distance from which he gazed, he could scarcely have seen anything so minute—it appeared to him, however, that a drop or two of moisture from the broken stem of the flower descended upon the lizard's head. For an instant, the reptile contorted itself violently, and then lay motionless in the sunshine. Beatrice observed this remarkable phenomenon, and crossed herself, sadly, but without surprise; nor did she therefore hesitate to arrange the fatal flower in her bosom. There it blushed, and almost glimmered with the dazzling effect of a precious stone, adding to her dress and aspect the one appropriate charm, which nothing else in the world could have supplied.

from "Rappaccini's Daughter"
Nathaniel Hawthorne

Literature MODEL

EXERCISE 26
1. *beautiful*—adjective
2. *singular*—adjective
3. *scarcely*—adverb
4. *minute*—adjective
5. *violently*—adverb
6. *motionless*—adverb
7. *sadly*—adverb
8. *fatal*—adjective
9. *precious*—adjective
10. *appropriate*—adjective

EXERCISE 27
1. Felicity's reserved and quiet nature belie her troubled inner spirit.
2. The rabbit moved too quickly for our aging bloodhound to catch it.
3. correct
4. Your sister is running really fast at this meet.
5. The woods grew ominously silent as we walked along.
6. Elizabeth whispered quietly to Allison during the lecture.
7. Her husband Jack is a rabid fan of the Pittsburgh Steelers.
8. If you can't treat your brother nicely you will have to take a nap.
9. Kelli asked her father hopefully if she could drive the car this weekend.
10. correct

EXERCISE 27

Understanding Modifiers

Rewrite the following sentences so that the adjectives and adverbs are used correctly. If the modifier or modifiers are used correctly, write *correct*.

1. Felicity's reserved and quietly nature belie her troubled inner spirit.
2. The rabbit moved too quick for our aging bloodhound to catch it.
3. The dark lord waved his sword menacingly at the defiant knight.
4. Your sister is running real fast at this meet.
5. The woods grew ominous silent as we walked along.
6. Elizabeth whispered quiet to Allison during the lecture.

7. Her husband Jack is a rabidly fan of the Pittsburgh Steelers.
8. If you can't treat your brother nice you will have to take a nap.
9. Kelli asked her father hopeful if she could drive the car this weekend.
10. The water in the cavern pool had a dull, eerie glow.

EXERCISE 28

Using Modifiers in Your Writing

Write a letter to the editor of your school newspaper expressing your disagreement with a school policy. As you explain your disagreement with the policy and propose an alternative to the issue, make sure that you use modifiers correctly. Use at least three adverbs and three adjectives in your letter.

EXERCISE 28
Responses will vary. Students should explain why they disagree with a certain school policy and propose an alternative. In doing so, they should use a variety of correctly chosen adjectives and adverbs.

COMMONLY CONFUSED WORDS

The modifiers *good*, *well*, *bad*, and *badly* can be confusing because the distinctions between *good* and *well* and between *bad* and *badly* are often not followed in conversation. Confusion can also occur because *well* can function as either an adjective or an adverb.

USAGE tip

Good, well, and *bad* form their comparative and superlative degrees irregularly: *good, better, best; well, better, best;* and *bad, worse, worst. Badly* becomes *more badly* and *most badly* in the comparative and superlative degrees.

EXAMPLES

Samuel felt **bad** about spilling juice on the carpet (*Bad* is an adjective. It follows a linking verb like *felt* and here modifies the subject *Samuel.*)

Debra sang **badly**, so she learned how to play the piano. (*Badly* is an adverb that modifies *sang.*)

Springfield has a **good** facility to host large conventions. (*Good* is an adjective that modifies the noun *facility.*)

He plays softball **well**. (*Well* is an adverb meaning "skillfully." It modifies the verb *plays.*)

If you feel **well** enough, we can go to the mall. (*Well* is an adjective meaning "healthy" or "state of satisfactory condition." It follows a linking verb like *feel.*)

Try It Yourself

EXERCISE 29

Identifying Commonly Confused Words

Choose the correct form of *good*, *well*, *bad*, and *badly* in the following sentences.

1. Bobby (bad, badly) wanted to join his teammates on the field.
2. Throughout this meeting I have heard (good, well) ideas about how to proceed.
3. The bargaining session has gone (well, good) up to this point.
4. Because Albert fields (well, good), he was added to the varsity roster.
5. Radio reception is especially (bad, badly) here in the valley.
6. The team played (bad, badly) tonight in its last regular season game.
7. Since you repaired the television set, the picture no longer looks (bad, badly).
8. Our high school drama club puts on a (good, well) show every year.
9. I believe Chester feels (well, good) enough to attend school today.
10. The board meeting went (badly, bad) after Bill yelled at Ed for dozing off.

EXERCISE 29
1. badly
2. good
3. well
4. well
5. bad
6. badly
7. bad
8. good
9. well
10. badly

EXERCISE 30

Understanding Commonly Confused Words

Correct any misuse of *good*, *well*, *bad*, and *badly* in the following sentences. If no modifiers are misused in the sentence, write *correct*.

1. Ever since he started taking lessons, Scott has become a good guitar player.
2. That cut above your right eye looks badly and should probably be treated.

EXERCISE 30
1. correct
2. That cut above your right eye looks bad and should probably be treated.

3. Teaching students to drive good is a primary goal of this class.
4. Gerald's hair was mussed bad by that last powerful gust.
5. Your new perfume smells well on you.
6. The doctors at this hospital have an excellent record at making sick patients well.
7. Gene felt badly after hearing about his brother's latest business failure.
8. Edith does not hear good enough to understand what the boy is saying.
9. Try to figure out from what source that bad odor is emanating.
10. One week after his surgery, Mark felt good enough to mow the lawn.

3. Teaching students to drive well is a primary goal of this class.
4. Gerald's hair was mussed badly by that last powerful gust.
5. Your new perfume smells good on you.
6. correct
7. Gene felt bad after hearing about his brother's latest business failure.
8. Edith does not hear well enough to understand what the boy is saying.
9. correct
10. One week after his surgery, Mark felt well enough to mow the lawn.

EXERCISE 31

Using Commonly Confused Words in Your Writing

Write a letter to a friend discussing a television show that you have watched recently. Describe the show's strengths and weaknesses and explain why you do or do not recommend watching it. Check to be sure that you have used the modifiers *good*, *well*, *bad*, and *badly* correctly.

EXERCISE 31

Responses will vary. Students' reviews should use the correct forms of *good, well, bad,* and *badly.*

UNIT 9 REVIEW

TEST YOUR KNOWLEDGE

EXERCISE 1

Identifying Adjectives and Adverbs

Identify each underlined word in the following sentences as either an *adjective* or an *adverb*. (10 points)

EXAMPLE

Louisiana is one of America's most diverse states. (adjective)

1. Many residents of the state benefit from the widely used Mississippi River.
2. The Mississippi originates in the northern state of Minnesota and forms a border between several states.
3. French explorer René-Robert Cavelier de La Salle first claimed Louisiana for his home country in 1682.
4. In 1755, the British forcibly transported 4,000 Cajuns from distant Nova Scotia to Louisiana.
5. In 1803, U.S. president Thomas Jefferson wisely purchased Louisiana from the French because of its strategic location.
6. Much commerce passed through New Orleans, an international port that serves America's most extensive river system.
7. Louisiana also has rich farmland and plentiful oil and gas reserves.
8. Today many are greatly concerned about the loosely regulated petrochemical plants that operate along the mighty Mississippi River.
9. Louisiana benefits from a very prosperous tourism industry.
10. The popular Mardi Gras festival in lively New Orleans attracts droves of visitors each year.

EXERCISE 1

1. *Many*—adjective; *widely*—adverb
2. *northern*—adjective; *several*—adjective
3. *French*—adjective; *first*—adverb
4. *forcibly*—adverb; *distant*—adjective
5. *wisely*—adverb; *strategic*—adjective
6. *Much*—adjective; *international*—adjective; *extensive*—adjective
7. *rich*—adjective; *plentiful*—adjective
8. *greatly*—adverb; *loosely*—adverb; *mighty*—adjective
9. *very*—adverb; *prosperous*—adjective
10. *popular*—adjective; *lively*—adjective; *each*—adjective

EXERCISE 2
1. Ermey—a Marine for twelve years
2. Francis Ford Coppola—director; *Apocalypse Now*—war epic
3. another powerful movie about the Vietnam War—*Full Metal Jacket*
4. a tough profane drill instructor who prepared raw recruits to go to war—gunnery sergeant Hartman
5. one of Stanley Kubrick's masterpieces—The film
6. *Toy Story* and *Toy Story 2*—movies; one of today's most popular actors—Tom Hanks
7. a thriller starring Danny Glover and Dennis Quaid—*Switchback*
8. a quirky comedy—*Saving Silverman*
9. a veteran of several television shows—Ermey; a program that answers viewer questions about weapons and military hardware—*Mail Call*
10. a cable channel that features programming on a variety of historical topics—the History Channel.

EXERCISE 2
Identifying Appositives

Identify the appositives and appositive phrases in the sentences below. Then tell which noun or pronoun the appositive identifies or modifies. (20 points)

EXAMPLE
Actor R. Lee Ermey served as a staff sergeant in the Marine Corps, a branch of the U.S. military.
(R. Lee Ermey, Actor; a branch of the U.S. military, Marine Corps)

1. Ermey, a Marine for twelve years, was wounded while serving in the Vietnam War.
2. In 1979, director Francis Ford Coppola cast Ermey in his war epic, *Apocalypse Now*.
3. Ermey is best known for his role in *Full Metal Jacket*, another powerful movie about the Vietnam War.
4. In the movie, he played gunnery sergeant Hartman, a tough profane drill instructor who prepared raw recruits to go to war.
5. The film, one of Stanley Kubrick's masterpieces, earned popular and critical acclaim.
6. Ermey later appeared in the movies *Toy Story* and *Toy Story 2* with Tom Hanks, one of today's most popular actors.
7. *Switchback*, a thriller starring Danny Glover and Dennis Quaid, provided Ermey with the opportunity to play a nonmilitary character.
8. In *Saving Silverman*, a quirky comedy, Ermey was cast as a crazed ex-football coach.
9. Ermey, a veteran of several television shows, is currently the host of *Mail Call*, a program that answers viewer questions about weapons and military hardware.
10. The show is on the History Channel, a cable channel that features programming on a variety of historical topics.

EXERCISE 3

Identifying Positives, Comparatives, and Superlatives

Identify the underlined words in the following sentences as positive, comparative, or superlative. (10 points)

EXAMPLE
My friend likes to visit several different stores to find the cheapest prices. (superlative)

1. The room looks worse after he painted it that awful color.
2. We have less money now than we did last year at this time.
3. That beverage has a sweet taste.
4. Buying a new appliance is the least attractive of the alternatives we are considering.
5. When the speaker asked for volunteers, I hesitantly raised my hand.
6. Larger watermelons can be difficult to carry from the store.
7. We need to throw off any unnecessary equipment to make the airplane lighter.
8. On the spur of the moment Don decided to climb the highest mountain in the state.
9. Bernice happily skipped to school since it was the last day of the semester.
10. After our loan was approved, I didn't care if interest rates climbed any higher.

EXERCISE 4

Understanding Modifiers

Rewrite the following sentences so that the adjectives and adverbs are used correctly. If the modifiers are used correctly in a sentence, write *correct*. (10 points)

EXERCISE 3
1. comparative
2. comparative
3. positive
4. superlative
5. positive
6. comparative
7. comparative
8. superlative
9. positive
10. comparative

EXERCISE 4
1. correct
2. Since Ethel is hard of hearing, you will need to knock on her door really hard.
3. You will not find a section of town that was hit more badly by the storm than here.
4. The students from the academy are the most charming boys I've ever met.
5. The lake at the resort has the bluest water I have ever seen.
6. Ken does not sing well enough to land one of the major roles in the musical.
7. After taking an aspirin, Otto felt really well and decided to go to school.
8. If you do not start swimming better, you will get cut from the team.

9. If Tom begins feeling worse, we will have to reschedule the appointment.
10. Mother yelled loudly to get her point across about taking out the trash.

EXERCISE 5
Responses will vary.
Sample responses:
1. She doesn't have any extra money to spend on such extravagances.
2. The manager said you can't stay here anymore.
3. Nobody in the stands saw anything unusual happening in the dugout.
4. There would be no more opportunities to heal the relationship.
5. She hardly ever puts her car in the garage.
6. correct
7. Although he could barely hear himself think, Doug completed the article on time.
8. Despite her disadvantages, Marie never asked anybody for help.
9. correct
10. I could scarcely see the road, but I drove on hoping to reach town by nightfall.

EXAMPLE
Upon returning from the expedition, he had become an exceeding rich young man. (Upon returning from the expedition, he had become an *exceedingly* rich young man.)

1. Not taking your medication will cause the pain to become sharper.
2. Since Ethel is hard of hearing, you will need to knock on her door real hard.
3. You will not find a section of town that was hit badder by the storm than here.
4. The students from the academy are the charmingest boys I've ever met.
5. The lake at the resort has the bluer water I have ever seen.
6. Ken does not sing good enough to land one of the major roles in the musical.
7. After taking an aspirin, Otto felt real well and decided to go to school.
8. If you do not start swimming gooder, you will get cut from the team.
9. If Tom begins feeling worst, we will have to reschedule the appointment.
10. Mother yelled loud to get her point across about taking out the trash.

EXERCISE 5

Understanding Negatives and Double Negatives

Rewrite the following sentences to remove the double negatives. Remember that you can either remove one of the negative words or replace it with a positive word. If a sentence does not contain a double negative, write *correct*. (10 points)

EXAMPLE
We don't have no time to take a break this morning.
(We don't have *any* time to take a break this morning.)

1. She doesn't have no extra money to spend on such extravagances.
2. The manager said you can't stay here no more.
3. Nobody in the stands saw nothing unusual happening in the dugout.
4. There wouldn't be no more opportunities to heal the relationship.
5. She hardly never puts her car in the garage.
6. Following school policy, I don't usually allow students to retake the final.
7. Although he couldn't barely hear himself think, Doug completed the article on time.
8. Despite her disadvantages, Marie never asked nobody for help.
9. He arrived at the train station hoping to catch her, but she was nowhere to be seen.
10. I couldn't scarcely see the road, but I drove on hoping to reach town by nightfall.

EXERCISE 6
Correcting Dangling and Misplaced Modifiers
Rewrite the following sentences so that the modifiers are placed as close as possible to the words they modify. You may need to add words to the sentences. (10 points)

EXAMPLE
After waking up in the morning, a cup of coffee is my strongest motivator to start the day. (After *I wake* up in the morning, a cup of coffee is my strongest motivator to start the day.)

EXERCISE 6
Responses will vary.
Sample responses:
1. When Pamela was sixteen, her grandfather moved in with the family.
2. From his warm bed, James heard the wolf howling outside.
3. As we were climbing the steps to the courthouse, rain cascaded down upon our heads.
4. With pink ribbons in her hair, Tina sang beautifully in front of all the parents and the principal.
5. The butler noticed the colonel's youngest son swimming in the river.
6. The distinguished professor with receding gray hair issued a challenge to the bright young student.
7. For workers completing their shift, bowling a couple of games is a great way to unwind.
8. While I was shoveling in the frigid wind, my nose grew rosy and my feet numbed.

9. Using a scooper and a bag, Laurel always picks up after her dog.
10. When you are working out in the sun, sunscreen is a necessity to avoid a painful burn.

EXERCISE 7
Responses will vary.
Sample responses:
1. The rich young widow purchased the elegant mink coat.
2. Twin brothers Phil and Shawn, after they finished scraping, painted the picket fence robin's egg blue.
3. A talented gymnast, Brooke skillfully jumps onto the balance beam to perform her routine.
4. Joel's oldest son, an honor roll student, plays goalie for his high school soccer team.
5. The evergreen bush shaped like a Christmas tree needs badly to be trimmed.
6. In front of the fireplace, a jet black housecat sleeps soundly on the oak floor.

1. At age sixteen, Pamela's grandfather moved in with the family.
2. James heard the wolf howling outside from his warm bed.
3. Climbing the steps to the courthouse, rain cascaded down upon our heads.
4. Tina sang beautifully in front of all the parents and the principal with pink ribbons in her hair.
5. Swimming in the river, the butler noticed the colonel's youngest son.
6. The distinguished professor issued a challenge to the bright young student with receding gray hair.
7. Bowling a couple of games for workers completing their shift is a great way to unwind.
8. Shoveling in the frigid wind, my nose grew rosy and my feet numbed.
9. Laurel always picks up after her dog using a scooper and a bag.
10. When working out in the sun, sunscreen is a necessity to avoid a painful burn.

EXERCISE 7

Using Modifiers

Expand each of the following sentences with modifiers. Choose colorful and precise adjectives and adverbs as well as appositives and degrees of comparison to bring your sentences to life. Be sure to place your modifiers as close as possible to the word or words they modify. (20 points)

EXAMPLE
The mouse ran under the bush. *(Hearing the swooping owl overhead, the diminutive brown mouse scurried in terror under the evergreen shrub.)*

1. The woman bought the coat.
2. Phil and Shawn painted the fence.
3. Brooke jumps.
4. Joel's son plays soccer.
5. The bush needs trimming.
6. A cat sleeps on the floor.
7. Andrew climbed the tree.
8. Kristen opened the door.
9. The cake was good.
10. Snow gathered.

EXERCISE 8

Using Appositives

Combine each pair of sentences below so that one of the two is used as an appositive. In combining the sentences, you may change the wording slightly. (10 points)

EXAMPLE

John Adams won a Pulitzer Prize. It is a biography of our nation's second president. (John Adams, *a biography of our nation's second president, won a Pulitzer Prize.)*

1. Independent films often feature well-known actors. They are a separate genre of moviemaking.
2. Clint Eastwood won a best director Oscar for a film released in 1992. It was called *Unforgiven*.
3. *Frasier* won the Emmy Award for best comedy five years in a row in the 1990s. The show is based on a character originally featured on *Cheers*.
4. One of the most popular comedies in television history is *Friends*. It depicts the lives of six young adults living in Manhattan.
5. We watched the movie to learn more about the Holocaust. The movie was *Schindler's List*.

7. Andrew, a longtime city firefighter, climbed the towering maple tree to rescue the frightened kitten.
8. A first-year graduate student in psychology, Kristen quietly opened the door to the lecture hall where the professor had already begun speaking.
9. The fresh-baked chocolate birthday cake was moist and delicious.
10. A mountain of snow, an impenetrable barrier, had gathered all around the log cabin.

EXERCISE 8

Responses will vary.

Sample responses:

1. Independent films, a separate genre of moviemaking, often feature well-known actors.
2. Clint Eastwood won a best director Oscar for *Unforgiven,* a film released in 1992.
3. *Frasier,* a show based on a character originally featured on *Cheers*, won the Emmy Award for best comedy five years in a row in the 1990s.

6. The Holocaust is also the setting for the film *Life Is Beautiful*. The Holocaust is one of the worst tragedies in human history.
7. Jonathon Nash is the subject of Sylvia Nasar's book *A Beautiful Mind*. He is a mathematician.
8. According to the American Film Institute, Humphrey Bogart and Katherine Hepburn are the top movie legends. Bogart and Hepburn starred in *The African Queen*.
9. *Patton* won the Oscar for best picture in 1970. It depicts the World War II career of a famous American general.
10. The Tony is named after Antoinette Perry. It is awarded for distinguished achievements in Broadway theater.

4. One of the most popular comedies in television history is *Friends*, a show depicting the lives of six young adults living in Manhattan.
5. We watched the movie *Schindler's List* to learn more about the Holocaust.
6. The Holocaust, one of the worst tragedies in human history, is also the setting for the film *Life Is Beautiful*.
7. Jonathon Nash, a mathematician, is the subject of Sylvia Nasar's book *A Beautiful Mind*.
8. According to the American Film Institute, Humphrey Bogart and Katherine Hepburn, stars in *The African Queen*, are the top movie legends.
9. *Patton*, a movie depicting the World War II career of a famous American general, won the Oscar for best picture in 1970.
10. The Tony, an award for distinguished achievements in Broadway theater, is named after Antoinette Perry.

UNIT *10* LINKERS AND JOINERS
Prepositions and Conjunctions

UNIT OVERVIEW

LINKERS AND JOINERS: PREPOSITIONS AND CONJUNCTIONS

PREPOSITIONS AND CONJUNCTIONS

Prepositions and conjunctions are the linkers of the English language. They are used to join words and phrases to the rest of a sentence. They also show the relationships between ideas. Prepositions and conjunctions help writers vary their sentences by connecting sentence parts in different ways.

A **preposition** is used to show how its object, a noun or a pronoun, is related to other words in the sentence. Some commonly used prepositions include *above*, *after*, *against*, *among*, *around*, *at*, *behind*, *beneath*, *beside*, *between*, *down*, *for*, *from*, *in*, *on*, *off*, *toward*, *through*, *to*, *until*, *upon*, and *with*.

EXAMPLES

Leif jumped **off** the cliff top and **into** the deep waters **of** the quarry.

I reached **for** the remote control **between** the sofa cushions.

A **conjunction** is a word used to link related words, groups of words, or sentences. Like a preposition, a conjunction shows the relationship between the words it links. Some of the most commonly used conjunctions are *and*, *but*, *for*, *nor*, *or*, *yet*, *so*, *if*, *after*, *because*, *before*, *although*, *unless*, *while*, and *when*. Some conjunctions are used in pairs, such as *both/and*, *neither/nor*, and *not only/but also*.

EXAMPLES

Lavender **and** jasmine are my two favorite scents.

When the Nazis occupied France, some brave Parisians joined the Resistance.

Not only did Jill recover from her disappointment, **but** she **also** went on to achieve great success.

Certain words can function as either conjunctions or prepositions. There are two important differences between a word used as a preposition and one used as a conjunction.

1. A preposition is always followed by an *object*, but a conjunction is not.

EXAMPLES

preposition We waited **for** the bus **for** thirty-five minutes! (The nouns *bus* and *minutes* are both objects of the preposition *for.*)

conjunction The buses are often late, **for** the bus company is in total disarray. (*For* is not followed by an object. It links two groups of words, each of which can stand as a sentence.)

2. A preposition links its object and modifiers of that object to some other word in the sentence. A conjunction connects words or groups of words.

EXAMPLES

preposition **Before** a trip, Dad compulsively readies the house for all sorts of disasters.

conjunction **Before we leave on a vacation**, Dad mows the lawn, trims the hedges, prunes the fruit trees, cleans the gutters, and double-checks the alarm system.

USAGE tip

Certain words can function as prepositions or as adverbs.

He climbed **up**. (adverb)

He climbed **up** the hill. (preposition)

Try It Yourself

EXERCISE 1

Identifying Prepositions and Conjunctions in Literature

Identify the underlined words in the literature passage as prepositions or conjunctions.

Because I could not stop for Death—
He kindly stopped for me—
The Carriage held but just Ourselves—
And Immortality.

CONTINUED

EXERCISE 1

1. *Because*—conjunction
2. *for*—preposition
3. *for*—preposition
4. *And*—conjunction
5. *And*—conjunction
6. *and*—conjunction
7. *For*—preposition
8. *where*—conjunction
9. *At*—preposition
10. *in*—preposition

Literature MODEL

11. *of*—preposition
12. *Or*—conjunction
13. *and*—conjunction
14. *For*—preposition

We slowly drove—He knew no haste
And I had put away
My labor and my leisure too,
For His Civility—

We passed the School, where Children strove
At recess—in the Ring—
We passed the Fields of Gazing Grain—
We passed the Setting Sun—

Or rather—He passed Us—
The Dews drew quivering and Chill—
For only Gossamer, my Gown—
My Tippet—only Tulle—

from "Because I could not stop for Death—"
Emily Dickinson

EXERCISE 2
Responses will vary. Students should write sentences that indicate their understanding of the use of prepositions and conjunctions.

LANGUAGELINK
Print exercise worksheets or have students complete exercises online with the LanguageLINK CD.

EXERCISE 2

Using Prepositions and Conjunctions

Write a sentence for each preposition or conjunction below.

1. and (conjunction)
2. over (preposition)
3. beside (preposition)
4. while (conjunction)
5. neither/nor (conjunction)
6. for (preposition)
7. for (conjunction)
8. among (preposition)
9. on account of (preposition)
10. in order that (conjunction)

PREPOSITIONS

A **preposition** shows the relationship that exists between its object, the noun or pronoun that follows it, and some other word or group of words in a sentence. Notice in the following sentences the number of different relationships shown between the verb *spoke* and the noun *delegates.*

EXAMPLES
The ambassador spoke **to** the delegates.
The ambassador spoke **with** the delegates.
The ambassador spoke **before** the delegates.
The ambassador spoke **for** the delegates.
The ambassador spoke **about** the delegates.

The noun or pronoun that follows the preposition is called the **object of the preposition**. Together, the preposition, the object of the preposition, and the modifiers of that object form a **prepositional phrase**. In the following sentence, *with a Halloween mask*, *of cash*, and *from the bank teller* are all prepositional phrases.

The thief **with** a Halloween mask grabbed the sack of cash **from** the bank teller.

To test a word to see if it is a preposition, ask questions like "with what?," "of what?," or "from whom?" The answers are "Halloween mask," "cash," and "bank teller." All three are objects of the preposition. Therefore, there are three prepositional phrases in the sentence.

These are the most commonly used prepositions. Remember, though, that any word on this list may not always be used as a preposition. If it is a preposition, it will always have an object.

USAGE tip

In some sentences, particularly those that ask a question, the preposition follows the object: *Whom did you debate against? Whom* is the object, and *against* is the preposition. Think: *Against whom did you debate?*

Prepositions			
aboard	behind	during	since
about	below	except	through
above	beside	for	throughout
across	besides	from	to
after	between	in	under
against	beyond	into	underneath
along	but (meaning "except")	like	until
amid	by	of	up
among	concerning	off	upon
around	down	on	with
at		over	within
before		past	without

A **compound preposition** contains more than one word. It functions in a sentence the same way that a single-word preposition functions. This allows writers to express relationships such as *in front of*, *on account of*, *along with*, *except for*, *on top of*, and *next to*. Some commonly used compound prepositions include *aside from*, *because of*, *in addition to*, *in place of*, *instead of*, *in spite of*, *according to*, *out of*, *as of*, and *in back of*.

EXAMPLES

Except for the cilantro, all of the ingredients are available at the produce market.

I may have to use another herb **instead of** cilantro.

Try It Yourself

EXERCISE 3

Identifying Prepositional Phrases in Literature

Identify the sixteen prepositional phrases in the literature passage below.

EXERCISE 3

The mass of men lead lives of quiet desperation. What is called resignation is confirmed desperation. From the desperate city you go into the desperate country, and have to console yourself with the bravery of minks and muskrats. A stereotyped but unconscious despair is concealed even under what are called the games and amusements of mankind. There is no play in them, for this comes after work. But it is a characteristic of wisdom not to do desperate things. When we consider what, to use the words of the catechism, is the chief end of man, and what are the true necessaries and means of life, it appears as if men had deliberately chosen the common mode of living because they preferred it to any other. Yet they honestly think there is no choice.

MODEL

The mass of men lead lives of quiet desperation. What is called resignation is confirmed desperation. From the desperate city you go into the desperate country, and have to console yourself with the bravery of minks and muskrats. A stereotyped but unconscious despair is concealed even under what are called the games and amusements of mankind. There is no play in them, for this comes after work. But it is a characteristic of wisdom not to do desperate things. When we consider what, to use the words of the catechism, is the chief end of man, and what are the true necessaries and means of life, it appears as if men had deliberately chosen the common mode of living because they preferred it to any other. Yet they honestly think there is no choice.

from *Walden*
Henry David Thoreau

EXERCISE 4

Understanding Prepositional Phrases

Rewrite each of the following sentences, supplying a preposition or a compound preposition and an object of the preposition in each blank. Some objects of the preposition may be more than one word. Some sentences may make the most sense with a compound preposition.

1. Reporters heard ___ when they arrived ___.
2. The problem ___ was lengthily analyzed ___.
3. All ___, excited bystanders have gathered ___.
4. The doctor advised Leslie to go ___ if the pain increased ___.
5. The hikers set out ___ and hoped to reach the campground ___.
6. After the energetic puppy squeezed ___ , it scampered ___.
7. The vase ___ was purchased ___.
8. Unfortunately, Uncle Jack fell asleep and snored ___.
9. A few headlights could be spotted ___ that had hung ___ all day.
10. ___ lie artifacts from the previous inhabitants ___.

EXERCISE 4

Responses will vary. Sample responses:

1. Reporters heard about the coup when they arrived in the capital.
2. The problem with the space mission was lengthily analyzed at command headquarters.
3. All along the parade route, excited bystanders have gathered with their cameras.
4. The doctor advised Leslie to go to the emergency room if the pain increased in her ear.
5. The hikers set out from Stockbridge and hoped to reach the campground by dusk.
6. After the energetic puppy squeezed out of its pen, it scampered across the street.
7. The vase behind the dishes was purchased at an estate sale.
8. Unfortunately, Uncle Jack fell asleep and snored during the concert.
9. A few headlights could be spotted through the fog that had hung over the city all day.
10. Underneath the streets lie artifacts from the previous inhabitants of the city.

EXERCISE 5

Using Prepositional Phrases in Your Writing

Assume that you are on a high school debate team and must take a stand on whether having an after-school job during high school is beneficial or whether it gets in the way of focusing on studies. Write a short position statement for or against after-school jobs. If possible, back up your argument with concrete examples from your own or friends' and siblings' experiences. In writing your position, use at least seven prepositional phrases, including at least one compound preposition.

EXERCISE 5
Responses will vary. Students should provide an argument that contains at least seven prepositional phrases, including at least one compound preposition.

COORDINATING CONJUNCTIONS

A **coordinating conjunction** is a word used to join words or groups of words of equal importance in a sentence. The most common coordinating conjunctions are *and*, *or*, *nor*, *for*, *but*, *yet*, and *so*.

Coordinating conjunctions can connect nouns, verbs, adjectives, adverbs, phrases, clauses, and sentences. Each coordinating conjunction shows a different relationship between the words that it connects.

When a coordinating conjunction joins two or more complete thoughts that could be independent sentences, then a **compound sentence** is formed. A comma is placed before the coordinating conjunction that joins the two complete thoughts.

USAGE tip

Note that a comma always comes before a coordinating conjunction that separates two complete sentences.

EXAMPLES

This movie was enjoyable **but** easily forgettable. (*But* shows the contrast between *enjoyable* and *forgettable*. The coordinating conjunction joins two adjectives.)

Will the prescription arrive by U.S. mail **or** a delivery service? (*Or* shows choice. The coordinating conjunction joins two objects of a preposition.)

You didn't respond to the invitation, **so** I assumed you weren't attending. (*So* is a coordinating conjunction that joins two complete sentences.)

By using coordinating conjunctions to connect words and groups of words, you can express the clear relationships between ideas without needless repetition. The following three sentences can be rewritten as one by using a coordinating conjunction between the verbs.

EXAMPLES

Callista focused on the bull's-eye. She pulled back the string of the bow. She let the arrow fly.

Callista focused on the bull's-eye, pulled back the string of the bow, **and** let the arrow fly.

Try It Yourself

EXERCISE 6

Identifying Coordinating Conjunctions in Literature

Identify the thirteen coordinating conjunctions in the literature passage below.

> A single knoll rises out of the plain in Oklahoma, north and west of the Wichita Range. For my people, the Kiowas, it is an old landmark, and they gave it the name Rainy Mountain. The hardest weather in the world is there. Winter brings blizzards, hot tornadic winds arise in the spring, and in summer the prairie is an anvil's edge. The grass turns brittle and brown, and it cracks beneath your feet. There are green belts along the rivers and creeks, linear groves of hickory and pecan, willow and witch hazel. At a distance in July or August the steaming foliage seems almost to writhe in fire. Great green and yellow grasshoppers are everywhere in the tall grass, popping up like corn to sting the flesh, and tortoises crawl about on the red earth, going nowhere in the plenty of time. Loneliness is an aspect of the land. All things in the plain are isolate; there is no confusion of objects in the eye, but *one* hill or *one* tree or *one* man.

from "The Way to Rainy Mountain"
N. Scott Momaday

EXERCISE 6

A single knoll rises out of the plain in Oklahoma, north and west of the Wichita Range. For my people, the Kiowas, it is an old landmark, and they gave it the name Rainy Mountain. The hardest weather in the world is there. Winter brings blizzards, hot tornadic winds arise in the spring, and in summer the prairie is an anvil's edge. The grass turns brittle and brown, and it cracks beneath your feet. There are green belts along the rivers and creeks, linear groves of hickory and pecan, willow and

Literature MODEL

witch hazel. At a distance in July or August the steaming foliage seems almost to writhe in fire. Great green and yellow grasshoppers are everywhere in the tall grass, popping up like corn to sting the flesh, and tortoises crawl about on the red earth, going nowhere in the plenty of time. Loneliness is an aspect of the land. All things in the plain are isolate; there is no confusion of objects in the eye, but *one* hill or *one* tree or *one* man.

EXERCISE 7
Responses will vary. Sample responses:

1. In the land near Rainy Mountain, the weather is bitterly cold or blisteringly hot.
2. The Kiowa Five showed their art in leading museums and universities of the United States.
3. The ancestors of today's Native Americans probably came here from Asia about 30,000 years ago, for that is when the Bering Strait was frozen.
4. The Kiowa needed a buffalo for their ceremony, but all the buffalo were gone.
5. The hunter searched for a track or other sign to show that an animal had passed by recently.
6. The Plains were utterly silent; the grasshoppers weren't sounding off, nor were the birds singing.

EXERCISE 7
Understanding Coordinating Conjunctions

Write the coordinating conjunction that best fits the blank in each item below by linking the words, phrases, or sentences.

1. In the land near Rainy Mountain, the weather is bitterly cold ____ blisteringly hot.
2. The Kiowa Five showed their art in leading museums ___ universities of the United States.
3. The ancestors of today's Native Americans probably came here from Asia about 30,000 years ago, ___ that is when the Bering Strait was frozen.
4. The Kiowa needed a buffalo for their ceremony, ___ all the buffalo were gone.
5. The hunter searched for a track __ other sign to show that an animal had passed by recently.
6. The Plains were utterly silent; the grasshoppers weren't sounding off, ___ were the birds singing.
7. We want to see the original homeland of the Kiowa, __ we are traveling to western Montana.
8. The old grandmother had lost her home and her traditions, ___ she bore the world no bitterness.
9. The old cabin was small, bare, ___ weather-beaten.
10. If your grandmother was a Native American from this part of Oklahoma, she was a Kiowa ___a Comanche.

7. We want to see the original homeland of the Kiowa, so we are traveling to western Montana.
8. The old grandmother had lost her home and her traditions, yet she bore the world no bitterness.

EXERCISE 8
Using Coordinating Conjunctions in Your Writing

Assume that your school counselor asks you what career you want to pursue after finishing your education. Think of two very different careers you are interested in pursuing. Write a paragraph describing each of these two paths and how they might result in entirely different lifestyles. Use as many coordinating conjunctions in your paragraph as you can. Check to be sure that you use a comma between any two complete sentences joined by a coordinating conjunction.

CORRELATIVE CONJUNCTIONS

Correlative conjunctions are words used in pairs to join parts of a sentence. The most common correlative conjunctions include *both/and*, *either/or*, *neither/nor*, and *not only/but also.*

EXAMPLES

Both the sari **and** the Western dress look flattering on Umaya.

Neither Mara **nor** Lauren can stand that shade of pink.

You can wear **either** a denim jacket **or** a sweatshirt to keep warm.

The salesperson tried to sell me **not only** a pair of shoes that didn't fit **but also** a jacket that had a small rip in the shoulder seam!

Because correlative conjunctions emphasize the equal relationship between ideas, it is important that all the sentence elements are parallel. The order of the elements after the second connector should match the elements after the first connector.

EXAMPLES

not parallel	Trevor both composes music and has written lyrics for the band.
parallel	Trevor both composes music and writes lyrics for the band.

Try It Yourself

EXERCISE 9

Identifying Correlative Conjunctions

Write the correlative conjunctions you find in the following sentences.

1. Running a small inn or bed and breakfast is both great fun and sheer drudgery.
2. Either the innkeeper or a reliable employee must always be on hand to take reservations.

9. The old cabin was small, bare, and weather-beaten.
10. If your grandmother was a Native American from this part of Oklahoma, she was a Kiowa or a Comanche.

EXERCISE 8

Responses will vary. Students should describe two specific careers and explore their ramifications. They should combine words, phrases, and complete sentences using coordinating conjunctions.

EXERCISE 9

1. Running a small inn or bed and breakfast is both great fun and sheer drudgery.
2. Either the innkeeper or a reliable employee must always be on hand to take reservations.

3. Neither fatigue nor a sullen mood can excuse a less than welcoming attitude.
4. Guests can be not only demanding but also occasionally dishonest.
5. Both published travel guides and websites list inns throughout the country.
6. Staying in a bed and breakfast instead of a big hotel not only can result in a more interesting experience but also can save the customer money.
7. Neither this inn nor the one down the road provides an outlet for plugging in your laptop.
8. Every morning, delectable scones were baked by either the owner or her daughter.
9. A good innkeeper not only loves talking to guests but also enjoys listening to them.
10. The route to the inn is neither direct nor scenic.

EXERCISE 10

Understanding Correlative Conjunctions

Combine each pair of sentences below with the correlative conjunction indicated in parentheses.

1. The roadside stand sells fresh produce. The roadside stand sells inexpensive cut flowers. (both/and)
2. Cork is used to make stoppers for bottles. Cork is used to make durable and affordable flooring. (not only, but also)
3. We will eat jambalaya in the little restaurant on the bayou. We will come home and cook some red beans and rice. (either/or)
4. Daniel doesn't put his dirty clothes in the hamper. Daniel doesn't put his clean clothes in the dresser. (neither/nor)
5. Soybeans are a good source of protein. Eggs are a good source of protein. (both/and)
6. Regular exercise improves physical health. Regular exercise promotes good mental health. (not only/ but also)
7. Singers need to breathe deeply. Runners need to breathe deeply. (both/and)

3. Neither fatigue nor a sullen mood can excuse a less than welcoming attitude.
4. Guests can be not only demanding but also occasionally dishonest.
5. Both published travel guides and websites list inns throughout the country.
6. Staying in a bed and breakfast instead of a big hotel not only can result in a more interesting experience but also can save the customer money.
7. Neither this inn nor the one down the road provides an outlet for plugging in your laptop.
8. Every morning, delectable scones were baked by either the owner or her daughter.
9. A good innkeeper not only loves talking to guests but also enjoys listening to them.
10. The route to the inn is neither direct nor scenic.

EXERCISE 10

Responses will vary. Sample responses:

1. The roadside stand sells both fresh produce and inexpensive cut flowers.
2. Cork is used not only to make stoppers for bottles but also to make durable and affordable flooring.
3. We will either eat jambalaya in the little restaurant on the bayou or we will come home and cook some red beans and rice.

8. Nate's mother doesn't have much patience with foolish questions. Nate's father doesn't have much patience with foolish questions. (neither/nor)
9. Lucia can juggle five balls at a time. Lucia can walk on stilts. (not only/but also)
10. You can use cornstarch to thicken the fruit mixture. You can use flour to thicken the fruit mixture. (either/or)

EXERCISE 11

Using Correlative Conjunctions in Your Writing

Write instructions to a classmate for a task that you know very well. It could be anything from how to put a resistant two-year-old to bed to how to program a computer. Think of something that has a number of steps, and for which there are some alternatives involved. Explain the steps and skills involved in performing this task, and use correlative conjunction pairs to link your thoughts. During revising, check your sentences for parallelism, making sure that the order of the elements that follows the second part of the conjunction pair is the same as the order of elements that follows the first part of the conjunction pair.

SUBORDINATING CONJUNCTIONS

Subordinating conjunctions introduce subordinate clauses (also known as dependent clauses)—clauses that cannot stand alone. Subordinating conjunctions like those in the following table are used to introduce subordinate clauses. These conjunctions connect the clauses to independent clauses, which can stand alone as complete sentences.

In the example sentence, the subordinating conjunction *after* introduces the subordinate clause *it has been used for approximately 760 hours. After* connects the subordinate clause to the independent clause, *An ordinary incandescent light bulb burns out.* The subordinating clause adds important information about how long an incandescent light bulb usually lasts.

4. Daniel neither puts his dirty clothes in the hamper nor puts his clean clothes in the dresser.
5. Both soybeans and eggs are good sources of protein.
6. Regular exercise improves not only

physical health but also mental health.
7. Both singers and runners need to breathe deeply.
8. Neither Nate's mother nor Nate's father has much patience with foolish questions.
9. Lucia not only can juggle five balls at a time but also can walk on stilts.
10. You can use either cornstarch or flour to thicken the fruit mixture.

EXERCISE 11

Responses will vary. Students should model their sentences after those in Exercise 9, using a variety of correlative conjunction pairs. Check their sentence structure for parallelism.

EXAMPLE

An ordinary incandescent light bulb burns out **after** it has been used for approximately 760 hours.

Subordinating conjunctions usually express relationships like these:

time	after, as, as long as, as soon as, before, since, until, when, whenever, while
place	where, wherever
manner	as, as if, as though
cause	because, as, since
condition	although, as long as, even if, even though, if, provided that, though, unless, while, wherever
comparison	as, than
purpose	in order that, so that, that

USAGE tip

Keep in mind that many of the words in this list can be used as other parts of speech. For example, *after, as, before, since,* and *until* can also be used as prepositions.

EXAMPLES

Because compact fluorescent bulbs last up to thirteen times longer, you should buy them instead of incandescent bulbs. (*Because* introduces the subordinating clause and expresses cause.)

We will continue to waste natural resources as well as money **as long as we use inefficient light bulbs.** (*As long as* introduces the subordinating clause and expresses a relationship of condition.)

USAGE tip

A subordinate clause may precede, interrupt, or follow an independent clause. Notice how the wording may change, however, so that all ideas are correctly modified:

Even though the rim is slightly chipped, that Cantonese export plate is still quite valuable.

That Cantonese export plate is still quite valuable *even though the rim is slightly chipped.*

That Chinese export plate, *even though it has a slightly chipped rim,* is still quite valuable.

Try It Yourself

EXERCISE 12

Identifying Subordinating Conjunctions in Literature

Identify the subordinating conjunctions in the following literature passage. Then identify both the subordinating clause and the independent clause in each of the sentences that contains one or more subordinating conjunctions.

At the Fair she was glad to be seen in his company as he was well dressed and a stranger. She knew that the fact of his presence would create an impression. During the day she was happy, but when night came on she began to grow restless. She wanted to drive the instructor away, to get out of his presence. While they sat together in the grandstand and while the eyes of former schoolmates were upon them, she paid so much attention to her escort that he grew interested. "A scholar needs money. I should marry a woman with money," he mused.

Helen White was thinking of George Willard even as he wandered gloomily through the crowds thinking of her. She remembered the summer evening when they had walked together and wanted to walk with him again.

from "Sophistication"
Sherwood Anderson

Literature MODEL

EXERCISE 12

1. *as* = subordinating conjunction; *At the Fair she was glad to be seen in his company* = independent clause; *as he was well dressed and a stranger* = subordinating clause
2. *that* = subordinating conjunction; *She knew* = independent clause; *that the fact of his presence would create an impression* = subordinating clause
3. *when* = subordinating conjunction; *During the day she was happy* = independent clause; *when night came on* = subordinating clause; *she began to grow restless* = independent clause
4. *While, while, that* = subordinating conjunctions; *While they sat together in the grandstand* = subordinating clause; *while the eyes of former schoolmates were upon them* = subordinating clause; *she paid so much attention to her escort* = independent clause; *that he grew interested* = subordinating clause
5. *even as* = subordinating conjunction; *Helen White was thinking of George Willard* = independent clause; *even as he wandered gloomily through the crowds thinking of her* = subordinating clause
6. *when* = subordinating clause; *She remembered the summer evening* = independent clause; *when they had walked together* = subordinating conjunction

EXERCISE 13

Responses will vary. The correctness of students' responses should be based on use and placement of the subordinating conjunction.

EXERCISE 13

Understanding Subordinating Conjunctions

Combine each pair of sentences below with the subordinating conjunction indicated in parentheses. You may need to reword the sentences slightly so that they make sense when combined. Try to express main ideas in independent clauses and less important ideas in subordinate clauses.

1. Before the hurricane, Mitchell put tape over the windows. The glass would not shatter all over the floor. (so that)
2. Lisa is apprehensive about the carpenter bees. These particular bees do not sting. (even though)
3. We will book the flights online. We know the date of the wedding. (as soon as)
4. Quay has to practice walking on spike heels. She is going to model dresses in her aunt's runway show. (since)
5. Traveling with Steve is enjoyable. You don't mind stopping every two hours for provisions. (provided that)
6. Gisele will study math with a tutor. Gisele will be on tour with the circus. (while)

7. Jake insisted on treating everyone to a lobster dinner. Jake is supposed to be saving money for college. (even though)
8. Alabama is known as the "Yellowhammer State." Its state bird is the yellowhammer. (since)
9. Adolescent girls need to eat sufficient calcium. Calcium builds strong bones and can help prevent osteoporosis later in life. (because)
10. Life in Japan changed dramatically after 1853. Japan opened its doors to Western visitors. (when)

EXERCISE 14

Using Subordinating Conjunctions

Write a sentence for each subordinating conjunction listed below. Use the kind of conjunction in parentheses as a guide for the relationship between the independent and subordinating clauses. Experiment with different placements of the subordinating clauses. You may need to reword the sentences slightly so that they make sense with each placement of the subordinate clause.

1. as long as (time)
2. wherever (place)
3. as though (comparison)
4. since (cause)
5. provided that (condition)
6. while (time)
7. where (place)
8. as if (manner)
9. as (cause)
10. even if (condition)

1. Before the hurricane, Mitchell put tape over the windows so that the glass would not shatter all over the floor.
2. Lisa is apprehensive about the carpenter bees even though these particular bees do not sting.
3. We will book the flights online as soon as we know the date of the wedding.
4. Quay has to practice walking on spike heels since she is going to model dresses in her aunt's runway show.
5. Traveling with Steve is enjoyable provided that you don't mind stopping every two hours for provisions.
6. Gisele will study math with a tutor while she will be on tour with the circus.
7. Jake insisted on treating everyone to a lobster dinner even though he is supposed to be saving money for college.
8. Alabama is known as the "Yellowhammer State" since its state bird is the yellowhammer.
9. It is important for adolescent girls to eat sufficient calcium because calcium builds strong bones and can help prevent osteoporosis later in life.
10. Life in Japan changed dramatically after 1853 when Japan opened its doors to Western visitors.

EXERCISE 14
Responses will vary. Students should vary the placement of the subordinating conjunction.

UNIT 10 REVIEW

TEST YOUR KNOWLEDGE

EXERCISE 1
Identifying Prepositions
Identify the prepositions and their objects in each of the following sentences. (10 points)

EXAMPLE
The dying woman lies in her bed, motionless. The children stand around her, their shoulders drooping with sadness, their eyes full of unshed tears. The clock on the wall has stopped ticking, but the silence is interrupted by rain dripping onto the tin roof. *(in/bed, around/her, with/sadness, of/tears, on/wall, by/rain, onto/roof)*

She is looking at the window, at Cash stooping steadily at the board in the failing light, laboring on toward darkness and into it as though the stroking of the saw illumined its own motion, board and saw engendered.

"You, Cash," she shouts, her voice harsh, strong, and unimpaired. "You, Cash!"

He looks up at the gaunt face framed by the window in the twilight. It is a composite picture of all time since he was a child. He drops the saw and lifts the board for her to see, watching the window in which the face has not moved. He drags a second plank into position and slants the two of them into their final juxtaposition, gesturing toward the ones yet on the ground, shaping with his empty hand in pantomime the finished box.

from *As I Lay Dying*
William Faulkner

EXERCISE 1
at/window, at/Cash, at/board, in/light; toward/darkness; into/it; of/saw; at/face; by/window; in/twilight; of/time; for/her; into/position; of/them; into/juxtaposition; toward/ones; on/ground; with/hand; in/pantomime

Literature MODEL

EXERCISE 2

1. *Since*, subordinating; *or*, coordinating; *and*, coordinating
2. *even though*, subordinating; *or*, coordinating
3. *both/and*, correlative
4. *although*, subordinating; *and*, coordinating
5. *and*, coordinating
6. *as if*, subordinating; *and*, coordinating; *and*, coordinating
7. *neither/nor*, correlative; *and*, coordinating
8. *but*, coordinating; *and*, coordinating
9. *not only/but also*, correlative
10. *because*, subordinating

EXERCISE 2
Identifying Conjunctions

Identify the conjunctions in the following sentences and then label them as *coordinating*, *correlative*, or *subordinating*. (10 points)

EXAMPLE
As you gently release the clutch with your left foot, press on the accelerator with your right foot and move forward with caution. (*as*, subordinating; *and*, coordinating)

1. Since the days of ancient Egypt, flags have been used to show loyalty to a king or a country and to send messages from far away.
2. Even though most contemporary flags are rectangular or square, flags of the past had a wide variety of shapes.
3. Both the vexillum, a squarish flag with a deeply scalloped bottom edge, and the gonfannon, a rectangle with notches along one side, were flown in the past.
4. Although modern technology can print designs easily and cheaply on fabric, people long ago had to embroider their flag designs, stitch by careful stitch.
5. Australia held a competition to design a new flag in 1900, and over 30,000 designs were submitted.
6. As if they had communicated by magic, five separate individuals submitted the identical design, and it was the winner.
7. Neither the red and orange flag of Spain nor the black, red, and yellow flag of Belgium is particularly attractive, in my opinion.
8. Before the French Revolution of 1789, the French flag was plain white, but the revolutionaries adopted a blue, white, and red banner.
9. There is a single star in the center of not only Somalia's flag but also Senegal's.
10. New Zealand's national flag contains the British Union Jack design because New Zealand was part of the British Empire.

EXERCISE 3

Identifying Prepositions and Conjunctions

Identify the underlined word in each of the following sentences as either a preposition or a conjunction. (10 points)

EXAMPLE

Why is there a stack of soccer and lacrosse equipment in the living room? (preposition)

1. Juliette kept having to blow her nose during the assembly.
2. The man secretly went to prison instead of his twin brother.
3. I'm planning to sleep late tomorrow, for the weather forecaster predicts a massive ice storm.
4. Aside from precalculus, Jaime feels confident about all of his subjects for this semester.
5. Mom thought she had taken care of the pantry moth infestation, but yesterday a moth fluttered out as soon as she opened the door.
6. No one may leave the banquet hall until the governor has finished his speech.
7. Firefighters cleared equipment from the stairwell so that people from the upper floors could be evacuated.
8. The person sitting behind me on the metro was wearing way too much aftershave.
9. The horses had not been groomed, nor had they been properly fed that day.
10. Nomadic people travel wherever they must to follow the food supply.

EXERCISE 4

Understanding Prepositions

Combine each group of sentences below into one sentence that includes one or two prepositional phrases. You may have to add, delete, or rearrange words. Some items have more than one possible answer. (10 points)

EXERCISE 3

1. preposition
2. compound preposition
3. coordinating conjunction
4. compound preposition
5. coordinating conjunction; subordinating conjunction
6. subordinating conjunction
7. subordinating conjunction
8. preposition
9. coordinating conjunction
10. subordinating conjunction

EXERCISE 4

Responses will vary.

Sample responses:

1. Bats make sounds in a range inaudible to the human ear.
2. Throughout the filming of the video, the singer was actually mute with laryngitis!
3. Some practical joker had planted plastic roses among the daffodils in the lawn.
4. Apparently an anonymous benefactor is sending the students to the Smithsonian Institution at spring break.

5. Some beautiful old yachts were sailing toward the harbor at dusk.
6. Roger knocked his croquet ball through the two final wickets and against the post for victory.
7. Many Greek works of art were rediscovered during the Renaissance.
8. Most experts except the state archaeologist believe these ruins were made by Paleolithic Indians.
9. Aunt Lucy borrowed the recorded version of *In the Frame* by Dick Francis.
10. Dad drove past the exit for downtown and into the industrial wasteland outside the city.

EXAMPLE

The decorator transformed the basement. The decorator transformed it with a mural. The mural showed a tropical beach scene. *(The decorator transformed the basement with a mural of a tropical beach scene.)*

1. Bats make sounds. These sounds are inaudible to the human ear. The sounds are in an inaudible range.
2. The video was filmed. Throughout the singer was mute. The muteness was from laryngitis.
3. Some joker had planted plastic roses. They were on the lawn. They were among the daffodils.
4. The students are being sent to the Smithsonian Institution. They are going during spring break. Apparently an anonymous benefactor is sending them.
5. Some beautiful old yachts were sailing. It was dusk. They were heading in the direction of the harbor.
6. Roger had victory. He knocked his croquet ball through the two final wickets. The ball was knocked into the post.
7. Many Greek works of art were rediscovered. This happened during the Renaissance.
8. Most experts believe these ruins were made by Paleolithic Indians. The state archaeologist does not believe this.
9. Aunt Lucy borrowed *In the Frame*. *In the Frame* is by Dick Francis. She borrowed the recorded version.
10. Dad drove. He drove past the exit for downtown. He drove into the industrial wasteland. It was outside the city.

EXERCISE 5

Responses may vary slightly. Sample responses:

1. Christopher Columbus intended to travel to Asia, but instead he traveled to the West Indies.
2. Thousands of Arawaks died, since they had no resistance to the diseases brought by Spanish explorers.

EXERCISE 5

Understanding Coordinating and Correlative Conjunctions

Combine each group of sentences below into one sentence that includes at least one coordinating or correlative conjunction. You may have to add, delete, or rearrange words. Some items have more than one possible answer. (20 points)

EXAMPLE

Before the arrival of Europeans, the Arawak Indians lived in the Caribbean islands. So did the Carib Indians. (*Before the arrival of Europeans, the Arawak and Carib Indians lived in the Caribbean islands.*)

1. Christopher Columbus intended to travel to Asia. He traveled to the West Indies.
2. Thousands of Arawaks died. They had no resistance to the diseases brought by Spanish explorers.
3. French sailors raided the Spanish Empire in the West Indies. Dutch sailors raided the Spanish Empire in the West Indies. English sailors raided the Spanish Empire in the West Indies.
4. Africans were transported to the Caribbean islands. They were forced to work as slaves.
5. The slave trade was outlawed in the British colonies in 1807. Slaves were still being sold in the British West Indies in 1829.
6. Some ex-slaves became traders. Some became crafts-people. Some became farmers.
7. Tourism is a major part of the West Indian economy. The islands have rich natural and cultural resources.
8. You can visit an island where the primary language is French. You can visit an island where the primary language is English.
9. Marcus Garvey was a famous political figure of the West Indies. Toussaint L'Ouverture was a famous political figure of the West Indies.
10. Tourists can go snorkeling in exquisite, azure waters. Tourists can listen to reggae music played by musicians on the beach.

3. French, Dutch, and English sailors raided the Spanish Empire in the West Indies.
4. Africans were transported to the Caribbean islands and forced to work as slaves.
5. The slave trade was outlawed in the British colonies in 1807, yet slaves were still being sold in the British West Indies in 1829.
6. Some ex-slaves became traders, while others became crafts-people and farmers.
7. Not only is tourism a major part of the West Indian economy, but the islands have rich natural and cultural resources.
8. You can visit an island where the primary language is French or one where the main language is English.
9. Both Marcus Garvey and Toussaint L'Ouverture were famous political figures of the West Indies.
10. Tourists can go snorkeling in exquisite, azure waters and listen to reggae music played by musicians on the beach.

EXERCISE 6
Responses will vary. Students should use an independent clause containing a related idea to complete each subordinate clause. Students should also show their understanding of the different positions available for both subordinate and independent clauses.

EXERCISE 6

Correcting Subordinate Clauses

Each of the subordinate clauses below is a sentence fragment. Even though each group of words has a subject and a verb, it is introduced by a subordinating conjunction; consequently, it must be combined with an independent clause to make sense. Rewrite each of the following clauses by attaching it to a complete sentence that can stand alone. Try to vary the placement of the subordinate clauses. (20 points)

EXAMPLE
Although we've lived in this house for ten years
(Although we've lived in this house for ten years, *we're still known as the new folks in town.*)

1. wherever the current carries it
2. provided that the teacher approves the topic
3. as though he had never been told not to
4. in order that the contents won't break
5. while our neighbors are away
6. after the flood waters recede
7. even though she could afford much
8. unless you can find some in the refrigerator
9. because she's so proud
10. even if I have to walk the entire way

EXERCISE 7
Responses will vary. Students' explanations should be detailed and conversational. Their ideas should flow relatively smoothly with the use of prepositional phrases and different types of conjunctions.

EXERCISE 7

Using Prepositional Phrases and Conjunctions in Your Writing

For a column in your school newspaper, describe one invention you wish had never been created. The object and your reasons for wishing it were nonexistent might be deadly serious (a certain weapon, for example) or more trivial (a certain snack food you just cannot resist). Describe the item to your readers, explain what you think is wrong with it, and tell how the world—or your life—would be better if the invention magically disappeared. Use prepositional phrases and the different kinds of conjunctions to link your ideas and help them flow. (20 points)

UNIT 11 INTERRUPTERS

UNIT OVERVIEW

INTERRUPTERS

INTERRUPTERS

An **interrupter** is a word or phrase that breaks, or interrupts, the flow of thought in a sentence. In your writing, you will sometimes want to use an interrupter to emphasize a point.

An interrupter is usually set off by commas from the rest of the sentence because it is not a basic part of the sentence or essential to its meaning. The commas that set off an interrupter indicate a pause before and after the interruption.

EXAMPLES

The new cost-saving measures, **I assume**, will also limit our travel budget this year.

Moreover, office supplies will now be distributed through a rationing system.

The president, **as you know**, is a stickler for efficiency.

USAGE tip

Sometimes dashes are used to set off interrupters.

McClellan's caution—*a quality that made him popular with his soldiers*—ultimately caused Lincoln to replace him.

Try It Yourself

EXERCISE 1

Identifying Interrupters in Literature

Identify the five interrupters in the passage below.

As he rose to the surface, gasping for breath, he saw that he had been a long time under water; he was perceptibly farther down stream—nearer to safety. The soldiers had almost finished reloading; the metal ramrods flashed all at once in the sunshine as they were drawn from the barrels, turned in the air, and thrust into their sockets. The two sentinels fired again, independently and ineffectually.

The hunted man saw all this over his shoulder; he was now swimming vigorously with the current. His brain was as energetic as his arms and legs; he thought with the rapidity of lightning.

CONTINUED

EXERCISE 1

As he rose to the surface, gasping for breath, he saw that he had been a long time under water; he was perceptibly farther down stream—nearer to safety. The soldiers had almost finished reloading; the metal ramrods flashed all at once in the sunshine as they were drawn from the barrels, turned in the air, and thrust into their sockets. The two sentinels fired again, independently and ineffectually. The hunted man saw all this over his shoulder; he was now swimming vigorously with the current. His brain was as energetic as his arms and legs; he thought with the rapidity of lightning.

"The officer," he reasoned, "will not make that martinet's error a second time. It is as easy to dodge a volley as a single shot. He has probably already given the order to fire at will. God help me, I cannot dodge them all!"

Literature MODEL

"The officer," he reasoned, "will not make that martinet's error a second time. It is as easy to dodge a volley as a single shot. He has probably already given the command to fire at will. God help me, I cannot dodge them all!"

from "An Occurrence at Owl Creek Bridge"
Ambrose Bierce

EXERCISE 2

Understanding Interrupters

Identify the interrupters in the following sentences. Then rewrite each sentence, correctly adding commas or dashes to set off each interrupter from the rest of the sentence.

1. Ambrose Bierce known as "Bitter Bierce" was born in Ohio in 1842.
2. An unhappy childhood contributed unfortunately to his cynicism, bitterness, and pessimism.
3. Bierce as a young man was exposed to the unimaginable brutality of the Civil War.
4. He joined the Union army rising to the rank of lieutenant and distinguished himself at several major battles.
5. His war experiences not surprisingly provided material for some of his best short stories.
6. Bierce later worked in San Francisco as a journalist establishing himself through witty, satirical columns.
7. While in San Francisco he became friends with Samuel Clemens better known as Mark Twain and Bret Harte.
8. Bierce later traveled to Mexico which was torn by civil war at the time and disappeared without a trace.
9. Steve have you read the story "Chickamuga" or *The Devil's Dictionary?*
10. Some of Bierce's stories "An Occurrence at Owl Creek Bridge" for example are influenced by Naturalism.

EXERCISE 2

1. Ambrose Bierce, known as "Bitter Bierce," was born in Ohio in 1842.
2. An unhappy childhood contributed, unfortunately, to his cynicism, bitterness, and pessimism.
3. Bierce, as a young man, was exposed to the unimaginable brutality of the Civil War.
4. He joined the Union army—rising to the rank of lieutenant—and distinguished himself at several major battles.
5. His war experiences, not surprisingly, provided material for some of his best short stories.
6. Bierce later worked in San Francisco as a journalist, establishing himself through witty, satirical columns.
7. While in San Francisco, he became friends with Samuel Clemens—better known as Mark Twain—and Bret Harte.
8. Bierce later traveled to Mexico, which was torn by civil war at the time, and disappeared without a trace.
9. Steve, have you read the story "Chickamuga" or *The Devil's Dictionary?*
10. Some of Bierce's stories, "An Occurrence at Owl Creek Bridge," for example, are influenced by Naturalism.

EXERCISE 3
Responses will vary. Students should correctly use at least five interrupters in their paragraph and set off each interrupter with commas or dashes.

EXERCISE 3

Using Interrupters in Your Writing

Write a narrative paragraph for a peer audience about a strange incident that happened to you or someone you know. Focus on mysterious or unexplained details, and use a suspenseful tone. Use at least five interrupters in your narrative paragraph.

INTERJECTIONS

LANGUAGELINK
Print exercise worksheets or have students complete exercises online with the LanguageLINK CD.

An **interjection** is a part of speech that expresses feeling, such as surprise, joy, relief, urgency, pain, or anger. Common interjections include *ah*, *aha*, *alas*, *bravo*, *dear me*, *goodness*, *great*, *ha*, *help*, *hey*, *hooray*, *hush*, *indeed*, *mercy*, *of course*, *oh*, *oops*, *ouch*, *phooey*, *really*, *say*, *see*, *ugh*, and *whew*.

EXAMPLES
Oh, no, we are not going to make it!
Ha! Your master plan has been foiled.
Argh! My car is wrecked!
Bravo, you did a wonderful job.

Interjections actually indicate different degrees of emotion. They may express intense or sudden emotion, as in *Wow! That was a surprise.* Notice that the strong expression of emotion stands alone in the sentence and is followed by an exclamation mark.

Interjections can also express mild emotion, as in *Well, we didn't have any other choice.* In this sentence, the interjection is part of the sentence and is set off only with a comma. Even when interjections are part of a sentence, they do not relate grammatically to the rest of the sentence.

Try It Yourself

EXERCISE 4

Identifying Interjections in Literature

Identify the interjections in the following sentences from literature passages.

1. Upon my recovery, too, I felt very—oh, inexpressibly sick and weak, as if through long inanition. —from "The Pit and the Pendulum" by Edgar Allan Poe
2. "Heaven forbid, signor!—unless it were fruitful of better pot-herbs than any that grow there now," answered old Lisabetta. —from "Rappaccini's Daughter" by Nathaniel Hawthorne
3. Ah, then, exclaim the aged ladies, you shall be sure to be misunderstood. —from "Self-Reliance" by Ralph Waldo Emerson
4. Well, children, where there is so much racket there must be something out of kilter. —from "Ain't I a Woman?" by Sojourner Truth
5. "Oh, no, they're stuffed and preserved, dozens and dozens of them. . . ." —from "A White Heron" by Sarah Orne Jewett
6. Ah, distinctly I remember it was in the bleak December, / And each separate dying ember wrought its ghost upon the floor. —from "The Raven" by Edgar Allan Poe
7. "What are you doing, Louise? For heaven's sake open the door." —from "The Story of an Hour" by Kate Chopin
8. Oh, my dear Lord, do wait a minute. I meant to do something about the Forty Acres, Jimmy doesn't need it and Lydia will later on, with that worthless husband of hers. —from "The Jilting of Granny Weatherall" by Katherine Anne Porter
9. "Goody goody! Pay'er back for all those "Rise an' Shines." —from *The Glass Menagerie* by Tennessee Williams
10. "All right. The doctor said as long as you came to get it, you could have it," said the nurse. —from "A Worn Path" by Eudora Welty

EXERCISE 4

1. Upon my recovery, too, I felt very—oh, inexpressibly sick and weak, as if through long inanition.
2. "Heaven forbid, signor!—unless it were fruitful of better pot-herbs than any that grow there now," answered old Lisabetta.
3. Ah, then, exclaim the aged ladies, you shall be sure to be misunderstood.
4. Well, children, where there is so much racket there must be something out of kilter.
5. "Oh, no, they're stuffed and preserved, dozens and dozens of them. . . ."
6. Ah, distinctly I remember it was in the bleak December, / And each separate dying ember wrought its ghost upon the floor.
7. "What are you doing, Louise? For heaven's sake open the door."
8. Oh, my dear Lord, do wait a minute. I meant to do something about the Forty Acres, Jimmy doesn't need it and Lydia will later on, with that worthless husband of hers.
9. "Goody goody! Pay'er back for all those "Rise an' Shines."
10. "All right. The doctor said as long as you came to get it, you could have it," said the nurse.

EXERCISE 5
Responses will vary. Students' sentences should be appropriately expressive and correctly punctuated.

EXERCISE 5

Understanding Interjections

For each interjection listed below, write a sentence that includes it and expresses the appropriate emotion. Use either a comma or an exclamation point to set off the interjection from the sentence.

1. alas
2. oops
3. my
4. humph
5. d'oh
6. drat
7. hooray
8. sweet
9. grrrrr
10. wow

EXERCISE 6
Responses will vary. Students' conversations should be as realistic as possible, and students should correctly use a variety of interjections.

EXERCISE 6

Using Interjections in Your Writing

Write the conversation that might take place between an individual and his or her friend the day after a job interview, a final exam, or some other stressful event. What transpired, what were the results, and what reaction did the friend have? Use a variety of appropriate interjections in your conversation.

PARENTHETICAL EXPRESSIONS

Parenthetical expressions are those words or groups of words that may explain, comment on, or qualify the ideas contained in a sentence.

Expressions such as *of course, after all, however, mind you, for instance, for example, by the way, furthermore, besides, in fact, to tell the truth, in my opinion, on the other hand, too, in addition,* and *as I was saying* may aid understanding but are not essential to meaning. They are set off from the rest of the sentence with a comma or commas.

EXAMPLES

On the other hand, owning a large dog might discourage prowlers.

This was not one of your wiser decisions, **in my opinion.**

The paint, **as you can see,** is starting to crack and peel.

Try It Yourself

EXERCISE 7

Identifying Parenthetical Expressions in Literature

Write the parenthetical expressions that you find in the excerpt from the following short story.

> His clothes, of course, were frightful. They had been made for him by a Greek tailor in Lima—in two days. He was young enough, too, to have explained this sartorial deficiency to Jonquil in his otherwise laconic note. The only further detail it contained was a request that he should *not* be met at the station.
>
> George O'Kelly, of Cuzco, Peru, waited an hour and a half in the hotel, until, to be exact, the sun had reached a midway position in the sky. Then, freshly shaven and talcum-powdered toward a somewhat more Caucasian hue, for vanity at the last minute had overcome romance, he engaged a taxicab and set out for the house he knew so well.

from "The Sensible Thing"
F. Scott Fitzgerald

EXERCISE 8

Understanding Parenthetical Expressions

Rewrite each of the following sentences by inserting a parenthetical expression into each. Try to vary your placement of these expressions, and be sure to punctuate them correctly with commas.

EXERCISE 7

His clothes, <u>of course</u>, were frightful. They had been made for him by a Greek tailor in Lima—in two days. He was young enough, <u>too</u>, to have explained this sartorial deficiency to Jonquil in his otherwise laconic note. The only further detail it contained was a request that he should *not* be met at the station.

George O'Kelly, of Cuzco, Peru, waited an hour and a half in the

Literature
MODEL

hotel, until, <u>to be exact</u>, the sun had reached a midway position in the sky. Then, freshly shaven and talcum-powdered toward a somewhat more Caucasian hue, <u>for vanity at the last minute had overcome romance</u>, he engaged a taxicab and set out for the house he knew so well.

EXERCISE 8

Responses will vary. Sample responses:

1. Computers are a necessity, in my opinion, but they can be aggravating.
2. Fortunately, the price of printers has declined in recent years.
3. A 56K modem, I have heard, will soon be outdated.
4. Our plan, barring unforeseen circumstances, is to buy a new computer system next spring.

5. Of course, I would like to compare prices from several different companies.
6. My hope, you see, is to find a powerful system that has been drastically marked down in price.
7. As you know, Ivan is an expert on computers and their manufacturers.
8. I would like to talk to him, as such, before I purchase a system.
9. He will be giving a lecture at University Hall next Tuesday, by the way.
10. Ivan has a great mind for technology and, moreover, can explain complex processes lucidly.

EXERCISE 9
Responses will vary. Students' choices of parenthetical expressions should be appropriate to the context of their sentences. They should experiment with placement of the expressions and punctuate them correctly.

1. Computers are a necessity, but they can be aggravating.
2. The price of printers has declined in recent years.
3. A 56K modem will soon be outdated.
4. Our plan is to buy a new computer system next spring.
5. I would like to compare prices from several different companies.
6. My hope is to find a powerful system that has been drastically marked down in price.
7. Ivan is an expert on computers and their manufacturers.
8. I would like to talk to him before I purchase a system.
9. He will be giving a lecture at University Hall next Tuesday.
10. Ivan has a great mind for technology and can explain complex processes lucidly.

EXERCISE 9

Using Parenthetical Expressions

Write a sentence for each of the parenthetical expressions below. Try to vary your placement of the expressions, and be sure to punctuate them correctly with commas.

1. in closing
2. I see
3. notwithstanding
4. anyway
5. to be frank
6. it seems
7. you understand
8. as I said
9. in the end
10. that is

NOUNS OF DIRECT ADDRESS

Nouns of direct address say the name of the person or group spoken to. A noun of direct address is *never* the subject of the sentence.

EXAMPLES

Boris, will you please remove your shoes? (*Boris* is the noun of direct address. *You* is the subject of the sentence.)

Mom, the Johnsons have returned home. (*Mom* is the noun of direct address. *Johnsons* is the subject of the sentence.)

A noun of direct address can appear at any place in a sentence. Notice in the following examples where each noun of direct address appears and how commas are used to set it off from the rest of the sentence.

EXAMPLES

Your python is dangerous, Jack, and you should not own such a pet in a crowded residential neighborhood. (*Jack* is the noun of direct address. *Python* and *you* are the subjects of the two independent clauses.)

Pass your assignments to the front, students. (*Students* is the noun of direct address. *You* is the understood subject of the sentence.)

USAGE tip

When the subject of a sentence is understood, or not stated, be careful not to confuse the understood subject with the noun of direct address.

Try It Yourself

EXERCISE 10

Identifying Nouns of Direct Address in Literature

Write the nouns of direct address that you find in the literature passage below.

> Better turn over, hide from the light, sleeping in the light gave you nightmares. "Mother, how do you feel now?" and a stinging wetness on her forehead. But I don't like having my face washed in cold water!
>
> Hapsy? George? Lydia? Jimmy? No, Cornelia, and

CONTINUED

EXERCISE 10

Better turn over, hide from the light, sleeping in the light gave you nightmares. "Mother, how do you feel now?" and a stinging wetness on her forehead. But I don't like having my face washed in cold water!

Hapsy? George? Lydia? Jimmy? No, Cornelia, and her features were swollen and full of little puddles. "They're coming, darling, they'll all be here soon." Go wash your face, child, you look funny.

Instead of obeying, Cornelia knelt down and put her head on the pillow. She seemed to be talking but there was no sound. "Well, are you tongue-tied? Whose birthday is it? Are you going to give a party?"

Literature MODEL

Cornelia's mouth moved urgently in strange shapes. "Don't do that, you bother me, daughter."

"Oh, no, Mother. Oh, no. . . ."

Nonsense. It was strange about children. They disputed your every word. "No what, Cornelia?"

"Here's Doctor Harry."

EXERCISE 11

1. In this closet, Jeff, you will find the office supplies. Subject = you
2. Edie, who will be performing at tonight's concert? Subject = who
3. Your bowler hat is old and dirty, Grandpa, but we can buy a new one for you. Subjects = hat, we
4. Can you finish the rest of this crossword puzzle, Kenneth? Subject = you
5. Soldiers, we need to take that hill by nightfall or the battle is lost. Subjects = we, battle
6. Dawn, please take the recyclables to the curb for pick-up. Subject = you
7. Nice going, Einstein, now we have to start the experiment all over again. Subject = we
8. Please stop arguing, both of you. Subject = you
9. John will drive you to the bus station, Hillary. Subject = John
10. As you can see, Mother, the house is neat and tidy, just as you left it. Subject = house

her features were swollen and full of little puddles. "They're coming, darling, they'll all be here soon." Go wash your face, child, you look funny.

Instead of obeying, Cornelia knelt down and put her head on the pillow. She seemed to be talking but there was no sound. "Well, are you tongue-tied? Whose birthday is it? Are you going to give a party?"

Cornelia's mouth moved urgently in strange shapes. "Don't do that, you bother me, daughter."

"Oh, no, Mother. Oh, no. . . ."

Nonsense. It was strange about children. They disputed your every word. "No what, Cornelia?"

"Here's Doctor Harry."

from "The Jilting of Granny Weatherall"
Katherine Anne Porter

EXERCISE 11

Understanding Nouns of Direct Address

Identify the nouns of direct address in each of the following sentences and set them off with commas. Then identify the subject of each independent clause.

1. In this closet Jeff you will find the office supplies.
2. Edie who will be performing at tonight's concert?
3. Your bowler hat is old and dirty Grandpa but we can buy a new one for you.
4. Can you finish the rest of this crossword puzzle Kenneth?
5. Soldiers we need to take that hill by nightfall or the battle is lost.
6. Dawn please take the recyclables to the curb for pick-up.
7. Nice going Einstein now we have to start the experiment all over again.
8. Please stop arguing both of you.
9. John will drive you to the bus station Hillary.
10. As you can see Mother the house is neat and tidy, just as you left it.

EXERCISE 12

Using Nouns of Direct Address in Your Writing

Sometimes a speaker will directly address his or her audience to emphasize a point or to convey a note of sincerity and familiarity. This is often the case when a speaker wants to impress upon his or her listeners the need to take specific action. Imagine that you are seeking to convince your neighborhood to support an improvement project. Write a brief speech in which you talk directly to your audience about the necessity of the project. Be sure to punctuate nouns of direct address correctly.

EXERCISE 12
Responses will vary. The subject of students' speeches should be appropriate for their purpose and audience. They should use nouns of direct address for effect but should not overuse them.

APPOSITIVES

An **appositive** is a word or a group of words that renames a noun. In the following sentence, the appositive *heavily armed mounted troups* renames the noun *dragoons.*

EXAMPLE
Dragoons, heavily armed mounted troups, were deployed by the British in the Revolutionary War.

If the information in an appositive specifically identifies the noun that precedes it, then the appositive is called **essential** (or *restrictive*) and is not set off with commas. In the sentence below, *Daniel Webster* specifically identifies which great orator served as secretary of state.

EXAMPLE
The great orator Daniel Webster served as secretary of state from 1841 to 1843.

If the information in the appositive is not necessary to identify the noun that precedes it, then the appositive is called **nonessential** (or *nonrestrictive*) and is set off with commas. This is the case in the first example above, where the appositive provides extra information about the noun *dragoons,* helping to define it. The following two sentences will help you see the difference between essential and nonessential information in an appositive.

USAGE tip

Before you examine appositives as interrupters, you may want to review appositives as modifiers in Unit 9 on pages 202–205.

EXAMPLES

essential appositive

Alan's friend Rex writes a column for the local newspaper. (The appositive *Rex* renames the noun *friend.* The appositive *Rex* is essential to the meaning of the sentence. Without it, you would not know which friend writes a column for the local newspaper.)

nonessential appositive

Alan's favorite uncle, Rex, writes a column for the local newspaper. (The appositive *Rex* is not essential to the meaning of the sentence. The adjective *favorite* tells you which uncle. You do not need the information in the appositive to tell you which uncle.)

USAGE tip

Do not use commas with an appositive when it is part of a proper name or when it is needed to identify the noun it follows: *my brother Robert, my teammate Caroline, King George III.*

EXERCISE 13

1. a rabbinical student at the Yeshiva University—Leo Finkle
2. a marriage broker—Pinye Salzman
3. a table near a window that overlooked the lamp-lit city—clear place

Try It Yourself

EXERCISE 13

Identifying Appositives

Identify the three appositives or appositive phrases in the literature passage below. Then write the noun or pronoun that the appositive identifies or renames.

MODEL

Not long ago there lived in uptown New York, in a small, almost meager room, though crowded with books, Leo Finkle, a rabbinical student at the Yeshiva University. Finkle, after six years of study, was to be ordained in June and had been advised by an acquaintance that he might find it easier to win himself a congregation if he were married. Since he had no present prospects of marriage, after two tormented days of turning it over in his mind, he called in Pinye Salzman, a marriage broker whose two-line advertisement he had read in the *Forward.* . . .

The two went to their business. Leo had led Salzman to the only clear place in the room, a table near a window that overlooked the lamp-lit city. He seated himself at the matchmaker's side but facing him, attempting by an act of will to suppress the unpleasant tickle in his throat.

CONTINUED

Salzman eagerly unstrapped his portfolio and removed a loose rubber band from a thin packet of much-handled cards.

from "The Magic Barrel"
Bernard Malamud

EXERCISE 14

Correcting Sentences with Appositives

Rewrite the sentences below, adding commas where necessary. If a sentence has no errors, write *correct.*

1. Macedonia an ancient kingdom north of present-day Greece once ruled the largest empire in the world.
2. Alexander the Great the son of Phillip II led the conquest of this great empire.
3. As a boy, Alexander was tutored by Aristotle, the famous Greek philosopher.
4. Alexander defeated Persia Macedonia's chief rival in a series of battles.
5. Persian forces were commanded by Darius IV, a military commander overmatched by Alexander.
6. Other enemies the Scythians, the Sogdians, and the Mallians also fell before the powerful Macedonian king.
7. In 327 B.C., Alexander married Roxane daughter of Spitamenes the leader of the Sogdian revolt.
8. Alexander's advance into India was eventually stopped by mutinies armed uprisings by his own soldiers.
9. In 323 B.C. Alexander succumbed to malaria a disease characterized by chills, fever, and sweating.
10. Alexander's military career a string of impressive victories on three continents remains unmatched by any other world leader.

EXERCISE 14

1. Macedonia, an ancient kingdom north of present-day Greece, once ruled the largest empire in the world.
2. Alexander the Great, the son of Phillip II, led the conquest of this great empire.
3. correct
4. Alexander defeated Persia, Macedonia's chief rival, in a series of battles.
5. correct
6. Other enemies, the Scythians, the Sogdians, and the Mallians, also fell before the powerful Macedonian king.
7. In 327 B.C., Alexander married Roxane, daughter of Spitamenes, the leader of the Sogdian revolt.
8. Alexander's advance into India was eventually stopped by mutinies, armed uprisings by his own soldiers.
9. In 323 B.C. Alexander succumbed to malaria, a disease characterized by chills, fever, and sweating.
10. Alexander's military career, a string of impressive victories on three continents, remains unmatched by any other world leader.

EXERCISE 15

Using Appositives in Your Writing

For a historical magazine, write a brief description of what you consider to be a legendary achievement that has occurred in your lifetime. Discuss the key figure(s) who brought about this noteworthy accomplishment and the challenges he, she, or they faced. Also consider how history might have been different if this achievement had never occurred. Use at least three appositives in your description to provide more information about the accomplishment and the person(s) involved. Be sure to punctuate your appositives correctly.

EXERCISE 15
Responses will vary. Students should include and correctly punctuate at least three appositives and/or appositive phrases in their paragraphs.

UNIT 11 REVIEW

TEST YOUR KNOWLEDGE

EXERCISE 1

Identifying Interrupters

Write the interrupters in the following sentences. Then indicate whether the interrupter is an interjection, a parenthetical expression, a noun of direct address, or an appositive or appositive phrase. (20 points)

EXAMPLE

The merger, in the end, proved to be a great financial success. (*in the end,* parenthetical expression)

1. Well, at least we don't have to write a research paper for this class.
2. You will not be taught by Mr. Tolson this semester; instead, Ms. Anderson will teach American history.
3. In my opinion, historians have overlooked the accomplishments of Chester Arthur.
4. Considering your ability to memorize names, Mark, I think you could easily list every U.S. president.
5. Grover Cleveland, as you know, is the only president to serve two nonconsecutive terms.
6. During the administration of Theodore Roosevelt, a bold, aggressive leader, the presidency was redefined.
7. The powers of the president are listed in the U.S. Constitution, a document written over two hundred years ago.
8. Rats! I can't remember the names of the presidents who served during the Gilded Age.
9. Theresa, please discuss the presidency of James Polk, the dark horse candidate who won the election of 1844.
10. John Quincy Adams, the sixth president of the United States, is the son of John Adams, the second president.
11. William Henry Harrison, tragically, caught pneumonia and died one month after his inauguration.

EXERCISE 1

1. *Well*—interjection
2. *instead*—parenthetical expression
3. *In my opinion*—parenthetical expression
4. *Mark*—noun of direct address
5. *as you know*—parenthetical expression
6. *a bold, aggressive leader*—appositive phrase
7. *a document written over two hundred years ago*—appositive phrase
8. *Rats!*—interjection
9. *Theresa*—noun of direct address; *the dark horse candidate who won the election of 1844*—appositive phrase
10. *the sixth president of the United States*—appositive phrase; *the second president*—appositive phrase
11. *tragically*—parenthetical expression
12. *Harry Truman*—appositive
13. *not surprisingly*—parenthetical expression
14. *I assume*—parenthetical expression
15. *Wow!*—interjection; *Sharon*—noun of direct address

16. *however*—parenthetical expression
17. *head of the state executive branch*—appositive phrase
18. *Clearly*—parenthetical expression
19. *Ah*—interjection
20. *Northern Democrats who opposed the Union war effort*—appositive phrase

EXERCISE 2
1. Tammy, will you be living in the city of Chicago or in one of the suburbs?
2. Chicago was incorporated in 1837, the year Andrew Jackson left office, and had a population of 4,170.
3. Say, I wonder if those early residents had any idea of how large their city would become.
4. A military stockade, Fort Dearborn, was first built here in 1803.
5. Chicago grew rapidly in the late 1800s, a period marked by rapid urbanization.
6. Holy cow! You once took the stairs to the top of the Sears Tower?

12. The underdog incumbent Harry Truman surprised the experts and won the presidential election of 1948.
13. Herbert Hoover, not surprisingly, lost the election of 1932 in a landslide.
14. Richard Nixon, I assume, would have easily defeated George McGovern in 1972.
15. Wow! I've never met anyone who knew so much about Millard Fillmore, have you, Sharon?
16. Ulysses S. Grant, however, did not enjoy great success while serving in the White House.
17. The governor, head of the state executive branch, does not have the same powers as the president.
18. Clearly, George Washington did not have any interest in serving as chief executive for a third term.
19. Ah, so you didn't actually meet the president, you just saw him on television.
20. Copperheads, Northern Democrats who opposed the Union war effort, created difficulties for Abraham Lincoln.

EXERCISE 2

Correcting Sentences with Interrupters

Rewrite the following sentences so that nouns of direct address, parenthetical expressions, interjections, and appositives are punctuated correctly. (10 points)

EXAMPLE

Chicago is located on the southwestern shoreline of Lake Michigan one of the five Great Lakes. *(Chicago is located on the southwestern shore of Lake Michigan, one of the five Great Lakes.)*

1. Tammy will you be living in the city of Chicago or in one of the suburbs?
2. Chicago was incorporated in 1837 the year Andrew Jackson left office and had a population of 4,170.
3. Say I wonder if those early residents had any idea of how large their city would become?

4. A military stockade Fort Dearborn was first built here in 1803.
5. Chicago grew rapidly in the late 1800s a period marked by rapid urbanization.
6. Holy Cow you once took the stairs to the top of the Sears Tower?
7. You could quite easily spend an entire week exploring the attractions of this city.
8. The Cubs by the way will be playing at Wrigley Field this weekend.
9. Comiskey Park home of the White Sox might also be of interest to you.
10. Did you know Lewis the Cubs last won the World Series in 1908?

7. You could, quite easily, spend an entire week exploring the attractions of this city.
8. The Cubs, by the way, will be playing at Wrigley Field this weekend.
9. Comiskey Park, home of the White Sox, might also be of interest to you.
10. Did you know, Lewis, the Cubs last won the World Series in 1908?

EXERCISE 3

Understanding Interrupters

Make the following sentences more interesting. Rewrite them, adding an appropriate interjection, parenthetical expression, appositive phrase, or noun of direct address. You may reword the sentences where necessary so that your additions make sense. Be sure to punctuate your interrupters correctly. (20 points)

EXAMPLE
Matthew has a tendency to be ornery.
(*As you can see, Jessica,* Matthew has a tendency to be ornery.)

1. I believe that you underestimated the cost of the car repairs.
2. Some people put salt on their tomatoes, while others put sugar on them.
3. Brandon has two left feet out on the dance floor.
4. We played five sets of tennis this afternoon.
5. Each aluminum can that you return is worth five cents.
6. When did you arrive?
7. Joe enjoyed his trip to Indianapolis.

EXERCISE 3
Responses will vary. At a minimum, students should add a single interjection, noun of direct address, appositive phrase, or parenthetical expression. Some sentences may have more than one interrupter. In all cases, students' additions of interrupters should improve the sentence by making it more interesting, more personal, or more specific.

EXERCISE 4
Responses will vary. Sample responses:

1. The 1920s were marked by Prohibition, a constitutional amendment prohibiting the manufacture or sale of alcohol.
2. In the 1920s the Fitzgeralds, part of a celebrated circle of American expatriates, lived in Paris, France.
3. Fitzgerald's collection *All the Sad Young Men*, a book containing stories with carefully crafted plots that often addressed the themes of love and loss, was published in 1926.
4. After 1930, Zelda Fitzgerald was frequently hospitalized for schizophrenia, a psychotic disorder involving delusions and a loss of contact with reality.
5. In the 1920s and 1930s many American writers adopted opinions critical of capitalism, ideals based on the theories of Karl Marx.
6. Modernism, a response to the perceived breakdown of modern culture, was an international literary and artistic movement that rejected the artistic conventions of the past.

8. Experts do not recommend adopting wild animals.
9. The car ran out of gas.
10. This rain is going to cause flooding downtown.

EXERCISE 4

Understanding Appositives

Combine each group of sentences below, creating one sentence that contains an essential or a nonessential appositive. You can change the language of the sentence so that the inserted appositive makes sense. Be sure to punctuate the appositives correctly. (20 points)

EXAMPLE
In 1925, F. Scott Fitzgerald published *The Great Gatsby*. Many critics consider it the greatest American novel.
(In 1925 F. Scott Fitzgerald published The Great Gatsby, *the greatest American novel according to many critics.)*

1. The 1920s were marked by Prohibition. It was a constitutional amendment prohibiting the manufacture or sale of alcohol.
2. In the 1920s, the Fitzgeralds lived in Paris, France. They were part of a celebrated circle of American expatriates.
3. Fitzgerald's collection *All the Sad Young Men* was published in 1926. The book contained stories with carefully crafted plots that often addressed the themes of love and loss.
4. After 1930, Zelda Fitzgerald was frequently hospitalized for schizophrenia. Schizophrenia is a psychotic disorder involving delusions and a loss of contact with reality.
5. In the 1920s and 1930s many American writers adopted ideals that were critical of capitalism. The ideals were based on the theories of Karl Marx.
6. Modernism was an international literary and artistic movement that rejected the artistic conventions of the past. It was a response to the perceived breakdown of modern culture.

7. Some modernist writers used stream-of-consciousness prose in their works. They presented the unedited thoughts and impressions of the characters.
8. Stream-of-consciousness writing is an example of subjectivism in Modernist literature. Subjectivism is a style that treats reality not as absolute and orderly but as dependent upon the point of view of the observer.
9. Modernist writers held a different credo than the writers who preceded them. Ezra Pound called this philosophy "make it new."
10. Some prominent writers in the 1920s and 1930s were regionalists. These authors wrote about the local and rural areas in which they had settled.

EXERCISE 5

Using Interrupters

Write a sentence for each of the interrupters listed below. (10 points)

EXAMPLE
a noun of direct address for the end of a sentence
(To be ready for tomorrow's exam, you should go to bed at an earlier hour, Jesse.)

1. an interjection showing mild emotion
2. an interjection showing sudden, intense emotion
3. a parenthetical expression for the beginning of a sentence
4. a parenthetical expression for the middle of a sentence
5. a noun of direct address for the beginning of a sentence
6. an essential appositive
7. a nonessential appositive
8. a parenthetical expression and a noun of direct address
9. a parenthetical expression and an appositive
10. an appositive and an interjection

7. In their works, some modernist writers used stream-of-consciousness prose, the unedited thoughts and impressions of the characters.
8. Stream-of-consciousness writing in Modernist literature is an example of subjectivism, a style that treats reality not as absolute and orderly but as dependent upon the observer's point of view.
9. Modernist writers held a different credo than the writers who preceded them, a philosophy that Ezra Pound called "make it new."
10. Some prominent writers in the 1920s and 1930s were regionalists, authors who wrote about the local and rural areas in which they had settled.

EXERCISE 5
Responses will vary. Students should create an appropriate sentence to illustrate each direction. They should punctuate their interrupters correctly in all cases.

EXERCISE 6
Responses will vary. Students should agree or disagree with one of the statements, using specific reasons and examples to express their viewpoint about school politics. They should use at least three of the four different kinds of interrupters. Overuse of interrupters should be allowed for the purposes of applying grammar to writing, but students should be cautioned about the "sputtering" effect of too many interrupters.

EXERCISE 6

Using Interrupters in Your Writing

Choose one of the following positions to support in a letter to the editor of your school newspaper: Our school leaders are or are not responsive to our needs. Use your specific observations of school politics to support your point of view. Use interrupters—interjections, nouns of direct address, parenthetical expressions, and appositives—where they will help to reinforce a point or achieve an effect. Be sure to punctuate correctly the interrupters you use. (20 points)

UNIT 12 PHRASES, CLAUSES, AND COMPLEX SENTENCES

UNIT OVERVIEW

PHRASES, CLAUSES, AND COMPLEX SENTENCES

PHRASES AND CLAUSES

Sometimes groups of words function as one part of speech. These groups of words are either *phrases* or *clauses*. Clauses have both subjects and verbs; phrases do not.

EXAMPLES

phrase	Aunt Glynis placed the porcelain elephant **on the mantel.**
phrase	The stunt double needed **to move exactly like the actor.**
clause	**Before we leave the cottage,** we must clean it from top to bottom.
clause	This best-selling advice book explains **how you can overcome all of your fears.**

LANGUAGELINK
Print exercise worksheets or have students complete exercises online with the LanguageLINK CD.

Try It Yourself

EXERCISE 1

Identifying Phrases and Clauses in Literature

Identify the underlined groups of words in the literature passage as phrases or clauses.

MODEL

EXERCISE 1
1. *As her words fell upon my new ears,* clause
2. *from somewhere within me,* phrase, phrase
3. *how Bluebeard had duped and married his seven wives,* clause
4. *in a dark closet,* phrase
5. *around me,* phrase
6. *As she spoke,* clause
7. *with magical presences,* phrase

She whispered to me the story of *Bluebird and His Seven Wives* and I ceased to see the porch, the sunshine, her face, everything. As her words fell upon my new ears, I endowed them with a reality that welled up from somewhere within me. She told how Bluebeard had duped and married his seven wives, how he had loved and slain them, how he had hanged them up by their hair in a dark closet. The tale made the world around me be, throb, live. As she spoke, reality changed, the look of things altered, and the world became people with magical presences.

from *Black Boy*
Richard Wright

EXERCISE 2

Using Phrases and Clauses

Write a complete sentence incorporating each phrase or clause below.

1. at the bottom of the well
2. whenever a delivery person comes to the house
3. to bounce on the trampoline
4. if he glimpses a speck of dust
5. as soon as the siren went off
6. until I find a summer job
7. behind the velvet curtain
8. which was not the story she told me
9. while the movie credits were rolling
10. whom we saw in the subway station

EXERCISE 2

Responses will vary. Sample responses:

1. The key glinted at the bottom of the well.
2. The dog hurls herself at the door whenever a delivery person comes to the house.
3. Laura loves to bounce on the trampoline.
4. Walker gets anxious if he glimpses a speck of dust on his dashboard.
5. As soon as the siren went off, the emergency medical technician jumped in his truck.
6. I really can't start spending money until I find a summer job.
7. Sammi hid behind the velvet curtain.
8. Mrs. Lane told the police that the car rolled into the street, a tale which was not the story she told me.
9. I left while the movie credits were rolling.
10. Is that the performer whom we saw in the subway station?

PHRASES

A **phrase** is a group of words used as a single part of speech—a noun, an adjective, or an adverb. A phrase lacks a subject, a complete verb, or both; therefore, it cannot be a sentence. There are three common kinds of phrases: prepositional phrases, verbal phrases, and appositive phrases. A fourth kind, the absolute phrase, is less common but can be useful as another way of adding information to a clause.

USAGE tip

You may want to review prepositions and prepositional phrases on pages 235–238 in Unit 10.

PREPOSITIONAL PHRASES

A **prepositional phrase** consists of a preposition, its object, and any modifiers of that object. A prepositional phrase adds information to a sentence by modifying another word in the sentence. It may function as an adjective or an adverb.

EXAMPLES

adjectives The boots **on the porch** are Ben's. (The prepositional phrase *on the porch* tells which boots are Ben's. The phrase is an adjective, modifying the noun *boots.*)

CONTINUED

	Shoes **with smooth, hard soles** can slip on ice. (The prepositional phrase *with smooth, hard soles* tell what kind of shoes can slip on ice. The phrase is an adjective, modifying the noun *shoes*.)
adverbs	A large comet appeared **in 1577**. (The prepositional phrase *in 1577* tells when the comet appeared. The phrase is an adverb, modifying the verb *appeared*.)
	The Danish astronomer Tycho Brahe proved that this comet was high **above the earth's atmosphere**. (The prepositional phrase *above the earth's atmosphere* tells how high the comet was. The phrase is an adverb, modifying the adjective *high*.)

USAGE tip

Remember that some words can function as either an adverb or a preposition, depending on the sentence. Prepositions never stand alone. They always have an object. If the word stands alone, it is an adverb.

adverb
Natasha spun *around*.

preposition
Natasha walked *around* the table.

Use prepositional phrases to create sentence variety. When every sentence in a paragraph starts with its subject, the rhythm of the sentences becomes boring. Revise your sentences, where it is appropriate, to start some with prepositional phrases.

EXAMPLE
Clarice pounded on the door **with increasing frustration.**
With increasing frustration, Clarice pounded on the door.

Try It Yourself

EXERCISE 3
Identifying Prepositional Phrases in Literature

Write the word that each underlined group of words modifies. Then label each prepositional phrase as an adjective or an adverb phrase.

I went to dances <u>at Chandlerville</u>,
And played snap-out <u>at Winchester</u>.
One time we changed partners,
Driving home in the moonlight <u>of middle June</u>,
And then I found Davis.
We were married and lived together <u>for seventy years</u>,

CONTINUED

EXERCISE 3
1. *dances—at Chandlerville*—adjective
2. *played—at Winchester*—adverb
3. *moonlight—of middle June*—adjective
4. *together—for seventy years*—adverb

Literature MODEL

5. *age—of sixty*—adjective
6. *Rambled—over the fields*—adverb
7. *gathering—by Spoon River*—adverb

Enjoying, working, raising the twelve children,
Eight of whom we lost
Ere I had reached the age of sixty.
I spun, I wove, I kept the house, I nursed the sick,
I made the garden, and for holiday
Rambled over the fields where sang the larks,
And by Spoon River gathering many a shell,
And many a flower and medicinal weed—
Shouting to the wooded hills, singing to the green valleys.
At ninety-six I had lived enough, that is all,
And passed to a sweet repose.
What is this I hear of sorrow and weariness,
Anger, discontent, and drooping hopes?
Degenerate sons and daughters,
Life is too strong for you—
It takes life to love Life.

from "Lucinda Matlock"
Edgar Lee Masters

EXERCISE 4

Understanding Prepositional Phrases

Rewrite the following sentences so that each begins with a prepositional phrase.

1. Franca works for a thrift shop after school.
2. Relics from basements and attics find their way to Rosie's Resale.
3. The elderly owner, Rosie Ramirez, greets her customers from a large, gold-painted throne.
4. She announces, in her deep, gravelly voice, that she rescued this magnificent chair from a dump!
5. Special daily sale items are located at the back of the store.
6. I once, to my great surprise, found an authentic Chanel handbag at Rosie's.
7. The bag, with its double-C logo, stood out from the rest of the battered items in the bargain bin.

8. *Shouting—to the wooded hills*—adverb
9. *I—At ninety-six*—adjective
10. *passed—to a sweet repose*—adverb
11. *strong—for you*—adverb

EXERCISE 4

1. After school Franca works for a thrift shop.
2. From basements and attics, relics find their way to Rosie's Resale.
3. From a large, gold-painted throne, the elderly owner, Rosie Ramirez, greets her customers.
4. In her deep, gravelly voice, she announces that she rescued this magnificent chair from a dump!
5. At the back of the store, special daily sale items are located.
6. To my great surprise, I once found an authentic Chanel handbag at Rosie's.
7. With its double-C logo, the bag stood out from the rest of the battered items in the bargain bin.
8. On the coldest winter days, Mom wears a warm, quilted coat from Rosie's.
9. From the local drama school, actors come to find materials for their costumes and sets.
10. With her gold-topped cane, Rosie points out an old apothecary jar made of wavy bluish glass.

8. Mom wears a warm, quilted coat from Rosie's on the coldest winter days.
9. Actors come from the local drama school to find materials for their costumes and sets.
10. Rosie points out with her gold-topped cane an old apothecary jar made of wavy bluish glass.

EXERCISE 5

Using Prepositional Phrases in Your Writing

For the school newspaper, write a description of a sporting event, cultural performance, or club activity. Use prepositional phrases to add lively details to your description. Make sure you include some phrases that function as adjectives and some that function as adverbs.

EXERCISE 5
Responses will vary. Students' descriptions should include specific details and prepositional phrases to give readers a clear idea of the type of performance or event. For variety, students should begin several sentences with prepositional phrases.

VERBAL PHRASES

Verbals are verb forms that act as namers or modifiers. There are three kinds of verbals: participles, gerunds, and infinitives.

Participial Phrases

A **participle** is a verb form ending in *–ing*, *–d*, or *–ed* that acts as an adjective, modifying a noun or a pronoun. A **participial phrase** is made up of a participle and all of the words related to the participle, which may include objects, modifiers, and prepositional phrases. The entire phrase acts as an adjective.

EXAMPLES

Singing loudly every song in her repetoire, Lucia tried to conquer her fears. (The participle *singing,* the adverb *loudly,* the direct object *every song,* and the prepositional phrase *in her repetoire* make up the participial phrase that modifies *Lucia.*)

Worried about the coming thunderstorm, Mom shut all the windows in the house but left all the car windows open. (The participle *worried* and the prepositional phrase *about the coming thunderstorm* make up the participial phrase that modifies *Mom.*)

For variety, begin some of your sentences with participial phrases. However, be sure to place the participial phrase close to the word it modifies. Otherwise, you may say something you do not mean.

EXAMPLES

misplaced participial phrase	Chugging along the tracks, we heard the train.
revised sentence	We heard the train chugging along the tracks.

Try It Yourself

EXERCISE 6

Identifying Participial Phrases in Literature

Identify the five participial phrases in the literature passage below. Beside each, identify the noun or pronoun the participial phrase modifies.

> Finally, to those nations who would make themselves our adversary, we offer not a pledge but a request—that both sides begin anew the quest for peace before the dark powers of destruction unleashed by science engulf all humanity in planned or accidental self-destruction. We dare not tempt them with weakness. For only when our arms are sufficient beyond doubt can we be certain beyond doubt that they will never be employed.
>
> But neither can two great and powerful groups of nations take comfort from our present course—both sides overburdened by the cost of modern weapons, both rightly alarmed by the steady spread of the deadly atom, yet both racing to alter that uncertain balance of terror that stays the hand of mankind's final war.
>
> So let us begin anew—remembering on both sides that civility is not a sign of weakness, and sincerity is always subject to proof.

from Inaugural Address
John F. Kennedy

EXERCISE 6
1. powers—unleashed by science
2. sides—overburdened by the cost of modern weapons
3. both—rightly alarmed by the steady spread of the deadly atom
4. both—racing to alter that uncertain balance of terror that stays the hand of mankind's final war
5. us—remembering on both sides that civility is not a sign of weakness, and sincerity is always subject to proof

Literature
MODEL

EXERCISE 7

Responses will vary. Sample responses:

1. Thumping up the stairs, Nita woke the rest of the family.
2. We were all tired of chicken for supper.
3. Snoring loudly, Vikram woke himself.
4. The quarrel, overheard by neighbors, lasted for hours.
5. Ransacking the file cabinets, the secretary finally located the file.
6. Perched on the birdfeeder, a chattering squirrel devoured the birdseed.
7. We saw Ann chatting with her friends.
8. Remembering a ridiculous moment, the teacher dissolved in laughter.
9. Surrounded by hysterical fans, the tennis player signed programs.
10. The apron, stained with blackberry juice, went into the washer

EXERCISE 8

Responses will vary. Students' descriptions of the event should feature a clear explanation aided by participial phrases. Check to be sure that they have placed their phrases correctly in the sentences. Look for sentence variety based on varying the placement of participial phrases.

EXERCISE 7
Understanding Participial Phrases

For each of the following participial phrases, write a complete sentence. Try to vary your sentence structure, but be sure to place the participial phrase close to the word it modifies.

1. thumping up the stairs
2. tired of chicken for supper
3. snoring loudly
4. overheard by neighbors
5. ransacking the file cabinets
6. perched on the birdfeeder
7. chatting with her friends
8. remembering a ridiculous moment
9. surrounded by hysterical fans
10. stained with blackberry juice

EXERCISE 8
Using Participial Phrases in Your Writing

Imagine that you write a weekly column called "The Camera's Eye" for the school newspaper. For one of your columns, describe an interesting or unexpected event that you have observed at school. Describe what happened, where and when it happened, and what different people did and said. Use participial phrases to describe the scene clearly.

Gerund Phrases

A **gerund phrase** is a phrase made up of a gerund (a verb form ending in *–ing*) and all of its modifiers and complements. The entire phrase functions as a noun. This means that it may be the subject, predicate nominative, direct object, indirect object, or object of the preposition in a sentence. A gerund's modifiers include adjectives, adverbs, and prepositional phrases.

EXAMPLES

Breathing deeply is a good way to calm one's nerves. (The gerund phrase functions as the subject of the sentence.)

Joanna's secret to serenity is **breathing deeply**. (The gerund phrase functions as the predicate nominative of the sentence.)

Before each basketball game, Colin practices **breathing deeply**. (The gerund phrase functions as the direct object of the sentence.)

We begin our yoga practice by **breathing deeply.** (The gerund phrase functions as the object of the preposition.)

Try It Yourself

EXERCISE 9

Identifying Gerund Phrases in Literature

Identify the three gerund phrases in the literature passage below. Beside each phrase, tell whether the gerund phrase is used as a subject, predicate nominative, direct object, indirect object, or object of the preposition.

EXERCISE 9

1. *going through*—object of preposition
2. *plain sailing for him in the future*—predicate nominative
3. *the beginning of their love affair*—direct object

MODEL

> And then a curious thing happened. George stepped aside to let Jonquil pass, but instead of going through she stood still and stared at him for a minute. It was not so much the look, which was not a smile, as it was the moment of silence. They saw each other's eyes, and both took a short, faintly accelerated breath, and then they went on into the second garden. That was all.

CONTINUED

The afternoon waned. They thanked the lady and walked home slowly, thoughtfully, side by side. Through dinner too they were silent. George told Mr. Cary something of what had happened in South America, and managed to let it be known that everything would be plain sailing for him in the future.

Then dinner was over, and he and Jonquil were alone in the room which had seen the beginning of their love affair and the end.

from "The Sensible Thing"
F. Scott Fitzgerald

EXERCISE 10
Responses will vary. Sample responses:
1. Daydreaming all the time gets Selina into trouble.
2. Ken's assignment is catching a spotted newt.
3. The blinking of the traffic light bothered my eyes.
4. Dad loves watching old movies.
5. The archaeologist spent weeks photographing the ruins.
6. Janet practiced dribbling the basketball in patterns around the floor.
7. Right now, finding a pair of warm socks is my first priority.
8. When you're really low, doing something for others is often the best solution.
9. Repairing the broken window is necessary before winter.
10. His constant coughing and sniffling annoyed the other bus passengers.

EXERCISE 11
Responses will vary. Students' speeches should follow the typical style for such events and should describe one or more performers' achievements. The entries should incorporate at least four gerund phrases. Make sure that students have not confused gerunds with participles or with verbs.

EXERCISE 10
Understanding Gerund Phrases

Write a sentence for each of the following gerund phrases. Be sure to use each phrase as the subject, predicate nominative, direct object, indirect object, or object of the preposition.

1. daydreaming all the time
2. catching a spotted newt
3. blinking of the traffic light
4. watching old movies
5. photographing the ruins
6. dribbling the basketball
7. finding a pair of warm socks
8. doing something for others
9. repairing the broken window
10. coughing and sniffling

EXERCISE 11
Using Gerund Phrases in Your Writing

Imagine that you are appearing on a music or movie awards show. Write a speech describing the achievements of one or more performers. In your paragraph, use at least four gerund phrases.

Infinitive Phrases

An **infinitive phrase** is made up of an infinitive (a verb form preceded by the word *to*) and all its modifiers and complements. Infinitive phrases can function as nouns, adjectives, or adverbs.

EXAMPLES

To tap dance in a Broadway musical is Marla's fondest dream. (The infinitive phrase functions as a noun, the subject of the sentence.)

Right now Marla is practicing **to get into the school talent show.** (The infinitive phrase functions as an adverb, telling why Marla is practicing.)

USAGE tip

When a modifier comes between *to* and the verb, the infinitive is said to be split. Avoid split infinitives unless doing so makes the sentence sound unnatural or awkward.

Sometimes the *to* of an infinitive phrase is left out; it is understood. This happens frequently after such verbs as *see*, *hear*, *feel*, *watch*, *help*, *know*, *dare*, *need*, *make*, *let*, and *please*.

EXAMPLES

Carlos helps **[to]** plaster the ceiling.

The customers in the laundromat let the machine **[to]** overflow.

EXERCISE 12

1. *to give a Wagner program*—noun
2. *to take my aunt*—noun
3. *to wish to venture out*—adverb
4. *to venture out*—adverb
5. *to leave instructions*—noun
6. *to tell her daughter*—noun

Try It Yourself

EXERCISE 12

Identifying Infinitive Phrases in Literature

Identify the six infinitive phrases in the literature passage below. Beside each phrase, tell whether it is used as a noun, adjective, or adverb.

MODEL

> At two o'clock the Symphony Orchestra was to give a Wagner program, and I intended to take my aunt; though, as I conversed with her, I grew doubtful about her enjoyment of it. I suggested our visiting the Conservatory and the Common before lunch, but she seemed altogether too timid to wish to venture out. She questioned me absently about various changes in the city, but she was chiefly concerned that she had forgotten to

CONTINUED

leave instructions about feeding half-skimmed milk to a certain weakling calf, "old Maggie's calf, you know, Clark," she explained, evidently having forgotten how long I had been away. She was further troubled because she had neglected to tell her daughter about the freshly-opened kit of mackerel in the cellar, which would spoil if it were not used directly.

from "A Wagner Matinee"
Willa Cather

EXERCISE 13
Responses will vary. Sample responses:

1. Reinalda plans to finish the marketing.
2. The principal looks as if she is about to lose her temper.
3. Jake is famous for his tendency to tell the same story again and again.
4. To win a trip to the Bahamas would be an unexpected thrill.
5. When it gets really cold, we plan to flood the backyard and make a skating rink.
6. This Halloween, I will definitely try to come up with a better costume.
7. To interrupt a speaker is extremely bad manners.
8. Every time you get in the car, you must remember to check the mileage.
9. That animal is able to open the door of its cage.
10. To hang out with that group is asking for trouble.

EXERCISE 13
Understanding Infinitive Phrases

Complete each of the following sentences with an infinitive phrase.

1. Reinalda plans ___.
2. The principal looks as if she is about ___.
3. Jake his famous for his tendency ___.
4. ___ would be an unexpected thrill.
5. When it gets really cold, we plan ___.
6. This Halloween, I will definitely try ___.
7. ___ is extremely bad manners.
8. Every time you get in the car, you must remember ___.
9. That animal is able ___.
10. ___ is asking for trouble.

EXERCISE 14
Using Infinitive Phrases in Your Writing

Write a set of instructions for junior high school students telling them how to succeed in high school. You might concentrate on succeeding academically, athletically, socially, or emotionally. Use at least five infinitive phrases in your directions.

EXERCISE 14
Responses will vary. Students' instructions should be concise, clear, and relevant. Check to be sure that students are not confusing infinitive phrases with prepositional phrases that begin with *to*.

ABSOLUTE PHRASES

An **absolute phrase** consists of a participle, a noun or pronoun that performs the action in the particle, and any modifiers of these two words. Either the *–ing* or the *–ed* form of the participle can appear in an absolute phrase, which belongs neither to the complete subject nor the complete predicate; it stands "absolutely" by itself in relation to the rest of the sentence. You can use absolute phrases to add information about time, reasons, and circumstances to the main clause of a sentence.

In the following examples, the absolute phrases appear in bold type and add information regarding the circumstances of Lee's surrender to Grant.

EXAMPLES

His forces surrounded by Union soldiers, Lee surrendered to Grant at Appomattox Court House.

History hanging in the balance, General Lee admitted defeat.

Try It Yourself

EXERCISE 15

Identifying Absolute Phrases

Identify the absolute phrase in each of the following sentences.

1. All options for victory closed, General Lee's surrender spared his few remaining, starving men.
2. The Civil War having ended, Lee worked tirelessly and peaceably to restore the South.
3. Wounded and exhausted soldiers returned home, many young bugle boys being among them.
4. The Emancipation Proclamation having laid the groundwork, Lincoln worked after the war for passage of the Thirteenth Amendment, which ended slavery in the United States once and for all.

EXERCISE 15

1. All options for victory closed, General Lee's surrender spared his few remaining, starving men.
2. The Civil War having ended, Lee worked tirelessly and peaceably to restore the South.
3. Wounded and exhausted soldiers returned home, many young bugle boys being among them.

USAGE tip

Be careful not to confuse an absolute phrase with a participial phrase. An absolute phrase contains a subject; a participial phrase does not. In a participial phrase, the verb form functions as an adjective.

absolute phrase
The surrender officially announced, Lee and Grant shook hands.

participial phrase
Surrendering to the Union commander, Lee shook Grant's hand.

4. The Emancipation Proclamation having laid the groundwork, Lincoln worked after the war for passage of

the Thirteenth Amendment, which ended slavery in the United States once and for all.

5. A troubled actor by the name of John Wilkes Booth, his anger fueled by the Confederacy's loss, shot President Lincoln at Ford's Theater.
6. People spilled into the aisles and onto the streets, faint whispers and cries revealing their concern.
7. The sad news conveyed, people stood in shock and disbelief in Washington.
8. A paper carrier, tears streaming down his face, hawked the news in the morning paper.
9. A train carried the dead president home to Illinois, its slow, sad route traveling from Washington to Springfield.
10. Their hearts broken by Lincoln's death, people of all ages gathered at the train stations, waiting for the funeral car to pass by.

EXERCISE 16
Responses will vary.

5. A troubled actor by the name of John Wilkes Booth, his anger fueled by the Confederacy's loss, shot President Lincoln at Ford's Theater.
6. People spilled into the aisles and onto the streets, faint whispers and cries revealing their concern.
7. The sad news conveyed, people stood in shock and disbelief in Washington.
8. A paper carrier, tears streaming down his face, hawked the news in the morning paper.
9. A train carried the dead president home to Illinois, its slow, sad route traveling from Washington to Springfield.
10. Their hearts broken by Lincoln's death, people of all ages gathered at the train stations, waiting for the funeral car to pass by.

EXERCISE 16

Understanding Absolute Phrases

Rewrite each of the following sentences, adding an absolute phrase to each.

1. The performance was satisfactory.
2. We went home.
3. Stars sparkled in the night sky.
4. My sister wanted a big celebration for her birthday.
5. The students studied speeches by other famous Americans.
6. He switched on the reading lamp.
7. I washed the dishes and cleaned the kitchen counter.
8. The author was pleased with the publicity tour.
9. Birdwatchers generally rely on high-powered binoculars.
10. A stray cat stood in the damp, dark alley.

EXERCISE 17

Using Absolute Phrases in Your Writing

For a special suspense issue of the school literary magazine, write a narrative that begins with the absolute phrase "My heart hammering in my chest, . . ." Focus on a suspenseful, thrilling, or surprising moment that you experienced, and include at least two additional absolute phrases in your paragraph.

EXERCISE 17 *Responses will vary.* Students should begin their narratives with the absolute phrase "My heart hammering in my chest" and should contain two additional absolute phrases.

APPOSITIVE PHRASES

An **appositive phrase** is a group of words made up of an appositive and all its modifiers. The phrase renames or identifies a noun or pronoun.

EXAMPLES

The corgi, **a herding dog**, originally came from Wales. (The appositive phrase renames the noun *corgi.*)

The ingredients **coriander, turmeric, and fennel** are fundamental to curry powder. (The appositive phrase identifies which ingredients are fundamental to curry powder.)

USAGE tip

Before reading this section, you may want to review coverage of appositives on pages 202–205 in Unit 9.

If the information in an appositive phrase specifically identifies the noun that precedes it, then the appositive phrase is called **essential** (or **restrictive**) and is not set off with commas. In the second example, *coriander, turmeric, and fennel* is an **essential appositive phrase**. It is necessary to identify which ingredients are fundamental to curry powder.

If the information in an appositive phrase is not necessary to identify the noun that precedes it, then the appositive phrase is called **nonessential** (or **nonrestrictive**) and is set off with commas. In first example above, *a herding dog* is a **nonessential appositive phrase.** It is not necessary to the meaning of the sentence; therefore, it is set off with commas.

Appositive phrases add variety to your writing because they can be placed at the beginning, in the middle, or at the end of a sentence. Using appositive phrases to combine sentences eliminates unimportant words and creates more fact-filled sentences. When you join two ideas with an appositive phrase, place the idea you wish to stress in the main clause and make the less important idea the appositive.

EXAMPLES

Ponce de Léon was a Spanish explorer. He set out to find the Fountain of Youth.

Ponce de Léon, **a Spanish explorer,** set out to find the Fountain of Youth.

Try It Yourself

EXERCISE 18
1. the people of the United States—we
2. the people—we
3. the white male citizens—we
4. the male citizens—we
5. the whole people—we

MODEL

EXERCISE 18

Identifying Appositive Phrases in Literature

Identify the five appositive phrases in the following literature passage. Then tell which noun or pronoun the appositive identifies.

"We, the people of the United States, in order to form a more perfect union, establish justice, insure domestic tranquillity, provide for the common defense, promote the general welfare, and secure the blessings of liberty to ourselves and our posterity, do ordain and establish this Constitution for the United States of America."

It was we, the people; not we, the white male citizens; nor yet we, the male citizens; but we, the whole people, who formed the Union.

from "Woman's Right to Suffrage"
Susan B. Anthony

EXERCISE 19

Identifying Appositive Phrases

Write the appositive phrases you find in the sentences below. Then tell the noun or pronoun each appositive phrase identifies.

1. Patrick Henry, a member of the Virginia House of Burgesses, gave many memorable speeches.
2. Demosthenes, an Athenian orator and diplomat, is reputed to have practiced speaking with marbles in his mouth to overcome a speech defect.
3. Susan B. Anthony, a leader of the nineteenth century women's movement in America, began her political life as an organizer of a temperance movement.
4. Anthony's motto, "Failure is impossible," reveals her iron will.
5. Mary Rose Oakar, a representative from Ohio, introduced a bill providing for the portrait of Susan B. Anthony on a silver dollar.
6. Sojourner Truth, a former slave, stunned the audience at the 1851 Women's Rights Convention with her powerful oratory.
7. Sojourner Truth's speech, "Ain't I a Woman?," used a brilliant mixture of colloquial language, direct questions, and emotional exclamations to sway listeners.
8. With the profits from her autobiography, *Narrative of Sojourner Truth: A Northern Slave*, the former Isabella Baumfree bought herself a home and supported herself.
9. Dr. Martin Luther King, Jr., a minister and leader of the Civil Rights movement, is considered one of the greatest speakers of recent decades.
10. Dr. King's voice, a deep and expressive instrument, was the perfect vehicle with which to deliver his stirring sentiments.

EXERCISE 19

1. a member of the Virginia House of Burgesses—Patrick Henry
2. an Athenian orator and diplomat—Demosthenes
3. a leader of the nineteenth century women's movement in America—Susan B. Anthony
4. "Failure is impossible"—motto
5. a representative from Ohio—Mary Rose Oakar
6. a former slave—Sojourner Truth
7. "Ain't I a Woman?"—speech
8. *Narrative of Sojourner Truth: A Northern Slave*—autobiography
9. a minister and leader of the Civil Rights movement—Dr. Martin Luther King, Jr.
10. a deep and expressive instrument—voice

EXERCISE 20
Responses will vary. Sample responses:
1. The bush baby, a nocturnal animal, has enormous eyes.
2. Many burrowing animals live on prairies or pampas, types of grassland.
3. Mole-rats feed on roots, bulbs, and tubers, underground plant parts.
4. Moles, solitary creatures, chase away any strangers that come into their burrows.
5. Bears are classified as carnivores, meat-eaters, but they also consume nonmeat products such as fruits and berries.
6. Mice, defenseless creatures, produce many young to replace those that are killed.
7. A stoat turns white in winter for camouflage, a method of blending in with surroundings.
8. The bat, a flying mammal, uses sound waves to figure out where it is going at night.
9. The Borneo bat, a mammal with a face like a fox, eats fruit.
10. The leaf-nosed bat, a hideous creature, has huge, curving fangs and a big, pointy snout.

EXERCISE 21
Responses will vary. Students' letters should outline an itinerary and explain or define the relevant concepts, vocabulary, and background. Check that students have punctuated their five essential and nonessential appositive clauses correctly.

EXERCISE 20
Understanding Appositive Phrases

Combine each pair of sentences with an appositive or an appositive phrase.

1. The bush baby is a nocturnal animal. The bush baby has enormous eyes.
2. Many burrowing animals live on prairies or pampas. Prairies and pampas are types of grassland.
3. Mole-rats feed on roots, bulbs, and tubers. Roots, bulbs, and tubers are underground plant parts.
4. Moles are solitary creatures. Moles chase away any strangers that come into their burrows.
5. A carnivore is a meat-eater. Bears are classified as carnivores, but they also consume nonmeat products such as fruits and berries.
6. Mice are defenseless creatures. Mice produce many young to replace those that are killed.
7. A stoat turns white in winter for camouflage. Camouflage is a method of blending in with surroundings.
8. The bat is a flying mammal. The bat uses sound waves to figure out where it is going at night.
9. The Borneo bat is a mammal with a face like a fox. The Borneo bat eats fruit.
10. The leaf-nosed bat has huge, curving fangs and a big, pointy snout. The leaf-nosed bat is a hideous creature.

EXERCISE 21
Using Appositives in Your Writing

Write a letter to an imaginary friend who lives in another country. Imagine that your friend speaks English but has a fairly limited vocabulary. Prepare your friend for a visit to the United States by describing the places you will take him or her and some of the phenomena she or he will observe while here. Use appositives to define or explain the things you describe. Include at least five appositive phrases in your letter.

CLAUSES WITHIN A SENTENCE

A **clause** is a group of words that contains a subject and verb and that functions as one part of speech—an adjective, an adverb, or a noun. There are two types of clauses—independent and subordinate.

An **independent clause,** sometimes called a *main clause*, has a subject and a verb and expresses a complete thought. Since it can stand alone as a sentence, it is called *independent.*

EXAMPLE
The calcium in milk helps to build strong teeth and bones.

A **subordinate clause** has a subject and a verb, but it doesn't express a complete thought. Unable to stand alone, it must be attached to or inserted into an independent clause. That's why subordinate clauses are also called *dependent clauses.* When you combine subordinate clauses with independent clauses, you form complete sentences.

EXAMPLES
Because the calcium in milk can help to build strong teeth and bones, physicians recommend that most young people include dairy products in their daily diet. (The subordinate clause *because the calcium in milk can help to build strong teeth and bones* is attached to an independent clause.)

The cheese **that I like best** comes from Caerphilly, Wales. (The subordinate clause *that I like best* is inserted into the independent clause *The cheese comes from Caerphilly, Wales.*)

Try It Yourself

EXERCISE 22

Identifying Independent and Subordinate Clauses in Literature

Write the independent and subordinate clauses you find in the following passage.

EXERCISE 22

1. *My brother, Caleb, was seventeen*—independent clause
2. *when I was ten*—subordinate clause
3. *We were very good friends*—independent clause
4. *In fact, he was my best friend and, for a very long time, my only friend*—independent clause
5. *I do not mean to say*—independent clause
6. *that he was always nice to me*—subordinate clause
7. *I got on his nerves a lot*—independent clause
8. *he resented having to take me around with him and be responsible for me*—independent clause
9. *when there were so many other things he wanted to be doing*—subordinate clause
10. *[that] he wanted to be doing*—subordinate clause
11. *his hand was often up against the side of my head*—independent clause
12. *my tears caused him to be punished many times*—independent clause

Literature MODEL

EXERCISE 23
Resonses may vary slightly.
Sample responses:
1. Subordinate—*We will continue to skate every day as long as the pond is frozen.*
2. Independent
3. Subordinate—*Millie turned down the radio and crept closer to the door so that she could hear the conversation better.*
4. Subordinate—*It's hard to believe that that prize-winning dog is a collie that had been rescued from a shelter.*
5. Independent
6. Subordinate—*Cranberries that are grown in Massachusetts are shipped nationwide in time for Thanksgiving.*
7. Subordinate—*Please don't emerge from the shelter until you are absolutely sure it's safe.*
8. Subordinate—*The younger players conferred on the bench while the first string took to the field.*
9. Independent
10. Independent

My brother, Caleb, was seventeen when I was ten. We were very good friends. In fact, he was my best friend and, for a very long time, my only friend.

I do not mean to say that he was always nice to me. I got on his nerves a lot, and he resented having to take me around with him and be responsible for me when there were so many other things he wanted to be doing. Therefore, his hand was often up against the side of my head, and my tears caused him to be punished many times.

from *Tell Me How Long the Train's Been Gone*
James Baldwin

EXERCISE 23

Understanding Independent and Subordinate Clauses

Label the following clauses as independent or subordinate. Then rewrite the subordinate clauses so that they are attached to or inserted into an independent clause.

1. as long as the pond is frozen
2. some oil was spilled on the floor
3. so that she could hear the conversation better
4. that had been rescued from a shelter
5. hail pitted the hood and the roof of the car
6. that are grown in Massachusetts
7. until you are absolutely sure
8. while the first string took to the field
9. sparrows chirped
10. Danelle wasn't there

ADJECTIVE CLAUSES

There are three types of subordinate clauses: adjective clauses, adverb clauses, and noun clauses.

An **adjective clause** is a subordinate clause that functions as an adjective. It modifies a noun or pronoun. Adjective clauses are introduced most frequently with words like the following: *that*, *which*, *who*, *whom*, *whose*, *after*, *before*, *since*, *than*, *when*, *why*, and *where*. An adjective clause follows the word it modifies.

EXAMPLES

The pink shirt **that is hanging on the line** belongs to Cecil.

Kyla is the girl **who once spilled tea on her homework and hung it on the clothesline to dry.**

When an adjective clause is essential to the meaning of a sentence, it should not be set off from the rest of the sentence with commas. When an adjective clause is nonessential, it is set off with commas.

EXAMPLES

essential	I prefer peanut butter **that is unsalted and chunky.**
	The lead singer is the girl **who has a pink Mohawk and black glasses.**
nonessential	Darjeeling, **which is a tea from India,** is brewing in the silver teapot.
	Mollie, **who has never been very dependable,** forgot to pick me up in time for the tennis match.

EXERCISE 24
For many days after the incident, the young man avoided the window that looked into Doctor Rappacini's garden, as if something ugly and monstrous would have

Literature MODEL

blasted his eyesight, had he been betrayed into a glance. He felt conscious of having put himself, to a certain extent, within the influence of an unintelligible power, by the communication which he had opened with Beatrice. The wisest course would have been, if his heart were in any real danger, to quit his lodgings and Padua itself, at once; the next wiser, to have accustomed himself, as far as possible, to the familiar and day-light view of Beatrice; thus bringing her rigidly and systematically within the limits of ordinary experience. Least of all, while avoiding her sight, should Giovanni have remained so near this extraordinary being, that the proximity and possibility even of intercourse, should give a kind of substance and reality to the wild vagaries which his imagination ran riot continually in producing. Guasconti had not a deep heart—or at all events, its depths were not sounded now—but he had a quick fancy, and an ardent southern temperament, which rose every instant to a higher fever-pitch.

Try It Yourself

EXERCISE 24

Identifying Adjective Clauses in Literature

Write the four adjective clauses in the following excerpt.

> For many days after the incident, the young man avoided the window that looked into Doctor Rappaccini's garden, as if something ugly and monstrous would have blasted his eyesight, had he been betrayed into a glance. He felt conscious of having put himself, to a certain extent, within the influence of an unintelligible power, by the communication which he had opened with Beatrice. The wisest course would have been, if his heart were in any real danger, to quit his lodgings and Padua itself, at once; the next wiser, to have accustomed himself, as far as possible, to the familiar and day-light view of Beatrice; thus bringing her rigidly and systematically within the limits of ordinary experience. Least of all, while avoiding her sight, should Giovanni have remained so near this extraordinary being, that the proximity and possibility even of intercourse, should give a kind of substance and reality to the wild vagaries which his imagination ran riot continually in producing. Guasconti had not a deep heart—or at all events, its depths were not sounded now—but he had a quick fancy, and an ardent southern temperament, which rose every instant to a higher fever-pitch.

from "Rappaccini's Daughter"
Nathaniel Hawthorne

EXERCISE 25

Correcting Adjective Clauses

Correct the punctuation of the adjective clauses in the following sentences. If a sentence has no punctuation errors, write *correct.*

1. Jean-Baptiste whose family comes from Haiti won a scholarship to art college.
2. Return those rotten blueberries to the fruit stand, where you bought them.
3. The months before my sister's wedding were full of hysterical scenes that embarrassed me.
4. My locket, which I inherited from my grandmother, contains a photograph of my great-grandparents in Hungary.
5. Dad is going to have to complain about the dog, that starts barking each morning at five.
6. Is that the telephone that starts buzzing and clicking, whenever you're in the middle of an important conversation?
7. The reason why Michelle is angry with Debbie remains a mystery to most of her friends.
8. The teacher whom everyone will miss when he retires is Mr. Garibaldi.
9. In the middle of the commercial strip, where all the car dealerships are located, looms a solitary Victorian mansion.
10. The microwave oven, which was invented in 1947, has drastically altered people's cooking habits.

EXERCISE 25

1. Jean-Baptiste, whose family comes from Haiti, won a scholarship to art college.
2. Return those rotten blueberries to the fruit stand where you bought them.
3. correct
4. correct
5. Dad is going to have to complain about the dog that starts barking each morning at five.
6. Is that the telephone that starts buzzing and clicking whenever you're in the middle of an important conversation?
7. correct
8. correct
9. In the middle of the commercial strip where all the car dealerships are located looms a solitary Victorian mansion.
10. correct

EXERCISE 26

Using Adjective Clauses in Your Writing

Write a proposal for the creation of a theme park or amusement park in your community. Let your imagination run wild as you invent rides, displays, and food courts for your new park. Describe this place in detail, using at least five essential or nonessential adjective clauses.

EXERCISE 26

Responses will vary. Students' proposals should be imaginative and coherent (but not necessarily realistic). Their essential and nonessential adjective clauses should be correctly punctuated.

ADVERB CLAUSES

An **adverb clause** is a subordinate clause that functions as an adverb. It modifies a verb, an adjective, or another adverb.

EXAMPLES
The dog barks **whenever the emergency siren goes off.** (*Whenever the emergency siren goes off* tells when the dog barks. The clause modifies the verb *barks.*)

Bettina is more philosophical **than the average high school student is.** (*Than the average high school student is* modifies the adverb *more.*)

Cal reacts quickly *when the hockey puck slides toward him.* (*When the hockey puck slides toward him* modifies the adverb *quickly.*)

When you use an adverb clause at the beginning of a sentence, follow it with a comma. If you use an adverb clause at the end of a sentence, you do not need to use a comma before it.

EXAMPLES
While the baby naps, the mother frantically does her aerobic routine in front of the TV.

The mother frantically does her aerobic routine in front of the TV while the baby naps.

Adverb clauses often, but not always, start with a subordinating conjunction such as *after, although, because, before, if, so that, unless, when, whether,* and *while.*

USAGE tip

You may want to review the section on subordinating conjunctions on pages 243–246 in Unit 10.

Try It Yourself

EXERCISE 27
Identifying Adverb Clauses in Literature
Identify the four adverb clauses in the following passage.

EXERCISE 27
As Mrs. Nakamura stood watching her neighbor, everything flashed whiter than any white she had ever seen. She did not notice what happened to the man next door; the reflex of a mother set her in motion toward her children. She had taken a single step (the house was 1,350 yards, or three-quarters of a mile, from the explosion) when something picked her up and she seemed to fly into the next room over the raised sleeping platform, pursued by parts of her house.

Timbers fell around her as she landed, and a shower of tiles pommelled her; everything became dark, for she was buried. The debris did not cover her deeply. She rose up and freed herself. She heard a child cry, "Mother help me!," and saw her youngest—Myeko, the five-year-old—buried up to her breast and unable to move. As Mrs. Nakamura started frantically to claw her way toward the baby, she could see or hear nothing of her other children.

As Mrs. Nakamura stood watching her neighbor, everything flashed whiter than any white she had ever seen. She did not notice what happened to the man next door; the reflex of a mother set her in motion toward her children. She had taken a single step (the house was 1,350 yards, or three-quarters of a mile, from the center of the explosion) when something picked her up and she seemed to fly into the next room over the raised sleeping platform, pursued by parts of her house.

Timbers fell around her as she landed, and a shower of tiles pommelled her; everything became dark, for she was buried. The debris did not cover her deeply. She rose up and freed herself. She heard a child cry, "Mother help me!," and saw her youngest—Myeko, the five-year-old—buried up to her breast and unable to move. As Mrs. Nakamura started frantically to claw her way toward the baby, she could see or hear nothing of her other children.

from *Hiroshima*, "A Noiseless Flash"
John Hersey

EXERCISE 28
Responses will vary. Sample responses:

1. Rodney feels sad each year until the robins return.
2. Since the king disappeared, various factions have been fighting for control of the government.
3. After the curtain fell, the actors scuttled around like cockroaches when you turned on a light.
4. As the vase crashed to the floor, the dog shot out of the room.
5. The kicker of the winning goal circled the field while the fans roared with delight.
6. An unearthly silence settled over the racecourse just before before the racecars started their engines.
7. The president has vowed to take action whether or not the legislation passes.
8. Everyone heads for the fairgrounds when the carnival comes to town.
9. If someone has just accidentally locked the keys in the car, check to make sure there are no children or pets at risk inside.
10. As long as the team keeps winning, this store will keep on selling T-shirts with the team's logo.

EXERCISE 28

Understanding Adverb Clauses

Write an independent clause to attach to each of the following adverb clauses. When you write out the complete sentences, be sure to punctuate the adverb clauses correctly.

1. until the robins return
2. since the king disappeared
3. after the curtain fell
4. as the vase crashed to the floor
5. while the fans roared with delight
6. before the racecars started their engines
7. whether or not the legislation passes
8. when the carnival comes to town
9. if someone has just accidentally locked the keys in the car
10. as long as the team keeps winning

EXERCISE 29

Responses will vary. Students should provide an explanation of skills and attitudes necessary to play the sport and the conditions that influence outcomes. Students should create sentence variety by placing their adverb clauses at the beginning or end of their sentences. Check to be sure that they have punctuated them correctly.

EXERCISE 29

Using Adverb Clauses in Your Writing

Interview someone at your school who plays a sport. Ask questions about what skills are necessary to succeed in the sport, what attitudes are helpful or unhelpful to the athlete, and what conditions (environmental, psychological, nutritional, and so on) influence the outcome of a game. Then write a summary of what you learned from the interview, using adverb clauses to help your peer readers understand the sport from the athlete's point of view.

NOUN CLAUSES

A **noun clause** is a subordinate clause that functions as a noun. This means that it can function as a subject, predicate nominative, direct object, indirect object, object of a preposition, or appositive. Notice that noun clauses can have modifiers and complements. They can come at the beginning, middle, or end of a sentence.

Words like these often introduce noun clauses: *how*, *if*, *that*, *what*, *whatever*, *when*, *where*, *whether*, *which*, *who*, *whoever*, *whom*, *whose*, and *why*.

EXAMPLES

subject	**How the boot ended up on the roof** is the question.
predicate nominative	That is **why I am so enraged!**
direct object	The hunter never revealed **where he had discovered the nest.**
indirect object	Ask **whomever was in the vicinity** if they heard mysterious noises.
object of the preposition	Uzma wandered into **what turned out to be trouble.**
appositive	Clare's secret fear, **that her asthma would keep her from playing college soccer,** turned out to be unfounded.

Too many noun clauses can make your writing sound wordy and overly formal, especially when the noun clauses are used as subjects.

EXAMPLES

Whoever hopes to become a true leader must learn to listen as well as give orders.

A true leader must learn to listen as well as give orders.

Try It Yourself

EXERCISE 30

Identifying Noun Clauses in Literature

Write the four noun clauses you find in the literature passage below. Beside each, identify its function in the sentence.

> When in the course of human events, it becomes necessary for one people to dissolve the political bonds which have connected them with another; and to assume, among the powers of the earth, the separate and equal station to which the laws of nature and of nature's God entitle them, a decent respect to the opinions of mankind requires that they should declare the causes which impel them to the separation.
>
> We hold these truths to be self-evident:—that all men are created equal; that they are endowed by their Creator with certain inalienable rights; that among these are life, liberty, and the pursuit of happiness.
>
> from Declaration of Independence
> Thomas Jefferson

EXERCISE 31

Understanding Noun Clauses

Write a sentence using each group of words below as a noun clause. Check your work to be sure that you have written a noun clause, not an adjective or adverb clause.

EXERCISE 30

1. *that they should declare the causes which impel them to the separation*—direct object
2. *that all men are created equal*—appositive
3. *that they are endowed by their Creator with certain inalienable rights*—appositive
4. *that among these are life, liberty, and the pursuit of happiness*—appositive

EXERCISE 31

Responses will vary. Sample responses:

1. The historical novel imagines how the Mongols overran Baghdad in 1258.
2. Why there was salad dressing on top of the ice cream is the question of the day in our house.
3. The magazine's article about how the ceramics were glazed was full of errors.
4. That we didn't realize there was a hole in the tent amused Dad.

5. The Centers for Disease Control and Prevention's main concern, where the epidemic originated, will be discussed on the talk show.
6. Where the Connecticut River enters Long Island Sound is one of the world's most unusual estuaries.
7. That the player repeatedly slam-dunked the ball was the topic of the lead article.
8. Until I saw that documentary, I didn't know how small the baby kangaroo is at birth.
9. The big mystery, why the actor retired at the top of her career, was the subject of the interview.
10. Gwen wants to know when her parents will return home from their trip.

EXERCISE 32
Responses will vary. The students' summaries should be succinct and should contain cogent details. Students should use at least four noun clauses appropriately so that they express their ideas as directly as possible.

1. how the Mongols overran Baghdad in 1258
2. why there was salad dressing on top of the ice cream
3. how the ceramics were glazed
4. that we didn't realize there was a hole in the tent
5. where the epidemic originated
6. where the Connecticut River enters Long Island Sound
7. that the player repeatedly slam-dunked the ball
8. how small the baby kangaroo is at birth
9. why the actor retired at the top of her career
10. when her parents will return

EXERCISE 32

Using Noun Clauses in Your Writing

Choose a current event. Look up several articles about the event online or in current newspapers or magazines. Take notes about the aspects of the event that you find most significant, and then write a news summary for your classmates. Use at least four noun clauses in your summary, and underline each one.

THE CLAUSES OF A SENTENCE: SIMPLE, COMPOUND, COMPLEX, AND COMPOUND-COMPLEX

Sentences are classified according to the number and kind of clauses they contain. Four types of sentence structures are *simple*, *compound*, *complex*, and *compound-complex*.

A **simple sentence** contains one independent clause and no subordinate clauses. It may have any number of phrases. It may also have a compound subject and a compound verb. A simple sentence is sometimes called an independent clause because it can stand by itself.

EXAMPLES

An opal is easily cracked.

The opal, a semiprecious stone, often includes swirls of different colors.

The jewelry store displayed opal rings, earrings, and pendants.

A **compound sentence** consists of two or more independent clauses that are joined together with a comma and a coordinating conjunction (*and*, *but*, *or*, *nor*, *for*, *yet*, or *so*).

EXAMPLES

Fulco di Verdura used brightly colored gemstones, **and** he created designs that were both classic and flamboyant.

Both topazes and citrines are yellow stones used in jewelry, **but** citrines are usually less expensive.

A **complex sentence** consists of one independent clause and one or more subordinate clauses. In the following examples, the subordinate clauses are italicized.

EXAMPLES

Before you buy something in an antique store, examine it carefully for repairs.

Read the Lovejoy mysteries *if you want to learn how many "antiques" are faked.*

A **compound-complex sentence** consists of two or more independent clauses and one or more subordinate clauses. In the following examples, the independent clauses are italicized.

EXAMPLES

Many immigrants came to the United States for economic reasons, but *the Covenanters,* who were persecuted in Scotland for religious reasons, *immigrated because of their principles.*

Because they were Catholic, *many Irish immigrants to America were discriminated against,* and *they had to take the most poorly paid and menial jobs to survive.*

EXERCISE 33

1. *I tried to relax; the chair was beautiful but hard—*compound
2. *Where had the man gone—*simple

Literature MODEL

3. *Had he shown any antagonism when he saw me—*complex
4. *I was annoyed that I had failed to see him first—*complex
5. *One had to watch such details—*simple
6. *Suddenly there came a harsh cry from the cage, and once more I saw a mad flashing as though the birds had burst into spontaneous flame, fluttering and beating their wings maliciously against the bamboo bars, only to settle down just as suddenly when the door opened and the blond man stood beckoning, his had upon the knob—*compound-complex
7. *I went over, tense inside me—*simple
8. *Had I been accepted or rejected—*simple

EXERCISE 34

Responses will vary.

Try It Yourself

EXERCISE 33

Identifying Sentence Structures in Literature

Identify each sentence in the literature passage below as *simple*, *compound*, *complex*, or *compound-complex*.

> I tried to relax; the chair was beautiful but hard. Where had the man gone? Had he shown any antagonism when he saw me? I was annoyed that I had failed to see him first. One had to watch such details. Suddenly there came a harsh cry from the cage, and once more I saw a mad flashing as though the birds had burst into spontaneous flame, fluttering and beating their wings maliciously against the bamboo bars, only to settle down just as suddenly when the door opened and the blond man stood beckoning, his hand upon the knob. I went over, tense inside me. Had I been accepted or rejected?

from *Invisible Man*
Ralph Ellison

EXERCISE 34

Understanding How to Use Clauses to Create Different Sentence Structures

Expand each of the following simple sentences into a compound, complex, or compound-complex sentence by adding subordinate clauses and/or independent clauses. Label each sentence type that you create.

1. Most people have a secret dream.
2. Some people expect to fulfill their fantasies.
3. Daydreams of wild success can release frustration.
4. Psychologists study dreams and fantasies.
5. Not all daydreams are positive.
6. People's aspirations reflect their culture.
7. Singing karaoke is a kind of wish fulfillment.
8. Young children often pretend.
9. Do you ever dream?
10. The astronaut had always dreamed of going into outer space.

EXERCISE 35

Using Different Sentence Structures in Your Writing

In a journal entry, analyze an inner conflict that you have experienced yourself or that you have observed others struggle with. One example might be the desire to be one of the crowd while at the same time experiencing the contrary wish to stand out as special and unusual in some way. In your analysis, use a variety of sentence structures—simple, compound, complex, and compound-complex.

EXERCISE 35
Responses will vary. In addition to identifying an inner conflict, the student should analyze it in some way, such as by explaining its roots. Check to see if students have used all four sentence structures and have achieved sentence variety.

UNIT 12 REVIEW

TEST YOUR KNOWLEDGE

EXERCISE 1
1. AB, PREP, INF
2. GER, PREP
3. APP, PART
4. PART, PREP
5. GER, APP
6. GER, APP, PREP, PREP
7. AB, PART, INF
8. PART, INF, GER
9. GER, PART
10. APP, PREP

EXERCISE 1

Identifying Phrases

Identify each underlined phrase by writing one of these abbreviations. (10 points)

PREP = prepositional phrase
PART = participial phrase
GER = gerund phrase
INF = infinitive phrase
APP = appositive phrase
AB = absolute phrase

EXAMPLE

Couscous, a North African dish made from semolina, is very popular in France. (APP)

1. Proof of identity in his hand, Josh arrived at the Department of Motor Vehicles to get his learner's permit.
2. Drumming loudly is the way Derek gets rid of his aggressions.
3. *Tosca*, a melodramatic opera by Giacomo Puccini, will be performed for two weeks, beginning the third of June.
4. Tattered by the wind, the kite hung in the oak tree.
5. Since visiting her cousins in Tennessee, Melissa plans to go to Vanderbilt, a college in that state.
6. Howling is a way that wolves, social animals, communicate with each other across long distances.
7. One paw held up off the ground, the wounded fox tried to make its way to safety.
8. With arms linked solidly together, the demonstrators formed a circle to keep workers from entering Town Hall.
9. Mom got credit for making the applesauce, but it was I who spent hours peeling the apples.
10. Adrian, the tallest student in eleventh grade, experienced an enormous growth spurt over the summer.

EXERCISE 2
Identifying Independent and Subordinate Clauses

Label each numbered item below by writing *I* for independent clause and *S* for subordinate clause. (10 points)

EXAMPLE
Some people explored unknown territory. (I)

1. who hoped to discover great riches
2. because they were persecuted in their home countries
3. the risk of death was extraordinarily high during the early voyages
4. when relying on verbal descriptions of coastlines and channels
5. Marco Polo grew rich because of his friendship with the Chinese emperor
6. ever since the Phoenicians founded colonies in what is now Tunisia
7. when sailing ships were becalmed on a windless ocean
8. Leif Ericson, a Viking, probably landed in the New World long before Columbus
9. who traveled around the Pacific in dugout canoes
10. if you seek the thrill of exploration today

EXERCISE 2
1. S
2. S
3. I
4. S
5. I
6. S
7. S
8. I
9. S
10. S

EXERCISE 3
Identifying Types of Clauses

Identify the underlined clauses in each sentence by writing *ADJ* for an adjective clause, *ADV* for an adverb clause, and *N* for a noun clause. (10 points)

EXAMPLE
The new shade of lipstick, which is called "Bizarre," is selling like crazy. (ADJ)

1. My parents won't let me buy a used car until I demonstrate that I can pay for the extra insurance and other costs.
2. If the river rises over the levee, thousands of city inhabitants will have to be evacuated.

EXERCISE 3
1. ADV, N
2. ADV

3. N
4. N
5. ADV
6. N
7. ADJ
8. ADJ
9. ADJ
10. N

3. Tell <u>whomever you encounter</u> that there is a going-out-of-business sale at the sporting goods store.
4. Rachel's greatest achievement, <u>that she was voted captain of the volleyball team</u>, has unfortunately threatened her friendship with Neisja.
5. Felicia kept bursting into laughter <u>as she tried to repeat the ridiculous story</u>.
6. <u>Why Marcus and Danielle broke up</u> is the burning question these days.
7. The year <u>since our dog died</u> has passed slowly and sadly, but we are starting to recover.
8. Joe loves the Indian restaurant <u>that is on 57th Street</u>.
9. Did the person <u>who called in the fake alarm</u> ever get caught by the police?
10. <u>How families can learn better communication skills</u> is the subject of the public television series.

EXERCISE 4
1. CD
2. CD-CX
3. S
4. CX
5. CD-CX
6. CX
7. CD
8. CX
9. S
10. CD

EXERCISE 4

Identifying Sentence Structure

Identify each of the following sentences as *S* for simple, *CD* for compound, *CX* for complex, and *CD-CX* for compound-complex. (10 points)

EXAMPLE
Melinda shucked the corn and washed the lettuce. (S)

1. Roger wanted the baseball game to be a surprise, but his nephews found the tickets.
2. Simone requested that her old car be painted dark green, but the painters lost the form she had filled out and they painted it red by mistake.
3. On their summer vacation, the Martins visited an alligator sanctuary in Florida, a nut museum in Connecticut, and a lighthouse in Maine.
4. As soon as Jennifer got over her sinus infection, she came down with mononucleosis.
5. When the thunderstorm hit, our cat streaked down to the basement, and our dog quivered in a corner.

6. The artist who sculpted the gigantic stone figure was Henry Moore.
7. Finland was part of Sweden for many hundreds of years, but it never lost its distinct culture.
8. Jared loves that old T-shirt even though it is faded and ripped.
9. Every morning, Justine does 100 abdominal crunches and 50 push-ups before breakfast.
10. The ferry pulled up to the dock, and all the passengers disembarked.

EXERCISE 5

Understanding Phrases

Use different kinds of phrases to combine the sentences in each numbered item. You may have to change the wording slightly so that your sentences make sense. Remember to punctuate your phrases correctly. (10 points)

EXAMPLE

Peter Dickinson writes children's books. He was born in Africa and grew up in England. *(Peter Dickinson, a writer of children's books, was born in Africa and grew up in England.)*

1. There are many kinds of folk songs. Some examples are work songs, lullabies, and love songs.
2. Venice may disappear under the waves. I dream of visiting it first.
3. Papua New Guinea gained independence in 1975. This ended a United Nations trusteeship under Australia.
4. A tsunami is caused by an undersea volcano or earthquake. Some people incorrectly call a tsunami a tidal wave.
5. John Wilkes Booth was Abraham Lincoln's assassin. John Wilkes Booth died of gunshot wounds.
6. In Norse mythology, the chief gods are the Aesir. They live in Asgard.
7. Thanksgiving is a national holiday. It is celebrated on the fourth Thursday in November. Thanksgiving became a national holiday in 1863.

EXERCISE 5

Responses will vary.

Sample responses:

1. There are many kinds of folk songs, including work songs, lullabies, and love songs.
2. To visit Venice before it disappears under the waves is my dream.
3. Papua New Guinea gained independence in 1975, ending a United Nations trusteeship under Australia.
4. A tsunami, sometimes incorrectly called a tidal wave, is caused by an undersea volcano or earthquake.
5. John Wilkes Booth, Lincoln's assassin, died of gunshot wounds.
6. In Norse mythology, the chief gods, the Aesir, lived in Asgard.
7. Thanksgiving, celebrated the fourth Thursday in November, became a national holiday in 1863.

8. In 1992, Kathryn Watt won an Olympic medal for cycling.
9. The story sells many kinds of olive oil from Spain, Italy, and Greece.
10. Currently the population is growing rapidly in India and falling in the former Soviet bloc.

EXERCISE 6
Responses will vary. Sample responses:
1. During the Middle Ages, learning declined in Europe but medicine and mathematics flourished in the Islamic world.
2. In the 1300s, the plague, which had been brought to Europe by Italian sailors, killed a third of the population.
3. The stonemasons who built the soaring cathedrals were highly respected medieval artisans.
4. In winter, when the weather was too cold to work outside, the stonemasons stayed in their lodge and designed pieces of stone.
5. A medieval foot soldier had to walk about six miles a day, and his stomach was often grumbling with hunger.

8. Kathryn Watt won an Olympic medal in 1992. Watt cycled.
9. The store sells many kinds of olive oil. The olive oil is from Spain, Italy, and Greece
10. Currently, the population is both rising and falling. The population is growing rapidly in India. It is falling in the former Soviet bloc.

EXERCISE 6
Understanding Clauses and Phrases

Use different kinds of clauses and phrases to combine the sentences in each numbered item. You may have to change the wording slightly so that your sentences make sense. Remember to punctuate your clauses correctly. (10 points)

EXAMPLE
In the fifth century, the Roman Empire collapsed. Germanic tribes from the north invaded the Roman Empire during this period. They destroyed Roman towns, and they destroyed Roman trade routes. *(In the fifth century, the Roman Empire collapsed when Germanic tribes from the north invaded, destroying Roman towns and trade routes.)*

1. Learning declined during the Middle Ages in Europe. During the Middle Ages, medicine and mathematics flourished in the Islamic world.
2. In the 1300s, the plague killed a third of Europe's population. This disease was brought to Europe from Asia by Italian sailors.
3. Stonemasons were highly respected medieval artisans. They built the soaring cathedrals.
4. In winter, the weather was too cold for stonemasons to work outside. They stayed in their lodge. They designed and marked pieces of stone.
5. A medieval foot soldier usually had to walk about six miles a day. His stomach was often grumbling with hunger.

6. An unmarried medieval woman could own property. A married medieval woman had to give all of her property to her husband.
7. Women wore thin-soled leather shoes. Sometimes the ground got very muddy. Then the women slipped wooden clogs over the leather shoes.
8. Most people in the Middle Ages slept on straw mattresses. A few wealthy people slept on feather-filled beds.
9. Common people worked for a lord. The lord protected the common people.
10. By 1400, most towns in Europe had a band of professional musicians. These musicians played in public processions and parades.

6. An unmarried medieval woman could own property, but if she married she had to give all of her property to her husband.
7. Women wore thin-soled leather shoes, but when the ground got muddy, they slipped wooden clogs over the shoes.
8. While most people in the Middle Ages slept on straw mattresses, a few wealthy people slept on feather-filled beds.
9. Common people worked for a lord, who protected them in return.
10. By 1400, most towns in Europe had a band of professional musicians who played in public processions and parades.

EXERCISE 7

Understanding How to Use Clauses to Create Different Sentence Structures

Expand each of the following sentences by adding subordinate and/or independent clauses to create compound, complex, or compound-complex sentences. Then identify the type of sentence you have written. Write at least two examples for each type of sentence structure. (20 points)

EXERCISE 7
Responses will vary.

EXAMPLE

simple sentence	Bats have a bad reputation.
complex sentence	Although bats have a bad reputation, they actually perform many helpful functions.

1. Max has decided to take swimming lessons.
2. All of the peaches had to be thrown out.
3. The attic was insulated, heated, and carpeted.
4. The helicopter flew low overhead.
5. Marie made an appointment with a physical therapist.
6. The otter slid gleefully down the muddy bank.
7. A bus was stalled in the middle of the street.
8. Francine couldn't get up this morning.
9. Deer devoured all of the new shrubs.
10. Winter jackets are on sale at Brigham's.

EXERCISE 8

Using Different Sentence Structures in Your Writing

Concepts of what constitutes appropriate adult behavior vary from one time period to another and among groups of people. What do you see as the privileges and responsibilities of adulthood? How do you think they vary from those of childhood, and why? Write a brief essay on this topic for a collection in your social studies class. Use a variety of sentence structures in your essay to maintain your peer readers' interest and to express yourself fully. (20 points)

EXERCISE 8
Responses will vary. Students should provide examples of the distinctions between adulthood and childhood. Students should use a variety of sentence structures punctuated correctly.

UNIT 13 DIAGRAMMING SENTENCES

UNIT OVERVIEW

DIAGRAMMING SENTENCES

SENTENCE DIAGRAMS

A sentence consists of different parts of speech that work together to form a complete thought. A good way to see the relationship between these parts of speech is to diagram them. A **sentence diagram** is a picture of the structure of a sentence. Using horizontal, vertical, and slanting lines, the diagram shows the role of every word and phrase in a sentence.

A few general rules apply to all sentence diagrams.

1. Start with a horizontal line. On this line you will write the sentence base.
2. In approximately the center of the line, you will draw a short vertical line cutting the horizontal one. This vertical line is the dividing point between the complete subject, which goes on the left, and the complete predicate, which goes on the right. Use this placement even if the predicate precedes the subject in the sentence, as in interrogative sentences.
3. Always capitalize the first word in the sentence.
4. Do not use sentence punctuation in the diagram.

SIMPLE SUBJECTS AND SIMPLE PREDICATES

Start with the basic diagram—a horizontal line divided approximately in the center by a vertical line. Write the simple subject to the left of the vertical line, and write the simple predicate to the right of the vertical line. Notice that the entire verb phrase is written on the horizontal line in the examples.

EXAMPLES

The crowd roared.

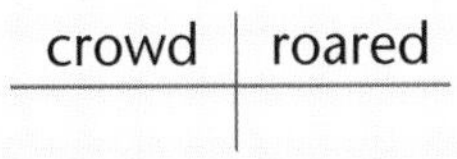

crowd | roared

Cindy had been painting.

Cindy | had been painting

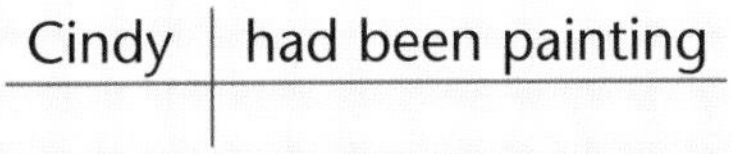

The dog yapped shrilly.

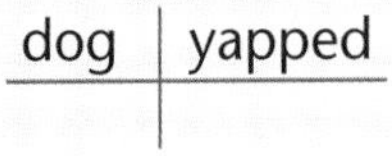

dog | yapped

Try It Yourself

EXERCISE 1

Diagramming Simple Subjects and Simple Predicates

Diagram the simple subject and simple predicate for each sentence below.

EXERCISE 1
Answers for sentence diagrams are available at www.emcp.com.

1. African violets bloomed on the windowsill.
2. Mom roasted a turkey.
3. Our dog loves cherry tomatoes.
4. Sheila met Jeremy at the corner.
5. Trees hid the house.
6. It took forever to download the software.
7. The backpack was much too heavy.
8. Breakfast is ready.
9. The symphony played outdoors.
10. No one noticed the time.

FOUR TYPES OF SENTENCES

In a sentence diagram, the order of simple subject and simple predicate is always the same, regardless of the order the words actually occur in the sentence.

Declarative and Exclamatory Sentences

EXAMPLES

The rain fell.

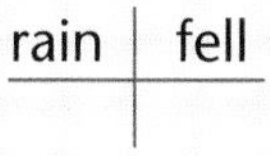

rain | fell

Josh is here!

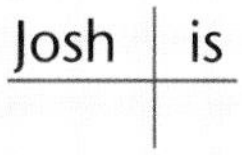

Josh | is

Interrogative Sentences

Notice that although the subject comes between the two parts of the verb phrase, it is diagrammed just like the declarative sentence.

EXAMPLES

Did the rain fall?

rain | Did fall

Is Josh here?

Josh | Is

Imperative Sentences

Notice that the simple subject is the understood *you.*

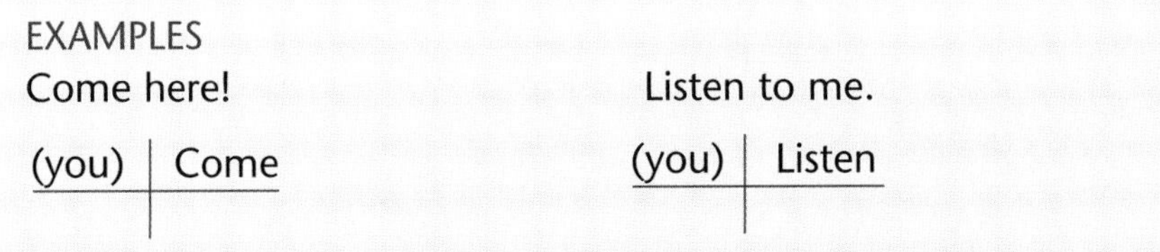

Try It Yourself

EXERCISE 2

Diagramming Four Types of Sentences

Diagram the simple subject and simple predicate for each sentence below.

EXERCISE 2
Answers for sentence diagrams are available at www.emcp.com.

1. Do I have a choice?
2. Help!
3. Everyone will be home soon.
4. That was a cheap shot!
5. Can you pick up the twins after school?
6. Cobalt Lake is the perfect name.
7. Do you enjoy riding horses?
8. Catch it!
9. Pitcher plants grow along the bog trail.
10. Don't fall in the water.

COMPOUND SUBJECTS AND COMPOUND PREDICATES

When a sentence has a compound subject or a compound verb or both, diagram them on separate horizontal lines. Write the conjunction that joins the subjects or verbs on a broken vertical line linking the horizontal lines.

EXAMPLES

compound subject

Greg and Gunther built a shed.

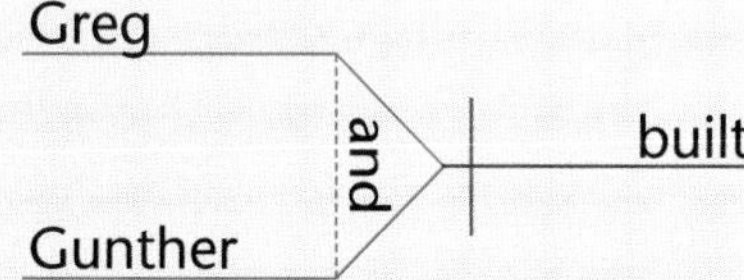

compound predicate

The air conditioner whistles and thumps.

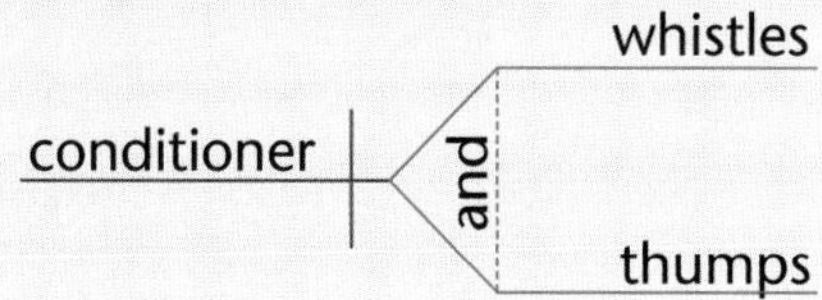

compound subject and compound predicate

Gloria and Dan cleaned the salmon and smoked it over mesquite.

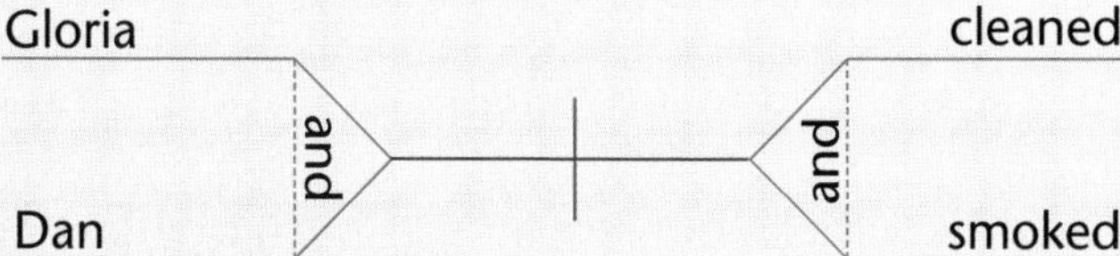

compound subject and compound predicate joined with correlative conjunction

Neither Irene nor Lynn gardens or swims.

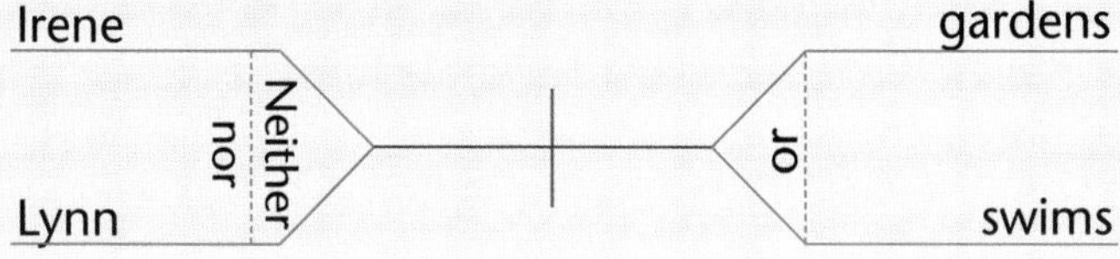

CONTINUED

Both Rick and Nelson hunt and fish.

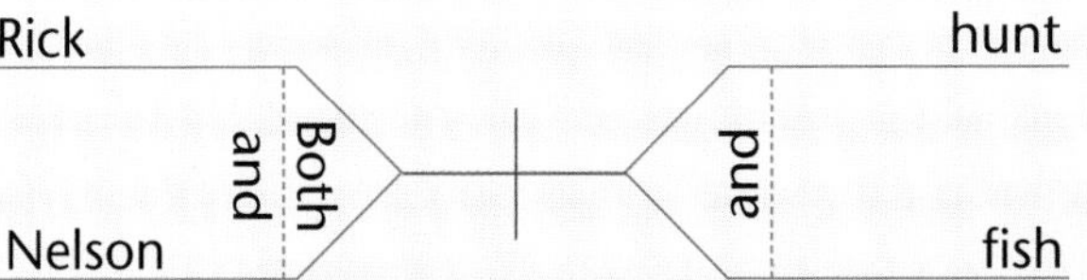

Notice how a compound verb is diagrammed when the helping verb is not repeated.

EXAMPLE

The men were chopping wood and digging a fire pit.

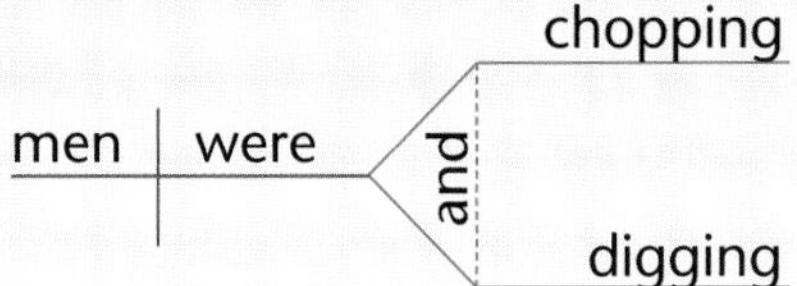

Try It Yourself

EXERCISE 3

Answers for sentence diagrams are available at www.emcp.com.

EXERCISE 3

Diagramming Compound Subjects and Compound Predicates

Diagram the compound subjects, the compound predicates, or both in the sentences below.

1. The cook lightly seasoned and pan-fried the trout.
2. Lupines and other wildflowers grew in the meadow.
3. Tall beargrass and low-growing vines can trip an unwary hiker.
4. Every brook, creek, and stream was bordered by plants and surrounded by granite boulders.
5. Both the marmots and the beavers had been busy.
6. Neither hikers nor campers were pleased with the weather.
7. Grizzly bears and black bears have killed or injured hundreds of campers.
8. Huckleberry branches rustled and shook as some animal snacked.
9. Either St. Mary's Lake or Two Medicine Lake is a good fishing spot.

10. Both the architecture of the building and its view made the trip worthwhile.

DIRECT AND INDIRECT OBJECTS

A direct object is part of the predicate and appears on the horizontal line after it. The direct object is separated from the predicate by a short vertical line. Notice that unlike the line that separates subject and predicate, the line that separates the predicate and the direct object does not extend below the horizontal line.

EXAMPLES

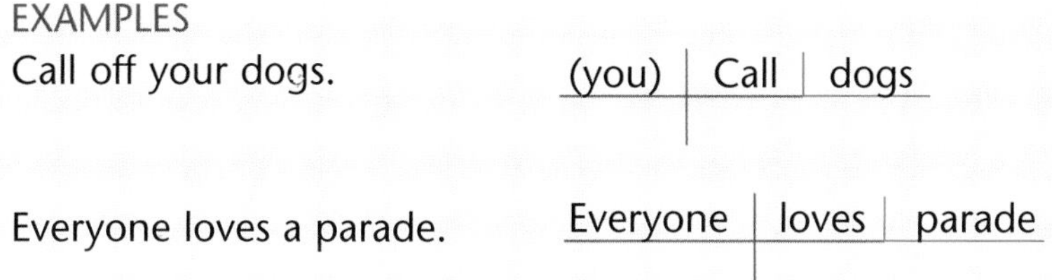

The indirect object is diagrammed on a horizontal line beneath the verb because it tells to whom or for whom the action of a verb is done. An indirect object comes before the direct object in a sentence. Connect the indirect object to the verb with a slanted line. Notice in the second example that the parts of a compound indirect object are diagrammed on horizontal parallel lines. The conjunction is placed on a broken line between them.

EXAMPLES

We sent Grandmother a rosebush for her birthday.

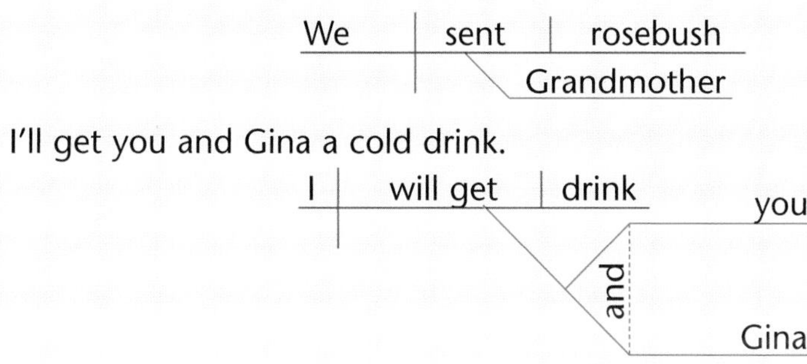

Try It Yourself

EXERCISE 4
Answers for sentence diagrams are available at www.emcp.com.

EXERCISE 4

Diagramming Direct and Indirect Objects

Diagram the direct and indirect objects in the following sentences.

1. Hobos and migrant farm workers populate the novels of John Steinbeck.
2. Californians have become devoted guardians of Steinbeck's legacy.
3. He gave us books such as *Cannery Row*, *The Grapes of Wrath*, and *Tortilla Flat*.
4. They offer people a chance to understand the depression.
5. Steinbeck conveys a love of those he called "the gathered and the scattered."
6. His graphic portrayal of landowners' cruelties brought him death threats and an FBI investigation.
7. Steinbeck won the Nobel Prize for literature in 1962.
8. A collector is displaying posters from the more than thirty films made from Steinbeck's works.
9. Steinbeck's understanding of the average human being transcends national boundaries.
10. He gives his readers simple, direct portraits of people from the inside out.

ADJECTIVES AND ADVERBS

In a sentence diagram an adjective is written on a slanting line below the noun or pronoun it modifies. When more than one adjective modifies a word, each is written on its own line. The articles *a*, *an*, and *the* and possessive pronouns such as *her* and *their* are also diagrammed in this way. Notice that a conjunction joining two adjectives is placed on a broken line between them.

EXAMPLES

Irregular flagstones curved invitingly through a rose arbor.

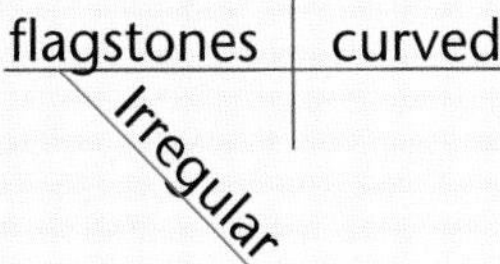

The elegant black dog wore his plaid coat and matching boots proudly.

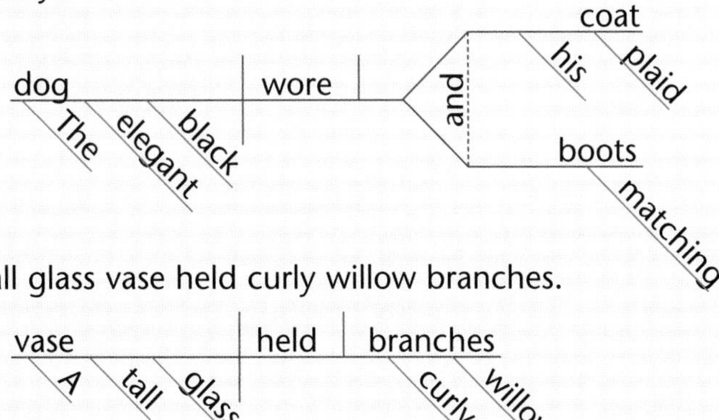

A tall glass vase held curly willow branches.

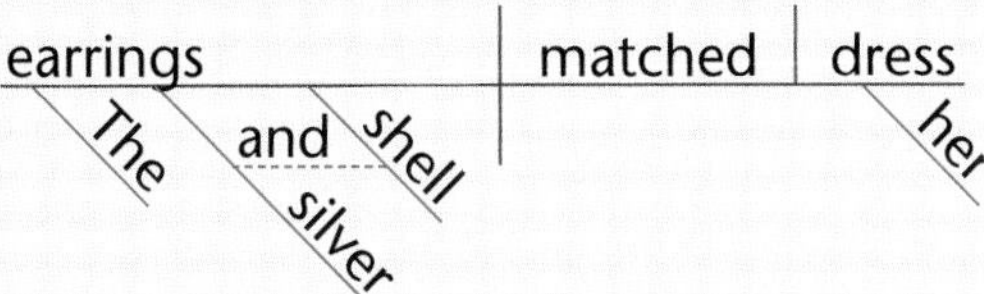

The silver and shell earrings matched her dress perfectly.

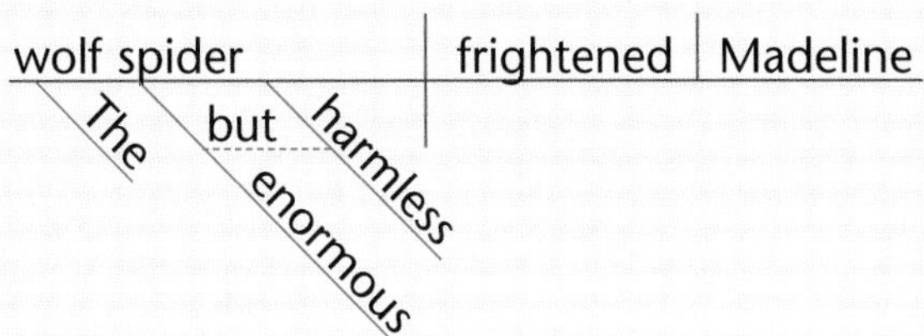

The enormous but harmless wolf spider frightened Madeline.

wolf spider | frightened | Madeline

The | but | harmless | enormous

Adverbs are also diagrammed on slanting lines. An adverb modifying a verb is placed below the verb. An adverb modifying an adjective or an adverb is placed on a slanting line attached to the word that is being modified. Notice that *not* and *never* are diagrammed as adverbs modifying the verbs with which they are used.

EXAMPLES

The audience applauded wildly.

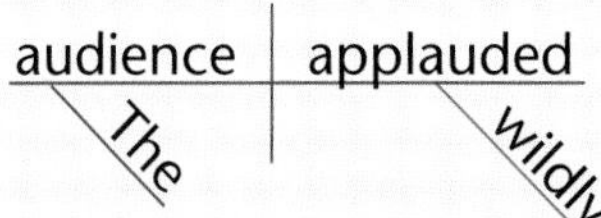

Calli's allergies did not bother her much.

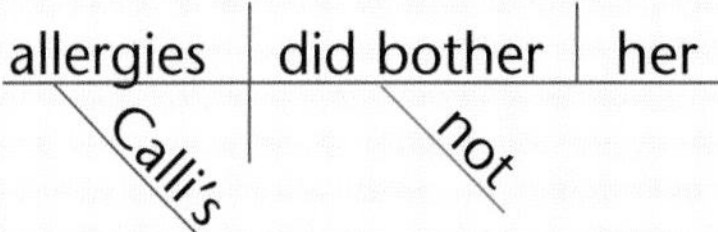

The architect drew a fairly rough sketch of the house he had in mind.

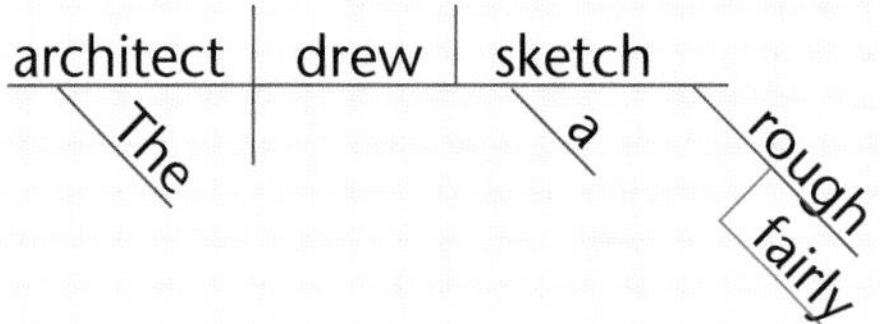

Food poisoning can nearly always be avoided.

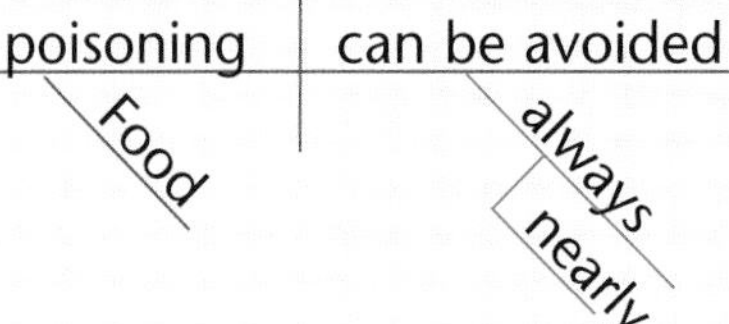

Try It Yourself

EXERCISE 5

EXERCISE 5
Answers for sentence diagrams are available at www.emcp.com.

Diagramming Adjectives and Adverbs

Diagram the adjectives and adverbs in the following sentences.

1. The vast tidal marshes of the United States have long provided sources of nourishment and a refuge to seafood and wildlife.
2. Nutrients in seawater are swished twice daily through the marshes by tides.
3. Snails need a fairly constant water level throughout the year.

4. Periwinkle snails can turn the world's most productive grassland to bare mud in as few as eight months.
5. The blue crabs that eat the snails have recently been overfished.
6. Higher densities of snails mean a faster destruction of marsh grass.
7. Rising global sea levels are also clearly influencing marsh disappearance.
8. Sea level rise might better explain the marsh losses.
9. Swallows, starlings, and other songbirds frequently use the marsh grass as overnight roosts.
10. Ultimately, scientists may discover ways to protect the marshes.

PREPOSITIONAL PHRASES

To diagram a prepositional phrase, draw a slanted line below the word that the phrase modifies. From the bottom of that line, draw a line parallel to the base line. Write the preposition on the slanted line and its object on the horizontal line. Write any words that modify the object of the preposition on slanted lines below the object.

EXAMPLES

Peregrine chicks were born in a nest box high above the clatter of New York traffic.

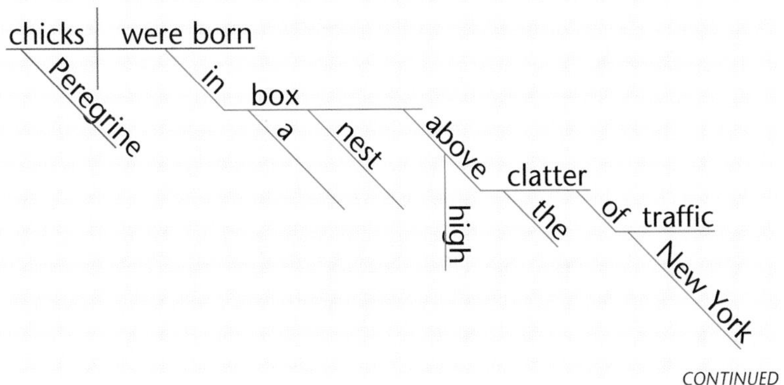

CONTINUED

The number of urban raptors has grown in recent years.

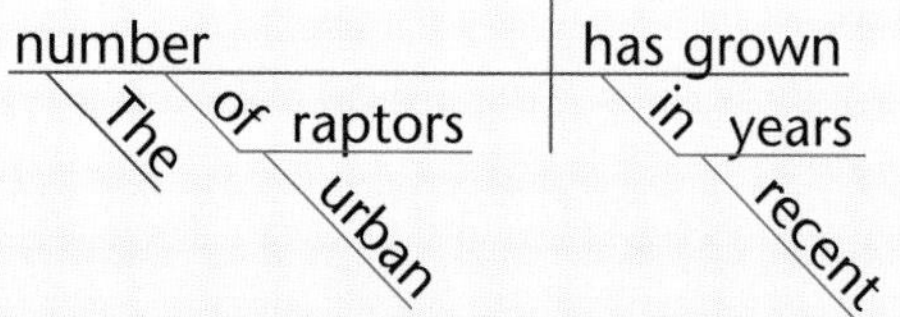

Try It Yourself

EXERCISE 6

Diagramming Prepositional Phrases

Diagram the prepositional phrases in each of the following sentences.

EXERCISE 6
Answers for sentence diagrams are available at www.emcp.com.

1. In 1995, residents of San Juan Capistrano worried about the return of the cliff swallows.
2. For centuries the birds had built their nests in crevices in the roofs of the old mission buildings.
3. The missions had been rebuilt against earthquake damage.
4. Many of the swallows' mud nests had been knocked down or replaced by towering steel beams and concrete.
5. Father Junipero Serra welcomed the birds to the mission over two centuries ago.
6. The swallows had returned to their same nests on March 19.
7. Children were let out of school for the occasion.
8. Volunteers created mud puddles as collection spots for new nests.
9. They also put insects in the shrubbery around the mission.
10. Large flocks of swallows came back to Capistrano.

PREDICATE NOUNS AND PREDICATE ADJECTIVES

Predicate nouns and predicate adjectives follow linking verbs. To diagram a sentence with a predicate noun or a predicate adjective, extend the base line to the right of the verb. From the base line, draw a line that extends upward and toward the subject. This line shows that the predicate noun or predicate adjective is closely related to the subject. Write the predicate noun or predicate adjective on the extended base line. Place any modifiers of the predicate noun or predicate adjective on the slanted lines below it.

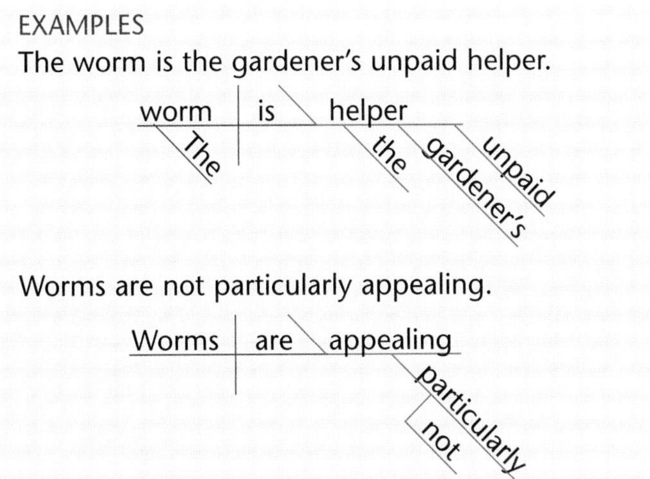

Try It Yourself

EXERCISE 7

Diagramming Predicate Nouns and Predicate Adjectives

Diagram the predicate nouns and predicate adjectives in the sentences below.

EXERCISE 7
Answers for sentence diagrams are available at www.emcp.com.

1. The Keystone Kops were bumbling, inefficient police officers.
2. Their creator was the "master of fun," according to W. C. Fields.
3. Mack Sennett's movies were funny with their pratfalls, chases, and pies in the face.

4. The Little Tramp was the creation of Charlie Chaplin.
5. He had also been an actor with Mack Sennett's Keystone Company.
6. *The Gold Rush* was Chaplin's masterpiece.
7. *Modern Times* was a satire on mechanization.
8. Chaplin was the greatest silent screen comedian of all time.
9. W. C. Fields was master of the comic aside.
10. His unusual voice and line delivery were successful in talking motion pictures.

VERBALS

A participle or a participial phrase acts as an adjective. To diagram a participle or a participial phrase, draw a slanted line and a horizontal line below the word that the participle or participial phrase modifies. Write the participle so that it starts on the slanted line and curves onto the horizontal line. If a direct object follows the participle, separate the two elements with a vertical bar. If a predicate noun follows the participle, separate the two elements with a slanted line.

EXAMPLES

Sinéad O'Connor is a musical recording artist.

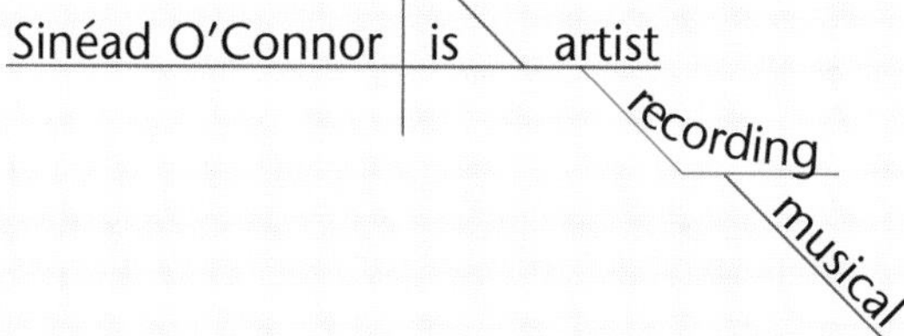

Invented by the Chinese, the rickshaw was used long before the Roman chariot.

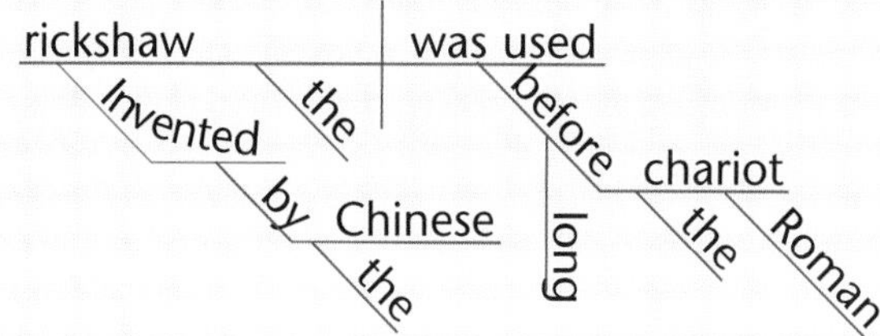

A gerund or a gerund phrase acts as a noun. To diagram a gerund or a gerund phrase, place the gerund on a step, and place the step on a standard or stilt. Write the gerund so that it starts on the slanted line and curves onto the horizontal line. Place the standard or stilt in the position in the main diagram that shows the function of the gerund or gerund phrase in the sentence. If the phrase has modifiers or complements, diagram them on the line extending from the step.

EXAMPLES

Cooking for guests was always a pleasure.

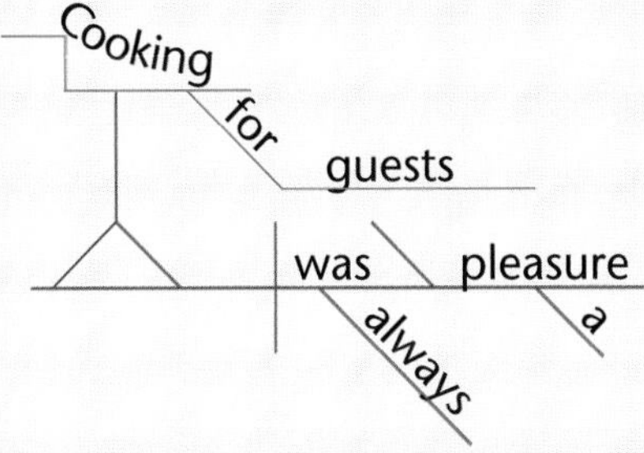

Mark's interest in swimming began during his first summer.

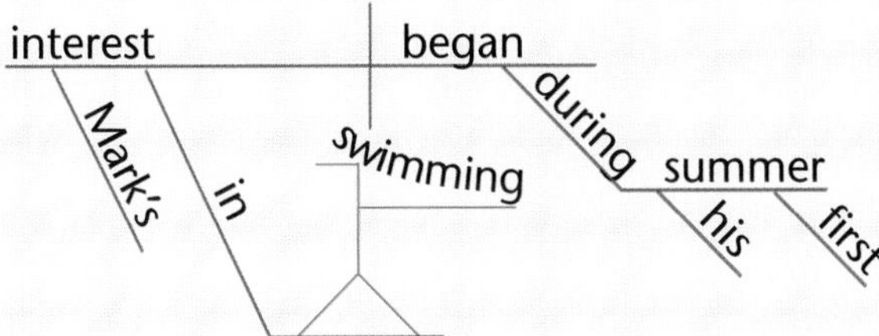

An infinitive or an infinitive phrase may be used as a noun, an adjective, or an adverb. To diagram an infinitive or an infinitive phrase, place it on a standard or stilt. Put the word *to* on a slanted line and the verb on a horizontal line. Diagram modifiers and complements as you would in a sentence. Then place the standard or stilt in a position in the main diagram that shows the function of the infinitive phrase in the sentence.

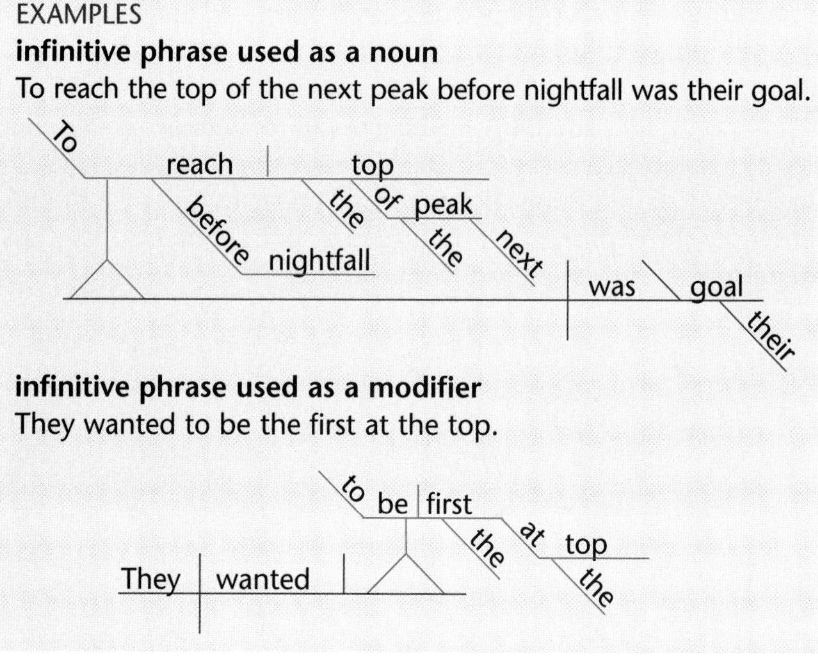

Try It Yourself

EXERCISE 8

Answers for sentence diagrams are available at www.emcp.com.

EXERCISE 8

Diagramming Verbals and Verbal Phrases

Diagram the verbals and verbal phrases in the following sentences. Some sentences may have more than one verbal or verbal phrase.

1. Missing the bus, Elise decided to walk the four miles to school.
2. Some fish can survive the winter in polar regions without freezing.
3. A telegram was sent to Eleanor Roosevelt from the 1939 World's Fair using only the current from electric eels.
4. James Whistler abandoned the telling of stories in favor of arousing sensation in portraits, landscapes, and nocturnal scenes.
5. Jessica refused to go to the meeting.
6. The flying snake of Java and Malaysia is able to flatten itself out like a ribbon and sail like a glider from tree to tree.

7. During the mating season, competing male porcupines bristle their quills at each other before attacking.
8. Rattlesnakes gather in groups to sleep through the winter.
9. Harley Davidson fans have their own vocabulary, describing their motorcycles as *flatheads*, *knuckleheads*, *panheads*, *shovelheads*, or *blockheads*, depending on the shape of the engine.
10. Aspiring to have their picture on a box of Wheaties cereal is the goal of many athletes.

APPOSITIVES AND APPOSITIVE PHRASES

To diagram an appositive or an appositive phrase, place the appositive in parentheses next to the word that it explains or identifies. Place any modifiers on slanted lines directly below the appositive.

EXAMPLES

Composer Stephen Foster wrote "Oh! Susanna" and "My Old Kentucky Home."

A famous 1930 art deco skyscraper, New York's Chrysler Building was modeled after the automobile's radiator cap.

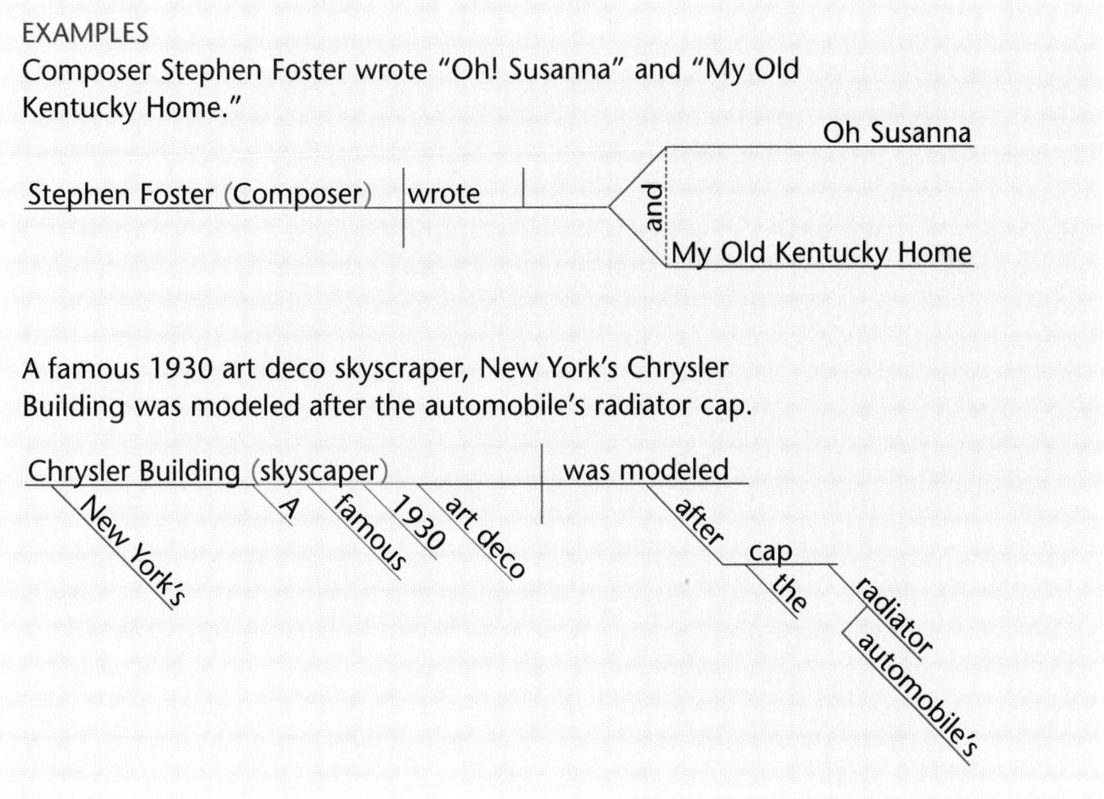

Try It Yourself

EXERCISE 9

Answers for sentence diagrams are available at www.emcp.com.

EXERCISE 9

Diagramming Appositives and Appositive Phrases

Diagram the appositives and appositive phrases in the following sentences.

1. The truffle, an underground mushroom harvested by pigs, is highly prized as a flavoring in French cuisine.
2. A rich chocolate candy, the truffle is a round ball coated with cocoa powder or chopped nuts.
3. Georgia O'Keeffe drew her inspiration from her feelings for the land, the flat midwestern landscape of her childhood.
4. "Kemo Sabe," the words used by Tonto to address the Lone Ranger, mean "white brother."
5. Union organizer Mother Jones led the crusade to lessen the exploitation of children in mills and mines.
6. She organized women into groups, "mop and bucket brigades," to encourage men to strike.
7. A monument was erected in Mount Olive, Illinois, in memory of Mother Jones, beloved labor leader for sixty years.
8. A war between two superpowers, Tikal and Calakmul, split the Mayan civilization.
9. Calakmul, the snake kingdom, was located in Mexico.
10. For the Maya, time and space, the physical and supernatural worlds, are one single continuous reality.

UNIT 13 REVIEW

TEST YOUR KNOWLEDGE

EXERCISE 1

Diagramming Subjects and Predicates

Diagram the simple and compound subjects and the simple and compound predicates in the following sentences. (20 points)

EXERCISE 1
Answers for sentence diagrams are available at www.emcp.com.

1. Please don't go.
2. No one made a sound.
3. Peppers, squash, and tomatoes were piled on the kitchen counter.
4. Go around the back.
5. Does anyone know what time it is?
6. The children screamed, giggled, and cheered.
7. Both Ricki and Jake paint.
8. Start now.
9. Either the chicken or the veal looks good.
10. Radullah and Sundiata stretched and yawned.

EXERCISE 2

Diagramming Modifiers

Diagram the adjectives and adverbs in the following sentences. (20 points)

EXERCISE 2
Answers for sentence diagrams are available at www.emcp.com.

1. The old engine stopped repeatedly.
2. Try harder now.
3. Baby birds drank thirstily from the birdbath.
4. The bleak, humid day was finally over.
5. Tiny red stones glistened on the baby's earlobes.
6. Sarcastic and mean, the reviewer's comments hurt many feelings.

7. Three fledgling falcons easily caught the next current of air.
8. The two boys raced their bikes competitively.
9. Patrick listened carefully and thoughtfully.
10. Both the children and the elderly waited quite impatiently.

EXERCISE 3
Answers for sentence diagrams are available at www.emcp.com.

EXERCISE 3

Diagramming Direct and Indirect Objects, Predicate Nouns, and Predicate Adjectives

Diagram the direct and indirect objects and the predicate nouns and predicate adjectives in the following sentences. (20 points)

1. Hand surgeons can sometimes reattach lost fingers.
2. A team of surgeons can reconnect the bones and sew together tendons, arteries, veins, and nerves.
3. Dr. Sean Simmons is an orthopedic surgeon.
4. The girls created their own Web pages and programmed a robot.
5. The workshop participants send each other e-mails to keep in touch.
6. Frozen cheese becomes rubbery.
7. Turquoise jewelry has become popular again.
8. Osteoarthritis is chronic and painful.
9. Metal clay is actually pure silver in an organic binder.
10. Shibori is a Japanese fabric art.

EXERCISE 4
Answers for sentence diagrams are available at www.emcp.com.

EXERCISE 4

Diagramming Phrases

Diagram the prepositional, appositive, and verbal phrases in the following sentences. (20 points)

1. Chopping vegetables and cleaning lawnmower blades can be dangerous for your fingers.
2. Shirrét is the art of crocheting and shirring fabric to create rugs and clothing.

3. Lady MacCready teaches the shirrét course at the handcraft center.
4. Temari balls are made by wrapping a styrofoam ball with layers of batting, yarn, and fine sewing.
5. Bruce Barton, a famous wood turner, will demonstrate his craft.
6. Participants will use their newly acquired knowledge to make a representative sculpture.
7. Darrell Pettit, our teacher, handworked the stone with hammer and chisel.
8. The garden obelisk, actually a teepee-shaped trellis, fell over during a windstorm.
9. *Tromp l'oeil*, "fool the eye," is an artistic technique to produce the grand illusion of reality.
10. Artemis considers drawing dull and repetitive.

EXERCISE 5

Diagramming Sentences

The following sentences contain various sentence parts and parts of speech that you have studied. Diagram each sentence to show where subjects, predicates, modifiers, phrases, objects, and complements go. (20 points)

EXERCISE 5
Answers for sentence diagrams are available at www.emcp.com.

1. America's first abstract painter, Arthur Dove, had a personal style, based on emotions and derived from nature.
2. Refusing to imitate reality, he emphasized color and shape.
3. Dove started his career by drawing illustrations for magazines.
4. His first paintings were filled with realistic images of the wild rural landscape of his childhood.
5. By reducing objects to patterns of color and shape, he eliminated representation in his work.
6. Dove's first attempts at abstraction were neither appreciated nor purchased.

7. He experimented with assemblage, found bits of materials glued to a wooden board.
8. In *Goin' Fishin'*, he uses denim shirtsleeves and pieces of a bamboo fishing pole.
9. Dove was never popular or successful as an artist during his lifetime.
10. He left an important legacy, a new way of looking at things.

Untitled Construction, c.1924. Arthur Dove.

UNIT 14 COMMON USAGE PROBLEMS

ASSESSMENT
Grammar and Usage Test is available at www.emcp.com.

UNIT OVERVIEW

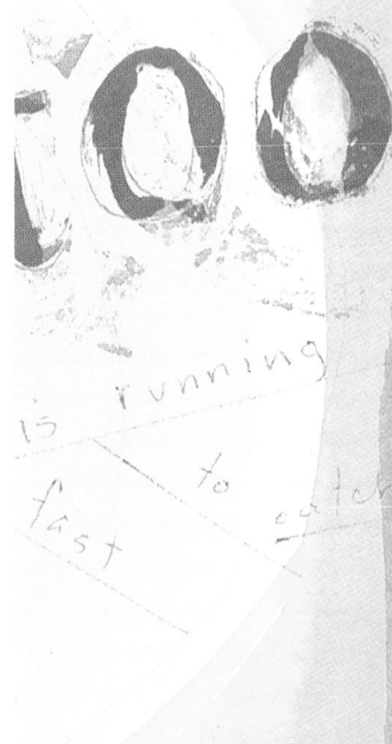

COMMON USAGE PROBLEMS

USAGE tip

Before beginning this section, you may want to review Unit 8, "Subject-Verb Agreement and Usage," pages 168–185

INCORRECT SUBJECT-VERB AGREEMENT

A subject and its verb must agree in number. Use singular verb forms with singular subjects and plural verb forms with plural subjects.

Intervening Words

A prepositional phrase that comes between a subject and a verb does not determine whether the subject is singular or plural.

EXAMPLES

The **shirt** on the clothesline **flaps** in the brisk wind. (*shirt flaps*, singular)

The **manager** of the rental units **recommends** that we fill out an application immediately. (*manager recommends*, singular)

The **singers**, along with their publicist, **hop** into the waiting limousine. (*singers hop*, plural)

The **salamanders** in the vernal pool **are** endangered. (*salamanders are,* plural)

When the subject is an indefinite pronoun, the object of the preposition sometimes controls the verb. This exception is covered on page 336 of this unit.

EXAMPLES

Most of the **floor** has been sanded.
Most of the **floors** have been sanded.

Compound Subjects

Use a plural verb with most compound subjects connected by *and*.

EXAMPLES

<u>Chris</u> and <u>Stewart</u> **referee** for junior soccer games.

<u>Streetlights</u>, automobile <u>headlights</u>, and the exterior <u>illumination</u> of buildings at night **obscure** the details of the night sky.

Use a singular verb with a compound subject that refers to one person or thing or that generally conveys the idea of a unit.

EXAMPLES
Bangers and mash **tastes** delicious, despite the absurd name. (one dish)

According to the firefighter, dropping and rolling often **puts** out flames on clothing. (one strategy)

Use a singular verb with a compound subject made up of singular nouns or pronouns connected by *or* or *nor.* Use a plural verb with a compound subject formed from plural nouns or pronouns.

EXAMPLES
singular
Neither Janine nor Kadeisha **tolerates** disorder.
Either the dog or the cat **has** been chewing on the afghan.

plural
Either journalists or VIPs **receive** the best seats in the stadium.
Neither roses nor phlox **flourish** in the shade garden.

When a compound subject consists of a singular subject and a plural subject connected by *or* or *nor*, use a verb that agrees in number with the subject that is closer to it in the sentence.

EXAMPLES
Either the guard or the residents **patrol** the apartment complex periodically. (*residents patrol,* plural)

Either the residents or the guard **patrols** the apartment complex periodically. (*guard patrols,* singular)

Indefinite Pronouns as Subjects

Indefinite pronouns are pronouns that refer to people or things in general. Some indefinite pronouns are always singular and take singular verbs: *anybody, anyone, anything, each, either, everybody, everyone, everything, much, neither, nobody, no one, nothing, one, other, somebody, someone, something.*

EXAMPLES

Everything that you do affects you in the end. (*everything affects,* singular)

Someone hangs paper butterflies all over the school during exam week. (*someone hangs,* singular)

Some indefinite pronouns are always plural and take plural verbs: *several*, *both*, *few*, *many*.

EXAMPLES

Many choose to earn modest salaries in order to have more free time. (*many choose,* plural)

Several called the news program to correct the pronunciation of Chechnya. (*several called,* plural)

Some indefinite pronouns can be either singular or plural, depending on their use in the sentence: *all*, *any*, *enough*, *more*, *most*, *none*, *plenty*, *some*. They are singular when they refer to a portion or to a single person, place, or thing. They are plural when they refer to a number of individual persons, places, or things. In some cases, the object of the preposition determines whether the verb is singular or plural.

EXAMPLES

None of the plot makes sense. (*None* refers to a portion of the plot and is therefore singular.)

None of the characters are believable. (*None* refers to multiple characters and is therefore plural.)

Inverted Word Order

In questions and in sentences beginning with *Here* or *There*, the verb appears before the subject. In these sentences with inverted word order, you must identify the subject and then make the verb agree with it in number. Saying the sentence to yourself in normal order often helps.

EXAMPLES

Where **does** the football team practice off-season? (*Team does practice*—singular)

There **goes** the balloon that was tied to the railing. (*balloon goes,* singular)

Here **are** the fossils that were embedded in the cliff. (*fossils are,* plural)

There **were** dozens of tree frogs clamoring in the valley. (*dozens were clamoring,* plural)

Try It Yourself

EXERCISE 1

Identifying Problems with Subject-Verb Agreement

Write the correct verb form in parentheses that agrees in number with the subject of the sentence.

1. The master of ceremonies usually (begins, begin) the evening with a few bad jokes.
2. Through the village square (marches, march) a German brass band.
3. Nailed to the door of the church (was, were) Luther's ninety-five theses.
4. Jason and a number of other students (has, have) difficulty expressing themselves in writing.
5. Either Gorgonzola or Stilton (complements, complement) the flavor of the pears.
6. Few of the tulips (blooms, bloom) for more than one or two springs.
7. Neither the play nor any of the filmed versions (lives, live) up to the quality of the original book.
8. A cell phone, as well as a laptop and a microwave, (is, are) now considered standard equipment for a first-year student to take to college.
9. There (is, are) the keys to the storage room in the basement.
10. Some of the carpeting in the school (has, have) suffered water damage and must be replaced.

EXERCISE 1
1. begins
2. marches
3. were
4. have
5. complements
6. bloom
7. live
8. is
9. are
10. has

LANGUAGELINK
Print exercise worksheets or have students complete exercises online with the LanguageLINK CD.

EXERCISE 2
1. enchants/drives
2. correct
3. are appearing
4. makes
5. stick
6. do
7. Do
8. correct
9. correct
10. correct

EXERCISE 3
Responses will vary. Sample responses:
1. Tumbleweeds roll across the highway.
   A tumbleweed is a symbol of the West.
2. Donuts are a calorie-filled but delicious snack.
   The donut was dusted with cinnamon.
3. Either Nina or Kate attends boarding school.
   Both Nina and Kate play bass guitar.
4. If you study classical music, you'll learn that some is quite wild and atonal.
   If you study dogs, you'll find that some are more nervous than others.
5. Both the Mississippi and the Ohio are mighty rivers with important histories.
   Neither the Mississippi nor the Ohio is west of the Rocky Mountains.

EXERCISE 2
Correcting Subject-Verb Agreement Problems

Correct the verb forms in each sentence so that subject and verb agree in number. If there are no subject-verb agreement problems in the sentence, write *correct*.

1. The hourly ringing of the bells enchant some guests and drive others mad.
2. On the eroding shoreline tilts an abandoned and crumbling lighthouse.
3. Kilts and burnooses, in addition to mukluks and stilettos, is appearing on the Paris runways this autumn.
4. The best of the archers routinely make nine bull's-eyes out of every ten shots.
5. All of the letters on the keyboard sticks because Naomi spilled lemonade while typing her term paper.
6. Where exactly does the bald eagles congregate along the lower Connecticut River?
7. Does Rachel and the twins attend conferences for home-schooled students?
8. Bagels and lox is a classic combination for breakfast.
9. In a period of inflation, the value of a currency falls and the amount needed to buy items rises.
10. Neither the yacht nor the Boston whaler is moored at the Westbrook marina.

EXERCISE 3
Using Correct Subject-Verb Agreement

Some of the following phrases are singular, and some are plural. Write a sentence using each of the following five phrases. Then change each phrase from singular to plural or from plural to singular and write five new sentences.

1. tumbleweeds roll
2. donuts are
3. either Nina or Kate attends
4. some is
5. both the Mississippi and the Ohio

INCORRECT USE OF APOSTROPHES

You may also want to refer to "Apostrophes" in Unit 15, pages 398–401.

Use an apostrophe to replace letters that have been left out in a contraction.

EXAMPLES
it's = it is wasn't = was not I'd = I would

Use an apostrophe to show possession.

Singular Nouns

Use an apostrophe and an *s* (*'s*) to form the possessive of a singular noun, even if it ends in *s*, *x*, or *z*.

EXAMPLES
ostrich's plume gem's luster
Jess's internship box's label

Plural Nouns

Use an apostrophe and an *s* (*'s*) to form the possessive of a plural noun that does not end in *s*.

EXAMPLES
geese's flight pattern children's literature oxen's diet

Use an apostrophe alone to form the possessive of a plural noun that ends in *s*.

EXAMPLES
prospectors' hopes captains' uniforms curries' flavors

Do not add an apostrophe or *'s* to possessive personal pronouns: *mine*, *yours*, *his*, *hers*, *its*, *ours*, or *theirs*. They already show ownership.

EXAMPLES
The association publishes its bylaws annually.
Is that backpack mine or hers?

EXERCISE 4
1. men's
2. river's
3. Somebody's
4. its, its
5. Lice's
6. elements'
7. bananas'
8. miners'
9. remedy's
10. his

EXERCISE 5
1. The boss's employees respect her commitment to their individual development.
2. Honestly, where's the Louisiana hot sauce I always add to my scrambled eggs?
3. The series of medieval paintings depicts the four seasons' progress in the life of the countryside.
4. In Shakespeare's play *Macbeth,* many think that the witches' predictions merely echo Macbeth's preexisting ambitions.
5. Even though my name is on the credit card, responsibility for those purchases is yours.
6. Is that Justine's scrawl on the sign-up sheet for the stair climber?

Try It Yourself

EXERCISE 4

Identifying Problems with Apostrophes

Choose the word in parentheses that represents the correct use of an apostrophe.

1. Hannah always buys her jeans from the (men's, mens') department.
2. The (river's, rivers') source is a tiny stream in the wilds of northern Canada.
3. (Somebody's, Somebodys') sunglasses had been placed on the nose of the statue.
4. A parrot often holds (it's, its) food in (it's, its) foot while eating.
5. (Lice's, Lices') reputation as a scourge of elementary schools is fully deserved.
6. Susan couldn't remember three (element's, elements') symbols for her chemistry test.
7. The (banana's, bananas') overripe state made them unsuitable for the fruit bowl but ideal for banana bread.
8. The (miner's, miners') union works to prevent accidents and to compensate workers for job-related illnesses.
9. That (remedy's, remedies') side effects are almost worse than the symptoms it is designed to treat.
10. Why does Erik have such a woebegone expression on (his, his') face?

EXERCISE 5

Correcting the Use of Apostrophes

Rewrite the following sentences to correct the use of apostrophes. If there are no errors in a sentence, write *correct.*

1. The boss' employees respect her commitment to their individual development.
2. Honestly, wheres the Louisiana hot sauce I always add to my scrambled eggs?

3. The series of medieval paintings depict the four season's progress in the life of the countryside.
4. In Shakespeare's play *Macbeth*, many think that the witches predictions merely echo Macbeth's preexisting ambitions.
5. Even though my name is on the credit card, responsibility for those purchases is yours.
6. Is that Justines' scrawl on the sign-up sheet for the stair climber?
7. The legislator's support for that piece of legislation is lukewarm because they think the cost would be exorbitant.
8. I ca'nt bear the sound of someone brushing his' teeth, but I actually don't mind the squeak of chalk on a chalkboard.
9. We giggled at all the ice cream variety's bizarre names.
10. In the past, many psychologists did not realize that childrens' grief was just as profound as that of adults, even though it was expressed differently.

7. The legislators' support for that piece of legislation is lukewarm because they think the cost would be exorbitant.
8. I can't bear the sound of someone brushing his teeth, but I actually don't mind the squeak of chalk on a chalkboard.
9. We giggled at all the ice cream varieties' bizarre names.
10. In the past, many psychologists did not realize that children's grief was just as profound as that of adults, even though it was expressed differently.

EXERCISE 6

Using Apostrophes Correctly

Write two sentences for the following words. The first sentence should use the singular possessive form of each noun. The second sentence should use the plural possessive form of each noun.

1. wilderness
2. comedy
3. somebody
4. fox
5. jazz
6. emissary
7. alto
8. monkey
9. cockroach
10. woman

EXERCISE 6
Responses will vary. Students may write the same or different sentences to show the singular possessive and the plural possessive of each noun.

AVOIDING DOUBLE NEGATIVES

USAGE tip

Before reading this section, you may want to review "Negatives and Double Negatives" in Unit 9, pages 210–213.

Make sure that you use only one of the following negatives in each sentence: *not, nobody, none, nothing, hardly, scarcely, can't, doesn't, won't, isn't, aren't.* A **double negative** is the use of two negative words together when only one is needed. Correct double negatives by removing one of the negative words or by replacing one of the negative words with a positive word.

EXAMPLES

double negative	I didn't hardly say a word during the whole interview.
corrected sentence	I hardly said a word during the whole interview. I didn't say much during the whole interview.
double negative	Amanda didn't recognize nobody at the dance.
corrected sentence	Amanda didn't recognize anybody at the dance. Amanda recognized nobody at the dance.

Try It Yourself

EXERCISE 7
Identifying Double Negatives

Choose the correct word in parentheses to complete each sentence. After you have completed the exercise, read each sentence aloud with the correct word in place.

EXERCISE 7
1. ever
2. is
3. anyone
4. any

1. Josefina didn't (ever, never) realize that the painting hanging in her living room was actually upside-down.
2. There (is, isn't) no way to convey how deeply your kind words affected me.
3. Couldn't (no one, anyone) in this family manage to get to the train station on time?
4. I called the box office to order some tickets for the musical, but they don't have (any, none) left!

5. Jacque (could, couldn't) hardly get out of bed the morning after she competed in the state gymnastics competition.
6. There didn't seem to be (anybody, nobody) available in the entire department store to ring up the sale and take my money.
7. Why isn't there (anything, nothing) in the refrigerator for dinner?
8. We couldn't decide whether to go somewhere exotic or somewhere close by for the holidays, so we didn't go (anywhere, nowhere).
9. Do you think Hal's mother will (ever, never) believe that he had no involvement in the prank?
10. Vi was sure the necklace was in her room, but when she looked she could find it (anywhere, nowhere).

5. could
6. anybody
7. anything
8. anywhere
9. never
10. nowhere

EXERCISE 8

Responses will vary. Sample responses:

1. There is no windshield wiper fluid in the reservoir. (OR There isn't any windshield wiper fluid in the reservoir.)
2. correct
3. During the school-sponsored trip to Spain, we students didn't speak any English. (OR During the school-sponsored trip to Spain, we students spoke no English.)
4. Hula and Irish step dancing couldn't be more different; one is based on hip movement while the other requires a stiff, upright torso. (OR Hula and Irish step dancing could hardly be more different; one is based on hip movement while the other requires a stiff, upright torso.)
5. If our town doesn't begin to preserve its open spaces, soon there won't be any left for the inhabitants to enjoy. (OR If our town doesn't begin to preserve its open spaces, soon there will be none left for the inhabitants to enjoy.)
6. correct

EXERCISE 8

Correcting Double Negatives

Rewrite the following sentences to remove the double negative. Remember that you can either remove one of the negative words or replace it with a positive word. If a sentence does not contain a double negative, write *correct*. After you have corrected the sentences, read each one aloud to train your ear to hear the correct usage.

1. There isn't no windshield wiper fluid in the reservoir.
2. The retriever will jump into the river to chase sticks until it can scarcely move from exhaustion
3. During the school-sponsored trip to Spain, we students didn't speak no English.
4. Hula and Irish step dancing couldn't hardly be more different; one is based on hip movement while the other requires a stiff, upright torso.
5. If our town doesn't begin to preserve its open spaces, soon there won't be none left for the inhabitants to enjoy.
6. Imperialism brought many benefits to whose who ran various empires, but few to those who were ruled.

7. Tim's antique car is an impressive-looking vehicle, but something tells me it won't go anywhere. (OR Tim's antique car is an impressive-looking vehicle, but something tells me it will go nowhere.)
8. The British prime minister can scarcely be heard at times because the members of Parliament are always shouting in encouragement or derision.
9. correct
10. Great excitement preceded the opening of the time capsule, but there wasn't anything inside. (OR Great excitement preceded the opening of the time capsule, but there was nothing inside.)

EXERCISE 9
Responses will vary. Students should correctly use each negative word in a sentence.

7. Tim's antique car is an impressive-looking vehicle, but something tells me it won't go nowhere.
8. The British prime minister can't scarcely be heard at times because the members of Parliament are always shouting in encouragement or derision.
9. Domestic cats spend an enormous amount of time sleeping because they don't need to hunt for survival.
10. Great excitement preceded the opening of the time capsule, but there wasn't nothing inside!

EXERCISE 9

Using Negatives Correctly

Write a sentence using each of the following negative words. Avoid using any double negatives in your sentences.

1. nowhere
2. scarcely
3. barely
4. nobody
5. nothing
6. not
7. not one
8. never
9. hardly
10. no

AVOIDING DANGLING AND MISPLACED MODIFIERS

USAGE tip

Before reading this section, you may want to review "Dangling and Misplaced Modifiers" in Unit 9, pages 215–218.

Place modifying phrases and clauses as close as possible to the words they modify; otherwise, your sentences may be unclear or unintentionally humorous.

A **dangling modifier** has nothing to modify because the word it would logically modify is not present in the sentence. In the following sentence, the modifying phrase has no logical object. The sentence says that an enormous parcel was looking into the mailbox.

EXAMPLE
Looking into the mailbox, an enormous parcel was seen.

You can eliminate dangling modifiers by rewriting the sentence so that an appropriate word is provided for the modifier to modify. You can also expand a dangling phrase into a full subordinate clause.

EXAMPLES
Looking into the mailbox, we saw an enormous parcel.
When we looked into the mailbox, we saw an enormous parcel.

A **misplaced modifier** is located too far from the word it should modify.

EXAMPLE
Revving its engine, I was awakened by the sound of a car.

You can revise a misplaced modifier by moving it closer to the word it modifies.

EXAMPLES
Revving its engine, a car awakened me.
I was awakened by a car revving its engine.

Try It Yourself

EXERCISE 10

Identifying Dangling and Misplaced Modifiers

Identify the dangling modifiers in the following sentences by writing *DM*. Identify the misplaced modifiers by writing *MM*.

1. By taking the elevator as far as it goes and then ascending a narrow staircase, the penthouse can be reached.
2. Father gave a lecture to the staff, which was almost an hour long.
3. The car sales executives went to two trade shows in Detroit wanting to learn more about the latest hybrid electric designs.
4. Dashing through the back alley, there were garbage cans and delivery trucks partially blocking the way.

EXERCISE 10
1. DM
2. MM
3. MM
4. DM

5. MM
6. MM
7. MM
8. DM
9. MM
10. MM

EXERCISE 11
Responses will vary.
Sample responses:
1. By taking the elevator as far as it goes and then ascending a narrow staircase, one can reach the penthouse.
2. Father gave the staff a lecture almost an hour long about conserving energy.
3. Wanting to learn more about the latest hybrid electric designs, the car executives went to the trade show in Detroit.
4. As I dashed through the alley, my way was blocked by garbage cans and delivery trucks.
5. Maria made with eloquence the case for attending vocational or technical school.
6. The mason, never taking his eyes off the wall he was building, conducted a lengthy conversation with the contractor.
7. I was given repeated standing ovations by the audience, who were dazzled by my tap dancing ability.
8. Making gravy without lumps, Terrence combined the flour with liquid before adding it to the pan.

5. Maria made the case for attending vocational or technical school with eloquence.
6. The mason conducted a lengthy conversation with the contractor, never taking his eyes off the wall he was building.
7. Dazzled by my tap dancing ability, I was given repeated standing ovations by the audience.
8. Making gravy without lumps, the flour was mixed with liquid before it was added to the pan.
9. While taking a luxury cruise through the Caribbean, influenza struck, and half of the passengers and crew had to be evacuated to the mainland for medical treatment.
10. Anahita sat entranced by the account of an outrageously expensive society wedding in the newspaper.

EXERCISE 11
Correcting Dangling and Misplaced Modifiers

Revise the sentences in Exercise 10 so that the modifiers are placed as close as possible to the words they modify.

EXERCISE 12
Using Modifiers Correctly

Expand each of the following sentences by adding a phrase or clause that provides detail. Be sure to place your phrases and clauses as close as possible to the words they modify.

1. The hikers requested bottled water.
2. The worker on duty turned on the gigantic frozen yogurt machine.
3. A swarm of bees descended on the orchard.
4. Small bits of gravel stuck in the soles of the shoes.
5. Blossoming mountain laurel festooned the hillside.
6. A dead branch dangled from the sycamore.
7. A roar erupted in the stadium.
8. Nobody could find the flashlight.
9. The mayor accused of corruption addressed the press.
10. Mati charged toward the trampoline.

AVOIDING SPLIT INFINITIVES

An **infinitive**, the base verb combined with *to*, should not be split under most circumstances. Infinitives such as *to save*, *to teach*, and *to hold* should not be interrupted by adverbs or other sentence components.

EXAMPLES

nonstandard	Dad wanted me to unobtrusively walk beside Grandma to keep her from falling.
standard	Dad wanted me to walk unobtrusively beside Grandma to keep her from falling.

In some cases, a modifier sounds awkward if it does not split the infinitive. In these situations, it may be best to reword the sentence to eliminate the split infinitive.

EXAMPLES

awkward	Theresa wanted to prevent diligently employees from slipping on wet floors.
revised	Theresa wanted to diligently prevent employees from slipping on wet floors.

In certain cases, you may want to use a split infinitive to change the meaning of the sentence.

EXAMPLES
I wanted merely to taste the soup.
I wanted to merely taste the soup.
I wanted to taste merely the soup.

Try It Yourself

EXERCISE 13
Correcting Split Infinitives
Revise the following sentences to eliminate any split infinitives.

1. Gordon was unable to quickly complete the online transaction in the required time period, so he was forced to start all over again.

USAGE tip

Before reading this section, you may want to review "Infinitive Phrases" in Unit 12, pages 283–284.

9. While taking a luxury cruise through the Caribbean, half of the passengers and crew were struck by influenza and had to be evacuated to the mainland for medical treatment.
10. Anahita sat entranced by the newspaper account of an outrageously expensive society wedding.

EXERCISE 12
Responses will vary. Students should add descriptive phrases and clauses as close as possible to the words that they modify.

EXERCISE 13
1. Gordon was unable to complete quickly the online transaction in the required time period, so he was forced to start all over again.
2. The truck driver was forced to brake abruptly when a large box flew off the flatbed in front of him.
3. Our financial advisor stressed that it is dangerous to reach automatically for a credit card when purchasing something.

4. Jaime started to babble an apology awkwardly, but I pointed out that I'm always forgetting birthdays myself.
5. It is possible to clone a farm animal, but it is impossible to do so economically.
6. As the deadline for the college placement tests approaches, Mali is starting to recite feverishly endless lists of arcane words.
7. The surgeon tried to remove gently the dirt embedded in Steve's chin, but ultimately he had to scrub quite hard to cleanse the wound completely.
8. The ceramicist had to rework the teapot design patiently again and again until the handle adhered during the firing process.
9. To pack safely for shipping an item as valuable and delicate as an eighteenth-century clock requires a high degree of expertise, dexterity, and patience.
10. One way to soothe a frightened animal quickly can be to cover its eyes gently.

2. The truck driver was forced to abruptly brake when a large box flew off the flatbed in front of him.
3. Our financial advisor stressed that it is dangerous to automatically reach for a credit card when purchasing something.
4. Jaime started to awkwardly babble an apology, but I pointed out that I'm always forgetting birthdays myself.
5. It is possible to clone a farm animal, but it is impossible to economically do so.
6. As the deadline for the college placement tests approaches, Mali is starting to feverishly recite endless lists of arcane words.
7. The surgeon tried to gently remove the dirt embedded in Steve's chin, but ultimately he had to scrub quite hard to completely cleanse the wound.
8. The ceramacist had to patiently rework the teapot design again and again until the handle adhered during the firing process.
9. To safely pack for shipping an item as valuable and delicate as an eighteenth-century clock requires a high degree of expertise, dexterity, and patience.
10. One way to quickly soothe a frightened animal can be to gently cover its eyes.

EXERCISE 14

Responses will vary. Students' sentences should exhibit their understanding of how to avoid splitting infinitives when writing their own sentences.

EXERCISE 14
Using Infinitives Correctly

Create a sentence for each of the following infinitives. Be careful not to split the infinitives.

1. to energize
2. to soar
3. to lament
4. to tighten
5. to mesmerize
6. to evacuate
7. to breathe
8. to ponder
9. to nibble
10. to complain

AVOIDING RUN-ON SENTENCES: COMMA SPLICES AND FUSED SENTENCES

A **run-on sentence** is made up of two or more sentences that have been run together as if they were one complete thought. A run-on sentence can confuse the reader about where a thought starts or ends.

USAGE tip

Identify run-on sentences by looking for subjects and verbs. This strategy will help you see where one complete thought ends and another one begins.

Take a look at the following examples of run-on sentences. In the first run-on, called a **fused sentence**, no punctuation mark is used between sentences. In the second run-on, called a **comma splice**, a comma is used to separate two complete thoughts.

EXAMPLES

fused sentence

Benjamin Franklin modeled his writing style after Neoclassical masters like the Neoclassicists Franklin valued reason and rational thought.

corrected sentence

Benjamin Franklin modeled his writing style after Neoclassical masters; like the Neoclassicists, Franklin valued reason and rational thought.

comma splice

Franklin wrote *The Autobiography of Benjamin Franklin* over a period of twenty years, many of the aphorisms that people associate with Franklin, however, actually appeared in Franklin's *Poor Richard's Almanac.*

corrected sentence

Franklin wrote *The Autobiography of Benjamin Franklin* over a period of twenty years. Many of the aphorisms that people associate with Franklin, however, actually appeared in Franklin's *Poor Richard's Almanac.*

Fused sentences and comma splices can be corrected by using a period or a comma to separate the two complete thoughts. Another alternative is to join the two thoughts with a comma followed by a coordinating conjunction such as *and*, *but*, *or*, *nor*, *yet*, or *for*.

Try It Yourself

EXERCISE 15
Responses may vary slightly.

EXERCISE 15

Correcting Comma Splices and Fused Sentences

Revise the following sentences to eliminate any run-on sentences.

1. The son of a soap and candle maker, Ben Franklin made many contributions during his lifetime, he was greatly respected for his wisdom and insight.
2. Franklin was a writer, scientist, inventor, and diplomat, in fact, he spent eighteen years in England as an unofficial ambassador for the American Colonies.
3. At the age of twelve he began work in the printing trade, at the age of sixteen he wrote and published a series of essays titled "Silence Dogood."
4. Franklin moved to Philadelphia and started his own printing shop his shop made paper currency and published the *Pennsylvania Gazette*.
5. Many of the aphorisms in his *Poor Richard's Almanac* stress hard work, frugality, and thrift these same virtues helped to make Franklin a wealthy man.
6. *Poor Richard's Almanac* was enormously successful, the almanac was published yearly for twenty-five years and many people still quote from it today.
7. "Creditors have better memories than debtors" was often quoted by my grandmother, she, too, believed in the virtues Franklin preached.
8. He pursued many interests, including his passion for science, which resulted in new inventions Franklin invented a cook stove, bifocal glasses, and the lightning rod.
9. Franklin helped write the Declaration of Independence, he also helped draft and signed the treaty that ended the Revolutionary War.
10. In the last years of his life Franklin wrote the last two sections of his autobiography the complete work, however, was not published until 1868.

COMMONLY MISUSED WORDS

The following pages contain an alphabetic list of words and phrases that often cause usage problems.

a, an Use *a* before words beginning with a consonant sound. Use *an* before words beginning with a vowel sounds, including a silent *h*.

EXAMPLES
Have you ever attended **a** classic country fair?
Deirdre made the daybed look cosy with **an** afghan, **a** velvet pillow, and **a** long bolster.
Is it true that our server is actually an **heir** to the Transylvanian throne?

accept, except *Accept* is a verb meaning "to receive willingly" or "to agree." *Except* is a preposition that means "leaving out" or "but."

EXAMPLES
Jared refused to **accept** full responsibility for the incident.
Everyone **except** my father decided to snorkel around the reef.

affect, effect *Affect* is a verb that means "to influence." The noun *effect* means "the result of an action." The verb *effect* means "to cause" or "to bring about."

EXAMPLES
It is widely accepted that greenhouse emissions do **affect** the global climate.
Shrieking at a naughty child seldom has a positive **effect**.
The experimental antibiotic may **effect** an immediate cure for the infection.

ain't This word is nonstandard English. Avoid using it in speaking and writing.

EXAMPLES

nonstandard	The snowblower **ain't** working.
standard	The snowblower **isn't** working.

all ready, already *All ready* means "entirely ready or prepared." *Already* means "previously."

EXAMPLES
I'm **all ready** to go out, but unfortunately my date won't arrive for hours.

Dad brought home takeout from the Thai restaurant, but Mom had **already** bought sushi for dinner.

all right *All right* means "satisfactory," "unhurt," "correct," or "yes, very well." The word *alright* is not acceptable in formal written English.

EXAMPLES

All right, it's time to haul out all of the trash that's accumulated in the basement.
Does Kris feel **all right**?

a lot *A lot* means "a great number or amount" and is always two words. Because it is imprecise, you should avoid it except in informal usage. *Alot* is not a word.

EXAMPLES

Alison manages to carry **a lot** in that slender handbag.
A lot of years must pass before the forest recovers from that devastating fire.

altogether, all together *Altogether* is an adverb meaning "thoroughly." Something done *all together* is done as a group or mass.

EXAMPLES

The heels on those shoes are **altogether** too high to carry you comfortably around the city all day.

The chaperones stressed that the students must stay **all together** when they got off the bus.

anywheres, everywheres, somewheres, nowheres Use these words and others like them without the *s: anywhere*, *everywhere*, *somewhere*, *nowhere*.

EXAMPLES

There should be some glue **somewhere** in that messy drawer.
I can't take you **anywhere** without you causing a fuss!

assure, ensure, insure These words all mean "To make certain, safe, or secure." Generally, they may be used interchangeably. However, use *assure* when referring to people or setting a person's mind at rest. Use *insure* when referring to the guarantee of life or property against risk.

EXAMPLES

We **assured** the frightened child that she was safe.

To **ensure** the program's success, volunteers contributed hundreds of hours of their time.

I would like to **insure** the antique diamond ring I inherited from my grandmother.

at Don't use this word after *where*.

EXAMPLE
Where did you store the skate guards?

bad, badly *Bad* is always an adjective, and *badly* is always an adverb. Use *bad* after linking verbs.

EXAMPLES
Be sure to discard any **bad** blueberries before you start to bake.

Jeremiah felt **bad** about implying that Jill's soliloquy was a failure.

Nell thinks she plays tennis **badly**, but actually she has the potential to be an excellent competitor.

beside, besides *Beside* means "next to." *Besides* means "in addition to." *Besides* can also be an adverb meaning "moreover."

EXAMPLES
The terriers bark and tussle all day, but at night they lie down placidly **beside** each other.

Is there anything **besides** another idiotic reality show on TV tonight?

I couldn't find that book at the library; **besides,** I have more than enough sources for that report.

between, among Use *between* when referring to two people or things. Use *among* when you are discussing three or more people or things.

EXAMPLES
The maid placed the vase on the mantel **between** two tall gilt candlesticks.
It's going to be difficult to divide eight biscuits **among** ten dinner guests!

bring, take Use *bring* when you mean "to carry to." It refers to movement toward the speaker. Use *take* when you mean "to carry away." It refers to movement away from the speaker.

EXAMPLES
Bring me the scissors so I can cut the tag off this ski jacket.
When you go on your trip, **take** a sketchbook instead of a camera.

bust, busted Do not use these nonstandard words as verbs to substitute for *break* or *burst.*

EXAMPLES

nonstandard	Leon **busted** the air-conditioner by trying to force the setting knob. If you overfill that helium balloon, it will **bust**.
standard	Leon **broke** the air-conditioner by trying to force the setting knob. If you overfill the helium balloon, it will **burst.**

can, may The word *can* means "able to do something." The word *may* is used to ask or give permission.

EXAMPLES

Can that enormous cat actually squeeze through the cat flap?
Clay **may** not participate in the Civil War reenactment until he purchases an authentic uniform.

choose, chose *Choose* is the present tense and *chose* is the past tense.

EXAMPLES

Connie gets to **choose** the first chocolate from the box because it is her birthday.
Ahmed **chose** raw umber for the background of his painting.

could of Use the helping verb *have* (which may sound like *could of*) with *could*, *might*, *must*, *should*, *ought*, and *would*.

EXAMPLES

nonstandard	No one could of predicted the victory given the team's record.
standard	No one **could have** predicted the victory.

doesn't, don't *Doesn't* is the contraction of *does not*. It is used with singular nouns and the pronouns *he*, *she*, *it*, *this*, and *that*. *Don't* is the contraction of *do not*. Use it with plural nouns and the pronouns *I*, *we*, *they*, *you*, *these*, and *those*.

EXAMPLES

Cilla **doesn't** like to contemplate the fact that she will someday be middle-aged.
Elephants **don't** have any predators other than humans.

farther, further Use *farther* to refer to physical distance. Use *further* to refer to greater extent in time or degree or to mean "additional."

EXAMPLES

Don't be discouraged by your first attempt at rowing; you'll be able to go **farther** next week.

Eileen thinks she can ace the exam without **further** study.

fewer, less Use *fewer*, which tells "how many," to refer to things that you can count individually. *Fewer* is used with plural words. Use *less* to refer to quantities that you cannot count. It is used with singular words and tells "how much."

EXAMPLES

There are **fewer** soccer players on the bench now that the school has formed a junior varsity team.

Why do some people think that **less** regulation is required for herbal remedies than for chemical compounds?

good, well *Good* is always an adjective. *Well* is an adverb meaning "ably" or "capably." *Well* is also a predicate adjective meaning "satisfactory" or "in good health." Don't confuse *feel good*, which means "to feel happy or pleased," with *feel well*, which means "to feel healthy."

EXAMPLES

Paige created a surprisingly **good** dish by randomly tossing ingredients into the stewpot.
Mrs. Park felt **good** [pleased] about finding a great bargain on gym socks.
Jenna sees **well** in daylight conditions, but her night vision is limited.
Kevin is not feeling **well** because of all the immunizations he has gotten for his trip.

had ought, hadn't ought The verb *ought* should never be used with the helping verb *had*.

EXAMPLES

nonstandard	You had ought to get adequate directions before taking off for the festival.
standard	You **ought** to get adequate directions before taking off for the festival.
nonstandard	Drivers **hadn't ought** to make phone calls while moving in traffic.
standard	Drivers **ought** not to make phone calls while moving in traffic.

hardly, scarcely Since both of these words have negative meanings, do not use them with other negative words such as *not*, *no*, *nothing*, and *none*.

EXAMPLES

nonstandard	Albinia can't hardly eat any desserts because of her allergies.
standard	Albinia **can hardly** eat any desserts because of her allergies.
nonstandard	The restaurant hadn't scarcely opened before it was hugely popular.
standard	The restaurant **had scarcely** opened before it was hugely popular.

he, she, they Do not use these pronouns after a noun. This error is called a double subject.

EXAMPLES

nonstandard	Labote he is going to get his degree in biology at the end of this year.
standard	Labote is going to get his degree in biology at the end of this year.

hisself, theirselves These are incorrect forms. Use *himself* and *themselves*.

EXAMPLES

nonstandard	Roxanne could not believe that the lead singer from her favorite band had raised his sister by hisself when he was younger.
standard	Roxanne could not believe that the lead singer from her favorite band had raised his sister by himself when he was younger.
nonstandard	The owner of the orchard invited visitors to help **theirselves** to any of the apples that had fallen to the ground.
standard	The owner of the orchard invited visitors to help **themselves** to any of the apples that had fallen to the ground.

how come Do not use in place of *why*.

EXAMPLES

nonstandard	I can never understand how come movie tickets cost so much.
standard	I can never understand **why** movie tickets cost so much.

in, into Use *in* to mean "within" or "inside." Use *into* to suggest movement toward the inside from the outside.

EXAMPLES
There was one faded rose **in** the antique hatbox.
Rain poured **into** the car through the open sunroof.

its, it's *Its* is a possessive pronoun. *It's* is the contraction for *it is.*

EXAMPLES
Each publishing house has **its** own way of indicating a first edition.
It's a good idea to wear protective clothing when walking in areas infested by ticks.

kind, sort, type Use *this* or *that* to modify the singular nouns *kind*, *sort*, and *type*. Use *these* and *those* to modify the plural nouns *kinds*, *sorts*, and *types*. *Kind* should be singular when the object of the preposition following it is singular. It should be plural when the object of the preposition is plural.

EXAMPLES
Which **kind** of saddle do you use on your horse?
Those **types** of shoes can cause bunions and other foot problems.

kind of, sort of Do not use these terms to mean "somewhat" or "rather."

EXAMPLES

nonstandard	It was kind of rude of Millie to take the best seat.
standard	It was rather rude of Millie to take the best seat.

lay, lie *Lay* means "to put" or "to place." *Lay* usually takes a direct object. *Lie* means "to rest" or "to be in a lying position." *Lie* never takes a direct object. (Note that the past tense of *lie* is *lay*.)

EXAMPLES
Lay the suit flat in the garment bag so it doesn't get wrinkled during the flight.

The mourners l**aid** wreathes on the poet's grave.

The little girl obstinately refused to **lie** down even though she was exhausted.

Jamie **lay** down on one of the mattresses in the department store and promptly fell asleep!

learn, teach *Learn* means "to gain knowledge." *Teach* means "to give knowledge." Do not use them interchangeably.

EXAMPLES

Aunt Martha **learned** classic Mexican cooking techniques from one of Diana Kennedy's books.

Once she had mastered the art of making a proper tortilla, she decided to **teach** others.

like, as *Like* is usually a preposition followed by an object. It generally means "similar to." *As*, *as if*, and *as though* are conjunctions used to introduce subordinate clauses.

EXAMPLES

The glass ornament looks just **like** a clear plastic bag with a goldfish swimming inside.
The goldfish looks **as though** it is alive.
As I said, Monica is not here.

of This word is unnecessary after the prepositions *inside*, *outside*, and *off*.

EXAMPLES

Did you hear that the balcony actually fell **off** the building?
Demonstrators gathered **outside** the Houses of Parliament.
In case of a tornado warning, try to go **inside** a sturdily built shelter immediately.

precede, proceed *Precede* means "to go or come before." *Proceed* means "to go forward."

EXAMPLES

Diagnosis must always **precede** treatment.
The match will begin in five minutes; you must **proceed** to your seat without delay.

quiet, quite Although these words sound alike, they have different meanings. *Quite* is an adverb meaning "positively" or "completely," whereas *quiet* is an adjective that means "making little or no noise."

EXAMPLES

Marina insists that it's impossible for her to study in a **quiet** environment.

Tommy became **quite** excited as the boat's speed increased and his parachute lifted into the air.

real, really *Real* is an adjective meaning "actual." *Really* is an adverb meaning "actually" or "genuinely." Do not use *real* to mean "very" or "extremely."

EXAMPLES
A **real** detective would never ask such silly questions.
The new magnet school is **really** successful.

reason . . . because *Reason is because* is both wordy and redundant. Use *reason is that* or simply *because.*

EXAMPLES

nonstandard	The reason their song is such a hit is because the video is hilarious.
standard	The reason their song is a hit is that the video is hilarious.
standard	Their song is a hit because the video is hilarious.
standard	Because the video is hilarious, their song is a hit.

regardless, irregardless Use *regardless*, *unmindful*, *heedless*, or *anyway*. *Irregardless* is a double negative and should never be used.

EXAMPLE

nonstandard	Some people continue to smoke irregardless of the proven risks to their health.
standard	Some people continue to smoke regardless of the proven risks to their health

rise, raise *Rise* is an intransitive verb that means "to move upward." It is an irregular verb and does not take a direct object. *Raise* is a transitive verb that means "to lift or make something go upward." It is a regular verb, and it takes a direct object.

EXAMPLES
After the horse fell, the spectators anxiously waited to see if it could **rise** to its feet.
When you **raise** the shades in the living room, please attempt to roll them up evenly.

scratch, itch *Scratch* means "to scrape lightly to relieve itching." *Itch* means "to feel a tingling of the skin, with the desire to scratch."

EXAMPLES
My mosquito bites **itch** more the second day than they did the first.
Therefore, I'm more likely to **scratch** the bites on the second day than on the first.

set, sit *Set* is a transitive verb meaning "to place something." It always takes a direct object. *Sit* is an intransitive verb meaning "to rest in an upright position." It does not take a direct object.

EXAMPLES
Don't **set** the hot teakettle on the kitchen counter.
Sit carefully in that chair; it's a bit rickety.

some, somewhat *Some* is an adjective meaning "a certain unspecified quantity." *Somewhat* is an adverb meaning "slightly." Do not use *some* as an adverb.

EXAMPLES

nonstandard	The ribs at that restaurant are **some** tender.
standard	The ribs at that restaurant are **somewhat** tender.
standard	Is there **some** wood to throw on the fire?

than, then *Than* is a conjunction used in comparisons. *Then* is an adverb that shows a sequence of events.

EXAMPLES
Hummingbirds are much more aggressive **than** you would ever guess from their size.
The wool was spun into yarn and **then** knitted into a garment.

their, there, they're *Their* is the possessive form of *they*. *There* points out a place or introduces an independent clause. *They're* is the contracted form of *they are*.

EXAMPLES
The Hepburns always remove **their** shoes before entering the house.
The twins achieve more than most people because **they're** remarkably energetic.
You really shouldn't go **there** after dark.

them *Them* is a pronoun. It should never be used as an adjective. Use *those*.

EXAMPLES

nonstandard	India really shouldn't have tried to hem **them** pants herself.
standard	India really shouldn't have tried to hem **those** pants herself.

this here, that there Do not use. Simply say *this* or *that.*

EXAMPLES

nonstandard	This here was a movie theater before being transformed into a skating rink.
standard	**This** was a movie theater before being transformed into a skating rink.
nonstandard	That there looks really expensive.
standard	**That** looks really expensive.

to, too, two *To* is a preposition that can mean "in the direction of." *Too* is an adverb that means both "extremely, overly" and "also." *Two* is the spelling for the number 2.

EXAMPLES

It can be difficult **to** decide whether or not to classify an animal as a crustacean.
The crustaceans known as woodlice live on land, but die if they get **too** dry.
A blue whale can consume over **two** tons of krill, a shrimplike crustacean.

try and Use *try to* instead.

EXAMPLES

nonstandard	Try and point your toes when you dive.
standard	**Try to** point your toes when you dive.

use to, used to Be sure to add the *d* to *used* to form the past participle.

EXAMPLES

nonstandard	Printers use to set type by hand.
standard	Printers used to set type by hand.

way, ways Do not use *ways* for *way* when referring to distance.

EXAMPLES

nonstandard	Karenna hopped off her bicycle and walked a ways.
standard	Karenna hopped off her bicycle and walked a **way**.

when, where When you define a word, don't use *when* or *where.*

EXAMPLES

nonstandard	A *potlatch* was where Northwest Indians gathered to give each other elaborate presents.
standard	A *potlatch* was an event at which Northwest Indians gathered to give each other elaborate presents.

where, that Do not use *where* to mean "that."

EXAMPLES

nonstandard	Did you hear where the Senate has refused to pass the appropriations bill?
standard	Did you hear **that** the Senate has refused to pass the appropriations bill?

which, that, who, whom *Which* is used to refer only to things. Use it to introduce nonessential clauses that refer to things or to groups of people. Always use a comma before *which* when it introduces a nonessential clause.

EXAMPLES

Downward dog, **which** is one of the most basic yoga positions, stretches the Achilles tendon and the hamstrings.

The lute, **which** is a stringed instrument, is shaped like a pear.

That is used to refer either to people or things. Use it to introduce essential clauses that refer to things or groups of people. Do not use a comma before *that* when it introduces an essential clause.

EXAMPLES

The arrowheads in the display case are the ones **that** Grandpa George found back in Ohio.

Micaela admitted **that** she was tone-deaf.

Who or *whom* is used to refer only to people. Use *who* or *whom* to introduce essential and nonessential clauses. Use a comma only when the pronoun introduces a nonessential clause.

EXAMPLES
Richard Trevithick was the English inventor **who** devised the first steam-powered locomotive.

Rafael, **whom** we had always thought humorless, had us laughing hysterically with his impersonations.

who, whom The pronoun *who* has two different forms. *Who* is used when it functions as a nominative pronoun. *Whom* is used when it functions as an objective pronoun.

EXAMPLES
Who put a five-dollar bill in the tip jar? (nominative pronoun)
For **whom** was that generous tip intended? (objective pronoun)

who's, whose *Who's* is a contraction for *who is* or *who has*. *Whose* is the possessive form of *who*.

EXAMPLES
Who's the Attorney General of Ohio?
Whose idea was it to paint a mural on the wall of the abandoned building?

without, unless Do not use the preposition *without* in place of the conjunction *unless*.

EXAMPLES

nonstandard	Ryan cannot accept that summer job without he gets some reliable transportation.
standard	Ryan cannot accept that summer job **without** some reliable transportation.
standard	Ryan cannot accept that summer job **unless** he gets some reliable transportation.

your, you're *Your* is a possessive pronoun. *You're* is a contraction for the words *you are*.

EXAMPLES
The scientific study begins with a painless study of **your** bone density.
After you finish the test, **you're** instructed to put down your pencil and wait quietly.

USAGE tip

Review the alphabetic list of Commonly Misused Words on pages 351–363 before completing these exercises.

EXERCISE 16
1. a lot
2. take
3. well
4. its
5. teach
6. set, sit
7. try to
8. you're
9. except
10. already
11. besides
12. fewer
13. why didn't you
14. proceeded

Try It Yourself

EXERCISE 16

Identifying Common Usage Problems

Choose the correct word in parentheses to complete the sentence.

1. It takes (alot, a lot) of determination to make it in the world of musical comedy.
2. Please don't forget to (bring, take) your casserole dish home at the end of the party.
3. Poor Mike—whenever he doesn't feel (good, well), he's sure he's contracted some deadly disease.
4. A male deer's position in the herd is indicated by the size of (its, it's) antlers.
5. Believe it or not, Jeff is trying to (learn, teach) his dog to sing.
6. (Set, Sit) a pillow on the seat before you (set, sit) on that uncomfortable chair.
7. (Try and, Try to) keep your eyes out for some rare lady-slipper orchids when you take your walk.
8. (Your, You're) very talented at mediating disputes among your peers.
9. All of the French IV students (accept, except) Lauren have been inducted into the French Honor Society.
10. Although Jane had (all ready, already) showered, she gleefully jumped back into the sea to body surf.
11. Nobody (beside, besides) the owner of the restaurant thinks the new neon sign is a good idea.
12. I unpacked (fewer, less) plums from the shopping bag than I remembered selecting from the bin.
13. (How come you didn't, Why didn't you) pick me up when you said you would?
14. We checked our backpacks and purses in the museum cloakroom and (preceded, proceeded) to the Egyptian exhibit.

15. Greta seems (real, really) arrogant and aloof, but she's just shy.
16. A tree-ripened pineapple has a much richer and more intense flavor (than, then) one that is harvested before it is ready.
17. She's of the opinion (that, where) everyone should take a year off after high school to figure out what they really want to do.
18. (Whose, Who's) rings were left next to the sink in the girls' room?
19. The (affect, effect) of the speech was the opposite of what the speaker intended.
20. You'll never get (anywhere, anywheres) in life if you don't learn a little self-discipline.
21. Kurt felt so (bad, badly) when he failed to recognize his kindergarten teacher!
22. After the ceremony, Lina distributed tiny handfuls of rice (between, among) the wedding guests.
23. Billy won't enjoy that car for long if he (doesn't, don't) start having the oil changed more frequently.
24. We (can hardly, can't hardly) wait to see how the ceramics look after the firing.
25. I'm sorry, but I explained that I don't like this (kind, kinds) of chunky peanut butter.

15. really
16. than
17. that
18. whose
19. effect
20. anywhere
21. bad
22. among
23. doesn't
24. can hardly
25. kind

EXERCISE 17

Correcting Common Usage Problems

Rewrite the following sentences to correct any mistakes in usage. If a sentence does not have any errors, write *correct*.

1. Proteus, which is one of Neptune's small satellites, reflects little of the light that strikes it.
2. If you are a heir to a nation's throne, you may live in luxury, but you have very little freedom.

EXERCISE 17
Responses will vary. Sample responses:

1. correct
2. If you are an heir to a nation's throne, you may live in luxury, but you have very little freedom.
3. The water isn't boiling because no one remembered to light the flame.
4. correct

5. I assure you there is nothing more difficult to furnish than an octagonal room.
6. The goal on a vacation is not always to travel farther and faster, but to savor the moment.
7. Some people never worry; others have trouble protecting themselves from anxiety.
8. In the foyer, a houndstooth jacket sits on top of an elegant little table.
9. It's rather late to check the lost-and-found for a scarf you misplaced last spring.
10. The reason your tea looks peculiar is that you added both lemon and milk, and they curdled!
11. The flight was fully booked, so that regardless of his preferences, Nick was given an aisle seat at the back of the plane.
12. Mom was upset that I laid the table with plastic forks and paper plates instead of silver and china.
13. If you scratch an insect bite, the relief lasts for just a second, and then the irritation gets worse.
14. When Rick entered the kitchen, the cat jumped off the table with a guilty expression.
15. Outside the castle stood a weary busload of tourists waiting to get in.
16. Mr. Liu said the weather was simply too glorious to hold English class indoors.
17. I chose this yarn because the hues remind me of brilliant autumn leaves.
18. correct

3. The water ain't boiling because no one remembered to light the flame.
4. There is nothing more comfortable than sleeping on a genuine featherbed.
5. I assure you there is nothing more difficult to furnish then an octagonal room.
6. The goal on a vacation is not always to travel further and faster, but to savor the moment.
7. Some people never worry; others have trouble protecting theirselves from anxiety.
8. In the foyer, a houndstooth jacket sets on top of a elegant little table.
9. Its kind of late to check the lost-and-found for a scarf you misplaced last spring.
10. The reason your tea looks peculiar is because you added both lemon and milk, and they curdled!
11. The flight was fully booked, so that irregardless of his preferences, Nick was given an aisle seat at the back of the plane.
12. Mom was upset that I lay the table with plastic forks and paper plates instead of silver and china.
13. If you itch an insect bite, the relief lasts for just a second, and then the irritation gets worse.
14. When Rick entered the kitchen, the cat jumped off of the table with a guilty expression.
15. Outside of the castle stood a weary busload of tourists waiting to get in.
16. Mr. Liu said the weather was simply to glorious to hold English class indoors.
17. I chose this here yarn because the hues remind me of brilliant autumn leaves.
18. Sylvester Graham, after whom the graham cracker was named, was an early health-food advocate.
19. Jackie use to run through the low-hanging wands of the willow tree, pretending she was a car going through a carwash.

20. Sometimes when he goes to the diner, Kyle orders breakfast and lunch, two.
21. Where did you get that amazing pair of tie-dyed jeans at?
22. The ceiling of the dining room was painted a heavenly shade of blue.
23. You hadn't ought to build a house in a floodplain if you're afraid of risk.
24. Yasmin is over the worst of mononucleosis, but she still needs to lay down for a few hours every afternoon.
25. He was quiet disturbed by the suggestions that he'd been unfair.

EXERCISE 18

Using Commonly Misused Words

Write an original sentence using each of the following groups of words correctly.

1. between Salma and Bill
2. as if no one paid attention
3. has affected you somewhat
4. affect the outcome
5. feel bad
6. feel good
7. look well
8. bring warm socks
9. further inspection
10. many fewer
11. studying all together
12. learn the tango
13. really valuable
14. besides a mulberry tree
15. altogether nasty
16. try to sympathize
17. which flavored the soup
18. can enter
19. may enter
20. accept the problem

19. Jackie used to run through the low-hanging wands of the willow tree, pretending she was a car going through a carwash.
20. Sometimes when he goes to the diner, Kyle orders breakfast and lunch, too.
21. Where did you get that amazing pair of tie-dyed jeans?
22. correct
23. You ought not build a house in a floodplain if you're afraid of risk.
24. Yasmin is over the worst of mononucleosis, but she still needs to lie down for a few hours every afternoon.
25. He was quite disturbed by the suggestions that he'd been unfair.

EXERCISE 18

Responses will vary. Students' sentences should be grammatically correct in addition to showing an understanding of common usage problems. Encourage students to create as many different contexts for these commonly confused words as they can.

ASSESSMENT
Grammar and Usage Test is available at www.emcp.com.

EXERCISE 1
1. is
2. count
3. hides
4. has
5. taste
6. are
7. make
8. taste
9. do
10. are

UNIT 14 REVIEW

TEST YOUR KNOWLEDGE

EXERCISE 1

Identifying Problems with Subject-Verb Agreement

Choose the verb in parentheses that agrees in number with the subject. (10 points)

EXAMPLE
If there (is, are) walnuts in that muffin, Delilah won't eat it.
(are)

1. What exactly (is, are) the definition of a nut?
2. Any fruits or seeds with a tough skin forming a shell (counts, count) as nuts.
3. Inside the hard shell (hides, hide) the tender, edible kernel.
4. An animal that feeds on nuts (has, have) strong teeth in order to crack the shell.
5. Either peanuts or cashews (tastes, taste) delicious when roasted and lightly salted.
6. What nutrients (is, are) contained in nuts?
7. Both protein and fat (makes, make) up the nutritional value of nuts.
8. Neither the hazelnuts nor the filberts (tastes, taste) quite fresh to me.
9. How (does, do) nuts get dispersed by animals?
10. The woody fibers of the coconut (is, are) manufactured into matting for floors.

EXERCISE 2

Identifying Problems with Apostrophes

Choose the word in parentheses that uses the apostrophe correctly. (10 points)

EXAMPLE

(It's, Its) true that a chameleon can change (it's, its) color, but only within a fairly narrow color range. *(It's, its)*

1. The four main Channel (Island's, Islands') names are Jersey, Guernsey, Alderney, and Sark.
2. I had to borrow (Rees's, Rees') phone when my parents didn't show up after the football game.
3. (Mice's, Mices') ability to produce many generations in a short period of time has made them invaluable to genetic researchers.
4. When a crowd gathers passively at an accident, it is (someone's, someones') responsibility to step forward and take action.
5. Please go through the closet and take out everything (thats, that's) (yours, your's).
6. All of the motorcycle (rider's, riders') jackets were decorated with the insignia of their club.
7. C. S. (Lewis's, Lewis') seven-book series about the fantasy world of Narnia is an allegory about the universal struggle between good and evil.
8. Yearbook pictures arrived today, and Erika burst into wild laughter when she saw (her's, hers).
9. The most sophisticated computer (cant, can't) always detect a fraudulent identification card.
10. According to the morning news, (theirs, there's) a terrible traffic jam on Route 84.

EXERCISE 2
1. Islands'
2. Rees's
3. Mice's
4. someone's
5. that's yours
6. riders'
7. Lewis's
8. hers
9. can't
10. there's

EXERCISE 3
1. isn't
2. among
3. take
4. already
5. really, bad
6. have
7. broken
8. further
9. fewer
10. This

EXERCISE 3
Identifying Commonly Misused Words

Choose the word in parentheses to complete each sentence correctly. (10 points)

EXAMPLE
Everyone could participate in the final round (accept, except) Lincoln, who hadn't scored a point. *(except)*

1. Public transportation (isn't, ain't) going to replace the automobile as Americans' preferred mode of traveling for many years, if ever.
2. The anonymous benefactor appeared from time to time with a briefcase full of ten-dollar bills, which he distributed (among, between) all those who quickly congregated.
3. In Wales, it's a good idea to (bring, take) an umbrella with you whenever you go out, because the weather can change from moment to moment.
4. When Goldie went to buy her niece a graduation card, the drugstore had (all ready, already) sold out of them.
5. Neal felt (real, really) (bad, badly) about backing his parents' car into a telephone pole.
6. Some critics say that law enforcement officials should (of, have) better communicated intelligence findings prior to the attacks.
7. I'd be happy to lend you my portable CD player; unfortunately, it is (broken, busted).
8. Many scientists had explored the phenomenon, but the Nobel Prize winner took her investigations (farther, further).
9. There are (fewer, less) pearls on this necklace than on that one, but the pearls on this necklace are bigger.
10. (This, These) kind of infomercial pretends to give an objective view of the product.

EXERCISE 4

Correcting Problems in Usage

Rewrite the following sentences to correct for errors in subject-verb agreement, apostrophes, double negatives, split infinitives, comma splices, fused sentences, and dangling and misplaced modifiers. If there are no usage errors in the sentence, write *correct*. (10 points)

EXAMPLE

The detective discovered the abandoned convertible climbing the hill. *(Climbing the hill, the detective discovered the abandoned convertible.)*

1. Mr. Marcos went to a conference in Turkey about a new treatment for skin cancer on the fourth of August.
2. The article didn't mention nothing about the environmental effects of allowing cruise ships to dock in the harbor.
3. After the 2000 election, Florida spent millions of dollars in an attempt to dramatically upgrade its voting system.
4. A tremendous bolt of lightning split the sky, and all of the students were ordered to immediately go into the school.
5. Running from one scheduled after-school activity to another, there is no time for leisurely thought or conversation.
6. Konrad, as well as his sisters Else and Heike, is an expert rider.
7. Danielle is very upset because she doesn't know which boots are hers'.
8. Either the president or his advisors has come up with a compromise solution to the impasse, the senators hope to vote on the compromise at tomorrow's session.
9. Both rose oil and shea butter is real soothing to very dry skin.
10. Carvings and statues cover buildings of the Gupta period with symbolical references.

EXERCISE 4

Responses may vary slightly.
Sample responses:

1. On the fourth of August, Mr. Marcos went to Turkey for a conference about a new treatment for skin cancer.
2. The article mentioned nothing about the environmental effects of allowing cruise ships to dock in the harbor. *OR* The article didn't mention anything about the environmental effects of allowing cruise ships to dock in the harbor.
3. After the 2000 election, Florida spent millions of dollars in an attempt to upgrade its voting system dramatically.
4. A tremendous bolt of lightning split the sky, and all of the students were ordered to go into the school immediately.
5. Running from one scheduled after-school activity to another, students have no time for leisurely thought or conversation.
6. correct
7. Danielle is very upset because she doesn't know which boots are hers.

8. Either the president or his advisors have come up with a compromise solution to the impasse. The senators hope to vote on the compromise at tomorrow's session.
9. Both rose oil and shea butter are really soothing to very dry skin.
10. correct

EXERCISE 5
Responses will vary. Look for essays that are creative responses to the question and that are free of common usage problems.

EXERCISE 5

Writing with Correct Usage

Write a brief essay for the op-ed page of your local newspaper about the conflicts high school students often feel between doing what other people (whether peers, parents, or teachers) think or imply is right, and doing what they want. To focus your essay, select a specific conflict. Analyze the pros and cons of both meeting others' expectations and resisting them in relation to that conflict. When you revise your essay, look for common usage problems, including subject-verb agreement, double negatives, split infinitives, run-on sentences, incorrect apostrophe use, and commonly misused words. (10 points)

PART THREE

UNIT 15 PUNCTUATION

ASSESSMENT
Style Pretest, Style Comprehensive Test, and Punctuation and Capitalization Test are available at www.emcp.com.

UNIT OVERVIEW

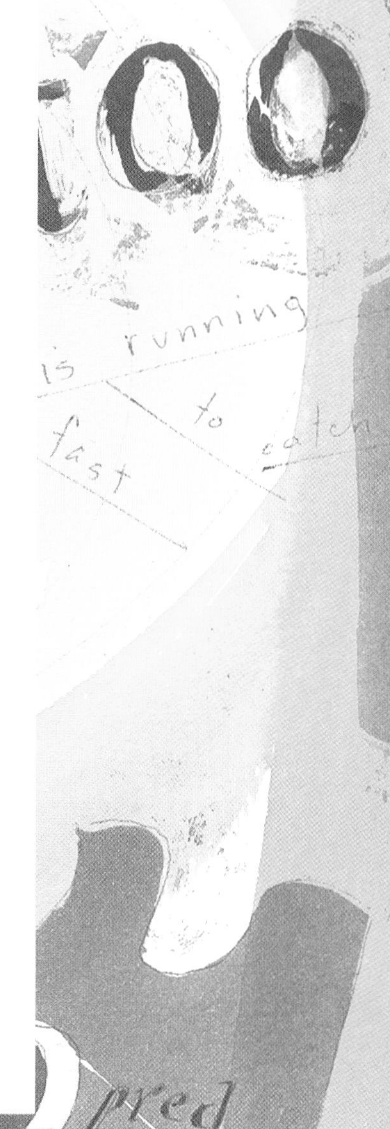

PUNCTUATION

EDITING FOR PUNCTUATION ERRORS

When editing your work, correct all punctuation errors. Several common punctuation errors to avoid are the incorrect use of **end marks**, **commas**, and **semicolons**.

END MARKS

An **end mark** tells the reader where a sentence ends. An end mark also shows the purpose of the sentence. The three end marks are the **period,** the **question mark**, and the **exclamation point.**

EXAMPLES

declarative sentence	The mark of good manners is thoughtfulness to others.
imperative sentence	Get inside.
interrogative sentence	Have you ever seen the northern lights?
exclamatory sentence	That was an incredible feat of strength!

A **declarative sentence** makes a statement and ends with a period.

EXAMPLE
A branch fell off the apple tree.

An **imperative sentence** gives a command or makes a request. Often, the understood subject of these sentences is *you*. An imperative sentence usually ends with a period. If the command or request is strong, the sentence may end with an exclamation point.

EXAMPLES
(You) Pass me the French bread, please.
(You) Don't touch that frayed cord!

An **interrogative sentence** asks a question. It ends with a question mark.

EXAMPLE
Where should I put this damp towel?

An **exclamatory sentence** expresses strong feeling and ends with an exclamation point.

EXAMPLES
How gorgeous that dress is!
I absolutely loathe meatloaf

USAGE tip

An indirect question ends with a period rather than a question mark.

Henry asked me if I liked Katherine Anne Porter's short stories.

USAGE tip

Do not confuse imperative and exclamatory sentences. Whereas an exclamatory sentence always ends with an exclamation point, an imperative sentence may end with either a period or an exclamation point. Remember that an imperative sentence always gives a command or makes a request.

Other Uses of Periods

As you know, periods are used at the end of all declarative sentences and most imperative sentences. Periods can be used in other ways, too.

Use a period at the end of most abbreviations or initials. An **abbreviation** is a shortened form of a word of phrase. (Learn more about abbreviations in Unit 16, pages 439–442.)

Personal Names

Use a period at the end of an abbreviated given name.

EXAMPLES
E. E. Cummings, General **J. E. B.** Stuart, Robert **E.** Lee

Titles

Use a period after abbreviated social and professional titles and degrees.

EXAMPLES

Mr. Victor Funk	**Mrs.** Sarah S. Wright
Ms. Steinem	**Dr.** Cairo-Smith
Sen. Gail Wood	**Gov.** Seth Taft
Capt. Queeg	**Prof.** Hamilton

USAGE tip

When you use a professional title or degree after a name, do not include the title at the beginning of the name.

Dr. Jaime Cairo or Jaime Cairo, **M.D.** (Not **Dr.** Jaime Cairo, **M.D.**)

USAGE tip

Spell out civil and military titles when they are used before last names alone.

Captain Miksis
Senator Lieberman

Business Names

Use a period after abbreviated business names.

EXAMPLES
Ashleigh's Fashions, **Inc.** The Xerxes **Corp.**
Jayne Zeller and **Co.**

Addresses

Use a period after abbreviated addresses.

EXAMPLES
Sheridan **Ave.** Hollywood **Blvd.** Union **Sq.**
Great River **Rd.** Empire State **Bldg.**

USAGE tip

Spell out the names of states and other geographical terms when you're using them in regular text.

The jazz festival was held in Chicago, **Illinois.**

Geographical Terms

Use a period after abbreviated geographical terms when you're using the abbreviated terms in notes, tables, and bibliographies.

EXAMPLES
London, **Eng.** Chicago, **Ill.** Marseilles, **Fr.**

Time

In notes, tables, and footnotes, use a period after abbreviations of dates. Abbreviations of time and year designations also take periods.

EXAMPLES
A.D. 1166 49 **B.C.** 3:20 **A.M.** 7:00 **P.M.**
2 **hrs.** 48 **min.**
Tues. morning **Mar.** 3

When names of months and days appear in regular text, however, do not abbreviate.

EXAMPLES
I have to be at school early on **Tuesday** morning.
The bridge was completed on **March** 3.

Units of Measurement

Use a period after abbreviations of units of measurement used in tables and notes.

EXAMPLES

1 tsp. baking powder
4 oz. baking chocolate
117 lbs.
2 c. cake flour
5 ft. 3 in.

When units of measurement appear in text, however, do not abbreviate. Spell out the names of units of measurement, whether they stand alone or follow a numeral.

EXAMPLES

The floodwater in the basement was nearly two feet deep.
How many pints are in a quart?
Our Labrador retriever needs to lose five pounds.

Abbreviations without Periods

Some abbreviations do *not* use a period. Do *not* use periods with metric measurements, state names in postal addresses, or directional elements.

EXAMPLES

metric measurements	cc, ml, km, g, L
state postal codes	CO, TN, AL
compass points	N, NW, S, SE

Do *not* use periods with acronyms or abbreviations that are pronounced letter by letter. Capitalize all the letters, but use no periods.

EXAMPLES

American Society for the Prevention of Cruelty to Animals—**ASPCA**
video jockey—**VJ**
John Fitzgerald Kennedy—**JFK**
television—**TV**

EXERCISE 1

1. AMANDA. Why are you trembling so, Laura? (interrogative)
2. LAURA. Mother, you've made me so nervous! (exclamatory)
3. AMANDA. Why, how have I made you nervous? (interrogative)

MODEL

4. LAURA. By all this fuss! (exclamatory)
5. You make it seem so important. (declarative)
6. AMANDA. I don't understand you at all, honey. (declarative)
7. Every time I try to do anything for you that's the least bit different you just seem to set yourself against it. (declarative)
8. Now look at yourself. (imperative)
9. No, wait! (imperative)
10. Wait just a minute— (imperative)
11. I forgot something. (declarative)

EXERCISE 2

1. Yikes, that police car is pulling us over!
2. What on earth have we done wrong?
3. I was going 33, and the speed limit is 35 on this stretch of road.
4. Excuse me, officer, but what is the problem?
5. Do you realize that you are driving with your lights off at night?
6. Oh my goodness, what an idiot I am!
7. Turn them on immediately so that I can make sure both of them work.
8. I'm sorry it's taking me a minute to comply; I'm just a little shaky.
9. Please don't give me a ticket, officer.

Try It Yourself

EXERCISE 1
Identifying Sentence Purposes in Literature

Identify each sentence in the following literature passage as declarative, interrogative, imperative, or exclamatory.

AMANDA. Why are you trembling so, Laura?
LAURA. Mother, you've made me so nervous!
AMANDA. Why, how have I made you nervous?
LAURA. By all this fuss! You make it seem so important.
AMANDA. I don't understand you at all, honey. Every time I try to do anything for you that's the least bit different you just seem to set yourself against it. Now look at yourself. (LAURA *starts for door R.*) No, wait! Wait just a minute—I forgot something.

from *The Glass Menagerie*
Tennessee Williams

EXERCISE 2
Understanding End Marks

Punctuate the end of each of the sentences with the correct mark of punctuation—a period, question mark, or exclamation point.

1. Yikes, that police car is pulling us over
2. What on earth have we done wrong
3. I was going 33, and the speed limit is 35 on this stretch of road
4. Excuse me, officer, but what is the problem
5. Do you realize that you are driving with your lights off at night
6. Oh my goodness, what an idiot I am
7. Turn them on immediately so that I can make sure both of them work
8. I'm sorry it's taking me a minute to comply; I'm just a little shaky
9. Please don't give me a ticket, officer
10. Well, I believe you made an honest mistake, but honest mistakes can still lead to accidents

EXERCISE 3

Correcting Punctuation of End Marks and Abbreviations

Rewrite each of the following sentences, correcting any errors or omissions in the punctuation of end marks and the use of abbreviations.

1. My impacted wisdom teeth were removed by Dr Murray Jackman, DMD
2. If you're coming to my party, please park in the lot behind Pee-Wee's Print Shop on Morehouse Blvd.!
3. How ridiculous that she thought that Toby Wilson, Jr was the father of Toby Wilson, Sr?
4. Meghan just learned that her mother has been relocated by her employer from Fla. to Ala.
5. Fabulous Floors, Inc, has been in business since Nov. 17.
6. Capt Rafael Semmes of the Confederate cruiser the *Alabama* captured over sixty Yankee merchant ships during the Civil War.
7. Did you know that just one oz. of saffron, a flavoring agent often used with rice, costs over $35.00.
8. Sen. Jones is on the Armed Services Committee!
9. How outrageous it was of you to wake me up at 6:00 A M on a Sunday.
10. When you read an ancient Greek play, you realize that although customs were very different in 500 B C, human nature was the same as it is now?

EXERCISE 4

Using End Marks in Your Writing

Assume that you witnessed a minor traffic accident at a city intersection and that the police have ased you to write a report of what you observed. Use correctly punctuated abbreviations to note the names of the streets involved, the nearby businesses, the drivers' names, and the exact time of the incident. Use sentences that end with periods, exclamation points, and question marks. (You may want to include comments from onlookers.)

---

10. Well, I believe you made an honest mistake, but honest mistakes can still lead to accidents.

EXERCISE 3

1. My impacted wisdom teeth were removed by Murray Jackman, D.M.D.
2. If you're coming to my party, please park in the lot behind Pee-Wee's Print Shop on Morehouse Blvd.
3. How ridiculous that she thought that Toby Wilson, Jr., was the father of Toby Wilson, Sr.
4. Meghan just learned that her mother has been relocated by her employer from Florida to Alabama.
5. Fabulous Floors, Inc., has been in business since November 17.
6. Capt. Rafael Semmes of the Confederate cruiser the *Alabama* captured over sixty Yankee merchant ships during the Civil War.
7. Did you know that just one ounce of saffron, a flavoring agent often used with rice, costs over $35.00?
8. Senator Jones is on the Armed Services Committee.
9. How outrageous it was of you to wake me up at 6:00 A.M. on a Sunday morning!

10. When you read an ancient Greek play, you realize that although customs were very different in 500 B.C., human nature was the same as it is now.

EXERCISE 4

Responses will vary.

COMMAS

A **comma** separates words or groups of words within a sentence. Commas tell the reader to pause at certain spots in the sentence. These pauses help keep the reader from running together certain words and phrases when they should be kept apart.

Use commas to separate items in a series. The items in a series may be words, phrases, or clauses.

EXAMPLES

words in a series	**India, Pakistan, and Bangladesh** are three of the nations in South Asia.
phrases in a series	Coach DiBenedetto said to the new players, "I want to see you **on the playing field, in your uniforms, at exactly 3:00 P.M.**"
clauses in a series	Unfortunately, the manual fails to explain **how you turn off the car alarm, how you placate your annoyed neighbors when you cannot, or how you explain the problem to the police.**

USAGE tip

Do not use a comma to separate the verb phrases of a compound predicate.

You should pay attention to bird calls and then start memorizing particular patterns of sound.

Make sure you use both a comma and a conjunction between independent clauses.

Avoid disturbing birds that are nesting, and contact experts if you think you have sighted a rare or endangered species.

Use commas when you combine sentences using *and*, *but*, *or*, *nor*, *yet*, *so*, or *for*. Place the comma before these words.

EXAMPLES

Bird watching is a hobby accessible to most people, **for** even in urban environments, many types of birds exist.

You can start by going outside and observing as many birds as possible, **or** you can begin by getting a bird identification guide and studying the major types of birds.

Use a comma after an introductory word, phrase, or clause.

EXAMPLES

Sadly, many bird populations are dropping because their traditional habitats are vanishing.

Possessed of a distinctive silhouette, the pelican is easy to recognize from a distance.

Use a comma to set off words or phrases that interrupt sentences. Use two commas if the word or phrase occurs in the middle of the sentence. Use one comma if the word or phrase comes at the beginning or at the end of a sentence.

EXAMPLES

Commonly called the passenger pigeon, the *ectopistes migratorius* sadly became extinct in 1900.

Birds' bills, believe it or not, are constantly growing.

Birds keep themselves clean in unexpected ways, such as "bathing" in dust or even chimney smoke!

Use a comma between two or more adjectives that modify the same noun.

EXAMPLES

The American wigeon is a duck with a rather long, pointed tail.

The low, soft hoot of the flammulated owl can be heard in the remote, quiet pine-forests of the southwestern mountains.

Use a comma to set off names used in direct address.

EXAMPLES

That bird, Jamie, is a juvenile whip-poor-will.

Kelly, you must avoid walking near that restricted area of the beach because the piping plovers nest there.

Use commas to separate parts of a date. Do not use a comma between the month and the year.

EXAMPLES
On October 7, 1959, a Russian spacecraft took the first photographs of the far side of the moon.

In October 1959, a Russian spacecraft took the first photographs of the far side of the moon.

Use commas to separate items in addresses. Do not use a comma between the state and the ZIP code.

EXAMPLES
After making the first nonstop trans-Atlantic flight, Charles Lindbergh received an uproarious welcome in Paris, France.

My mother's former college roommate lives at 2997 Mountain Way, Boise, Idaho 83712.

Do not use unnecessary commas. Too many commas can make a sentence's meaning unclear and its style choppy.

EXAMPLES

confusing	The most popular girls' name, for babies born in 2001, is Emily, which comes from the Gothic name *Amala*, meaning "industrious one."
clear	The most popular girls' name for babies born in 2001 is Emily, which comes from the Gothic name *Amala,* meaning "industrious one."

Try It Yourself

EXERCISE 5

Identifying Commas in Literature

Identify the use of the comma in each sentence of the literature passage below as one of the following: to separate items in a series; to combine sentences; to set off interrupters, introductory words or phrases, or direct address; or to separate two or more adjectives that modify the same noun.

EXERCISE 5

1. . . . the people filed out of the hall chattering and laughing, glad to relax and find the living level again, but my kinswoman made no effort to rise. (interrupter, combining sentences)
2. . . . the men of the orchestra went out one by one, leaving the stage to the chairs and music stands, empty as a winter cornfield. (interrupter)
3. "I don't want to go, Clark, I don't want to go!" (direct address, combining sentences)
4. For her, just outside the concert hall, lay the black pond with the cattle-tracked bluffs; the tall, unpainted house, with weather-curled boards, naked as a tower; the crook-backed ash seedlings where the dishcloths hung to dry; the gaunt, moulting turkeys picking up refuse about the kitchen door. (introductory phrase, interrupter, two or more adjectives modifying the same noun)

The concert was over; the people filed out of the hall chattering and laughing, glad to relax and find the living level again, but my kinswoman made no effort to rise. The harpist slipped the green felt cover over his instrument; the flute-players shook the water from their mouthpieces; the men of the orchestra went out one by one, leaving the stage to the chairs and music stands, empty as a winter cornfield.

I spoke to my aunt. She burst into tears and sobbed pleadingly. "I don't want to go, Clark, I don't want to go!"

I understood. For her, just outside the concert hall, lay the black pond with the cattle-tracked bluffs; the tall, unpainted house, with weather-curled boards, naked as a tower; the crook-backed ash seedlings where the dishcloths hung to dry; the gaunt, moulting turkeys picking up refuse about the kitchen door.

from "A Wagner Matinee"
Willa Cather

EXERCISE 6

Correcting Comma Use

Rewrite the following sentences so that they are correctly punctuated with commas.

1. Some woodwind instruments have a single reed but others have a double reed.
2. The reason the tube of a French horn is so elaborately coiled Genevieve is that if straight the tube would extend to an unmanageable distance.
3. Reeds are manufactured from plastic metal or thin pieces of cane.
4. The eager inexperienced violin student produces sounds like the screeches of a feline in agony.
5. The harpist watched tensely as her instrument was placed on the concert stage seated herself on a low bench and began tentatively to strum the strings.

EXERCISE 6
1. Some woodwind instruments have a single reed, but others have a double reed.
2. The reason the tube of a French horn is so elaborately coiled, Genevieve, is that, if straight, the tube would extend to an unmanageable distance.
3. Reeds are manufactured from plastic, metal, or thin pieces of cane.
4. The eager, inexperienced violin student produces sounds like the screeches of a feline in agony.
5. The harpist watched tensely as her instrument was placed on the concert stage, seated herself on a low bench, and began tentatively to strum the strings.

6. Franz Josef Haydn wrote over sixty works for the string quartet, an ensemble composed of two violins, a viola, and a cello.
7. The organ pipe that produced the lowest note, a behemoth as tall as a house, was for some mysterious reason failing to function properly.
8. The xylophone, Jacob, is classified as a percussion instrument, but unlike most of the other instruments in that category, the xylophone can play a tune.
9. Miraculously, the missing Stradivarius violin was recovered intact in an alley.
10. On October 18, 2002, Wagner's *Rhinegold* was performed at the Barbican Theatre, London, England.

EXERCISE 7
Responses will vary. Students should use commas to separate items in a series, to combine sentences, to indicate interrupters and modifiers, and to separate parts of geographical items, locations, and dates.

6. Franz Josef Haydn wrote over sixty works for the string quartet an ensemble composed of two violins, a viola, and a cello.
7. The organ pipe that produced the lowest note a behemoth as tall as a house was for some mysterious reason failing to function properly.
8. The xylophone Jacob is classified as a percussion instrument but unlike most of the other instruments in that category the xylophone can play a tune.
9. Miraculously the missing Stradivarius violin was recovered intact in an alley.
10. On October 18 2002 Wagner's *Rhinegold* was performed at the Barbican Theatre London England.

EXERCISE 7

Using Commas in Your Writing

Write a letter to a friend describing a memorable event you attended. The event could have been a concert, a play, a school assembly, or an over-the-top wedding. Include complex and compound sentences, lists, introductory phrases, and phrases that interrupt a sentence. Check to make sure you have used commas correctly.

SEMICOLONS

A **semicolon** joins two closely related sentences.

EXAMPLE
Electronic wonders are not the essence of espionage; human intelligence is.

Use a semicolon to join the independent clauses of a compound sentence if no coordinating conjunction is used.

Coordinating conjunctions such as *and, but, so, or, nor, for,* and *yet* can be used to combine two related sentences. A semicolon is a punctuation mark that also joins two closely related sentences. A semicolon used in place of the comma and conjunction adds emphasis to the second clause. The semicolon signals a pause that is longer than that of a comma but shorter than that of a period.

EXAMPLES

two separate sentences	Spies have been around for as long as civilization. Great kings and emperors from Babylon to Rome employed spies to find out what their enemies were plotting.
joined with semicolon	Spies have been around for as long as civilization; great kings and emperors from Babylon to Rome employed spies to find out what their enemies were plotting.

Use a semicolon between independent clauses joined by a conjunction if either clause contains commas.

EXAMPLE
Microdots are minuscule photographs of documents, photographs, or other sources of information; they can be concealed in everyday objects such as rings and pens.

Use a semicolon between items in a series if the items contain commas.

EXAMPLE
Motivated by a deep belief in communism, Kim Philby became one of the Soviet Union's spies in Britain; motivated by a desire for money, Aldrich Ames turned over American secrets to the KGB; and motivated by vanity, the professor Hugh Hambleton betrayed his country to Moscow.

Use a semicolon between independent clauses joined by a conjunctive adverb or a transitional phrase.

EXERCISE 8

1. For the period from the end of World War II in 1945 to the fall of the communist system in the early 1990s, the Soviet Union and the United States were involved in a cold war; consequently, each country was in avid pursuit of military information about the other.
2. The city of Berlin, which was divided into democratic West Berlin and communist East Berlin, was a center of espionage; as a matter of fact, the CIA and British intelligence dug a tunnel from West Berlin to a point just under some important military telephone lines in the east.
3. Subminiature cameras have been inserted into a number of devices; for instance, there are cigarette pack cameras, cigarette lighter cameras, and wristwatch cameras.
4. An early surveillance camera was in the shape of a matchbox; it could be camouflaged by a label from any country so that it would look natural when used in that country.
5. Mordecai Louk, an Israeli double agent, was captured by Egyptian intelligence in Rome; then he was drugged and put in a special trunk, which was mailed to Cairo.

EXAMPLES

conjunctive adverb

Colditz Castle in eastern Germany was considered to be an inescapable fortress; however, helped by a team of fellow prisoners who manufactured false identity papers and other necessities, a British officer named Airey Neave escaped from Colditz in 1942.

transitional phrase

American spy Christopher Boyce was convicted of selling secrets about the United States' satellite system; **as a result**, he was sentenced to forty years in prison.

Common Conjunctive Adverbs			
accordingly	furthermore	meanwhile	otherwise
also	however	moreover	still
besides	indeed	nevertheless	then
consequently	instead	next	therefore

Common Transitional Phrases			
as a result	for instance	in fact	in spite of
for example	in conclusion	in other words	that is

Try It Yourself

EXERCISE 8

Understanding Semicolons

Combine each pair of clauses by correctly placing a semicolon between them. Some clauses may be independent, while others begin with a conjunctive adverb or a transitional phrase.

1. For the period from the end of World War II in 1945 to the fall of the communist system in the early 1990s, the Soviet Union and the United States were involved in a cold war consequently, each country was in avid pursuit of military information about the other.

2. The city of Berlin, which was divided into democratic West Berlin and communist East Berlin, was a center of espionage, as a matter of fact, the CIA and British intelligence dug a tunnel from West Berlin to a point just under some important military telephone lines in the east.
3. Subminiature cameras have been inserted into a number of devices for instance, there are cigarette pack cameras, cigarette lighter cameras, and wristwatch cameras.
4. An early surveillance camera was in the shape of a matchbox it could be camouflaged by a label from any country, so that it would look natural when used in that country.
5. Mordecai Louk, an Israeli double agent, was captured by Egyptian intelligence in Rome, then he was drugged and put in a special trunk, which was mailed to Cairo.
6. The drugs wore off while the trunk was still in the Rome airport, Louk began to yell and was freed by customs officers.
7. Christopher Clayton Hutton was a British intelligence officer who designed numerous aids to espionage, for example, he invented a way of lighting secret airstrips that made them just barely visible to incoming pilots but easily overlooked by passersby on the ground.
8. Robert Baden-Powell, the man who founded the Boy Scouts, had another career, he was a British spy.
9. Baden-Powell went to the Balkans in 1890 disguised as an entomologist, he carried a sketchbook in which he drew the local butterflies.
10. The sketches contained more than first met the eye, for instance, on one drawing the veins on the butterfly's wings actually represented a plan of some fortifications.

EXERCISE 9

Using Semicolons

Each independent clause that follows is the first half of a sentence. Add a semicolon and a second independent clause per the directions. Make sure that your second thought is also independent and is related to the first thought.

6. The drugs wore off while the trunk was still in the Rome airport; Louk began to yell and was freed by customs officers.
7. Christopher Clayton Hutton was a British intelligence officer who designed numerous aids to espionage; for example, he invented a way of lighting secret airstrips that made them just barely visible to incoming pilots but easily overlooked by passersby on the ground.
8. Robert Baden-Powell, the man who founded the Boy Scouts, had another career; he was a British spy.
9. Baden-Powell went to the Balkans in 1890 disguised as an entomologist; he carried a sketchbook in which he drew the local butterflies.
10. The sketches contained more than first met the eye; for instance, on one drawing the veins on the butterfly's wings actually represented a plan of some fortifications.

EXERCISE 9

Responses will vary. Sample responses:

1. Katha is studying Russian, physics, and calculus; her best friend is taking courses in French, chemistry, and art history.

2. The hemlocks are suffering from a blight; pesticides seem to offer some hope of saving them.
3. The principal had canceled the orientation for first-year students; in spite of that fact, many students arrived at the school at the designated time.
4. Garth filled the trunk of his car with sports equipment; he took a volleyball and net, a lacrosse stick, and his tennis racquet.
5. I expected my parents to be furious when I arrived home late after getting a flat tire; however, they were just relieved to see me home safe.
6. Evan installed a fantastic rope swing that flies out over the pond; subsequently, everyone lined up to take a turn.
7. Several residents returned to their homes to assess the flood damage; they discovered mud-covered carpets, saturated upholstery, and ruined appliances.
8. Our cat Welly can become really vicious when you try to pick him up; as a result, I put on oven mitts to give him medicine.
9. Ulla submitted a large painting to the community art show; furthermore, she entered a sculpture in a state competition.
10. Greg bought the strangest items at the garage sale; he recently purchased some old Russian postcards, a broken microscope, and some tiny Victorian children's shoes.

1. Katha is studying Russian, physics, and calculus. (second independent clause with items in a series)
2. The hemlocks are suffering from a blight. (second independent clause)
3. The principal had canceled the orientation for first-year students. (second independent clause with transitional phrase)
4. Garth filled the trunk of his car with sports equipment. (second independent clause with commas)
5. I expected my parents to be furious when I arrived home late after getting a flat tire. (second independent clause with a conjunctive adverb)
6. Evan installed a fantastic rope swing that flies out over the pond. (second independent clause with a conjunctive adverb)
7. Several residents returned to their homes to assess the flood damage. (second independent clause with items in a series)
8. Our cat Welly can become really vicious when you try to pick him up. (second independent clause with transitional phrase)
9. Ulla submitted a large painting to the community art show. (second independent clause with conjunctive adverb)
10. Greg bought the strangest items at the garage sale. (second independent clause with commas)

COLONS

A **colon** is a punctuation mark used to mean "note what follows."

Use a **colon** to introduce a list of items.

EXAMPLES

Before he became one of America's best-loved humorists, Mark Twain had several different jobs: printer's assistant, riverboat pilot, and reporter.

CONTINUED

Some of Twain's most famous books are the following: *The Adventures of Tom Sawyer, Life on the Mississippi,* and *The Adventures of Huckleberry Finn.*

Sadly, Twain's later life was marked by a series of unhappy events, including the following: failed investments, the death of one daughter, and the illnesses of another daughter and his wife.

Use a colon to introduce a long or formal statement or a quotation. The first word of the statement or quotation should be capitalized.

EXAMPLES

One of Twain's most celebrated short stories begins:

> In compliance with the request of a friend of mine, who wrote me from the East, I called on good-natured, garrulous old Simon Wheeler, and inquired after my friend's friend, Leonidas W. Smiley, as requested to do, and I hereunto append the result. I have a lurking suspicion that *Leonidas W.* Smiley is a myth; that my friend never knew such a personage; and that he only conjectured that if I asked old Wheeler about him, it would remind him of his infamous *Jim* Smiley, and he would go to work and bore me to death with some exasperating reminiscence of him as long and as tedious as it should be useless to me. If that was the design, it succeeded.

Soon enough, old Wheeler appears in the story and begins to tell the tale of "The Notorious Jumping Frog of Calaveras County" in the following dialect:

> Rev'd Leonidas W. H'm, Reverend Le—well, there was a feller here once by the name of *Jim* Smiley, in the winter of '49—or maybe it was the spring of '50—I don't recollect exactly, somehow, though what makes me think it was one or the other is because I remember the big flume warn't finished when he first come to the camp; but any way, he was the curiousest man. . . .

Use a colon between two independent clauses when the second clause explains or summarizes the first clause. If the element following the colon consists of more than one sentence, then it should begin with a capital letter. If the second clause consists of only one sentence, then it may begin with a lowercase letter.

EXAMPLES

Mark Twain headed west in the 1860s with a clear goal in mind: he wanted to get rich quickly.

Twain became a licensed riverboat pilot on the Mississippi in 1859 and might have remained on the river if not for the following: In 1861, the Civil War broke out. North-south traffic on the river was cut off, and there was no longer need for Twain's services.

Colons are also used between numbers that tell hours and minutes, after the greeting in a business letter, and between chapter and verse of religious works.

EXAMPLES

The actor will give his impersonation of Mark Twain in the State Theater this Sunday at 3:00 P.M.

Dear Sir or Madam:
I Corinthians 3:3–7

USAGE tip

Avoid using a colon after a form of the verb *to be* or after a preposition.

In the following situations, do not use a colon: after a verb, between a preposition and its object(s), or after *because* or *as*.

EXAMPLES

after a verb

incorrect Two of the popular newspaper stories that Twain revealed as hoaxes were: "The Petrified Man" and "The Empire City Massacre."

correct Twain revealed the following newspaper stories to be hoaxes: "The Petrified Man" and "The Empire City Massacre."

CONTINUED

between a preposition and its object(s)

incorrect Although he is often considered a lighthearted humorist, Twain revealed his pessimistic view of human nature in: *The Adventures of Huckleberry Finn, The War Prayer,* and *Letters from Earth.*

correct Although he is often considered a lighthearted humorist, Twain revealed his pessimistic view of human nature in the following works: *The Adventures of Huckleberry Finn, The War Prayer,* and *Letters from Earth.*

after *because* or *as*

incorrect Twain was forced to work extremely hard toward the end of his life because: he had suffered devastating financial losses as the result of investing in an invention that proved to be an utter failure.

correct Twain was forced to work extremely hard toward the end of his life because of the following problem: He had suffered devastating financial losses as the result of investing in an invention that proved to be an utter failure.

Try It Yourself

EXERCISE 10

Correcting Colons

Rewrite the following sentences by adding or deleting colons. Use capitalization correctly.

1. Mark Twain was a success as all of the following a newspaper reporter, a humorous lecturer, a travel writer, and a novelist.
2. Twain made the following memorable comment on the subject of parents

   When I was a boy of fourteen, my father was so ignorant I could hardly stand to have the old man around. But when I got to be twenty-one, I was astonished at how much he had learned in seven years.

EXERCISE 10

1. Mark Twain was a success as all of the following: a newspaper reporter, a humorous lecturer, a travel writer, and a novelist.
2. Twain made the following memorable comment on the subject of parents:

   When I was a boy of fourteen, my father was so ignorant I could hardly stand to have the old man around. But when I got to be twenty-one, I was astonished at how much he had learned in seven years.
3. Twain had this opinion of classic literature: "A classic is something that everybody wants to have read but nobody wants to read."
4. I opened my copy of *The Adventures of Huckleberry Finn* at 9:00 P.M. and was unable to put it down until 2:00 A.M.
5. Twain's public persona was composed of the following carefully presented characteristics: gruffness, honesty, and good humor.
6. At the end of his life, Twain gained enormous respect by the way he responded to his financial troubles: Instead of declaring bankruptcy, he worked like a dog to pay each of his creditors in full.
7. As a boy growing up on the Mississippi, Twain had been enchanted by the physical presence of the river itself, the charming and unreliable characters who washed up along the shore, and the various boats that plied the river.

8. In 1847, an event occurred that caused the happy-go-lucky young boy to grow up suddenly: His father died and Twain needed to help support his mother and numerous siblings.
9. Some of the writers who influenced Twain's literary development were Bret Harte, Artemus Ward, and Josh Billings.
10. In his travel book *The Innocents Abroad*, Mark Twain blended many contrasting elements because he wanted to include both serious observations of European culture and extravagant accounts of laughable misadventures.

EXERCISE 11
Responses will vary. Students should accurately use as many colons as possible in their accounts of a trip.

3. Twain had this opinion of classic literature "A classic is something that everybody wants to have read but nobody wants to read."
4. I opened my copy of *The Adventures of Huckleberry Finn* at 900 P.M. and was unable to put it down until 200 A.M.
5. Twain's public persona was composed of the following carefully presented characteristics gruffness, honesty, and good humor.
6. At the end of his life, Twain gained enormous respect by the way he responded to his financial troubles Instead of declaring bankruptcy, he worked like a dog to pay each of his creditors in full.
7. As a boy growing up on the Mississippi, Twain had been enchanted by: the physical presence of the river itself, the charming and unreliable characters who washed up along the shore, and the various boats that plied the river.
8. In 1847, an event occurred that caused the happy-go-lucky young boy to grow up suddenly His father died and Twain needed to help support his mother and numerous siblings.
9. Some of the writers who influenced Twain's literary development were: Bret Harte, Artemus Ward, and Josh Billings.
10. In his travel book *The Innocents Abroad*, Mark Twain blended many contrasting elements because: he wanted to include both serious observations of European culture and extravagant accounts of laughable misadventures.

EXERCISE 11

Using Colons in Your Writing

For a school literary magazine, write a humorous account of a real or imagined excursion you have taken. Include Twainian exaggeration, colloquial language, extravagant descriptions, and any other techniques to make your peer audience laugh. Make frequent use of colons.

ELLIPSIS POINTS

Ellipsis points are a series of three spaced points. Ellipsis points are used to show that material from a quotation or a quoted passage has been left out. Read the following literature model, then note how the underlined material is omitted and replaced with ellipsis points in the second model.

Literature MODELS

He was not conscious of an effort, but a sharp pain in his wrist apprised him that he was trying to free his hands. He gave the struggle his attention, as an idler might observe the feat of a juggler, without interest in the outcome. What splendid effort!—what magnificent, what superhuman strength! Ah, that was a fine endeavor! Bravo! The cord fell away; his arms parted and floated upward, the hands dimly seen on each side in the growing light. He watched them with a new interest as first one and then the other pounced upon the noose at his neck. They tore it away and thrust it fiercely aside, its undulations resembling those of a watersnake.

from "The Pit and the Pendulum"
Edgar Allan Poe

He was not conscious of an effort, but a sharp pain in his wrist apprised him that he was trying to free his hands. He gave the struggle his attention . . . without interest in the outcome. What splendid effort. . . . Ah, that was a fine endeavor! Bravo! The cord fell away; his arms parted and floated upward. . . . He watched them with a new interest as first one and then the other pounced upon the noose at his neck. They tore it away and thrust it fiercely aside. . . .

from "The Pit and the Pendulum"
Edgar Allan Poe

To use ellipsis points correctly, follow these guidelines:

USAGE tip

Other punctuation may be used on either side of the ellipsis points if it helps the sense of the sentence or better shows what has been omitted.

I was at the mercy of savage predators! A pool of crocodiles seethed on one side of me and a ravening tiger approached on the other! I had reached the tragic end to a glorious existence.

. . . savage predators!. . . A pool of crocodiles . . . a ravening tiger! . . . I had reached the tragic end to a glorious existence.

- If material is left out at the beginning of a sentence or passage, use three points with a space between each point.

EXAMPLE

. . . All I knew what that something dreadful, unimaginable, and inescapable had happened, and I had reached the end.

- If material is left out in the middle of a sentence, use three points with a space between each point.

EXAMPLE

All I knew was that something . . . had happened, and I had reached the end.

- If material is left out at the end of a sentence, use an end mark after the ellipsis points.

EXAMPLE

All I knew was that something dreadful, unimaginable, and inescapable had happened. . . .

Try It Yourself

EXERCISE 12

1. A man stood upon a railroad bridge . . . looking down into the swift water. . . .
2. The man's hands were behind his back, the wrists bound. . . .
3. A rope . . . encircled his neck.
4. It was attached to a stout cross timber above his head. . . .

EXERCISE 12
Understanding Ellipsis Points

Rewrite each of the following sentences, correctly adding ellipsis points in place of the underlined material.

1. A man stood upon a railroad bridge in northern Alabama, looking down into the swift water twenty feet below.
2. The man's hands were behind his back, the wrists bound with a cord.
3. A rope closely encircled his neck.
4. It was attached to a stout cross timber above his head and the slack fell to the level of his knees.

5. Some loose boards <u>laid upon the sleepers supporting the metals of the railway</u> supplied a footing for him and his executioners—<u>two private soldiers of the Federal army, directed by a sergeant who in civil life may have been a deputy sheriff</u>.
6. At a short remove <u>upon the same temporary platform</u> was an officer in the uniform of his rank, arm. He was a captain.
7. A sentinel at each end of the bridge stood with his rifle in the position known as "support," <u>that is to say, vertical in front of the left shoulder, the hammer resting on the forearm thrown straight across the chest</u>—a formal and unnatural position, enforcing and erect carriage of the body.
8. <u>It did not appear to be the duty of these two men to know what was occurring at the center of the bridge</u>; they merely blockaded the two ends of the foot planking that traversed it.
9. <u>Beyond one of the sentinels nobody was in sight</u>; the railway ran straight away into a forest for a hundred yards, then, <u>curving</u>, was lost to view.
10. Doubtless there was an outpost <u>farther along</u>.

from "An Occurrence at Owl Creek Bridge"
Ambrose Bierce

5. Some loose boards . . . supplied a footing for him and his executioners. . . .
6. At a short remove . . . was an officer in the uniform of his rank, arm. He was a captain.
7. A sentinel at each end of the bridge stood with his rifle in the position known as "support," . . . a formal and unnatural position, enforcing and erect carriage of the body.
8. . . . they merely blockaded the two ends of the foot planking that traversed it.
9. . . . the railway ran straight away into a forest for a hundred yards, then . . . was lost to view.
10. Doubtless there was an outpost. . . .

EXERCISE 13

Using Ellipsis Points in Your Writing

Select a favorite passage from a work of literature. Write the passage in its complete form. Then rewrite the passage, indicating omissions with ellipsis points. Compare your work to that of a classmate.

EXERCISE 13

Responses will vary. Students should correctly use ellipsis points to show omissions of material from a quoted passage.

APOSTROPHES

An **apostrophe** is used to form the possessive of nouns and pronouns; to form contractions; and to form the plurals of numerals, symbols, and words referred to as words.

- Use an apostrophe to form the possessive case of a singular or plural noun. To form the possessive of a singular noun, add an apostrophe and an *s* to the end of the word.

EXAMPLES
a kangaroo's pouch
Liz's trust fund
the duchess's taxes

USAGE tip

To make pronunciation easier, add only an apostrophe after historical names of more than one syllable: *Pegasus' wings, Perseus' adversary, Dædalus' maze, and Cyrus' empire.*

The possessive of a plural noun is formed two different ways. If the plural noun does not end in *s*, you add an apostrophe and an *s* to the end of the word. If the plural noun ends with an *s*, add only an apostrophe.

EXAMPLES
tresses' color
roses' thorns
buses' exhaust
children's games

- Use an apostrophe to show joint or separate ownership. If two nouns are used to show joint ownership, form only the last noun in the possessive.

EXAMPLES
Punch and Judy's quarrel
the cup and saucer's pattern
Lerner and Lowe's musical
the architect and builder's agreement

If two or more nouns are used to show separate ownership, form each noun in the possessive.

EXAMPLES
Maury's and Nell's shell collections
Labradors' and Spaniels' coats
Jack's and Jim's toothbrushes
measles' and mumps' symptoms

USAGE tip

Do not use an apostrophe with possessive singular or plural pronouns. You may want to review possessive pronouns in Unit 5, pages 97–100.

- Add an apostrophe and an *s* to form the possessive of an indefinite pronoun.

EXAMPLES

someone's anorak	another's idea
everybody's hopes	somebody's outline

- Use an apostrophe to form a contraction to show where letters, words, or numerals have been omitted.

EXAMPLES

I'm = I am	you're = you are
who's = who is	should've = should have
there're = there are	o'clock = of the clock
can't = cannot	we'd = we would
didn't = did not	they'll = they will
ma'am = madam	won't = will not

- Use an apostrophe to form the possessive of only the last word in a compound noun, such as the name of an organization or a business.

EXAMPLES
vice president's background
Sun Records' output
the East India Company's influence

- Use an apostrophe to form the possessive of an acronym.

EXAMPLES
CEO's investments
MADD's mission
NBC's fall lineup

- Use an apostrophe to form the plural of letters, numerals, and words referred to as words.

EXAMPLES
p's and *q*'s
a row of *3*'s
repeated "*like*'s"

• Use an apostrophe to show the missing numbers in a date.

EXAMPLES
the stock market crash of '29
the hurricane of '32
the swinging '60s

• Use an apostrophe to form the possessive of time and money.

EXAMPLES
a day's wait
a dollar's worth
five dollars' worth

USAGE tip

To review how to form the possessives of nouns, see Unit 4 Nouns, pp. 74–76.

EXERCISE 14
1. tuxedo's, tuxedoes'
2. epithet's, epithets'
3. brother-in-law's, brothers-in-law's
4. penny's, pennies'
5. flamingo's, flamingos'
6. louse's, lice's
7. emissary's, emissaries'
8. James's, Jameses'
9. man's, men's
10. mattress's, mattresses'

Try It Yourself

EXERCISE 14

Understanding the Use of Apostrophes

Use apostrophes to form the singular and plural possessive forms of each of the following words.

EXAMPLE
botanist
(*botanist's,* singular possessive; *botanists',* plural possessive)

1. tuxedo
2. epithet
3. brother-in-law
4. penny
5. flamingo
6. louse
7. emissary
8. Yeats
9. man
10. mattress

EXERCISE 15
Correcting the Use of Apostrophes

Rewrite the following sentences, correcting any errors in the use of apostrophes. If a sentence contains no errors, write *correct*.

1. Odysseus wits saved his men from the Cyclops wrath; they escaped by hiding under some sheeps bellies.
2. Shanice really shouldn't be so devastated just because she got a couple of B's on her report card.
3. I always forget that there are two *m*s in *accommodation*.
4. It's important to understand that viruses and bacterias methods of attacking the body are very different.
5. Keller loves to go down to the marina just to look at all the boat's names.
6. Hank couldnt sleep well because of the fusillade of acorns' hitting his car roof all night long.
7. Is it true that the last verified sighting of an ivory-billed woodpecker was in Cuba in 1987?
8. Otis sent his application and a check to the American' Automobile' Association's state office.
9. Childrens' literature seldom receives the serious critical attention it deserves.
10. Joan Baez and the Band's covers of the Bob Dylan song "I Shall Be Released" have very different feels and tempos.

EXERCISE 16
Using Apostrophes in Your Writing

Write a brief music review for your school newspaper comparing three new CD releases. Use apostrophes correctly in your singular and plural possessive nouns and your contractions.

EXERCISE 15

1. Odysseus' wits saved his men from the Cyclops' wrath; they escaped by hiding under some sheep's bellies.
2. correct
3. I always forget that there are two *ms* in *accommodation*.
4. It's important to understand that viruses' and bacteria's methods of attacking the body are very different.
5. Keller loves to go down to the marina just to look at all the boats' names.
6. Hank couldn't sleep well because of the fusillade of acorns hitting his car roof all night long.
7. Is it true that the last verified sighting of an ivory-billed woodpecker was in Cuba in 1987?
8. Otis sent his application and a check to the American Automobile Association's state office.
9. Children's literature seldom receives the serious critical attention it deserves.
10. Joan Baez's and the Band's covers of the Bob Dylan song "I Shall Be Released" have very different feels and tempos.

EXERCISE 16

Responses will vary. Students should include several singular and plural possessive nouns and pronouns, punctuated correctly with apostrophes. They should also use apostrophes correctly in contractions.

UNDERLINING AND ITALICS

Italics are a type of slanted printing used to make a word or phrase stand out. In handwritten documents or in forms of printing in which italics are not available, underlining is used.

EXAMPLE

italics	Jean Rhys's twentieth-century novel *The Wide Sargasso Sea* is a reworking of some of the characters in Charlotte Bronte's earlier masterpiece *Jane Eyre.*
underlining	Jean Rhys's twentieth-century novel The Wide Sargasso Sea is a reworking of some of the characters in Charlotte Bronte's earlier masterpiece Jane Eyre.

USAGE tip

Italic type is available in most word-processing software. When using a computer, you can set words in italics yourself.

- Use italics (or underlining) for the titles of books, plays, long poems, periodicals, works of art, movies, radio and television series, videos, computer games, comic strips, and long musical works and recordings.

USAGE tip

Italicize and capitalize the articles *a, an,* and *the* when they are written before a title and are part of the official title.

The Atlantic Monthly
An American Tragedy

EXAMPLES

books	*The Mill on the Floss; The Possessed*
plays	*Death of a Salesman; No Exit*
long poems	*Paradise Lost; Orlando Furioso*
periodicals	*Vogue; Newsweek; Rolling Stone*
works of art	*The Peaceable Kingdom; Les Demoiselles d'Avignon, The Scream*
movies	*Casablanca; You Can Count on Me; Taxi Driver*
radio/television series	*All Things Considered; Friends; Nightline*
videos	*Tales of Beatrix Potter; Wall Glazing*
computer games	*Hover; Oregon Trail; Tony Hawk's Pro Skater 2*
comic strips	*Calvin and Hobbes; For Better or For Worse; Heathcliff*
long musical works/recordings	*La Traviata; Peter Grimes; Peter and the Wolf*

USAGE tip

Do not use italics for sacred books, such as the Bible and the Koran; for public documents, such as the Constitution and the Magna Carta; or for the titles of your own papers.

• Use italics for the names of trains, ships, aircraft, and spacecraft.

EXAMPLES

trains	*Lake Shore Limited; Orient Express*
ships	*Titanic; Lusitania*
aircraft	*Spirit of St. Louis; Concorde*
spacecraft	*Apollo; Soyuz*

• Use italics for words, letters, symbols, and numerals referred to as such.

EXAMPLES

Flannel is one of the few English words derived from the Welsh language.

I tell people my name is spelled *Stacey*, but they often leave out the *e*.

Florencia meant to produce the symbol %, but she forgot to hit the shift button and produced a *5* instead.

• Use italics to set off foreign words or phrases that are not common in English.

EXAMPLES

Once in a while Americans need to embrace the Italian practice of *dolce far niente*, literally the "sweet doing of nothing," or pleasant inactivity.

The Greek word *xenia* expresses the concept, so important to ancient Greek culture, of the duty of the host to the guest.

• Use italics to place emphasis on a word.

EXAMPLES

The plot of that movie was *absurd*.

Jacqueline will absolutely *not* tell a lie, even to save her own skin.

USAGE tip

Borrowed words that have become part of the English vocabulary are not italicized.

We sat on the patio and devoured burritos and enchiladas.

The casserole was even better heated up the second day.

EXERCISE 17

1. Elvis Costello's <u>My Aim Is True</u> was one of the greatest albums of the late seventies.
2. I can't believe you booked a flight to Paris, stood in line for an hour to get into the Louvre, marched up to the <u>Mona Lisa</u>, stared at it for ten minutes, and flew home.
3. Mrs. Rioux loves it when the hygienist is late for her dental appointment because then she gets a chance to read <u>Style</u> in the waiting room.
4. In 1985, Palestinian terrorists hijacked the <u>Achille Lauro</u>, an Italian cruise ship.
5. The superb British revival of <u>Oklahoma!</u> has surprised everyone who doubted British actors could bring to life such a quintessentially American musical.
6. The Talmud contains a collection of writings on Jewish religious law.
7. Situation comedies such as <u>Grounded for Life</u> are much more expensive to produce than the so-called reality shows.
8. He was talking about <u>Tom Thumb</u> the train, not the tiny hero of the old folktale.

Try It Yourself

EXERCISE 17

Understanding Correct Usage of Underlining and Italics

Underline any words in the following sentences that should be italicized.

1. Elvis Costello's My Aim Is True was one of the greatest albums of the late seventies.
2. I can't believe you booked a flight to Paris, stood in line for an hour to get into the Louvre, marched up to the Mona Lisa, stared at it for ten minutes, and flew home.
3. Mrs. Rioux loves it when the hygienist is late for her dental appointment because then she gets a chance to read Style in the waiting room.
4. In 1985, Palestinian terrorists hijacked the Achille Lauro, an Italian cruise ship.
5. The superb British revival of Oklahoma! has surprised everyone who doubted British actors could bring to life such a quintessentially American musical.
6. The Talmud contains a collection of writings on Jewish religious law.
7. Situation comedies such as Grounded for Life are much more expensive to produce than the so-called reality shows.
8. He was talking about Tom Thumb the train, not the tiny hero of the old folk tale.
9. William Styron's devastating novel about the Holocaust and its repercussions, Sophie's Choice, was made into an Academy Award-winning movie.
10. Bart was sitting at the breakfast table, hunched over the newspaper and guffawing at Jump Start.

EXERCISE 18

Using Italics and Underlining in Your Writing

For your yearbook entry, list at least five of your favorites, including movies, books, TV shows, CDs, and comic strips or video games. Give a one-sentence description of each. Use italics correctly.

QUOTATION MARKS

Quotation marks are used to set off direct quotations, titles of short works, slang, and unusual expressions.

• Use quotations marks at the beginning and end of a direct quotation. When you use a person's exact words in your writing, you are using a **direct quotation.**

EXAMPLES

"If the cat heads to the cellar before a storm, I generally follow him," stated Miss King.

"I adore a nice, violent thunderstorm," said Jeanne, "but I have a morbid fear of tornadoes."

A direct quotation should always begin with a capital letter. Separate a direct quotation from the rest of the sentence with a comma, a question mark, or an exclamation point. Do not separate the direct quotation from the rest of the sentence with a period. When a quoted sentence is interrupted, the second part begins with a lowercase letter. All punctuation marks that belong to the direct quotation itself should be placed inside the quotation marks.

EXAMPLES

"How absurdly large your SUV is!" exclaimed Martin.

Letitia snapped, "Have you tried driving six teenagers to a soccer game in a regular car?"

"No!" Martin shouted in alarm. "I would rather eat worms than do such a thing!"

"Oh, Martin," sighed Letitia, "you are such an unbearable misanthrope."

9. William Styron's devastating novel about the Holocaust and its repercussions, Sophie's Choice, was made into an Academy Award-winning movie.
10. Bart was sitting at the breakfast table, hunched over the newspaper and guffawing at Jump Start.

EXERCISE 18

Responses will vary. Students should supply the titles requested and should correctly use five examples of italics or underlining in their reviews.

Place colons and semicolons outside the closing quotation marks.

EXAMPLES
Grandmother finds the following behaviors "beyond the pale": resting elbows on the table, using paper napkins, and saying "pardon."

Aunt Amy always calls me "honeybunch"; I think it's embarrassing but sweet.

USAGE tip

Use a lowercase letter when a quoted fragment of the original quotation is inserted in a sentence.

I hate to be impatient, but I get weary of Nana's constant references to "the good old days."

Place exclamation points and question marks outside the closing quotation marks if the quotation itself is not an exclamation or a question.

EXAMPLES
What is the meaning of the proverb "Butter wouldn't melt in his mouth"?

When he stepped on your foot, I can't believe you said, "Excuse me"!

Place exclamation points and question marks inside the closing quotation marks if both the sentence and the quotation are exclamations or questions.

EXAMPLES
Was it Shakespeare who wrote, "What's in a name?"
Oh no, someone just screamed, "Fire!"

When a quoted sentence is interrupted, the second part begins with a lowercase letter, unless the first word of the second part begins a new sentence. Use quotation marks to enclose both parts of a divided quotation.

EXAMPLES
"If you ever feel lonely or desperate," Mika told me, "you must promise to call me."

"I will," I responded. "You must promise me to do the same."

Use only one set of quotation marks when a direct quotation of two or more sentences by the same speaker is not divided or interrupted.

EXAMPLE
The ballet teacher addressed her new students. "I understand that as dancers you want to remain slender so as to show a beautiful line. However, I will not tolerate students who drive themselves to become emaciated. A dancer needs to be strong and healthy; he or she needs to eat a healthful diet with sufficient nutrients and calories. If I have worries about any of you, I will talk to your parents and send you to a nutritionist."

- Don't use quotation marks to set off an **indirect quotation**. An indirect quotation is a rewording of a person's exact words.

EXAMPLES

direct quotation	"Don't leave anything behind in the taxi," said the recording.
indirect quotation	The recording reminded us not to leave anything behind in the taxi.

- Use single quotation marks to enclose a quotation within a quotation.

EXAMPLE
Mrs. Hemphill said, "I cry every time I read Churchill's words, '. . . we shall fight on the beaches, we shall fight on the landing grounds, we shall fight in the fields and in the streets, we shall fight in the hills; we shall never surrender.'"

- In dialogue, enclose each speaker's words in quotation marks, and begin a new paragraph every time the speaker changes.

Literature MODEL

"I'm sorry, Mrs. Wilson," Ella stammered, rising. "But he asked me—"

"He's just a foolish child and you know it!" Granny blazed.

Ella bowed her head and went into the house.

"But, Granny, she didn't finish," I protested, knowing that I should have kept quiet.

She bared her teeth and slapped me across my mouth with the back of her hand.

"You shut your mouth!" she hissed. "You don't know what you're talking about!"

from *Black Boy*
Richard Wright

- Sometimes a direct quotation from an author's work may be several paragraphs in length. If so, place quotation marks at the beginning of each paragraph and at the end of only the last paragraph.

EXAMPLE

The Declaration of Independence gave a list of reasons why the colonists felt justified in throwing off the yoke of British governance:

"For quartering large bodies of armed troops among us;

"For protecting them, by a mock trial, from punishment for any murders which they should commit on the inhabitants of these States;

"For cutting off out trade with all parts of the world. . . ."

- Do not use quotation marks if you are quoting a long passage. Instead, set off the entire passage from the rest of the text by indenting and single-spacing it.

EXAMPLE

In this selection from *The Autobiography of Benjamin Franklin*, Franklin tells about an occasion in which his brother, a newspaper publisher, was imprisoned:

> One of the Pieces in our Newspaper, on some political Point which I have now forgotten, gave Offense to the Assembly. He was taken up, censured, and imprisoned for a Month by the Speaker's Warrant. I suppose because he would not discover his author. I too was taken up and examined before the Council; but though I did not give them any Satisfaction, they contented themselves with admonishing me, and dismissed me, considering me perhaps as an Apprentice who was bound to keep his Master's Secrets. During my Brother's Confinement, which I resented a good deal, notwithstanding our private Differences, I had the Management of the Paper, and I made bold to give our Rulers some Rubs in it, which my Brother took very kindly, while others began to consider me in an unfavorable Light, as a young Genius that had a Turn for Libeling and Satire.

- Use quotation marks to enclose the titles of short works such as short stories, poems, articles, essays, parts of books and periodicals, songs, and episodes of TV series.

EXAMPLES

short stories	"The Garden-Party," "White Dump"
poems	"Sailing to Byzantium," "Sonnet XXX"
articles	"Unbuilding the World Trade Center," "Picking Up Terror's Trail,"
essays	"Odysseus' Scar," "On Genius and Common Sense"
parts of books	"Novels of Detection, Crime, Mystery, and Espionage," "Life in an Early Castle"
songs	"Sweet Jane," "London Calling,"
episodes of TV series	"Dagger of the Mind," "Bart the Genius"

- Use quotation marks to set off slang, technical terms, unusual expressions, invented words, and dictionary definitions.

EXAMPLES

When asked to describe the crazy period of getting ready for work and/or school in the morning, Barbara Wallraff came up with "pandemornium" in an *Atlantic Monthly* article titled "Word Fugitives."

According to *Webster's New World Dictionary*, the word *gobo* is an Americanism meaning "a black screen used to reduce light falling on a camera lens."

Try It Yourself

EXERCISE 19

Understanding the Correct Use of Quotation Marks

Add the appropriate quotation marks, commas, question marks, exclamation points, and periods to the sentences.

1. The boxer Mohammed Ali is known as The Greatest.
2. Like all of the great poets, Yeats conjured up inexplicable yet gorgeous images such as that dolphin-torn, that gong-tormented sea.
3. Hilary screeched, You've no right to read my e-mails
4. Percy Bysshe Shelley's essay A Defence of Poetry was written in response to a humorous attack on poetry by Thomas Love Peacock.
5. Li-Young Lee's poem Mnemonic contains these lines: I won't last. Memory is sweet. / Even when it's painful, memory is sweet.
6. I opened *Phoenix II*, a collection of D. H. Lawrence's writings, and I turned to the section Reflections on the Death of a Porcupine.
7. The German word Weltanschauung means a comprehensive personal philosophy about the world.

EXERCISE 19

1. The boxer Mohammed Ali is known as "The Greatest."
2. Like all of the greatest poets, Yeats conjured up inexplicable yet gorgeous images such as "that dolphin-torn, that gong-tormented sea."
3. Hilary screeched, "You've no right to read my e-mails!"
4. Percy Bysshe Shelley's essay "A Defence of Poetry" was written in response to a humorous attack on poetry by Thomas Love Peacock.
5. Li-Young Lee's poem "Mnemonic" contains these lines: "I won't last. Memory is sweet. / Even when it's painful, memory is sweet."
6. I opened *Phoenix II*, a collection of D. H. Lawrence's writings, and I turned to the section "Reflections on the Death of a Porcupine."
7. The German word *Weltanschauung* means a comprehensive personal philosophy about the world.

8. Were you frightened when Gina shouted to the mountain guide, What just happened
9. For some reason, her constant iteration of the phrase long story short makes me want to scream.
10. Did the subway guard tell me Take the E train to Second Avenue

8. Were you frightened when Gina shouted to the mountain guide, "What just happened?"
9. For some reason, her constant iteration of the phrase "long story short" makes me want to scream.
10. Did the subway guard tell me, "Take the E train to Second Avenue"?

EXERCISE 20

Using Quotation Marks

Write a sentence or more in response to each direction below. Be sure to use quotation marks correctly.

1. Identify a newspaper article and explain how it affected you.
2. Name a poem you've read, and describe your reaction to it.
3. Quote a phrase that gets on your nerves, and tell what you wish people would say instead.
4. Recite a quotation of 100 words or more by your favorite writer, and explain the reasons why it is memorable.
5. Nominate the song you would vote "Best of the Year" and explain why.

EXERCISE 20

Responses will vary. Students should write a sentence or more explaining each of their choices and correctly using quotation marks and their accompanying punctuation.

HYPHENS AND DASHES

Hyphens

Hyphens are used to make a compound word or compound expression.

EXAMPLES

compound nouns	a movie tie-in, great-aunts, boogie-woogie
compound adjectives used before a noun	well-intentioned nuisance, a horror-struck onlooker
compound numbers	sixty-two cents, twenty-two uniforms
spelled-out fractions	one-third cup, four-fifths of the wood

USAGE tip

Use a dictionary to find out if a compound word or expression is hyphenated or written as one word or two words.

If a word must be divided at the end of a line, here are a few rules to help you know when and how to hyphenate a word at a line break.

- Divide an already hyphenated word at the hyphen.

EXAMPLE
Although she is only sixty-five, my **great-**
aunt has traveled around the world twice.

- Divide a word only between syllables. If you are uncertain of a word's syllables, look up the word in a dictionary.

USAGE tip

A word containing double consonants usually may be divided between the double consonants.

flur-ry
tas-sel

EXAMPLES

incorrect	The latest reports place the hur- ricane just off the east coast of Florida.
correct	The latest reports place the hurri- cane just off the east coast of Florida.

- Do not divide a one-syllable word.

EXAMPLES

incorrect	Some people are quick to assign bla- me instead of accepting responsibility.
correct	Some people are quick to assign blame instead of accepting responsibility.

- Do not divide a word so that one letter stands alone.

EXAMPLES

incorrect	It's not a good idea to place a penn- y on the railroad tracks.
correct	It's not a good idea to place a penny on the railroad tracks.

- Use a hyphen with the prefixes *all–*, *ex–*, *great–*, *half–* and *self–* and with all prefixes before a proper noun or proper adjective.

EXAMPLES

pre-election squabbling	all-powerful deity
ex-husband	self-image
great-grandmother	anti-intellectual
non-native	pro-mayor coalition
half-timbered house	co-edition

- Use a hyphen with the suffixes *–free*, *–elect*, and *–style*.

EXAMPLES
fat-free yogurt
president-elect Moriarty
southwestern-style clothing

USAGE tip

The prefix *half* is sometimes used without a hyphen, as part of a single word, or as a separate word, such as *halfhearted*, *halfway*, and *half gainer*. Double-check the spelling of a compound word containing *half* by looking up the word in a dictionary.

Dashes

A **dash** is used to show a sudden break or change in thought. Note that a dash is longer in length than a hyphen. Dashes sometimes replace other marks of punctuation, such as periods, semicolons, or commas.

USAGE tip

On your word processor, you can create a dash by typing two hyphens without a space between them.

In the first example below, the first dash sets off a long series (the compound subject) from the rest of the sentence. In the second example, both dashes set off a descriptive phrase about Mr. Tanimoto from a description of the Japanese people in general.

Literature MODEL

> Mr. Tanimoto cooked his own breakfast. He felt awfully tired. The effort of moving the piano the day before, a sleepless night, weeks of worry and unbalanced diet, the cares of his parish—all combined to make him feel hardly adequate to the day's work. There was another thing, too: Mr. Tanimoto had studied theology at Emory College, in Atlanta, Georgia; he had graduated in 1940; he spoke excellent English; he dressed in American clothes; he had corresponded with many American friends right up to the time the war began; and among a people

CONTINUED

obsessed with being spied upon—perhaps almost obsessed himself—he found himself growing increasingly uneasy.

from *Hiroshima*, "A Noiseless Flash"
John Hersey

A dash can also be used to mean *namely*, *that is*, or *in other words*.

EXAMPLES

Sadly there is only one topic that is of interest to Rebekah—herself!

Anthony Hopkins says he is overjoyed to exchange the climate of his native Wales—cool and rainy—for the dry heat and abundant sunlight of the American southwest.

EXERCISE 21

1. You won't believe Jacob's idea for the Thanksgiving centerpiece—a rubber chicken disguised as a turkey.

USAGE tip

Do not use the dash when commas, semicolons, and periods are more appropriate. Too many dashes can create a jumpy style in writing.

2. Endless repetitions of such mind-numbing classics as "Ninety-Nine Bottles of Beer on the Wall" and "Found a Peanut" amused us kids during long field trips in the prevideo days.
3. I might be able to accept Fernando's holier-than-thou attitude if I hadn't heard so many stories about him from his ex-girlfriend.
4. Hannah invited everyone to her house—what an amazing place that is—for a postgame pasta dinner.
5. A large gourmet restaurant—a capital-intensive business—is not the right choice for a student just out of culinary college.

Try It Yourself

EXERCISE 21

Understanding the Correct Use of Hyphens and Dashes

Rewrite the following sentences, adding hyphens and dashes where they are appropriate.

1. You won't believe Jacob's idea for the Thanksgiving centerpiece a rubber chicken disguised as a turkey.
2. Endless repetitions of such mind numbing classics as "Ninety nine Bottles of Beer on the Wall" and "Found a Peanut" amused us kids during long field trips in the prevideo days.
3. I might be able to accept Fernando's holier than thou attitude if I hadn't heard so many stories about him from his ex girlfriend.
4. Hannah invited everyone to her house what an amazing place that is for a postgame pasta dinner.
5. A large gourmet restaurant a capital intensive business is not the right choice for a student just out of culinary college.

6. An *objet d'art* that's an art object to those of you who can't speak French may have value only to the person who bought it, or it may continue to appreciate in the open market.
7. Greta's great grandmother says it's never too late in life to hop on a merry go round.
8. At the press conference a host of proenvironment activists Campbell, Shinohara, and Schrenk spoke out eloquently about the need to protect the aquifer.
9. Members of the club can pick up a one day pass for nonmembers for just $4.00 a pretty reasonable arrangement.
10. Mark swears his vintage bell bottoms were designed for but never picked up by a member of Jimi Hendrix's band.

6. An *objet d'art*—that's an art object to those of you who can't speak French—may have value only to the person who bought it, or it may continue to appreciate in the open market.
7. Greta's great-grandmother says it's never too late in life to hop on a merry-go-round.
8. At the press conference a host of proenvironment activists—Campbell, Shinohara, and Schrenk—spoke out eloquently about the need to protect the aquifer.

9. Members of the club can pick up a one-day pass for nonmembers for just $4.00—a pretty reasonable arrangement.
10. Mark swears his vintage bell-bottoms were designed for—but never picked up by—a member of Jimi Hendrix's band.

EXERCISE 22

Using Hyphens and Dashes in Your Writing

Imagine you have entered a writing contest called "Dreams—Real and Imagined." If you are one of those people who can remember your dreams, describe a dream sequence. If you can't remember a dream in detail, make one up. Use dashes to describe the sudden shifts in time and space so typical of dreams. Use hyphens to describe the sorts of compound entities that appear only in dreams (a woman-eagle, for instance). Refer to the rules in this section to come up with other ways to incorporate hyphens and dashes in your writing.

EXERCISE 22

Responses will vary. Students' dreams should reflect correct use of hyphens and dashes.

PARENTHESES AND BRACKETS

Use **parentheses** around material that is added to a sentence but is not considered of major importance. This material might include explanations, facts, minor digressions, and examples that aid understanding but are not essential to meaning.

USAGE tip

Parentheses are often used in place of dashes or commas.

USAGE tip

Common parenthetical expressions include *after all, by the way, for example, furthermore, however, I believe, in fact, nevertheless, of course,* and *therefore.*

EXAMPLES

The poet Charlotte Mew (1869–1928) received little recognition during her lifetime.

Bertie Wooster (the inane upper-class hero of many of P. G. Wodehouse's comic novels) is utterly dependent upon the advice of his sage gentleman's gentleman, Jeeves.

The buffet table was loaded with high-calorie treats (for example, guacamole, a bean-and-sour-cream dip, Brie, and some crab dip).

Parentheses are also used to punctuate a parenthetical sentence contained within another sentence. Do not capitalize the parenthetical sentence, unless it begins with a word that should be capitalized. Do not end the parenthetical sentence with a period, but you may end it with a question mark or exclamation point.

EXAMPLES

Although I get good grades in school, I'm totally clueless (it's a real challenge for me to operate a vending machine) at real-life tasks.

Take good care of my car (please don't park it on the street) when you borrow it over the weekend.

When Dawn came out of the water (do you remember that incredible spectacle?) there was pondweed draped all over her shoulders and mingled with her long, wet hair.

Commas, dashes, and parentheses may all be used to enclose words or phrases that interrupt the sentence and are not considered essential to meaning. Notice in the following sentences how each punctuation mark increases the emphasis.

EXAMPLES

She added unusual elements, feathers and shells, to the bouquet. (a short pause)

She added unusual elements—feathers and shells—to the bouquet. (a stronger break in the sentence)

She added unusual elements (did you think the effect was a bit pretentious?) to the bouquet. (minor digression)

Use **brackets** to enclose information that explains or clarifies a detail in quoted material.

EXAMPLES

The writer states unequivocally, "Caerphilly [a castle in south Wales] is not only the largest castle in Britain, but it is the most astounding."

The sports writer wrote, "In the race at Charles Town last night, the jockey [James Thornton, one of the few African-American riders on the circuit back in 1970] who started the race on Native Bird came over the finish line on a different horse [Kandi Arm]!"

Try It Yourself

EXERCISE 23

Understanding Parentheses and Brackets

Rewrite the following sentences, adding parentheses and brackets where they are needed.

1. Jake spends all of his free time I think he's a bit obsessive, don't you? researching obscure South American coins on the Internet.
2. The poet Milton wrote, "Sweet is the breath of morn, her rising sweet / With charm meaning song of earliest birds. . . ."
3. For breakfast, Michel made crepes very flat French pancakes which we filled with strawberries and drenched with melted butter.

EXERCISE 23

1. Jake spends all of his free time (I think he's a bit obsessive, don't you?) researching obscure South American coins on the Internet.
2. The poet Milton wrote, "Sweet is the breath of morn, her rising sweet / With charm [meaning song] of earliest birds. . . ."
3. For breakfast, Michel made crepes (very flat French pancakes) which we filled with strawberries and drenched with melted butter.
4. The fork in the road (do you remember the one just after the Ivoryton Playhouse?) is where everyone gets lost on the way to our house.
5. In 1932, Babe Didrikson (one of the greatest athletes of all time) was the sole member of an amateur track and field team known as the Golden Cyclones.
6. To the amazement of all of the onlookers at the 1932 National AAU Women's Track and Field Championship (an event that also served as the Olympic Team Trials) Didrikson won six gold medals and broke three world records in a single afternoon!

7. Captain Kira Falconetti announced, "We [she meant the members of the varsity girls' soccer team] have to set a good example to the junior varsity team."
8. Mei-Su assured us that being a vegan (is that the diet in which you don't eat anything cooked or just the one that avoids any animal products?) has reduced her allergies and improved her overall health.
9. Franklin Delano Roosevelt (1882–1945) shepherded the United States through the depression years and then through World War II.
10. "He [the gypsy guitarist Django Reinhardt] played exquisitely despite having burned his left hand so badly that he could barely move two of the fingers," said Ben reverentially.

4. The fork in the road do you remember the one just after the Ivoryton Playhouse is where everyone gets lost on the way to our house.
5. In 1932, Babe Didrikson one of the greatest athletes of all time was the sole member of an amateur track and field team known as the Golden Cyclones.
6. To the amazement of all of the onlookers at the 1932 National AAU Women's Track and Field Championship an event that also served as the Olympic Team Trials Didrikson won six gold medals and broke three world records in a single afternoon!
7. Captain Kira Falconetti announced, "We she meant the members of the varsity girls' soccer team have to set a good example to the junior varsity team."
8. Mei-Su assured us that being a vegan is that the diet in which you don't eat anything cooked or just the one that avoids any animal products? has reduced her allergies and improved her overall health.
9. Franklin Delano Roosevelt 1882–1945 shepherded the United States through the depression years and then through World War II.
10. "He the gypsy guitarist Django Reinhardt played exquisitely despite having burned his left hand so badly that he could barely move two of the fingers," said Ben reverentially.

EXERCISE 24
Responses will vary. Students should use parentheses and brackets correctly to set off details, explanations, and digressions in their essays.

EXERCISE 24

Using Parentheses and Brackets in Your Writing

For the school newspaper, write an informal essay about curious habits—yours and those of people you know. These can all be habits of a certain type (such as odd eating habits) or they can be very disparate behaviors (ways of talking, superstitions, ways of interacting with others). Use brackets and parentheses to set off details, explanations, and digressions.

UNIT 15 REVIEW

TEST YOUR KNOWLEDGE

EXERCISE 1

Identifying Sentence Purposes

Identify the following sentences as imperative, declarative, interrogative, or exclamatory. (10 points)

EXAMPLE
Will this detour really get us to the airport? (interrogative)

1. Flee for your life!
2. Spam, the potted meat, is extremely popular in Hawaii.
3. Please trim the stems of the roses with a knife, not with scissors.
4. Is a fjord the same thing as a bight?
5. Oh no, my jacket just split all the way down the back!
6. Renee wondered whether the current inhabitants would allow her to photograph her childhood home.
7. Yikes—the movie already started!
8. Dams, which were once seen as the ideal solution to certain irrigation and electricity problems, are now viewed with disfavor by many planning experts.
9. Do you think that an elm that is truly resistant to disease will be successfully developed and propagated?
10. Have a licensed electrician inspect the old house's wiring before you start plugging in appliances.

EXERCISE 2

Understanding Commas and End Marks of Punctuation

Proofread the following sentences to add end punctuation marks and commas where appropriate. (10 points)

1. No the springer spaniel is not a good breed for families with small children
2. The Skahans had a magical time on their trip to Vietnam

EXERCISE 1
1. imperative
2. declarative
3. imperative
4. interrogative
5. exclamatory
6. declarative
7. exclamatory
8. declarative
9. interrogative
10. imperative

EXERCISE 2
1. No, the springer spaniel is not a good breed for families with small children.
2. The Skahans had a magical time on their trip to Vietnam.
3. The tailor measured the length of Edward's leg seam, drew a chalk mark where the hem should be, and promised to have the trousers ready before graduation.
4. Did you know that it was once thought medically sensible to "bleed" sick patients with leeches?
5. How terrifying it was when that eighteen-wheeler swerved into the lane just ahead of us!
6. Fedoras, cloches, and berets are all different types of hats.
7. On June 17, 1972, five men were caught trying to break into Democratic National Headquarters in the Watergate complex.
8. The electric pencil sharpener is malfunctioning, but you can use the small plastic sharpener instead.
9. The nurse said, "Matthew, I'm just going to take your blood pressure before the doctor comes in."

10. The rag doll in that museum case, believe it or not, dates back to Roman-occupied Egypt in the first century A.D.

EXERCISE 3

1. In the ancient Mesopotamian kingdom of Uruk, a shekel of silver could buy the following: three measures of barley, three measures of sesame oil, or twelve measures of wool.
2. For money, people have used such items as feathers, beads, and shells.
3. One step in the manufacture of a modern coin is a complex process called "electrotyping."
4. Yikes, winning $27 million is just too much for me even to contemplate!
5. Criminals have made counterfeit money for centuries; ancient Greek forgers plated cheap copper coins with gold.
6. The international banker laughed and ironically quoted the lines from John Keats: "Much have I travell'd in the realms of gold, / And many goodly states and kingdoms seen."
7. Didn't you hear the cashier just ask you, "Do you have a smaller bill than a twenty?"

3. The tailor measured the length of Edward's leg seam drew a chalk mark where the hem should be and promised to have the trousers ready before graduation
4. Did you know that it was once thought medically sensible to "bleed" sick patients with leeches
5. How terrifying it was when that eighteen-wheeler swerved into the lane just ahead of us
6. Fedoras cloches and berets are all different types of hats
7. On June 17 1972 five men were caught trying to break into Democratic National Headquarters in the Watergate complex
8. The electric pencil sharpener is malfunctioning but you can use the small plastic sharpener instead
9. The nurse said "Matthew I'm just going to take your blood pressure before the doctor comes in"
10. The rag doll in that museum case believe it or not dates back to Roman-occupied Egypt in the first century A.D

EXERCISE 3

Correcting Punctuation Errors

Rewrite the following sentences to correct any errors in end marks, commas, colons, and semicolons. If a sentence is punctuated correctly, write *correct.* (10 points)

1. In the ancient Mesopotamian kingdom of Uruk, a shekel of silver could buy the following three measures of barley three measures of sesame oil or twelve measures of wool.
2. For money people have used such items as: feathers, beads, and shells.
3. One step in the manufacture of a modern coin is a complex process called "electrotyping."
4. Yikes, winning $27 million is just too much for me even to contemplate
5. Criminals have made counterfeit money for centuries ancient Greek forgers plated cheap copper coins with gold.

6. The international banker laughed and ironically quoted the lines from John Keats "Much have I travell'd in the realms of gold, / And many goodly states and kingdoms seen."
7. Didn't you hear the cashier just ask you, "Do you have a smaller bill than a twenty"
8. Ancient Chinese coins were made of bronze and cast in irregular shapes in A.D. 621 round coins were introduced.
9. For a tour, contact the United States Mint at 151 North Independence Mall East Philadelphia, Pennsylvania 19106-1886.
10. The largest banknote ever issued was Chinese it was nine by thirteen inches.

EXERCISE 4

Correcting the Use of Apostrophes

Identify each word that needs an apostrophe in the following sentences. Then correctly write the word. (10 points)

EXAMPLE

In my opinion, Calvin Trillins humor is more charming than Dave Barrys. *(Trillin's, Barry's)*

1. If you were cold, you shouldve borrowed Lewis sheepskin jacket.
2. In Roman mythology, Venus son was Cupid, the mischievous boy-god of love.
3. In the large telemarketing center, innumerable workers voices combined to create one gigantic, persuasive hum.
4. The reason those pants don't fit you is that they are a childrens medium, not a womens size!
5. The IRSs newly stated policy is to audit the tax returns of fewer low-income workers and focus more on the wealthiest individuals and corporations.
6. The brothers and sisters rooms reveal their different personalities; hers is chaotic, while his is neat.
7. I could tell by the way the pharmacist wrote her 7s and 2s that she had been educated in Europe rather than in the United States.

8. Ancient Chinese coins were made of bronze and cast in irregular shapes; in A.D. 621 round coins were introduced.
9. For a tour, contact the United States Mint at 151 North Independence Mall, East Philadelphia, Pennsylvania 19106-1886.
10. The largest banknote ever issued was Chinese; it was nine by thirteen inches.

EXERCISE 4
1. If you were cold, you should've borrowed Lewis's sheepskin jacket.
2. In Roman mythology, Venus' son was Cupid, the mischievous boy-god of love.
3. In the large telemarketing center, innumerable workers' voices combined to create one gigantic, persuasive hum.
4. The reason those pants don't fit you is that they are a children's medium, not a women's size!
5. The IRS's newly stated policy is to audit the tax returns of fewer low-income workers and focus more on the wealthiest individuals and corporations.
6. The brother's and sister's rooms reveal their different personalities; hers is chaotic, while his is neat.
7. I could tell by the way the pharmacist wrote her 7's and 2's that she had been educated in Europe rather than in the United States.

8. United Airlines' flight schedule is available on the Web.
9. The highlight of Julio and Reinalda's wedding reception was the fireworks display at midnight.
10. Somebody's opal ring has fallen into the mice's cage.

EXERCISE 5

1. A horseman slowly ascended the trail. In the fresh, open face of the newcomer, Mr. Oakhurst recognized Tom Simson. . . . —Bret Harte, from "The Outcasts of Poker Flat"
2. The cow stopped long at the brook to drink. . . ,and Sylvia stood still and waited, letting her bare feet cool themselves in the shoal water. . . . —Sarah Orne Jewett, from "A White Heron"
3. She was young, with a fair, calm face, whose lines bespoke repression. . . . But now there was a dull strength in her eyes. . . . It . . . indicated a suspension of intelligent thought. —Kate Chopin, from "The Story of an Hour"

8. United Airlines flight schedule is available on the Web.
9. The highlight of Julio and Reinaldas wedding reception was the fireworks display at midnight.
10. Somebodys opal ring has fallen into the mices cage.

EXERCISE 5

Understanding Ellipsis Points

Rewrite each of the following sentences, correctly adding ellipsis points in place of the underlined material. (10 points)

EXAMPLE

Once school started I looked for him in all my classes, but P.S. 13 was a huge, overpopulated place and it took me days and many discreet questions to discover that Eugene was in honors classes for all his subjects, classes that were not open to me because English was not my first language, though I was a straight A student. —Judith Ortiz Cofer, "American History"

(. . . I looked for him in all my classes, but P.S. 13 was a huge, overpopulated place and it took me days . . . to discover that Eugene was in honors classes for all his subjects, classes that were not open to me because English was not my first language, though I was a straight A *student.)*

1. A horseman slowly ascended the trail. In the fresh, open face of the newcomer, Mr. Oakhurst recognized Tom Simson, otherwise known as "The Innocent" of Sandy Bar. —Bret Harte, from "The Outcasts of Poker Flat"
2. The cow stopped long at the brook to drink, as if the pasture were not half a swamp, and Sylvia stood still and waited, letting her bare feet cool themselves in the shoal water, while the great twilight moths struck softly against her. —Sarah Orne Jewett, from "A White Heron"
3. She was young, with a fair, calm face, whose lines bespoke repression and even a certain strength. But now there was a dull strength in her eyes, whose gaze was fixed away off yonder on one of those patches of blue sky. It was not a glance of reflection but rather indicated a suspension of intelligent thought. —Kate Chopin, from "The Story of an Hour"

4. She was stretched on her back beneath the pear tree soaking in the alto chant of the visiting bees, the gold of the sun and the panting breath of the breeze when the inaudible voice of it all came to her. —Zora Neale Hurston from *Their Eyes Were Watching God*
5. Late Saturday afternoon, conscious of Salzman, Leo Finkle walked with Lily Hirschorn along Riverside Drive. He walked briskly and erectly, wearing with distinction the black fedora he had that morning taken with trepidation out of the dusty hatbox on his closet shelf, and the heavy black Saturday coat he had thoroughly whisked clean. —Bernard Malamud, from "The Magic Barrel"

4. She was stretched on her back beneath the pear tree . . . when the inaudible voice of it all came to her. —Zora Neale Hurston, from *Their Eyes Were Watching God*
5. Late Saturday afternoon . . . Leo Finkle walked with Lily Hirschorn along Riverside Drive. He walked briskly and erectly, wearing . . . the black fedora he had that morning taken with trepidation out of the dusty hatbox on his closet shelf, and the heavy black Saturday coat he had thoroughly whisked clean. — Bernard Malamud, from "The Magic Barrel"

EXERCISE 6
1. Agatha Christie's crime novel And Then There Were None is called a tour de force by Jacques Barzun and Wendell Hertig Taylor in A Catalogue of Crime, an annotated bibliography.
2. "Willow," a song on Joan Armatrading's album Show Some Emotion, contains the lines: "Come running to me / When it's more than you can stand / Running to me / When things get out of hand."
3. Both in Roddy Doyle's novel The Woman Who Walked Into Doors and Iris Murdoch's novel The Sea, The Sea, the author assumes the voice and point of view of a character of the opposite sex—with brilliant results.
4. Lord Chesterfield said, "An injury is much sooner forgotten than an insult."

EXERCISE 6

Understanding Apostrophes, Underlining, Italics, and Quotation Marks

Proofread the following sentences to add apostrophes, underlining or italics, and quotation marks where appropriate. (10 points)

EXAMPLE

Tori Amos's song Jackie's Strength is both a tribute to Jackie Onassis and a song about typical teenage angst.

(Tori Amos's song "Jackie's Strength" is both a tribute to Jackie Onassis and a song about typical teenage angst.)

1. Agatha Christies crime novel And Then There Were None is called a tour de force by Jacques Barzun and Wendell Hertig Taylor in A Catalogue of Crime, an annotated bibliography.
2. Willow, a song on Joan Armatradings album Show Some Emotion, contains the lines: Come running to me / When its more than you can stand / Running to me / When things get out of hand.
3. Both in Roddy Doyles novel The Woman Who Walked Into Doors and Iris Murdoch's novel The Sea, The Sea, the author assumes the voice and point of view of a character of the opposite sex—with brilliant results.

5. Iona spelled *broccoli* with too few *c*s and too many *l*s.
6. The article "Women on the Waves" appeared in the San Francisco Chronicle sometime in 2002, I believe.
7. "[T]he imperative of a free and unfettered press," wrote Chief Justice Burger in 1971, "comes into collision with another imperative, the effective functioning of a complex modern government. . . ."
8. In their book The Lore and Language of Schoolchildren, Peter and Iona Opie include the chapter "Unpopular Children: Jeers and Torments."
9. A common jeer that British children apply to someone who doesn't know how to take a joke is the following: "Roses are red / Violets are blue / Lemons are sour / And so are you."
10. "Will this endless rain never stop?" groaned Mrs. Beich.

EXERCISE 7
Responses may vary slightly.
Sample responses:
1. When children are very young, they think their parents are all-knowing and all-powerful.
2. Call me cheap, but I think a dollar seventy-five is too much to spend for one tiny chocolate truffle.
3. Let's go out beachcombing—I'm really hoping to find some rare, blue sea glass before breakfast tomorrow morning.

4. Lord Chesterfield said, An injury is much sooner forgotten than an insult.
5. Iona spelled *broccoli* with too few *c*s and too many *l*s.
6. The article Women on the Waves appeared in the San Francisco Chronicle sometime in 2002, I believe.
7. [T]he imperative of a free and unfettered press, wrote Chief Justice Burger in 1971, comes into collision with another imperative, the effective functioning of a complex modern government. . . .
8. In their book The Lore and Language of Schoolchildren, Peter and Iona Opie include the chapter Unpopular Children: Jeers and Torments.
9. A common jeer that British children apply to someone who doesn't know how to take a joke is the following: Roses are red / Violets are blue / Lemons are sour / And so are you.
10. Will this endless rain never stop? groaned Mrs. Beich.

EXERCISE 7
Understanding Hyphens, Dashes, Parentheses, and Brackets

Proofread the following sentences to add hyphens, dashes, parentheses, or brackets where appropriate. (10 points)

EXAMPLE
I don't have much money right now my checking account is overdrawn because I haven't gotten paid in two weeks.
(I don't have much money right now—my checking account is overdrawn—because I haven't worked at the flower shop this semester.)

1. When children are very young, they think their parents are all knowing and all powerful.
2. Call me cheap, but I think a dollar seventy five is too much to spend for one tiny chocolate truffle.
3. Let's go out beachcombing I'm really hoping to find some rare, blue sea glass before breakfast tomorrow morning.
4. Martin Van Buren 1782–1862 was not one of the most sparkling U.S. presidents.

5. Who won the 400 meter relay in the 1912 Olympics?
6. Is it nepotism if a mayor hires his sister in law for a job for which she is highly qualified?
7. Mel buys fragrance free detergent, low fat crackers, and nondairy creamer.
8. A parent came to the School Board Meeting and said, "It the high school building contains asbestos ceiling tiles that must be removed as soon as possible."
9. The *Vallery Courier* the newest weekly newspaper on the shoreline is delivered free because the parent company derives so much money from the advertising that appears in the paper.
10. What Madeline so proudly considers self esteem is considered somewhat more negatively by the rest of us to be self centeredness.

4. Martin Van Buren (1782–1862) was not one of the most sparkling U.S. presidents.
5. Who won the 400-meter relay in the 1912 Olympics?
6. Is it nepotism if a mayor hires his sister-in-law for a job for which she is highly qualified?
7. Mel buys fragrance-free detergent, low-fat crackers, and nondairy creamer.
8. A parent came to the School Board Meeting and said, "It [the high school building] contains asbestos ceiling tiles that must be removed as soon as possible."
9. The *Vallery Courier*—the newest weekly newspaper on the shoreline—is delivered free because the parent company derives so much money from the advertising that appears in the paper.
10. What Madeline so proudly considers self-esteem is considered somewhat more negatively by the rest of us to be self-centeredness.

EXERCISE 8

Using Correct Punctuation

Write a sentence for each direction below. (10 points)

EXAMPLE

Commas to set off an appositive, a compound adjective, and a dash

(Teddy Johnson, a shy, unassuming high school boy, tied a game with no time left in a second overtime and then made the winning basket at the buzzer in the third overtime—a mind-boggling performance!)

1. commas in a series and quotation marks
2. a declarative sentence and a colon
3. a semicolon and a transitional expression
4. two sentences joined by a semicolon
5. quotation marks for a direct quotation and brackets
6. a compound sentence and parentheses
7. an exclamatory sentence and a dash or dashes
8. a singular possessive noun and a colon
9. a long quotation, a colon, and a hyphen
10. an imperative sentence and a dash

EXERCISE 8

Responses will vary. Students should double-check their punctuation. You may want students to read some of their sentences aloud so that the class can see the many different ways the directions can be followed.

EXERCISE 9

Using Correct Punctuation in Your Writing

Imagine that you have the opportunity to pose one question to four famous artists or writers from different places. Write your question, and then draft the responses that you believe each individual would provide. Use quotation marks, commas, and end punctuation correctly in dialogue. Correctly punctuate the titles of the authors' and artists' works. In addition, use each of the following at least once: semicolon, colon, apostrophe, hyphen, dash, parentheses, and brackets. (20 points)

EXERCISE 9
Responses will vary. Students should correctly and effectively use at least one example of each punctuation mark covered in the unit.

UNIT 16 CAPITALIZATION

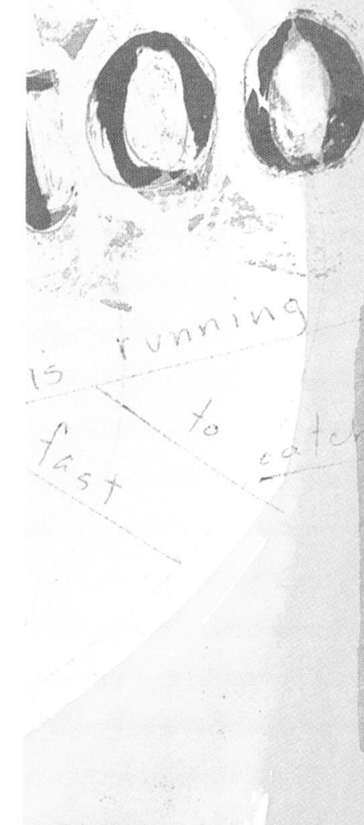

ASSESSMENT
Style Pretest, Style Comprehensive Test, and Punctuation and Capitalization Test are available at www.emcp.com.

UNIT OVERVIEW

CAPITALIZATION

EDITING FOR CAPITALIZATION ERRORS

To avoid capitalization errors, check your draft for proper nouns and proper adjectives; geographical names, directions, and historical names; and titles of artworks and literary works.

Proper nouns and proper adjectives are capitalized. A **proper noun** names a specific person, place, or thing.

EXAMPLES
Venus Williams   South America   Gulf of California

A **proper adjective** is an adjective formed from a proper noun.

EXAMPLES
Gordian knot   Scottish highlands   Federalist architecture

Geographical names of specific places are capitalized, including terms such as *lake*, *mountain*, *river*, or *valley* if they are used as part of a name. Do not capitalize general names for places.

EXAMPLES

capitalized	Lake Ontario Missouri River	Laurentian Mountains
not capitalized	a lake	the mountains

Geographical directions are capitalized if they are part of a specific name of a commonly recognized region. Do not capitalize such words as *east(ern)*, *west(ern)*, *north(ern)*, and *south(ern)* if they are used only to indicate direction.

EXAMPLES

capitalized	Far East Southeast Asia	Eastern Europe Midwest
not capitalized	north of Springfield west shore of the lake	southern rivers

Historical events are capitalized, as are special events and recognized periods of time.

EXAMPLES

Age of Enlightenment	World Series
Bataan Death March	Taiping Rebellion

The first and last words and all major words in between are capitalized in the **titles of artworks and literary works, including short stories, songs, and poems.** Articles, conjunctions, and prepositions are not capitalized unless they follow colons in titles.

EXAMPLES

"O Captain! My Captain!"
The Scarlet Letter
"The Notorious Jumping Frog of Calaveras County"
The Belfry of Bruges and Other Poems
"Trees in Bloom"

Try It Yourself

EXERCISE 1

Identifying Capitalized Words in Literature

For each underlined word in the following passage, identify the capitalization rule.

Neither have I so much of the infidel in me as to suppose that He has relinquished the government of the world, and given us up to the care of devils; and as I do not, I cannot see on what grounds the King of Britain can look up to heaven for help against us: a common murderer, a highwayman, or a housebreaker has as good pretense as he.

'Tis surprising to see how rapidly a panic will sometimes run through a country. All nations and ages have been subject to them: Britain has trembled like an ague at the report of a French fleet of flat-bottomed boats, and in the fourteenth century the whole English

CONTINUED

EXERCISE 1
1. proper noun
2. proper noun
3. proper adjective
4. proper adjective
5. proper noun
6. proper noun
7. proper adjective

Literature MODEL

LANGUAGELINK
Print exercise worksheets or have students complete exercises online with the LanguageLINK CD.

army, after ravaging the kingdom of France, was driven back like men petrified with fear; and this brave exploit was performed by a few broken forces collected and headed by a woman, Joan of Arc. Would that heaven might inspire some Jersey maid to spirit up her countrymen, and save her fair fellow sufferers from ravage and ravishment!

from *Crisis, No. 1*
Thomas Paine

EXERCISE 2

Correcting Capitalization

Rewrite each sentence, correcting it for errors in capitalization.

1. The first shots in the american revolution were fired at lexington and concord in april 1775.
2. George washington, a veteran of the french and indian war, commanded the continental army.
3. King george iii placed british forces under the command of general william howe.
4. After a series of defeats, on christmas night in 1776, washington crossed the delaware river and routed the british and their hessian allies at trenton and princeton.
5. Hoping to rally the loyalists, in 1777, howe captured philadelphia and forced the continental congress to move into exile.
6. On october 17, 1777, american forces led by horatio gates and benedict arnold captured a large british army at saratoga, new york.
7. The colonists' success helped benjamin franklin convince france to support the revolution.
8. The english later shifted their efforts to the south and captured charleston, south carolina, on may 12, 1780.
9. After suffering heavy losses in the carolinas, lord cornwallis moved his british army to yorktown, virginia.
10. Washington and his french allies forced cornwallis to surrender in october 1781, ensuring the survival of the united states.

EXERCISE 2

1. The first shots in the American Revolution were fired at Lexington and Concord in April 1775.
2. George Washington, a veteran of the French and Indian War, commanded the Continental army.
3. King George III placed British forces under the command of General William Howe.
4. After a series of defeats, on Christmas night in 1776, Washington crossed the Delaware River and routed the British and their Hessian allies at Trenton and Princeton.
5. Hoping to rally the Loyalists, in 1777, Lowe captured Philadelphia and forced the Continental Congress to move into exile.
6. On October 17, 1777, American forces led by Horatio Gates and Benedict Arnold captured a large British army at Saratoga, New York.
7. The colonists' success helped Benjamin Franklin convince France to support the revolution.
8. The English later shifted their efforts to the South and captured Charleston, South Carolina, on May 12, 1780.
9. After suffering heavy losses in the Carolinas, Lord Cornwallis moved his British army to Yorktown, Virginia.
10. Washington and his French allies forced Cornwallis to surrender in October 1781, ensuring the survival of the United States.

EXERCISE 3

Using Capitalization in Your Writing

Assume you are the leader of a third-world country. You have been asked by a national newspaper to write a brief narrative of what steps you intend to take to increase the wealth and the income of your people. In your narrative note the rules for capitalization: proper noun, proper adjective, geographical name, geographical direction, historical name, the title of an artwork, the title of a literary work, the pronoun *I*, the first word in a sentence, and the title of a person. Include at least one capitalized word for each rule listed above.

EXERCISE 3 *Responses will vary.* Narratives should reflect proper capitalization and include one example of at least four of the rules governing proper nouns, proper adjectives, geographical names, geographical directions, historical names, titles of artwork, title of literary works, the pronoun *I*, the first word in a sentence, and the title of a person.

PROPER NOUNS AND PROPER ADJECTIVES

Proper Nouns

A **proper noun** names a specific person, place, or thing. The following kinds of proper nouns should be capitalized.

Names of people

EXAMPLES

Oprah Winfrey   John F. Kennedy   Ken Griffey, Jr.

USAGE tip

Middle initials and the abbreviations *Jr.* and *Sr.* should also be capitalized.

Months, days, and **holidays**

EXAMPLES

April   Thursday   Labor Day

USAGE tip

Do not capitalize the names of seasons: *spring, summer, fall, winter.*

Names of religions, languages, races, and **nationalities**

EXAMPLES

Lutheran   Gnosticism

Norwegian   French

Swedish   Latino/Latina

Greek   Native American

Capitalize words referring to the Deity: *Our Father, God, Yahweh, Allah.* Do not capitalize the word *god* referring to deities in ancient mythologies: *Mars was the god of war.*

USAGE tip

Do not capitalize words such as *school, college,* or *theater* unless they are part of a name: *Brown University, The Grier School, Schubert Theater.*

Names of clubs, organization, businesses, and **institutions**

EXAMPLES

Disabled American Veterans
Hershey Foods Corporation
General Hospital
Daughters of the American Revolution

Names of awards, prizes, and **medals**

EXAMPLES

Nobel Prize
National Book Award
McPhee Fellowship
The Newbery Medal

Proper Adjectives

A **proper adjective** is either an adjective formed from a proper noun or a proper noun used as an adjective.

USAGE tip

Check a dictionary if you have any questions about whether a proper adjective formed from a proper noun should be capitalized.

Proper adjectives formed from proper nouns

EXAMPLES

German chocolate
Japanese literature
French class
Irish setter

Proper nouns used as adjectives

EXAMPLES

Democratic Party conference
Roman candle
Swiss steak
Arizona mountains

Some adjectives derived from names or nationalities are no longer capitalized because of common use: *venetian blinds, scotch whiskey, french dressing.*

Brand names are used as proper adjectives. Capitalize the name used as an adjective, but do not capitalize the common noun it modifies unless the word is part of the product name: *Xerox copier, DeMarini softball bat.*

Try It Yourself

EXERCISE 4

Identifying Proper Nouns and Proper Adjectives in Literature

Identify the proper nouns and proper adjectives in the following sentences, and cite the appropriate rule that governs their capitalization.

> At exactly fifteen minutes past eight in the morning, on August 6, 1945, Japanese time, at the moment when the atomic bomb flashed above Hiroshima, Miss Toshiko Sasaki, a clerk in the personnel department of the East Asia Tin works, had just sat down at her place in the plant office and was turning her head to speak to the girl at the next desk. At that same moment, Dr. Masakazu Fujii was settling down cross-legged to read the Osaka *Asahi* on the porch of his private hospital, overhanging one of the seven deltaic rivers which divide Hiroshima; Mrs. Hatsuyo Nakamura, a tailor's widow, stood by the window of her kitchen, watching a neighbor tearing down his house because it lay in the path of an air-raid-defense fire lane; Father Wilhelm Kleinsorge, a German priest of the Society of Jesus, reclined in his underwear on a cot on the top floor of his order's three-story mission house, reading a Jesuit magazine, *Stimmen der Zeit*; . . .
>
> from *Hiroshima*, "A Noiseless Flash"
> John Hersey

EXERCISE 4
1. *Japanese*—proper adjective
2. *Hiroshima*—proper noun/geographic location
3. *Miss Toshiko Sasaki*—proper noun, person
4. *East Asia Tin*—proper adjective formed from proper noun, organization name

Literature MODEL

5. *Dr. Masakazu Fujii*—proper noun, person
6. *Osaki Asahi*—proper noun, newspaper title
7. *Hiroshima*—proper noun/geographic location
8. *Mrs. Hatsuyo Nakamura*—proper noun, person
9. *Father Wilhelm Kleinsorge*—proper noun, person
10. *German*—proper adjective
11. *Society of Jesus*—proper noun, organization name
12. *Jesuit*—proper adjective
23. *Stimmen der Zeit*—proper noun, magazine title

EXERCISE 5

Correcting Capitalization for Proper Nouns and Adjectives

Correct any capitalization errors in the following sentences.

1. During world war II, the United States government initiated the manhattan project to develop an Atomic bomb.
2. J. robert oppenheimer directed the scientists who constructed the bomb at los alamos, New Mexico.

EXERCISE 5
1. During World War II, the United States government initiated the Manhattan Project to develop an atomic bomb.
2. J. Robert Oppenheimer directed the scientists at Los Alamos, New Mexico, who constructed the bomb.

3. On july 16, 1945, they tested the first atomic weapon in the desert near Alamogordo, new Mexico.
4. President Harry s Truman was informed of the successful Test while he was in potsdam, germany.
5. Truman issued an Ultimatum to the japanese demanding that they surrender or face total devastation.
6. Japan refused to surrender and many american soldiers feared they would have to invade the Islands.
7. On august 6, 1945, a u.s. B-29, the *enola gay*, dropped an Atomic bomb on hiroshima.
8. The Japanese Government was slow to respond, so America dropped an atom bomb on nagasaki on august 9, 1945.
9. Japan agreed to give up, and officials from both sides met on board the American Battleship *missouri* to sign the articles of Surrender.
10. Scholars such as John W. Dower, who wrote *war without mercy*, have questioned truman's motives for dropping the atomic bomb at the end of the War.

EXERCISE 6

Using Capitalization of Proper Nouns and Proper Adjectives in Your Writing

Describe a difficult decision that you have had to make. Provide details in your description about where you were, the problem you faced, the people who might be affected by the decision, the options you were considering, and what finally prompted your decision. Be sure to capitalize correctly proper nouns and proper adjectives.

I and First Words

Capitalize the pronoun ***I***.

EXAMPLE
I walked to the grocery store.

Capitalize the **first word** of each sentence.

EXAMPLE
My car will be in the shop until Friday.

3. On July 16, 1945, they tested the first atomic weapon in the desert near Alamogordo, New Mexico.
4. President Harry S Truman was informed of the successful test while he was in Potsdam, Germany.
5. Truman issued an ultimatum to the Japanese demanding that they surrender or face total devastation.
6. Japan refused to surrender and many American soldiers feared they would have to invade the islands.
7. On August 6, 1945, a U.S. B-29, the *Enola Gay*, dropped an atomic bomb on Hiroshima.
8. The Japanese government was slow to respond, so America dropped an atomic bomb on Nagasaki on August 9, 1945.
9. Japan agreed to give up, and officials from both sides met on board the American battleship *Missouri* to sign the articles of surrender.
10. Scholars such as John W. Dower, who wrote *War Without Mercy*, have questioned Truman's motives for dropping the atomic bomb at the end of the war.

EXERCISE 6
Responses will vary. Students should provide numerous examples of correctly capitalized proper nouns and proper adjectives in their descriptions.

Capitalize the first word of a **direct quotation**. Do not capitalize the first word of a direct quotation, however, if it continues after the identification tag for who is speaking. Do not capitalize the beginning of an indirect quotation.

EXAMPLES

direct quotation

"You effortlessly excelled in nearly every subject in high school, but you must not become complacent and expect such easy success in college," cautioned the counselor.

direct quotation interrupted

"Your grade point average will stand out to admissions counselors," the teacher commended, "but you still need a stellar performance on the SAT to gain acceptance at the school of your choice."

indirect quotation

The counselor told me that I should participate in more extracurricular activities.

When citing **poetry,** follow the capitalization of the original poem. Although most poets capitalize the first word of each line in a poem, as is the case in the first set of lines below, some poets do not. The second example shows how the poet uses a combination of uppercase and lowercase letters at the beginning of lines. Also note that the author has chosen to capitalize certain words within the poem that would not normally be capitalized.

Literature MODELS

Hoarse, booming drums of the regiment,
Little souls who thirst for fight,
These men were born to drill and die.
The unexplained glory flies above them,
Great is the Battle-God, great, and his Kingdom—
A field where a thousand corpses lie.

from "Do not weep, maiden, for war is kind"
Stephen Crane

CONTINUED

My tongue, every atom of my blood, form'd from this soil,
    this air.
Born here of parents born here from parents the same, and
    their parents the same,
I, now thirty-seven years old in perfect health begin,
Hoping to cease not till death.

from "Song of Myself"
Walt Whitman

Capitalize the first word in a **letter salutation** and the **name or title of the person** addressed.

EXAMPLES

Dear Father	My sweet Aunt Lynda	Dear Ms.

Capitalize only the first word in **letter closings**.

EXAMPLES

Sincerely yours	Yours truly
Love	Best wishes

Try It Yourself

EXERCISE 7

Correcting Capitalization for the Pronoun *I* and First Words

Correct any errors in capitalization you find in each of the following sentences. If there are no errors in the sentence, write *correct.*

1. After greg noticed the flat tire, he exclaimed, "why does this always happen to me?"
2. While filling my plate with more pretzels, i overheard shelly ask Terrell, "when can we leave this boring party?"
3. At the end of his letter to the governor, David added the closing, "your obedient servant."

EXERCISE 7

1. After Greg noticed the flat tire, he exclaimed, "Why does this always happen to me?"
2. While filling my plate with more pretzels, I overheard Shelly ask Terrell, "When can we leave this boring party?"
3. At the end of his letter to the governor, David added the closing, "Your obedient servant."

4. As you will recall, i told you in no uncertain terms to Take out the garbage.
5. Brad wrote, "i can no longer serve as mayor of this town and must resign immediately," and signed his letter "regretfully, Brad Jefferson."
6. Vanessa was proud when her mother won the pulitzer prize.
7. The sun was high in the sky when Jessica suggested, "Let's go to the beach."
8. Herman Melville begins *moby dick* with the famous line, "call me ishmael."
9. My grandmother always closed her letters with, "fondly, nana."
10. Harry used to say about his brother-in-law, "i'd like to buy him for what he's worth and sell him for what he thinks he's worth."

4. As you will recall, I told you in no uncertain terms to take out the garbage.
5. Brad wrote, "I can no longer serve as mayor of this town and must resign immediately," and signed his letter "Regretfully, Brad Jefferson."
6. Vanessa was proud when her mother won the Pulitzer Prize.
7. correct
8. Herman Melville begins *Moby Dick* with the famous line, "Call me Ishmael."
9. My grandmother always closed her letters with, "Fondly, Nana."
10. Harry used to say about his brother-in-law, "I'd like to buy him for what he's worth and sell him for what he thinks he's worth."

EXERCISE 8

Using Capitalization of *I* and First Words

Write a response for each of the directions below. Be sure to capitalize any proper nouns and proper adjectives in addition to the pronoun *I* and first words in sentences and in quotations.

1. Quote two sentences from a newspaper or magazine article that you have read recently. Include the title of the work and its author.
2. Quote a character from a television show who always uses the same word, phrase, or expression to describe someone or something.
3. Restate in an indirect quotation the person's meaning from number 2.
4. Write several sentences summarizing your most recent summer vacation.
5. Write a short note you might leave for a family member.

EXERCISE 8

Responses will vary. By following each direction, students will be provided practice in capitalizing first words, the pronoun *I*, proper nouns, and proper adjectives.

FAMILY RELATIONSHIPS AND TITLES OF PERSONS

Capitalize the **titles** or **abbreviations** that come before the names of people.

EXAMPLES

Colonel Mike Anderson	Ms. Marie Franklin
Senator Harkin	Dr. Louis
Mr. and Mrs. Sweeney	President Jackson

Capitalize a person's title when it is used as a proper noun.

EXAMPLES

The eulogy will be delivered by Reverend Larson.
This patient needs attention, Doctor.

Capitalize words showing **family relationships** when used as titles or as substitutes for a name.

EXAMPLES

Uncle Leonard	Grandma
Father	Cousin Samuel

Try It Yourself

EXERCISE 9
1. correct
2. Pastor Gibson
3. Governor Huey Long
4. his nephew and grandson
5. Princess Grace of Monaco
6. Senator Hillary Clinton

EXERCISE 9

Understanding Capitalization of Titles and Family Relationships

Correct the capitalization in the following items. If the item is correct as written, write *correct.*

1. Queen Elizabeth II
2. pastor gibson
3. governor huey long
4. his Nephew and Grandson
5. princess Grace of Monaco
6. senator hillary clinton

7. Bishop O'Connor
8. inspector townsend
9. aunt phyllis
10. president James Buchanan

7. correct
8. Inspector Townsend
9. Aunt Phyllis
10. President James Buchanan

EXERCISE 10

Using Titles and Family Relationships in Your Writing

Write a letter to a friend describing a family reunion or a class party that you attended. Answer all the *who, what, when, where, why,* and *how* questions about the event. Use a variety of capitalized and lowercase titles and family relationships in your entry.

EXERCISE 10
Responses will vary. Students' letters should illustrate their understanding of when capitalization is used for titles, family relationships, or names at class parties.

ABBREVIATIONS

Abbreviate titles such as those of **organizations, parts of the government, businesses, address elements,** and **personal titles.**

Abbreviate social titles when they appear before a proper name. The most common social titles are *Mr.* (stands for Mister) and *Mrs.* (stands for Missus). Other common titles include *Dr.* (Doctor), *Prof.* (Professor), *Rep.* (Representative), and *Gov.* (Governor).

Social titles can appear after a name as well: *Jr.* for "Junior" and *Sr.* for "Senior," as well as abbreviations that indicate a person's educational standing (*R.N.* for Registered Nurse). Other common abbreviations for after names include: *B.S.* (Bachelor of Science), *M.D.* (Doctor of Medicine), *Esq.* (Esquire), *Ph.D.* (Doctor of Philosophy), and *J.P.* (justice of the peace). Capitalize the first letter of these abbreviations and follow them with a period.

USAGE tip

Everyone uses certain standard abbreviations because they are convenient and readily understood. Not all abbreviations are acceptable in formal writing.

USAGE tip

Miss is not an abbreviation so it needs no period. *Ms.* is not an abbreviation but is still followed by a period. You may use *Ms.* for married or unmarried women, while *Miss* is reserved for unmarried women only.

EXAMPLES

My algebra teacher is **Mr.** Tolari.

Rep. Osborne was quoted in the local newspaper.

Abbreviate the titles of organizations such as *Brothers (Bros.* or *Bro.), Company (Co.)*, and *Limited (Ltd.)*. Other commonly abbreviated organization words include *RR* (railroad), *Corp.* (Corporation), *Inc.* (Incorporated), *Mfg. (Manufacturing)*, and *Assoc. or Assn. (Association)*.

EXAMPLES

Sampson & **Bros.**	Roofing Sampson & Brothers Roofing
Iowa Calf Ropers **Assn.**	Iowa Calf Ropers Association

Abbreviate parts of government with the initials of each word in the title. Capitalize all the letters and use no periods. This rule also applies to some company titles.

EXAMPLES

Agency for International Development	**AID**
Environmental Protection Agency	**EPA**
Columbia Broadcasting System	**CBS**

Abbreviate address titles such as *Blvd.* (Boulevard), *Ct.* (Court), *Dr.* (Drive), *Ln* or *La.* (Lane), *Pl.* (Place). Capitalize the first letter in road titles and follow with a period. Abbreviate state titles with the official postal service abbreviations. Capitalize both letters in a postal service abbreviation and use no period following.

USAGE tip

Treat directional parts of addresses as you would state abbreviations: *NW, NE, SE*, and *SW.*

EXAMPLES

Street	**St.**
Road	**Rd.**
Avenue	**Ave.**

State Titles/Postal Service Abbreviations			
Alabama	AL	Montana	MT
Alaska	AK	Nebraska	NE
Arizona	AZ	Nevada	NV
Arkansas	AR	New Hampshire	NH
California	CA	New Jersey	NJ
Colorado	CO	New Mexico	NM
Connecticut	CT	New York	NY
Washington, D.C.	DC	North Carolina	NC
Delaware	DE	North Dakota	ND
Florida	FL	Ohio	OH
Georgia	GA	Oklahoma	OK
Hawaii	HI	Oregon	OR
Idaho	ID	Pennsylvania	PA
Illinois	IL	Rhode Island	RI
Indiana	IN	South Carolina	SC
Iowa	IA	South Dakota	SD
Kansas	KS	Tennessee	TN
Kentucky	KY	Texas	TX
Louisiana	LA	Utah	UT
Maine	ME	Vermont	VT
Maryland	MD	Virginia	VA
Massachusetts	MA	Washington	WA
Michigan	MI	West Virginia	WV
Minnesota	MN	Wisconsin	WI
Mississippi	MS	Wyoming	WY
Missouri	MO		

Try It Yourself

EXERCISE 11

Correcting Capitalization of Abbreviations

Correct any capitalization errors in each of the following sentences.

1. The soccer game will be carried by most nbc affiliates.
2. The sign on my uncle's mailbox reads, "Paul Murphy, esq."
3. While in the capitol building, we met rep. Neil Smith.
4. In the classroom, mr. Thompson is a strict disciplinarian.
5. We drove down Griffin blvd. and turned left on Bismarck dr., before stopping to ask for directions.

EXERCISE 11

1. The soccer game will be carried by most NBC affiliates.
2. The sign on my uncle's mailbox reads, Paul Murphy, Esq.
3. While in the capitol building, we met Rep. Neil Smith.
4. In the classroom, Mr. Thompson is a strict disciplinarian.
5. We drove down Griffin Blvd. and turned left on Bismarck Dr., before stopping to ask for directions.
6. My advisor, Prof. Turgison, earned his Ph.D. at Vanderbilt University.
7. Mrs. Williams said that the CIA is working covertly in at least one NATO country.
8. Based on his experience with the NLRB, Gov. Underwood is unlikely to favor either side in the contract negotiations.
9. The James Bros. firm will be representing us in this case.
10. A representative of the Pine Lake Development Assn. met with Mr. Carlson today.

6. My advisor, prof. Turgison, earned his phd at Vanderbilt University.
7. Mrs. Williams said that the cia is working covertly in at least one nato country.
8. Based on his experience with the nlrb, gov. Underwood is unlikely to favor either side in the contract negotiations.
9. The James bros. firm will be representing us in this case.
10. A representative of the Pine Lake Development assn. met with mr. Carlson today.

EXERCISE 12
1. AL
2. FL
3. WA
4. MO
5. ME
6. IN
7. GA
8. PA
9. MI
10. KY

EXERCISE 12

Understanding State Abbreviations

For each state below, write the two-letter postal abbreviation. Make sure you capitalize it correctly.

1. Alabama
2. Florida
3. Washington
4. Missouri
5. Maine
6. Indiana
7. Georgia
8. Pennsylvania
9. Michigan
10. Kentucky

EXERCISE 13
Responses will vary. Students should use abbreviations correctly. However, in the process of comparing character sketches, they will probably realize that not all abbreviations are instantly clear and identifiable. You may want to clarify that when using certain abbreviations, they use them first as an accompaniment to the fully spelled out words, as in Central Intelligence Agency (CIA).

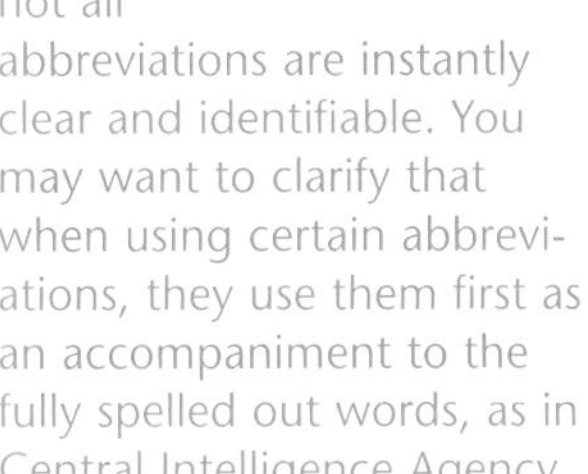

EXERCISE 13

Using Abbreviations in Your Writing

Write a letter of application, including a resume, for positions that might interest you with a local, state, or federal agency in your area. Describe the kinds of jobs you have had, including official titles of employers or companies for whom you have worked in the past. Use as many appropriate abbreviations as you can to illuminate your work experience and the position in which you are interested. Exchange your letter with a classmate and compare results. Were the abbreviations immediately clear or did they take time and attention away from your explanation?

TIME DESIGNATIONS

Capitalize the time abbreviations **B.C., A.D., A.M.,** and **P.M.** When these abbreviations appear in type, they usually are printed in small capital letters.

The abbreviation **B.C.** refers to the time before Christ. When using the abbreviation B.C., place it after the date.

EXAMPLE
In 546 B.C. an exiled aristocrat named Pisistratus defeated his opponents and established his rule in Athens.

USAGE tip

You may also see *C.E.* (of the common era) and *B.C.E.* (before the common era) used instead of *B.C.*

The abbreviation **A.D.** refers to the time after Christ. When using the abbreviation A.D., place it before the date.

EXAMPLE
Jerusalem fell to the attacking Romans in A.D. 70.

The abbreviation **A.M.** refers to time within the 12-hour period of midnight and noon. The abbreviation **P.M.** refers to time within the 12-hour period of noon and midnight.

EXAMPLE
During summer break the library will be open from 9 A.M. until 8 P.M.

USAGE tip

Never use the terms *morning, evening,* or *o'clock* with either *A.M.* or *P.M.*, since the time has already been indicated.

Try It Yourself

EXERCISE 14

Understanding Capitalization of Time Designations

Answer each of the following questions with a time designation. Be sure to capitalize the time abbreviations correctly. You may use words such as *about* or *approximately* if you're unsure of exact times.

1. What time do you eat breakfast on a school day?
2. What time do you eat breakfast a weekend day?
3. What time does your second class begin?
4. What time does your school day end?

EXERCISE 14
Responses will vary except for numbers 9 and 10.

9. 470–399 B.C. (These are the correct dates for Socrates. Do not deduct points for an incorrect date. Grade only for correct capitalization and placement of *B.C.*)
10. A.D. 64 (This is the correct date of the Great Fire of Rome. Do not deduct points for an incorrect date. Grade only for correct capitalization and placement of *A.D.*)

5. What time do any of your extracurricular activities begin? Name the activity in your response.
6. What time does your family eat supper?
7. During what hours at night do you sleep?
8. In what year will you graduate from high school?
9. Approximately when did Socrates, the Greek philosopher, live?
10. In what year after Christ did the Great Fire of Rome occur?

EXERCISE 15

1. My history class starts at 8:00 A.M. and ends at 9:55 A.M.
2. correct
3. The bus for Albuquerque departs at 9:45 A.M. and the bus for Little Rock leaves at 12:15 P.M.
4. A plague of typhoid fever killed thousands in Athens from 430 B.C.E. to 427 B.C.E.
5. Without the urging of Theodora, Justinian would have abandoned Constantinople during the Nika Revolt in A.D. 532.
6. The meteor shower will begin tonight sometime between 10:00 P.M. and 1:00 A.M.
7. In 216 B.C., during the Second Punic War, Hannibal crushed the Romans at the Battle of Cannae.
8. Constantinople fell to the Turks in A.D. 1453, ending the Byzantine Empire.
9. Earthquakes caused A.D. 1693 to be known as a year of destruction in Italy.
10. On Sundays I usually stay up until 2:00 A.M., even though I have to be at work the next day at 9:00 A.M.

EXERCISE 15

Correcting Capitalization Errors in Time Designations

Correct any capitalization and usage errors in time designations in the following sentences. If the sentences are correct as written, write *correct.*

1. My history class starts at 8:00 am and ends at 9:55 am.
2. Sicily's Mount Etna erupted in 1226 B.C., 1170 B.C., 1149 B.C. and 525 B.C.
3. The bus for Albuquerque departs at 9:45 A.M. and the bus for Little Rock leaves at 12:15 pm.
4. A plague of typhoid fever killed thousands in Athens from 430 bce to 427 bce.
5. Without the urging of Theodora, Justinian would have abandoned Constantinople during the Nika Revolt in ad 532.
6. The meteor shower will begin tonight sometime between 10:00 pm and 1:00 am .
7. In 216 bc, during the Second Punic War, Hannibal crushed the Romans at the Battle of Cannae.
8. Constantinople fell to the Turks in 1453 A.D. ending the Byzantine Empire.
9. Earthquakes caused ad 1693 to be known as a year of destruction in Italy.
10. On Sundays I usually stay up until 2:00 a.m., even though I have to be at work the next day at 9:00 a.m.

EXERCISE 16

Using Time Designations in Your Writing

Assume that you are living in Greece in A.D. 300 and that you keep a journal that you wish to pass down to your ancestors. Write an entry describing a typical day. In your entry, use date and time designations correctly.

EXERCISE 16
Responses will vary. Students should correctly use and capitalize time designations in their paragraphs.

GEOGRAPHICAL NAMES, DIRECTIONS, AND HISTORICAL NAMES

Capitalize the **names of cities, states, countries, islands,** and **continents**.

EXAMPLES

cities	Montgomery	Saigon
	Managua	
states	Massachusetts	Tennessee
	California	
countries	Norway	Saudi Arabia
	Panama	
islands	Guam	Iceland
	Mauritius	
continents	Europe	Australia
	North America	

Capitalize the **names of bodies of water** and **geographical features**.

EXAMPLES

Indian Ocean — Rio Grande River

Negev Desert — Great Dismal Swamp

Do not capitalize prepositions such as *of* or *upon* used in geographical names: *Stratford-upon-Avon.* This applies also to prepositions in other languages, such as *de: Rio de Janiero.*

Capitalize **names of buildings, monuments,** and **bridges.**

EXAMPLES

Eiffel Tower — Taj Mahal

Washington Monument — Golden Gate Bridge

USAGE tip

Do not capitalize general names for places: *Stay on the interstate until you reach exit 403, then take a right and follow the highway until you reach the river.*

USAGE tip

Do not capitalize directions of the compass: *Matt pedaled south as the sun set behind the mountains. He found the campsite near the western edge of the forest.*

Capitalize the **names of streets** and **highways**.

EXAMPLES

42nd Street	Sunset Boulevard
Coal Ridge Turnpike	Martin Luther King, Jr. Parkway

Capitalize **sections of the country**.

EXAMPLES

the Western Shore	the Corn Belt
the Highlands	the Midwest

Capitalize the **names of historical events, special events, documents,** and **recognized periods of time.**

EXAMPLES

historical events	Spanish Inquisition
	Defenestration of Prague
special events	Sundance Film Festival
	Election Day
documents	Magna Carta
	Treaty of Guadalupe Hidalgo
historical periods	Age of Reason
	Reconstruction

Try It Yourself

EXERCISE 17

Identifying Capitalization in Literature

Identify the rule that applies to each of the underlined words or groups of words in the following literature passage.

MODEL

A few facts about shopping centers. The "biggest" center in the United States is generally agreed to be Woodfield, outside Chicago, a "super" regional or "leviathan" two-million-square-foot center with four major tenants.

The "first" shopping center in the United States is generally agreed to be Country Club Plaza in Kansas City, built in the twenties. There were some other earlier

CONTINUED

EXERCISE 17

1. *United States*—country
2. *Woodfield*—place name
3. *Chicago*—city
4. *Country Club Plaza*—place name
5. *Kansas City*—city

centers, notably Edward H. Bouton's 1907 Roland Park in Baltimore, Hugh Prather's 1931 Highland Park Shopping Village in Dallas, and Hugh Potter's 1937 River Oaks in Houston, but the developer of Country Club Plaza, J. C. Nichols, is referred to with ritual frequency in the literature of shopping centers, usually as "pioneering J. C. Nichols" or "J. C. Nichols, father of the center as we know it."

from "On the Mall"
Joan Didion

6. *Roland Park*—place name
7. *Baltimore*—city
8. *Highland Park Shopping Village*—place name
9. *Dallas*—city
10. *River Oaks*—place name
11. *Houston*—city

EXERCISE **18**

Correcting Capitalization of Geographical and Historical Names and Directions

Rewrite the following using correct capitalization. If an item is correctly capitalized, write *correct.* You may need to consult a dictionary for some items.

1. promontory point
2. southern florida
3. nicholas channel
4. bay of biscay
5. tang dynasty
6. monroe doctrine
7. a northern province
8. memorial day
9. stanley cup finals
10. west of the Mississippi River
11. council of trent
12. great schism
13. belmont stakes
14. far west
15. the rosetta stone
16. empire state building
17. the potsdam conference
18. waterloo bridge
19. Great Wall of China
20. second great awakening

EXERCISE 18

1. Promontory Point
2. southern Florida
3. Nicholas Channel
4. Bay of Biscay
5. Tang Dynasty
6. Monroe Doctrine
7. correct
8. Memorial Day
9. Stanley Cup Finals
10. correct
11. Council of Trent
12. Great Schism
13. Belmont Stakes
14. Far West
15. the Rosetta Stone
16. Empire State Building
17. the Potsdam Conference
18. Waterloo Bridge
19. Great Wall of China
20. Second Great Awakening

EXERCISE 19

Using Capitalization in Your Writing

Write a paragraph or two for a foreign pen pal about a major turning point in American history, such as the Civil War or attacks on the World Trade Center. Explain what happened, including important groups, events, places, and people involved in or affected by the turning point. Be sure to check your capitalization when you are editing and proofreading.

EXERCISE 19
Responses will vary. Students should capitalize all proper nouns, not just those terms related to the historical turning point they are explaining.

TITLES OF ARTWORKS AND LITERARY WORKS

Capitalize the first and last words and all important words in the titles of artworks and literary works, including books, magazines, short stories, poems, songs, movies, plays, paintings, and sculpture. Do not capitalize articles (*a*, *an*, and *the*), conjunctions, and prepositions that are less than five letters long.

USAGE tip

Titles of complete works, such as books, magazines, movies, and plays, should also be italicized or underlined.

EXAMPLES

Car and Driver (magazine)
"A White Heron" (short story)
"Come Sail Away" (song)
The Grapes of Wrath (book)
"Boy Sitting in the Grass" (painting)
Saving Private Ryan (movie)

Capitalize the titles of **religious works**.

EXAMPLES

Torah	Koran	New Testament
Dead Sea Scrolls	Vedas	Upanishads

Try It Yourself

EXERCISE 20

Identifying and Correcting Errors in Capitalization of Titles of Artworks and Literary Works

Write the words that should be capitalized in the following sentences.

1. In F. Scott Fitzgerald's short story "the sensible thing," the main character discovers that love is not repeatable.
2. From 1868 to 1870, Susan B. Anthony and Elizabeth Cady Stanton published a newspaper *the revolution*, which called for equal rights for women.
3. Sinclair Lewis depicted the worst excesses of materialism in his novels *babbitt* and *elmer gantry*.
4. Frank Wildhorn's musical *the civil war* features the songs "brother, my brother," "the day the sun stood still," and "if prayin' were horses."
5. *apocalypse now*, set in vietnam and cambodia, is based on the novel *the heart of darkness*.
6. The cartoon strip *sherman's lagoon* depicts a turtle, a hermit crab, and two sharks named megan and sherman.
7. Abraham Lincoln's most famous writings include "the gettysburg address," "a house divided," and a letter he wrote to mrs. bixby in boston, massachusetts.
8. Although best known for his portrayal of sergeant hartman in *Full Metal Jacket*, R. Lee Ermey displayed his comedic talents in *saving silverman* and *toy story*.
9. In *common sense*, Thomas Paine brings a harsh indictment against the concept of a divine-right monarchy.
10. Ralph Waldo Emerson's essay "self-reliance" is considered the finest expression of his beliefs on individualism.

EXERCISE 20
1. "The Sensible Thing"
2. *The Revolution*
3. *Babbitt, Elmer Gantry*
4. *The Civil War,* "Brother, My Brother," "The Day the Sun Stood Still," "If Prayin' Were Horses"
5. *Apocalypse Now,* Vietnam, Cambodia, *The Heart of Darkness*
6. *Sherman's Lagoon,* Megan, Sherman
7. "The Gettysburg Address," "A House Divided," Mrs. Bixby, Boston, Massachusetts
8. Sergeant Hartman, *Saving Silverman, Toy Story*
9. *Common Sense*
10. "Self-Reliance"

EXERCISE 21

Using Correct Capitalization in Your Writing

How much do you know about the time period in which your grandparents, parents, aunts, and uncles grew up? Choose an older relative to interview about popular culture when he or she was a young adult. First, make a list of books, movies, television shows, magazines, short stories, album, songs, poems, and paintings popular in that time period. Then, beside each reference, write a sentence explaining why your relative particularly enjoyed, disliked, or was unfamiliar with it. In exchange, provide your relative with a short list of some of your favorite products of contemporary culture. Be sure to capitalize your references correctly.

EXERCISE 21

Responses will vary. Students should capitalize titles of artworks and literary works correctly as well as any other proper nouns they include in the assignment.

UNIT 16 REVIEW

TEST YOUR KNOWLEDGE

EXERCISE 1

1. *Nathaniel Hawthorne*—proper noun; *American*—proper adjective; *Liverpool*—proper noun; *Manchester*—proper noun
2. *World War II*—proper noun; *Axis*—proper adjective; *German*—proper noun; *Italy*—proper noun; *Japan*—proper noun
3. *Detroit Lions*—proper noun; *Dallas Cowboys*—proper noun; *Thanksgiving Day*—proper noun
4. *Sojourner Truth*—proper noun; *New York State Anti-Slavery Act*—proper noun
5. *Siamese*—proper adjective
6. *July*—proper noun; *Louis Armstrong*—proper adjective
7. *Wimbledon*—proper noun; *Serena Williams*—proper noun; *Sports Illustrated*—proper adjective
8. *Muslim*—proper adjective; *U.S.*—proper adjective; *Middle East*—proper noun
9. *Xerox*—proper adjective; *Union Bank*—proper adjective
10. *Labor Day*—proper noun; *Jerry Lewis MDA Telethon*—proper noun; *NFL*—proper adjective

EXERCISE 1

Identifying Proper Nouns and Proper Adjectives

Write the proper nouns and proper adjectives that appear in the following sentences. (10 points)

EXAMPLE

Professor Jefferson gave a lecture on Sojourner Truth at the Kimble Auditorium. (*Professor Jefferson*, proper noun; *Sojourner Truth*, proper noun; *Kimble Auditorium*, proper noun)

1. Writer Nathaniel Hawthorne served as American counsel at Liverpool and Manchester in the 1850s.
2 During World War II, the Axis nations consisted of Germany, Italy, and Japan.
3. The Detroit Lions and Dallas Cowboys usually host football games on Thanksgiving Day.
4. Sojourner Truth was freed from slavery in 1828 by the New York State Anti-Slavery Act.
5. Our Siamese cat always hides under the bed when guests arrive.
6. Attendance at the jazz festival in July was boosted by the Louis Armstrong exhibit.
7. After her victory at Wimbledon, Serena Williams appeared on the cover of *Sports Illustrated* magazine.
8. The Muslim students at the university organized a discussion forum on U.S. foreign policy in the Middle East.
9. I believe that the Xerox machine in the Union Bank lobby has finally been repaired.
10. On Labor Day weekend, we usually watch the Jerry Lewis MDA Telethon and NFL football games.

EXERCISE 2

Correcting Errors in Capitalization of Proper Nouns, Proper Adjectives, and Abbreviations

Rewrite the following sentences to correct any capitalization errors. (10 points)

EXAMPLE

In january our office will be closed on martin luther king, jr. day. *(In January, our office will be closed on Martin Luther King, Jr. Day.)*

1. Although she holds an m.a. degree, sheila did not impress me with her knowledge of psychology.
2. On halloween this year, my nephew plans to dress up like a power ranger.
3. Fred Witney jr. had a long and distinguished government career, serving in both the cia and the fbi.
4. A boy scout troop visited the white house the tuesday following memorial day.
5. Alan lives on n. Stetson avenue. and has a yellow mailbox that reads "dr. Hanson."
6. Oliver Wendell Holmes, sr. earned an m.d. degree from harvard in 1836.
7. I wrote a note to mr. and mrs. Graeve apologizing for denting their ford taurus.
8. Hans left his position at the Bank so he could work as a translator for the un.
9. In history class today, dr. wilt lectured about fdr and the creation of the aaa and nra.
10. Ken and millie watched the super bowl highlights on espn.

EXERCISE 2

1. Although she holds an M.A. degree, Sheila did not impress me with her knowledge of psychology.
2. On Halloween this year, my nephew plans to dress up like a Power Ranger.
3. Fred Witney, Jr. had a long and distinguished government career, serving in both the CIA and the FBI.
4. A Boy Scout troop visited the White House the Tuesday following Memorial Day.
5. Alan lives on N. Stetson Avenue and has a yellow mailbox that reads "Dr. Hanson."
6. Oliver Wendell Holmes, Sr. earned an M.D. degree from Harvard in 1836.
7. I wrote a note to Mr. and Mrs. Graeve apologizing for denting their Ford Taurus.
8. Hans left his position at the bank so he could work as a translator for the UN.
9. In history class today, Dr. Wilt lectured about FDR and the creation of the AAA and NRA.
10. Ken and Millie watched the Super Bowl highlights on ESPN.

EXERCISE 3
1. Historians call Calvin Coolidge "The Silent President."
2. Henry Wadsworth Longfellow published "The Village Blacksmith" in his 1841 collection *Ballads and Other Poems*.
3. Before she left, I told Patricia, "Don't forget to write once you get settled in at Princeton."
4. Archie and I traveled with his brother to the Pacific Northwest.
5. In 1865, Abraham Lincoln told a war-weary nation, "Let us strive on to finish the work we are in."
6. correct
7. correct
8. Cotuilla is located on the Nueces River in the southern part of Texas.
9. The English king Henry VIII, though opposed to Lutherans, severed his realm from the Catholic Church in 1532.
10. In the Rush song "Free Will," Geddy Lee sings, "If you choose not to decide, you still have made a choice."

EXERCISE 3

Correcting Errors in Capitalization of Proper Nouns, Family Relationships, *I*, and First Words

Rewrite the following sentences to correct any capitalization errors. If no added capitals are needed, write *correct*. (20 points)

EXAMPLE

After i saw him leave the office, father must have driven straight to the stadium. *(After I saw him leave the office, Father must have driven straight to the stadium.)*

1. Historians call calvin coolidge "the silent president."
2. Henry Wadsworth Longfellow published "the village blacksmith" in his 1841 collection *ballads and other poems.*
3. Before she left, i told Patricia, "don't forget to write once you get settled at princeton."
4. Archie and I traveled with his Brother to the pacific northwest.
5. In 1865, Abraham Lincoln told a war-weary Nation, "let us strive on to finish the work we are in."
6. My sister and my second cousin look eerily similar in their graduation pictures.
7. A professor from the University of Minnesota was awarded the Pulitzer Prize for poetry.
8. Cotuilla is located on the nueces river in the southern part of texas.
9. The english king Henry VIII, though opposed to lutherans, severed his realm from the catholic church in 1532.
10. In the Rush song "free will," Geddy Lee sings, "if you choose not to decide, you still have made a choice."

EXERCISE 4

Correcting Errors in Capitalizing Titles, Time Designations, and Geographical and Historical Names

Rewrite the following sentences to correct any capitalization errors. If no added capitals are needed, write *correct*. (20 points)

EXAMPLE

In 1946 the winecoff hotel in atlanta, georgia, burned down.
(In 1946, the Winecoff Hotel in Atlanta, Georgia, burned down.)

1. My father once met jfk at a fundraiser in boston, massachusetts.
2. On all saints' day in 1755, an earthquake destroyed lisbon, portugal.
3. On May 13, you need to appear at the Calhoun County Courthouse at 8:00 A.M.
4. Daphne's grandfather fought the german luftwaffe during the battle of britain.
5. In 1687, the parthenon in Athens was destroyed during the fighting between venetians and turks.
6. The Keokuk historical preservation assn. is sponsoring a lecture by prof. Pope.
7 Between 87 B.C. and 80 B.C., thousands died in a series of massacres in Rome.
8. In A.D. 410 King Alaric led the visigoths in a six-day pillage of Rome.
9. In 538 b.c., the famed hanging gardens of babylon were destroyed when a fire leveled the city.
10. On Tuesday night, dr. Leslie Phelps will discuss the reign of Augustus, the Roman emperor from 27 b.c. to a.d. 14.

EXERCISE 4

1. My father once met JFK at a fundraiser in Boston, Massachusetts.
2. On All Saints' Day in 1755, an earthquake destroyed Lisbon, Portugal.
3. correct
4. Daphne's grandfather fought the German Luftwaffe during the Battle of Britain.
5. In 1687, the Parthenon in Athens was destroyed during the fighting between Venetians and Turks.
6. The Keokuk Historical Preservation Assn. is sponsoring a lecture by Prof. Pope.
7 correct
8. In A.D. 410, King Alaric led the Visigoths in a six-day pillage of Rome.
9. In 538 B.C, the famed Hanging Gardens of Babylon were destroyed when a fire leveled the city.
10. On Tuesday night, Dr. Leslie Phelps will discuss the reign of Augustus, the Roman emperor from 27 B.C. to A.D. 14.

EXERCISE 5
Responses will vary. Students should capitalize all relevant words in their sentences.

EXERCISE 5

Using Capitalization

For each item listed below, write the name of someone or something that is your favorite. Then write a short explanation of the importance of the person, place, thing, or idea. Be prepared to compare your choices with those of a classmate, and be sure to use capitalization correctly. (20 points)

EXAMPLE
president
(Franklin Delano Roosevelt, often referred to as FDR, led the nation through two great crises, the Great Depression and World War II.)

1. author
2. sport
3. beverage
4. month
5. musical
6. animal
7. celebrity
8. recreation activity
9. family tradition
10. television show

EXERCISE 6
Responses will vary. In their news articles, students should correctly capitalize first words, proper nouns and proper adjectives, times and days, and any other terms they include that fit the rules in the unit.

EXERCISE 6

Using Capitalization in Your Writing

A club to which you belong has decided to sponsor a guest lecture from an expert or popular figure in the field with which the club is affiliated. Write a brief newspaper article about the forthcoming lecture to arouse interest and support. Who is the person giving the lecture? When and where will it be held? What topics will he or she discuss? What are the potential benefits for the audience? Be sure to capitalize correctly. (20 points)

UNIT 17 SPELLING

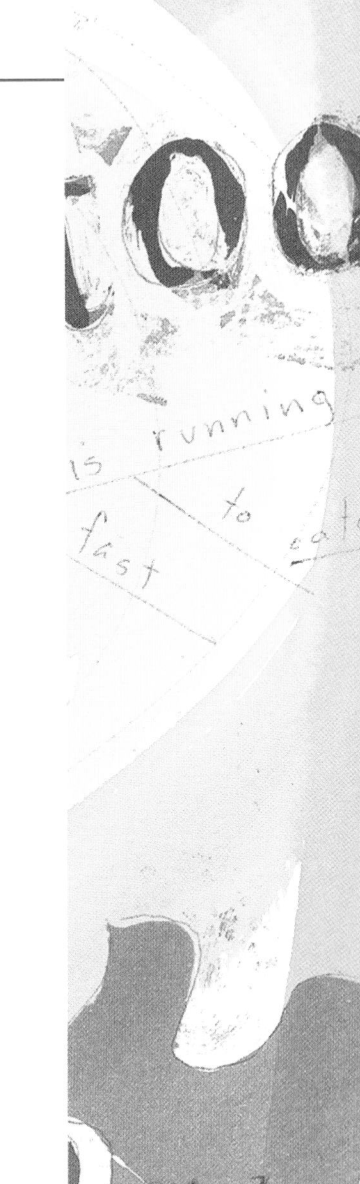

UNIT OVERVIEW

ASSESSMENT
Spelling Test is available at www.emcp.com.

SPELLING

EDITING FOR SPELLING ERRORS

Always check your writing for spelling errors, and try to recognize the words that give you more trouble than others. Use a dictionary when you think you may have misspelled a word. Keep a list in a notebook of words that are difficult for you to spell. Write the words several times until you have memorized the correct spelling. Break down the word into syllables, and pronounce each individual syllable carefully.

Some spelling problems occur when adding prefixes or suffixes to words or when making nouns plural. Other spelling problems occur when words follow certain patterns, such as those containing *ie/ei*. The following spelling rules can help you spell many words correctly.

SPELLING RULES I: PREFIXES AND SUFFIXES

Prefixes

A **prefix** is a letter or a group of letters added to the beginning of a word to change its meaning.

When adding a prefix, do not change the spelling of the word itself.

EXAMPLES
pre– + fabricate = prefabricate
im– + perishable = imperishable
in– + tolerant = intolerant
com– + patriot = compatriot
bi– + lateral = bilateral

Suffixes

A **suffix** is a letter or a group of letters added to the end of a word to change its meaning.

The spelling of most words is not changed when the suffix *–ness* or *–ly* is added.

EXAMPLES
graceful + –ness = gracefulness
blind + –ness = blindness
wicked + –ness = wickedness
leisure + –ly = leisurely
certain + –ly = certainly
sly + –ly = slyly

If you are adding a suffix to a word that ends with *y* and that *y* follows a vowel, usually leave the *y* in place.

EXAMPLES

destroy	destroys	destroying	destroyed
portray	portrays	portraying	portrayal
enjoy	enjoys	enjoying	enjoyment

If you are adding a suffix to a word that ends with *y* and that *y* follows a consonant, change the *y* to *i* before adding any ending except *–ing*.

EXAMPLES

murky	murkier	murkiness
apply	appliance	applying
giddy	giddiness	giddily
rely	reliable	reliant

USAGE tip

Note that this rule will sometimes form *ie* combinations after *c*. In these cases, it is correct for *ie* to follow *c*.

fancy **fancier**
saucy **saucier**

Double the final consonant before adding a suffix beginning with a vowel (such as *–ed*, *–en*, *–er*, *–ing*, *–ence*, *–ance*, or *–y)* in words ending in a single consonant preceded by a single vowel and if the word is either a single syllable or ends in a stressed syllable.

EXAMPLES	
remit	remittance
flap	flapper
swab	swabbing
thug	thuggish
regret	regrettable
gad	gadded
prim	primmest

If you are adding a suffix that begins with a vowel to a word that ends with a silent *e*, usually drop the *e*.

EXAMPLES	
dazzle	dazzling
tribe	tribal
secure	security
contribute	contributor

If you are adding a suffix that begins with a consonant to a word that ends with a silent *e*, usually leave the *e* in place.

EXAMPLES	
hate	hateful
incite	incitement
austere	austerely
blame	blameless

USAGE tip

With some words, the *e* becomes an *i* when you add the suffix.

caprice + –ous = capricious

office + –ial = official

EXCEPTIONS	
argue	argument
true	ruly
nine	ninth
judge	judgment

If the word ends in a soft *c* (spelled *ce*) or a soft *g* (spelled *ge*) sound, keep the *e* when adding the suffixes *–able* or *–ous.*

EXAMPLES	
courage	courageous
change	changeable
trace	traceable

Try It Yourself

EXERCISE 1

Identifying Incorrect Spelling with Prefixes and Suffixes

Write the correct spelling of the words that are misspelled in the following sentences. If no words are misspelled in the sentence, write *correct.*

1. The defense attorney tried to convince the jury that the new evidence was imaterial and should be completly ignored.
2. Agatha is one of those people who consider any dissagreement an unforgiveable betrayal.
3. The cheeryness of the song's melody is offset by the deep sadness of the lyrics.
4. On her ninth birthday, Erika asked for and received the world's bounciest trampoline.
5. The hotel clerk duely noted the customer's name and address but omitted to take down the phone number.
6. Simplifiing a long novel for a screenplay inevitabley results in the loss of some truly important details.
7. I'm afraid my brother mispoke when he said it would be advantagous for you to offer to teach me to ski.
8. The officious behavior of the bodyguard was deemed truly unforgivable by all of the fans who had waited for hours to get the star's autograph.
9. Nigel noted plaintivly that the response to his manuscript had been distinctly maliceous.
10. The Irish potato famine caused mass starveation and led to mass imigration to the United States from Ireland.

EXERCISE 1
1. immaterial, completely
2. disagreement, unforgivable
3. cheeriness
4. correct
5. duly
6. simplifying, inevitably
7. misspoke, advantageous
8. correct
9. plaintively, malicious
10. starvation, immigration

LANGUAGELINK
Print exercise worksheets or have students complete exercises online with the LanguageLINK CD.

EXERCISE 2

Understanding Spelling with Prefixes and Suffixes

Combine the prefix and root word or the root word and the suffix. Write each new word and be sure to spell it correctly.

EXERCISE 2
1. immature
2. enchantment
3. phoniness
4. prioritize
5. irradiate
6. delaying
7. jogger
8. retrievable
9. coyness
10. artificial

1. im– + mature
2. enchant + –ment
3. phony + –ness
4. priority + –ize
5. ir– + radiate
6. delay + –ing
7. jog + –er
8. retrieve + –able
9. coy + –ness
10. artifice + –al

EXERCISE 3
Using Prefixes and Suffixes Correctly in Your Writing
Choose at least ten words from this lesson or group of exercises. Using the words you've selected, write a brief narrative about a journey you have taken or hope to take. Be sure to spell each word correctly according to its rule about adding a prefix or suffix, and be prepared to share your paper with a classmate.

EXERCISE 3
Responses will vary. Students' narratives should be loosely tied together. More credit should be given for correctly spelled words than for a well-crafted narrative.

SPELLING RULES II: PLURAL NOUNS AND SPELLING PATTERNS

Plural Nouns

Most noun plurals are formed by simply adding *–s* to the end of the word.

EXAMPLES
autocrat + –s = autocrats
cupful + –s = cupfuls
panorama + –s = panoramas
decimal + –s = decimals

The plural of nouns that end in *o*, *s*, *x*, *z*, *ch*, or *sh* should be formed by adding *–es*.

EXAMPLES
volcano + –es = volcanoes
caress + –es = caresses
jinx + –es = jinxes
buzz + –es = buzzes
speech + –es = speeches
bulrush + –es = bulrushes

USAGE tip

Some nouns have plural forms that are exceptions to the rules:

ox	**oxen**
man	**men**
child	**children**
tooth	**teeth**
mouse	**mice**

The exception to the rule above is that musical terms and certain other words that end in *o* are usually made plural by adding *–s*. Check a dictionary if you aren't sure whether to add an *–s* or an *–es*.

EXAMPLES

cello + –s = cellos	stereo + –s = stereos
piccolo + –s = piccolos	bronco + –s = broncos
ratio + –s = ratios	tango + –s = tangos

Form the plural of nouns that end in *y* following a consonant by changing the *y* to an *i* and adding *–es*.

EXAMPLES

histories	anchovies	calumnies
balconies	memories	banalities

Nouns that end in *f* or *fe* must be modified, changing the *f* or *fe* to *v*, before adding *–es* to the plural form.

EXAMPLES

calf	calves
shelf	shelves
scarf	scarves
knife	knives
wife	wives

The *ie/ei* Spelling Pattern

When a word is spelled with the letters *i* and *e* and has a long *e* sound, it is usually spelled *ie* except after the letter *c*.

EXAMPLES

frieze	ceiling
diesel	deceit
shield	conceive

USAGE tip

This rhyme may help you remember the *ie/ei* rule:

Put *i* before *e*
Except after *c*
Or when sounded like *a,*
As in *neighbor* and *weigh.*

EXCEPTIONS

either neither weird seize

Use *ei* when the sound is not long *e.*

EXAMPLES

foreign sleight freight

EXCEPTIONS

friend fief handkerchief

If the vowel combination has a long *a* sound (as in *eight*), always spell it with *ei.*

EXAMPLES

weight sleigh deign rein

When two vowels are pronounced separately in a word, spell them in the order of their pronunciation.

EXAMPLES

helium chaos society poetic

The "Seed" Sound Pattern

The "seed" ending sound has three spellings: *–sede*, *–ceed*, and *–cede*.

EXAMPLES

Only one word ends in *–sede: supersede*
Three words end in *–ceed: proceed, succeed, exceed*
All other words end in *–cede: accede, concede, recede, precede, secede*

Silent Letters

Some spelling problems result from letters that are written but not heard when a word is spoken. Becoming familiar with the patterns in letter combinations containing silent letters will help you identify other words that fit the patterns.

- Silent *b* usually occurs with *m*.

EXAMPLES

lamb	catacomb	succumb	climb

- Silent *b* also appears in *debt* and *doubt*.

- Silent *c* often appears with *s*.

EXAMPLES

science	scissors	scenic	crescent

- Silent *g* often appears with *n*.

EXAMPLES

malign	design	reign	campaign

- Silent *gh* often appears at the end of a word, either alone or in combination with *t (–ght)*.

EXAMPLES

caught	drought	height	delight

- Silent *h* appears at the beginning of some words.

EXAMPLES

heir	honest	honorable	heirloom

- Silent *h* also appears in a few other words, as in *rhododendron* and *ghastly*.

- Silent *k* occurs with *n*.

EXAMPLES

knickknack	knavery	knockout	knee high

- Silent *n* occurs with *m* at the end of some words.

EXAMPLES

hymn column solemn

- Silent *p* occurs with *s* at the beginning of some words.

EXAMPLES

psoriasis psylla psychosomatic psychedelic

- Silent *s* occurs with *l* in some words.

EXAMPLES

aisle isle island

- Silent *t* occurs with *s* in a few words.

EXAMPLES

fasten castle jostle

- Silent *w* occurs at the beginnings of some words.

EXAMPLES

wrapping wreckage wreath wrist watch

- Silent *w* also occurs with *s* in a few words, such as *sword* and *answer*.

Letter Combinations

Some letter combinations can cause spelling problems because when combined, the letters have a different pronunciation.

- The letters *ph* produce the *f* sound.

EXAMPLES

graph choreograph
phosphorescent hieroglyph

- The letters *gh* produce the *f* sound usually at the end of a word. (Otherwise they are silent.)

EXAMPLES

tough	cough	enough	autograph

- The letter combination *tch* sounds the same as *ch*.

EXAMPLES

thatch	wretch	snatch	pitch
ostrich	detach	enrich	approach

Letter Combinations

If the letters *c* and *g* have soft sounds (of *s* and *j*), they will usually be followed by *e*, i, or *y*.

EXAMPLES

cylinder	gerbil
circulate	agility
precipice	gingerly
recess	degenerate
certainly	geologist

If the letters *c* and *g* have hard sounds (of *k* and *g*), they will usually be followed by *a*, *o*, or u.

EXAMPLES

corrosive	garner
cartridge	geyser
caftan	garage
capacity	gully
cordon	gobble

Spelling Patterns of Borrowed Words

Many words borrowed from other languages follow the spelling patterns of the original language. For example, some English words borrowed from French, Spanish, and Italian follow letter patterns of the language of origin.

- The final *t* is silent in many words borrowed from French.

EXAMPLES
ricochet
crochet
filet

- The letter combinations *eur* and *eau* appear at the end of many words with French origin.

EXAMPLES

amateur	bureaucrat
masseur	plateau
hauteur	chateau

- The letter combination *oo* appears in many words borrowed from the Dutch language.

EXAMPLES
spook
cookie
snoop

Many plural Italian words end in *i*.

EXAMPLES
confetti
ravioli
biscotti

Many words of Spanish origin end in *o*.

EXAMPLES
poncho
burrito
rodeo

Compound Words

A **compound word** consists of two or more words used together to form a single word. Sometimes they are written as one word *(basketball, downtown)*. Sometimes they are written separately *(grocery store, police officer)*. Still other compound words are connected with hyphens *(father-in-law, self-esteem)*. Consult a good dictionary when you are not sure of the form of compounds.

USAGE tip

The word *and* is unnecessary in writing numbers, including those between one hundred one and one hundred ten, two hundred one and two hundred ten, and so forth: *Michelle wrote two hundred six postcards while she was in Europe.*

Numerals

Spell out numbers of *one hundred* or less and all numbers rounded to hundreds. Larger round numbers such as *nine thousand* or *two million* should also be spelled out.

EXAMPLES

Aunt Angela owns **twenty** racehorses and over **thirty** polo ponies.

Lanssen Volcanic National Park is over **a hundred thousand** acres of volcanic phenomena.

Use a hyphen to separate compound numbers from twenty-one through ninety-nine.

EXAMPLES

forty-nine icicles
seventy-two chinchillas
one hundred volumes
sixty thousand entries

Use a hyphen in a fraction used as a modifier, but not in a fraction used as a noun.

EXAMPLES

Hank selected a **three-quarter** inch bolt for the job.

Gideon devoured **seven eighths** of the pizza before anyone else could grab a bite.

USAGE tip

Use commas to separate series of five or more figures into thousands, millions, and so on. No comma is necessary for four-digit numerals.

Use Arabic numerals for numbers greater than one hundred that are not rounded numbers.

EXAMPLES

The most dangerously active volcano in Central America is Santa Maria Quezaltenango, which is **12,361 feet**, or **3,768 meters**, tall.

With an area of **31,820 square miles**, Lake Superior is the world's largest freshwater lake.

If a number appears at the beginning of a sentence, spell it out or rewrite the sentence.

EXAMPLES

incorrect	1765 was the birth date of Eli Whitney, inventor of the cotton gin.
correct	**Seventeen sixty-five** was the birth date of Elli Whitney, inventor of the cotton gin.
correct	The birth date of Eli Whitney, inventor of the cotton gin, was **1765**.

USAGE tip

When numbers are used infrequently in a piece of writing, spell out those that can be expressed in one or two words and use figures for the others. When numbers are used frequently in a piece of writing, spell out numbers from one to ten and use figures for all others. Above all, be consistent in the way you use words or numerals to express numbers in writing.

Use words to write the time unless you are writing the exact time (including the abbreviation A.M. or P.M.). When the word *o'clock* is used for time of day, express the number in words.

EXAMPLES

The press conference begins at **quarter past ten**.
My airplane didn't land until about **one-thirty** this morning.
Dinah was born at **3:01 P.M.** on September 29, 1985.
The beading workshop begins at **seven o'clock**.

Use numerals to express dates, street numbers, room numbers, apartment numbers, telephone numbers, page numbers, exact amounts of money, scores, and percentages. Spell out the word *percent*. Round dollar or cent amounts of only a few words may be expressed in words.

EXAMPLES

February 26, 1928	(216) 555-1212
7566 Sprague Road	pages 136–139
fifty cents	fifteen hundred dollars
Apartment 600	92 percent
$2.5 million (or $2,500,000)	$1,751

When you write a date, do not add *–st*, *–nd*, or *–th*.

EXAMPLES

incorrect	March 6th, 1972	August 2nd
correct	March 6, 1972	August 2 or the second of August

Try It Yourself

EXERCISE 4

Identifying Words with Spelling Patterns

Write the correct spelling for misspelled words in the following sentences.

1. The bureu chief in Tel Aviv was nearly killed when a bullet ricocheted and struck him in the back.
2. You ought not to leave a cooked roast sitting out for hours; refrijerate whatever is not served immediately.
3. In his final colum, the sportswriter described the first knockout punch he ever witnessed.
4. The eir to the throne did not dain to look up when the multitudes shouted his name.
5. The farmer wraped the newborn lamb in a blanket to keep it warm in the drafty old barn.
6. Jessica mournfuly announced that in humid weather, her curly hair becomes totally unmanagable!
7. During the late ninteenth and early twentyeth centuries, the migrateon of millions of Sicilians to the United States changed the demographics of both countries.
8. The little boy watched in fasination as some tadpoles riggled in the muddy pond.

EXERCISE 4
1. bureau
2. refrigerate
3. column
4. heir, deign
5. wrapped
6. mournfully, unmanageable
7. nineteenth, twentieth, migration
8. fascination, wriggled

9. extremely, immature, annoying
10. juicier, unforgettable

9. It was extremly imature of Ryan to give his grandmother that annoiing card.
10. Of the two types of oranges, this one is juicyer, but that one has an unforgetable flavor.

EXERCISE 5
1. deceit
2. weird
3. freight
4. handkerchief
5. shield
6. succeed
7. proceedings
8. supersede
9. concede
10. precede
11. rhythm
12. qualm
13. feign
14. psychology
15. trough
16. notch
17. wreath
18. sleigh
19. hygiene
20. veil

EXERCISE 5

Understanding Words with Spelling Patterns

Complete the following words by filling in the blanks with the letters *ie* or *ei*.

1. the spy's history of dec_ _ t
2. a very w_ _ rd witch costume
3. hauling fr_ _ ght
4. the lace-edged handkerch_ _ f
5. the warrior's sh _ _ ld

Add the correct *–sede*, *–ceed*, or *–cede* ending to these words.

6. suc_ _ _ _ in business
7. dubious pro _ _ _ _ ings
8. super _ _ _ _ the legislation
9. con_ _ _ _ victory
10. pre_ _ _ _ the rest of the group

Complete each word by adding the correct silent letter or letter combination.

11. driving _ _ _thm
12. without a qu _ _ _
13. fe_ _ _ a headache
14. study _ _ _chology
15. a trou_ _ for the pigs
16. a no_ _ _ on the belt
17. the _ _ eath on the front door
18. riding in a sl _ _ _ _
19. oral hyg_ _ ne
20. the bride's gauzy v _ _ l

EXERCISE 6

Understanding Noun Plurals

Make the following words plural by adding the correct ending.

1. piano
2. box
3. array
4. minx
5. echo
6. controversy
7. ox
8. wrench
9. child
10. knife

EXERCISE 6
1. pianos
2. boxes
3. arrays
4. minxes
5. echoes
6. controversies
7. oxen
8. wrenches
9. children
10. knives

EXERCISE 7

Understanding Compound Words

Match a word in the right column with a word in the left column to form a compound. Make sure you write and punctuate your compounds correctly. Check a dictionary if you're not certain whether the compound should be written as one word, two or more words, or if it should be hyphenated.

Column A	Column B
1. fire	piece
2. master	president
3. junk	tape
4. vice	escape
5. video	bond

EXERCISE 7
1. fire escape
2. masterpiece
3. junk bond
4. vice president
5. videotape

EXERCISE 8

Understanding Numbers in Writing

Shorten each of the following items by using numbers where it is appropriate to do so. If the item is expressed correctly, write *correct*.

EXERCISE 8
1. correct
2. 40,012 pounds
3. correct
4. at the beginning of her fourth month
5. correct
6. correct
7. $261.89
8. December 7, 1941
9. at exactly 11:12 P.M.
10. pages 178 and 179

1. in the second year of the new millennium
2. forty thousand and twelve pounds
3. two o'clock in the morning
4. at the beginning of her 4th month
5. at the third station on the subway line
6. the governor's four-year term
7. two hundred sixty-one dollars and eighty-nine cents
8. December seventh, nineteen hundred and forty-one
9. at exactly eleven twelve P.M.
10. pages one hundred seventy-eight and one hundred seventy-nine

EXERCISE 9
Responses will vary. Students' advertisements should contain detailed descriptions. Either response to the assignment should make use of words in the *ie/ei* pattern, the "seed" sound pattern, silent letters, letter combinations, noun plurals, compound words, and numerals that follow different rules.

EXERCISE 9

Using Spelling Patterns in Your Writing

Think of some items you would like to get rid of. Write a poster for a tag sale or garage sale. Tell where and when the sale will take place and describe some of the more interesting items you hope to sell and at what price. Use as many words from the unit as you can to show your understanding of letter and sound patterns.

COMMON SPELLING ERRORS

Pronunciation is not always a reliable guide for spelling because words are not always spelled the way they are pronounced. However, by paying attention to letters that spell sounds and letters that are silent, you can improve some aspects of your spelling. Always check a dictionary for the correct pronunciations and spellings of words new to your experience.

Extra Syllables

Sometimes people misspell a word because they include an extra syllable in it. For example, *monstrous* is easily misspelled if it is pronounced *monsterous*, with four syllables instead of three. Pay close attention to the number of syllables in these words.

EXAMPLES

two syllables	hindrance	business
	grievous	
three syllables	mischievous	jewelry
	nuclear	

Omitted Sounds

Sometimes people misspell a word because they do not sound one or more letters when they pronounce the word. Be sure to include the underlined letters of these words even if you don't pronounce them.

EXAMPLES

arctic	extraordinary	February
mathematics	mortgage	privilege
probably	restaurant	temperamental
nuisance		

Homophones

Words that have the same pronunciation but different spellings and meanings are called **homophones.** An incorrect choice can be confusing to your readers. Knowing the spelling and meaning of these groups of words will improve your spelling.

EXAMPLES

allowed/aloud	compliment/complement	sole/soul
alter/altar	hear/here	some/sum
ascent/assent	lead/led	threw/through
bear/bare	night/knight	wait/weight
brake/break	pair/pear	weak/week
buy/bye/by	peace/piece	who's/whose
capital/capitol	plain/plane	
coarse/course	site/sight/cite	

Commonly Confused Words

Some other groups of words are not homophones, but they are similar enough in sound and spelling to create confusion. Knowing the spelling and meaning of these groups of words will also improve your spelling. You'll find other groups of these commonly confused words in Unit 14, pages 351–363.

EXAMPLES

access/excess	formally/formerly
accede/exceed	literal/literally
accept/except	loose/lose
alternate/alternative	nauseous/nauseated
desert/dessert	passed/past
dissent/descent	principle/principal
eminent/imminent	regimen/regiment
farther/further	stationary/stationery

Try It Yourself

EXERCISE 10
1. monstrous
2. realtor
3. adjourn
4. grocery
5. acquire
6. veteran
7. literature
8. nuclear
9. subtle
10. library

EXERCISE 10

Identifying Words with Extra Syllables and Omitted Sounds

Write the word in each group that is spelled correctly.

EXAMPLE

jewelry	jewlry	jewlery	*(jewelry)*

1.	monsterous	monstrous	monstris
2.	relator	reltor	realtor
3.	ajourn	adjourn	adjurn
4.	grocry	grocrey	grocery
5.	aquire	acquire	acqire
6.	veteran	vetran	vetrean
7.	literature	litrature	litterature
8.	nucular	nuclar	nuclear
9.	suttle	subtle	suptle
10.	library	libarry	libry

EXERCISE 11

Understanding Common Spelling Problems

Choose the appropriate spelling of the word in parentheses to complete the meaning of the following sentences. If necessary, use a dictionary to find the meanings of the two words before making your choice.

1. The (sheer, shear) chiffon skirt must be worn over another layer of clothing.
2. Millie lost control of her horse when she pulled hard on the (rain, rein) and it broke.
3. Every month, the Jenkins pay a little extra toward the (principal, principle) on their car loan.
4. A democracy thrives on (descent, dissent) in the long run.
5. A (healthy, healthful) diet does not need to be tasteless or repetitive.
6. Sadly, those great (canvas, canvass) shoes I bought in Spain are beginning to fall apart.
7. The entire country was in (mourning, morning) after the dire events of September 11.
8. The marathon (coarse, course) begins at the old Grange building on Main Street and ends at the corner of Dressler and Cockaponssett Streets.
9. It is rude to (pier, peer) through keyholes, no matter what the temptation.
10. The couple slowly approached the (alter, altar) and knelt to take their vows.

EXERCISE 11
1. sheer
2. rein
3. principal
4. dissent
5. healthful
6. canvas
7. mourning
8. course
9. peer
10. altar

EXERCISE 12

Using Commonly Confused Words Correctly in Your Writing

Assume that you have been asked to write a short comic sketch for a class assembly. Choose at least five pairs of commonly confused words, and write a dialogue between two characters in which they confuse the various meanings of the words. In your dialogue, use one or both of the words in each pair. Underline the words that you use, and be sure to check your spelling.

EXERCISE 12
Responses will vary. Students should select their pairs of words so that they can maintain some sense in their dialogue while still spelling the words correctly.

COMMONLY MISSPELLED WORDS

Some English words are often misspelled. Here is a list of 150 commonly misspelled words. If you master this list, you will avoid many errors in your spelling.

Commonly Misspelled Words		
absence	conceivable	magnificent
abundant	conscientious	manageable
academically	conscious	maneuver
accessible	consistency	meadow
accidentally	deceitful	mediocre
accommodate	descendant	miniature
accurate	desirable	mischievous
acknowledgment	disastrous	misspell
acquaintance	discipline	mortgage
adequately	efficiency	mysterious
adolescent	eighth	naïve
advantageous	embarrass	necessity
advisable	enormous	nickel
ancient	enthusiastically	niece
annihilate	environment	noticeable
anonymous	exhaust	nucleus
answer	existence	nuisance
apparent	fascinating	nutritious
article	finally	obedience
attendance	forfeit	occasionally
bankruptcy	fulfill	occurrence
beautiful	guerrilla	orchestra
beggar	guidance	outrageous
beginning	hindrance	pageant
behavior	hypocrite	parallel
biscuit	independent	pastime
breathe	influential	peasant
business	ingenious	permanent
calendar	institution	persistent
camouflage	interference	phenomenon
catastrophe	irrelevant	physician
cellar	irresistible	pneumonia
cemetery	judgment	prestige
changeable	league	privilege
clothes	leisure	procedure
colossal	license	prophesy
column	lightning	prove
committee	liquefy	receipt

CONTINUED

referred	significance	unmistakable
rehearsal	souvenir	unnecessary
relieve	sponsor	vacuum
resistance	succeed	vehicle
resources	surprise	vengeance
responsibility	symbol	villain
rhythm	synonymous	vinegar
schedule	temperature	weird
seize	tomorrow	whistle
separate	transparent	withhold
sergeant	twelfth	yacht
siege	undoubtedly	yield

Try It Yourself

EXERCISE 13
Identifying Commonly Misspelled Words

Choose the correct spelling of each of the following words.

1.	consceintous	conscientious	conscientous
2.	leauge	leage	league
3.	villain	villan	villin
4.	twelth	twelf	twelfth
5.	orkestra	orcestra	orchestra
6.	yacht	yaht	yacth
7.	noticeable	notissable	noticable
8.	embaras	embarrass	embarass
9.	acknowledgment	acknowledgement	acknoledgment
10.	colossal	collosal	collossal

EXERCISE 13
1. conscientious
2. league
3. villain
4. twelfth
5. orchestra
6. yacht
7. noticeable
8. embarrass
9. acknowledgment
10. colossal

EXERCISE 14
Using Commonly Misspelled Words Correctly in Your Writing

Choose from the list of Commonly Misspelled Words ten words that you find difficult. Write a short letter to a friend in which you discuss the importance of spelling and use all of the words you selected.

EXERCISE 14
Responses will vary. In addition to spelling correctly the words they choose, students should use their choices correctly in their letters.

ASSESSMENT
Spelling Test is available at www.emcp.com.

UNIT 17 REVIEW

TEST YOUR KNOWLEDGE

EXERCISE 1
1. correct
2. pageant
3. humming, illuminating
4. extremely, artificial
5. human beings, truly
6. crochet, embroidery
7. slotted, gently, simmering
8. sneezing, approach
9. agility
10. deployed, terrorism

EXERCISE 1

Identifying Incorrectly Spelled Words

Find the spelling errors in the following sentences and rewrite the incorrectly spelled words. If there are no misspelled words, write *correct.* (10 points)

EXAMPLE

The reck of the *Mary Rose* contained a horde of treasure, including weapons, herbs and spices, leather boots, and combs for dealing with louses. *(wreck, hoard, lice)*

1. Without specialized training, you can find it difficult to perceive whether or not a certain bill is counterfeit.
2. Do we have sufficient costumes for all of the people who want to be in the pagant?
3. When the generator started huming, the garage lights clicked back on, iluminating the car that was up on the lift.
4. The extremly artifishal flavor of that pudding puts me in mind of cheap saltwater taffy.
5. The psychiatrist and the philosopher debated the question of whether or not humanbeings trully have free will.
6. My mother loves to croshay, my sister loves to knit, and I like to relax with embroidry.
7. With a sloted spoon, gentley lift the fatty part of the meat out of the simmerring broth.
8. Putting scented paper on the shelves seemed like a good idea, but I keep sneezeing whenever I approatch it.
9. Nana's fingers are gnarled, but they still move with remarkable ajility.
10. The fleet has been deploied in the Persian Gulf because of the threat of further terrism.

EXERCISE 2
Understanding Prefixes and Suffixes
Put the words and their prefixes or suffixes together correctly. Correctly spell the new word. (20 points)

EXAMPLE
incidental + –ly *(incidentally)*

1. gay + –ly
2. dis– + heartening
3. dis– + satisfaction
4. conspire + –ing
5. cancel + –ation
6. soliloquy + –ize
7. dismay + –ing
8. tune –ful
9. office + –al
10. re– + emphasize
11. il– + literate
12. embody + –ment
13. grace + –ous
14. lace + –y
15. red + –en
16. respire + –ation
17. pre– + dominant
18. noble + –ly
19. prestige + –ous
20. describe + –able

EXERCISE 2
1. gaily
2. disheartening
3. dissatisfaction
4. conspiring
5. cancellation
6. soliloquize
7. dismaying
8. tuneful
9. official
10. reemphasize
11. illiterate
12. embodiment
13. gracious
14. lacy
15. redden
16. respiration
17. predominant
18. nobly
19. prestigious
20. describable

EXERCISE 3
Understanding Noun Plurals
Write the plural form of each of the following nouns. (10 points)

EXAMPLE
loss *(losses)*

1. ilex
2. mattress
3. goulash

EXERCISE 3
1. ilexes
2. mattresses
3. goulashes

4. patios
5. jackknives
6. vetoes
7. wives
8. moose
9. jinxes
10. sisters-in-law

4. patio
5. jackknife
6. veto
7. wife
8. moose
9. jinx
10. sister-in-law

EXERCISE 4
1. friendly
2. reign
3. neither
4. ebullient
5. feigned
6. society
7. deify
8. yield
9. heirloom
10. retrieval
11. intercede
12. concede
13. secede
14. recede
15. accede
16. precede
17. exceed
18. supersede
19. succeed
20. proceed

EXERCISE 4

Understanding Words with Letter or Sound Patterns

Write each word, adding *ie* or *ei*. (20 points)

EXAMPLE
n _ _ ce *(niece)*

1. fr _ _ ndly
2. r _ _ gn
3. n _ _ ther
4. ebull _ _ nt
5. f _ _ gned
6. soc _ _ ty
7. d _ _ fy
8. y _ _ ld
9. h _ _ rloom
10. retr _ _ val

Write each word, adding *–sede*, *–ceed*, or *–cede*.

11. inter_ _ _ _
12. con _ _ _ _
13. se_ _ _ _
14. re_ _ _ _
15. ac _ _ _ _
16. pre_ _ _ _
17. ex _ _ _ _
18. super_ _ _ _
19. suc_ _ _ _
20. pro_ _ _ _

EXERCISE 5

Correcting Words with Silent Letters or Letter Combinations

Using the rules for silent letters or letter combinations, write the correct spelling for each of the following words. (10 points)

EXAMPLE
lam *(lamb)*

1. undoutable
2. senario
3. nowledge
4. onorarium
5. rathful
6. soverenty
7. sploch
8. colum
9. sychic
10. arrain

EXERCISE 6

Correcting Numerals

Rewrite the following sentences so that the numbers are written and punctuated correctly. If there are no errors in the sentence, write *correct*. (10 points)

1. The lower limit of an aurora is about fifty miles above the earth, and the upper limit is approximately four hundred miles.
2. In eighteen one, Ceres, one of the first 10 minor planets, or asteroids, was discovered.
3. 1849 marked the discovery of Hygeia, an asteroid two hundred and twenty two million miles from the sun.
4. On May 24th, nineteen sixty-four, over three hundred soccer fans died when a riot erupted at a Peru versus Argentina soccer game.

EXERCISE 5
1. undoubtable
2. scenario
3. knowledge
4. honorarium
5. wrathful
6. sovereignty
7. splotch
8. column
9. psychic
10. arraign

EXERCISE 6
1. correct
2. In 1801, Ceres, one of the first ten minor planets, or asteroids, was discovered.
3. Eighteen forty-nine marked the discovery of Hygeia, an asteroid 222 million miles from the sun.
4. On May 24, 1964, over three hundred soccer fans died when a riot erupted at a Peru versus Argentina soccer game.
5. The lowest temperature recorded in the United States was –79.8 degrees Fahrenheit in northern Alaska on January 23, 1971.
6. correct
7. correct
8. Sixty-two people failed to respond by the date mentioned at the bottom of the invitation.

9. In 1994, Greece contributed $3,560,503 to the United Nations budget.
10. The necklace contains one hundred ten perfect black pearls.

EXERCISE 7
Responses will vary. An example of a memory device to help students remember the exceptions to the *i* before *e* rule: *Either weird people enjoy leisure or they are seized by regret.* Students might also create a memory device to help them spell a specific troublesome word: *There's a rat in separate.*

EXERCISE 8
Responses will vary. Students' reviews should contain at least ten words based on spelling rules from the unit that fit the context of their work.

5. The lowest temperature recorded in the United States was –seventy-nine point 8 degrees Fahrenheit in northern Alaska on January 23, 1971.
6. When I won the online auction, I sent a check for $16.75 to Terrific Tees, 6542 Appleton Way, Olmsted Falls, OH 44138.
7. My sister paid me eight dollars, so she now owns nearly a one-half share of the tee-shirt.
8. 62 people failed to respond by the date mentioned at the bottom of the invitation.
9. In 1994, Greece contributed three million, five hundred sixty thousand, five hundred three dollars to the United Nations' budget.
10. The necklace contains one hundred and ten perfect black pearls.

EXERCISE 7

Understanding Spelling Rules

Make a list of the spelling errors you commonly make. You might also review writing assignments that your teacher has already graded and check for spelling errors. Once you have a list of twenty-five words or so, group them according to the spelling rules in this unit. Include both the correct and incorrect spelling, the spelling rule, and a memory device that will help you recall the correct spelling. Keep your spelling list in your notebook or writing folder and add to it regularly. Once you feel that you have mastered the spelling of a difficult or unfamiliar word, cross it off your list. (10 points)

EXERCISE 8

Using Correct Spelling in Your Writing

Assume that you are the arts and letters editor for your school newspaper. Write a brief review of a current television show. Describe the show's premise and main characters, evaluate its quality and success, and indicate whether you would recommend it for viewing. Use at least ten words from this unit in your essay. Then proofread carefully to be sure that you've spelled all words correctly. (10 points)

UNIT *18* ELECTRONIC COMMUNICATIONS
Etiquette and Style

UNIT OVERVIEW

ELECTRONIC COMMUNICATIONS: ETIQUETTE AND STYLE

NETIQUETTE FOR COMMUNICATING ON THE INTERNET

Netiquette, a blend of the words *Internet* and *etiquette*, refers to the courtesies writers use when communicating with others online. Given the flexibility, speed, and low cost of communicating on the Net, people sometimes forget how very public and permanent e-mail actually is.

Judith Martin, who writes about etiquette as Miss Manners, highlights some of the reasons for netiquette in cyberspace.

Literature MODEL

> Freedom without rules doesn't work. And communities do not work unless they are regulated by etiquette. It took about three minutes before some of the brighter people discovered this online. We have just as many ways, if not more, to be obnoxious in cyberspace and fewer ways to regulate them. So, posting etiquette rules and looking for ways to ban people who violate them is the way sensible people are attempting to deal with this.
>
> from "Manners Matter"
> Kevin Kelly and Judith Martin

Whether you're chatting online with a friend, requesting information from an organization, or writing a complaint letter about an order that went awry, use netiquette that is appropriate for your purpose and audience.

Dos and Don'ts

Do use e-mail

- to ask quick questions.
- to exchange information and to send newsy updates to friends.
- to schedule events and activities.
- to praise a group, especially when you want to send a copy to others.

Not all messages should be electronic, however. Don't use e-mail

- to replace a formal thank-you note.
- to share controversial or personal information.
- to send bad news.
- to convey anything that if forwarded or read by others could be harmful or embarrassing.

Guidelines for Communicating on the Internet

Know the rules. Make sure that you understand the policies of the online services you are using. In listservs, chat rooms, and other group discussions, check the new subscriber information or ask other participants for guidance. In a chat room, if you feel your privacy is being compromised, ask a responsible adult for help or simply sign off.

State your topic. Always fill in the subject line. Flag your message with a clear, informative header. If your problem is urgent, write SOS. If it's a quick question, say so. This allows the user to locate and deal with the message quickly.

Be brief. Lengthy e-mails—those longer than one screen—can be daunting and annoying. Even though friendly exchanges can be chatty, a screen filled with solid type can overwhelm readers. If you want a quick reply, be concise. Break long thoughts into separate paragraphs or numbered lists.

Use a limited number of acronyms. Acronyms like the ones listed below are frequently used to shorten communications on the Internet. However, keep in mind that messages filled with these abbreviations can be both confusing and annoying.

EXAMPLES
IMHO = in my humble (or honest) opinion
LOL = laughing out loud
ROFL = rolling on the floor laughing
BTW = by the way
F2F = face to face
BCNU = be seeing you
FWIW = for what it's worth
G, D, & R = grinning, ducking, and running
J/K = just kidding
L8R = later
IOW = in other words
OTOH = on the other hand
OIC = Oh, I see!

Know what the buttons mean. The most destructive use of e-mail can occur when you reply "back to all" when your intention is to reply to the sender only.

Watch what you say. E-mail can be printed, forwarded, and filed. Even worse, deleted e-mails can be retrieved and used as evidence in a court of law. Use common sense, and try not to put anything in an e-mail that you wouldn't want published in the local newspaper. Avoid writing when angry. Avoid personal attacks, known as **flaming**. Keep in mind that sarcasm and humor may be misinterpreted. Without the benefit of facial expression, body language, and tone of voice, your joke may come across as criticism or an insult.

LANGUAGELINK
Print exercise worksheets or have students complete exercises online with the LanguageLINK CD.

Use conventional capitalization. Using all capital letters in a message comes across online as SHOUTING and can be irritating or even offensive to your readers. Using all lowercase letters can make a message harder to read. Use **asterisks** before and after a word or phrase to make your point more evident, or use more conventional methods of emphasis, such as boldface and underlining. If your e-mail software doesn't allow type styles such as italic or underlining, it is appropriate to use all caps for titles of books or films, for example.

Edit your writing. Reread your message before sending it to be sure it says what you want it to. Check for the kinds of careless errors you may make when your mind operates faster than your fingers can type—left-out words and reversed letters. If your e-mail carrier has a spell checker, use it before you press the send button.

Try It Yourself

EXERCISE 1

Identifying Netiquette

For a humor column in your school newspaper, write a paragraph about a fictional person who violated two of the points on the Dos and Don'ts list with disastrous results. You may draw from real-life situations that have happened to you or to someone you know.

EXERCISE 2

Understanding Netiquette

Suppose that a relative is considering signing up with an Internet provider and has asked you about benefits and drawbacks of using e-mail. Drawing from your own personal experience, write a response explaining the positive and negative aspects of e-mail and communicating on the Internet. Tell whether you think e-mail will continue to be a popular form of communication. If so, why?

EXERCISE 3

Using Netiquette in Your Writing

Suppose you are the head of a unit at a company and have several people working for you. Write an e-mail message to your staff to schedule a meeting about an important project. Make sure to include all of the important information, such as time, date, place, and what each person needs to bring. If you do not have access to e-mail, you may write out the message on a piece of paper.

EXERCISE 1
Responses will vary. You may want students to share the points in their paragraphs in pairs or in small groups so that they can get a larger view of real-life applications of the Dos and Don'ts.

EXERCISE 2
Responses will vary. Students should cover positive and negative aspects of using e-mail and generalize about whether e-mail will continue to be a popular form of communication.

EXERCISE 3
Responses will vary. Sample response:
From: Cole Thomason <cthomason@company.com>
To: Marketing <mkt.hawkseye@company.com>
Date: Thursday, November 4, 2003, 9:43 A.M.
cc: Ms. Barber
Subject: Orr Project

Marketing Staff:
We will be meeting on November 8, 2003, at 2:30 P.M. in the west conference room. This meeting is to discuss strategies and ideas to pursue with the Orr

project. If you have a scheduling conflict, please let me know as soon as possible. Otherwise, I will see you Monday afternoon.
Cole

SEARCHING THE INTERNET

The Internet is an enormous collection of computer networks that can open a whole new world of information. With just a couple of keystrokes, you can access libraries, government agencies, high schools and universities, nonprofit and educational organizations, museums, user groups, and individuals around the world.

Evaluating Your Sources

Keep in mind that no one owns or regulates the Internet. Just because you read something online doesn't mean it's true or accurate. Because anyone can publish something on the Internet without having to verify facts or guarantee quality, it's always a good idea to confirm facts from the Internet against another source. In addition, to become a good judge of Internet materials, do the following:

- **Consider the domain name of the resource.** Be sure to check out the sites you use to see if they are commercial (.com or .firm), educational (.edu), governmental (.gov), or organizational (.org or .net). Ask yourself questions like these: What bias might a commercial site have that would influence its presentation of information? Is the site sponsored by a special-interest group that slants or spins information to its advantage?

Key to Internet Domains	
.com	commercial entity
.edu	educational institution
.firm	business entity
.gov	government agency or department
.org or .net	organization

- **Consider the author's qualifications.** Regardless of the source, ask these questions: Is the author named? What expertise does he or she have? Can I locate other online information about this person?

- **Check the date posted.** Is the information timely? When was the last time the site was updated?

Keeping Track of Your Search Process

Because the Internet allows you to jump from one site to the next, it's easy to lose track of how you got from place to place. A research journal, kept in a separate electronic file or in a notebook, is an excellent tool for mapping how you find information. The example on page 490 shows one way to set up a research log.

- Write a brief statement of the topic of your research.
- Write key words or phrases that will help you search for this information.
- Note the search engines that you will use.
- As you conduct a search, note how many "hits" or Internet sites the search engine has accessed. Determine whether you need to narrow or expand your search. Write down new key words and the results of each new search.
- Write down all promising sites. As you access them, evaluate the source and nature of the information and jot down your assessment.
- As you find the information you need, document it carefully according to the directions in "Citing Internet Resources," pages 493–496.
- Keep a list of favorite websites, either in your research journal or in your browser software. This feature may be called *bookmark* or *favorites.* You can click on the name of the site in your list and return to that page without having to retype the URL (Uniform Resource Locator).

Internet Research Log

Topic: ______________________________

Key words: ______________________________

Search engine: ______________________________

Promising hits (titles and summary of sources): __________

____

____

New key words or phrases tried: ______________________________

____

Promising hits (titles and summary of sources):

____

____

Complete web addresses of most promising sites:

____

____

____

____

____

Search Tools

A number of popular and free search engines allow you to find topics of interest. Keep in mind that each service uses slightly different methods of searching, so you may get different results using the same key words.

All the Web at http://www.alltheweb.com
AltaVista at http://www.altavista.com
Go at http://www.go.com
Yahoo at http://www.yahoo.com
Excite at http://www.excite.com
HotBot at http://www.hotbot.com
WebCrawler at http://www.webcrawler.com
Google at http://www.google.com

Search Tips

- To make searching easier, less time consuming, and more directed, narrow your subject to a key word or a group of key words. These key words are your search terms. Key search connectors, or Boolean commands, can help you limit or expand the scope of your topic.

AND (or +)	narrows a search by retrieving documents that include both terms. For example: *John Steinbeck* AND *Grapes of Wrath.*
OR	broadens a search by retrieving documents that include any of the terms. For example, *John Steinbeck* OR *Grapes of Wrath* OR *East of Eden.*
NOT	narrows a search by excluding documents containing certain words. For example: *John Steinbeck* NOT *Grapes of Wrath.*

- If applicable, limit your search by specifying a geographical area by using the word *near*. For example, *American Legion posts near Peoria*.

- When entering a group of key words, present them in order, from the most important to the least important key word.

EXERCISE 4

1. *Responses will vary.* Sample responses:
   http://www3.uakron.edu/english/richards/edwards/crane.html
   http://www.classicnote.com/ClassicNotes/Authors/about_stephen_crane.html
2. *Responses will vary.* Sample responses:
   The first site is maintained by a British botanist. It provides introductory information and basic facts about mosses and liverworts. It was revised most recently in January 2001. While the information is substantive, it applies only to Wales.
   The second site is a university website and provides information, including important terminology, about the two types of liverworts. No date is provided about when it was last revised. The material found on the site is academic but limited in range.
   The third site, revised in 2000, appears to be the work of a botanist in New Zealand. Its presentation is more polished and professional than that in the other two sites. It also provides general and specific material in a well-organized manner. The photographs of different types of liverworts are another strength of this site.
3. *Responses will vary.* Sample responses:
   http://www.google.com
   http://fireant.tamu.edu
   http://ipmworld.umn.edu/chapters/lockley.htm
   http://www.hotbot.com
   http://www.tpwd.state.tx.us/nature/wild/insects/fireants.htm
   http://www.antcolony.org/fire_ants.htm

- If the terms of your search are not leading you to the information you need, try using synonyms. For example, if you were looking for information about psychology, you might use these terms: *behaviorism*, *applied psychology*, *clinical psychology*, and *developmental psychology*.

- Avoid opening the link to every page in your results list. Search engines typically present pages in descending order of relevancy or importance. The most useful pages will be located at the top of the list. However, skimming the text of lower order sites may give you ideas for other key words.

- If you're not getting the desired results, check your input. Common search mistakes include misspelling search terms and mistyping URLs. Remember that URLs must be typed exactly as they appear, using the exact capital or lowercase letters, spacing, and punctuation.

Try It Yourself

EXERCISE 4

Understanding the Internet

Follow the directions for each item.

1. Use the Internet to locate information about Stephen Crane. Write down two URLs that you find.
2. Your topic is liverworts. You've found three sites:
   http://home.clara.net/adhale/bryos/
   http://www.hcs.ohio-state.edu/hcs300/liver1.htm
   http://www.hiddenforest.co.nz/bryophytes/liverworts/intro.htm
   Evaluate them in terms of where the data comes from, who wrote it, and when it was written.
3. Choose two of the search engines listed on page 491 and do a search on fire ants. List two relevant hits you get from each search engine.
4. You are interested in doing a report on the Trojan War. What key terms might you use to narrow your search?

5. Where would you expect to get the most unbiased information about the potential negative side effects of using Creatine—a site that has the suffix .com, .edu, .gov, .org, or .net? Why?

4. *Responses will vary.* Sample responses:

Troy	Trojan Horse
Achilles	Apollo
Hector	Odyssey

5. A .gov site on this topic should contain information that is not biased for or against any muscle-building supplements. A .org or .net site that is from a consumer protection group might also be unbiased in its evaluation of such supplements.

EXERCISE 5

Using the Internet

Use the Internet and the searching tips in this section of the unit to find the answers to these questions.

1. What is the largest turtle in the world? Give its length, its weight, and its place of residence. Name one site where you found the answer.
2. Which U.S. president had the shortest term in office, and how many days did he serve?
3. What are two websites where you can read excerpts from upcoming novels?
4. What is the URL of a site with a map of Winona, Minnesota?
5. What are the URLs of two websites with information about the Rosetta Stone?

EXERCISE 5

Responses will vary. Sample responses:

1. The leatherback turtle can reach a length of 2.1 meters and a weight of 365 kg. It is a rare sea turtle that lives in the warm sea waters near the West Indies, Florida, northeastern South America, Senegal, Natal, Madagascar, Ceylon, and Malaya. http://www.nature.ca/notebooks/english/leathert.htm

2. William Henry Harrison, 32 days. http://www.americanpresident.org/KoTrain/Courses/WHH/WHH_In_Brief.htm
3. http://www.lobin.freeserve.co.uk/online-novels; http://www.awe-struck.net/PREVIEWS/previews.html
4. http://www.mapquest.com http://www.randmcnally.com
5. http://pw1.netcom.com/~qkstart/rosetta.html http://www.ba.dlr.de/ne/pe/virtis/stone1.htm

EXERCISE 6

Using the Internet in Your Writing

Imagine you are preparing a report on Eli Whitney, the inventor of the cotton gin. Conduct a search on this individual and create a research journal to track your process. Include key words or phrases for searching, the search engines you use, promising sites and an evaluation of each, and a summary of what each site or article contains.

CITING INTERNET SOURCES

Plagiarism means to claim someone else's words or thoughts as your own. Whenever you use someone else's words or ideas, you must be careful either to put the ideas in your own words or to use quotation marks. In either case, you must give credit to the person whose ideas you are using. This is as true for Internet resources as it is for print resources, such as encyclopedias, books, and magazines. Giving such credit to others is called documenting your sources.

To document your sources, use your research journal to record each site you visit, or make bibliography cards as you search. An entry should include the following general pieces of information:

- Name of the author, if available, last name first, followed by a period.

- Title of the source, document, file, or page in quotation marks, followed by a period.

- Date of the material if available, followed by a period.

- Name of the database or online source, underlined, and followed by a period.

- Date the source was accessed (day month year), followed by a period. Although MLA (Modern Language Association) style does not require the insertion of the words *retrieved* or *accessed* before the access date, you may want to include one of these words to distinguish a retrieval date from a publication date.

- Electronic address, enclosed in angle brackets (< >), followed by a period. MLA style suggests that writers avoid showing network and e-mail addresses as underlined hyperlinks. Note that when line length forces you to break a Web address, always break it after a slash mark.

The *Modern Language Association Style Manual* acknowledges that all source tracking information may not be obtainable. Therefore, the manual recommends that if you cannot find some of this information, cite what is available.

EXERCISE 6

Responses will vary. Sample responses:

Search terms: Ely Whitney, cotton gin

http://www.alltheweb.com

Steward, Robin. "The History of the Cotton Gin." PageWise Inc. 2001. A brief biography of Whitney and a short discussion of the cotton gin and its historical impact. No links to other sites, no information about the author. Accessed on 8 September 2003. <http://sc.essortment.com/ cottongin_rciv.htm>. A commercial site with a disclaimer about not reviewing author's material for accuracy. Use with caution.

"Eli Whitney: Inventor of the Cotton Gin." The Whitney Research Group. 1999. Contains encyclopedia articles about Whitney and the cotton gin. Accessed on 8 September 2003. <http://www.whitneygen.org/ archives/biography/eli.html>.

Probably reliable since the encyclopedia information is drawn from respected historical monographs.

USAGE tip

The Modern Language Association of America website answers basic questions about MLA documentation of Web sources. From the home page, select "MLA Style."

http://www.yahoo.com

"Eli Whitney." Eli Whitney Museum. No update

Examples of Bibliography Cards

EXAMPLES

Shankland, Stephen. "Intel's Madison Chip on Parade." 6 September 2002. CNET Networks, Inc. Accessed 5 September 2003.
<http://news.com.com/2100-1001-956973.html?tag=fd_top>.

This site has no name of the database or online source:

McShaffrey, Dave. "Box Turtles Are Lousy Pets." 23 October 1996. Accessed 7 September 2003.
<http://www.marietta.edu/~mcshaffd/boxt/lousy.html>.

This site has no author:

"September 11's Historical Significance." 8 September 2002. CBS News. Accessed 9 September 2003.
<http://www.cbsnews.com/stories/2002/09/06/sunday/main521095.shtml>.

This is the citation for an e-mail message:

Matt Klaus (mklaus@corsair.net) "Future Shows." E-mail to Sidney Rich (sdrich@jackrabbit.com). 25 August 2003.

Try It Yourself

EXERCISE 7

Understanding Internet Documentation

Visit the following websites about Amelia Earhart and write a bibliography card for each site.

http://www.ameliaearhart.com/
http://www.capnhq.gov/nhq/cp/cpr/earhart.htm
http://www.womeninaviation.com/amelia.html

information. Contains full history, complete with illustrations, of the economic impact of the cotton gin. Accessed 8 September 2003. <http://www.eliwhitney.org/ew.htm>.

No author or contact information provided, but contains bibliography. Probably accurate since the material is drawn from a variety of well-known secondary sources. Bias is possible since this is an official Whitney site.

Taylor, Norris. "Eli Whitney." 1998. Contains brief biography drawn from an online encyclopedia, links, and lineage information for Whitney. Accessed 8 September 2003. <http://members.aol.com/~ntgen/baldwi/whit_eli.html. No information about the author provided. May or may not be reliable since neither database nor online source information is provided.

EXERCISE 7

"The Official Site of Amelia Earhart." 1996–2002. Estate of Amelia Earhart. Accessed 8 September 2003. <http://www.ameliaearhart.com>.

Smith, Robert B. "Civil Air Patrol Amelia Earhart Award." 3 October 2001. National Headquarters Civil Air Patrol. Accessed 8 September 2003. <http://www.capnhq.gov/nhq/cp/cpr/earhart.htm>.

"Amelia Earhart: First Woman to Solo the Atlantic." 1998. Aviation Archives. Accessed 8 September 2003. <http://www.womeni-naviation.com/amelia.html>.

EXERCISE 8

Understanding Internet Documentation

You were intrigued by the first site in Exercise 7, http://www.ameliaearhart.com/. Choose one of the links listed in the site, such as Naval Historical Center, Amelia Earhart Birthplace Museum, or Freedom of Information Act, and write a bibliography card for it.

EXERCISE 9

Using Internet Documentation in Your Writing

Using the information you found about Eli Whitney in Exercise 6, create four bibliography cards for sites you would use in your report.

EXERCISE 8
"Amelia Earhart Information." Naval Historical Center. 14 March 2002. Accessed 8 September 2003. <http://www.history.navy.mil/faqs/faq3-1.htm>.

EXERCISE 9
Responses will vary. Students should create bibliography cards for four different sites about Eli Whitney. They should model their bibliography cards after those shown in Unit 18, p. 495.

UNIT 18 REVIEW

TEST YOUR KNOWLEDGE

EXERCISE 1
Identifying Netiquette
Tell whether each of the following is a "do" or "don't" when communicating on the Internet. (10 points)

EXAMPLE
edit your writing (do)

1. frequently use acronyms
2. write short e-mails
3. fill in the subject line
4. share personal information
5. schedule events for a group
6. write when angry
7. send bad news
8. write SOS in subject line for urgent problems
9. praise a group
10. chat with friends

EXERCISE 2
Understanding Netiquette
Based on your own experience with Internet communication, what netiquette guidelines do you think are the most important to follow? Choose three such guidelines and explain why you think each is important. (10 points)

EXERCISE 3
Understanding Proper Netiquette
Rewrite the following e-mail, correcting any improper netiquette and changing the tone from informal to formal. (10 points)

EXERCISE 1
1. don't
2. do
3. do
4. don't
5. do
6. don't
7. don't
8. do
9. do
10. do

EXERCISE 2
Responses will vary.

EXERCISE 3
Responses will vary.
Sample response:
From: Dave Huffman <dhuffman@company.org>
To: Julie Underwood <junderwood@company.org>
Date: Tuesday, May 14, 2003 1:44 P.M.
Subject: Discussion Meeting
Dear Julie,
I will be leading a meeting to discuss the new motivational manual that the vice president recommended for the employees. Please ask the members of your unit to read the booklet and to be ready to discuss its main points.
I have reserved Conference Room B on Thursday at 2:00 P.M. for the meeting. Please let me know if this time conflicts with your schedule.
Dave Huffman

EXERCISE 4
Responses will vary.
Sample responses:
1. An ocelot is a wild cat, twice as large as a housecat, marked by dark spots and rings on tawny-yellow fur. http://www.pbs.org/kratts/world/sa/ocelot
2. A .gov, or .edu site would provide the most unbiased advice. A .org, .net, or .com site is more likely to be connected with the sale of siding.
3. http://www.google.com
   http://mc04.equinox.net/wdsmuseum/deanehouse.html
   http://members.tripod.com/~ntgen/bw/part_deane.html
   http://www.yahoo.com
   http://www.bartleby.com/65/de/Deane-Si.html
   http://www.infoplease.com/ce6/people/A0814875.html
4. http://www.baseballalmanac.com/teamstats/roster.php?y=1929&t=PHA
5. http://www.gohawaiianvacations.com/oahu_main.htm

From: Dave Huffman <dhuffman@company.org>
To: Julie Underwood <junderwood@company.org>
Date: Tuesday, May 14, 2003 1:44 P.M.
Subject: <<no subject>>

Yo Jules,

The bossman has really done it this time. He wants me to lead a discussion meeting on that new employee motivational manual we all received last week. The vice president is really high on this booklet as a morale booster. IMHO that rah-rah garbage is mindless drivel and a complete waste of time.

OTOH, we could have some fun at this meeting. I've already got some great jokes based on the "Teamwork" section. I could even read some passages in the vp's nasally voice. Maybe it will be a fun time after all. Anyhow, how does Thursday at 2:00 P.M. in Conference Room B sound? Inform the drones in your unit, will ya?

L8R

Dave

EXERCISE 4
Understanding Internet Searches and Sources

Follow the directions for each item. (20 points)

1. What is an ocelot? Write down one Internet site where you located information.
2. You are considering putting siding on your house and want advice on how to approach this task. Where would you expect to get the most unbiased advice—from a .com, .edu, .gov, .org, or .net? Why?
3. Choose two search engines and do a search on *Silas Deane*. List two relevant hits you get from each search engine.

4. What is the URL of a site that lists the roster of the 1929 Philadelphia Athletics?
5. What is the URL of a site that provides an online tour of the U.S.S. *Arizona Memorial*?
6. Who invented the hula hoop? When and where? List one URL site where you found your information.
7. Your topic is the Krakatoa volcano. You've found two sites:
   http://www.geocities.com/CapeCanaveral/Lab/1029/Vocano1883Krakatoa.html
   http://windows.arc.nasa.gov/cgi-bin/tour_def/earth/interior/Krakatoa.html
   Write a brief evaluation, comparing and contrasting the two sites.
8. How would you cite the following e-mail message?

> From: Betty Gisolo <batter4@corsair.net>
> To: Karla Krandle <kkrandle@schoool.edu>
> Date: Sunday, November 1, 2002 8:41 P.M.
> Subject: Book Quotes
>
> Karla:
>
> I appreciate your interest in my book, *Women and the Diamond*. You may use the quotations you cited from Chapters 3, 5, and 6. Feel free to cite any other quotes from my book if you have such a need.
>
> Good luck on your history thesis. I'd be interested in reading the finished product. Please mail a copy to me when you are done.
>
> Betty Gisolo

9. Use the Internet to locate information about the Old Kingdom in ancient Egypt. List five different Old Kingdom Pharaohs and two relevant sites.
10. What is the URL of a site that allows you to read the short story "Bartelby the Scrivener" by Herman Melville?

6. The hula hoop was first invented in ancient times. Richard Knerr and Arthur "Spud" Melin reinvented it in 1957 in California. http://web.mit.edu invent/www/inventors I-Q/hulahoop.html
7. The first site is written by an expert on natural disasters, George Pararas-Carayannis. Though under construction, the site provides a wealth of historical and scientific information about the Krakatoa volcano and its devastating eruption in 1883. The site also contains pictures, diagrams, and a bibliography. Information on when the site was last updated is unavailable.

   The second site is professionally produced by the University Corporation for Atmospheric Research (University of Michigan). It was last updated on February 15, 1997, and contact information is provided. Though more limited it its coverage, the site provides an impressive scientific discussion of the Karaktoa eruption of 1883.

8. Betty Gisolo (batter4@corsair.net). "book quotes." E-mail to Karla Krandle (kkrandle@school.edu). 1 November 2002.
9. Snofru, Khufu, Djedefre, Khafre, Bikheris. http://www.arab.net/egypt/history/et_oldkingdom.html. http://www.thepharaohs.net/Ancient/old_kingdom/pharaohs.cfm

EXERCISE 5

Understanding Internet Searches

List two or three key terms you might use to narrow a search on each of the following topics. (10 points)

EXAMPLE
tire repair *(tires + radial + patches)*

1. Model T automobiles
2. the Jazz Age
3. baseball musicals
4. Jesse James
5. Franklin D. Roosevelt

10. http://www.cwrl.utexas.edu/~daniel/amlit/bartleby/bartleby.html

EXERCISE 5
Responses will vary.
Sample responses:
1. tin lizzie + Henry Ford
2. F. Scott Fitzgerald + *The Great Gatsby* + expatriate writers
3. *Take Me Out to the Ballgame, Damn Yankees*
4. bank robbers, train robbers, outlaws, James-Younger Gang
5. New Deal policies + Social Security + unemployment insurance

EXERCISE 6
Responses will vary.

EXERCISE 7
Responses will vary.

EXERCISE 6

Using the Internet in Your Writing

Imagine you are preparing a report on British commanders in the Revolutionary War. Conduct a search on this topic, narrowing your search to one specific aspect of the topic, such as the Howe brothers (William and Richard) or Lord Cornwallis. Create an Internet Research Log to track your process. Include key words or phrases for searching, the search engines you use, and a list of promising sites you locate. (20 points)

EXERCISE 7

Using Internet Documentation in Your Writing

Using the information you found on British Revolutionary War commanders in Exercise 6, create four bibliography cards for sites you would use in your report. (20 points)

PART FOUR

Writing

UNIT 19 WRITER'S WORKSHOP
Building Effective Sentences

UNIT OVERVIEW

WRITER'S WORKSHOP: BUILDING EFFECTIVE SENTENCES

SENTENCE FRAGMENTS

A sentence contains a subject and a verb and should express a complete thought. A **sentence fragment** is a phrase or clause that does not express a complete thought but that has been punctuated as though it did.

Writing tip

When reading a sentence fragment, ask yourself, "What is missing?" A sentence fragment is usually missing either a subject, a verb, or both subject and verb.

EXAMPLES

complete sentence	A burly logger gave Phyllis directions to the courthouse.
sentence fragment	Gave Phyllis directions to the courthouse. (The subject is missing.)
sentence fragment	A burly logger. (The verb is missing.)
sentence fragment	To the courthouse. (The subject and verb are missing.)

Try It Yourself

LANGUAGELINK
Print exercise worksheets or have students complete exercises online with the LanguageLINK CD.

EXERCISE 1

Identifying Sentence Fragments in Literature

As a rule, sentence fragments should be avoided. For stylistic reasons, however, authors sometimes include sentence fragments in their work. Identify each of the following items as either a sentence or a sentence fragment.

MODEL

EXERCISE 1
1. sentence
2. sentence fragment
3. sentence
4. sentence fragment
5. sentence fragment
6. sentence
7. sentence fragment
8. sentence
9. sentence fragment

1. I want you to find George.
2. The last.
3. Everything came in good time.
4. Nothing left out, left over.
5. Better.
6. The light was blue from Cornelia's silk lampshades.
7. No sort of light at all, just frippery.
8. You'll see Hapsy again.
9. What about her?

CONTINUED

10. What then?

excerpts from "The Jilting of Granny Weatherall"
Katherine Anne Porter

10. sentence fragment

EXERCISE 2

1. Subject is missing.
2. Subject and verb are missing.
3. Verb is missing.
4. Verb is missing.
5. Subject and verb are missing.
6. Subject is missing.
7. Subject is missing.
8. Subject and verb are missing.
9. Subject is missing.
10. Verb is missing.

EXERCISE 3

Responses will vary. Each sentence should include a subject and a verb and express a complete thought. Sample responses are provided.

1. Sunlight slipped through the partially opened window.
2. The little girl enjoyed the breeze blowing through her hair.
3. An autumn gust shuffled the fallen leaves.
4. The gray shadow in the corner took on an ominous shape.
5. A parade of relatives danced across her hazy memories of years gone by.
6. A funny story lightened the atmosphere.
7. The green rug in the study concealed the trapdoor.
8. A brown mouse scurried under the old cedar chest.
9. The child saw lightning and heard thunder.
10. He rested his head on the soft pillow.

EXERCISE 2

Understanding Sentence Fragments

Tell what is missing in each of the following sentence fragments—subject, verb, or subject and verb.

1. Warned the doctor.
2. At the foot of the bed.
3. Her ailing grandmother.
4. Hushed whispers from the hallway.
5. On the crowded pantry shelves.
6. Collected dust in the attic.
7. Rummaged through the box of letters.
8. On her last birthday.
9. Packed up and moved back to her own house.
10. My daughter and her ideas.

EXERCISE 3

Correcting Sentence Fragments

Correct each of the following sentence fragments. Make each fragment into a complete sentence by supplying the missing element(s).

1. through the partially opened window
2. enjoyed the breeze blowing through her hair
3. shuffled the fallen leaves
4. the gray shadow in the corner
5. across her hazy memories of years gone by
6. a funny story
7. the green rug in the study
8. under the old cedar chest
9. saw lightning and heard thunder
10. on the soft pillow

RUN-ON SENTENCES

A **run-on sentence** is made up of two or more sentences that have been run together as if they were one complete thought. A run-on sentence can confuse the reader about where a thought starts or ends.

Take a look at the following examples of run-on sentences. In the first run-on, called a **fused sentence**, no punctuation mark is used between two complete thoughts. In the second run-on, called a **comma splice**, a comma rather than an end mark or semicolon separates the sentences.

EXAMPLES

The gambler slowly rode away from the town the citizens cast him out as an unsavory character. (fused sentence)

Three other outcasts accompanied the gambler, they vocalized their displeasure at being forced to leave the town. (comma splice)

You can correct a run-on by dividing it into two separate sentences. Mark the end of each idea with a period, question mark, or exclamation point. Capitalize the first word of each new sentence.

EXAMPLE

The gambler slowly rode away from the town. The citizens cast him out as an unsavory character.

You can also correct a run-on by using a semicolon. The second part of the sentence is not capitalized. Use a semicolon to join two sentences only if the thoughts are closely related.

EXAMPLE

Three other outcasts accompanied the gambler; they vocalized their displeasure at being forced to leave the town.

Try It Yourself

EXERCISE 4

Identifying Run-on Sentences

Identify each of the following items as either a sentence or a run-on sentence.

1. The travelers set out for another town which was a day's journey away.
2. One of the women eventually became tired of riding and dismounted her horse she needed to stop and rest.
3. The party pitched camp in a wooded canyon they did not have many provisions.
4. Three of the travelers drank whiskey, it sent them into a deep sleep.
5. A man called out to the gambler from the trail he was an old friend.
6. In a stroke of luck, the man had discovered a log cabin not far from the trail.
7. One of the travelers disappeared in the night he stole the party's mules.
8. Fortunately for the party, they had stored their provisions inside the cabin.
9. The gambler made another discovery in the morning it had snowed heavily during the night.
10. The surrounding wall of snow, an impenetrable barrier, did not immediately discourage the travelers.

EXERCISE 4
1. sentence
2. run-on
3. run-on
4. run-on
5. run-on
6. sentence
7. run-on
8. sentence
9. run-on
10. sentence

EXERCISE 5

Understanding Run-on Sentences

Correct each of the following run-on sentences. Decide whether the run-on sentence can be corrected by dividing it into two separate sentences or by using a semicolon to form one sentence.

1. The outcasts played music and told stories during the evening they enjoyed themselves despite their circumstances.

EXERCISE 5
Responses will vary. Sample responses:
1. The outcasts played music and told stories during the evening; they enjoyed themselves despite their circumstances.

2. Snow continued to fall throughout the week; it formed a barrier that stretched twenty feet into the sky.
3. One of the party succumbed to illness and died; she had not eaten for over a week.
4. The group buried their friend in the snow. They mournfully forsook music and story-telling that day.
5. The gambler fashioned a crude pair of snow-shoes. The snow had not melted in the past week.
6. After saying goodbye, one of the men set out to find help. He faced great difficulty traveling through the deep snow.
7. At camp, the fire slowly died away; its embers gradually blackened.
8. The winter storm increased its fury during the night; snow broke through the roof of the cabin.
9. The gambler never returned to camp; realizing his fate, he decided not to wait for nature to finish the job.
10. Eventually warmer weather reduced the blanket of snow. When spring arrived, people from the town discovered the camp.

2. Snow continued to fall throughout the week it formed a barrier that stretched twenty feet into the sky.
3. One of the party succumbed to illness and died she had not eaten for over a week.
4. The group buried their friend in the snow they mournfully forsook music and story-telling that day.
5. The gambler fashioned a crude pair of snow-shoes the snow had not melted in the past week.
6. After saying goodbye, one of the men set out to find help he faced great difficulty traveling through the deep snow.
7. At camp, the fire slowly died away its embers gradually blackened.
8. The winter storm increased its fury during the night snow broke through the roof of the cabin.
9. The gambler never returned to camp realizing his fate he decided not to wait for nature to finish the job.
10. Eventually warmer weather reduced the blanket of snow when spring arrived, people from the town discovered the camp.

WORDY SENTENCES

A **wordy sentence** includes extra words and phrases that can be difficult, confusing, or repetitive to read. When you write, use only words necessary to make your meaning clear. Revise and edit your sentences so that they are not wordy or complicated. Review the following examples to learn about three different ways to correct wordy sentences.

Replace a group of words with one word.

EXAMPLES

wordy My grandmother traveled by train **because of the fact that** she is afraid to fly.

revised My grandmother traveled by train **because** she is afraid to fly.

Replace a clause with a phrase.

EXAMPLES

wordy	**After Grandmother bought her ticket at the ticket counter**, she quickly boarded the train.
revised	**After buying her ticket at the counter,** Grandmother quickly boarded the train.

Delete a group of unnecessary or repetitive words.

When revising, read your sentences aloud to check for wordiness. A wordy sentence will not only sound awkward, but it also will feel like an unnecessary mouthful.

EXAMPLES

wordy	**What I believe is that** flying is one of the safest forms of transportation.
revised	Flying is one of the safest forms of transportation.
wordy	Betty's description of the trip was interminable, **and it continued with no end in sight.**
revised	Betty's description of the trip was interminable.

Do not confuse a wordy sentence with a lengthy sentence. Writers vary their sentence lengths to create rhythm and add variety and liveliness to their work. Note the lengthy sentence underlined in the following excerpt. Even though the sentence is long, it does not contain "extra words." Precise word choices make its meaning clear and create a vivid picture.

Literature MODEL

> <u>This communication, worn and rubbed, looking as if it had been carried for some days in a coat pocket that was none too clean, was from my Uncle Howard, and informed me that his wife had been left a small legacy by a bachelor relative, and that it would be necessary for her to go to Boston to attend to the settling of the estate</u>. He requested me to meet her at the station and render her whatever services might be necessary. On examining the date indicated as that of her arrival, I found it to be no later than tomorrow. He had characteristically delayed writing until, had I been away from home for a day, I must have missed my aunt altogether.

from "A Wagner Matinee"
Willa Cather

EXERCISE 6

1. My aunt traveled to Boston because of the fact that she had to attend the settling of a relative's estate.
2. She was exhausted after her long trip and was really tired after arriving.
3. Her duster was black with soot and dirt was all over the coat she wore.
4. Dawn's first light roused me from my sleep and I woke up early in the morning.
5. My aunt seemed to be in a somnambulant state and moved around like a sleepwalker.
6. Many years ago she moved to Nebraska with my uncle Howard, the man she married.
7. As a youth my aunt lived in Boston, the city where she was raised.
8. The women in the audience wore dresses of many different colors, red, mauve, pink, blue, purple, rose, and yellow.
9. My aunt was moved by the concert, and she heard many songs at the concert that had a deep meaning for her.
10. After the last song ended, she remained in her seat and did not leave after the concert.

EXERCISE 7

Responses will vary. Sample response:

Try It Yourself

EXERCISE 6
Identifying Wordy Sentences

Read the following sentences. Underline any unnecessary words and phrases in each of the sentences.

1. My aunt traveled to Boston because of the fact that she had to attend the settling of a relative's estate.
2. She was exhausted after her long trip and was really tired after arriving.
3. Her duster was black with soot and dirt was all over the coat she wore.
4. Dawn's first light roused me from my sleep and I woke up early in the morning.
5. My aunt seemed to be in a somnambulant state and moved around like a sleepwalker.
6. Many years ago she moved to Nebraska with my uncle Howard, the man she married.
7. As a youth my aunt lived in Boston, the city where she was raised.
8. The women in the audience wore dresses of many different colors, red, mauve, pink, blue, purple, rose, and yellow.
9. My aunt was moved by the concert, and she heard many songs at the concert that had a deep meaning for her.
10. After the last song ended, she remained in her seat and did not leave after the concert.

EXERCISE 7
Understanding Wordy Sentences

The following paragraph contains some wordy sentences. Revise the paragraph by correcting the wordy sentences and making the meaning clear.

> When I wake up each day, I am often reminded of the past in the morning. Sometimes I can still hear the music I played at concerts long ago. I remember performing

CONTINUED

before concert halls that were sold out and did not have any available seats the night of the performance. The audience seemed mesmerized by my music. After the last song, the cheering masses always rose to their feet, stood, and called for an encore. Five years ago I had to retire because of the fact that an illness deprived me of the stamina needed to perform a concert. I still very much enjoy listening to the music of the classical composers, including for example, Bach, Beethoven, and Wagner.

When I wake up, I am often reminded of the past. Sometimes I can still hear the music I played at concerts long ago. I remember performing before sold-out concert halls. The audience seemed mesmerized by my music. After the last song, the cheering masses always rose to

their feet and called for an encore. Five years ago I had to retire because an illness deprived me of the stamina needed to perform a concert. I still very much enjoy listening to the music of the classical composers, including Bach, Beethoven, and Wagner.

EXERCISE 8

Using Only Necessary Words in Your Writing

Write a paragraph about a memory that you treasure. The memory may involve a special place or event, a meaningful friendship, or an important accomplishment. Describe the memory and explain what it means to you. After writing, read your paragraph aloud to yourself; then ask a classmate to read it aloud while you listen. Correct any sentences that sound wordy.

EXERCISE 8

Responses will vary. Students' paragraphs should be about a special memory and should avoid wordy sentences.

COMBINING AND EXPANDING SENTENCES

A series of short sentences in a paragraph can make your writing sound choppy and boring. The reader might also have trouble understanding how your ideas are connected. By **combining and expanding sentences,** you can connect related ideas, make sentences longer and smoother, and make a paragraph more interesting to read.

One way to combine sentences is to take a key word or phrase from one sentence and insert it into another sentence.

Writing tip

When you insert a key word from one sentence into another, you might need to change the form of the word.

The doe darted into the woods. She was **swift**.

The doe **swiftly** darted into the woods.

Writing tip

When combining two related sentences to form a compound sentence, you need to insert a comma before the coordinating conjunction.

Writing tip

When you form a compound subject, make sure the compound subject agrees with the verb in number.

EXAMPLES

short, choppy sentences	The soldiers charged up the rocky hill. They were brave.
combined sentence (with key word)	The **brave** soldiers charged up the rocky hill.
short, choppy sentences	I will probably see my great-uncle at the reunion. He lives in Mobile.
combined sentence (with key phrase)	I will probably see my great-uncle from Mobile at the reunion.

Another way of combining sentences is to take two related sentences and combine them by using a coordinating conjunction—*and*, *but*, *or*, *so*, *for*, *yet*, or *nor*. By using a coordinating conjunction, you can form a compound subject, a compound verb, or a compound sentence.

EXAMPLES

two related sentences	Roger teaches carpentry at the community college. He paints houses to earn extra money during the summer.
combined sentence	Roger teachers carpentry at the community college, **and** he paints houses to earn extra money during the summer. (compound sentence)
two related sentences	Wealthy alumni called for the coach's removal. Students at the university also wanted the coach fired.
combined sentence	Wealthy **alumni** and the **students** at the university called for the coach's removal. (compound subject)

CONTINUED

two related sentences	Fire swept through the heart of the city. It destroyed two bridges downtown.
combined sentence	Fire **swept** through the heart of the city and **destroyed** two bridges downtown. (compound verb)

Try It Yourself

EXERCISE 9

Understanding How to Combine and Expand Sentences

Combine each of the following sentence pairs by taking the underlined word or phrase from the second sentence and inserting it into the first sentence. Remember: You might need to change the form of words when combining sentences.

1. The Great Depression brought hardship to millions of Americans. It occurred during the 1930s.
2. Herbert Hoover and Franklin Roosevelt struggled to deal with the economic crisis. They were presidents.
3. Roosevelt's New Deal programs created thousands of jobs. The programs were ambitious.
4. The president's allies in Congress usually supported his agenda. These allies were Democrats.
5. The Supreme Court struck down several of Roosevelt's programs. The Court found the programs to be unconstitutional.
6. Because of his ambitious agenda, Roosevelt faced vocal critics. These critics were from the left and the right.
7. Some people believed that the radical "Share Our Wealth" program was needed to save the country. This program was proposed by Huey Long.
8. Many big business leaders thought Roosevelt's programs went too far. These leaders were conservative.
9. Roosevelt proposed a controversial idea during his second term. The idea was to increase the number of Supreme Court justices.

EXERCISE 9

Responses may vary slightly.

Sample responses:

1. The Great Depression brought hardship to millions of Americans during the 1930s.
2. Presidents Herbert Hoover and Franklin Roosevelt struggled to deal with the economic crisis.
3. Roosevelt's ambitious New Deal programs created thousands of jobs.
4. The president's Democratic allies in Congress usually supported his agenda.
5. The Supreme Court struck down several of Roosevelt's programs as unconstitutional.
6. Because of his ambitious agenda, Roosevelt faced vocal critics from the left and the right.
7. Some people believed that Huey Long's radical "Share Our Wealth" program was needed to save the country.
8. Many conservative big business leaders thought Roosevelt's programs went too far.
9. Roosevelt proposed a controversial idea during his second term—to increase the number of Supreme Court justices.
10. The New Deal brought rapid and dramatic growth to the national government.

EXERCISE 10
Responses may vary slightly.
Sample responses:

1. During his presidency, Roosevelt had to confront the Great Depression and deal with World War II.
2. In 1940 Roosevelt campaigned on a pledge to keep America out of war, but in 1941 he sought to bring the United States into the struggle against Nazi Germany.
3. The United States supplied Great Britain with military equipment and supplies and with 50 destroyers.
4. After December 10, 1941, the United States was at war with Japan and Germany, and also with Italy.
5. Japan won a series of victories over the Americans in early 1942 but was soundly defeated at the Battle of Midway in June 1942.
6. In the fall of 1942, Germany and Italy occupied much of North Africa, so the United States and Britain launched an invasion of North Africa in November 1942.
7. The war had not ended when Roosevelt's third term expired, so he ran for a fourth term in 1944.
8. Roosevelt died in April of 1945, and his vice president Harry Truman succeeded to the presidency.
9. To defeat Japan, the United States would have to invade the home islands or drop an atomic bomb.
10. Roosevelt helped lead the nation through the terrible crisis of World War II but did not live to see its final victorious conclusion.

10. The New Deal brought growth to the national government. The growth was <u>rapid and dramatic</u>.

EXERCISE 10

Using Coordinating Conjunctions to Combine Sentences

Combine each of the following sentence pairs by using one of the following coordinating conjunctions—*and*, *but*, *or*, *so*, *for*, *yet*, or *nor*. Remember to insert a comma if necessary.

1. During his presidency, Roosevelt had to confront the Great Depression. He also had to deal with World War II.
2. In 1940 Roosevelt campaigned on a pledge to keep America out of war. In 1941 he sought to bring the United States into the struggle against Nazi Germany.
3. The United States supplied Great Britain with military equipment and supplies. It also delivered 50 destroyers to the British.
4. After December 10, 1941, the United States was at war with Japan and Germany. The country was also at war with Italy.
5. Japan won a series of victories over the Americans in early 1942. It was soundly defeated at the Battle of Midway in June 1942.
6. In the fall of 1942, Germany and Italy occupied much of North Africa. The United States and Britain launched an invasion of North Africa in November 1942.
7. The war had not ended when Roosevelt's third term expired. He ran for a fourth term in office in 1944.
8. Roosevelt died in April of 1945. His vice president Harry Truman succeeded him to the presidency.
9. To defeat Japan, the United States would have to invade the home islands. The United States could drop an atomic bomb to end the war.
10. Roosevelt helped lead the nation through the terrible crisis of World War II. He did not live to see its final victorious conclusion.

MAKING PASSIVE SENTENCES ACTIVE

A verb is **active** when the subject of the verb performs the action. It is **passive** when the subject of the verb receives the action.

EXAMPLES

active	The report of the cannon **deafened** the private.
passive	The private **was deafened** by the report of the cannon.

***Writing* tip**

Overusing passive verbs in sentences makes your writing dull and weak. Active verbs engage your reader's attention and make your sentences sound more natural, alive, and interesting.

Try It Yourself

EXERCISE 11

Identifying Active and Passive Verbs in Sentences in Literature

Indicate whether the underlined verbs in the passage below are active or passive.

> Objects were represented by their colors only; circular horizontal streaks of color—that was all he saw. He had been caught in a vortex and was being whirled on with a velocity of advance and gyration that made him giddy and sick. In a few moments he was flung upon the gravel at the foot of the left bank of the stream—the southern bank—and behind a projecting point which concealed him from his enemies. The sudden arrest of his motion, the abrasion of one of his hands on the gravel, restored him, and he wept with delight.
>
> from "An Occurrence at Oak Creek Bridge"
> Ambrose Bierce

EXERCISE 12

Understanding Passive and Active Sentences

Identify each of the verbs in the following sentences as being either passive or active. Then make each of the passive verbs into an active verb.

EXERCISE 11

1. *were represented*—passive
2. *saw*—active
3. *had been caught*—passive
4. *was being whirled*—passive
5. *made*—active
6. *was flung*—passive

MODEL

7. *concealed*—active
8. *restored*—active
9. *wept*—active

EXERCISE 12

Responses will vary. Sample responses:

1. *began*—active; *was shelled*—passive; the Civil War began when Confederate troops shelled Fort Sumter in April 1861.
2. *was offered*—passive; Abraham Lincoln offered Virginian Robert E. Lee command of the Union Army.
3. *refused*—active
4. *was blockaded*—passive; the Union Navy blockaded the Confederacy.

5. *were defeated*—passive; Lee defeated several Union generals in 1862 and 1863.
6. *was commanded*—passive; in 1864 and 1865, Ulysses S. Grant commanded the Union Army.
7. *gained*—active
8. *dug*—active
9. *was taken*—passive; Union troops took Richmond, the Confederate capital, in April 1865.
10. *was assassinated*—passive; a few days after Lee's surrender, John Wilkes Booth assassinated President Lincoln.

1. The Civil War began when Fort Sumter was shelled by Confederate troops in April 1861.
2. Virginian Robert E. Lee was offered command of the Union Army by Abraham Lincoln.
3. Lee, though opposed to secession, refused the offer, not wanting to fight against his home state.
4. The Confederacy was blockaded by the Union Navy.
5. Several Union generals were defeated by Lee in 1862 and 1863.
6. In 1864 and 1865, the Union Army was commanded by Ulysses S. Grant.
7. Grant gained recognition for his brilliant siege of Vicksburg.
8. Lee's army dug in at Petersburg to resist Grant's assault.
9. Richmond, the Confederate capital, was taken by Union troops in April 1865.
10. A few days after Lee's surrender, President Lincoln was assassinated by John Wilkes Booth.

EXERCISE 13
Responses will vary. Students should underline the active verbs.

EXERCISE 13

Using Active Verbs in Your Writing

Write a short letter to a pen pal described an important challenge that you recently met. In your letter describe the nature of the challenge, any other people involved, and how meeting the challenge affected you. Use at least five active sentences in your letter. Underline the active verb(s) in each sentence.

Writing tip

When revising for parallelism, read your sentences aloud. Any errors in parallelism will sound awkward.

ACHIEVING PARALLELISM

A sentence has **parallelism** when the same forms are used to express ideas of equal—or parallel—importance. Parallelism can add emphasis and rhythm to a sentence. Words, phrases, and clauses that have the same form and function in a sentence are called **parallel**.

EXAMPLES

not parallel	The frog **leaped** out of the box, **jumped** onto the lily pad, and **had splashed** into the pond. (The highlighted verbs are not in the same tense.)
parallel	The frog **leaped** out of the box, **jumped** onto the lily pad, and **splashed** into the pond.
not parallel	The old man was **monotonous, longwinded,** and **frowns**. (The three highlighted words include two adjectives and one verb.)
parallel	The old man was **monotonous, longwinded,** and **cranky**.

Try It Yourself

EXERCISE 14

Identifying Parallelism in Literature

Identify examples of parallelism in the following passage.

> Simon Wheeler backed me into a corner and blockaded me there with his chair, and then sat down and reeled off the monotonous narrative which follows this paragraph. He never smiled, he never frowned, he never changed his voice from the gentle-flowing key to which he tuned his initial sentence, he never betrayed the slightest suspicion of enthusiasm; but all through the interminable narrative there ran a vein of impressive earnestness and sincerity, which showed plainly that, so far from his imagining that there was anything ridiculous or funny about his story, he regarded it as a really important matter, and admired its two heroes as men of transcendent genius in *finesse*.
>
> from "The Notorious Jumping Frog of Calaveras County"
> Mark Twain

EXERCISE 14

Simon Wheeler backed me into a corner and blockaded me there with his chair, and then sat down and reeled off the monotonous narrative

Literature MODEL

which follows this paragraph. He never smiled, he never frowned, he never changed his voice from the gentle-flowing key to which he tuned his initial sentence, he never betrayed the slightest suspicion of enthusiasm; but all through the interminable narrative there ran a vein of impressive earnestness and sincerity, which showed plainly that, so far from his imagining that there was anything ridiculous or funny about his story, he regarded it as a really important matter, and admired its two heroes as men of transcendent genius in *finesse*.

EXERCISE 15

1. Mr. Smiley likes to bet on dogfights, wager on frog races, and gamble on any occasion.
2. Listening to the story, the narrator fidgeted, squirmed, and started to nod off.
3. correct
4. Are you starting another story or adding an epilogue to the last tale?
5. He saw little hope in distracting the man, slipping out the back door, and escaping into the alleyway.
6. The storyteller never paused for effect, displayed enthusiasm, or tried to make the story interesting.
7. correct
8. correct
9. At one point in the twentieth century, Twain's books were panned by critics, banned by libraries, and excluded from school curriculums.
10. Today, Twain is popular, revered, studied, and analyzed.

EXERCISE 15

Understanding Parallelism

Some of the following sentences contain errors in parallelism. Rewrite each flawed sentence by making sentence parts parallel. If a sentence is already parallel, write *correct*.

1. Mr. Smiley likes to bet on dogfights, wager on frog races, and will gamble on any occasion.
2. Listening to the story, the narrator fidgeted, squirmed, and was starting to nod off.
3. The other tavern patrons ordered drinks, played pooled, and ignored our conversation.
4. Are you starting another story or will you add an epilogue to the last tale?
5. He saw little hope in distracting the man, slipping out the back door, and escape into the alleyway.
6. The storyteller never paused for effect, displayed enthusiasm, or had tried to make the story interesting.
7. Finally, Mr. Wheeler heard his name called, rose from his chair, and walked out to the front yard.
8. Mark Twain's stories are often humorous, ironic, and witty.
9. At one point in the twentieth century, Twain's books were panned by critics, banned by libraries, and had been excluded from school curriculums.
10. Today, Twain is popular, revered, studied, and has been analyzed.

EXERCISE 16

Responses will vary. Students should include five examples of parallelism in their letters.

EXERCISE 16

Using Parallelism in Your Writing

Imagine that you lived during Mark Twain's time. Write a letter to the celebrated author in which you describe something humorous that happened to you. You may include understatement, hyperbole, or irony in your description. Use five examples of parallelism in your letter.

ADDING COLORFUL LANGUAGE TO SENTENCES

When you write, use words that tell your readers exactly what you mean. **Colorful language**—such as precise and lively nouns, verbs, and modifiers—tells your readers exactly what you mean and makes your writing more interesting.

Writing tip

Think of colorful language as a way to help your readers see, hear, smell, taste, and/or feel what you are describing.

Precise nouns give your reader a clear picture of who or what is involved in the sentence.

EXAMPLES

original sentence	The **man** sat alone in the **room**.
revised sentence	The **prisoner** sat alone in the **dungeon**.

Colorful, vivid verbs describe the specific action in the sentence.

EXAMPLES

original sentence	The odor **bothered** the guards.
revised sentence	The odor **nauseated** the guards.

Modifiers—adjectives and adverbs—describe the meaning of other words and make them more precise. Colorful or surprising modifiers can make your writing come alive for your readers.

EXAMPLES

original sentence	Escaping seemed a difficult task for the inmate.
revised sentence	Escaping seemed an **insuperable** task for the **scrawny** inmate.

Try It Yourself

EXERCISE 17

Identifying Colorful Language in Literature

Identify examples of colorful language in the following passage. Think about how each example makes the meaning of a sentence more precise and vivid.

EXERCISE 17

Responses will vary. Sample responses:

What I had taken for masonry seemed now to be iron, or some other metal, in huge plates, whose sutures or joints occasioned the depression. The entire surface of this metallic enclosure was rudely daubed in all the hideous and repulsive devices to which the charnel superstition of the monks has given rise. The figures of fiends in aspects of menace, with skeleton forms, and other more really fearful images, overspread and disfigured the walls.

Literature MODEL

What I had taken for masonry seemed now to be iron, or some other metal, in huge plates, whose sutures or joints occasioned the depression. The entire surface of this metallic enclosure was rudely daubed in all the hideous and repulsive devices to which the charnel superstition of the monks has given rise. The figures of fiends in aspects of menace, with skeleton forms, and other more really fearful images, overspread and disfigured the walls.

from "The Pit and the Pendulum"
Edgar Allan Poe

EXERCISE 18
Responses will vary. Sample responses:
1. The bespectacled judge berated the accused.
2. The captive trembled with terror when he saw the dungeon.
3. An eerie darkness pervaded the cell.
4. Faceless guards tortured the ragged prisoner.
5. A dingy stone corridor wound to the torture chamber.
6. The inmate was exhausted and thirsty.
7. A sharp metallic blade waved menacingly back and forth above him.
8. The rats crawled on the man.
9. A sulfuric stench permeated the prison.
10. A thunderous blast echoed through the halls.

EXERCISE 18
Understanding Colorful Language

Revise each of the following sentences, using precise nouns, vivid verbs, and colorful modifiers.

1. The judge spoke to the man.
2. The man was afraid when he saw the cell.
3. Darkness filled the room.
4. Guards hurt the prisoner.
5. A stone hallway led to the chamber.
6. The man was tired and thirsty.
7. A blade waved back and forth above him.
8. The small animals were on the man.
9. A bad smell was in the prison.
10. A loud noise went through the halls.

EXERCISE 19
Using Colorful Language in Your Writing

Imagine that you will be hosting a bonfire for a group of sixth graders. Write the opening paragraph for a spooky story to tell around the campfire. In your opening paragraph, establish the setting and use a first-person narrator. Be sure to use precise nouns, vivid verbs, and colorful modifiers to create a suspenseful mood.

EXERCISE 19
Responses will vary. Students should use precise nouns, vivid verbs, and colorful modifiers in their paragraphs.

VARYING SENTENCE BEGINNINGS

Just as you probably wouldn't like to eat the same thing for breakfast every morning, your readers wouldn't enjoy reading the same sentence pattern in every paragraph. By **varying sentence beginnings**, you can give your sentences rhythm, create variety, and keep your readers engaged.

Sentences often begin with a subject. To vary sentence beginnings, start some sentences with a one-word modifier, a prepositional phrase, a participial phrase, or a subordinate clause.

EXAMPLES

subject	**She** sometimes watches the children play from the front porch.
one-word modifier	**Sometimes,** she watches the children play from the front porch.
prepositional phrase	**After breakfast** she reads the paper.
participial phrase	**Rummaging through the closet,** Sally searched for her old bowling ball.
subordinate clause	**Because a storm is threatening,** all games scheduled for today are cancelled.

Try It Yourself

EXERCISE 20

Identifying Varying Sentence Beginnings in Literature

Underline the varying sentence beginnings in the following passage. Read the passage aloud to hear the rhythm and interest that the variety creates.

> Before six o'clock that morning, Mr. Tanimoto started for Mr. Matsuo's house. There he found that their burden was to be a *tansu,* a large Japanese cabinet, full of clothing and household goods. The two men set out. The morning was perfectly clear and so warm that the day

CONTINUED

EXERCISE 20

Before six o'clock that morning, Mr. Tanimoto started for Mr. Matsuo's house. There he found that their burden was to be a *tansu,* a large Japanese cabinet, full of clothing and household goods. The two men set out. The morning was perfectly clear and so warm that the day promised to be uncomfortable. A few minutes after they started, the air raid siren went off—a minute-long blast that warned of approaching planes but indicated to the people of Hiroshima only a slight degree of danger, since it sounded every morning at this time, when an American weather plane came over.

Literature MODEL

promised to be uncomfortable. A few minutes after they started, the air raid siren went off—a minute-long blast that warned of approaching planes but indicated to the people of Hiroshima only a slight degree of danger, since it sounded every morning at this time, when an American weather plane came over.

from "A Noiseless Flash"
John Hersey

EXERCISE 21
Responses will vary. Sample response:
Keith is preparing to write a term paper for his history class. While in middle school, he first became interested in World War II history. To learn more about his topic, he checked out several books from the library. Keith narrowed his research focus to the Battle of Iwo Jima. While searching the Internet, he found a wealth of information about the battle. This information helped him complete an outline and determine the main idea for his paper. With a fast-approaching due date, Keith had to work evenings and weekends to complete the project on time.

EXERCISE 21
Understanding How to Vary Sentence Beginnings
Revise the following paragraph to vary sentence beginnings.

Keith is preparing to write a term paper for his history class. He first became interested in World War II history while in middle school. He checked out several books from the library in order to learn more about his topic. Keith narrowed his research focus to the Battle of Iwo Jima. He found a wealth of information about the battle while searching the Internet. This information helped him complete an outline and determine the main idea for his paper. Keith, with a fast-approaching due date, had to work evenings and weekends to complete the project on time.

EXERCISE 22
Responses will vary. Students should use varying sentence beginnings.

EXERCISE 22
Using Varying Sentence Beginnings in Your Writing
Select an event in modern history, such as the assassination of President John F. Kennedy, the fall of the Berlin Wall, or the collapse of the Twin Towers, and imagine you are a reporter on the scene of the event. Write the opening paragraph of your eyewitness news article, describing with sensory detail what you see. Vary sentence beginnings in the paragraph.

UNIT 19 REVIEW

TEST YOUR KNOWLEDGE

EXERCISE 1

Identifying Sentence Fragments and Run-on Sentences

Identify each of the following items as a complete sentence, a sentence fragment, or a run-on sentence. (10 points)

1. He attended the conference and addressed the delegates.
2. The speaker rambled.
3. A hot, stuffy, August afternoon.
4. Opposition members shifted in their seats they were already planning their responses.
5. Eyeing the clock on the wall.
6. Mercifully, the speaker brought his address to a close.
7. Before hearing any others, the delegates approved a recess they needed a break.
8. Realizing the time of day.
9. The door opened.
10. Shuffled out to the street.

EXERCISE 1
1. complete sentence
2. complete sentence
3. sentence fragment
4. run-on sentence
5. sentence fragment
6. complete sentence
7. run-on sentence
8. sentence fragment
9. complete sentence
10. sentence fragment

EXERCISE 2

Identifying Passive and Active Verbs

Identify each of the following sentences as having either a passive or an active verb. (10 points)

1. Emile excitedly raced toward the phone.
2. An invitation to a party was extended to her by Frank.
3. A light drizzle peppered the town.
4. A popular jazz band was hired by the hosts to perform at the event.
5. Guests were led into the ballroom by tuxedoed servants.
6. Frank cautiously led Emile on to the dance floor.
7. The caterers had provided a variety of culinary delights for the guests.

EXERCISE 2
1. active
2. passive
3. active
4. passive
5. passive
6. active
7. active
8. passive
9. active
10. passive

8. Food and drinks were enjoyed by all in attendance.
9. Outside, gaslights cast a pale glow into the misty night.
10. Automobiles were brought around by dutiful valets.

EXERCISE 3

Understanding Fragments, Run-ons, and Wordy Sentences

Correct the following fragments, run-ons, and wordy sentences. (10 points)

1. Across the dusty field.
2. The bank foreclosed on our farm we had three weeks to leave the property.
3. We decided to travel to California because of the fact that jobs were available there.
4. Loaded the old truck.
5. Members of the impoverished family remained optimistic though they had little money.
6. Desert heat oppressed the travelers they still maintained a steady pace across New Mexico and Arizona.
7. The steaming radiator under the hood.
8. Do you understand the plight of the Okies they struggled to find a better life in the midst of economic despair?
9. Received a rude awakening in California.
10. Until the end of the Great Depression.

EXERCISE 4

Combining and Expanding Sentences

Combine the following sentence pairs. (10 points)

1. Natalie studied all week for her calculus test. She did not feel adequately prepared.
2. The new quarterback ignored the sportswriters' criticisms. He also ignored the coach's insults.
3. Tamara delivered the pizza to the mansion. The pizza was pepperoni.
4. Nate was too tired to watch the entire baseball game. He went to bed after the seventh inning.

EXERCISE 3
Responses will vary. Sample responses:
1. Tumbleweeds blew across the dusty field.
2. The bank foreclosed on our farm; we had three weeks to leave the property.
3. We decided to travel to California because jobs were available there.
4. Three men loaded the old truck.
5. Members of the impoverished family remained optimistic.
6. Desert heat oppressed the travelers. They still maintained a steady pace across New Mexico and Arizona.
7. The steaming radiator under the hood was just one of many causes of concern.
8. Do you understand the plight of the Okies? They struggled to find a better life in the midst of economic despair.
9. Many travelers received a rude awakening in California.
10. They endured great hardships until the end of the Great Depression.

EXERCISE 4
Responses will vary. Sample responses:
1. Natalie studied all week for her calculus test, but she did not feel adequately prepared.
2. The new quarterback ignored the sports-writers' criticisms and the coach's insults.

5. The students went on a fall field trip. The field trip was to the arboretum.
6. Dr. Ackley is a brilliant scholar. He has no teaching skills.
7. Paul battled the rain for over 100 miles. The rain was relentless and driving.
8. The trainees must understand company policies before having any contact with customers. Company policies must be thoroughly understood.
9. Wake the dog and take him for a walk. He is sleeping in the basement.
10. I sat and looked upon the lake for three hours. The lake was peaceful.

EXERCISE 5

Understanding Parallelism

Correct any errors in parallelism in the following sentences. If a sentence contains no errors in parallelism, write *correct.* (10 points)

1. Geoff stretched his muscles, focused his thoughts, and moving into position at the starting blocks.
2. At dawn, the boy rode to the dropoff point, rolled the newspapers, and loaded them into his bag.
3. Her friend is arrogant, annoying, and never stops talking.
4. Tyler studied for hours in the library and passing all his finals.
5. Tomorrow Fran will drive to the courthouse and give her testimony to the judge.
6. Before he returns to the house Colin milks the cows and feeding the sheep.
7. The professor lectured, taught, and was inspiring the students.
8. Jana's cat jumped out of her lap, shot across the room, and hid under the bed.
9. Hannah climbed the tree, scouted the neighborhood, and plotting her strategy.
10. The bear gazed into the stream, eyed an unsuspecting salmon, raised its paw, and scooping the fish out of the water.

3. Tamara delivered the pepperoni pizza to the mansion.
4. Too tired to watch the entire baseball game, Nate went to bed after the seventh inning.
5. The students went on a fall field trip to the arboretum.
6. Dr. Ackley is a brilliant scholar, yet he has no teaching skills.
7. Paul battled the relentless and driving rain for over 100 miles.
8. The trainees must thoroughly understand company policies before having any contact with customers.
9. Wake the dog sleeping in the basement and take him for a walk.
10. I sat and looked upon the peaceful lake for three hours.

EXERCISE 5

Responses will vary. Sample responses:

1. Geoff stretched his muscles, focused his thoughts, and moved into position at the starting blocks.
2. correct
3. Her friend is arrogant, annoying, and loquacious.
4. Tyler studied for hours in the library and passed all his finals.
5. correct
6. Before he returns to the house Colin milks the cows and feeds the sheep.

7. The professor lectured, taught, and inspired the students.
8. correct
9. Hannah climbed the tree, scouted the neighborhood, and plotted her strategy.
10. The bear gazed into the stream, eyed an unsuspecting salmon, raised its paw, and scooped the fish out of the water.

EXERCISE 6
Responses will vary. All ten sentences should be active. Students should underline the active verb(s) in each sentence.

EXERCISE 7
Responses will vary. Students' paragraphs should include precise nouns, vivid verbs, and colorful modifiers describing a sports or entertainment figure.

EXERCISE 8
Responses will vary. Students' paragraphs should include varying sentence beginnings to describe a significant achievement.

EXERCISE 6

Using Active Sentences in Your Writing

Write ten active sentences in an introductory paragraph about an important political leader, past or present. The paragraph should serve as the introduction for an article in a magazine that covers politics. Underline the active verb(s) in each sentence. (10 points)

EXERCISE 7

Using Colorful Language in Your Writing

Write a paragraph for a school newspaper column describing a sports or entertainment figure who inspires young people in your community. In your paragraph, use precise nouns, vivid verbs, and colorful modifiers to describe this person and to tell what he or she does that inspires others. Try to make your word portrait as clear and interesting as possible. (20 points)

EXERCISE 8

Using Varying Sentence Beginnings in Your Writing

Write a paragraph for a chapter in an autobiography to be passed down in your family. In your paragraph, describe one of your first significant achievements. Vary sentence beginnings in your paragraph. (20 points)

UNIT 20 WRITER'S WORKSHOP
Building Effective Paragraphs

UNIT OVERVIEW

WRITER'S WORKSHOP: BUILDING EFFECTIVE PARAGRAPHS

THE PARAGRAPH

In Unit 19, you learned how words are organized to create effective sentences. In this unit, you'll learn how sentences work together to create effective paragraphs.

A **paragraph** is a carefully organized group of related sentences that focus on or develop one main idea. As the sentences within a paragraph are connected—like links in a chain—so are a series of paragraphs connected to create a longer piece of writing, whether an essay, short story, or research paper.

Most effective paragraphs have a **main idea** or point that is developed with **supporting details**—such as examples, sensory details, facts, anecdotes, and quotations. Paragraphs can serve different purposes—to narrate, to describe, to persuade, or to inform—but all effective paragraphs share two key elements: unity and a logical method of organization.

Read the following paragraph from *Narrative of the Life of Frederick Douglass, an American Slave, Written by Himself.* The paragraph is unified because every sentence contributes to the paragraph's main idea—that slaves sang to express their unhappiness and sorrow.

Literature MODEL

> I have often been utterly astonished, since I came to the north, to find persons who could speak of the singing, among slaves, as evidence of their contentment and happiness. It is impossible to conceive of a greater mistake. Slaves sing most when they are most unhappy. The songs of the slave represent the sorrows of his heart; and he is relieved by them, only as an aching heart is relieved by its tears. At least, such is my experience. I have often sung to drown my sorrow, but seldom to

CONTINUED

express my happiness. Crying for joy, and singing for joy, were alike uncommon to me while in the jaws of slavery. The singing of a man cast away upon a desolate island might be as appropriately considered as evidence of contentment and happiness, as the singing of a slave; the songs of the one and of the other are prompted by the same emotion.

from *Narrative of the Life of Frederick Douglass, an American Slave, Written by Himself*
Frederick Douglass

EXAMINING THE *Model*

Notice how the main idea of this paragraph is developed with specific details so that readers get a clear idea of how the singing of slaves is a manifestation of their discontentment.

Try It Yourself

EXERCISE 1

Identifying Main Ideas in Paragraphs in Literature

Read each of the following paragraphs, all of which are literary excerpts. Then tell what the main idea is of each paragraph.

1. This seemingly empty land is busy with inhabitants. Low to the ground are bullsnakes, rattlers, mice, gophers, moles, grouse, prairie chickens, and pheasant. Prairie dogs are more noticeable, as they denude the landscape with their villages. Badgers and skunk lumber busily through the grass. Jackrabbits, weasels, and foxes are quicker, but the great runners of the Plains are the coyote, antelope, and deer. Meadowlarks, killdeer, blackbirds, lark buntings, crows and seagulls dart above the fields, and a large variety of hawks, eagles and vultures glide above it all, hunting for prey.

from "Seeing"
Kathleen Norris

2. This [Hispaniola] was the first land in the New World to be destroyed and depopulated by the Christians, and here they began their subjection of the women and children, taking them away from the Indians to use them and ill use them, eating the food they provided with their

CONTINUED

Literature MODELS

EXERCISE 1

Responses will vary. Sample responses:

1. main idea: The Plains are alive with the activities of a plethora of creatures.
2. main idea: The Christians ruthlessly exploited the native inhabitants of Hispaniola.
3. main idea: Each person can and should create meaning in his or her life.
4. main idea: Slavery was based on a cruelly self-sustaining logic.

LANGUAGELINK
Print exercise worksheets or have students complete exercises online with the LanguageLINK CD.

sweat and toil. The Spaniards did not content themselves with what the Indians gave them of their own free will, according to their ability, which was always too little to satisfy enormous appetites, for a Christian eats and consumes in one day an amount of food that would suffice to feed three houses inhabited by ten Indians for one month. And they committed other acts of force and violence and oppression which made the Indians realize that these men had not come from Heaven. And some of the Indians concealed their foods while others concealed their wives and children and still others fled to the mountains to avoid the terrible transactions of the Christians.

from *The Very Brief Relation of the Devastation of the Indies*
Bartolomé de las Casas

3. We must learn to reawaken and keep ourselves awake, not by mechanical aids, but by an infinite expectation of the dawn, which does not forsake us in our soundest sleep. I know of no more encouraging fact than the unquestionable ability of man to elevate his life by a conscious endeavor. It is something to be able to paint a particular picture, or to carve a statue, and so to make a few objects beautiful; but it is far more glorious to carve and paint the very atmosphere and medium through which we look, which morally we can do. To affect the quality of the day, that is the highest of arts. Every man is tasked to make his life, even in its details, worthy of the contemplation of his most elevated and critical hour. If we refused, or rather used up, such paltry information as we get, the oracles would distinctly inform us how this might be done.

from *Walden*
Henry David Thoreau

4. We first debase the nature of man by making him a slave, and then very coolly tell him that he must always remain a slave because he does not know how to use freedom. We first crush people to the earth, and then claim the right of trampling on them forever, because they are prostrate. Truly, human selfishness never invented a rule which worked out so charmingly both ways!

from *An Appeal in Favor of That Class of Americans Called Africans*
Lydia Maria Child

EXERCISE 2

Understanding Main Ideas and Supporting Details in a Paragraph

Write two supporting sentences for each of the following main ideas. Make sure that each supporting sentence develops the main idea and that all the sentences are related.

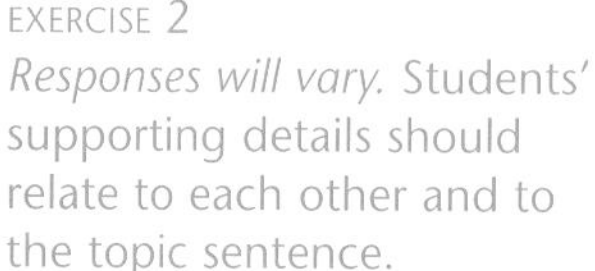
EXERCISE 2
Responses will vary. Students' supporting details should relate to each other and to the topic sentence.

1. The minimum wage should (should not) be raised.
2. ___ is one of our state's most important leaders.
3. Owning a car is a substantial responsibility.
4. ___ is a short story every high school junior should read.
5. Reinstating the draft will not improve our national security.

EXERCISE 3

Using Related Sentences to Develop a Main Idea in a Paragraph

For an entertainment column in your student newspaper, write a review of a movie, play, or television show. Write a clear topic sentence that explains why you recommend or do not recommend the subject of your review. Then supply details that support your recommendation.

EXERCISE 3
Responses will vary. Students' paragraphs should include a clear topic sentence and details that all work together to develop the main idea.

THE TOPIC SENTENCE

The main idea of a paragraph is often stated directly in a **topic sentence**. The topic sentence can be placed at the beginning, middle, or end of a paragraph. Usually the topic sentence appears at the beginning of a paragraph and is followed by one or more supporting sentences. In the following example, the first sentence introduces the subject. The second sentence states the main idea that will be developed in the passage.

Literature MODEL

> Another reason for my optimism is in American history. The exhilarating features of our history and culture have in the past been captured in the idea of "American Exceptionalism."
>
> from "Why I Am Optimistic about America"
> Daniel J. Boorstin

In many paragraphs, however, the main idea is implied rather than stated in a topic sentence. This means that the sentences in the paragraph work together to suggest—rather than directly state—the main idea.

Literature MODEL

> In those days, and later as a young man, I used to try to picture in my imagination the feelings and ambitions of a white boy with absolutely no limit placed upon his aspirations and activities. I used to envy the white boy who had no obstacles placed in the way of his becoming a Congressman, Governor, Bishop, or President by reason of the accident of his birth or race. I used to picture the way that I would act under such circumstances; how I would begin at the bottom and keep rising until I reached the highest round of success.
>
> from *Up from Slavery*
> Booker T. Washington

Notice how, in the excerpt from *Up from Slavery*, the implied main idea is that, in America, white people had far greater opportunities than African Americans. The author does not directly state the main idea; instead, he provides details and examples that lead readers to this conclusion.

When writing a topic sentence, consider the point you wish to make in your paragraph and the details that will support, explain, or describe your point. It might be helpful to think of your main idea as a problem or state it in the form of a question.

EXAMPLES
Wild animals are the unwanted guests of many homeowners.

How can I remove the possum family living in the hole underneath my garage?

The statement of the main idea as a problem or a question can lead you to refine the main idea into a specific topic sentence.

EXAMPLE
Like most urban homeowners, I have little interest in sharing my yard with a family of possums. Although wild animals are unlikely to respond to legal threats of eviction, there are several other strategies one may pursue to remove furry squatters from your backyard.

Try It Yourself

EXERCISE 4

Identifying Stated and Unstated Topic Sentences in Paragraphs in Literature

Read each of the following paragraphs, all of which are excerpts from literature. If the paragraph has a stated topic sentence, identify it. If the paragraph has an implied topic sentence or main idea, tell what it is in your own words.

Exercise 4

1. stated topic sentence: *What I must do, is all that concerns me, not what the people think.*
2. unstated topic sentence: African-American women are not given equal consideration.
3. stated topic sentence: *In your hands, my fellow citizens, more than mine, will rest the final success or failure of our course.*
4. unstated topic sentence: I arrived early for my interview to improve my chances of getting the job.

Literature MODELS

1. What I must do, is all that concerns me, not what the people think. This rule, equally arduous in actual and in intellectual life, may serve for the whole distinction between greatness and meanness. It is the harder, because you will always find those who think they know what is your duty better than you know it. It is easy in the world to live after the world's opinion; it is easy in solitude to live after our own; but the great man is he who in the midst of the crowd keeps with perfect sweetness the independence of solitude.

from "Self-Reliance"
by Ralph Waldo Emerson

2. That man over there says that women need to be helped into carriages, and lifted over ditches, and to have the best place everywhere. Nobody ever helps me into carriages, or over mud-puddles, or gives me any best place! And ain't I a woman? Look at me! Look at my arm! I have ploughed and planted, and gathered into barns, and no man could head me! And ain't I a woman? I could work as much and eat as much as a man—when I could get it—and bear the lash as well! And ain't I a woman? I have born thirteen children, and seen most all sold off to slavery, and when I cried out with my mother's grief, none but Jesus heard me! And ain't I a woman?

from "Ain't I a Woman?"
Sojourner Truth

3. In your hands, my fellow citizens, more than mine, will rest the final success or failure of our course. Since this country was founded, each generation of Americans has been summoned to give testimony to its national loyalty. The graves of young Americans who answered the call to service surround the globe.

from Inaugural Address
John F. Kennedy

CONTINUED

4. When I reached the door of Mr. Emerson's office it occurred to me that perhaps I should have waited until the business of the day was under way, but I disregarded the idea and went ahead. My being early would be, I hoped, an indication of both how badly I wanted work, and how promptly I would perform any assignment given me. Besides, wasn't there a saying that the first person of the day to enter a business would get a bargain? Or was that said only of Jewish business? I removed the letter from my brief case. Was Emerson a Christian name or a Jewish name?

from *Invisible Man*
Ralph Ellison

EXERCISE 5

Understanding Topic Sentences

Think about what each group of details has in common—what they are describing or explaining. Then write a topic sentence for each group.

EXAMPLE

Details: Before the onset of winter, make sure your car has adequate coolant protection in its radiator. Change the oil to an all-weather viscosity such as 10W-30 or 5W-30. Also, fill the washer fluid reservoir so you are not caught short when driving on slushy streets. Finally, to minimize starting problems, use the lowest octane fuel that your car will take.
(Topic sentence: *Automobile owners need to take several precautions to prepare their cars for the cold winter weather.*)

1. In August 1862, Robert E. Lee's Confederate Army defeated a Union force led by John Pope at the Second Battle of Bull Run. In September 1862, Union General George McClellan failed to defeat Lee's outnumbered army at Antietam. The following December, Lee routed General Burnside's troops at Fredericksburg. In May 1863, Lee's army emerged victorious at Chancellorsville over Union forces commanded by Joseph Hooker.

EXERCISE 5
Responses will vary. Sample responses:
1. In 1862 and 1863 Robert E. Lee bested several Union generals in a series of battles.
2. In the 1950s, the movement to repeal segregation made great progress.
3. The game of chess features several different pieces that vary in power.
4. Several U.S. presidents were successful wartime commanders.

2. In 1954, the Supreme Court ruled that segregated schools were unconstitutional. The following year, a boycott in Montgomery, Alabama, attracted national attention and ended the segregation of the city's buses. In 1957, President Eisenhower sent federal troops to Little Rock, Arkansas, to protect African Americans seeking to attend a formerly all-white school. In 1959, African-American students started a sit-in movement to desegregate lunch counters throughout the South.
3. On the chessboard, the King is the most important piece. The object of the game is to capture your opponent's King. The Queen, able to move in any direction, is the most powerful piece. The Rook is next in the chess power hierarchy. Bishops and Knights, though very different in their movements, are nearly equal in power. Finally, the Pawn is the least powerful of the combatants on a chessboard.
4. George Washington, the nation's first president, successfully commanded the Continental Army during the Revolutionary War. Andrew Jackson, who served in the White House from 1829 to 1837, led American troops to victory at the Battle of New Orleans, which concluded the War of 1812. Ulysses S. Grant was elected president three years after accepting Robert E. Lee's surrender at the end of the Civil War. Less than a decade after commanding the successful invasion of Normandy during World War II, Dwight Eisenhower became the president and commander in chief of all U.S. forces.

EXERCISE 6
Responses will vary. Students should write five topic sentences that express five of their main ideas.

EXERCISE 6
Using Topic Sentences

Write down at least five ideas about a historical event that you have studied or would like to learn more about. Review your list and write five effective topic sentences—one for each of five different paragraphs you might develop about the historical event.

CREATING UNITY IN A PARAGRAPH

In the novel *The Three Musketeers*, Alexandre Dumas wrote, "All for one, one for all, that is our motto." The motto of the Three Musketeers—good friends and renowned swordsmen—could very well serve as the motto for a group of sentences within a paragraph. To create **unity** in a paragraph, all the sentences within the paragraph work to support one main idea. You can create unity in a paragraph through the use of supporting details and transitions.

Supporting details include examples or illustrations, sensory details, anecdotes, facts, and quotations. By using supporting details that best develop or explain your main idea, you can help your reader understand what you are trying to say.

Each of the different kinds of details listed below supports the following topic sentence: *In the 1730s and 1740s, a Great Awakening brought a spirit of religious fervor to the American colonies.* Of course, depending on the purpose of your paragraph or longer piece of writing, one kind of supporting detail may be more appropriate or effective than another.

EXAMPLES

example/illustration	One English preacher, George Whitfield, arrived in the colonies in 1739 and electrified crowds from New England to Georgia with his powerful sermons.
sensory details	The preacher's booming voice echoed across the field where a great assembly had gathered. Throughout the crowd, wails of repentant grief periodically pierced the air. Three women in drab-colored dresses arose and stretched their hands up to the sky.
anecdote	One preacher warned his congregation that they were like a spider in God's hand being held above a fire.

CONTINUED

Sensory details that convey how things look, taste, smell, feel, and sound can make a description come alive for your readers.

tip

Remember to use quotation marks when including someone else's exact words.

fact	Jonathon Edwards served as president of the College of New Jersey, present-day Princeton University.
quotation	Jonathon Edwards warned, "The bow of God's wrath is bent, and the arrow made ready on the string, and justice bends the arrow at your heart, and strains the bow, and it is nothing but the mere pleasure of God, and that of an angry God, without any promise or obligation at all, that keeps the arrow from being made drunk with your blood."

A **transition** is a word or phrase that is used to connect ideas and to show relationships between them. Transitions can show time/chronological order, place/spatial order, cause and effect order, comparison and contrast order, and order of importance. The following examples include some of the more common transitions.

EXAMPLES

time/chronological order	first, next, before, after, then, later, finally
place/spatial order	above, behind, next to, on top of, near, to the left
cause and effect	therefore, because, since, as a result, consequently
comparison and contrast	on the other hand, similarly, in contrast
order of importance	of least importance, more important, most importantly

Try It Yourself

EXERCISE 7
Identifying Supporting Details and Transitions in Literature

Identify the topic sentence or the main idea in the following paragraph. Then identify one example of sensory detail, one example of illustration, and one example of transition.

> Here, the eye learns to appreciate slight variations, the possibilities inherent in emptiness. It sees that the emptiness is full of small things, like grasshoppers in their samurai armor clicking and jumping as you pass. This empty land is full of grasses: sedges, switch grass, needlegrass, wheatgrass. Brome can grow waist-high by early summer. Fields of wheat, rye, oats, barley, flax, alfalfa. Acres of sunflowers brighten the land in summer, their heads alert, expectant. By fall they droop like sad children, waiting patiently for the first frost and harvest.
>
> from "Seeing"
> Kathleen Norris

EXERCISE 7
Responses will vary. Sample responses:
1. Main idea: The Dakota plains are alive with details that often go unnoticed.

Literature MODEL

2. Sensory detail: *Acres of sunflowers brighten the land in summer, their heads alert, expectant.*
3. Illustration: *It sees that the emptiness is full of small things, like grasshoppers in their samurai armor clicking and jumping as you pass.*
4. Transitions: *By fall. . . .*

EXERCISE 8
Understanding How to Create Unity in a Paragraph

Follow the directions to provide supporting details and/or transitions for each topic sentence.

EXAMPLE
Topic sentence: Donating blood is one way a person can give back to the community.
(one example, one cause and effect transition)
(Donors recline back in a chair and squeeze a rubber ball. Although donating blood involves being stuck with a needle, the pain is brief and the process is uncomplicated.)

1. The sudden blizzard surprised even the weather forecasters. (one sensory detail, one place/spatial transition)

EXERCISE 8
Responses will vary. Students should choose details and transitions that follow the directions and that support the topic sentence effectively.

2. College athletics are more entertaining than professional sports. (one example/illustration, one comparison and contrast transition)
3. The forest near my uncle's house inspired many childhood adventures. (one example/illustration, one order of importance transition)
4. Holding a part-time job in high school requires discipline and responsibility. (one quotation, one time/chronological order transition)

EXERCISE 9
Responses will vary. Students should further develop one of the topic sentences they worked with in Exercise 8. Check to be sure that they have used a minimum of three different kinds of supporting details and two different transitions.

EXERCISE 9

Using Supporting Details and Transitions in Your Writing
Choose one of the topic sentences in Exercise 8 and develop it by adding more supporting details and transitions. Use at least three different kinds of supporting details and at least two different transitions in your paragraph.

TYPES OF PARAGRAPHS

Paragraphs can serve different purposes—to describe, to narrate, to persuade, or to inform. If you wanted to introduce a character, for example, you could write a descriptive paragraph and create a picture in your reader's mind of the character's physical features and personality. If you wanted to tell about a series of events, you could write a narrative paragraph to relate the events in the order in which they happened.

Type of Paragraph	Purpose
descriptive	to describe, to set a scene, to create a mood, to appeal to the readers' senses
narrative	to tell a story, to relate a series of events, to tell about people's lives
informative	to inform, to present or explain an idea, to explain a process
persuasive	to persuade, to present an argument, to suggest a course of action

Try It Yourself

EXERCISE 10

Identifying Types of Paragraphs in Literature

Identify each of the following excerpts as either a descriptive, narrative, persuasive, or informative paragraph.

EXERCISE 10
1. informative
2. narrative
3. descriptive
4. persuasive

Literature MODELS

1. The "first" shopping center in the United States is generally agreed to be Country Club Plaza in Kansas City, built in the twenties. There were some other earlier centers, notably Edward H. Bouton's 1907 Roland Park in Baltimore, Hugh Prather's 1931 Highland Park Shopping Village in Dallas, and Hugh Potter's 1937 River Oaks in Houston, but the developer of Country Club Plaza, J. C. Nichols, is referred to with ritual frequency in the literature of shopping centers, usually as "pioneering J. C. Nichols" or "J. C. Nichols, father of the center as we know it."

   from "On the Mall"
   Joan Didion

2. As Mrs. Nakamura stood watching her neighbor, everything flashed whiter than any white she had ever seen. She did not notice what happened to the man next door; the reflex of a mother set her in motion toward her children. She had taken a single step (the house was 1,350 yards, or three-quarters of a mile, from the center of the explosion) when something picked her up and she seemed to fly into the next room over the raised sleeping platform, pursued by parts of her house.

   from "A Noiseless Flash"
   John Hersey

3. My grandmother was nearly white as a Negro can get without being white, which means that she was white. The sagging flesh of her face quivered; her eyes, large, dark, deep-set, wide apart, glared at me. Her lips narrowed to a line. Her high forehead wrinkled. When she was angry her eyelids drooped halfway down over her pupils, giving her a baleful aspect.

   from *Black Boy*
   Richard Wright

CONTINUED

4. No man, who seriously considers what human nature is, and what it was made for, can think of setting up a claim to a fellow-creature. What! own a spiritual being, a being made to know and adore God, and who is to outlive the sun and the stars? What! chain to our lowest uses a being made for truth and virtue? convert into a brute instrument that intelligent nature, on which the idea of Duty has dawned, and which is a nobler type of God than all outward creation! Should we not deem it a wrong which no punishment could expiate, were one of our children seized as property, and driven by the ship to toil? And shall God's child, dearer to him than an only son to a human parent, be thus degraded?

from *Slavery*
William Ellery Channing

EXERCISE 11
Responses will vary. Students should analyze the text from the newspaper articles, identify the different kinds of paragraphs included, and identify the purpose of each paragraph. Students should also identify one supporting detail that develops, explains, or describes the main idea in each paragraph.

EXERCISE 11
Understanding Different Types of Paragraphs
Look through a section of the newspaper. Identify paragraphs that illustrate the four different purposes. For each paragraph, identify one supporting detail that develops, explains, illustrates, or describes the main idea.

EXERCISE 12
Responses will vary. Students should support their main idea or topic sentence with appropriate details. Students should compare and contrast the two paragraphs and the differences among the supporting details.

EXERCISE 12
Using Different Types of Paragraphs in Your Writing
Choose an object in your house. Write an informative, descriptive, narrative, or persuasive paragraph about the object. Then use the same object as a prompt to write a second paragraph, using one of the other three types. After writing the two paragraphs, compare with a classmate the main ideas and supporting details you used in each. How do they differ?

METHODS OF ORGANIZATION

As you've learned, supporting details and transitions develop and explain the main idea or topic sentence in a paragraph. Those same elements can be organized in different ways to show the relationships or connections among ideas. These different methods, or patterns, of organization include time/chronological order, place/spatial order, order of importance, comparison and contrast order, and cause and effect order.

Chronological Order

Events are arranged in the time order in which they happened. This method of organization is used to tell a story, to present a series of events, or to describe the steps in a process. Transition words and phrases, such as *at the beginning*, *next*, *then*, and *finally*, are used to show the order of events. In the following passage, the chronological order transitions are underlined.

Literature MODEL

> Very suddenly there came back to my soul motion and sound—the tumultuous motion of the heart, and, in my ears, the sound of its beating. Then a pause in which all is blank. Then again sound, and motion, and touch—a tingling sensation pervading my frame. Then the mere consciousness of existence, without thought—a condition which lasted long. Then, very suddenly, *thought*, and shuddering terror, and earnest endeavor to comprehend my true state. Then a strong desire to lapse into insensibility. Then a rushing revival of soul and a successful effort to move. And now a full memory of the trial, of the judges, of the sable draperies, of the sentence, of the sickness, of the swoon. Then entire forgetfulness of all that followed; of all that a later day and much earnestness of endeavor have enabled me vaguely to recall.
>
> from "The Pit and the Pendulum"
> Edgar Allan Poe

Spatial Order

Details are described in the order of their location in space, such as from back to front, left to right, or top to bottom. Transition words and phrases such as *next to*, *beside*, *above*, *below*, and *beyond* are used to connect the descriptions. This method of organization is used to set a scene, to establish a location, and to place the reader's mind in a specific setting. In the following passage, spatial organization transitions are underlined.

An appalling splash within two yards of him was followed by a loud, rushing sound, *diminuendo*, which seemed to travel back through the air to the fort and died in an explosion which stirred the very river to its deeps! A rising sheet of water curved over him, fell down upon him, blinded him, strangled him! The cannon had taken a hand in the game. As he shook his head free from the commotion of the smitten water he heard the deflected shot humming through the air ahead, and in an instant it was cracking and smashing the branches in the forest beyond.

from "An Occurrence at Owl Creek Bridge"
Ambrose Bierce

Order of Importance

Ideas are organized from least important to most important or from most important to least important. Transition words and phrases such as *first*, *best*, *worst*, *more/most important*, *less/least important*, and *to a greater/lesser degree* are used to show the ranking among the ideas, people, places, objects, and events being discussed. The order of importance transitions are underlined in the following example.

EXAMPLE
In the opening of a chess game, development in the center is the most important objective. A player's first concern should be to move pawns and minor pieces to control the center squares. Advancing the Queen is less important during the opening and should be postponed until the Knights and Bishops are developed. After the minor pieces and pawns are in position, the next step is to castle the King to safety. The final goal in the opening is to move the Rooks to cover the open files.

Comparison and Contrast Order

The similarities and differences between two subjects are organized in one of two ways. In the first method, the characteristics of one subject are presented, followed by the characteristics of the second subject. In the second method, both subjects are compared and contrasted characteristic by characteristic. Transition words and phrases such as *also*, *like*, *both*, *similarly*, and *in the same way* show similarities. Transition words and phrases such as *in contrast*, *however*, *but*, *yet*, and *on the other hand* show differences. In the following excerpt, comparison and contrast transitions are underlined.

Literature MODEL

We have been seduced by the rise of our country as a "superpower." For while power is quantitative, the uniqueness of the United States is not merely quantitative. We have suffered, too, from the consequences of our freedom. Totalitarian societies exaggerate their virtues. But free societies like ours somehow seize the temptation to exaggerate their vices. The negativism of our press and television reporting are, of course, the best evidence of our freedom to scrutinize ourselves. Far better this than the chauvinism of self-righteousness which has been the death of totalitarian empires in our time.

from "Why I Am Optimistic about America"
Daniel J. Boorstin

Cause and Effect Order

The causes and effects of events are organized in one of two ways to show the relationships between events and their results. In the first method, one or more causes are stated in the topic sentence, then details about the effects are presented. In the second method, one or more effects are presented followed by a discussion of the cause or causes of those effects. Transition words and phrases such as *one cause*, *another effect*, *as a result*, *consequently*, *therefore*, *since*, *because*, and *if . . . then* show cause and effect.

Literature MODEL

My own line of reasoning is to myself as straight and clear as a ray of light. Not all the treasures of the world, so far as I believe, could have induced me to support an offensive war, for I think it murder; but if a thief breaks into my house, burns and destroys my property, and kills or threatens to kill me, or those that are in it, and to "bind me in all cases whatsoever" to his absolute will, am I to suffer it? What signifies it to me, whether he who does it is a king or a common man; my countryman or not my countryman; whether it be done by an individual villain, or an army of them? If we reason to the root of things we shall find no difference; neither can any just cause be assigned why we should punish in the one case and pardon in the other. Let them call me rebel, and welcome, I feel no concern from it; but I should suffer the misery of devils were I to make a whore of my soul by swearing allegiance to one whose character is that of a sottish, stupid, stubborn, worthless, brutish man. I conceive likewise a horrid idea in receiving mercy from a being, who at the last day shall be shrieking to the rocks and mountains to cover him, and fleeing with terror from the orphan, the widow, and the slain of America.

from *Crisis, No. 1*
Thomas Paine

Problem and Solution Order

In this method of organization, a problem is stated and then a solution is explained. Problem and solution order is often used in a piece of writing that calls for specific action or promotes change.

Literature
MODEL

> And what have we to oppose them [the British]? Shall we try argument? Sir, we have been trying that for the last ten years. Have we anything new to offer upon the subject? Nothing. We have held the subject up in every light of which it is capable; but it has been all in vain. Shall we resort to entreaty and humble supplication? What terms shall we find which have not been already exhausted? Let us not, I beseech you, sir, deceive ourselves longer. Sir, we have done everything that could be done to avert the storm which is now coming on. We have petitioned; we have remonstrated; we have supplicated; we have prostrated ourselves before the throne, and have implored its interposition to arrest the tyrannical hands of the ministry and Parliament. Our petitions have been slighted; our remonstrances have produced additional violence and insult; our supplications have been disregarded; and we have been spurned with contempt from the foot of the throne! In vain, after these things, may we indulge the fond hope of peace and reconciliation. There is no longer any room for hope. If we wish to be free, if we mean to preserve inviolate those inestimable privileges for which we have been so long contending, if we mean not basely to abandon the noble struggle in which we have been so long engaged, and which we have pledged ourselves never to abandon until the glorious object of our contest shall be obtained—we must fight! I repeat it, sir, we must fight! An appeal to arms and to the God of Hosts is all that is left us!
>
> from Speech in the Virginia Convention
> Patrick Henry

Deductive Organization

A deductive argument begins with a general statement, presents a specific situation illustrating that statement, and then draws a specific conclusion about that situation. Carefully state your argument; a deductive argument must be correctly structured to be valid. In other words, the conclusion must follow logically from the argument's premise.

EXAMPLE

general statement	A state law that violates natural law can only be enforced within that state's borders.
specific premise	State laws enforcing slavery are in violation of natural law.
specific conclusion	A slave becomes free after leaving a state that upholds slavery for one that does not.

Literature MODEL

The law of the Creator, which invests every human being with an inalienable title to freedom, cannot be repealed by any inferior law, which asserts that man is property. Such a law may be enforced by power; but the exercise of the power must be confined within the jurisdiction of the state, which establishes the law. It cannot be enforced—it can have no operation whatever—in any other jurisdiction. The very moment a slave passes beyond the jurisdiction of the state, in which he is held as such, he ceases to be a slave; not because any law or regulation of the state which he enters confers freedom upon him, but because he continues to be a man and leaves behind him the law of force, which made him a slave.

from *Argument before the Supreme Court in the Case of Wharton Jones v. John Vanzandt, 1846*
Salmon P. Chase

Inductive Organization

Whereas a deductive argument proceeds from the general to the specific, an inductive argument is organized from the specific to the general. An inductive argument begins with specific facts and examples. Use the inductive method to lead your readers to a general conclusion drawn from the facts and examples you've presented.

EXAMPLE

specific facts

fact 1 Booker T. Washington founded the Tuskegee Institute.

fact 2 Washington's "Atlanta Compromise" was approved by radicals for being a complete surrender of demands for political and social equality.

fact 3 Washington's "Atlanta Compromise" was approved by conservatives for providing a working basis for mutual understanding.

general conclusion

Booker T. Washington is one of the most distinguished Southerners since Jefferson Davis.

Literature MODEL

To gain the sympathy and cooperation of the various elements comprising the white South was Mr. Washington's first task; and this, at the time Tuskegee was founded, seemed, for a black man, well-nigh impossible. And yet ten years later it was done in the word spoken at Atlanta: "In all things purely social we can be as separate as the five fingers, and yet one as the hand in all things essential to mutual progress." This "Atlanta Compromise" is by all odds the most notable thing in Mr. Washington's career. The South interpreted it in different ways: the radicals received it as a complete surrender of the demand for civil and political equality; the conservatives, as a generously conceived working basis for mutual

CONTINUED

understanding. So both approved it, and today its author is certainly the most distinguished Southerner since Jefferson Davis, and the one with the largest personal following.

from *The Souls of Black Folk*
W. E. B. Du Bois

Try It Yourself

EXERCISE 13

EXERCISE 13
1. cause and effect order—*because, Moreover, since*

2. chronological order—*then, for a minute, then*
3. order of importance—*interesting, more important still*
4. spatial order—*center, around, along, onto, around*
5. comparison and contrast order—*compared with, than*

Identifying Methods of Organization in Literature

Identify the method of organization used in each of the following literature excerpts. List the transitions that emphasize the method of organization being used.

1. He remarked in passing that the function of the marriage broker was ancient and honorable, highly approved in the Jewish community, because it made practical the necessary without hindering joy. Moreover, his own parents had been brought together by a matchmaker. They had made, if not a financially profitable marriage—since neither had possessed any worldly goods to speak of—at least a successful one in the sense of their everlasting devotion to each other. Salzman listened in embarrassed surprise, sensing a sort of apology. Later, however, he experienced a glow of pride in his work, an emotion that had left him years ago, and he heartily approved of Finkle.

from "The Magic Barrel"
Bernard Malamud

2. And then a curious thing happened. George stepped aside to let Jonquil pass, but instead of going through she stood still and stared at him for a minute. It was not so much the look, which was not a smile, as it was the moment of silence. They saw each other's eyes, and both

CONTINUED

took a short, faintly accelerated breath, and then they went on into the second garden. That was all.

from "The Sensible Thing"
F. Scott Fitzgerald

3. The interesting fact that there are *five hundred thousand* free persons of color, one half of whom might peruse, and the whole benefitted by the publication of the Journal; that no publication, as yet, has been devoted exclusively to their improvement—that many selections from approved standard authors, which are within the reach of few, may occasionally be made—and more important still, that this large body of our citizens have no public channel—all serve to prove the real necessity, at present, for the appearance of the FREEDOM'S JOURNAL.

from *Freedom Journal* March 16, 1827
John B. Russwurm

4. The road narrows until it is hardly more than a lane. Grass has begun to grow in its center. As the river twists and turns, so does the road twist and turn, curving around hills that consist of enormous boulders, bare of all trees and plants, covered only in patches by a dull, brown lichen that is unfamiliar to you. Along one stretch rocks of varying sizes have fallen down onto the road, so that you are forced to drive around them with great caution.

from "Journey"
Joyce Carol Oates

5. Some are dinning in our ears that we Americans, and moderns generally, are intellectual dwarfs compared with the ancients, or even the Elizabethan men. But what is that to the purpose? A living dog is better than a dead

CONTINUED

lion. Shall a man go and hang himself because he belongs to the race of pygmies, and not be the biggest pygmy that he can? Let every one mind his own business, and endeavor to be what he was made.

from *Walden*
Henry David Thoreau

EXERCISE 14
Responses will vary. Sample responses:
1. chronological order
2. comparison and contrast order or order of importance
3. spatial order
4. chronological order, order of importance, or cause and effect order
5. comparison and contrast order
6. chronological order
7. order of importance
8. cause and effect order or chronological order
9. spatial order
10. inductive order

EXERCISE 14

Understanding Methods of Organization

Tell which method of organization you think would be best for each of the following writing purposes.

1. to explain how to fly a kite
2. to present three different strategies for solving a national problem
3. to describe a busy train station
4. to explain the president's latest economic initiative
5. to compare the original version of a movie with a remake
6. to explain how to vaccinate cattle
7. to defend your position on a controversial issue
8. to evaluate weekly progress toward a long-term goal
9. to describe a defensive alignment in football
10. to explain the need for stricter gun laws

EXERCISE 15
Responses will vary. After suitably narrowing the topic, students should use one of the methods of organization effectively in their paragraph.

EXERCISE 15

Using Different Methods of Organization in Your Writing

Select one of the general topics from Exercise 14 and narrow and focus it. Then write a paragraph using the method of organization that you think will best present the subject matter.

UNIT 20 REVIEW

TEST YOUR KNOWLEDGE

EXERCISE 1

Identifying the Main Idea in a Paragraph

Identify the stated or unstated main idea in each of the following paragraphs, all of which are literary excerpts. If the main idea is stated in a topic sentence, identify the topic sentence. If the main idea is unstated, write the main idea in your own words. (20 points)

1. In point of fact, Poker Flat was "after somebody." It had lately suffered the loss of several thousand dollars, two valuable horses, and a prominent citizen. It was experiencing a spasm of virtuous reaction, quite as lawless and ungovernable as any of the acts that had provoked it. A secret committee had determined to rid the town of all improper persons. This was done permanently in regard of two men who were then hanging from the boughs of a sycamore in the gulch, and temporarily in the banishment of certain other objectionable characters. I regret to say that some of these were ladies. It is but due to the sex, however, to state that their impropriety was professional, and it was only in such easily established standards of evil that Poker Flat ventured to sit in judgment.

from "The Outcasts of Poker Flat"
Bret Harte

2. The tyranny exercised by the Spaniards against the Indians in the work of pearl fishing is one of the most cruel that can be imagined. There is no life as infernal and desperate in this century that can be compared with it, although the mining of gold is a dangerous and burdensome way of life. The pearl fishers dive into the

CONTINUED

EXERCISE 1

Responses for unstated main ideas will vary. Sample responses are provided.

1. Topic sentence(s): *It was experiencing a spasm of virtuous reaction, quite as lawless and ungovernable as any of the acts that had provoked it. A secret committee had determined to rid the town of all improper persons.*
2. Topic sentence: *The tyranny exercised by the Spaniards against the Indians in the work of pearl fishing is one of the most cruel that can be imagined.*
3. Unstated main idea: I will someday tell my daughter the truth about what I did during the war.
4. Unstated main idea: If you continue to deny women power, someday it will come back to haunt you.

Literature MODELS

sea at a depth of five fathoms, and do this from sunrise to sunset, and remain for as many minutes without breathing, tearing the oysters out of their rocky beds where the pearls are formed. They come to the surface with a netted bag of these oysters where a Spanish torturer is waiting in a canoe or skiff, and if the pearl diver shows signs of wanting to rest, he is showered with blows, his hair is pulled, and he is thrown back into the water, obliged to continue the hard work of tearing out the oysters and bringing them again to the surface.

from *The Very Brief Relation of the Devastation of the Indies*
Bartolomé de las Casas

3. When she was nine, my daughter Kathleen asked if I had ever killed anyone. She knew about the war; she knew I'd been a soldier. "You keep writing these war stories," she said, "so I guess you must've killed somebody." It was a difficult moment, but I did what seemed right, which was to say, "Of course not," and then to take her onto my lap and hold her for a while. Someday, I hope, she'll ask again. But here I want to pretend she's a grown-up. I want to tell her exactly what happened, or what I remember happening, and then I want to say to her that as a little girl she was absolutely right. This is why I keep writing war stories:

from "Ambush"
Tim O'Brien

CONTINUED

4. I cannot say that I think you very generous to the ladies, for whilst you are proclaiming peace and good will to men, emancipating all nations, you insist upon retaining an absolute power over wives. But you must remember that arbitrary power is like most other things which are very hard, very liable to be broken—and notwithstanding all your wise laws and maxims, we have it in our power not only to free ourselves but to subdue our masters and without violence throw both your natural and legal authority at our feet—

from Letter to John Adams, May 7, 1776
Abigail Adams

EXERCISE 2
1. unity
2. the details and examples the writer gives
3. Transitions
4. Accept any reasonable transition for each method of organization listed in number 10 below.
5. false
6. main idea
7. topic sentence
8. Accept any two of the following answers: example/illustration, sensory details, anecdote, fact, quotation
9. to inform, to describe, to narrate, to persuade
10. Accept any three of the following answers: time/chronological, place/spatial, order of importance, comparison and contrast, cause and effect

EXERCISE 2

Understanding the Paragraph

Complete each of the following sentences, or answer the questions. (20 points)

1. A paragraph has ______________ when all the sentences relate to the topic sentence.
2. To determine the unstated topic sentence, draw a conclusion about ______________
3. ______________ show the relationships between ideas.
4. List one word or phrase that links ideas for each method of organization.
5. True or false? Every paragraph must have a topic sentence.
6. To work effectively, a paragraph should be built around a(n) ______________.
7. A(n) ______________ often contains the main idea of a paragraph.
8. What are two ways that writers can support their main ideas? ______________
9. What are the four most common purposes for paragraphs? ______________
10. Name three methods of organizing paragraphs.

    ____

EXERCISE 3
Responses will vary.
Sample responses:
1. The Confederate Army is surrendering to Union forces today.
2. The mall is opening for business.
3. It is very easy for a swimmer to receive a painful sunburn.
4. Abraham Lincoln successfully led the country through four years of crisis.
5. Contrary to myth, Abner Doubleday did not invent the game of baseball.
6. Union Army losses continued to mount. Northern public tired of war. Stalemate existed on major fronts.
7. World Series and playoffs broadcast on primetime television. Baseball games receive heavy media attention. Several teams draw more than three million fans each year.
8. Large crowds in stores and malls. Long lines at the checkouts. Usually tired and full after eating too much on Thanksgiving.

EXERCISE 3

Understanding Topic Sentences and Supporting Details

For items 1–5, write a topic sentence for each group of supporting details. For items 6–10 write two supporting details for each topic sentence. (20 points)

1. The gray-clad soldiers sit around the fires, most staring vacantly at the flames or off into the distance. They have had little to eat for the past month. The low thunder of far-off cannons barely registers in their ears. News of Lee's meeting with Grant has already spread throughout the camp. The somber mood hangs over the men like a dark cloud.
2. Lights clicked on, illuminating shops up and down the long corridor. Gates slowly rose and disappeared. A large center fountain sprang to life. Security personnel and sales clerks moved into place. Finally, doors to the massive building were unlocked. A line of shoppers slithered into the main corridor before fragmenting in different directions.
3. The sun smiles deceptively upon swimmers. The cool water offsets the heat of the powerful rays. It takes less than an hour for a painful burn to occur. A person does not feel the burn while it is happening. Swimmers should never spend time in the sun without sunscreen.
4. Abraham Lincoln was elected president in 1860. The slavery issue divided the nation. Eleven states left the Union in the months following the election. The Confederate states mobilized to resist any attempts to bring them back into the Union. Heavy casualties and a series of defeats weakened support for the war in the North. In 1865, after four years of bitter war, the conflict ended with the Union preserved.

5. Abner Doubleday was not in Cooperstown, New York, in 1839. He was at West Point that year. American boys played a variety of bat and ball games long before 1839. These games, including "rounders," were English in origin. Rounders and baseball had nearly identical rules at early points in their evolution. In the early 1900s, baseball officials wanted to establish the game's American origins.
6. In the summer of 1864, the reelection of Abraham Lincoln did not look likely.
7. Baseball is still popular in America today.
8. I do not like to go shopping the day after Thanksgiving.
9. The army of northern Virginia fought courageously during the Civil War.
10. The sun poses a greater health risk for humans today than it did one hundred years ago.

9. Despite being outnumbered, the army won a series of battles against the Army of the Potomac. It held out for four years in adverse conditions. Many men wanted to continue the fight even after Lee decided to surrender.

10. The ozone layer is being depleted. More ultraviolet radiation reaches the planet. People now have less protection from harmful UV rays.

EXERCISE 4

Understanding Different Kinds of Supporting Details

For each kind of supporting detail, write a sentence that supports the topic sentence: Education doesn't come by bumping your head against the schoolhouse. (20 points)

1. example/illustration
2. sensory details
3. anecdote
4. fact
5. quotation

EXERCISE 4

Responses will vary. Check students' details for their applicability to the topic sentence.

EXERCISE 5

Using Different Types of Paragraphs and Methods of Organization in Your Writing

EXERCISE 5
Responses will vary. Students' editorials should reflect their understanding of different types of unified paragraphs, different types of details, the need for a strong topic sentence, and methods of organization and the use of transitions.

Imagine that you are writing a letter to the editor to support a referendum that would increase funding for your school district. Using the quotation in Exercise 4 as a starting point, write a paragraph in which you explain what it means and how it's relevant to you and your experience. Begin by writing a topic sentence that states your position on the quotation. Then choose a purpose for writing, a method of organization, and several kinds of details to make your point. For example, you might want to entertain your audience with a chronologically organized anecdote about a humorous experience, or you might want to inform your readers with an explanation organized in cause and effect order. Be sure to use transitions to connect ideas, and check your paragraph for unity after you have completed your draft. (20 points)

UNIT 21 THE WRITING PROCESS

UNIT OVERVIEW

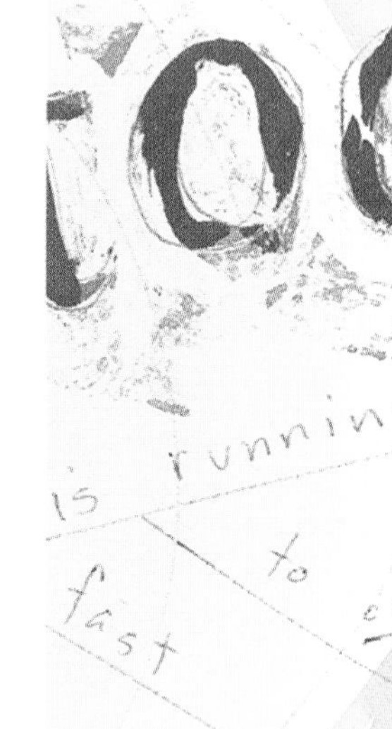

THE WRITING PROCESS

Writing tip

Before reading this unit, you may want to review the sections "Types of Paragraphs" and "Methods of Organization" in Unit 20 on pages 540–552.

THE SIX STAGES IN THE WRITING PROCESS

How do you begin to tackle a new writing project? Do you bravely dive in with both hands on the keyboard? Do you grab pen and paper and start jotting down ideas? Or, do you let an idea simmer for a few days? All writers—whether they are beginning writers, famous published writers, or somewhere in between—go through a process that leads to a complete piece of writing. The specifics of each writer's process may be unique, but for every writer, writing is a series of steps or stages. In this unit you'll learn about the six stages in the writing process and about strategies and ideas for putting them into action.

Quotables

"When you first start writing—and I think it's true for a lot of beginning writers—you're scared to death that if you don't get that sentence right that minute it's never going to show up again. And it isn't. But it doesn't matter—another one will, and it'll probably be better."
—Toni Morrison

SIX STAGES IN THE WRITING PROCESS

Stage	Tasks
1. Prewriting	Plan your writing; choose a topic, audience, purpose, and form; gather ideas; and arrange them logically.
2. Drafting	Get your ideas down on paper.
3. Self- and Peer Evaluation	Evaluate, or judge, the writing piece and suggest ways to improve it. Judging your own writing is called self-evaluation. Judging a classmate's writing is called peer evaluation.
4. Revising and Proofreading	Work to improve the content, organization, and expression of your ideas. Check your writing for errors in spelling, grammar, capitalization, and punctuation. Correct these errors, make a final copy of your paper, and proofread it again.
5. Publishing and Presenting	Share your work with an audience.
6. Reflecting	Think through the writing process to determine what you learned as a writer, what you accomplished, and what you would like to strengthen the next time you write.

Writers move through these stages when creating a work, but writing is also a continuing cycle. For example, you may need to return to a previous stage before proceeding to the next one. Returning to a previous stage will often strengthen your final work. Understanding the six stages of the writing process—from prewriting to reflecting—will help you to become a better writer.

---

1 PREWRITING

Think of prewriting—the first step in the writing process—as the stage that helps you answer the question, "Where do I begin?" During the prewriting stage, you identify your topic, purpose, audience, and mode of writing.

Identifying and Focusing a Topic

In school, writing topics are often assigned to you, or you may be instructed to choose your own topic. When you're unsure of what to write about, here are some techniques you can use to find an interesting topic.

WAYS TO FIND A WRITING TOPIC	
Check your journal	Search through your journal for ideas that you jotted down in the past. Many professional writers get their ideas from their journals.
Think about your experiences	Think about people, places, or events that affected you strongly. Recall experiences that taught you important lessons or that you felt strongly about.
Look at reference works	Reference works include printed or computerized dictionaries, atlases, almanacs, and encyclopedias.
Browse in a library	Libraries are treasure houses of information and ideas. Simply looking around in the stacks of a library can suggest good writing ideas.

Writing tip

Start off your writing with the best advantage of all—a topic that interests you. Even if the topic has been assigned to you, identify a facet or angle of the topic that truly captures your interest. Without your interest to fuel the process, the final product will sound flat and uninspired.

EXAMPLES
writing topic ideas
nutrition and fitness
European environmentalists
polar ice caps
handheld communication devices
post-Reconstruction race relations
mountain climbers
training German Shepherds
women aviators

Often a new writing topic is too general and broad or becomes too big to handle—especially if you're excited about the topic and gushing with ideas about what you'd like to say. Here are a few ways you can focus your writing topic.

Break the Topic into Parts. Break down your topic into a series of smaller parts or subtopics.

EXAMPLE

general topic	Post-Reconstruction race relations
possible subtopics	Booker T. Washington; W. E. B. Du Bois; Tuskegee Institute; Jim Crow laws; *Plessy v. Ferguson* (1896) decision; sharecropper narratives; African-American education; lynchings; southern politics

Quotables

"Getting started is partly stalling, stalling by way of reading and of listening to music, which energizes me and also makes me restless. Feeling guilty about not writing. . . ."
—Susan Sontag

Ask Questions about the Topic. Write down questions about your topic. Begin your questions with the words *who*, *what*, *where*, *when*, *why*, and *how*. Then ask yourself what stands out about the topic and what interests you most.

EXAMPLES
Who was Booker T. Washington?
What was the purpose of the Tuskegee Institute?
Where was segregation practiced?
When were the first Jim Crow laws passed?
Why did W. E. B. Du Bois criticize Booker T. Washington?
How is Booker T. Washington remembered today?

Make a Cluster Chart. Write your general topic in the middle of a piece of paper. Draw a circle around this topic. Draw more circles branching out from your center circle, and fill them with subtopics related to your main topic.

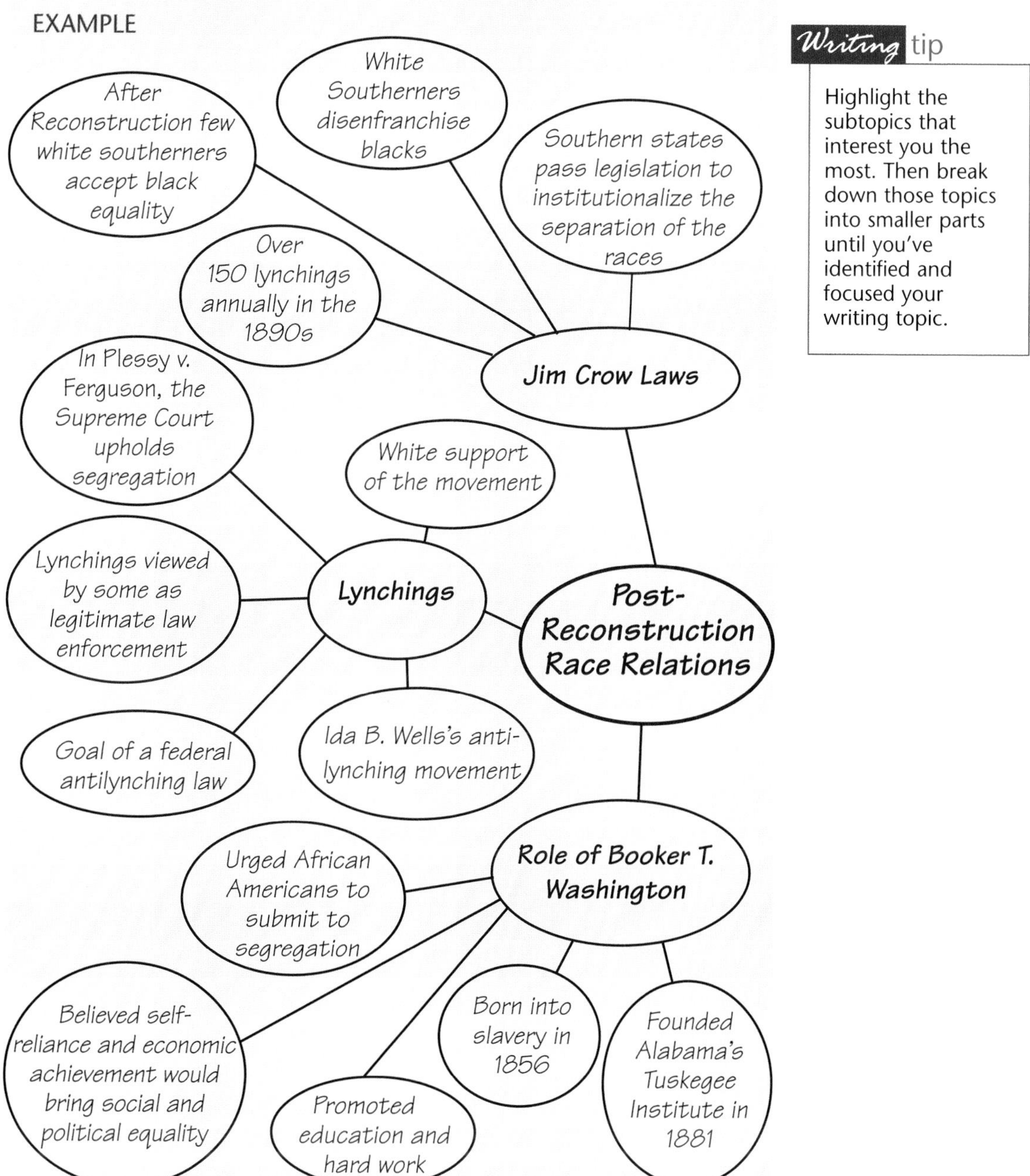

Writing tip

Highlight the subtopics that interest you the most. Then break down those topics into smaller parts until you've identified and focused your writing topic.

Try It Yourself

EXERCISE 1
Responses will vary. Students' responses should reflect their understanding of the different ways to find a writing topic and how to focus a writing topic.

EXERCISE 1

Understanding How to Identify and Focus a Topic

Scan your personal journal, think about recent events and experiences, let your mind wander a bit, and ask yourself questions beginning with *who*, *what*, *where*, *when*, *why*, and *how*. Make a list of at least five writing topic ideas. Select one of these topics and focus it by making a cluster chart.

Identifying Your Purpose for Writing

Writing tip

Ask yourself: *Why am I writing?* The answer to this question will help you identify your purpose.

The goal of your writing is to accomplish a **purpose**, or aim. For example, your purpose for writing might be to reflect on a personal experience, to tell a story, to entertain, to inform, or to persuade. Your writing might have more than one purpose. For example, a piece of writing might inform your readers about an important event while persuading them to respond in a specific way.

Quotables

"But it is part of the business of the writer—as I see it—to examine attitudes, to go beneath the surface, to tap the source."
—James Baldwin

MODES AND PURPOSES OF WRITING

MODE	PURPOSE	WRITING FORMS
personal/ expressive writing	to reflect	diary entry, personal letter, autobiography, personal essay
imaginative/ descriptive writing	to entertain, to describe, to enrich, and to enlighten	poem, character sketch, play
narrative writing	to tell a story, to narrate a series of events	short story, biography, legend, myth, history
informative/ expository writing	to inform, to explain	news article, research report, expository essay, book review
persuasive/ argumentative writing	to persuade	editorial, petition, political speech, persuasive essay

Try It Yourself

EXERCISE 2

Understanding How to Identify Your Purpose for Writing

Review the list of five general topics you identified in Exercise 1. For each of the general topics and for your focused topic, identify a suitable purpose and mode.

EXERCISE 2
Responses will vary. Students should choose a mode and a purpose that are appropriate for their topic.

Identifying Your Audience

An **audience** is the person or group of people intended to read what you write. For example, you might write for yourself, a friend, a relative, or your classmates. The best writing usually is intended for a specific audience. Choosing a specific audience before writing will help you make important decisions about your work. For an audience of young children, for example, you would use simple words and ideas. For an audience of athletic teammates, you would use jargon and other specialized words that your peers already know. For an adult audience, you would use more formal language.

LANGUAGELINK
Print exercise worksheets or have students complete exercises online with the LanguageLINK CD.

Use the following questions to help identify your audience.

- Who will be most interested in my topic? What are their values?
- How much do they already know about the topic?
- What background information do they need in order to understand my ideas and point of view?
- What words, phrases, or concepts will I need to define for my audience?
- How can I capture my audience's interest from the very start?

Quotables

"The room where I work has a window looking into a wood, and I like to think that these earnest, loveable, and mysterious readers are in there."
—John Cheever

Try It Yourself

EXERCISE 3

Understanding How to Identify Your Audience

Keep your focused topic in mind. Then write down your answers to each of the questions above. After answering the questions, write a brief description of your audience.

EXERCISE 3
Responses will vary. Students should write thoughtful responses to the questions and lead themselves to a logical and appropriate identification of their audience.

Choosing a Form of Writing

Another important decision that a writer needs to make is what form his or her writing will take. A **form** is a kind of writing. Once you've identified your topic, your purpose for writing, and your audience, a particular form of writing may become immediately obvious as the perfect one to convey your ideas. But, sometimes, an unexpected choice of form may be even more effective in presenting your topic. The following chart lists some of the many different forms of writing.

FORMS OF WRITING		
Adventure	Experiment	Petition
Advertisement	Fable	Play
Advice column	Family history	Police/Accident report
Agenda	Fantasy	Poster
Apology	Greeting card	Proposal
Appeal	Headline	Radio or TV spot
Autobiography	History	Rap
Biography	Human interest story	Recipe
Book review	Instructions	Recommendation
Brochure	Interview questions	Research report
Calendar	Invitation	Résumé
Caption	Itinerary	Schedule
Cartoon	Joke	Science fiction
Character sketch	Journal entry	Short story
Cheer	Letter	Slide show
Children's story	Magazine article	Slogan
Comedy	Memorandum	Song lyric
Consumer report	Menu	Speech
Debate	Minutes	Sports story
Detective story	Movie review	Statement of belief
Dialogue	Mystery	Summary
Directions	Myth	Tall tale
Dream report	Narrative	Thank-you note
Editorial	Newspaper article	Tour guide
Epitaph	Obituary	Want ad
Essay	Parable	Wish list
Eulogy	Paraphrase	

Quotables

"Essays, however, hang somewhere on a line between two sturdy poles: this is what I think, and this is what I am."
—Edward Hoagland

Try It Yourself

EXERCISE 4

Understanding How to Choose a Form of Writing

Now that you've identified your topic, purpose, and audience, select from the chart two possible forms of writing that you think would work best. Select one form that seems obvious. For example, if your purpose is to inform readers about a local event, select the news article as a form. Then, for your second choice, select a form that is unexpected or surprising. Write a brief explanation of why you think both of the forms would work well.

EXERCISE 4
Responses will vary. Students' choice of forms should be appropriate to their topic, purpose, audience, and mode. Their explanations should be logical and complete.

EXERCISE 5

Understanding Different Forms of Writing

Sometimes what you know first about a piece of writing is its form. You may have a class assignment, want to participate in a writing contest, or wish to experiment with a new writing form. Select one of the writing forms from the chart, perhaps one that you've never used before or one that especially interests and intrigues you. Then, apply what you've learned so far about prewriting to identify a topic, purpose, and audience specifically for that form of writing.

EXERCISE 5
Responses will vary. Students should exhibit an understanding of the prewriting steps of identifying a topic, purpose, and audience.

Gathering Ideas

After you have identified your topic, purpose, audience, and form, the next step in the prewriting stage is to gather ideas. There are many ways to gather ideas for writing. This section will introduce you to some of the most useful strategies.

tip

When you brainstorm in a group, one person's idea will often help another person to build on that concept. Welcome all ideas with an encouraging response.

Brainstorming. When you **brainstorm**, you think of as many ideas as you can, as quickly as you can, without stopping to evaluate or criticize the ideas. Anything goes—no idea should be rejected in the brainstorming stage. Sometimes even silly-sounding ideas can lead to productive results.

Learning from Professional Models. Professional models are works by published authors. They can be an excellent way to shape your own ideas. For example, if you are interested in topics related to post-Reconstruction race relations, you might read W. E. B. Du Bois's classic work *The Souls of Black Folk*. Notice how Du Bois includes different perspectives when describing how an important speech by Washington was received.

Literature MODEL

> To gain the sympathy and cooperation of the various elements comprising the white South was Mr. Washington's first task; and this, at the time Tuskegee was founded, seemed, for a black man, well-nigh impossible. And yet ten years later it was done in the word spoken at Atlanta: "In all things purely social we can be as separate as the five fingers, and yet one as the hand in all things essential to mutual progress." This "Atlanta Compromise" is by all odds the most notable thing in Mr. Washington's career. The South interpreted it in different ways: the radicals received it as a complete surrender of the demand for civil and political equality; the conservatives, as a generously conceived working basis for mutual understanding. So both approved it, and today its author is certainly the most distinguished Southerner since Jefferson Davis, and the one with the largest personal following.
>
> from *The Souls of Black Folk*
> W. E. B. Du Bois

Quotables

"It is fit for the beginner and learner to study others and the best. For the mind and memory are more sharply exercised in comprehending another man's things than our own."
—Ben Jonson

Keeping a Journal. A **journal** is a record of your ideas, dreams, wishes, and experiences. Composition books, spiral notebooks, loose-leaf binders, and bound books with blank pages all make excellent journal books. You may want to use a journal to write thoughts, to collect ideas for writing, to organize tasks, or to keep a learning log. A journal is very handy to return to when you're looking for writing ideas.

Freewriting. Freewriting is simply taking a pencil and paper and writing whatever comes into your mind. Try to write for several minutes without stopping and without worrying about spelling, grammar, usage, or mechanics. If you get stuck, just repeat the last few words until something new pops into your mind.

EXAMPLE

White southerners fought idea of black equality. Passed laws to separate races. Supreme Court approved. Black voting declined. Washington wanted education and hard work rather than resistance to slavery—adopt white middle class values to get ahead. Many disagreed. Lynchings increased. African Americans were too poor to get a leg up. Slavery is gone but the South hasn't changed its values.

Clustering. Another good way to tap into what you already know is to make a **cluster chart**. To make a cluster chart, draw a circle in the center of your paper. In it write a topic you want to explore. Draw more circles branching out from your center circle, and fill them with subtopics related to your main topic. (Review the example in "Identifying and Focusing a Topic" on page 563.)

Questioning. Ask the **reporting questions** *who*, *what*, *where*, *when*, *why*, and *how* about your topic. This questioning strategy is especially useful for gathering information about an event or for planning a story.

Imagining. If you are doing imaginative or creative writing, ask questions that begin with the words *what if*. "What if" questions can spark your imagination and lead you down unexpected and interesting paths. They can also help you to see another side of events and issues.

Quotables

"I surround myself with objects that carry with them a personal history—old books, bowls and boxes, splintering chairs and benches from imperial China. I imagine the people who once turned the pages or rubbed their palms on the surfaces. While they were thinking—thinking what?"
—Amy Tan

EXAMPLES

What if Lincoln had not been assassinated prior to Reconstruction?

What might have happened if the Supreme Court had struck down segregation in 1896?

What if Booker T. Washington had been more defiant?

What if W. E. B. Du Bois had developed a larger following?

Completing Venn Diagrams. If you are writing a comparison and contrast essay, one of the best ways to gather ideas is by completing a Venn diagram. A **Venn diagram** shows two slightly overlapping circles. The outer part of each circle shows what aspects of two things are different from each other. The inner or shared part of each circle shows what aspects the two things share.

Venn Diagram
Washington and Du Bois: Post-Reconstruction African-American Leaders

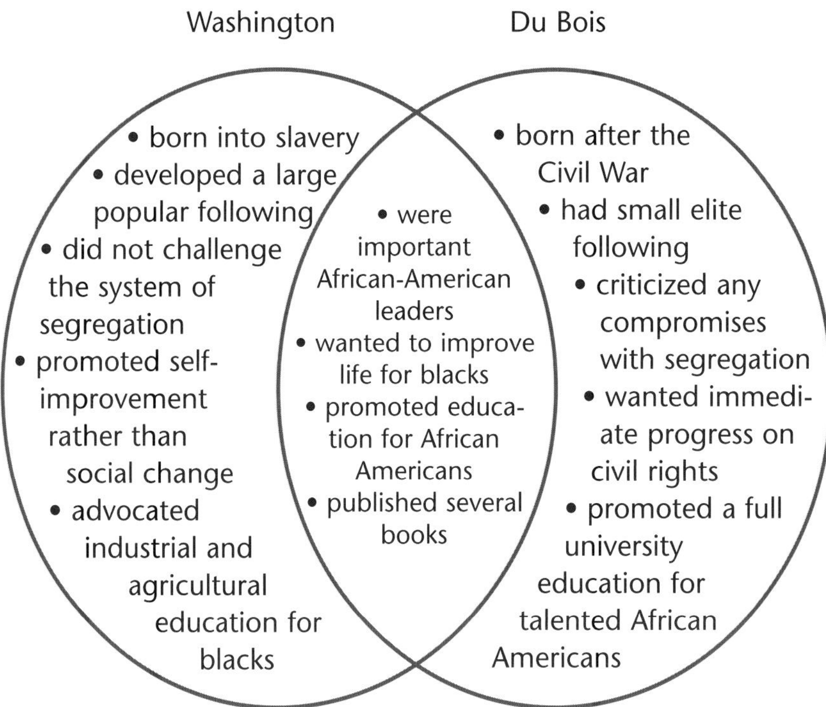

Creating a Sensory Detail Chart. A **sensory detail chart** helps you to collect information about details that you can describe through the use of the five major senses: sight, sound, touch, taste, and smell.

Sensory Detail Chart for Post-Reconstruction Race				
SIGHT	SOUND	TOUCH	TASTE	SMELL
"Whites Only" signs at public parks and restaurants Sharecroppers toiling in a field A lynch mob with torches and a rope	Booker T. Washington speaking to a crowd Singing and music from inside a church Sharp words from proprietors denying service to African Americans Angry curses of a lynch mob Cries from the victims' family members	Rough, calloused hands Oppressive humidity of the fields Insect bites Hard, coarse fibers of a rope	Dust Salt fish Hominy grits	Farm animals Smoke from a lynch mob's torches Fear

Creating a Time Line. Putting events in their order of occurrence can be useful when you are planning to write a story or a historical account. A **time line** gives you an overview of the sequence of events during a particular time period. To make one, draw a line on a piece of paper and divide it into equal parts. Label each part with a date or a time. Then add key events at the correct places along the time line.

Time Line

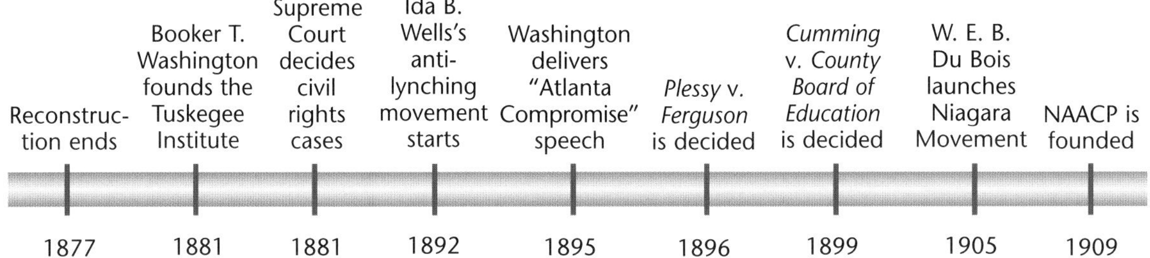

Creating a Story Map. A **story map** is a chart that shows the various parts of a fable, myth, tall tale, legend, short story, or other fictional work. Most story maps include the following elements:

Elements of a Story Map

Element	Description
setting	the time and place in which the story occurs
mood	the emotion created in the reader by the story
conflict	a struggle between two forces in the story
plot	the series of events taking place in the story
characters	the people (or sometimes animals) who play roles in the story
theme	the main idea of the story

Creating a Pro and Con Chart. A **pro and con** chart shows arguments for and against taking a particular position on some issue. To create a pro and con chart, begin by writing a statement, called a proposition, at the top of a piece of paper.

Under the proposition, make two columns, one labeled *Pro* and the other, *Con*. In the *Pro* column, list arguments in favor of the proposition. In the *Con* column, list arguments against the proposition.

Pro and Con Chart	
Proposition: Booker T. Washington's "Atlanta Compromise" hindered the quest for racial equality.	
Pro	**Con**
—supporters of segregation applauded Washington's message —Washington urged blacks not to challenge system of segregation —African Americans were further deprived of political, social, and civil rights in the years following the "Compromise"	—Washington helped African Americans make educational and economic progress —Washington gained a measure of acceptance among white southerners, helping to promote racial cooperation —prevailing racial attitudes in the 1890s suggested that a more defiant stance by Washington may have brought violent reprisals (e.g., revival of KKK activities) against African Americans

Interviewing. In an **interview**, you meet with someone and ask him or her questions. Interviewing people who are experts or authorities on a particular topic is an excellent way to gain information. When planning an interview, list the questions you would like to ask, including some about the person's background as well as about your topic. Other questions may occur to you as the interview proceeds.

Researching for Ideas. No matter what your topic is, you can probably find information about it by doing research in **reference works**. Reference works include encyclopedias, dictionaries, almanacs, atlases, indexes, Internet sites, and others.

Try It Yourself

EXERCISE 6

Using Strategies to Gather Ideas

Select two of the strategies to gather ideas about your writing topic—one strategy for the more obvious form and another strategy for the more unexpected or surprising form of writing you selected in Exercise 4. Carry out both strategies to gather ideas for your topic.

Quotables

"... all your elegant sentences will add up to chaos if you don't remember that writing is linear and sequential, that logic is the glue that holds it together, that tension and pace are crucial. Every component in a piece of writing must do new work, and the transitions must pull the reader from one sentence to the next without his noticing the tug."
—William Zinsser

EXERCISE 6
Responses will vary.

Organizing Ideas

How will you present the information you've gathered? After you have gathered ideas for a piece of writing, the next step is to organize these ideas in a useful and reader-friendly way. The most basic organization of ideas occurs in forming paragraphs. As you learned in Unit 20, a good paragraph is a carefully organized unit of writing. Review Unit 20 for information on topic sentences, paragraph unity, main ideas and supporting details, and methods of organization.

Outlining. Outlines can also help you organize your ideas. An **outline** is often an excellent framework for highlighting main ideas and supporting details. Rough and formal outlines are the two main types of outlines writers commonly use. To create a **rough outline**, simply list your main ideas in some logical order. Under each main idea, list the supporting details set off by dashes. A **formal outline** has headings and subheadings identified by numbers and letters. One type of formal outline is the **topic outline**. Such an outline has entries that are words or phrases rather than complete sentences. In the following topic outline, the student writer has listed a progression of ideas to include in an essay analyzing post-Reconstruction race relations.

tip

Many of the graphic organizers that you learned to use for gathering information, such as the Venn diagram and the story map, are also very helpful in organizing information. They can help you to organize points to compare and contrast, to put events in sequential order, and to record facts in order of importance.

EXAMPLE

Racism institutionalized
—Reconstruction ends in 1877
 —southern states fall under the control of conservative white oligarchies

CONTINUED

—Civil rights cases are heard (1883)
  —Civil Rights Act of 1875 is declared unconstitutional
  —private organizations and individuals may discriminate against people because of race
—Jim Crow laws are passed
  —separate accommodations are instituted in restaurants, trains, parks, etc.
  —schools are segregated
—Supreme Court endorses segregation
  —*Plessy* v. *Ferguson* upholds with "separate but equal" doctrine
  —*Cumming* v. *County Board of Education* finds towns do not have to establish schools for blacks
—African Americans are disfranchised

Washington's Leadership
—Encourages education at trade and agricultural schools for African Americans
—Founds Tuskegee Institute in 1881
  —provides technical and industrial education for black men
—Promotes self-improvement and education to bring about equality
  —recommends adoption of white middle-class values to gain respect
  —urges acceptance of the system of segregation
—Gains acceptance from whites
  —is invited to the White House by President Theodore Roosevelt

Du Bois's Leadership
—Is leader of the black elite
    —is first African American to earn a doctorate at Harvard University
—Criticizes Washington for selling out black political, civil, and social rights
—Promotes university education for blacks
—Campaigns for immediate progress on civil rights
  —launches Niagara Movement in 1905
  —helps found NAACP in 1909

Try It Yourself

EXERCISE 7
Responses will vary. Students should select a method of organizing their details that is appropriate for their topic, purpose, audience, mode, and form of writing.

EXERCISE 7

Understanding How to Organize Your Ideas

Use what you learned about paragraphs in Unit 20 and the information you gathered in Exercise 6 to create a rough outline or topic outline for the subject you've been exploring in this unit's exercises. List your main ideas, using an appropriate method of organization, such as time/chronological, place/spatial, order of importance, comparison and contrast, or cause and effect.

Writing tip

If you've selected a structured form of writing—such as a research paper or a problem-solution essay—you may want to create your draft from a carefully constructed plan, such as a formal outline.

2 DRAFTING

After you have gathered your information and organized it, the next step in writing is to produce a draft. A **draft** is simply an early attempt at writing—at getting your ideas down on paper. Different writers approach drafting in different ways. Some prefer to work slowly and carefully from a plan or to create a careful draft that is perfected, part by part. Others like to see where their ideas lead them by writing a discovery draft in which they get all their ideas down on paper in rough form and then go back over the ideas to shape and focus them.

Drafting an Introduction.

The purpose of an introduction is to capture your reader's attention and establish what you want to say. Think about the kinds of things that capture your attention when you're reading and hook you to keep on reading. Some effective introduction openers include quotes, questions, anecdotes, facts, or descriptions. The following literature model is the opening paragraph from a section on Booker T. Washington in W. E. B. Du Bois's *The Souls of Black Folk.* Notice how Du Bois establishes the historical context for the portrait that he will paint. The background of race relations in the 1800s helps readers see Washington's place in history.

Easily the most striking thing in the history of the American Negro since 1876 is the ascendancy of Mr. Booker T. Washington. It began at the time when war memories and ideals were rapidly passing; a day of astonishing commercial development was dawning; a sense of doubt and hesitation overtook the freemen's sons,—then it was that his leading began. Mr. Washington came, with a simple definite program, at the psychological moment when the nation was a little ashamed of having bestowed so much sentiment on Negroes, and was concentrating its energies on Dollars. His program of industrial education, conciliation of the South, and submission and silence as to civil and political rights, was not wholly original; the Free Negroes from 1830 up to war-time had striven to build industrial schools, and the American Missionary Association had from the first taught various trades; and Price and others had sought a way of honorable alliance with the best of the Southerners. But Mr. Washington first indissolubly linked these things; he put enthusiasm, unlimited energy, and perfect faith into this program, and changed it from a bypath into a veritable Way of Life. And the tale of the methods by which he did this is a fascinating study of human life.

from *The Souls of Black Folk*
W. E. B. Du Bois

Literature MODEL

EXAMINING THE *Model*

Introductions are like billboards: they must attract and entice the reader. This section of Du Bois's text is an example of informative writing about a historical figure. The author extends his subject's importance beyond his recognizable role as an African-American leader in the late 1800s. Du Bois establishes historical context and then pulls his readers in to find out more about the famous leader.

In the following draft of an introduction, the student writer uses an excerpt of a poem to introduce a historical essay and to establish a perspective for evaluating racism in the late 1800s.

EXAMPLE

We wear the mask that grins and lies,
It hides our cheeks and shades our eyes—
This debt we pay to human guile;
With torn and bleeding hearts we smile,
And mouth with myriad subtleties.

CONTINUED

In his poem "We Wear the Mask," Paul Laurence Dunbar expresses the frustration that African Americans felt in the segregated South. Unjustly denied political and civil rights, blacks were nonetheless expected to "wear a mask" by hiding their feelings and accepting treatment as second-class citizens. Even the noted African American leader Booker T. Washington urged blacks to submit to segregation and adopt the values of the white middle class.

Try It Yourself

EXERCISE 8
Responses will vary. Students should write an introductory paragraph using an element such as a quote, fact, anecdote, or description to capture their readers' attention.

EXERCISE 8

Understanding How to Draft an Introduction

Draft an introduction for your topic, using a quotation, a fact, a question, an anecdote, or a description.

Drafting Body Paragraphs

When writing the body of an essay or another form of structured writing, refer to the outline you created in Exercise 7. Use each heading in your outline as the main idea of one of your paragraphs. To connect ideas for your reader and to move smoothly from one idea to the next, use transitions. Whether you are writing a persuasive essay or a narrative poem, include details—in the form of evidence, facts, sensory description, and so on—to support and develop your main idea.

The following example is a body paragraph for the student's historical essay. Notice how the writer incorporates cause and effect into a description of Washington's personal history and uses a transition to link his topic to the larger cultural context.

EXAMPLE

Personal and cultural values shaped Booker T. Washington's view of how his race could advance. He was born a slave and emancipated into poverty. Forced to rely on his own efforts, Washington worked as a janitor to pay for his schooling. His education at Virginia's Hampton Institute and Wayland Seminary in Washington, D.C., facilitated his escape from

CONTINUED

poverty. He then became a school instructor and later founded Alabama's Tuskegee Institute, where he served as principal for three decades. Moreover, the Victorian culture that prevailed in America during Washington's lifetime valued hard work and self-reliance. It is thus little surprise that Washington, a product of his experience and his times, espoused education, self-improvement, and economic advancement as the keys to overcoming the political and social inequality that African Americans faced.

Writing tip

Transitions are words and phrases that help you connect and move smoothly from one idea to the next in your writing. Before writing Exercise 9, you may want to review transitions in Unit 20 on page 538

Try It Yourself

EXERCISE 9

Understanding How to Draft Body Paragraphs

Write two body paragraphs to follow your introduction. Use transitions to connect your ideas and use a method of organization to present your ideas effectively.

Drafting a Conclusion

In the conclusion, bring together the main ideas you included in the body of your essay and create a sense of closure to the topic you presented. There is no single right way to conclude a piece of writing. Possibilities include:

- making a generalization
- restating the main idea and supporting ideas in different words
- summarizing the points made in the rest of the essay
- drawing a lesson or moral
- calling on the reader to adopt a point of view or to take action
- expanding on your main idea by connecting it to the reader's own interests
- linking your topic to a larger issue or concern

In the closing paragraph of his section on Booker T. Washington in *The Souls of Black Folk*, W. E. B. Du Bois uses a quote from the Declaration of Independence to link his topic to the larger struggle for human equality.

"Finishing, like beginning, is more careful work."
—John Irving

EXERCISE 9

Responses will vary. Students' body paragraphs should use a method of organization and transitions to convey and connect their ideas.

The black men of America have a duty to perform, a duty stern and delicate,—a forward movement to oppose a part of the work of their greatest leader. So far as Mr. Washington preaches Thrift, Patience, and Industrial Training for the masses, we must hold up his hands and strive with him, rejoicing in his honors and glorying in the strength of this Joshua called of God and of man to lead the headless host. But so far as Mr. Washington apologizes for injustice, North or South, does not rightly value the privilege and duty of voting, belittles the emasculating effects of caste distinctions, and opposes the higher training and ambition of our brighter minds,—so far as he, the South or the Nation, does this,—we must unceasingly and firmly oppose them. By every civilized and peaceful method we must strive for the rights which the world accords to men, clinging unwaveringly to those great words which the sons of the Fathers would fain forget: "We hold these truths to be self-evident: That all men are created equal; that they are endowed by their Creator with certain inalienable rights; that among these are life, liberty, and the pursuit of happiness."

from *The Souls of Black Folk*
W. E. B. Du Bois

USAGE tip

Remember to use quotation marks when directly quoting a statement.

Try It Yourself

EXERCISE 10

Understanding How to Draft a Conclusion

Draft a conclusion for your topic. Even though you haven't yet written all the body paragraphs, use your outline to guide you in writing your conclusion.

EXERCISE 10
Responses will vary. Students' conclusions should bring together their main ideas and create a sense of closure.

3 SELF- AND PEER EVALUATION

When you evaluate something, you examine it carefully to find its strengths and weaknesses. Evaluating your own writing is called **self-evaluation**. A **peer evaluation** is an evaluation of a piece of writing done by classmates, or peers. The following tips can help you to become a helpful peer reader, to learn to give and receive criticism, and to improve your writing.

Tips for evaluating a piece of writing:

- **Check for content.** Is the content, including the main idea, clear? Have any important details been left out? Do unimportant or unrelated details confuse the main point? Are the main idea and supporting details clearly connected to one another?
- **Check for organization.** Are the ideas in the written work presented in a logical order? Is one sentence clearly linked or related to the next?
- **Check the style and language.** Is the language appropriately formal or informal? Is the tone appropriate for the audience and purpose? Have unfamiliar but important terms been defined?

Tips for delivering helpful criticism:

- **Be focused.** Concentrate on content, organization, and style. At this point, do not focus on proofreading matters such as spelling and punctuation; they can be corrected during the proofreading stage.
- **Be positive.** Respect the writer's feelings and genuine writing efforts. Tell the writer what you like about his or her work. Answer the writer's questions in a positive manner. In a tactful and positive manner, present any changes you are suggesting.
- **Be specific.** Give the writer concrete ideas for improving his or her work.

Writing tip

It's a good idea to set aside your writing for a day or two. Then read your work with a fresh pair of eyes.

Writing tip

Ask a peer to summarize briefly the main idea(s) of your piece of writing. This is a good test to find out if you've expressed your ideas clearly.

ASSESSMENT
Writing rubrics and evaluation forms are available at www.emcp.com.

EXERCISE 11
Responses will vary. Students should work through the self- and peer evaluation process to identify strengths and weaknesses in a completed draft or the current draft-in-progress.

Tips for benefiting from helpful criticism:

- **Tell your peer evaluator your specific concerns and questions.** If you are unsure whether you've clearly presented an idea, ask the evaluator how he or she might restate the idea.
- **Ask questions to clarify comments that your evaluator makes.** When you clarify, you make sure you understand your evaluator's comments.
- **Accept your evaluator's comments graciously.** Criticism can be helpful, but you don't have to use any or all of the suggestions.

Quotables

"Trust your material—it's stronger than you think. But it's only as strong as the structure you build for it and the control you maintain over it from the first sentence to the last."
—William Zinsser

Try It Yourself

EXERCISE 11

Understanding How to Evaluate Writing

Select a completed work or your current draft-in-progress to exchange with another student for evaluation. Provide your peer evaluator with a clean copy of your writing, and give your evaluator enough time to read and respond to your work. While the peer evaluator is reviewing your work, self-evaluate the same piece of writing. Compare your own comments with those of the peer evaluator. What strengths did each of you recognize? What weaknesses did each of you identify?

Quotables

"The first draft is in my head. The next draft is in longhand on paper, and after that, I type it. All along the way I make changes. The final draft bears very little resemblance to whatever it was I had in my head."
—Ann Petry

4 REVISING AND PROOFREADING

After identifying weaknesses in a draft through self-evaluation and peer evaluation, the next step in the process is to **revise** and **proofread** the draft. Here are four basic ways to revise your writing to improve meaning and content.

Adding or Expanding. Sometimes writing can be improved by adding details, examples, or transitions to connect ideas. Often a single detail will provide the necessary support for an idea, or a strong adjective or verb can make a piece of writer clearer or more vivid.

EXAMPLE

draft

Du Bois opposed Washington's ideas for compromise.

revision

Du Bois believed the ideas set forth in Washington's "Atlanta Compromise" would encourage segregation and block progress toward attaining black equality.

Cutting or Condensing. Often writing can be improved by cutting unnecessary or unrelated material. For example, combining related ideas into one sentence can have a larger impact than presenting them separately.

Quotables

". . . the essence of writing is rewriting."
—William Zinsser

EXAMPLE

draft

Washington believed that progress depended upon taking steps to bring about self-improvement. He called for African Americans to learn technical and industrial skills. He also felt blacks should refine their speech, dress well, and bathe regularly. Washington furthermore called for African Americans to forsake agitating for immediate political change.

revision

Washington believed that progress depended upon self-improvement. He promoted education, refinement, and patience among African Americans.

Replacing. Replace weak writing with words and phrases that are active, concrete, vivid, and precise.

EXAMPLE

draft

African Americans suspected of a crime were sometimes lynched.

revision

Occasionally, white people in rural areas formed mobs to hunt down and lynch African Americans suspected of a crime.

Moving. Often you can improve the organization of your writing by moving part of it so that related ideas appear near one another.

EXAMPLE

draft

The national government did not work for political and social equality for blacks in the late nineteenth century. The Supreme Court upheld segregation with its *Plessy* v. *Ferguson* decision in 1896. Presidents serving in the 1880s and 1890s showed little interest in the plight of oppressed southern blacks. Congress distanced itself from racial issues as well. In *Cumming* v. *County Board of Education* the Court ruled that communities were free to establish all-white schools, even if no comparable schools existed for African Americans.

revision

The national government did not work for political and social equality for blacks in the late nineteenth century. The Supreme Court upheld segregation with its *Plessy* v. *Ferguson* decision in 1896. In *Cumming* v. *County Board of Education* the Court ruled that communities were free to establish all-white schools, even if no comparable schools existed for African Americans. Presidents serving in the 1880s and 1890s showed little interest in the plight of oppressed southern blacks. Congress, as well, distanced itself from racial issues.

After you've revised the draft, ask yourself a series of questions. Think of these questions as your "revision checklist."

REVISION CHECKLIST

Content
- Does the writing achieve its purpose?
- Are the main ideas clearly stated and supported by details?

Organization
- Are the ideas arranged in a sensible order?
- Are the ideas connected to one another within paragraphs and between paragraphs?

Style
- Is the language appropriate to the audience and purpose?
- Is the mood appropriate to the purpose of the writing?

When you proofread your writing, you read it through to look for errors and mark corrections. When you mark corrections to your writing, use the standard proofreading symbols as shown in the following chart.

PROOFREADER'S SYMBOLS	
Symbol and Example	**Meaning of Symbol**
The very first time	Delete (cut) this material.
cat's cradle	Insert (add) something that is missing.
George	Replace this letter or word.
All the horses king's	Move this word to where the arrow points.
french toast	Capitalize this letter.
the vice-President	Lowercase this letter.
housse	Take out this letter and close up space.
book keeper	Close up space.
gebril	Change the order of these letters.
end. "Watch out," she yelled.	Begin a new paragraph.
Love conquers all	Put a period here.
Welcome friends.	Put a comma here.
Getthe stopwatch	Put a space here.
Dear Madam	Put a colon here.
She walked he rode.	Put a semicolon here.
name brand products	Put a hyphen here.
cats meow	Put an apostrophe here.
cat's cradle stet	Let it stand. (Leave as it is.)

After you have revised your draft, make a clean copy and proofread it for errors in spelling, grammar, and punctuation. Use the following proofreading checklist.

PROOFREADING CHECKLIST	
Spelling	• Are all words, including names, spelled correctly?
Grammar	• Does each verb agree with its subject? • Are verb tenses consistent and correct? • Are irregular verbs formed correctly? • Are there any sentence fragments or run-ons? • Have double negatives been avoided? • Have frequently confused words, such as *affect* and *effect*, been used correctly?
Punctuation	• Does every sentence end with an end mark? • Are commas used correctly? • Do all proper nouns and proper adjectives begin with capital letters?

After proofreading your draft, you will want to prepare your final manuscript. Follow the guidelines given by your teacher or the guidelines provided here. After preparing a final manuscript according to these guidelines, proofread one last time for errors.

- Keyboard your manuscript using a typewriter or word processor, or write it neatly using blue or black ink.
- Double-space your paper.
- Use one side of the paper.
- Leave one-inch margins on all sides of the text.
- Indent the first line of each paragraph.
- Make a cover sheet listing the title of the work, your name, the date, and the class.
- In the upper right-hand corner of the first page, put your name, class, and date, On every page after the first, include the page number in the heading, as follows:

EXAMPLE
Vicky Miguel
English 11
April 18, 2003
p. 3

Try It Yourself

EXERCISE 12

Understanding How to Revise a Draft

Use one or more of the four basic ways discussed above to revise your draft. After revising, take your draft through the revision checklist.

EXERCISE 12
Responses will vary. Students' revisions should reflect an understanding of the revision process and the four basic ways to improve a piece of writing.

EXERCISE 13

Using Proofreading Marks

Proofread your revision for errors in spelling, grammar, punctuation, and capitalization. If you are unsure about a word's spelling, check it in a dictionary or use the spell-check on your computer. After proofreading your revision, prepare your final manuscript. Then proofread your manuscript one last time for errors.

EXERCISE 13
Responses will vary. Students should use proofreading symbols to mark errors in spelling, grammar, punctuation, and capitalization. After proofreading, students should prepare a final manuscript.

---

5 PUBLISHING AND PRESENTING

In the **publishing and presenting stage**, you share your work with an audience. Some writing is done just for oneself—journal writing, for example. Most writing, however, is meant to be shared with others. There are many ways to share your work. Here are several ways in which you can publish your writing or present it to others:

- Submit the work to a local publication, such as a school literary magazine, school newspaper, or community newspaper.
- Submit the work to a regional or national publication.
- Enter the work in a contest.
- Read your work aloud to classmates, friends, or family members.
- Work with other students to prepare a publication—a brochure, online literary magazine, anthology, or newspaper.
- Prepare a poster or bulletin board, perhaps in collaboration with other students, to display your writing.

Writing tip

Keep in a writing portfolio a collection of all the pieces that you write. From time to time, examine the pieces in your portfolio and identify the improvements you've been making in your writing.

- Make your own book by typing or word processing the pages and binding them together.
- Hold an oral reading of student writing as a class or school-wide project.
- Share your writing with other students in a small writers' group.

Try It Yourself

EXERCISE 14
Responses will vary. Students should select one way in which to share their work with others, either through publishing or presenting.

EXERCISE 14

Publishing and Presenting Your Work

After you've prepared your final manuscript, decide how you will share your work with others. Select one of the ways listed above in which to publish your work or present it to others.

Quotables

"It always leaves you feeling great. In short, you've made sense of your life."
—John Cheever

 REFLECTING

In the **reflecting** stage, you think through the writing process to determine what you learned as a writer, what you learned about your topic, how the writing process worked or didn't work for you, and what skills you would like to strengthen. Reflection can be done on a self-evaluation form, in small-group discussion, or simply in your own thoughts. By keeping a journal, however, you'll be able to keep track of your writing experience and pinpoint ways to make the writing process work better for you. Here are some questions to ask as you reflect on the writing process and yourself as a writer:

- Which part of the writing process did I enjoy most and least? Why? Which part of the writing process was most difficult? least difficult? Why?
- What would I change about my approach to the writing process next time?
- What have I learned in writing about this topic?
- What have I learned by using this form?
- How have I developed as a writer while writing this piece?
- What strengths have I discovered in my work?
- What aspects of my writing do I want to strengthen? How can I strengthen them?

Try It Yourself

EXERCISE 15

Reflecting on Your Writing

Take yourself back through your experience with the writing process as you identified, focused, wrote, revised, and published and presented your manuscript. Did your feelings or thoughts about the topic change during the writing process? Why, or why not? What did you learn about the topic, or about yourself, that you didn't anticipate? What did you learn that could lead to further writing? Write the answers to these questions and those listed above as you reflect on the manuscript you wrote for this unit.

EXERCISE 15
Responses will vary. Students should express thoughtful reflection on their experience with the writing process as they've developed their manuscript in this unit.

ASSESSMENT
Writing Comprehensive Test, Writing Rubrics, and Writing Evaluation Forms are available at www.emcp.com.

UNIT 21 REVIEW

TEST YOUR KNOWLEDGE

EXERCISE 1
1. D
2. B
3. E
4. A
5. F
6. C

EXERCISE 1
Identifying the Stages in the Writing Process
Match each stage in the writing process with a description of the tasks involved. (10 points)

__1. Prewriting
__2. Drafting
__3. Self- and Peer Evaluation
__4. Revising and Proofreading
__5. Publishing and Presenting
__6. Reflecting

A. Work to improve the content and organization. Check for errors in spelling, grammar, and capitalization.
B. Get your ideas down on paper.
C. Think through the writing process.
D. Identify your topic, purpose, form, audience; gather ideas; organize your ideas.
E. Review your own work or a classmate's and suggest ways to improve it.
F. Share your work with an audience.

EXERCISE 2
Responses may vary slightly. Sample responses:
1. to reflect, to record personal thoughts and experiences
2. to describe, to entertain, to enrich, to enlighten
3. to tell a story
4. to inform, to explain a process
5. to persuade, to call readers to action

EXERCISE 2
Understanding Modes and Purposes of Writing
Write a brief description of the purpose(s) for each of the following modes of writing. (10 points)

1. personal/expressive writing
2. imaginative/descriptive writing
3. narrative writing
4. informative/expository writing
5. persuasive/argumentative writing

EXERCISE 3

Understanding Different Forms of Writing

For each of the following modes of writing, list five examples of different forms of writing. (20 points)

1. personal/expressive writing
2. imaginative/descriptive writing
3. narrative writing
4. informative/expository writing
5. persuasive/argumentative writing

EXERCISE 4

Understanding How to Gather Ideas

Use each of the following strategies to gather ideas about the assigned topic. (20 points; 5 points each)

1. strategy: pro and con chart; topic: raising the minimum wage one dollar higher than its current level
2. strategy: time line; topic: the United States' involvement in the Vietnam War
3. strategy: Venn diagram; topic: attending a large university versus attending a small college
4. strategy: questioning; topic: building a memorial site to honor those who died in the attacks on September 11, 2001

EXERCISE 5

Understanding How to Draft an Introduction

Select one of the topics in Exercise 4. Use the ideas that you gathered to write an introduction. Identify your purpose, mode, form, and audience. (20 points)

EXERCISE 3

Responses will vary.

Sample responses:

1. personal letter, thank-you note, song lyric, diary or journal entry, family history
2. character sketch, brochure, poem, menu, tour guide
3. detective story, mystery, myth, cartoon, comedy
4. advice column, consumer report, book review, research report, instructions
5. advertisement, appeal, petition, slogan, recommendation

EXERCISE 4

Responses will vary. Students should pursue several different lines of thinking at this point of the writing process. They should provide five or six details for each topic or each aspect of the topic.

EXERCISE 5

Responses will vary. Students should use one of the methods for writing an introduction suggested in the

chapter—a quotation, question, anecdote, fact, or description. In addition to identifying their purpose, mode, form, and audience, students may also want to specify the main method of organizing that will control the essay.

EXERCISE 6
Responses will vary. Students should use at least two of the basic revision methods to improve the meaning and content of their writing.

EXERCISE 6

Using Revising Methods

Select a piece of writing from your writing portfolio. Revise to improve the work's meaning and content by using at least two of the following methods: adding or expanding, cutting or condensing, replacing, or moving. (20 points)

UNIT 22 MODES AND PURPOSES OF WRITING

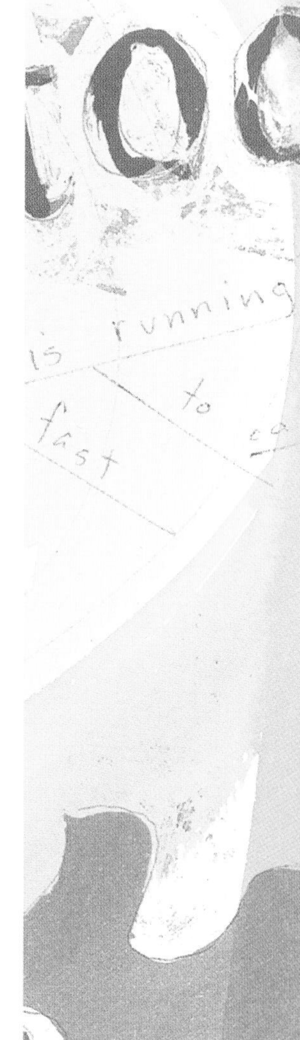

UNIT OVERVIEW

ASSESSMENT
Writing Comprehensive Test, Writing Rubrics, and Writing Evaluation Forms are available at www.emcp.com.

MODES AND PURPOSES OF WRITING

IDENTIFYING YOUR PURPOSE

A **purpose,** or **aim**, is the goal that you want your writing to accomplish. As explained in Unit 21, The Writing Process, you need to determine your purpose in order to choose the correct mode and style for your writing. You might write to reflect (personal/expressive writing), to entertain (imaginative/descriptive writing), to tell a story (narrative writing), to inform (informative/expository writing), or to persuade (persuasive/argumentative writing.) Your writing might have more that one purpose. For example, a piece of writing might inform about an important event while persuading the audience to respond in a specific way.

Writing tip

Before reading this unit, you may want to review the Modes and Purposes of Writing chart in Unit 21 on page 564.

PERSONAL/EXPRESSIVE WRITING

Writing a Personal Essay

The purpose of **personal/expressive writing** is to reflect about your thoughts and feelings. Sometimes personal writing may be writing that you do for yourself, perhaps in a journal or a diary, that you do not want others to read. If you want to share your thoughts and feelings with others, you might write a letter, a personal narrative, or a personal essay.

A **personal essay** is a short nonfiction work on a single topic related to the life of the writer. It is one of the most powerful forms of writing because the writer can share his or her personal insights with others.

The following literature model is an excerpt from a personal essay written by Ralph Waldo Emerson, a leading nineteenth-century American intellectual.

Quotables

"The essayist arises in the morning and, if he has work to do, selects his garb from an unusually extensive wardrobe: he can pull on any sort of shirt, be any sort of person, according to his mood or his subject matter—philosopher, scold, jester, raconteur, confidant, pundit, devil's advocate, enthusiast."
—E. B. White

Society everywhere is in conspiracy against the manhood of every one of its members. Society is a joint-stock company in which members agree for the better securing of his bread to each shareholder, to surrender the liberty and culture of the eater. The virtue in most request is conformity. Self-reliance is aversion. It loves not realities and creators but names and customs.

Whoso would be a man must be a nonconformist. He who would gather immortal palms must not be hindered by the name of goodness, but he must explore if it were goodness. Nothing is at last sacred but the integrity of our own mind.

What I must do, is all that concerns me, not what the people think. This rule, equally arduous in actual and in intellectual life, may serve for the whole distinction between greatness and meanness. It is the harder, because you will always find those who think they know what is your duty better than you know it. It is easy in the world to live after the world's opinion; it is easy in solitude to live after our own; but the great man is he who in the midst of the crowd keeps with perfect sweetness the independence of solitude.

from "Self-Reliance"
Ralph Waldo Emerson

Literature MODEL

EXAMINING THE *Model*

In this excerpt, Emerson describes his belief in the importance of relying on one's own ideas and avoiding conformity.

Try It Yourself

LANGUAGELINK
Print exercise worksheets or have students complete exercises online with the LanguageLINK CD.

Writing a Personal Essay

In this assignment, you will write a personal essay about an experience you have had. Before you begin this assignment, ask yourself how you think you will benefit from writing your personal essay. How will your readers benefit from reading it?

1. Prewriting

Select a topic to write about in your personal essay. Freewrite for a few minutes to tell the story about what happened to you. Write about your experience, your reaction to the experience, and what you learned from your experience. What do you

Writing tip

Voice is the way a writer uses language to reflect his or her personality and attitude toward topic, form, and audience. You can make your essay inviting to read by using your natural, personal voice as you share your experience and perspective. Think of your reader as an attentive friend with whom you are having a conversation.

know now that you did not know at the time? What would you like others to know? Use your thoughts to come up with a single, controlling idea to develop in your personal essay. A graphic organizer is often helpful when determining the controlling idea of your personal essay. Copy the graphic organizer below onto your own paper. First, list details about your experience and your perspective on it. From this information, identify the controlling idea—the main point—that you want to use in your personal essay.

Graphic Organizer

Topic: The Lone Ranger

Experience	***Perspective***
history final tomorrow	*heavy pressure to join friends*
friends going to a late-night party	*disappointment at missing party*
parents out of town	*happy with grade*
great opportunity to have fun	*learned an important lesson*
stay home and study	
pass exam with a good grade	
three friends fail	

Controlling Idea

It is wiser to rely upon one's own ideas than to conform to the opinions and wishes of others.

2. Drafting

Since your personal essay tells a narrative, or a story about your experience, you can use **chronological order** to organize your essay. Start with an introduction that includes your controlling idea. In the body paragraphs, relate what happened and explain how the experience helped you develop your perspective. In the conclusion, summarize what you learned from you experience and perspective. Also provide some direction for you audience about the experience. Should they experience this, too? Should they approach the experience in a different manner? Should they avoid the experience altogether?

You do not need to focus on mechanics, grammar, or spelling at this writing stage. You can go back later and check for errors. For now, focus on the big picture—the single controlling idea that you have in mind. Each sentence you write should contribute to your controlling idea.

Use a **first-person point of view** since you are telling about your own experience and perspective. Use words like *I*, *my*, *me*, and *mine*. Your readers want to hear about what happened to you and your insight about it.

tip

To start your draft, you might begin by stating your controlling idea. For example, "It is wiser to rely upon one's own ideas than to conform to the opinions and wishes of others. I found this out last spring when I faced a difficult final exam in my American history class."

Language, Grammar, and Style

CORRECTING RUN-ON SENTENCES

Identifying Run-on Sentences. Although there is nothing wrong with long sentences, they must be grammatically correct. Sentences that have multiple independent clauses joined without appropriate conjunctions or punctuation are called *run-ons*, and are grammatically incorrect.

EXAMPLE

Emerson was one of the leading champions of radical individualism he also promoted the Transcendentalist Movement.

Revise a run-on sentence by adding appropriate conjunctions or punctuation. The above run-on sentence could be fixed a few different ways:

CONTINUED

REVISED EXAMPLES

Divide it into two independent clauses separated by a period:

Emerson was one of the leading champions of radical individualism. He also promoted the Transcendentalist Movement.

Divide it into two independent clauses separated by a semicolon:

Emerson was one of the leading champions of radical individualism; he also promoted the Transcendentalist Movement.

Make one clause subordinate to the other:

Although Emerson was one of the leading champions of radical individualism, he also promoted the Transcendentalist Movement.

Insert a conjunction:

Emerson was one of the leading champions of radical individualism, and he also promoted the Transcendentalist Movement.

Correcting Run-on Sentences. Read each of the following sentences. If it is a run-on, rewrite it correctly. If it is not a run-on, write *correct.*

1. Emerson trained to be a minister for years when he began his ministry he found that it had lost its meaning.
2. After visiting Europe, Emerson's spirits were revived, and he was inspired to write his first book.
3. Emerson lectured on many topics he always included a discussion of the moral principles that underlay his thinking.
4. Believing that slavery was an abomination, Emerson delivered lectures against it even when he was emotionally involved with his subject he kept his dignity.
5. Emerson's optimism is obvious in most of his works he believed that people have within themselves everything they need to know about the meaning of their own existence.

Using Sentences Effectively in Your Writing. Read through your personal essay and look for run-ons. If you find any, fix them according to the directions in this lesson.

3. Self- and Peer Evaluation

After you finish your draft, complete a self-evaluation of your writing. You may also want to get one or two peer evaluations if you have time. As you evaluate your essay or that of a classmate, answer the following questions:

- What personal experience does the essay relate? What insight or perspective does the author have about the experience? What could be added to clarify the perspective?
- What technique does the essay use to hook the reader in the introduction? How effectively is it used?
- How thoroughly does the essay elaborate on the controlling idea? What additional information might be included to further develop the author's perspective? What might be deleted?
- How does the information in each paragraph contribute to the controlling idea?
- What descriptive words and specific details could be added to make the essay more interesting to the reader?
- What changes in sentence structure—such as a greater variety of sentence structures or correction of run-on sentences and fragments—might improve the writing?
- What type of information does the conclusion provide for the reader? What might be added or deleted?

4. Revising and Proofreading

If possible, give yourself some "wait time" after you complete your self- and peer evaluations. Then you will be able to look at your essay in a new light. Review your notes from the evaluations, then revise your essay. Concentrate on improving the organization of the essay. Be sure your have an introduction, a body, and a conclusion to your essay. Let your readers understand your controlling idea by focusing on your experience, your perspective, and the story you tell.

Writing rubrics and evaluation forms are available at www.emcp.com.

CORRECTING RUN-ON SENTENCES
Responses will vary. Sample responses:

1. Emerson trained to be a minister for years, but when he began his ministry he found that it had lost its meaning.
2. correct
3. Emerson lectured on many topics, and he always included a discussion of the moral principles that underlay his thinking.
4. Believing that slavery was an abomination, Emerson delivered lectures against it. Even when he was emotionally involved with his subject he kept his dignity.
5. Emerson's optimism is obvious in most of his works. He believed that people have within themselves everything they need to know about the meaning of their own existence.

Writing tip

When you proofread your writing, mark your corrections using the standard proofreading symbols. (See the Proofreader's Symbols chart in Unit 21 on page 585). With just a little practice you'll find them very easy and convenient to use.

ASSESSMENT
Writing rubrics and evaluation forms are available at www.emcp.com.

5. Publishing and Presenting

Rewrite your final copy in ink or print it from the computer. You may want to create a cover that illustrates part of your story or that you personalize in some other way. Decide how you will present your personal essay to other students. You may want to meet in small reading groups and read the essays aloud. Or, you may want to prepare a class book of all the essays.

If you have written your essays for your family or other adults, decide how you will pass along the essay from one person to the next. You might send a photocopy or an e-mail with your essay included.

6. Reflecting on Your Writing

As you reflect on your expressive writing, ask yourself these questions:

1. What have I learned in writing this essay?
2. What kind of voice does my writing have?
3. What strengths have I discovered in my work? in myself?

IMAGINATIVE/DESCRIPTIVE WRITING

Writing a Focused Description

The purpose of **imaginative/descriptive writing** is to entertain, enrich, and enlighten by using a form such as fiction or poetry to share a perspective. Poems, short stories, and plays are examples of imaginative or creative writing. **Imaginative writing** is created from the writer's imagination. **Descriptive writing** uses visual and other sensory details to evoke an emotional response. Descriptive writing is used to describe something, to set a scene, to create a mood, to appeal to the readers' senses.

Quotables

"I like to think of some scene, it doesn't matter how crazy, and work backward and forward from it until eventually it becomes quite plausible. . . ."
—P. G. Wodehouse

A **focused description** is a type of writing that portrays a character, an object, or a scene. Sensory details describe how things look, sound, smell, taste, or feel. Effective descriptions contain precise nouns, verbs, adverbs, and adjectives. In addition to imagery, descriptions often use figurative language.

The following passage by Kathleen Norris describes the landscape of western Dakota.

Literature MODEL

> Once, when I was describing to a friend from Syracuse, New York, a place on the plains that I love, a ridge above a glacial moraine with a view of almost fifty miles, she asked, "But what is there to see?"
>
> The answer, of course, is nothing. Land, sky, and the everchanging light. Except for a few signs of human presence—power and telephone lines, an occasional farm building, the glint of a paved road in the distance—it's like looking at the ocean.
>
> The landscape of western Dakota is not as abstract as the flats of Kansas, but it presents a similar challenge to the eye that appreciates the vertical definition of mountains or skyscrapers; that defines beauty in terms of the spectacular or the busy: hills, trees, buildings, highways, people. We seem empty by comparison.
>
> from "Seeing"
> Kathleen Norris

EXAMINING THE *Model*

In this passage, the author effectively uses words and phrases to set the scene of the Dakota plains.

Try It Yourself

Writing a Focused Description

In this assignment, you will write a description of a favorite place where you frequently spend time, have visited, or would like to visit. Work from a photograph or from your memory of the place.

1. Prewriting

LANGUAGELINK
Print exercise worksheets or have students complete exercises online with the LanguageLINK CD.

To start, think about how to depict your scene from a variety of different perspectives. Revisit the scene in your memory if you do not have a photograph or are unable to return to the place. Take note of what a person can see from various perspectives. Record the emotions you feel as you look at the scene. Ask yourself which details will most effectively depict the scene to your audience. What do you want your audience to feel as they read your description? Use the answers to these questions to help you decide which specific perspective you want to use for your description.

Use a sensory detail chart like the one below to assist with your recollection and recording of the details of the scene.

Writing tip

Use metaphors, similes, and personification in the notes you take about the scene. Using figurative language will help make the place come alive to your readers.

Graphic Organizer

Sensory Detail Chart

Sight	Sound	Smell	Taste	Touch
grasses; wheat fields; sunflowers blanketing the land; vast blue sky; prairie dogs	wind rushing through the grass; clicking of grasshop-pers; buzz of insects; howl of coyotes	fragrance of wild-flowers; smell of oats, barley, and alfalfa	wild berries	soft blades of tall grass; bristly plants

2. Drafting

Before writing a draft, you will need to decide how your description will be organized. You may wish to depict the place spatially, describing what a person would see as he or she slowly scans the area. Another method of organization is order of importance, in which the description begins with the most prominent and most important details.

Use your introduction to inspire an appreciation for the scene in your readers. Allow them to see the place as you see it. Follow your chosen organizational method in the body paragraphs of your description. At this point, you may decide to try another mode of organization if your first one isn't working. As you draft, think about how your words create mood and appeal to the readers' senses. For the conclusion, decide what final impression you would like to leave with your audience. This may be your emotions about the place, an enduring image from the scene, or some other sensory detail.

Quotables

"What impels the writer is a deep love for and respect for language, for literary forms, for books. It's a privilege to muck about in sentences all morning."
—Annie Dillard

Language, Grammar, and Style

EXPANDING SENTENCES

Identifying Short Sentences. Writers should avoid the repeated use of short, boring sentences. Such writing is dull, lifeless, and uninspiring.

EXAMPLE
The empty land is covered with grass.

There are many ways to expand sentences to achieve smooth writing and sentence variety. These include using modifiers, prepositional phrases, appositives, independent clauses, and subordinate clauses.

REVISED EXAMPLES

modifiers	The expansive, empty land rustles with waist-high emerald grass.
prepositional phrase	On the Dakota plains, the empty land is covered with grass.

CONTINUED

appositive	The empty land is covered with grass—a green, waving ocean.
independent clause	The empty land is covered with grass, and acres of wildflowers add an array of colors.
subordinate clause	The empty land, which has remained unchanged for decades, is covered with grass.

Expanding Short Sentences. Expand each of the following sentences by adding modifiers, prepositional phrases, appositives, independent clauses, or subordinate clauses, as indicated.

1. There is nothing to see—only land, sky, and light. (modifier)
2. Norris's friend from Boston proposed to a woman he knew. (prepositional phrase)
3. A friend asked what there was to see. (appositive)
4. Norris attended a Native American drum ceremony. (independent clause)
5. Hills, trees, buildings, highways, and people are absent from the Great Plains landscape. (subordinate clause).

Using Expanded Sentences in Your Writing. Read through your focused description and look for short, boring sentences. If you find any, expand them according to the directions in this lesson.

EXPANDING SHORT SENTENCES
Responses will vary. Sample responses:
1. There is nothing to see—only land, sky, and the everchanging light.
2. Norris's friend from Boston proposed to a woman he knew in his hometown.
3. A friend, Billy Watson, asked what there was to see.
4. Norris attended a Native American drum ceremony, and he later wrote about the experience.

3. Self- and Peer Evaluation

After you finish your first draft, complete a self-evaluation of your writing. If time allows, you may want to get one or two peer evaluations. As you evaluate your draft or a classmate's draft, ask these questions:

- What is the vantage point of the description? Is it similar to what would be depicted in a photograph?
- Are vivid details and figurative language used to make the scene come alive and inspire an emotional reaction?
- Is the writing organized in a manner that effectively conveys the purpose of the description?
- Is the description clear and unified?
- Does the description effectively use expanded sentences?

4. Revising and Proofreading

Based on your self- and peer edit, make changes to your draft. Reading the draft aloud is an excellent technique for hearing as well as seeing where you need to make revisions. Think about the strengths and weaknesses identified in the evaluation comments. Using these comments, decide how to revise your draft so that the final description is clear, detailed, and alive.

tip

After you have made changes to your description, proofread your writing for errors in spelling, grammar, punctuation, and capitalization. If you are unsure about a word's spelling, check it in a dictionary. Correct any punctuation errors you find.

5. Publishing and Presenting

If one is available, post a photograph of the place you wrote about, along with a copy of your description, in your classroom. You might work with several classmates or your entire class to create an exhibit that includes all of your class's descriptions and pictures. Students may decide to preserve their work in a class catalog.

5. Hills, trees, buildings, highways, and people, which define beauty in terms of the spectacular or the busy, are absent from the Great Plains landscape. (subordinate clause)

6. Reflecting on Your Writing

Reflect on what you learned from this assignment. What did you like the most about writing a focused description? What was the most difficult part of the experience? Did you gain any new insights from your writing? from the writing of your classmates?

ASSESSMENT
Writing rubrics and evaluation forms are available at www.emcp.com.

NARRATIVE WRITING

Writing a Narrative Essay

Narrative writing tells a story or relates a series of events. Narrative writing can be used to entertain, to make a point, or to introduce a topic. Describing an event, or narrating, involves the dimension of action over time. Narrative writing uses time, or *chronological order*, as a means of organization. It requires you to observe carefully, or recall vividly a series of moments. Narrative writing answers these questions:

Quotables

"With each story—and by story I mean anything I write—I am trying simply to work something out for myself."
—Roxana Robinson

Who was involved?
What happened?
When did it occur?
Where did it take place?
Why and *how* did the events unfold the way they did?

Using the **5 *W*s and an *H*** questioning strategy is especially helpful for gathering information about an event or for planning a story. Narrative writing is much like telling stories out loud. It requires you to give your readers enough information to understand what is happening—but not so much that they cannot follow the story. You decide which details to include based on your purpose and your audience.

Narratives are often used in essays, reports, and other nonfiction forms because stories are entertaining and fun to read. Just as important, they are a good way to make a point. Biographies, autobiographies, and family histories are also examples of narrative writing.

A **narrative essay** combines a series of events into a complete story. The following excerpt is taken from Mark Twain's classic work *Life on the Mississippi*.

After all these years I can picture that old time to myself now, just as it was then: the white town drowsing in the sunshine of a summer's morning; the streets empty, or pretty nearly so; one or two clerks sitting in front of the Water Street stores, with their splint-bottomed chairs tilted back against the wall, chins on breasts, hats slouched over their faces, asleep—with shingle shavings enough around to show what broke them down; a sow and a litter of pigs loafing along the sidewalk, doing a good business in watermelon rinds and seeds; two or three lonely freight piles scattered about the levee; a pile of skids on the slope of the stone-paved wharf, and the fragrant town drunkard asleep in the shadow of them; two or three wood flats at the head of the wharf, but nobody to listen to the peaceful lapping of the wavelets against them; the great Mississippi, the majestic, the magnificent Mississippi, rolling its mile-wide tide along, shining in the sun; the dense forest away on the other side; the point above the town, and the point below, bounding the river-glimpse and turning it into a sort of sea, and withal a very still and brilliant and lonely one. Presently a film of dark smoke appears above one of those remote points; instantly a Negro drayman, famous for his quick eye and prodigious voice, lifts up the cry, "S-t-e-a-m-boat a-comin'!" and the scene changes! The town drunkard stirs, the clerk wakes up, a furious clatter of drays follows, every house and store pours out a human contribution, and all in a twinkling the dead town is alive and moving. Drays, carts, men, boys, all go hurrying from many quarters to a common center, the wharf. Assembled there, the people fasten their eyes upon the coming boat as upon a wonder they are seeing for the first time.

from *Life on the Mississippi*
Mark Twain

Literature MODEL

EXAMINING THE *Model*

This excerpt describes events in a town on the Mississippi River in the nineteenth century.

ASSIGNMENT

Try It Yourself

Writing a Narrative Essay

For this assignment, you will be writing a narrative essay based on your own experience, a true story from your own life.

The voice you choose for your narrative should fit the nature of your story. Before you begin writing, think about how to match your voice with the general mood of the events in your essay.

Sensory details are critical in helping your reader experience the event you are relating. At the same time, your assignment is not to write pure description, but to use it to enhance your narrative.

1. Prewriting

There are several prewriting activities that can make your search for a topic fun and productive. One activity is to tap into the recorded history of your life that already exists. Talk to parents, siblings, and other relatives about important events. Look through old photo albums, watch family videos, or look back at old calendars to see what you were doing, when, and with whom. Finally, make a "*A time when* ______" list by filling in the blank with whatever comes to mind: "*A time when* I was afraid. *A time when* I was forced to make a difficult choice."

LANGUAGELINK
Print exercise worksheets or have students complete exercises online with the LanguageLINK CD.

After you have chosen a range of topics, narrow the list by freewriting a few minutes on each one to jog your memory. This will help you to find a topic that is important to you and possibly to others, and will eliminate the topics that don't spark your immediate interest. A graphic organizer like the one on the next page may help you keep track of details in your narrative essay.

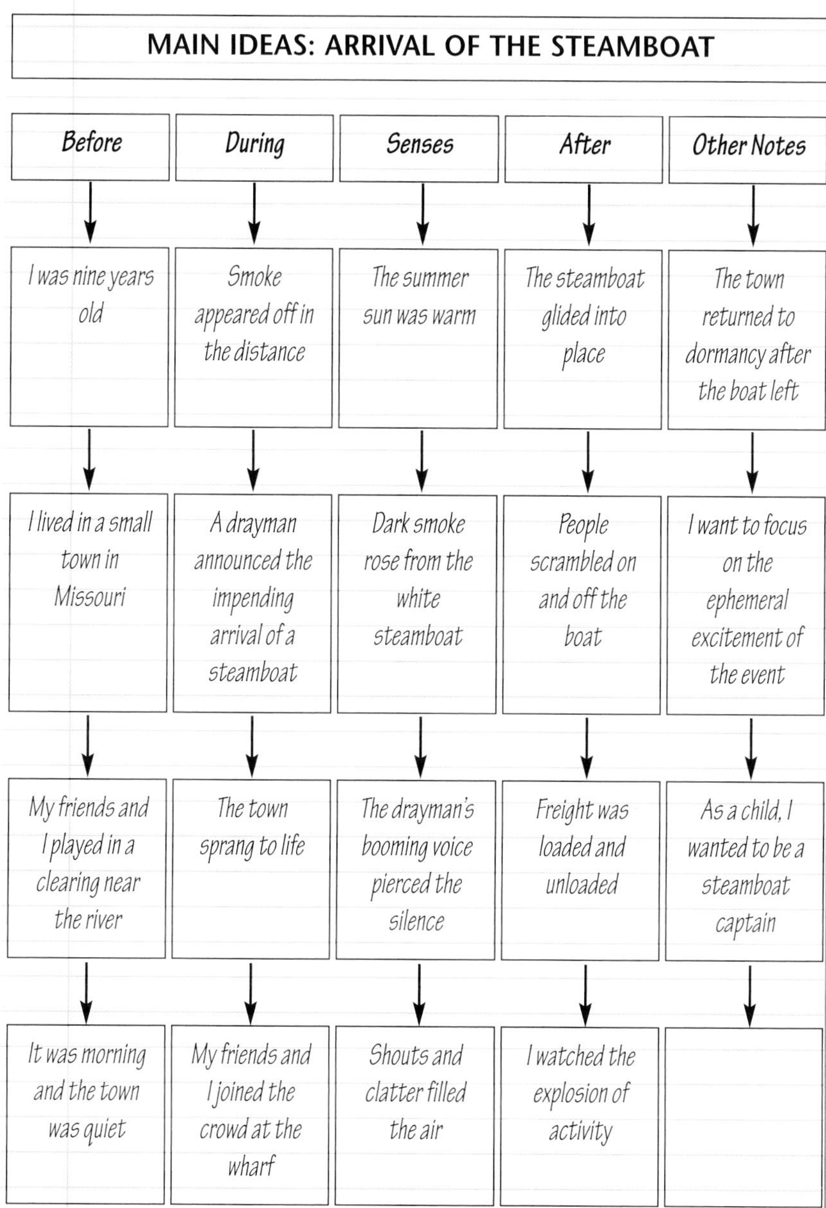

MAIN IDEAS: ARRIVAL OF THE STEAMBOAT

Before	*During*	*Senses*	*After*	*Other Notes*
I was nine years old	*Smoke appeared off in the distance*	*The summer sun was warm*	*The steamboat glided into place*	*The town returned to dormancy after the boat left*
I lived in a small town in Missouri	*A drayman announced the impending arrival of a steamboat*	*Dark smoke rose from the white steamboat*	*People scrambled on and off the boat*	*I want to focus on the ephemeral excitement of the event*
My friends and I played in a clearing near the river	*The town sprang to life*	*The drayman's booming voice pierced the silence*	*Freight was loaded and unloaded*	*As a child, I wanted to be a steamboat captain*
It was morning and the town was quiet	*My friends and I joined the crowd at the wharf*	*Shouts and clatter filled the air*	*I watched the explosion of activity*	

2. Drafting

Drafting a narrative is like reconstructing a real experience with words. As with all essays or stories, you need an inviting first paragraph that provides background information and introduces the story. Don't get into the plot of your narrative until you reach the first body paragraph.

 tip

As the paragraphs unfold and as you reconstruct your story, keep this question in mind: Am I *telling* or am I *showing?*

Before you move to the second paragraph, take a minute to look back at the graphic organizer and remind yourself of where your story really needs to start. If the event in your narrative takes place on a particular day, will you begin the first body paragraph at the beginning of that day, or will you need to give a little background information that wouldn't work in the introduction? If the event takes place in the evening, can you start the story at that time? Asking these questions helps to eliminate the needless baggage that can make a narrative drag.

You'll need to test the details. One effective way to do this is to read through your draft, highlighting in different colors images that use different senses: sight, hearing, smell, taste, and touch. Just the right details will show your reader the experience, not just tell about it.

Language, Grammar, and Style

PRONOUN-ANTECEDENT AGREEMENT

Identifying Agreement in Pronouns and Antecedents. A **pronoun** is a word that takes the place of a noun or stands in for an unknown noun. The noun that the pronoun replaces is called its antecedent. A pronoun must agree with or match its antecedent in gender, case, and number because it substitutes for the noun.

EXAMPLE
The town remained in a quiescent state prior to the arrival of the steamboat. Whenever it rounded the bend in the river, however, an explosion of activity always followed.

In this example, the pronoun comes in the second sentence. *It* is the pronoun, and the antecedent—the person, place, or thing *it* replaces—is *steamboat*. In this case the pronoun agrees with the antecedent in case and number. "It" refers to only one thing, not many.

CONTINUED

Correcting Pronoun-Antecedent Agreement. Correct the disagreement between the pronouns and antecedents in the following sentences.

1. The mates worked diligently to unload the freight as quickly as possible. The anxious throngs on the wharf rarely appreciated his efforts.
2. Two steamboats arrived and departed today, but I was sick and did not see it.
3. Our town is a dull, depressing place for most of the day. They depend upon the surge of excitement that comes with the arrival of the boats.
4. A person really can't appreciate the phenomenon unless they see it in person.

Using Pronouns and Antecedents Correctly in Your Writing. Read through your narrative essay and look for pronouns. Make sure that each pronoun agrees in case and number with its antecedent.

3. Self- and Peer Evaluation

Once you have finished your draft, read over your work. Let one or two of your peers do the same. Ask these questions about the essay:

- How many different senses are described in the draft?
- What is the climax of the narrative?
- What is the source of tension, good or bad, in the story?
- Underline a sentence that shows more than it tells.
- Which sentences use sensory details effectively?
- Is the story told in chronological order, or does it use a flashback?
- Is the order of events clear and logical?
- Find five sentences with pronouns and antecedents and check to see that they agree.
- What "things" in the narrative have distinctive shapes, sounds, or colors?

CORRECTING PRONOUN-ANTECEDENT AGREEMENT

1. The mates worked diligently to unload the freight as quickly as possible. The anxious throngs on the wharf rarely appreciated their efforts.
2. Two steamboats arrived and departed today, but I was sick and did not see them.
3. Our town is a dull depressing place for most of the day. It depends upon the surge of excitement that comes with the arrival of the boats.
4. A person really can't appreciate the phenomenon unless he or she sees it in person.

4. Revising and Proofreading

Check your draft against the questions above and make the necessary additions and deletions from your narrative. Keep in mind your goal of *showing your audience the story*, and of using sensory detail in your narrative.

5. Publishing and Presenting

tip

If your school has a literary publication, consider submitting your narrative to the nonfiction editor.

The best part about writing stories is that it's always easy to find readers. Share your narrative with those who participated in the experience with you, or classmates who know the people in your story. Send a copy of your story to interested relatives, or keep a book of your narratives and start developing a family history from your perspective. In class, share your story in a small reading group and ask for comments about your detail and organization.

ASSESSMENT
Writing rubrics and evaluation forms are available at www.emcp.com.

6. Reflecting on Your Writing

Your narrative is part of a vivid history of who you were at an important moment of your life. Add to it by starting a collection. Keep a journal about memorable moments and about people who experienced life with you. Spend some quiet time reflecting on the stories that you want to pass along to others.

INFORMATIVE/EXPOSITORY WRITING

Analyzing a Plot

The purpose of **informative** or **expository** writing is to inform, to present or explain an idea, or to explain a process. News articles and research reports are examples of informative expository writing.

One function of expository writing is to define, since a definition explains what something is. Another function of expository writing is to analyze and interpret. For example, a book review is writing that analyzes and interprets a piece of literature. Writers oftentimes explore the **plot**, a series of events related to a central **conflict,** or struggle, of a story. The following student model examines the plot of "American History," a short story by Judith Ortiz Cofer.

Quotables

"In most good stories it is the character's personality that creates the action of the story. . . . If you start with a real personality, a real character, then something is bound to happen. . . . You ought to be able to discover something from your stories. If you don't, probably nobody else will."

—Flannery O' Connor

Student MODEL

Her Own "American History"
by Patríce Williams

In Judith Ortiz Cofer's short story "American History" the plot unfolds as the narrator, a teen Puerto Rican girl, tells about her memories of the day President John F. Kennedy died. First, the author establishes the exposition and setting in the introduction as she provides background information about the time and place in which the story occurs. The time is November 22, 1963. The place is a tenement building, El Building, "a monstrous jukebox," in Paterson, New Jersey. Juxtaposed against this area with little vegetation is Eugene's house with its yard and trees. The two buildings are separated by a chain-link fence. Snow falls like gray slush in Paterson. Next, the inciting incidents occur with the death of President Kennedy and the arrival of Eugene. The action rises as the narrator prepares to meet Eugene by changing clothes and putting on pink lipstick and confronts her mother's grief at Kennedy's death. Finally, the climax of "American History" occurs toward the end of the story, when the narrator is rejected by Eugene's

EXAMINING THE *Model*

In the student model, Patríce explains the plot elements that comprise "American History."

CONTINUED

mother and told she cannot study with him. The author resolves the conflict by expressing the narrator's grief over the loss of Eugene through her tears. The narrator looks up at the white falling snow and refuses to look down to see it turning gray, acknowledging her need to ignore her depressing environment for the moment.

Try It Yourself

Analyzing a Plot

What makes a good story? Why do some stories "work" while others do not? Are there certain elements that all stories have in common? Your assignment is to analyze a short story using the elements of a plot that you will learn about in this unit. The assignment should help you understand what makes a good story.

1. Prewriting

Be sure that you understand each of the seven plot elements. Each element has a different purpose.

1. The **exposition,** or **introduction,** sets the tone and mood, introduces the characters and the setting, and provides the necessary background information.
2. The **inciting incident** is the event that introduces the central conflict.
3. The **rising action,** or **complication,** develops the conflict to a high point of intensity.
4. The **climax** is the high point of interest or suspense in the plot.
5. The **falling action** is all the events that follow the climax.
6. The **resolution** is the point at which the central conflict is ended, or resolved.
7. The **dénouement** is any material that follows the resolution and ties up loose ends.

Identifying Your Audience. Keep in mind that some members of your audience may not have read the story you chose to analyze. Be sure to provide enough examples in your paper to make your analysis understandable to anyone.

Obviously it is necessary to read the story that you plan to analyze first. You should plan to reread it, or parts of it, while you do your analysis. After you have read it the first time, go back over it and skim it to search for the different plot elements and to look for quotes that you might use in your writing. Next, complete a plot chart like the one below that is specific to your story. Your analysis should refer to each of the seven plot elements, so your plot chart will help ensure that you discuss them all.

Consider the following completed plot chart for "American History."

Graphic Organizer

Introductory Paragraph: *title and author (Judith Ortiz Cofer, "American History"); hook the reader's interest (link to the Kennedy assassination); explain how the plot elements work (Cofer skillfully weaves the rising action with the setting)*

1. ***Exposition:*** *The characters: teenage Puerto Rican girl (the narrator), her mother, and Eugene. Mood: cold and gray. Setting: tenement building in Paterson, New Jersey.*
2. ***Inciting Incident:*** *Eugene moves into a neighboring house; President Kennedy assassinated.*
3. ***Rising Action:*** *The narrator prepares to visit Eugene at his house; her mother grieves over the death of the president.*
4. ***Climax:*** *The narrator is turned away by Eugene's mother and not allowed to study with him.*
5. ***Falling Action:*** *The narrator returns home.*
6. ***Resolution:*** *The narrator lies in bed crying over the loss of Eugene.*
7. ***Dénouement:*** *The narrator looks out at the falling snow, refusing to look down and watch it turn gray.*

Conclusion: *Wrap up what I've done: assess how the plot elements worked together to pull the story along. (Refer back to the introduction.)*

tip

Work through the graphic organizer to help identify your thesis, build points of support, and establish your conclusion.

Quotables

"Every component in a piece of writing must do new work, and the transitions must pull the reader from one sentence to the next without his noticing the tug."
—William Zinsser

2. Drafting

Concentrate on getting your ideas down on paper. Don't worry about mechanics at this point. Your analysis will consist of your thoughts about how the different elements worked together in this story. In other words, how did the exposition successfully set the mood? Where did the rising action increase the level of intensity to make the climax the true high point of the story? Was the conflict resolved in a believable and creative way in the resolution? Your draft should expand on the list you completed in your graphic organizer. Try to combine elements, quotes, and analysis into a fluid piece of writing.

LANGUAGELINK
Print exercise worksheets or have students complete exercises online with the LanguageLINK CD.

Another important part of a plot analysis is using quotes from the story. When you use quotes, you use the story itself to support your analysis. Write down two or three quotes from your story that you may use in your analysis. Don't forget to use quotation marks, and copy the quoted message word for word as it appears in the story.

Language, Grammar, and Style

USING TRANSITIONS EFFECTIVELY

Identifying Transitions. A **transition** is a word or phrase that is used to connect ideas and to show relationships between them. Transitions can show time/chronological order, place/spatial order, cause and effect order, comparison and contrast order, and order of importance. The following examples include some of the more common transitions.

EXAMPLES

time/chronological order	first, next, before, after, then, later, finally
place/spatial order	above, behind, next to, on top of, near, to the left
cause and effect order	therefore, because, since, as a result, consequently
comparison and contrast order	on the other hand, similarly, in contrast
order of importance	of least importance, more important, most importantly

CONTINUED

Identifying Effective Transitions. Notice how transitions are used in the student model.

EXAMPLE

First, the author establishes the exposition and setting in the introduction as she provides background information about the time and place in which the story occurs.

Next, the inciting incidents occur with the death of President Kennedy and the arrival of Eugene.

Finally, the climax of "American History" occurs toward the end of the story, when the narrator is rejected by Eugene's mother and told she cannot study with him.

Correcting Ineffective Transitions. Add to the following sentences by using the type of transition listed in parentheses.

1. Only one house in our neighborhood had a yard and trees. (one place/spatial order transition)
2. There are several steps to making friends at school. (two order of importance transitions)
3. I prepared for my study date with my friend. (three time/chronological order transitions)
4. Nobody could have imagined what would happen today. (one cause and effect transition)
5. My mother and I both felt terrible. (one comparison and contrast transition)

Using Transitions in Your Writing. Reread your own writing and examine each of your paragraphs. Did you use transitions to connect ideas and show relationships? Look for places where you could more effectively use transitions.

3. Self- and Peer Evaluation

Use the following questions to complete a self- and peer evaluation:

- Where in the introduction are the title of the story and the author mentioned?
- How does the writer capture interest in the introduction?

CORRECTING INEFFECTIVE TRANSITIONS

Responses will vary. Sample responses:

1. Only one house in our neighborhood had a yard and trees. Behind the house stood our apartment.

2. There are several steps to making friends at school. Most important, remember to be yourself. Less important is trying to impress people with your accomplishments.
3. I prepared for my study date with my friend. First, I picked out my clothes and got dressed. Next, I combed my hair. Finally, I brushed and flossed my teeth.
4. Nobody could have imagined what happened today. As a result of the assassination, we were dismissed from school.
5. My mother and I both felt terrible. She cried because the president died. In contrast, I felt bad because I could not see a friend.

- Does the paper discuss all seven of the plot elements?
- Where does the writing seem to flow from one paragraph to another?
- Is there a place where the writing could be revised to be more fluent?
- Where are the insights of the writer clear?
- Do quotes fit into the piece without being awkward?
- Are transitions used effectively?
- Is the analysis written in such a way that someone who has not read the story could still understand it?
- How does the conclusion wrap up the paper?

4. Revising and Proofreading

Based on the responses of your self- and peer evaluations, make changes in your essay that will help your audience better understand your analysis. Don't hesitate to tweak your thesis so it says what you want it to say. When you are finished revising, proofread your paper for errors in conventions such as spelling and punctuation.

5. Publishing and Presenting

You will be expected to share your essays with other students in a read-aloud in class. Your analysis contains a fair amount of your insights, so each person's essay should be different. Discuss each story again after hearing one another's insights.

ASSESSMENT
Writing rubrics and evaluation forms are available at www.emcp.com.

6. Reflecting on Your Writing

What things did you discover about the story when you looked at it a second and third time that you missed the first time through? What did you learn when you heard others' reactions to the same story? Have your insights deepened even further? How might being an insightful reader help you to become a better writer?

PERSUASIVE/ARGUMENTATIVE WRITING

Writing a Letter to the Editor

The purpose of **persuasive/argumentative writing** is to persuade readers or listeners to respond in some way, such as to agree with a position, change a view on an issue, reach an agreement, or perform an action. Examples of persuasive writing are editorials, petitions, political speeches, and essays.

Many people seek to persuade others by writing a **letter to the editor**. The author of such a letter expresses an opinion and often tries to convince readers of a newspaper that some type of change needs to be effected. The following literature model is an excerpt from a letter written by poet Robert Frost to a college newspaper.

Quotables

"And while I try not to take myself too seriously, I take my work seriously. Because I know the power of words, I know the good they can do."

—Veronica Chambers

Literature MODEL

It is very, very kind of the *Student* to be showing sympathy with me for my age. But sixty is only a pretty good age. It is not advanced enough. The great thing is to be advanced. Now ninety would be really well along and something to be given credit for.

But speaking of ages, you will often hear it said that the age of the world we live in is particularly bad. I am impatient of such talk. We have no way of knowing that this age is one of the worst in the world's history. Arnold claimed the honor for the age before this. Wordsworth claimed it for the last but one. And so on back through literature. I say they claimed the honor for their ages. They claimed it rather for themselves. It is immodest of a man to think of himself as going down before the worst forces ever mobilized by God.

from Letter to *The Amherst Student*
Robert Frost

EXAMINING THE *Model*

In this excerpt, Frost expresses his opinion that people often exaggerate the problems of the age in which they are living.

Try It Yourself

Writing a Letter to the Editor

In this assignment, you will be writing a letter to the editor of a local or school newspaper. In your letter, you will define a problem, discuss its causes, and suggest possible solutions to the problem. A letter to the editor needs to be forceful and persuasive. You must persuade your readers that the problem you are writing about is important and that they need to take action.

1. Prewriting

The readers of your letter may be both students and adult members of the community. As you write, think about the information that is appropriate for this audience. What information will your audience need to understand the problem and your solution? What objections might they raise to your solution? What proofs for your solution will be most effective?

You may already have a topic that you would like to write about. If you do not, try the following process: First, brainstorm a list of ideas. Next, copy the graphic organizer below onto your own paper. Fill in the organizer with the three most interesting topics on your list. List consequences, causes, and best solutions for the problems. Then decide which topic you could write about most persuasively in a letter to the editor.

Writing tip

Voice. For this assignment you will want to use a compelling, forthright voice. Practice writing sentences that are compelling, reasonable, honest, and straightforward statements about the problem and its solution.

Graphic Organizer

Problem →	*Consequences* →	*Causes* →	*Solution*
people today believe the age they live in is the worst ever	*people will overreact to current problems*	*lack of knowledge about other time periods and cultures*	*revise school curriculum to stress historical perspectives*

2. Drafting
Use the information in your graphic organizer to guide you as you write the rough draft of your letter. Start by writing your **thesis statement**, the main idea of the letter. Add statements that help to clarify and define the problem. Next, identify the consequences and the causes of the problem. Finally, offer your solution. If part of your solution includes a request for your readers to contact an agency about a problem, provide the address and telephone number of that agency. Make it as easy as possible for your readers to respond and be part of the solution you suggest.

LANGUAGELINK
Print exercise worksheets or have students complete exercises online with the LanguageLINK CD.

Remember that you are writing for a real newspaper. This is your chance to influence others and bring about change. Express your opinion with a compelling, reasonable, and honest voice; support your ideas by offering facts and listing solutions.

Language, Grammar, and Style

AVOIDING DOUBLE NEGATIVES

Identifying Double Negatives. A negative is a "no" word. Using two negatives in a sentence when only one is needed is called using a **double negative**. Some languages, including Spanish, use double negatives. Standard English, however, does not use double negatives in any given sentence.

Check your writing to be sure that you have not used a negative word such as *not*, *nobody*, *nothing*, *hardly*, *barely*, *can't*, *doesn't*, *won't*, *isn't*, or *aren't* with another negative word. Change double negatives by replacing one of the negative words in the sentence with a positive word.

In the following examples, underline the negatives words. Identify the sentences that have double negatives by writing *incorrect*. If a sentence does not have a double negative, write *correct*.

CONTINUED

1. Without a strong grasp of history, you won't have any perspective with which to judge your own era.
   Without a strong grasp of history, you won't have no perspective with which to judge your own era.

2. Most of the people living today don't have no idea what the nineteenth century was like.
   Most of the people living today don't have any idea what the nineteenth century was like.

3. I couldn't find nobody in my class who understood the intensity of the Great Depression.
   I couldn't find anybody in my class who understood the intensity of the Great Depression.

Correcting Double Negatives. Look at the sentences below. Correct any double negatives by replacing one of the negatives in the sentence with a positive word. You may need to reword the sentence.

1. I couldn't scarcely understand the political issues in this book that was published in 1759.

2. None of our representatives aren't looking to the past to understand the problems of today.

3. If this situation continues, it isn't hardly likely that tomorrow's students will understand the issues that we are dealing with today.

Using Negatives Correctly in Your Writing. Examine each sentence in your letter to the editor. Check to see if you have used any double negatives. Correct any sentences that contain such errors.

IDENTIFYING DOUBLE NEGATIVES

1. Without a strong grasp of history, you <u>won't</u> have any perspective with which to judge your own era. (correct) Without a strong grasp of history, you <u>won't</u> have <u>no</u>

3. Self- and Peer Evaluation

After you finish your rough draft, complete a self-evaluation of your writing. Since your goal is for others to read your letter and be motivated to make changes because of it, try to get one or two peer reviews. As you evaluate your letter, answer the following questions. Take notes on your rough draft to use later when you write your final copy.

- How convincing is the letter?
- What improvements might be needed in the thesis statement to more clearly identify and define the problem?
- What consequences are identified? How seriously will the reader view these consequences? What additional consequences might be included?
- How does the letter refute other solutions that readers may have to offer?
- Which words and sentences present the most honest, reasonable, and convincing voice? Which words and sentences present the least honest, reasonable, and convincing voice?
- What action to solve the problem does the letter suggest?
- Check each sentence for double negatives. How could the sentences be rewritten correctly?
- Check the letter for a proper heading, inside address, salutation, body, complimentary closing, and signature.

tip

A good way to finish a piece of writing is to read it aloud and listen for problems. Does your letter say what you want it to say?

perspective with which to judge your own era. (incorrect)

2. Most of the people living today don't have no idea what the nineteenth century was like. (incorrect)
   Most of the people living today don't have any idea what the nineteenth century was like. (correct)
3. I couldn't find nobody in my class who understood the intensity of the Great Depression. (incorrect)
   I couldn't find anybody in my class who understood the intensity of the Great Depression. (correct)

CORRECTING DOUBLE NEGATIVES

Responses will vary. Sample responses:

1. I could scarcely understand the political issues in this book that was published in 1759.
2. None of our representatives are looking to the past to understand the problems of today.
3. If this situation continues, it isn't likely that tomorrow's students will understand the issues that we are dealing with today.

4. Revising and Proofreading

Look at your self- and peer evaluations. Use your notes and your peers' comments to make decisions about how to revise your letter. If there are any gaps in the letter, go back and fill them in. Take out any information that you feel distracts from the letter. Finally, proofread your revised draft for errors in spelling, grammar, usage, and mechanics.

5. Publishing and Presenting

You can write your final copy in ink or you may print it from a computer. Before you send your letter, check to see that you have included the following information:

1. heading
2. inside address
3. standard salutation
4. body
5. complimentary closing
6. signature

ASSESSMENT
Writing rubrics and evaluation forms are available at www.emcp.com.

If you are writing a letter to the school newspaper, check to see if your teacher wants you to use your school address rather than your home address. If you are sending your letter to a local newspaper, address the envelope neatly and include your return address in the upper left-hand corner of the envelope. Add postage and mail your letter promptly.

6. Reflecting on Your Writing

Have you ever met someone who could talk someone into doing something that wasn't in his or her best interests? Have you ever watched a television commercial or read an advertisement in a magazine that persuaded you to buy something you didn't need or even want? What do you think the difference is between being good at persuasion and being a good persuader? What might someone who is a good at persuasion try to influence you to do? What kind of language might this person use? What kinds of causes might someone who is a good persuader take up? What kind of language might this person use?

THE RESEARCH PAPER

Writing an Informative Research Paper

A **research paper** is a large writing project that requires an organized approach. A research paper is similar to an essay, but there are key differences. An essay tends to be shorter than a research paper. An essay usually contains one or more opinions supported by some facts, while a research paper may present many facts, from a variety of sources, as evidence in support of one major opinion. The main idea of a work of nonfiction such as an essay or a research paper is called the **thesis.**

Quotables

"I'm driven by a nomadic curiosity. . . . I try to give myself passionately to the subject with as much affectionate curiosity as I can muster. The information, the facts themselves, fuel my work but are really secondary to my rage to learn about the human condition."
—Diane Ackerman

To support your thesis, you will need to do a considerable amount of research. You need to know where to look and how to focus your search. Documentation of your sources is critical because it gives proper credit and it leads other researchers to the sources you found useful.

A research paper may be narrative or persuasive writing. It could also be an informative paper with the purpose of presenting clear information to others. Read the model informative research paper on pages 635–638.

Try It Yourself

Writing an Informative Research Paper
For an **informative research paper** you will research information from a variety of reliable sources. Then, in your paper, you will present the information in a clear and logical way for your readers. Finally, you will document the sources that you used to support your argument.

LANGUAGELINK
Print exercise worksheets or have students complete exercises online with the LanguageLINK CD.

1. Prewriting
Finding a topic is your first task. What topics come to mind from the personal experiences you have had? What topics are you learning about in chemistry, art, history, language arts, music, and math? On another piece of paper, brainstorm a list of topics that you could research. Remember to use your curiosity: *What do you want to know more about?*

After you have selected your topic, you will need to find out what information is available. Gather information from the library and your electronic sources and start reading. A primary source is a firsthand account. You should try to use at least one primary source. If you do not have three or four good sources of information including at least one primary source, you may need to think of a different topic

Next, write a thesis statement that states your topic and your focus on that topic. Organize the information you have gathered around the main points that support your thesis. Writers frequently organize their research in an outline to give their paper structure and order. If you favor a structure that is more visual or spatial, you may instead prefer to use a graphic organizer such as the one below.

Graphic Organizer

Keeping Track of Your Sources. Take your graphic organizer to the library, and collect your source material. In a research journal like the one below, write down the title, author, the publishing company, the place and date of publication, the location, and the call number for each book. Write down the addresses of any reliable Internet websites you plan to use. Record the names of articles in magazines, along with the magazine titles, dates, and volume numbers. You will need your list of sources when you write your bibliography.

tip

For more information on conducting Internet research see Unit 18, pages 488–499.

RESEARCH JOURNAL

1. Author ______________________
   Title ______________________
   Place, Publisher, Date ______________________
   Location, Call Number, or URL ______________________
2. Author ______________________
   Title ______________________
   Place, Publisher, Date ______________________
   Location, Call Number, or URL ______________________
3. Author ______________________
   Title ______________________
   Place, Publisher, Date ______________________
   Location, Call Number, or URL ______________________
4. Author ______________________
   Title ______________________
   Place, Publisher, Date ______________________
   Location, Call Number, or URL ______________________

Taking Notes. Look through your sources for information that is relevant to the items included on your graphic organizer. When you find pertinent material you can paraphrase, summarize, or quote the information on a piece of paper or on a note card. Do not copy the author's exact words unless you are quoting the author. To copy another person's words without crediting that person as your source is unethical. You want your research paper to reflect your clear and natural voice. Your notes should be specific, accurate, and brief. You will use your notes later to help you write your draft.

Use a separate card or piece of paper for each note you write. Include the question you are answering, the name of the source you are using, and the page number where you found the information. Try to include two or three important quotations from authors. Write the author's exact words on a note card and put quotation marks around them. Reference the quotation with the author's last name and the page number in parentheses.

Preparing Note Cards

- Identify the source at the top right corner of the card. (Use the source numbers from your Research Journal or bibliography cards.)
- Identify the subject or topic of the note on the top line of the card.
- Use a separate card for each fact or quotation.
- Write the pertinent source page number or numbers after the note.

Arranging Note Cards. Before you start writing, you need to decide on the best order for presenting the information in your paper. To help decide the order, ask yourself what is the most important or logical thing for my audience to learn first, second, third, and fourth. Put a number 1 next to the question on your graphic organizer that you will write about first in your research paper. Number the other questions according to the order in which you plan to write about them.

Now gather all your note cards together that go with question number 1. Arrange these cards in the order that you plan to use them. Number them as 1-1, 1-2, 1-3, and so on. Continue the same process for the note cards that go with the questions numbered 2, 3, and 4. You can write your rough draft from your ordered note cards or you may use your note cards to write an outline first.

SAMPLE NOTE CARD

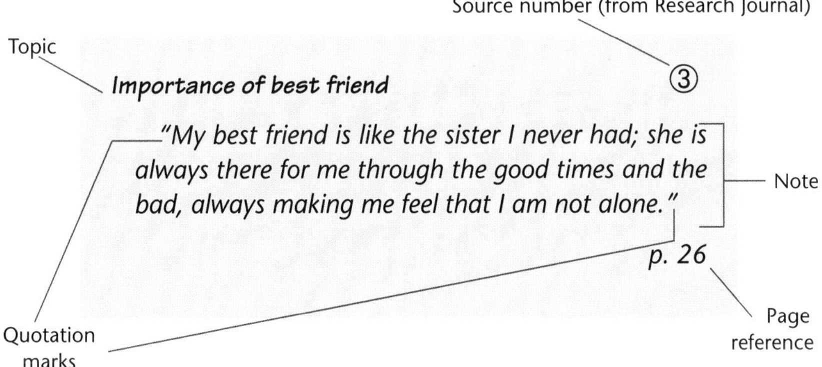

As you do research, your notes will include **quotations**, **paraphrases**, and **summaries**.

Type of Note	When to Use	What to Watch For
Quotation	When the exact wording of a primary source is important to your topic	Copy spelling, capitalization, punctuation, and numbers exactly as in the source.
	When you are providing a definition	Place quotation marks around all direct quotations.
Paraphrase	When the idea of a secondary source is particularly memorable or insightful, but you want to say it in your own words	Record, when appropriate, explanatory background information about the speaker or the context of a quotation.
	Most of the time	Focus on your main purpose, and note only points related to your topic.

CONTINUED

Summary	When the point you are making does not require the detail of a paraphrase	Place quotation marks around any quoted words or phrases. Reread the source after writing your summary to be sure that you have not altered the meaning.

2. Drafting

It is easier to write a good introduction for your paper if you wait until the body of the paper is written; then you know what your paper says, and what you need to finalize it. Begin instead with your thesis statement: What do you want to say about your topic? What are you trying to show your audience? Starting with a thesis will give your paper some direction.

From the thesis write about the main points that will support it. Write about only one point at a time. Insert the necessary parenthetical documentation as you quote or paraphrase specific information from your sources. After you finish a point, take a break before you go on to the next. Keeping a fresh mind is important while you are writing; otherwise, you may forget to include key information. Documenting sources as you go along will ultimately save you time later.

After you have developed all of the main points and their supporting information, read through your draft to see if the points are coherent. Then draft an introduction that uses an appropriate technique to develop interest in your topic. Include your thesis in the introduction. Finally, draft a conclusion that summarizes the essence of your paper.

At the end of the paper you will need to include a bibliography telling where you got your information. A **bibliography** is a list of sources used for the writing. (For more information on preparing your bibliography, see "Documenting Sources" in the following Language, Grammar, and Style section.)

Language, Grammar, and Style

DOCUMENTING SOURCES

Identifying Proper Documentation. As you research your writing, you must document your sources of information. Remember to:

- Credit the sources of all ideas and facts that you use.
- Credit original ideas or facts that are expressed in text, tables, charts, and other graphic information.
- Credit all artistic property, including works of literature, song lyrics, and ideas.

As you work on your paper, you should be writing down on note cards the information for each source that you use. Include all of the information shown on the sample bibliography card. Be sure to punctuate correctly and to capitalize proper nouns and the titles of print and online resources.

SAMPLE BIBLIOGRAPHY CARD

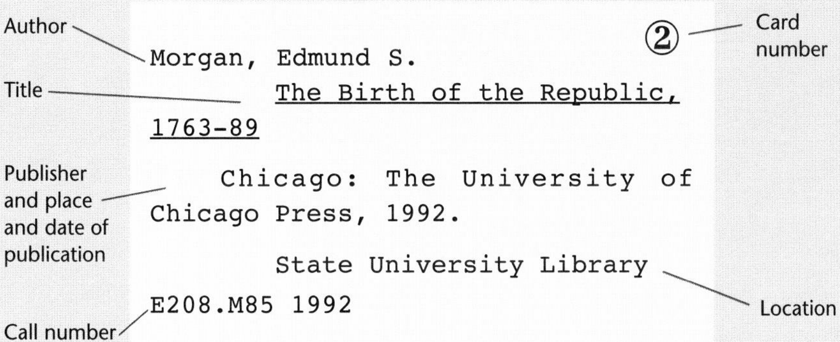

Author
Morgan, Edmund S.
②
Card number
Title
The Birth of the Republic, 1763-89
Publisher and place and date of publication
Chicago: The University of Chicago Press, 1992.
State University Library
Location
E208.M85 1992
Call number

Forms for Bibliographic Entries

- **A book**

  Morgan, Edmund S. *The Birth of the Republic, 1763–89* (3rd ed.). Chicago: University of Chicago Press, 1992.

- **A magazine article**

  Whitfield, Stephen J. "A Century and a Half of French Views of the United States." *The Historian.* April 1994: 531–542.

- **An encyclopedia entry**

  "Hamilton, Alexander." *The Harper Encyclopedia of Military Biography.* Dupuy, Trevor N. 1995 ed.

- **An interview**
  Dempsey, Christine. Personal interview. 13 November 2002.
- **An Internet page**
  Carlson, Wayne. "Were the Anti-Federalists Wrong?" The Sierra Times. 7 August 2001. <http://www.sierratimes.com/archive/files/aug/07/carlson.htm>.

Understanding Parenthetical Documentation. Parenthetical documentation is currently the most widely used form of documentation. To use this method to document the source of a quotation or an idea, place a brief note identifying the source in parentheses immediately after the borrowed material. This type of note is called a **parenthetical citation,** and the act of placing such a note is called **citing a source.** The first part of a parenthetical citation refers the reader to a source in your bibliography. The second part of the citation refers the reader to a specific page or place within the source. If the source is clearly identified in the text, omit if from the citation and give only the page number.

- **For works listed by author or editor, use the author's or editor's last name.**
  Sample bibliographic entry
  McGuinn, Taro. *East Timor: Island in Turmoil.* Minneapolis: Lerner, 1988.
  Sample citation
  "It's unlikely that the problem in East Timor will be solved militarily" (Brown 364).
- **For works listed by title, use the title (abbreviate if necessary).**
  Sample bibliographic entry
  "East Timor." Encyclopedia Britannica. 2000 ed.
  Sample citation
  Indonesia's rule over East Timor is disputed by the United Nations ("East Timor" 632).
- **When the author's name is used in the text, cite only the page number.**
  McGuinn believes that military forces cannot end the problems in East Timor (80).

Using Proper Documentation in Your Writing. Read your informative research paper again. Are there places where you paraphrased an author's ideas that you need to reference? Are there exact quotations that you need to reference? Fix any documentation in the body of your paper. Then look at your bibliography. Be sure each source is documented correctly and that you have punctuated and capitalized correctly.

3. Self- and Peer Evaluation

After you finish your first draft, complete a self-evaluation of your research paper. Try to read your draft as though you were uninformed about the topic. Identify background information or support that may be missing. As time allows, obtain one or more peer evaluations. As you evaluate your draft or that of a classmate, respond to the following questions:

- What additional information is needed for the reader to have a more thorough understanding?
- What would make the introduction more interesting or more focused?
- How clearly does the thesis statement present the issue?
- What main point is developed in each of the body paragraphs?
- How does each body paragraph relate to the thesis?
- How logically do the main points support the thesis? What points might be missing? Which points might be extraneous to the issue?
- What do direct quotations add? What additional quotations would add meaningful support? Which quotations seem unnecessary?
- How effective is the conclusion?
- Where, if anywhere, does the documentation fail to follow correct MLA form?

4. Revising and Proofreading

Review your self- and peer evaluations. Revise your writing after considering those comments. Check that each paragraph has a topic sentence that relates to your thesis statement. Proofread your revised draft for spelling, mechanical, and usage errors. Invite one or two friends to proofread your writing as well. Be sure that each source is referenced correctly in the paper and that the bibliography is also done correctly. Remember that each source listed at the end of the paper must be cited internally at least once. Finish the paper by including a title page. Finally, give your teacher a double-spaced paper as your final product.

USAGE tip

The Modern Language Association of America website answers basic questions about MLA documentation style, particularly documentation of Web sources. From the home page, select "MLA Style."

ASSESSMENT

Writing rubrics and evaluation forms are available at www.emcp.com.

5. Publishing and Presenting

Your final product should be a paper that you are proud to present. When you have done your best, share your work. Your may wish to publish the papers as an anthology. Your high school library might wish to shelve a copy—or you might post it on your school's website.

6. Reflecting on Your Writing

Writing a good research paper is one of the more difficult tasks asked of students. What was the most challenging part of the project for you? What do you wish you would have done differently? What did you learn about your research and organizational skills? the subject matter? What future reading or research might you be compelled to do?

A model informative research paper appears on pages 635–638.

RESEARCH PAPER MODEL

The Bill of Rights

by Tyrone Ramsey
English 11
September 21, 2003
p. 1

The Constitution is the foundation of the United States government. Today, it seems unimaginable that this cannonized document once aroused strong opposition from a sizeable percentage of Americans. In fact, after it was introduced in the fall of 1787, ratification did not look likely. Not until supporters of the Constitution promised to add individual protections in the form of a bill of rights did ratification have a chance. Thus, the Bill of Rights, the first ten amendments to the Constitution, was the crucial factor in propelling the document through the ratification process to become the supreme law of the land.

Following their victory in the Revolutionary War, the former colonists still had to prove they could govern themselves. The first attempt at a national government, the Articles of Confederation, contained fatal flaws. After a series of events in the 1780s revealed the unacceptable weaknesses of this initial national government, America's leaders realized the necessity of creating a new governmental framework (McLaughlin). Twelve of the thirteen states sent delegates to Philadelphia in May 1787 to complete this task. After working, debating, and sweating through a long hot summer, the delegates produced a constitution by the end of September (Johnson).

The document needed to be ratified by nine of the thirteen states before it could take effect. Across the new nation, Americans divided into factions.

Those supporting the Constitution were called Federalists; those in opposition were known as Anti-Federalists. Each state elected delegates to a state convention called for the specific purpose of deciding on the document. The well-organized Federalists effectively parried most of the arguments of their opponents. However, the charge that the Constitution would open the door for tyranny by the central government proved a difficult charge to counter (Johnson).

Leading Anti-Federalists warned that ratification would create an oppressive national leadership similar to the British government, which the Americans had just thrown off. The Constitution's opponents feared that a strong central government could trample the rights of the individual (Carlson). The debate eventually centered on the necessity of a bill of rights. Federalists such as James Wilson saw a bill of rights as unnecessary and impracticable. Their opponents strongly disagreed. At Pennsylvania's ratifying convention, Anti-Federalist John Smilie warned that without a bill of rights

> . . . there will be no check [on government] but the people, and their exertions must be futile and uncertain; since it will be difficult indeed, to communicate to them, the violation that has been committed and their proceedings will be neither systematical nor unanimous. It is said, however, that the difficulty of framing a bill of rights was insurmountable: but Mr. President, I can not agree in this opinion. Our experience, and the numerous precedents before us, would have furnished a very sufficient guide. At present there is no security, even for the rights of conscience, and under the sweeping force of the sixth article, every principle of a bill of rights, every stipulation

> for the most sacred and invaluable privileges of man, are left to the mercy of government. (Johnson)

In the face of strong opposition, leading Federalists had to admit that the absence of a bill of rights was a defect. Without an explicit protection of individual liberties, the Constitution was vulnerable to defeat. To avoid this fate, leading Federalist James Madison promised that, if ratified, the first task of the new government would be to pass a bill of rights to protect individual liberties. This promise countered the most important Anti-Federalist objections to the Constitution. By January 1788, five states had ratified the document. Over the following two years, the remaining eight states approved the Constitution on the condition that it would quickly be amended with a bill of rights (Johnson).

In 1789, James Madison produced drafts of ten amendments. The First Amendment grants citizens the freedom of religion, speech, press, assembly, and the right to petition. The next seven amendments protect the right to bear arms, property rights, and the rights of individuals who have been accused of a crime. The Tenth Amendment reserves for the people those powers not otherwise specifically delegated to the national government. Congress approved the ten amendments in September 1789. They were then sent to the states for ratification, which was completed on December 15, 1791. The Bill of Rights had become part of the Constitution (Johnson).

The Bill of Rights assuaged the fears of many of the Constitution's initial opponents. The protections included in the first ten amendments persuaded Americans to accept a strong national government. Considering their recent experience with a strong British government, this is a remarkable accomplishment. The Federalists' concession to include a bill of rights proved the decisive factor in the ratification process of the Constitution. Without its first ten amendments, the Constitution would have long ago been relegated to the trash bin of history.

Bibliography

Carlson, Wayne. "Were the Anti-Federalists Wrong?" The Sierra Times. 7 August 2001. <http://www.sierratimes.com/archive/files/aug/07/carlson.htm>.

Johnson, Paul. *A History of the American People.* New York: HarperCollins Publishers, 1997.

McLaughlin, Andrew. "The Articles of Confederation." *Essays on the Making of the Constitution*. Ed. Leonard W. Levy. New York: Oxford University Press, 1969.

Wilson, James, and John Smilie. "Debating the Need for a Bill of Rights." *Our Nation's Archive: A History of the United States in Documents.* Eds. Erik Bruun and Jay Crosby. New York: Black Dog and Leventhal Publishers, 1999.

UNIT 22 REVIEW

TEST YOUR KNOWLEDGE

ASSESSMENT
Writing Comprehensive Test, Writing Rubrics, and Writing Evaluation Forms are available at www.emcp.com.

EXERCISE 1
Identifying Writing Modes in Literature
Identify the following excerpt as *personal/expressive*, *imaginative/descriptive*, *narrative*, *informative/expository*, or *persuasive/argumentative* writing. (10 points)

> Man, who was created in the image of his Maker, never can properly be termed a thing, though the laws of the Slave States do call him a "chattel personal"; Man, I assert, never was put under the feet of men by the first charter of human rights which was given by God. . . . It has been justly remarked that "God never made a slave," he made man upright, his back was not made to carry burdens, nor his neck to wear a yoke, and the man must be crushed within him, before his back can be fitted to the burden of perpetual slavery; and that his back is not fitted to it, is manifest by the insurrections that so often disturb the peace and security of slaveholding countries. . . . Slavery always has, and always will produce insurrections wherever it exists, because it is a violation of the natural order of things, and no human power can much longer perpetuate it.
>
> from *Appeal to the Christian Women of the Southern States*
> Angelina Grimké

EXERCISE 1
persuasive/argumentative writing

EXERCISE 2
Identifying Writing Modes
Identify the following writing forms as *personal/expressive*, *imaginative/descriptive*, *narrative*, *informative/expository*, or *persuasive/argumentative* writing. (10 points)

EXERCISE 2
1. narrative writing
2. persuasive/argumentative writing
3. narrative writing
4. informative/expository writing
5. personal/expressive writing
6. narrative writing
7. personal/expressive writing
8. persuasive/argumentative writing
9. imaginative/descriptive writing
10. persuasive/argumentative, personal/expressive, or narrative writing

EXERCISE 3

1. personal/expressive
2. persuasive/argumentative
3. narrative
4. informational/expository
5. imaginative/descriptive

EXERCISE 4

In addition to the information listed below, students should also number each bibliography card and provide a library where the information was found and a call number if appropriate.

Shaara, Jeffrey M. *Rise to Rebellion*. New York: Ballantine Books, 2001.

Cronon, William. *Changes in the Land*. New York: Hill and Wang, 1983.

Gerstle, Gary. "Liberty, Coercion, and the Making of Americans." *The Journal of American History* 84, no. 2 (September 1997): 524–558.

Kimmel, Michael S. "Baseball and the Reconstitution of American Masculinity, 1880–1920." *Baseball History* 3 (1990): 98–112.

Smith, Stephen R. "Malpractice." *Encyclopedia of Psychology,* 2000 ed.

"Prohibition." *Encyclopedia of the 20th Century,* 1991 ed.

Caple, Jim. "From 3-Year-Olds to 30-Year-Olds." 24 October 2002. ESPN. Accessed 28 October 2003.

1. biography
2. editorial
3. short story
4. report
5. diary entry
6. family history
7. personal letter
8. petition
9. poem
10. essay

EXERCISE 3
Understanding the Purposes of Writing

Complete the following sentences by writing the correct mode of writing. (10 points)

1. The purpose of _______________ writing is to allow the writer to reflect about his or her thoughts and feelings.
2. Writing that convinces readers or listeners to respond in some way is called _______________ writing.
3. The purpose of _______________ writing is to share a story about an event.
4. Writing that informs is called _______________ writing.
5. The purpose of _______________ writing is to entertain, enrich, and enlighten.

EXERCISE 4
Understanding Proper Documentation

Using the facts below, write a bibliography card for each reference. Be sure to include a call number and library location where appropriate. Check your cards for correct punctuation and capitalization. (20 points)

Author	Title	Publication Facts
Books		
Jeffrey M. Shaara	*Rise to Rebellion*	Ballantine Books, New York, 2001
William Cronon	*Changes in the Land*	Hill and Wang, New York, 1983
Magazines		
Gary Gerstle	"Liberty, Coercion, and the Making of Americans"	*The Journal of American History* 84, no. 2 (September 1997): 524–558
Michael S. Kimmel	"Baseball and the Reconstitution of American Masculinity, 1880–1920"	Baseball History 3 (1990): 98–112
Encyclopedias		
Stephen R. Smith	"Malpractice"	*Encyclopedia of Psychology*, 2000 ed.
Not given	"Prohibition"	*Encyclopedia of the 20th Century*, 1991 ed.
Internet		
Jim Caple	"From 3-Year-Olds to 30-Year-Olds"	ESPN, <http://espn.go.com/mlb/columns/caple_jim/1450828.html> 24 October 2002
Not given	"ISU Animal Science Professor Named Iowa Inventor of the Year"	Iowa State University, <http://www.iastate.edu/~nscentral/releases/2002/oct/rothschild.shtml> 23 October 2002

<http://espn.go.com/mlb/columns/caple_jim/1450828.html>.

"ISU Animal Science Professor Named Iowa Inventor of the Year." 23 October 2002. Iowa State University. Accessed 3 November 2003. <http://www.iastate.edu/~nscentral/releases/2002/oct/rothschild.shtml>.

EXERCISE 5

Correcting Documentation

Prepare a bibliography card for each of the following sources. Be sure to check your cards for correct punctuation and capitalization. (10 points)

1. Larry M. Logue, *To Appomattox and Beyond: The Civil War Soldier in War and Peace*, 1996, Ivan R. Dee, Inc., Chicago
2. "Jimmy Carter: Man of His Words," Jerome V. Kramer, *Book* (November/December 2001), 30–36
3. "Montagnais-Naskapi" by Amanda Irene Seligman in *Encyclopedia of North American Indians*, pp. 392–393, 1996 edition

EXERCISE 5

Logue, Larry M. *To Appomattox and Beyond: The Civil War Soldier in War and Peace.* Chicago: Ivan R. Dee, Inc., 1996.

Kramer, Jerome V. "Jimmy Carter: Man of His Words," *Book* (November/December 2001), 30–36.

Seligman, Amanda Irene. "Montagnais-Naskapi." *Encyclopedia of North American Indians,* 1996 ed., pp. 392–393.

EXERCISE 6
Responses will vary. Students should select one of the writing prompts and provide a brief example of one of the corresponding writing modes.

EXERCISE 6
Using Writing Modes

Choose one of the following short writing prompts and write a brief example demonstrating this writing mode. (20 points)

1. a story about a surprising turn of events (narrative)
2. a journal entry (personal expressive)
3. a persuasive letter appealing a parking ticket (persuasive/argumentative)
4. a review of a novel (informative)
5. a poem about a beloved pet (imaginative)

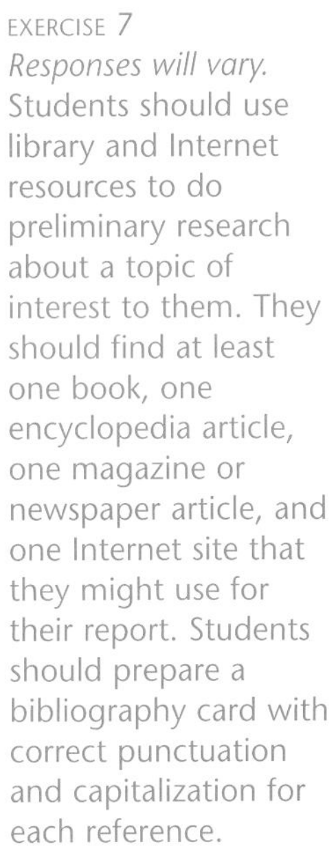

EXERCISE 7
Responses will vary. Students should use library and Internet resources to do preliminary research about a topic of interest to them. They should find at least one book, one encyclopedia article, one magazine or newspaper article, and one Internet site that they might use for their report. Students should prepare a bibliography card with correct punctuation and capitalization for each reference.

EXERCISE 7
Using Proper Documentation in Your Writing

Choose a topic that has always interested you. Use library and Internet resources to do preliminary research about it. Find at least one book, one encyclopedia article, one magazine or newspaper article, and one Internet site that you might use for your report. Prepare a bibliography card for each reference. Be sure to punctuate and capitalize correctly. (20 points)

INDEX OF TOPICS

D

H

I

O

P

Q

R

S

Y

INDEX OF LITERATURE MODELS

W

ACKNOWLEDGMENTS

Photo Acknowledgments

22 © Getty Images/Artville; **26** © Creatas/PictureQuest; **43** © Duncan Smith/Getty Images/Photodisc; **47** © Getty Images/Photodisc; **52** © Creatas/PictureQuest; **64** © Getty Images/Eyewire; **81** © Getty Images/Eyewire; **120** © Chris Hellier/CORBIS; **185** © Getty Images/Eyewire; **222** © Getty Images/PhotoDisc; **230** © AP WorldWide Photo; **266** © Stockbyte/PictureQuest; **272** © Anderson Ross/Photodisc/PictureQuest; **303** © Stockbyte/PictureQuest; **310** © Stockbyte/PictureQuest; **332** Untitled Construction, Arthur Dove. © Philadelphia Museum of Art/CORBIS; **372** © Getty Images/PhotoDisc; **496** © Kevin Fleming/CORBIS; **526** © Getty Images/PhotoDisc; **552** © Stockbyte/PictureQuest; **558** © Harald Sund/Brand X Pictures/PictureQuest; **589** © Getty Images/Eyewire; **592** © Nicole Katano/Brand X Pictures/PictureQuest; **634** © SW Productions/PhotoDisc/PictureQuest; **642** © Jeff Maloney/PhotoDisc/PictureQuest.